WINDOWS

WINDOWS

Exploring Personal Values Through Reading and Writing

Jeff Rackham Olivia Bertagnolli
University of North Carolina at Asheville

HarperCollins*CollegePublishers*

Acquisitions Editor: Lisa Moore
Developmental Editor: Leslie Taggart
Project Editor: Steven Pisano
Design Supervisor: Dorothy Bungert
Text and Cover Design: Paul Agresti
Cover Illustration:
Day Dream by Dante Gabriel Rossetti,
1828–1882 English/Italian, by courtesy
of the Board of Trustees of the Victoria &
Albert Museum, London/Superstock,
Inc./Bridgeman Art Library, London
Photo Researcher: Kelly Mountain
Production Administrator: Kathleen Donnelly
Compositor: Waldman Graphics, Inc.
Printer and Binder: R. R. Donnelley & Sons Company
Cover Printer: The Lehigh Press, Inc.

For permission to use copyrighted material, grateful acknowledgment is made to the copyright holders on pp. 741–744, which are hereby made part of this copyright page.

Library of Congress Cataloging-in-Publication Data

Rackham, Jeff.
Windows : exploring personal values through reading and writing / Jeff Rackham, Olivia Bertagnolli.
p. cm.
ISBN 0-06-043808-8
1. English language—Rhetoric. 2. College readers.
I. Bertagnolli, Olivia. II. Title.
PE1408.R14 1992
808'.0427—dc20 92-11049
CIP

95 9 8 7 6 5 4

We do not choose to be born. We do not choose our parents. We do not choose our historical epoch, the country of our birth, or the immediate circumstances of our upbringing. We do not, most of the time, choose to die; nor do we choose the time or conditions of our death. But within all this realm of choicelessness we do choose how we shall live: courageously or in cowardice, honorably or dishonorably, with purpose or in drift. We decide what is important and what is trivial in life. We decide that what makes us significant is either what we do or what we refuse to do. But no matter how indifferent the universe may be to our choices and decisions, these choices and decisions are ours to make. We decide and choose, so are our lives formed.

—JOSEPH EPSTEIN

CONTENTS

• PART 2 *Readings on Personal Values*

CHAPTER 6 PASSIONATE ATTENTION 168

CHAPTER 7 MAKERS OF MUSIC, DREAMERS OF DREAMS 239

▲ PART 3 *Larger Perspectives*

Alternate Contents

Essays

Fiction

PREFACE

Windows is a new kind of anthology. Frankly, we set out to create a text that wouldn't sound like a text. We asked ourselves, why shouldn't a book on reading and writing strive to be at least as interesting as many of the essays it has anthologized? Why not use a personal voice and recount actual stories of students and friends we've known as they have struggled with their own reading, their own writing? Why not show students how to read with both feeling and critical insight, instead of merely urging them to do so? And why not simultaneously lead students toward different ways of exploring values and concerns that directly inform their lives? Why not provide them with all the cultural richness that different windows on experience might reveal to them?

In Part I, "Reading Through Writing," we've been unashamedly eclectic in our attempt to answer our own questions. Reader response theory has influenced us, as has rhetorical and cultural criticism. Yet we've been unable entirely to abandon our earlier training in close reading. Our goal, then, has been to combine those best portions of contemporary theory with our own long-term experience teaching. We have been far more concerned about finding methods that succeed with students than with adhering to any single theoretical purity.

Windows also differs from other conventional readers in offering significantly more than an introductory overview of "how to read and write." Because we're convinced the act of writing contributes to and enlivens the act of critical reading, we've organized each chapter in Part I to illustrate what we see as five primary stages of a single integrated process.

1. **Thoughtful Reading**—emphasizes both the emotional and intellectual interaction of a reader with a text.
2. **Private Exploration**—asks the student to explore initial ideas and feelings in writing.
3. **Public Exploration**—illustrates how sharing one's views, either in class or in small groups, opens up even more windows on the reading experience.
4. **Private Reflection**—shows how writing—as a way of thinking through the response of other readers—may reveal new perspectives, or when possible, how a second reading of the text may lead to richer insights.
5. **Focused Writing**—provides examples of how initial student writing can lead directly into drafting, revising, and editing a formal essay.

Because Chapters 1–5 guide students through each of these stages at increasingly more complex levels, each chapter serves as a complete minicourse in the reading, thinking, and writing process. Depending on the level of student experience, instructors may lead their students through several chapters, beginning at a level that seems most appropriate, or guide them through only a single chapter, then spend the remainder of the term studying individual readings found in Part II. Still others may want to focus on the anthology of readings from the start, integrating selected portions of various chapters as needed.

In Part II, "Readings on Personal Values," we have attempted to select works that balance new and old, male and female, and ethnic and cultural backgrounds. In every case our primary concern has been to present lively, provocative, engaging—and always well-written—examples of literature. Instead of grouping readings according to great themes such as "War and Peace" or 'Science vs. Humanism" or "Man and Nature" (as important as those might be), we've focused on private concerns and on those conflicts that arise out of them: the different meanings of love, the relation of work to personal happiness, the power of imagination, the courage necessary for survival in a world in which the very concept of values is under debate.

Throughout the readings, we've mixed genres (essay, poetry, fiction, and drama) because genre does not seem as important to an exploration of values as does the human voice coming through each text. In our own class testing of this material, we sometimes encouraged students to reflect upon or synthesize different points of view and attitudes found in various genres, genders, and cultures: for example, an essay by Bruno Bettelheim and a poem by Linda Pastan, both on the subject of Anne Frank. At other times, we asked students to explore voices in related genders or cultures: for example, three works by Native American authors, Tom Whitecloud, Leslie Silko, and William Least Heat Moon. One of our most successful assignments came from asking our students to look at how two plays (Sophocles' *Antigone* and Jean Anouilh's *Antigone*) might focus on the same myth yet provide different perspectives and raise different questions of value.

Because we believe that each individual's reading of a text is shaped by history, culture, and personal experience, we've omitted those now-conventional headnotes or footnotes that provide information on the author or the reading. Such notes clearly influence any interaction the reader has with the text itself and may distort the more natural and honest response of less-experienced readers. When a headnote reveals that Gloria Steinem is a major American feminist, that William Blake was a mystic, or that Erich Fromm was a Marxist, first-year students may react to the text quite differently than if they approach it without the interference of well-intentioned editors.

At the same time, after students complete a first reading, we encourage them to investigate (on their own) the author and his or her historical and cultural background, then to reread and reconsider. We believe college students should be engaged in at least limited scholarship from the first year. One of the early acts of scholarship that leads to clear critical thinking is the uncovering of those cultural, historical, or personal influences that shape a text. Because such research might appear in a student's formal essay, we've also emphasized careful in-text documentation. A detailed Appendix answers many of the basic questions students might have about manuscript preparation.

Questions that reinforce the process detailed in Part I follow each essay, story, and poem in Part II. "Private Exploration" questions encourage students to write about initial feelings or thoughts by focusing attention on specifics in the text or by asking students to relate some aspect of the text to their own experience. "Public Exploration" questions (for in-class or small-group discussion) encourage students to share their diverse perspectives on the same reading. "Private Reflection" questions usually assume a second reading or a follow-up to group discussion, asking students to reflect on or revise initial reactions, and guiding them toward a focus of interest that might develop into a formal essay.

We've attempted to avoid standard questions that presuppose a specific answer: "What is the author's purpose?" or "Why does Harriet refuse to go to work?" We've also tried to avoid more formalistic questions that center on style, structure, or genre. Our experience shows that students become interested, even excited, when they understand that a text might actually have some direct connection to their own lives. (And isn't that why most of us were first attracted to the pleasures of reading?) Our questions, therefore, are open-ended, calling for responses that can only arise from a partnership between reader and text. At times, we've pointed to a specific scene or idea in an essay or story, or offered a short quotation, followed with nothing more than "What do you make of this?" Some instructors might fear that students will flounder with so little direction, but after three years of class testing, we've found that such broad questions give students an opportunity to write on what matters most to them—often for the first time in their lives.

In Part III, "Larger Perspectives," we anthologize plays and longer works of fiction, this time without prefacing categories such as Love or Imagination or Conscience, and without follow-up exercises.

In their richness and complexity, each of the longer works offers a variety of possible values for students to explore, and a number of additional options for instructors. Novellas like *Theft*, for example, can be incorporated into almost any of the earlier thematic sections. In turn, either could be assigned independently as a final term project for students to negotiate their own entrance into a text, exploring a particular value that seems important to their own lives.

Overall then, the text is meant to work both pedagogically and philosophically as an integrated whole. Yet we hope instructors will find a great deal of freedom within the structure we've created. Our own experience has shown that it is valuable to assign Chapter 1 and the first half of Chapter 2 together. Both illustrate how individuals bring their own cultural background and personal experience into operation when reading a text. For students who have never encountered this kind of freedom of response, we have found the concept provokes excited discussion. We have then followed up with selections of readings from one of the value units in Part II, asking students to write about their initial experiences with a specific text. After small-group or in-class discussions, we have asked them to write again on their own, this time with more reflection on the views others have brought to the text. After that, each of us has used the material differently, depending on the level of the class and our own best inclinations. Neither of us has used the same units in the same order or followed any prescribed pattern in the way we have integrated portions of pedagogical chapters into various readings selected from the anthology sections. In other words, we hope we've designed a text that offers both structure and flexibility in organizing a full semester of challenging new material.

ACKNOWLEDGMENTS

We are indebted to our students for their perceptive comments and contributions. Thanks to our many reviewers: Addison Amos, *Duke University*; Manuel B. Blanco, *Laredo Junior College*; Bill Cain, *Wellesley College*; Marvin Diogenes, *University of Arizona*; Jim Dubinsky, *West Point Military Academy*; Elinor C. Flewellan, *Santa Barbara City College*; Chrysanthy M. Grieco, *Seton Hall*; Robert Hill, *Middlebury College*; Ruth Jenkins, *California State University-Fresno*; Jeffrey Jeske, *Guilford College*; Janet Madden, *El Camino College*; Patricia Morgan, *University of Louisiana-Baton Rouge*; Toni J. Morris, *University of Indianapolis*; John Osbourne, *Butte College*; Virginia Parsons, *Northeastern University*; Gerald Pike, *University of California-Davis*; Sally Barr Reagan, *University of Missouri-St. Louis*; Marjorie Roemer, *University of Cincinnati*; Kate Ronald, *University of Nebraska*; David Shimkin, *Queensboro Community College*; Judith Stanford, *Rivier College*; and Howard Winn, *Dutchess Community College*. Special thanks to our colleagues at the University of North Carolina-Asheville for their support and enlightening criticism: Peter Caulfield, Dee James, David Hopes, Peggy Parris, and Arnold Wengrow. Finally, we want to acknowledge our exceptional editors at HarperCollins, Lisa Moore, Leslie Taggart, and Steven Pisano.

Jeff Rackham
Olivia Bertagnolli

PART 1

Reading Through Writing

CHAPTER 1

A THOUGHTFUL SPIRIT, AN INQUIRING MIND

THE STORY

Two friends of ours told us this story. Steve and Meg had been married only a few months. For a delayed honeymoon they traveled to Varanas, India, the oldest city in the world. The air lay over them like oily steam. A ceiling fan turned slowly in their hotel room. At night they had to leave the window open. A rush of traffic, the distant cry of street vendors, horns and far-off bells, all the sour smells and muffled sounds of a foreign place at night kept them awake. They tossed and turned on the damp sheets for hours. Finally, toward four o'clock in the morning, Steve realized the sounds he thought were keeping him awake were no longer there. No taxis, no mopeds buzzing like bees beneath the hotel window. Something else seemed to hover in his ears, a new sound he could not identify. He'd been listening to it for hours without being conscious of it: a nervous shuffle, like a snake shedding dry skin. He began to pace the floor in his underwear. Even then the heat pressed down on him. He found himself standing at the window. In the distance he could see the Ganges with flickering oil lamps floating on the water. At the window the strange shuffling noise was louder, yet hardly more than a whisper. The sound shimmered everywhere over the hushed streets below.

Then he realized what it was. Thousands and thousands of homeless people, whole families, slept on the streets, as they do in many countries, but here most of them slept on strips of cardboard. Each time they rolled over or turned in their sleep, the cardboard rustled. Throughout the steamy night, old men in loin cloths and children in thin cotton shirts turned on their cardboard mats, thousands and thousands of them on every sidewalk, in every alley. It was as if he could literally hear the city breathing.

Meg heard the sound too. She had known immediately what caused it. For her the sound came as a relief to earlier cries and shouts along the dark streets. It seemed almost natural to her ears, soothing and restful: a whole nation asleep. But she confessed she settled into uneasy dreams, one of those restless turnings when you're still half-conscious of what's going on around you.

Our friends told us this story several times. They couldn't agree on what it meant. Steve seemed haunted by the experience. He couldn't get a good read on it, he said. He was sure that deep within him something changed because of what he experienced. Meg argued that what happened had nothing to do with him personally—nor with her. The meaning was simple. Half the world lives in poverty. That was the tragedy. We couldn't realize the magnitude of such a terrible situation until it haunted us in our sleep. Governments must be held responsible. Mandatory birth control should be enforced. Meg is a chemist and she insisted Steve should look at the experience objectively: you observed, she said, then you analyzed and interpreted. But you were not involved.

No, Steve insisted. It was more than that. He had grown up in a well-to-do family in Colorado. He had seen sick migrant workers huddled around the steps of Catholic shelters. Yet he had travelled halfway around the world to recognize the need for human dignity. He couldn't put his finger on it, but he felt a responsibility hung over him.

READING THE STORY

For our purposes here, perhaps the key phrase is Steve's. We were all sitting on our summer porch and Steve leaned back in the wicker chair. "I just can't get a good read on it," he said. The phrase is a common cliche, yet it illustrates an important point. Almost all of us try to *read* our experiences. We attempt to *read* a lover's eyes; we *read* bad news on our supervisor's face; we *read* our parents' efforts at trying to influence choices we make about our future. And of course we read newspapers, photographs of drug dealers, hair styles on teenage girls, "body language," and novels. Reading, in the general way we're using it here, is simply the effort to construe meaning or understanding from a text. And a text can be any artifact or experience that engages your attention—a statue, an off-the-shoulder dress, a stockbroker wearing an earring, a novel, graffiti on subway walls, or a waterfall in Yosemite National Park.

Ralph Waldo Emerson advised us all to go into nature and to read it, arguing that if we did so, our new-found understanding would lead us to higher spiritual values. But Emerson's advice suggests the difficulty of reading. A text is seldom so simple that "meaning" can be immediately, generally, or universally construed. Most of us will remember that time in school when an enthusiastic teacher asked, "What is the meaning in *Hamlet*?". If you were like us, you felt a sinking panic. You felt certain there was a "right meaning" and the instructor knew what it was. Your job was to make guesses until you found it. But a better response might have been to ask, "Which meaning?" Hamlet's? The Queen's? Rosencrantz and Gildenstern's? The meaning found by British aristocrats who viewed a performance in the 17th century? Or by Chinese peasants who watched a touring production of the play in the Peoples' Republic of China in 1978? Obviously who reads the text, as well as the context it's read in, affects the "meaning."

Emerson read nature and found spiritual values. But Ben Franklin read nature with a stop watch in his hand. He wanted to know how long it would take two men with axes to chop down a tree three feet in diameter. Franklin was concerned with the practical consideration of clearing a forest. Each man brought to the text—the forest—a different personal and cultural background. Each read the same forest and found a different meaning.

Our friends, Steve and Meg, shared a common experience in Asia. Meg wanted to read the experience for its "facts": much of the population of third-world countries is devastatingly poor. Meg felt she was interpreting the experience objectively. Her personal background as a scientist probably influenced her method of construing experience. Steve reacted differently. For him, the facts were important because they related to a personal memory—his childhood in Colorado. Steve's reading of the experience was shadowed by guilt.

Yet Meg's use of the term *tragic* suggests that in spite of her objectivity, the experience contained an emotional element. She was acknowledging an implicit value. Perhaps the value could be phrased like this: when millions of human lives are reduced to poverty, when life seems to be nothing more than a desperate struggle to survive, then life itself, and the meaning of being human, is reduced to little more than wasted potential.

Steve probably would have agreed with our interpretation of Meg's response. But he would continue to insist that in this particular case, his own personal responsibility—or rather, the lack of it over all these years—was the more important meaning to be found in the experience. Steve had ignored human degradation as a young man. He had been consumed with his own future and career. And then on one single night, while standing at an open window looking out over an ancient city, his lungs filled with the odor of charcoal fires, he had sensed something unexpected. Poverty was not a fact, not a statistic, but a personal reality that insisted upon his own commitment to action.

Learning how to read a "text" well, as Steve and Meg are trying to do, or even as Emerson and Ben Franklin did, requires a special attitude. Reading actively and critically is not something limited to the classroom. Reading actively is especially not something limited to a course in composition or critical thinking. Active reading is nothing more nor less than engaging your mind with any text you find yourself confronting. Active, thoughtful reading attempts to identify significant details (within their context) which help you construe a meaning. In the academic world, most of those texts will involve written words—essays, autobiographies, fiction, poetry, journal articles, case histories, and textbooks. The *context* for such reading includes among many other possibilities, your own history of reading, where you've worked and lived, and the values held by those who raised you. Even the purpose for which you are reading can affect your response.

When we use the term *reading,* then, we are in essence using it as a code word for a special kind of thinking, for reflecting upon, for considering and puzzling about the experience in front of our eyes, as well as for the transformation of that experience in our imagination. Steve and Meg attempted to *read* their common experience. As we listened to their story, we attempted to *read* both their telling of it and their reasons—spoken and unspoken—which led them to see and understand the events differently.

You in turn have been reading, puzzling over, and attempting to construe meaning from what we've written here. You may have asked silent questions: *"What do the authors mean by text and context?" "What's the connection?" "Is reading really this complicated?"* Or you may have made silent observations: *"That's not how I would see it." "I don't think this is true." "Their interpretation is sure different from mine."* Any of these responses would show you are reading thoughtfully. You've become silently engaged in a dialogue with the text, attempting to construe meaning, to interpret and understand.

WRITING THE STORY

Meg went on to other things in her life. Steve felt something important had happened to him and he wanted to write it all down. He purchased a spiral notebook and tried describing the trip to India. The event seemed to be fading away from him and he wanted to keep it fresh, wanted to hold the moment. He wrote about the sights and smells, the night in the hotel, the spicy food and the diarrhea he had for two weeks. But merely describing his experience didn't satisfy him. The point wasn't to retell the story. He wanted to clarify it, discover its secret. He found himself writing off the subject, about his childhood and his two years at a private school where the boys played lacrosse on grassy fields. He began taking notes on *The Children of Sanchez,* a book about hunger in Mexico. Later he read Elie Wiesel's *Night,* an autobiographical account of Jewish experience in a concentration camp in Germany. In a way Steve couldn't explain, both accounts seemed to press upon his own, and again, he began writing about it, asking questions, exploring possibilities. In the evenings on our summer porch, Steve read passages to us. Meg rolled her eyes. She'd heard it all before. But after awhile all of us would be arguing, interpreting, disagreeing. Meg pretended to hold back, but she always seemed to ask just the right questions. I talked about my experience in the Peace Corps and Olivia talked about two Vietnamese students in her class who were children of refugees. Sometimes none of our points connected and other times we'd get so excited we talked over the top of each other. Meg told us afterward that Steve would go home and write even more, fleshing out ideas he'd heard that evening. He would try each one, as if taste testing new varieties of cheese.

Later he tried to write a book about it. He outlined several chapters but nothing came together. He was a slow writer. He had to revise again and again. Often, in the act of writing, he discovered new thoughts and insights that forced him to revise one more time. In the end, he did publish a small article in a respectable journal. Several readers wrote and thanked him. They said the essay moved them deeply. One reader said the way she looked at life had been changed. Steve was grateful for the response, but the struggle to write down what he felt and thought had been as important—perhaps more important—than the responses he received from others. Writing it down made him see the experience in ways that went beyond talking about it. Only in the act of writing itself had he found a way to explore and give shape to all the conflicting feelings and ideas that haunted him.

Both Emerson and Franklin spent much of their lives writing about their experiences, their ideas, and their values. So did Winston Churchill, the Prime Minister of England during World War II, and so did Georgia O'Keeffe, a major American artist. In fact, the list of those who have used writing as a tool for recording discoveries and exploring ideas in journals is astonishing. It includes those you would expect—poets like Theodore Roethke (17 board feet of notebooks)—but it also includes Charles Darwin, Margaret Mead, Loren Eiseley, Thomas Wolfe, Leonardo da Vinci, Tchaikovsky, Degas, and thousands of scientists, government leaders, psychologists, artists, and ordinary individuals whose names we never know.

We said above that reading, as we've been using the word, is in essence a code word for thinking. Writing is much the same. It's true that sometimes writing is merely an act of recording data or information, and sometimes merely a way of giving instructions (*Attach hexnut to the 2 inch bolt*). But clearly writing is also an act of the reflective mind.

PUTTING IT ALL TOGETHER

So what can we learn from this? We might phrase it like this: the act of reading (in the larger sense we've been speaking of) and writing (as an act of inquiry and exploration) are interrelated with thinking, learning, and growing as educated human beings. Reading is not limited to absorbing information. Writing is not a cosmetic skill applied to the surface of experience. At their highest level, both reading and writing are ways of using language to discover and investigate ideas, concepts, insights, values—give it whatever name you will. We've found that this kind of higher thinking process follows a general pattern.

1. ***Thoughtful*** (***or active***) ***reading*** begins with identifying details in a text that seem important. In a personal experience, such details might consist of special sounds heard in the night, a shuffling noise that seems distinct from all others. For Steve and Meg, it was exactly such an odd point that set them on a path of questioning. In a written text, key details might be special words, sentences, or passages. In this chapter, key words for most readers would probably be the terms *reading* and *writing*. We're using the terms in ways that might not at first be obvious. Identifying such words or phrases, questioning them, puzzling over them is the first stage in a journey.

2. *Private exploration* must follow. Mulling over what you've read or experienced, tracking down those buzzing disturbances that say, "I don't understand," is essential. No one else can understand it for you. This is where writing helps. Jotting down questions, ideas, thoughts, or even scribbling mini-essays to yourself in a notebook may clarify. Writing in this sense is writing as inquiry, writing to probe and discover rather than writing to communicate with someone else. Private writing is a means of thinking things through on paper.

3. *Public exploration* can also help. Just as Steve needed someone to talk to about his concerns, someone to test ideas against, to argue with, most of us find that hearing others' views, and sharing our own, become part of the mechanism of thinking itself. Others help place our views in perspective, help us see flaws in logic, help us rethink and revise.

4. *Private reflection* isn't over, however. After listening, debating, discussing, we almost always need to return to writing. The journal or notebook provides an opportunity to revise, refine, and sometimes reaffirm our thoughts with more confidence. This return to the journal may be a stage where the whole issue comes into clearer focus, where you sense the first glimmer of how your reflections could be organized and developed into something to share with others.

5. *Focused writing* is the final stage—the movement from journal exploration and reflection toward an organized essay. In college, this may be the only stage an instructor reads. Yet this is ultimately important for a larger reason. Only when ideas and values are shared in this organized fashion do we complete an intellectual process begun in stage one. That is, just as some other writer has struggled through the process to share one small portion of his or her life with us, our attempt to express ideas and insights with someone else completes the cycle. One person reaches out to another in an ever enlarging circle. We share and partake in the intellectual heritage of humankind. We become part of a dialogue that has been going on since Socrates.

Does everyone move through such a process? Obviously not. Yet the process exists because it has worked again and again over many generations. In the case of our friends, Meg felt comfortable with her first understanding of the experience in Asia. She would have thought no more about it if Steve hadn't sensed a need to explore further. Over the following year or so, Steve moved back and forth through each stage described above. Both friends found "meaning" in the experience. Steve probed deeper and seems to have found a deeper value, one that made him see his life in a new light. Some other experience, some other *text*, might have moved Meg to do the same. The *context*—the total life experience we bring to a work, as well as the frame in which the work presents itself—always affects our reading.

If we share the story with you now, it's because it also affected us. Through hearing the story, our own ideas on human worth evolved, not merely because of Steve's and Meg's insights about the waste of life caused by poverty and hunger, not merely because of their need to accept a new sense of responsibility, but because we had the opportunity of watching them struggle their way through to a final understanding. It was their own effort that seemed courageous. Wanting to know, wanting to learn, wanting to become more than they had been—that too affected us.

CHAPTER 2

ENGAGING THE IMAGINATION

THOUGHTFUL READING

Our friends seldom came by without bringing something that excited them. They were always bringing a new book or a poem to share with us. Once they spent two hours showing us a collection of photographs called *The Family of Man.* On another fall evening, while we sat on the porch watching light soften the woods, Steve read the first sentence of "Marrakech," an essay by George Orwell.

> As the corpse went past, the flies left the restaurant table in a cloud and rushed after it, but they came back a few minutes later.

We were delighted. What a wonderful opening. Hilarious, macabre, ironic. Meg said it sounded like something Woody Allen might have written.

We wanted to hear the rest of the essay. But while we listened our perception and understanding of the lead sentence changed. As we heard Orwell describe the painful condition of life in Morocco, the sentence took on new light. If there was humor, it was dark humor, and more painful than funny. We discovered levels of significance we hadn't recognized at first. As we talked later, we found each of us now saw something different in the sentence.

But if the sentence meant different things to different people, did that mean Orwell's sentence had no inherent meaning? Or that meaning can change at the reader's will? That a sentence or essay or history text can mean anything we want it to mean? Of course not. The word *fly* does not mean *elephant;* the word *corpse* does not mean *Eiffel Tower.* Authors struggle to express something with precision. We can't substitute our own words for the actual words on the page, just as we can't invent our own scenarios for events described. We have an obligation to read a work within the frame of its own context. The *context* of a work includes all the author has attempted to express, from title to final sentence. Shakespeare's *Hamlet,* for example, includes the appearance of a ghost. We can't arbitrarily decide the ghost walks because he ate Italian spaghetti sauce. Nothing in the context—none of the words, images, or actions in the play—suggests that spaghetti sauce is a factor.

As we listened to George Orwell's essay, as we considered the images and thoughts that followed his introduction, as we heard certain phrases repeated for emphasis, and as we recognized the serious tone, it quickly became apparent Orwell had not written something humorous and witty. It was the context that changed our response to the first sentence.

Yet the *context* for reading, as we pointed out in Chapter 1, does involve something outside the frame. We read an author's work—whether Orwell's or Shakespeare's—in light of just about everything we've ever read before. We read it in light of our own cultural experience and beliefs, in light of our sex and age and our emotional feelings at the time. Even knowing who Orwell was, or the audience he was writing for, or the era in which he published, might affect how we construe meaning from the work.

So all this suggests we're performing two actions simultaneously. We read a text with attention to the words, the sentences, the interior context of the piece, attempting as best we can to shape meaning from the author's own language, while at the same time, we test the author's words, ideas, and implications against all we've known before. Frank Smith, a nationally known expert on reading, observes that comprehension is a matter of "relating what we attend to in the world around us—the visual information of print in the case of reading—to what we already have in our heads."

After listening that evening to Steve read Orwell's "Marrakech," we decided to test an excerpt from it on our students. We were curious. Would they respond as we had? We passed out copies in class and asked the students to read it seriously, pencil in hand, marking those portions that seemed important to them. "Take notes in the margins," we said. "Jot down what seems to come across for you. Ask questions, if you have any. Make brief notes to yourself on thoughts or reflections you have as you go along."

Here is how Dale Weaver, a first-year student majoring in environmental studies, read and marked the excerpt.

> All people who work with their hands are partly invisible and the more important the work they do, the less visible they are. Still, a white skin is always fairly conspicuous. In northern Europe, when you see a labourer ploughing a field, you probably give him a second glance. In a hot country, anywhere south of Gibraltar or east of Suez, the chances are that you don't even see him. I have noticed this again and

Invisible people—why are those with more important work less visible?

again. In a tropical landscape one's eye takes in everything except the human beings. It takes in the dried-up soil, the prickly pear, the palm tree and the distant mountain, but it always misses the peasant hoeing at his patch. He is the same colour as the earth, and a great deal less interesting to look at.

It is only because of this that the starved countries in Asia and Africa are accepted as tourist resorts. No one would think of running cheap trips to the Distressed Areas. But where the human beings have brown skins their poverty is simply not noticed. What does Morocco mean to a Frenchman? An orange-grove or a job in Government service. Or to an Englishman? Camels, castles, palm trees, Foreign Legionnaires, brass trays, and bandits. One could probably live there for years without noticing that for nine-tenths of the people the reality of life is an endless, back-breaking struggle to wring a little food out of an eroded soil.

Why do we see the beauty and miss the poverty? (Or do we? or Is this still true? Would it be true today? Do tourists see New York and miss the Bronx?)

Most of Morocco is so desolate that no wild animal bigger than a hare can live on it. Huge areas which were once covered with forest have turned into a treeless waste where the soil is exactly like broken-up brick. Nevertheless a good deal of it is cultivated, with frightful labour. Everything is done by hand. Long lines of women, bent double like inverted capital L's, work their way slowly across the fields, tearing up the prickly weeds with their hands, and the peasant gathering lucerne for fodder pulls it up stalk by stalk instead of reaping it, thus saving an inch or two on each stalk. The plough is a wretched wooden thing, so

Lucerne: a plant like alfalfa

frail that one can easily carry it on one's shoulder, and fitted underneath with a rough iron spike which stirs the soil to a depth of about four inches. This is as much as the strength of the animals is equal to. It is usual to plough with a cow and a donkey yoked together. Two donkeys would not be quite strong enough, but on the other hand two cows would cost a little more to feed. The peasants possess no harrows, they merely plough the soil several times over in different directions, finally leaving it in rough furrows, after which the whole field has to be shaped with hoes into small oblong patches to conserve water. Except for a day or two after the rare rainstorms there is never enough water. Along the edges of the fields channels are hacked out to a depth of thirty or forty feet to get at the tiny trickles which run through the subsoil.

Every afternoon a file of very old women passes down the road outside my house, each carrying a load of firewood. All of them are mummified with age and the sun, and all of them are tiny. It seems to be generally the case in primitive communities that the women, when they get beyond a certain age, shrink to the size of children. One day a poor old creature who could not have been more than four feet tall crept past me under a vast load of wood. I stopped her and put a five-sou piece (a little more than a farthing) into her hand. She answered with a shrill wail, almost a scream, which was partly gratitude but mainly surprise. I suppose that from her point of view, by taking any notice of her, I seemed almost to be violating a law of nature. She accepted her status as an old

The people are invisible so that to see them violates a law of nature.

woman, that is to say as a beast of burden. When a family is travelling it is quite usual to see a father and a grown-up son riding ahead on donkeys, and an old woman following on foot, carrying the baggage.

But what is strange about these people is their invisibility. For several weeks, always at about the same time of day, the file of old women had hobbled past the house with their firewood, and though they had registered themselves on my eyeballs I cannot truly say that I had seen them. Firewood was passing—that was how I saw it. It was only that one day I happened to be walking behind them, and the curious up-and-down motion of a load of wood drew my attention to the human being beneath it. Then for the first time I noticed the poor old earth-coloured bodies, bodies reduced to bones and leathery skin, bent double under the crushing weight. Yet I suppose I had not been five minutes on Moroccan soil before I noticed the overloading of the donkeys and was infuriated by it. There is no question that the donkeys are damnably treated. The Moroccan donkey is hardly bigger than a St. Bernard dog, it carries a load which in the British Army would be considered too much for a fifteen-hands mule, and very often its pack-saddle is not taken off its back for weeks together. But what is peculiarly pitiful is that it is the most willing creature on earth, it follows its master like a dog and does not need either bridle or halter. After a dozen years of devoted work it suddenly drops dead, whereupon its master tips it into the ditch and the village dogs have torn its guts out before it is cold.

See opening sentence—Laborers are invisible to us—what does he mean?

The animals are not invisible, only the humans.

> This kind of thing makes one's blood boil, whereas—on the whole—the plight of the human beings does not. I am not commenting, merely pointing to a fact. People with brown skins are next door to invisible. Anyone can be sorry for the donkey with its galled back, but it is generally owing to some kind of accident if one even notices the old woman under her load of sticks.

Why do we not see brown skin? Do we block out what we don't want to see?

Is this something psychological in us?

Actually, like many of the students, Dale read through the excerpt once, picking up a general idea of the whole but feeling unsure of himself and finding little to respond to. Only after a second reading could he identify what for him were key passages and images. Only the second time through did he begin to question what he read.

That's not unusual. Almost all serious reading requires a second reading. The written word, unlike the spoken, remains permanently in place. You can return to it, mull over it, challenge it. Only on a second reading—sometimes a third or fourth or even tenth on a difficult text such as a poem by Dante—only on rereading can you approach a work with a full sense of the context created by the author.

This is the reading you need to deliberate on with pencil in hand. The use of a pencil—underlining passages, circling important words or phrases, jotting down questions or ideas—engages the mind actively with the text. Thoughtful reading requires that you invest something of yourself. Without that effort, it's unlikely you'll find much value in the work. Little in life has meaning if you've invested nothing in it. Nothing makes for nothing.

In other words, thoughtful reading demands effort and attention; what we call study. The pencil in your hand reminds you of that. Your job is not merely to scan the text. You must respond, question, and evaluate. You must take an active part. You must engage in an imaginative but silent dialogue with the author.

Yet how do you know what to mark? Which are the key passages and ideas? This is where your background, and especially your previous reading experience, affect your judgment. The way Dale has marked George Orwell's essay may not seem to catch the most significant points—at least not as you read it. And Dale's reactions, jotted in the margins, may not be even close to yours.

Consider the difference between how Dale read the text and how Kawana White, a transfer student from Washington D.C., marked one of the same paragraphs.

> Every afternoon a file of very old women passes down the road outside my house, each carrying a load of firewood. All of

Women do the labor of animals.

them are mummified with age and the sun, and all of them are tiny. It seems to be generally the case in primitive communities that the women, when they get beyond a certain age, shrink to the size of children. One day a poor old creature who could not have been more than four feet tall crept past me under a vast load of wood. I stopped her and put a five-sou piece (a little more than a farthing) into her hand. She answered with a shrill wail, almost a scream, which was partly gratitude but mainly surprise. I suppose that from her point of view, by taking any notice of her, I seemed almost to be violating a law of nature. She accepted her status as an old woman, that is to say as a beast of burden. When a family is travelling it is quite usual to see a father and a grown-up son riding ahead on donkeys, and an old woman following on foot, carrying the baggage.

They shrivel into tiny mummies—(women have always been slaves).

Women accept being "beasts of burden."

But what is strange about these people is their invisibility. For several weeks, always at about the same time of day, the file of old women had hobbled past the house with their firewood, and though they had registered themselves on my eyeballs I cannot truly say that I had seen them. Firewood was passing—that was how I saw it. It was only that one day I happened to be walking behind them, and the curious up-and-down motion of a load of wood drew my attention to the human being beneath it. Then for the first time I noticed the poor old earth-coloured bodies, bodies reduced to bones and leathery skin, bent double under the crushing weight.

He doesn't see women. They are invisible!

"earth-coloured" bodies—dark skin & old women—make you invisible.

Can you identify key differences between the two responses? Although Kawana has picked up on similar points to Dale's, she's seen those points—

invisibility, women's burden, and the role of "dark skinned" laborers—in light of her own background, as a woman and an African-American. Kawana finds Orwell's insights more emotionally personal, more cutting. Dale's notes react to the inner context of the essay, to how the poor in North Africa are made invisible. Kawana reacts to how Orwell's perceptions apply to her and to America. Is one reaction "correct" and the other "wrong"? Absolutely not. Both students have studied the text carefully; neither is reading into it something that isn't there; both are perceptive to the observations reported on by Orwell; yet each has begun the process of negotiating his or her own relationship to the text.

PRIVATE EXPLORATION

Studies in creativity reveal that the very act of writing generates ideas. For that reason we asked our students to keep reading notebooks, a place where they could explore thoughts and feelings further than the margins of their text allowed.* We explained that merely thinking about what has happened to you, what you're feeling, or what you've read may have a benefit, but writing about it stimulates the imagination. Words call up more words; vague notions develop into specific concepts; a puzzling feeling forms itself into focused questions. "Some of the things that happen to us in life seem to have no meaning," writes Chinese-American author Maxine Hong Kingston, "but when you write them down you find the meanings for them; or, as you translate life into words, you force a meaning. Meaning is intrinsic in words and stories."

Here's a portion of the reading-notebook entry Dale Weaver wrote on Orwell's essay. (We've left in Dale's punctuation and spelling because at this point such things are not yet important; only exploring ideas is important.)

> I have to admit Orwell's "Maraketch" passed right over me the first time I read it--It was about as interesting as a National Geographic special--I also got a feeling from it about people being invisible even though you could see the animals and

*Not all instructors will necessarily ask you to keep a reading notebook, and not all will want to read such a notebook even if required. Yet the value of taking notes on what you read is still essential to an intelligent and imaginative act of reading, whether you do so on your own or as part of an assignment. Throughout this text, then, we will encourage you to keep an ongoing notebook or journal. Your instructor will advise you on whether the notes you take should be considered a private activity, or whether you will be required to submit them as part of a course requirement.

orange groves--maybe I began to see his point. We ignore (avoid? block-out?) things we don't want to see--and we don't want to see people suffer.

"All people who work with their hands are partly invisible . . . "

" . . . what is strange about these people is their invsibility."

Why would you see the beauty of tropical landscapes, the palms, the mountains, or whatever and not see the people? I wonder if this is still true? When was this written? Do old lady's still carry wood on their backs anywhere in the world today? But that's the whole thing--We wouldn't see it even if they do--you don't see old people. We put them away in nursing homes. Mentally retarded people are the same way--we put them in special schools or half way houses. You don't even have to look at the dead anymore--when my grandmother died they put powder on her face and put her in a satin lined casket and said she's sleeping.--So why would you see "a labourer ploughing a field," or a "peasant gathering fodder." We're trained not to see anything that isn't Disney World clean and sparkly. They had a Live Aid Concert to raise money for people in Africa. I watched a few hours of it but the part I watched just showed rock stars in $100 levis and jewel-studded shirts playing on $2500 guitars--it was great. I could feel sorry for starving Africans and not have to even look at them. They were invisible.

How do Dale's notebook explorations move beyond his marginal notations? What kind of questions is he raising here? Many readers might agree that invisibility is clearly one of Orwell's key points. For Dale, at this stage, it seems to be the emerging focus of his interest.

For Kawana, however, invisibility is significant only in its relationship to other ideas. Here is Kawana's first reading-notebook entry in its entirety.

> After completing this (powerful) story by George Orwell, my first overall emotion is getting mad. Then after I read it again, I just felt bitterness. Not just for the way dark skinned people are treated, worse than animals, or at least no better than animals, but because Mr. Orwell is right when he says that the treatment of donkeys "makes one's blood boil," but the "plight of human beings does not." These "earth-colored bodies" are reduced to the level of slaves. Brown skinned men plow with wooden tools for almost no food. Old women carry firewood on their backs. I wonder how old they even are. Maybe they're leather skinned and hump backed by the age of 30. I'd be toothless and twisted too if I had a dozen kids and too much work and no medicine.
>
> I feel stunned by the women in this. "Long lines of women, bent double like inverted capital L's" pulling up weeds. Women who "shrink to the size of children" after a certain age, "mummified with age and sun." Who just accept that they're "a beast of burden." It makes me so mad. I don't even know who to be mad at. The women walk and carry baggage while men ride in front on donkeys. It's the women who stagger under loads of firewood, who about faint over a penny he puts in their hand.

Dark skinned people and women.

Dark skin and women.

Women with dark skin.

But look at this sentence--"I am not commenting, merely pointing to a fact."

He is not commenting. The treatment of women and blacks is a fact. What comment is needed from a white man? Except about the poor donkeys. Those old donkeys just make your blood boil. No comment on women and backs. Just pointing to the fact for informational purposes. Women and blacks are invisible, they suffer, they starve, they grow old while they're still young. Animal rights groupies in American bomb laboratories to protest the terrible cruel treatment of mice. In Washington, only a few blocks from the White House, black men die on the sidewalks without jobs, hooked on coke because their lives are shit. Black women sell their bodies while whites are chauffeured to the capital building to discuss lowering taxes for oil men.

"I am not commenting, merely pointing to a fact." Facts don't a need comment. The donkeys and the laboratory mice need a comment, the oil men need a comment. The way we treat them makes your blood boil. It really does. Women with dark skin are just facts. Dark skinned women. Earth colored bodies. No comment needed there, sister, No sir. No comment at all.

Thoughtful, active reading is always a transaction with the text, that is, a place where we act on printed words and they act on us. Clearly we need to be thinking, questioning, observing, taking notes while we read. But for many, the follow-up stage immediately after reading—the first writing down of ideas, emotions, reactions, and more questions—for many the private exploration that begins in a reading journal becomes the first place where thinking gains focus and clarity. The reading notebook offers an opportunity for private reflection.

Yet taking effective notes may not come easily. Two classmates of Dale and Kawana wrote the following in their journals:

> I didn't see much to this. Where is this place anyway? I like to read stories with action in them like Stephen King, nothing much happens here. I tried to read it like you asked but I don't see anything to write about. There were a lot of words I didn't know.

> This made me so sad. I hurt inside, like stars falling in the night. I feel lost and scared at so much suffering. How can it happen. The question I have to ask is, WHY??? Jews and Arabs will never solve their problem without loving each other like brothers. If only we could communicate better and share our love for each other we might be able to create heaven here on earth. A little love goes a long way! By suffering for these poor people in the middle East we can share their burdens. We can only lift our eyes to the dark sky above and cry out our pain!!

What's going on here? Why were Dale and Kawana able to respond so much more fully to the Orwell reading? The first student admits to not knowing many of the words or even where Morocco is. Clearly the material is foreign to him, as it was to many students in our class. Admitting difficulty with a text is a sound place to begin. There's nothing to be ashamed of. All of us have experienced the same frustration. But stopping at that point is like saying, "I don't know how to drive a car with a stick shift, therefore I won't try to learn." Driving with an automatic transmission may be easier (like reading action stories by Steven King), but we place limits on our own growth if we do not seek to discover more than we already know. This student probably needs to read Orwell a second time with a good dictionary at hand. If he doesn't create some meaning for those words, the text itself can have no meaning.

Yet other problems may also exist. Many students are simply unfamiliar with the kind of reading expected in an academic world. This student likes a good plot, he likes stories with action. Yet very few of the texts you'll ever read in college have either (unless you happen to major in literature). Academic reading is not for adventure but for ideas. And it requires a different attitude, a different mind-set. It requires you to slow down, to reflect, and to question or challenge. Quite simply, that translates into a willingness to give more of your time, to puzzle out difficulties, perhaps by talking them through with others, or by reading a sentence or a paragraph aloud to "hear" the meaning, or by copying out a passage by hand, forcing yourself to slow down and concentrate on individual words and phrases—which probably leads back to using a dictionary again.

The second student seems to have a different set of problems. She has described her emotional response, and again, that's usually a valuable place to begin. Both Dale and Kawana also start at that point (Dale was bored, Kawana was angry). Yet this time, the student has allowed a heightened emotion to lead her away from the text itself. For example, Orwell does not mention Jews and Arabs. And Morocco is in West Africa, not the "middle east." Such confusion is not unnatural. The student need not feel embarrassed that she has misunderstood the setting. But she does need to investigate further. A good essay or story or poem should always stimulate emotion. The next step is to follow up with reasoned questioning, as Kawana does, searching out details that stimulate those emotions and pondering over them.

In fact, the conscious effort by both Dale and Kawana to seek out specifics in the text, noting them in the margins and discussing them in their journals, helped focus their concerns. Only by paying attention to the details—the facts, the sensory images, the actions, the repeated words and phrases—only by consciously calling them to our attention can we begin to reflect upon them and consider various connections or insights. Only by consciously studying the text, can we integrate our emotional responses with our reasoned reactions.

Dale saw the word "invisible." He found that Orwell repeated it three times. Presumably Dale didn't actually count the number of repetitions, he simply made himself aware of it. And Kawana saw repeated references to women and dark skin. By focusing on specifics, we make sure we're reading the actual words the author has put on the page. And by questioning the specifics in their context—their relationship to each other and to other points in the text, as well as to why the author might have emphasized them—we can begin to form a hypothesis about their meaning. It is as simple as this, and as complex: all thoughtful, active reading moves from details to generalizations.

Kawana admitted to us that she paused in writing her journal response to reread the Orwell essay (for a third time). Only on the third reading did she discover the sentence, "I am not commenting, merely pointing to a fact." For her, that single sentence, that detail, became the means by which all other ideas and emotions suddenly pulled together for her.

Thoughtful writing follows thoughtful reading. Both require effort, concentration, and a willingness to explore and question possibilities. Both require curiosity and a sense of inquiry—a silent voice in the back of the mind that says, *Why does it make me feel the way it does? Is there any kind of truth coming at me here? What can I learn from this?* You don't need a reading journal for that. Some great minds do it all in their heads. For many of us, however, the reading notebook provides an opportunity to explore those questions in private, to speculate, revise, scribble, cross out, and otherwise stumble around until ideas begin to surface. For our friend Steve—because his experience in India had been so overwhelming for him—the private-exploration phase took more than a year of further reading and note taking. For Dale and Kawana, working with only a short essay, paying close attention to it, and being willing to reread, the effort took only an hour or so.

For all of them, the process to date was valuable, but not yet complete.

PUBLIC EXPLORATION

The year Steve worked on his book, he talked over his thoughts with us on several occasions. He talked with his wife Meg even more. The desire to share one's views, test them on others, and in turn, listen to how a different intelligence can be brought to bear on the same set of facts and details—all of that seems a normal and necessary part of intellectual growth. In turn then, after our students had read Orwell's essay, we suggested they form small groups and review their insights. We asked one person in each group to get things moving by reading from his or her reading notebook.

Dale and Kawana happened to be in the same group with two other students—Margerie Panhower, an adult returning to college after getting divorced, and Dee Styles, a sophomore from Dade County, Florida. Although we didn't make a tape recording of the session, here's an approximate reconstruction of what happened as we listened in.

> "I don't want to read first," Dale said.
>
> Margerie reached over and patted his hand. "I think you should go first because we need a strong male to lead the way."
>
> "Nothing doing."
>
> "I second it," said Dee Styles. She brushed her hair back over her shoulder. "Anyway, I forgot to bring my notebook."
>
> "I'm a terrible writer," Dale pleaded.
>
> Kawana pressed her own journal to her chest. "I'll tell you this, I'm not going first. I don't want anybody to hear this stuff."
>
> "We're all terrible writers," Margerie said. "That's why our courageous male is going to accept the burden."

Dale rolled his eyes and stared at what he had scribbled in pencil on loose sheets of paper. "It probably doesn't make sense, but here goes."

All of them listened politely. By the end, Kawana was leaning forward, her face intent. Dee Styles spoke first, however.

"I saw that Live Aid concert," she said. "The part I saw they did show pictures of Africa. There were those pictures of African babies with their bellies all swollen from worms or something. It was gross."

"That only proves my point," Dale said. "You just wanted to see the concert right? You didn't want to see the suffering. We block it out. That's the part where you probably got up to make more popcorn."

Margerie laughed. "I think Dale's right. We make these people invisible if we can. I guess I'm thinking along the same track. I spent a year with my husband—my ex-husband—in Venezuela, and when we saw campesinos planting crops by punching a stick in the ground to make a hole, I remember we said it was quaint. Colorful. I remember feeling pleased I had seen such a charming, old-world culture."

Dale nodded in agreement. "Even when we see them, the truth is still invisible to us, right? Either we don't see them at all, or we don't see what's really going on. We don't see the meaning behind it."

Dee Styles was rummaging through her purse for something. "I still thought it was gross. Why should I have to look at that? It's not my fault people are poor. I don't think they should mix politics with music."

Kawana had been leaning forward listening. Finally she shook her head and sat back. "I think I'm in the wrong group. You people didn't read the same essay I did."

"So let's hear what you wrote," Dale said. "If this essay isn't about invisibility, what's it about?"

"I don't want to read."

"None of us do," Margerie pointed out. "But if you saw it differently, we have to know what you think."

Kawana looked at each one of them, as if testing to see whether they could be trusted. Finally she sighed and began to read from a spiral notebook with a picture of Snoopy on the front. She read slowly at first, so softly the others could barely hear. As she read, her voice became more heated. At the finish she slammed her notebook shut and sat back defiantly.

"Wow!" Dale said. "That was great."

"Hell, I missed all of that," Margerie said. "I should've been the one who saw the emphasis on women. I'm the feminist."

Dee Styles shook her head. "It doesn't have anything to do with being black. He's writing about people in Morocco. This isn't a racist thing at all."

"It has everything to do with being black," Kawana said. "Listen to this line." She searched through her notebook and read a sentence she'd underlined. "Listen: ' . . . where the human beings have brown skins their poverty is simply not noticed.' "

"It says brown! Not black!"

"Wait a minute," Margerie said. "Racism isn't something directed only at blacks. The essay could have been about yellow skin and it would still apply to other races."

"Look," Kawana interrupted. "Even that's not the point I'm getting at anyway. It isn't just racist because it's women, too. It's a whole attitude that says if you're not white and male, you're only part of the scenery. A fact, but not worth commenting on."

"And poor," Margerie said. Dale agreed reluctantly. Of course the essay was about all that, but he insisted invisibility was still a main focus.

"What Orwell is doing is trying to get us to see what's invisible to us."

"Ok, ok," Kawana said. "I can see why you think so. But you're looking at it from a white male point of view. You're saying you 'block out' what you don't want to see. And I'm looking at it from the point of view of one of those people you're blocking out. I'm not invisible. My mother and sisters are not invisible. I don't have to be taught to see.

"That's just your point of view. That doesn't make you right and me wrong."

Margerie interrupted. "Look. Maybe what's going on here is that Orwell is making each of us have an insight of some kind into ourselves. Don't you think that's what's happening?"

She turned to Kawana. "You *are* being taught to see something, Kawana. You're being asked to see how white males can look at people who are dark skinned and female and poor, and not even see them. You're *seeing* how others are looking—or not looking—at you: as a fact, a statistic, something in the background.

"And Dale, you're being shown you don't see and don't want to see. You're being shown how white males make part of the world invisible."

"What's all this white male stuff?" he asked. "Didn't you admit the campesinos in South America were just part of the scenery to you? If you'd seen an old lady carrying wood, wouldn't you have said, 'How quaint'?"

Margerie sat back and blushed. Everyone was quiet for a moment. Dale and Kawana looked at each other.

Dee Styles gathered up her books to leave. "I don't care what anybody says. They shouldn't mix politics and music."

When someone critiques our ideas—or sees the point in a totally different light—it's only natural to feel frustration, even resentment. Yet differing views can illuminate our own insights and enrich our intellectual lives. They force us to reconsider and revise. Only in such a way can we begin to grow and change. The goal of such sharing is not to see who can "win," or prove himself more clever than the other, as in a debate. The goal is to work cooperatively rather than competitively, to seek understanding wherever it may lead us.

Everyone in Dale's and Kawana's study group left the first meeting dissatisfied. Yet each, in his or her own way, had been forced to reconsider initial attitudes. Each needed to re-see not only Orwell's essay, but his or her own responses to the essay. It is this circling around, this slow dancing of the mind, that enables us to sharpen judgment and increase critical discrimination.

PRIVATE REFLECTION

After talking about their ideas with others, we asked our students to write again in their reading notebooks. Pick up on any idea or aspect of discussion that seemed important, we suggested. Compare or contrast what you heard to your own thoughts. Use the act of writing to refine and reflect on your ideas further.

Here's a portion of Kawana's second journal entry.

> OK, I read the damn thing again. (The fourth time) And maybe it's not just race or women--although it's both of them too. Orwell gives as much space to the incredibly hard work the people do. The "wretched" wooden plough. The cow and donkey yoked together. The little scrapings on soil like "broken-up brick." And worst of all when you think about it, digging channels thirty feet deep to catch a tiny trickle of water. The women are "beasts of burden." Are the men's lives that much better? What makes them invisible is their "earth-coloured" bodies. They are like part of the earth. When Orwell gives the wood carrier a penny she screams because it's like "violating a law of nature." What does he mean by that? Like they're all beasts of the field--of nature, old women, men, cows and donkeys. But something makes us feel sympathy for the animals and not the people. Something. What is it? Does he ever really give the answer? What's wrong with people?

And here is Dale's second entry.

> I still think the essay's about invisibility, Orwell even says the more important the work, the

"less visible." Why is that? Kawana thinks it all has to do with sexism and racism. I don't know. Margerie says she thought the peasants in South America were "quaint." She never thought about punching holes in the ground as hard work--she saw it as colorful. And so does Orwell! He says a Frenchman would see Morocco as "an orange grove and government service." And an Englishman would see "camels, castles, palm trees, Foreign Legionnaires, brass trays, and bandits." That's it. We see what we expect to see. Maybe race or sex is part of it, but I think it's only because we already have steri-otypes. We don't see what's really there because we

Reminders

We don't want to make the reading process seem unnecessarily complicated. Here are some suggestions to keep it as simple as possible.

Thoughtful Reading

- If possible, always read the text twice, the first time to gain overall perspective, the second time to focus on details and meaning.
- Read with questions hovering in the back of your mind: What's going on here? Why does this make me feel the way it does? Am I being shown something I haven't seen before? Is there a truth coming at me?
- Read with a pencil in hand; annotate the text, marking key passages and jotting questions in the margins.
- Do not lose sight of the context of the work.
- Relate the text to your own previous reading, cultural experiences, and beliefs.

Private Exploration

- Keep a reading notebook to explore reactions, emotions and ideas.
- Let writing generate ideas.
- Focus on details in the text (the facts, sensory images, key actions, repeated words or phrases).
- Question details within their context.

```
see our steriotypes.--Everything else is invisible.
That's why when one of them is doing important work
we see it even less, because it doesn't fit the
steriotype, we don't want it to. Women and dark
skinned people are steriotyped for us so we
don't see them--is that racism? it's certainly
invisibility.
```

Dale and Kawana reveal something important here: the serious student is always involved in a continuous act of vision and revision. We read and respond, look again and reconsider. Answers that at first seemed right become less satisfactory. As we compare one passage in the text to another passage, or as we bring to bear on it our own experience, or the ideas of others, a good work of literature becomes richer and more complex.

Earlier we quoted Frank Smith on reading. Smith said reading comprehension is a matter of attending to the world around us, of relating it "to what

- Question the relationship of details to each other.
- Question the relationship of details to the whole.
- Let details lead you to generalizations.
- Make comparisons to other experiences or other reading.

Public Exploration

- Discuss your "reading" of the text with others.
- Question and challenge other readings, but only to clarify and seek insight, not to engage in competitive debate.
- Accept questions and challenges to your own reading as good faith attempts to clarify thinking.
- Allow the possibility of different "readings" so long as they do not violate the context of the work.
- Be willing to modify your views as you acquire new perspectives.

Private Reflection

- If possible, read the text a third time, keeping in mind the variety of reactions and feelings expressed by others.
- Reflect in your reading notebook on how you now see and understand the text.
- Allow intellectual energy generated by writing to evoke further ideas and insights.
- Use your writing to revise and sharpen your focus, moving from detail to generalization.

we already have in our heads." But *learning,* Smith observes, goes one step further: learning is a process of "modifying what we already have in our heads as a consequence of attending to the world around us. We learn to read, and we learn through reading, by adding to what we already know." The distinction here is significant.

Reading is not just an act of passively absorbing information, not just an act of acquiring facts or data. Reading is an act of *relating* what we see on the page to ideas and values we already possess. And learning is an act of *modifying* those ideas or values, or at least adding new concepts and points of view to the store of knowledge and experience in our heads. Relating and modifying are intellectual activities. They demand sustained effort. They require openness and a desire to grow. They flourish when the mind is curious, when we ask questions, reflect on answers, and show a willingness to reconsider pre-set attitudes.

Kawana and Dale possess those qualities. Their work shows they're well on the way toward bringing ideas into focus, toward giving shape and energy to them. They bring liveliness and sympathy to their reading. They engage not only their minds but their spirits. In such a way, human beings enlarge their capacity for living.

FOCUSED WRITING

> A writer is not so much someone who has something to say as much as he is someone who has found a process that will bring about new things he would not have thought of if he had not started to say them.
>
> —WILLIAM STAFFORD

The first book we ever wrote began with a story about Korean teapots. The book was about writing. It had nothing to do with teapots.

The truth was, we didn't know how to begin. We were working then in a basement apartment. For days we stared at the cinderblock walls. I took up pipe smoking, hoping it would make me look like a writer. Olivia drank black coffee and stacked rubber bands according to color and size. Nothing happened. Sometimes we paced the floor and scowled, waiting for profound thoughts. We owned an old Royal electric typewriter that growled when you turned it on. One of us would sit in front of the typewriter, roll in a sheet of blank paper, and let the typewriter growl and rumble for a while. The sound gave us an illusion of power. Only nothing happened. No writing came forth. We had a fairly good idea of what we wanted to say. We'd studied on it for years. We even had a detailed outline. But the white page remained blank.

Finally Olivia recalled the story of how in the last century Korean teapots were considered the most beautiful pottery in the world. A committee from Japan studied the pots. The committee analyzed form, symmetry, color, density of clay. Everything. But for some reason the Japanese teapots looked liked something you'd find in K-Mart. By contrast, the Korean pots hummed with deep, authentic beauty. Here was the problem: the committee from Japan studied the pots only after they were finished. No one realized the true cause of their beauty lay in the process used by the Korean masters in their daily work. For the Koreans it was the process, a Zen-like attitude toward working, that mattered most, not the finished product.

We realized in our own way we were making the same mistake. We were thinking about the book we wanted to write—the finished product. We felt paralyzed. We knew what books looked like. We had analyzed them: their heft, the big ideas, the hundreds of pages. We were trying to write a book instead of a sentence.

So we started over. Forget the end product. Get words on the page. Anything. Words generate more words. Sentences generate more sentences. Ideas stimulate more ideas.

Drafting

We found later that others already knew the secret. To do anything truly authentic for yourself, you have to forget the goal (at least for awhile) and immerse yourself in the act, the doing. You can't worry about what the critic may say, or your college professor, or your mother. After all, the first draft (sometimes called a discovery draft) is only a rough sketch. Much of it may be badly written, awkward, wordy, and without direction. Much of it probably will be. Yet no one else need ever see it. Novelist Kurt Vonnegut tells how he began each day of writing by typing *Mary Had a Little Lamb* or describing what he ate for breakfast. Such things never appeared in his novels. They were devices for jumpstarting his imagination. Each individual must find his or her own best process for working. For most, it's best to write fast and commit yourself wholly to the moment—to the subject at hand. It's probably best, for the time being, to ignore grammar and spelling, anything that might slow down the process. Let words and sentences lead you to ideas. There will be plenty of time later for revising, reorganizing, and correcting.

We don't mean to say, of course, that your discovery draft is a matter of flinging empty words at the page. No one can write out of ignorance. Most writing in college derives from books and essays you read, from lectures you hear, from experiments in the sciences, case studies in the social sciences, or from combinations of all these opportunities. In other words, long before you write, you're expected to engage in various kinds of preparation: reading, listening, asking questions, reflecting. Few of us can retain in our heads all the various possibilities we encounter—thus the need for keeping a notebook or journal.

Most students who maintain the type of reader's notebook we've been looking at are already immersed in a subject. After all, they've been copying out passages or quoting key phrases and sentences, asking questions, writing down definitions of words from the dictionary, exploring new ideas and relating them to their own experiences, values, and beliefs, or to other readings. Without knowing it, they've long been engaged in the primary act of preparation for writing. The problem should not be so much one of what to write, but where to begin.

We began our first book on writing with the story about Korean teapots because it led directly to a key confusion so many people have about writing—and it got us started. If *Mary Had a Little Lamb* can get you started, then use it. But the place to begin is probably already scribbled somewhere in your reader's notebook. We would suggest you look back over it (and back over the essay, story, poem—whatever you've been studying). Find the key concept, action, or feeling that provokes you most, the one thing that disturbs you, enlightens you, inspires you, angers you. If you're working with a fairly long text, it's also best to take time at the beginning to search for evidence or examples in the work that would justify developing your ideas further. Or jot down a short list of evidence and examples from personal experience, history, other works of literature, whatever is necessary. No need to begin writing if you can't come up with more than a paragraph before you hit a dead end.

Kawana White had strong feelings about Orwell's "Marrakech." How to organize those feelings, how to find a focus for them was a different matter. She glanced over her annotations on the essay and then over her two notebook responses. She was still disturbed by Orwell's sentence: "I am not commenting, merely pointing to a fact." She also found herself puzzling over another phrase copied out in her last notebook entry: "violating a law of nature." The questions it raised also seemed worth following. Here, then, is how she began her discovery draft, not even thinking she was "writing a paper" so much as letting language lead her toward insight.

On the surface it's all very clear. A white English tourist visits Morocco, enjoys palm trees, orange groves and bazaars. [~~He feels sympathy for~~] Later he realizes that he's [~~been~~] also been seeing brown-skinned peasants plowing fields behind a cow and a donkey. He feels sympathy for way the animals are being treated but hasn't paid attention to the people. He's seen "earth-coloured" women bent and shriveled up like "mummies." He was walking behind them carrying loads of wood that would have overloaded a British mule. But yet he's not really seen them. The people have been invisible to him. They have expected to be invisible. [~~But one day he~~] when he drops a "five-sou" coin in the hands of one old woman, and she screams, does he begin to reflect. He says, "I suppose that from her point of view, by taking any notice of her, I seemed almost to be violating a law of nature." But that's a strange [~~phrase~~] observation. What does he mean? Why was he violating a law of nature? Why does the old lady cry out? Because he took notice of her. What does it mean to "notice" someone? He gives her a sou and she screams. Out of surprise and gratitude, he says.

He <u>supposes</u> it's out of gratitude?

He <u>supposes</u>.

But what if he's wrong?

The writing here is obviously rough, yet Kawana has begun a focus by narrowing her topic to only two key phrases. By beginning with lists of questions, she clearly uses the act of writing as a means of inquiry, as a device for thinking and exploring in more depth a subject she's already reflected on for some time. Kawana told us later that the first sentences came haltingly, but once she hit upon the word "supposes," ideas began to flow faster than she could write them down. In two hours she wrote seven handwritten pages. Because she had read, reread, written about, and discussed the original text, her mind had been incubating on different aspects of it for a week. The act of focusing in and then letting the words lead her further into a topic revealed the power of writing for discovering ideas we don't even know we have. A character in a novel by E.M. Forster once said, "How do I know what I think until I see what I say?" Kawana would not have thought of the things she wrote—not even the questions—if she had "not started to say them."

On the other hand, Dale Weaver was fairly certain about his focus. He remained convinced that "invisibility" was the key insight to Orwell's work. He even had a title. Here's the first page of his discovery draft.

SEEING THE INVISIBLE

When George Orwell wrote "Maraketch" he saw something no one else ever saw--he saw invisible people.

But not right a way. "All people who work with

their hands are partly invisible, and the more important the work they do, the less visible they are." (George Orwell, par. 1) ~~To me this is the most important significant key statement in the essay. What it means is that we create steriotypes of people—we see the steriotype instead of the person. We have an image of old people This is especially true of people who anything unpleasant—We don't like to see People are individuals who have feelings too and we don't see them if we have a~~

To me this is the most important key statement in the essay. What I think this quote clearly means is that we probably create steriotypes of people and instead of seeing the person himself we stubstitute the steriotype we have created for the individual--We see the steriotype instead of the person--the person is invisible to us as a human being--as someone with feelings and one who suffers or would like to have a better life.

In many ways, Dale's discovery draft is even rougher than Kawana's. Dale plods forward, circles back, and sets off again. But always in the same direction. Dale claimed that for him the writing of the first draft was not so much an act of discovery as an attempt to find words that expressed what he already thought. But Dale also had a confession. When he reached his conclusion, the final paragraph came as a surprise. An idea he had never anticipated took over and expanded the significance. "I just sat and stared at it," he told us. "I knew it was right and I never even knew it was there."

Revising

For some authors, the difference between drafting and revising is almost indistinguishable. They push forward, hesitate, revise, and push on again. Others see revision as a totally separate act. Like Kawana, they compose a discovery draft at top speed, never looking back, letting energy generate ideas. Only when they've reached a conclusion of sorts do they stand back with a more critical stance and consider what they've written. Either way, revision is a matter of re-seeing the subject—as it now stands, as you've expressed and organized it. No matter how much revision you may have done as you worked on the first draft, we believe it's good advice to set material aside and return to it later—several hours, or even several days later if possible—to gain distance and objectivity. Most of us need to see (re-see) our early drafts with fresh eyes. We need to consider our own writing as our audience might see it.

And now we've added a new factor. The *audience.*

We've been proposing that writing is an act of discovery, a way of exploring ideas and insights for yourself. The time arrives, however, when all writing must express something to another reader. In fact, most forms of writing are affected by knowledge of your potential reader's expectations right from the beginning: you write a letter to your mother differently from a letter to a bank president; you write a note to Professor Harris in the History Department differently than you write a note to your roommate. The tone, vocabulary, even organization is often determined by the reader's requirements rather than yours. Yet the ideas must come from you. That's why we've left out audience until this point. We wanted to keep attention focused on how to use writing as a thinking tool, without the distraction or pressure of audience needs.

Revision now requires you to consider both elements simultaneously. You must continue to explore the subject, and you must begin to question whether you're shaping the subject well enough for someone else to understand. Have you found a focus? Have you offered convincing examples, details, or evidence from the text? Have you quoted or paraphrased selected passages? Have you left out anything? Can you say it better?

When you're deeply involved in writing, it may not be possible to see clearly. Sometimes, asking someone else to read what you've written is the only solution. Both Dale and Kawana revised several times on their own, then shared their essays with members of their group. They knew they'd reached a stage where they could go no further without suggestions from more objective readers. In the past we've found some students uncomfortable about letting others read their papers, or about trying to "criticize" the work of their friends. Yet most professional authors provide copies of their writing to colleagues or editors for criticism and suggestions. Olivia and I certainly share our own drafts with each other. All of us need an audience to respond to our efforts, to tell us where we've done something right as well as where we can improve. The critic must point to specific phrases, sentences, concepts where you share your ideas effectively: *your introduction is exactly right; the way you've phrased this argument is clean and forceful; the transition here is really necessary.* The point is not to criticize the writer personally, but to ask questions and make suggestions about the writing: *Did you mean to say this or that? Can you find a better example to support your point? Is the first paragraph necessary?* The goal is not to hurt each other, but to help each other. After all, a university is intended, in part, to be a place where ideas are shared, tested, argued over, and refined. Offering up early drafts for examination by fellow students is an important step into the life of the mind. Admitting the need for help is an act of maturity. Being able to learn from others is an act of intellectual vitality.*

Everyone liked Dale's essay. No one disagreed with his ideas, but several said the points were difficult to follow, mainly because he hadn't included enough evidence. He had tended to speculate abstractly without providing concrete examples. Kawana pointed out that Dale had written about "concepts" (stereotyping and invisibility) without relating them clearly to Orwell's essay.

Kawana's essay stirred more controversy. Her final insights were totally unexpected. Both Dale and Margerie Panhower argued that to be convincing, Kawana had to slow down and show—step by step—how she came to her conclusions. And Margerie suggested the essay would be stronger if Kawana tied it into the black experience in America.

Neither Dale nor Kawana were too pleased about having to rewrite one more time, but both later agreed that their final essays were much improved because of it. Many have argued that real writing doesn't begin until revision begins. We're not certain about that. We are certain that until you've revised—usually several times—you haven't acted in a professional manner. The work you do always represents who you are to others. To submit a discovery draft as a final draft is simply unacceptable. The act of revising signals you've committed yourself to a higher level of intellectual integrity.

THE FORMAL ESSAY

We once served as advisors to several students selected as interns by a major publishing house. The students had been among our very best in a sixteen-week freshman writing course. To our surprise, after serving only four weeks as assistants to professional copyeditors, our students improved as writers far beyond what we had taught. Of course we shouldn't have been surprised, but at that time we were not aware of the vital importance editing can play in improving the quality of a manuscript.

The line between revising and editing is seldom clear. Both stages are concerned with effectiveness in writing. For our purpose here, it's best to think of revision as focusing on what you say, on content, while editing is more concerned with how you say it. Editing pays close attention to details of language: sentence variety, paragraphing, unnecessary words, active verbs, and so on. Although some professional authors edit as they go along, concern for such details can sometimes overwhelm new writers. Stopping to consider whether you've chosen the perfect word can slow down the flow of ideas, even freeze the mind. It seems better for most students to hold off editing until

*We are indebted to William C. Coles, Jr. for these insights, and for numerous others throughout this text which we have no doubt absorbed from his various works, especially, *Seeing Through Writing*, Harper & Row, 1988.

the subject has been given shape and form. The mind can then concentrate on finding the most polished way of expressing the subject.

Editing

The first and most basic level of editing involves cutting unnecessary words. In drafting we often write twice as much as we need. To discover what we want to say, the mind tosses out all kinds of words. We circle about, duplicate, backtrack. And somewhere buried in there lurks an idea worth polishing.

Here's a single paragraph from Dale's zero draft. (Again, we've left in the misspellings. Proofreading will come later.)

```
What I think this quote clearly means is that we
probably create steriotypes of people and instead of
seeing the person himself we stubstitute the sterio-
type we have created for the individual--We see the
steriotype instead of the person--the person is in-
visible to us as a human being--as someone with
feelings and one who suffers or would like to have a
better life.
```

No two editors would necessarily reshape these thoughts the same way. Right and wrong answers are not at issue. But most readers would agree that by simply cutting extra words the ideas could be expressed more effectively.

Here are three possible ways of editing the first sentence:

Option one:

> ~~What I think~~ this quote ~~clearly means~~ is that we probably create steriotypes of people and instead of seeing ^a ~~the~~ person ^for himself we stubstitute ^a ~~the~~ steriotype ~~we have created~~ for the individual . . .

> What this means is that we probably create stereotypes of people and instead of seeing a person for himself, we substitute a stereotype for the individual . . .

Option two:

> ~~What~~ I think this ~~quote clearly~~ means is that we ~~probably~~ create steriotypes of people and instead of seeing ^an individual ~~the person~~ himself we stubstitute the steriotype ~~we have created for the individual~~ . . .

> I think this means that we create stereotypes of people and instead of seeing an individual for himself, we substitute the stereotype . . .

Option three:

> ~~What I think this quote~~ Orwell clearly means ~~is~~ that ~~we probably create steriotypes of people and~~ instead of seeing ~~the~~ each person for himself we stubstitute ~~the~~ a steriotype ~~we have created for the individual~~ . . .

> Orwell clearly means that instead of seeing each person for himself, we substitute a stereotype . . .

We prefer the last version. By eliminating excess words (more than half in Option Three) the original idea is expressed more economically and with greater strength. Unnecessary words are natural in a zero draft. Some may be struck down during the revision stage. But all excess—all that weedy verbiage that smothers your ideas—must be hacked away in the final editing stage. However, editing always occurs in the context of your total essay. Rigid rules seldom apply. Sometimes a preposition is grammatically necessary, sometimes it's necessary for emphasis, and sometimes it should be flung to the wind. Learn to trust your own ear. Literally. The best way to *see* problems in your writing is to *listen* to your paper. Lock yourself in a private room where no one will think you're crazy. Then read aloud, pencil in hand. The ear usually knows a weak sentence when it hears one. Or read your essay aloud to a group of your peers. Ask them to signal when a line or a phrase isn't clear or well-expressed. In general, a good essay sounds like good conversation.

The sad truth is that even the best ideas can be lost in poor prose. All the work you've done in the preparation phase—in reading thoughtfully, annotating a text, exploring questions and ideas in a notebook, discussing with others, drafting and revising—all of it can still fail to show strength of mind and effort if you fail to give final attention to small details.

Manuscript Preparation and Proofreading

Henry David Thoreau lived an odd life by most standards. He dressed to suit himself, refused to work at a steady job, and defied the advice of his friends by living alone at Walden Pond. Most people thought he was a crank. Yet when it came to his writing, Thoreau worked hard to ensure that every sentence he wrote was as perfect as he could make it. In the long run, it was the quality of his work by which people judged him.

Even if your ideas are odd or nonconforming, as Thoreau's were, the presentation of those ideas must be as clear as possible. A sloppy manuscript, careless spelling, or nonstandard grammar that fails to meet socially accepted conventions, rightly or wrongly, distracts a reader from the content—or worse—causes the reader to discount the content altogether.

There's nothing unusual or unfair about this. Few of us would pay $38,000 for a new Mercedes, or even $10,000 for a new Geo, if we discovered flawed paint, an upside down tape deck, and a missing manifold. From others we

Here's a Brief List of Simple Editing Actions You Can Take:

Cut Unnecessary Adjectives

She wore a ~~pretty~~, ~~soft~~, delicate ~~beige colored~~, angora sweater.

She wore a delicate angora sweater.

or

She wore an angora sweater.

Cut Unnecessary Adverbs

The man was ~~very~~ old and strangely dressed in ~~really~~ odd polka-dot trousers.

The man was old and dressed in odd polka-dot trousers.

or

The old man wore polka dot trousers.

Cut Unnecessary Prepositions & Articles

The university sponsors scholarships ~~to~~ assist ~~in~~ providing ~~for~~ financial aid ~~to the~~ better students.

The university sponsors scholarships for better students.

or

The university assists better students with financial aid.

Cut Unnecessary Whos, Whichs, and Thats

Dr. Kelly ~~was a man who~~ believed firmly ~~that~~ we must listen to our conscience.

Dr. Kelly firmly believed we must listen to our conscience.

expect quality in even the smallest detail. We should not be surprised when others expect quality from us.

Here's a paragraph taken from one of Dale's and Kawana's classmates, a paragraph that illustrates how even a few errors create problems for a reader:

> The thing is Orwell has not even to,d us whether we are in 20th century, I think it is. So how can we judge the accuracy of his report. This could be a limited observation that does not repressent the entire Culture. Whose to say.

The reader can only struggle along, tripping over typing errors, repeated spelling problems, and faulty syntax. Yet the student author admitted that she could have caught and corrected most of these errors if she had only reread her paper before turning it in.

In other words, the final stage in the reading and writing process requires a careful, detailed check of every word and sentence you've written. Standard usage, grammar, punctuation, and spelling, as well as proper manuscript form (described in the Appendix), will be expected of you. Dictionaries, English handbooks, and tutors are almost always available for assistance. All of us make mistakes. We have no reason to feel guilty. But the greatest error is the failure to identify and correct our mistakes.

After two weeks' work, Dale and Kawana completed their papers on Orwell's "Marrakech." Here are their final, revised, edited, and proofread copies. (And yes, Dale, with help from the writing center, did correct his spelling.) Neither paper is perfect, of course, but each in its own way reveals an attempt at growth and understanding we find commendable.

SEEING THE INVISIBLE

Dale Weaver

When George Orwell wrote "Marrakech" he saw something no one else ever saw. He saw invisible people.

But not right away.

Like other tourists he saw the scenery first. He saw the prickly pear palm, distant mountains, and desolate fields that were hard as bricks. Like other Englishmen, he saw camels, castles, the Foreign Legion, and brass trays. He saw what he went there to see. And Orwell points out that a Frenchman travelling to Marrakech would also see what he wanted to see--orange groves and a job in government service.

Orwell admits that he did not see the people. "One could probably live there for years without noticing that for nine-tenths of the people the reality of life is an endless, backbreaking struggle to wring a little food out of an eroded soil" (par. 2). In Europe you would see a farmer ploughing, but in North Africa, for some reason, you wouldn't.

Two important things happened to Orwell before he became aware of this. First, he became aware that he was feeling "his blood boil" because of how badly animals were being treated. He writes that he had not been there for five minutes when he saw donkeys treated cruelly. They were overloaded and overworked until they dropped dead. Then, one day, he saw an old lady, only four feet tall, "under a vast load of wood" (par. 4), and he gave her a penny. She was so surprised she cried out, and he realized that old ladies had been staggering past his house for days under loads of wood. "But what is strange about these people is their invisibility" (par. 5).

This statement is the key to understanding the essay. Orwell, and the other tourists, see what they have come prepared to see. But they block out anything that does not fit the pre-set picture in their mind. We create stereotypes of places and then when we visit there we don't see the real place, only the picture we have created of it. If you've ever visited New York, you set out to see the Statue of Liberty, Rockefeller Center, and Times Square--all those places you already have pre-set pictures of. The Statue of Liberty will look just like your stereotype. So will Rockefeller Center and Times Square. You will see them, check them off your list and hurry on to see the Empire State Building. You will probably also have heard of "street people" and you will see them sleeping on sidewalk grates, and because that is exactly what they do in your stereotype of them, you will mentally, unconsciously, check them off your list and hurry on by. You do not see the real New York, and you do not see the real street people.

George Orwell did not see Morocco and he did not see the condition of the Arab peasants. He says that ". . . though they had registered themselves on my eyeballs I cannot truly say that I had seen them" (par. 5). What this means is that we create stereotypes of people and then we substitute the stereotype for the individual. The actual person, whether the street person in New York, or the old lady carrying wood in Marrakech, is invisible to us as a human being with feelings. We don't see them as someone who suffers or would like to have a better life.

Only after Orwell realized that he was upset about cruel treatment to animals and that he was not upset about cruel treatment of people, did he realize that "the plight of human beings" (par. 6) did not affect him in the same way. When the old lady cried out, it was because he had noticed her. He had seen her. She was as surprised as he was because she too had accepted the stereotype of herself. It probably never occurred to her that she should or could be treated like anything other than a beast of burden.

We all know that stereotypes blind us to others, but Orwell shows us that they blind us to ourselves! The real thing that keeps us from knowing other human beings, and from knowing ourselves as whoever we really are, is a pre-set mental picture we have created of almost everything. As long as we see only pictures in the mind, the world will be invisible to all of us. I don't know how to change this, but I know it's the first step.

Dale's insight into George Orwell's essay has expanded greatly from his first notebook entry in which he said that "Marrakech" was about as interesting as *National Geographic.* In the long process of reading and rereading, writing and rewriting, discussing, and revising, Dale saw relationships and values he had never anticipated.

Here, for comparison, is Kawana's final revised and edited paper:

VIOLATING THE LAWS OF NATURE
Kawana White

On the surface, Mr. George Orwell's essay, "Marrakech," is all very clear. An Englishman visits Morocco. He enjoys palm trees and orange groves, and feels sympathy for the way donkeys are treated, and then he realizes, after "several weeks" that the dark-skinned people are far worse off than the donkeys. "Earth colored women" who are bent and shriveled up "like mummies" have filed passed his house every day carrying loads of firewood. "Brown skinned" laborers have been plowing earth as hard as broken-up bricks with "wretched wooden" ploughs. Mr. Orwell has not really been conscious of them. He saw the condition of the donkeys in five minutes but it has taken weeks for him to see the condition of human beings.

His awakening occurs one day when he sees "a poor old creature who could not have been more than four feet tall" carrying a "vast load of wood." He puts a five-sou piece ("little more than a farthing") into her hand and she responds by crying out. He calls it "a shrill wail, almost a scream" (par. 4). It is her cry that makes him begin to see her as a human being instead of just another tourist attraction. He has broken through his own prejudices. Mr. Orwell clearly means for us to be impressed by him at this point. The reader is expected to approve his actions. Unlike the other blind white men who visit Morocco, he has at least eventually *seen* the real condition of the native Arabs.

But this is the point that bothers me. I keep asking, why does this poor old woman scream? Mr. Orwell says, "I suppose that from her point of view, by taking any notice of her, I seemed almost to be violating a law of nature" (par. 4). He says "she accepted" her status as "a beast of burden," just as she accepts walking behind carrying baggage while her husband and son get to ride on donkeys. He believes she cries out because by noticing her he has failed to *accept* her condition. He thinks the cry is "partly gratitude, but mainly surprise" (par. 4) because he has not accepted her status. For the brown skinned peasants it is a law of nature that the women are subservient. They shrivel to the size of children under their treatment and they accept it in the same way the donkey's accept their treatment. And the brown skinned men also accept as part of nature that white men are in turn superior to them. I believe Mr. Orwell does not think these things are true laws of nature, but only the result of racial and sexual prejudice. That is why he points them out.

But the violation of the law of nature may not be what Mr. Orwell thinks. What if it isn't her passive acceptance that has been violated by Mr. Orwell noticing her? He writes, "I *suppose*" that she screams because he violated her passive acceptance. And he now feels superior to all those who have not discovered the same "truth." This is where he rises to his statement: "I am not commenting, merely pointing to a fact." He has discovered that dark skinned people, and especially dark skinned women, are "invisible" to white men. His discovery makes him superior. He expects our admiration for calling attention to everyone else's blindness.

But what is really going on here? Mr. Orwell, the very white English tourist has seen this poor woman's scream as gratitude and surprise for his generous act. He has seen it exactly as a white man who is suddenly superior to other white men by his act of *seeing*. But he never thinks that maybe her scream was not gratitude. That maybe her "shrill wail" was a cry of anger. Mr. Orwell says he gave her a "little more than a farthing," which is one-fourth of a penny. One-fourth of a penny! That is like Donald Trump giving a dime to the doorman of his hotel. Maybe her scream *was* partly surprise, but maybe it was also partly despair and resentment. He *supposes* she screamed because he took notice of her. But isn't the whole concept of "taking notice" of someone a concept of smug superiority? (The Queen chooses to "notice" the commoner at the ball. The commoner is supposed to feel grateful.) Doesn't Mr. Orwell's response show how distant he still is from seeing beyond the dark-skinned surface? He has *supposed* her cry was made to his generosity. But I think her response was made to his condescension and the insulting worth of his gift.

As an Afro-American woman growing up in Washington D. C., I have seen white congressmen dressed in dark suits drive through the slums in chauffeur driven limousines. These are liberals publicly outraged over black unemployment statistics. They are men who look out from behind their tinted glass windows at black men curled up on street corners and overdosed on crack. They propose 100 million dollar solutions like public housing and welfare. Then they go home feeling superior to other whites who have not *seen* the real conditions of the poor. They go home to their air-conditioned houses and swimming pools in Virginia and believe that blacks must certainly feel gratitude for what they've done. (Of course the millions for public housing goes to white contractors, and the housing is merely prefabricated slums; and the millions for welfare ensures that black women will remain below the poverty line by "giving" each of them just enough to make sure she never forgets that she's poor and black and dependent on white "generosity.") So when blacks give out a "shrill wail" the white liberals *suppose* it is one of surprise and gratitude. They have seen the truth and they have felt superior over others of their race who do not.

But the real violation of nature, for Mr. Orwell as well as for the white liberal in America, is in failing to see more than the surface conditions, and in failing to act on more than the surface, with one-fourth of a penny or 100 million dollars. Poverty and degradation are not going to be solved by "noticing" that it exists. No matter how sincere they are, a trivial generosity only embitters the people. It does not create gratitude. And an air of smug superiority over others who fail to see the poverty may be a step above blindness, but it is still myopia. Poverty and degradation destroy people's insides. You can't *see* it. You have to feel it. Mr. Orwell is not "commenting" about this, only pointing to facts. Here are his facts: "earth colored bodies," "back-breaking struggle," "frightful labour." Just the facts. Just pointing to the facts for informational purposes. But not the feelings. The feelings are inside the people; feelings of despair, shame, suffering, hopelessness and hatred.

I think the real violation of nature is Mr. Orwell's violation of his own humanness; he never *feels* the deep and painful sympathy he ought to feel, which ought to make him want to make a comment, a very loud and angry comment from the rooftops. Something like a shrill wail.

The acts of reading and writing are part of an integrated process of thinking, reflecting, revising. Our understanding of a text evolves, just as our understanding of ourselves must evolve if we are to be fully alive. Writing is central to the process because it engages our imagination. Only when we imaginatively interact with the original author's words and images, only when we immerse ourselves in a process of exploration, opening our minds to opportunity for growth in perception and feeling, can we reach a fuller understanding of who we are now, and what we believe.

Reminders

The writing process is not mysterious. It takes only a willingness to explore ideas with an open mind, and a commitment to hard work.

- Begin by getting words on the page. Whether you make lists, draw diagrams, or write doggerel, let writing activate the mind.
- Focus in on what you care about; if the idea is dull to you, it will be dull to your reader. The quality of your work will be determined by the spirit you invest in it.
- Revise, revise, revise.
- Consider your audience; anticipate their needs and expectations.
- Ask friends to critique your working copy; consider their suggestions as good faith efforts to help you improve.
- Revise again if necessary.
- Edit to improve the flow and strength of every sentence.
- Cut unnecessary words.
- Prepare your manuscript by proofreading for spelling, grammar, usage and other socially expected standards.

CHAPTER 3

HABITS OF MIND

THOUGHTFUL READING

Imagine a key. The key lies at the edge of a carpet, silver in the moonlight. A few feet away, in dark blue shadows, lies the body of a woman. A figure bends over her. He wears a mask and black gloves. In the distance, through open balcony doors, the sound of waves lap against a dock. The figure hurries onto the balcony. He glances back and hesitates, caught in sudden moonlight. Near the carpet's edge he sights the key. For a moment it's clear he plans to return. The latch of a doorway opening somewhere in the house stops him. He hears laughter from two young girls coming down a hall. One last time he looks at the key and then springs over the side of the balcony.

Such a scene could easily be taken from the first page of a mystery novel. In reading it, most of us would perform certain mental acts. We would probably question the meaning of the key at the edge of the carpet, even before we knew there was a body. Then we would question who the body belonged to. Was she dead or drugged? Had she merely fainted? We would surely be suspicious of the masked figure. We might hypothesize obvious possibilities: a murder or burglary. And who are the girls coming down the hall? Their laughter suggests innocence, although that may be a ploy. One of them could be in on the crime. Either way, we anticipate they'll discover the body. The key near the carpet seems to suggest more than a random break-in: the dark figure clearly wants it, was perhaps searching for it. Something has preceded this event. The key will figure later, although we have no idea why.

All these questions and hypotheses occur silently and almost simultaneously. As we move from sentence to sentence, we form predictions of what we expect in future pages. And we make connections back to what we've just been shown. The truth is we don't really know what's going on, yet we accept the suspense, usually enjoying the delay of answers, the confusion, doubts, and surprises. We participate eagerly in the text, playing our mind against the writer's. A mystery novel may seem the simplest of formulas, yet the manner in which we "read" such a work illustrates the manner we ought to engage in when reading almost anything—from a dialogue of Socrates to a poem by Tennyson. We must become involved in scrutinizing clues offered up to us, in predicting or hypothesizing, in anticipating, questioning, and looking for relationships. The fact that we do most such acts unconsciously while reading a mystery novel, means we need learn only how to convert these natural actions of the mind to a conscious strategy of study.

Repetition and Pattern

You may remember in high school when an instructor told you never to repeat the same word twice. A good thesaurus was a must, he said. And there was much truth to what you heard. Unnecessary repetition dulls the brain, like a drum beat without variation: *dum, dum, dum, dum, dum.* But controlled repetition, *with* variation, forms the quintessential shaping of all art. You can see it most obviously in something like a plaid shirt where certain red stripes are alternated with smaller pink and black lines; the size or color is then altered for variety, only to have the original red stripes, with smaller pink and black, predictably repeated. A dancer performs a series of movements, departs from them entirely, then repeats with slight variations. A painter shapes a central curve, then in smaller and less obvious ways, repeats the curve elsewhere on the canvas. And the same is true of literature. We can say it very simply: good writers repeat. Good writers use the same word or similar words again and again to achieve shape and coherence, to reinforce ideas and emotions, and to establish the beginnings of rhythm. In an essay, the function of repetition is to communicate both clarity of idea and strength of emotion. In imaginative literature, the function may lean toward evoking feeling, but it also points toward those values and elements the author considers important.

As readers we respond to repetition and use it to hypothesize or predict. In our mystery paragraph above, the word "key" is repeated three times. No good writer would do that without expecting us to anticipate that the key will play an important role later. If the key had been mentioned only once, it might still form a significant element of the scene, but it would constitute a single clue among many, perhaps no more important than black gloves or the dock outside the balcony. As readers, we would have no way to predict which clue, if any, would ultimately prove most significant. By the third repetition, however, we have every right to anticipate that the key is crucial.

One of the first moves toward developing higher reading skills is to become conscious of this device. Consider the following excerpt from D.H. Lawrence's *The Phoenix.*

> Never shall I forget the deep singing of the men at the drum, swelling and sinking, the deepest sound I have heard in all my life, deeper than thunder, deeper than the sound of the Pacific Ocean, deeper than the roar of a deep waterfall: the wonderful deep sound of men calling to the unspeakable depths.

What do you sense going on here? If at first the repetition seems too obvious, when does the word "deep" change into something more than a mere adjective attached to sound? When does it strike you that Lawrence is not merely describing an event but attempting to share a profound emotion? Repetition in essays and in most fiction is usually less dramatic, of course. But you may remember in Chapter 2 that Dale Weaver noticed Orwell's repetition of the word "invisible." By focusing on it, Dale pried open a path into Orwell that led to his understanding of the text.

The pattern of a work, the shape of it, in part or as a whole, points toward a significant end. And all pattern is composed of repetitions of some nature—words, images, concepts, events, and so on. By making ourselves sensitive to pattern, we make our mind alert to the direction in which a writer is sending us.

Opposition and Conflict

Most human experience evolves around a struggle between individuals, between women and men, between those with money and those without, between those with power and those who seek power. Or we struggle with conflicts in ourselves: with the desire to leave home and the sense of obligation to our parents; with the temptation to seduce or be seduced and concern over the consequences of it; with the need to believe in something meningful and the difficulty of finding values in a fragmented world. Opposition and conflict then, by their very nature, are almost always the subject of essays, movies, opera, and other forms of art. Our mystery paragraph at the beginning of this chapter suggests that some kind of conflict may have just occurred and that more is to come.

Learning to identify opposing forces or ideas in a work of literature can be one of the most immediate ways into a text. Here's an excerpt from an essay by philosopher Richard Taylor in which he attempts to define "faith."

> Faith is not reason, else religion would be, along with logic and metaphysics, a part of philosophy, which it assuredly is not. Nor is faith belief resting on scientific or historical inquiry, else religion would be part of the corpus of human knowledge, which it clearly is not. More than that, it seems evident that by normal, common sense criteria of what is reasonable, the content of Christian faith is *un*reasonable.

How does Taylor use opposing functions of the mind here to draw you in? Do you agree with each point as you move from sentence to sentence? Do you accept his conclusion? More likely, you find yourself saying, Wait a minute! What does he mean here? Is this true? By shaping each sentence around opposing ideas, Taylor immediately involves you in the conflict. The entire structure—the pattern—of his essay seems established from the beginning. Or at least, as readers, we anticipate that Taylor will elaborate on what he sees as inherently opposing concepts: faith and reason.

You may recall that in Chapter 2 Kawana White focused on George Orwell's recognition that a white visitor to Morocco would not "see" a brown-skinned laborer. She might have built her own essay entirely about that opposition: dark is invisible to white. But Kawana, bringing her personal experience to bear, found what she believed to be a contradiction in Orwell's perception of events. Contradiction is another form of opposition. Kawana was therefore able to double the level of conflict, and thus doubled the resonance of her insight.

These two strategies—seeking pattern and repetition, and focusing on the opposition or conflict found in most works of literature—are strategies for increasing our ability to discriminate and make judgments about a text. Consider the following selection from *Out of Africa,* by Isak Dinesen, a Danish woman who lived most of her life in Kenya.

The Iguana

ISAK DINESEN

In the Reserve I have sometimes come upon the Iguana, the big lizards, as they were sunning themselves upon a flat stone in a river-bed. They are not pretty in shape, but nothing can be imagined more beautiful than their coloring. They shine like a heap of precious stones or like a pane cut out of an old church window. When, as you approach, they swish away, there is a flash of azure, green and purple over the stones, the color seems to be standing behind them in the air, like a comet's luminous tail.

Once I shot an Iguana. I thought that I should be able to make some pretty things from his skin. A strange thing happened then, that I have never afterwards forgotten. As I went up to him, where he was laying dead upon his stone, and actually while I was walking the few steps, he faded and grew pale, all color died out of him as in one long sigh, and by the time that I touched him he was grey and dull like a lump of concrete. It was the live impetuous blood pulsating within the animal, which had radiated out all that glow and splendor. Now that the flame was put out, and the soul had flown, the Iguana was as dead as a sandbag.

Often since I have, in some sort, shot an Iguana, and I have remembered the one of the Reserve. Up at Meru I saw a young Native girl with a bracelet on, a leather strap two inches wide, and embroidered all over with very small turquoise-colored beads which varied a little in color and played in green, light blue and ultramarine. It was an extraordinarily live thing; it seemed to draw breath on her arm, so that I wanted it for myself, and made Farah buy it from her. No sooner had it come upon my own arm than it gave up the ghost. It was nothing now, a small, cheap, purchased article of finery. It had been the play of colors, the duet between the turquoise and the "nègre",—

that quick, sweet, brownish black, like peat and black pottery, of the Native's skin,—that had created the life of the bracelet.

In the Zoological Museum of Pietermaritzburg, I have seen, in a stuffed deep-water fish in a showcase, the same combination of coloring, which there had survived death; it made me wonder what life can well be like, on the bottom of the sea, to send up something so live and airy. I stood in Meru and looked at my pale hand and at the dead bracelet, it was as if an injustice had been done to a noble thing, as if truth had been suppressed. So sad did it seem that I remembered the saying of the hero in a book that I had read as a child: "I have conquered them all, but I am standing amongst graves."

In a foreign country and with foreign species of life one should take measures to find out whether things will be keeping their value when dead. To the settlers of East Africa I give the advice: "For the sake of your own eyes and heart, shoot not the Iguana."

We asked our class to read and write about Dinesen's experience. Here's how Marianne Clampitt explored the piece in her reading notebook. (Marianne had raised a family and returned to college to complete a degree in art history, begun some twenty years earlier.)

This reminds me of a grand uncle of mine who lived in the Smokey Mountains. He took me squirrel hunting once and I was excited (I was six or seven) and I thought the squirrels were wonderful and beautiful. But after my uncle shot one of the squirrels, I got sick to my stomach. The eye of the squirrel was all bloody and I hadn't realized that shooting it would mean it would die.

Dinesen has this same experience. First with the Iguana and then with the bracelet. Although one thing I don't understand is where the fish comes in. The three examples ought to reinforce each other, but the fish doesn't seem to work. She says that it was a stuffed fish in a museum--hence good and dead--but that the coloring (which I think she means was the same as the bracelet) "had survived death." So here something has been killed and all the life has not gone out of it. I'm not sure what's going on.

Dinesen gives us a concept about destroying beauty by capturing it, by taking it out of its natural setting, or by literally killing it. The last line hits us over the head with the point: "For the sake of your own eyes and heart, shoot not the Iguana." But the fish contradicts it all. And the fish is inserted in the middle of the example about the bracelet. So doesn't it prove her wrong even while she's trying to make her point? There's something I just don't get, I suppose. What ought to be a simple little moral is either botched, or more complex than I understand.

How is Marianne approaching the text here? Why does she begin with a brief memory of her own, so totally outside the context of Dinesen's essay? And why does she seem puzzled about the pattern within the context? Why not ignore the fish since other examples seem to prove the point?

To find answers, Marianne may need to allow the essay to incubate for awhile in the back of her mind, or discuss the text with others. In either case, we think Marianne is doing two things right.

First, she brings her own experience to bear on the text, testing it against something from her past. And that experience seems to confirm Dinesen's: an inherent opposition exists between certain forms of beauty and the attempt to capture or preserve it.

Second, she consciously relates the pattern of the text to what the words seem to say on the surface. Marianne finds a traditional structure of three examples. For some reason, three seems to be a magic number. Authors have been using three examples to prove a point since Aristotle. Marianne's instincts are correct: three examples form a pattern of repetition, signaling the direction the author is moving in. But only if all three support each other. What seems to be a break or "variation" in the pattern will either prove to strengthen the essay—if it can be demonstrated that the variation expands our insight—or to weaken the essay—if in fact it does not adequately support the theme.

Key Passages

Somehow, from our own college experience, we always thought that to talk about a text well, we had to talk about all of it. We thought a good critic started at the beginning and worked through to the last line. In fact, a better way into any text lies in focusing on a "key passage," one that illuminates the work as a whole.* A key passage may consist of almost anything: a single sentence, a phrase, an image, an event, an exchange of dialogue, even a paragraph of description. Kawana White, you'll remember, began with one passage ("I am not commenting, merely pointing to a fact") and found that after seeing it in light of another ("I seem to be violating a law of nature") she had discovered a whole new way into Orwell's essay.

But how do you locate one of these seemingly magic passages? How do you choose one to work with? How do you know you've selected the best one? Authors don't place stars around them.

The answer is, there's no answer. No single line or phrase is the correct key to the work. Instead, you choose a passage because in some way it affects you. It evokes in you personally a strong response: anger, deep feeling, confirmation of beliefs, disagreement, bewilderment. You begin with the center in yourself and then you test it against other parts of the text. *Why does this passage make me feel the way it does? What is it about me (or the text) that calls up such a feeling? What am I really being shown here? Why is it phrased like this? Does it have meaning at all? Does it connect to the opening scene? How does it relate to X later? How does it relate to Y at the beginning? Or to the dialogue spoken by Z? What truth am I being shown? Is it a truth? Is the author (or character) mistaken? Does it cast light on why the author later says A or B or C? Does the author mean what he or she says? Is it irony or sleight-of-hand? Does this remind me of something I've read elsewhere? How does it connect to my own life? To what I've always thought was true? Am I being shown something here that makes me reconsider?*

Only by pushing questions beyond what you think your mind can answer will you find deeper and more important relationships, the ones that go beyond mere surface polishing. Only by allowing the questions themselves to modify and change as you go along, following new paths (sometimes dead-end paths) will you cut through the conventional answers of popular culture and find those answers that are significant to your own heart.

At times, of course, nothing will come of it. The passage may lead nowhere. Or your questions may need further revision. You may need to talk about the passage with others. You may need to give it time to incubate in the back of your mind before pushing forward.

In any case the goal is not so much to make brief comments about the passage itself, but to use the passage as a lever that pries open entry into the complete text. The key passage, charged with possibilities, becomes a focus for an extended exploration. The goal is to probe all possible ways in which the selected passage reaches forward or back in the text, to discover how it relates to other actions, events, ideas or emotions, and how, by seeing such relationships, we come to know the text better.

*For this highly valuable strategy we want to acknowledge Benjamin DeMott, a nationally known teacher and writer, who has been using the concept of "key passages" for over twenty years.

Here's a brief short story that might illustrate how it's done. Sherwood Anderson was one of a new generation of writers at the beginning of the 20th century who inspired authors such as Hemingway and Faulkner. We asked our class to read the story thoughtfully.

Paper Pills

SHERWOOD ANDERSON

He was an old man with a white beard and huge nose and hands. Long before the time during which we will know him, he was a doctor and drove a jaded white horse from house to house through the streets of Winesburg. Later he married a girl who had money. She had been left a large fertile farm when her father died. The girl was quiet, tall, and dark, and to many people she seemed very beautiful. Everyone in Winesburg wondered why she married the doctor. Within a year after the marriage she died.

The knuckles of the doctor's hand were extraordinarily large. When the hands were closed they looked like clusters of unpainted wooden balls as large as walnuts fastened together by steel rods. He smoked a cob pipe and after his wife's death sat all day in his empty office close by a window that was covered with cobwebs. He never opened the window. Once on a hot day in August he tried but found it stuck fast and after that he forgot all about it.

Winesburg had forgotten the old man, but in Doctor Reefy there were the seeds of something very fine. Alone in his musty office in the Heffner Block above the Paris Dry Goods Company's Store, he worked ceaselessly, building up something that he himself destroyed. Little pyramids of truth he erected and after erecting knocked them down again that he might have the truths to erect other pyramids.

Doctor Reefy was a tall man who had worn one suit of clothes for ten years. It was frayed at the sleeves and little holes had appeared at the knees and elbows. In the office he wore also a linen duster with huge pockets into which he continually stuffed scraps of paper. After some weeks the scraps of paper became little hard round balls, and when the pockets were filled he dumped them out upon the floor. For ten years he had but one friend, another old man named John Spaniard who owned a tree nursery. Sometimes, in a playful mood, old Doctor Reefy took from his pockets a handful of the paper balls and threw them at the nursery man. "That is to confound you, you blithering old sentimentalist," he cried, shaking with laughter.

The story of Doctor Reefy and his courtship of the tall dark girl who became his wife and left her money to him is a very curious story. It is delicious, like the twisted little apples that grow in the orchards of Winesburg. In the fall one walks in the orchards and the ground is hard with frost underfoot. The apples have been taken from the trees by the pickers. They have been put in barrels and shipped to the cities where they will be eaten in apartments that are filled with books, magazines, furniture, and people. On the trees are only a few gnarled apples that the pickers have rejected. They look like the knuckles of Doctor Reefy's hands. One nibbles at them and they are delicious. Into a little round place at the side of the apple has been gathered all of its sweetness. One runs from tree to tree over the frosted ground picking the gnarled, twisted apples and filling his pockets with them. Only the few know the sweetness of the twisted apples.

The girl and Doctor Reefy began their courtship on a summer afternoon. He was forty-five then and already he had begun the practice of filling his pockets with the scraps of paper that became hard balls and were thrown away. The habit had been formed as he sat in his buggy behind the jaded grey horse and went slowly along country roads. On the papers were written thoughts, ends of thoughts, beginnings of thoughts.

One by one the mind of Doctor Reefy had made the thoughts. Out of many of them he formed a truth that arose gigantic in his mind. The truth clouded the world. It became terrible and then faded away and the little thoughts began again.

The tall dark girl came to see Doctor Reefy because she was in the family way and had become frightened. She was in that condition because of a series of circumstances also curious.

The death of her father and mother and the rich acres of land that had come down to her had set a train of suitors on her heels. For two years she saw suitors almost every evening. Except two they were all alike. They talked to her of passion and there was a strained eager quality in their voices and in their eyes when they looked at her. The two who were different were much unlike each other. One of them, a slender young man with white hands, the son of a jeweler in Winesburg, talked continually of virginity. When he was with her he was never off the subject. The other, a black-haired boy with large ears, said nothing at all but always managed to get her into the darkness where he began to kiss her.

For a time the tall dark girl thought she would marry the jeweler's son. For hours she sat in silence listening as he talked to her and then she began to be afraid of something. Beneath his talk of virginity she began to think there was a lust greater than in all the others. At times it seemed to her that as he talked he was holding her body in his hands. She imagined him turning it slowly about in the white hands and staring at it. At night she dreamed that he had bitten into her body and that his jaws were dripping. She had the dream three times then she became in the family way to the one who said nothing at all but who in the moment of his passion actually did bite her shoulder so that for days the marks of his teeth showed.

After the tall dark girl came to know Doctor Reefy it seemed to her that she never wanted to leave him again. She went into his office one morning and without her saying anything he seemed to know what had happened to her.

In the office of the doctor there was a woman, the wife of the man who kept the bookstore in Winesburg. Like all old-fashioned country practitioners, Doctor Reefy pulled teeth, and the woman who waited held a handkerchief to her teeth and groaned. Her husband was with her and when the tooth was taken out they both screamed and blood ran down on the woman's white dress. The tall dark girl did not pay any attention. When the woman and the man had gone the doctor smiled. "I will take you driving into the country with me," he said.

For several weeks the tall dark girl and the doctor were together almost every day. The condition that had brought her to him passed in an illness, but she was like one who has discovered the sweetness of the twisted apples, she could not get her mind fixed again upon the round perfect fruit that is eaten in the city apartments. In the fall after the beginning of her acquaintanceship with him she married Doctor Reefy and in the following spring she died. During the winter he read to her all of the odds and ends of thoughts he had scribbled on the bits of paper. After he had read them he laughed and stuffed them away in his pockets to become round hard balls.

After our students had completed Anderson's story, we asked them to write a brief initial response in their reading notebooks, then to read the story again with pencil in hand, annotating it fully. As an exercise we asked them—on the second reading—to select one or two key passages, anything that struck them personally which they could explore in their reading notebooks. We stressed there were no right answers here. We were not "testing" them to see if they could find "hidden" meanings. We were only asking that each individual plunge into the story and explore its possibilities. Here is how Esther Stein wrote about it. (Esther was a freshman from a well-to-do community near San Francisco.)

First reading

My first response to Sherwood Anderson's "Paper Pill" is not very positive. The story is ancient history. It hasn't got much to do with today. Country doctors who pull teeth, girls who get "in the family way." I mean, come on! This story may have meant something when virginity was golden, but what can it mean to us? It's even hard for me to think this is the way it was in earlier times. I kind of like the doctor although I don't have any idea why he stuffs paper in his pockets, but I liked him for pulling out that old bag's tooth and getting blood on her white dress. The girl, I just don't understand, I guess she couldn't get an abortion. After she marries the doctor she dies in childbirth. The story doesn't say what happened to the baby. Maybe the doctor stuffed it in his pocket and forgot it. Several of my friends in high school had abortions before the end of our senior year. It's hard to take this horse-and-buggy stuff seriously.

Second reading

She had a miscarriage. I missed that the first time. I just realized she doesn't have a name. Is that significant? I liked the doctor even more. He didn't have to marry her. He married her for reasons that aren't clear, but I think are there.

I'm not sure what the best key passage is but I think the one about the gnarled apples is interesting.

> On the trees are only a few gnarled apples that the pickers have rejected. They look like the knuckles of Doctor Reefy's hands. One nibbles them and they are delicious. Into a little round place at the side of the apple has been gathered all of its sweetness. . . . Only the few know the sweetness of the twisted apples.

This passage comes at the end of a paragraph that starts with the author saying the courtship of the girl and Doctor Reefy is curious and delicious, like "the twisted little apples." So I think the story itself relates to the apples. But so do the

Doctor's knuckles which are swollen up like the apples. At the end the girl loves the doctor because she "has discovered the sweetness of the twisted apples." But I'm not sure why. (Maybe she has a fetish for knuckles.) And what do they have to do with paper pills? Are the thoughts he writes on them sweet thoughts? And if so, why does he throw them away? Why not show them to the girl? Why is the baby lost in a miscarriage, and then the girl dies without explanation? The author could have made her die from childbirth if he needed to bump her off. And what does it have to do with the two lovers, the virgin superman and the dark little fellow who bites her on the shoulder? (Why do I never meet that kind?)

—How are the apples like paper pills? Maybe because they are rejects with sweet thoughts inside.

—How are the apples like the girl? They are sweet but rejected (pregnant).

—How are the apples like the doctor? Maybe because they are sweet inside but old and strange outside (he was 45 and unmarried)

—Why does the doc throw away the paper pills? They contain truths, but he knows no one will accept them, like the twisted apples, people only want the bright shiny apples, so his thoughts are rejected

—Because both the girl and the doc are rejected, they find the sweetness in each other

—But how does it all connect to the truths written on the papers? What truths? What is the truth in this?

I'm exhausted.

Esther has taken the plunge and found more than she expected. In fact, after discussing the story with her group, she wrote several more pages in her reading notebook, using her key passage to comment on almost every aspect of the story. Other students chose different passages and found different relationships. The details for many became rich and meaningful. The values of the story began to seem charged with larger implications.

Reminders

All these approaches to reading thoughtfully are means to a single goal: to give you additional strategies for improving critical discrimination and judgment.

- Train yourself to be sensitive to controlled repetition: key words, phrases, or ideas that acquire significance and alert you to an author's central concerns.
- Watch for structural patterns, often revealed through repetition and variation. The pattern of a work (the organization of ideas, examples, events, or emotions) often provides deeper insights or—when it's lacking—may reveal weaknesses in the author's thinking.
- Identify opposition or conflict when it exists (and it almost always does). Such patterns can serve as a focus for clarifying the text.
- After you annotated a text, use a key passage to open up the fullness of it:

  *—**Select** a passage (conversation, phrase, description, sentence) that evokes in you a special responsiveness: anger, puzzlement, sorrow, enlightenment. Which passage seems at the center of the work for you? Or focuses your feelings about the text?*

  *—**Question** how the passage connects to events, actions, or ideas throughout the rest of the text. Push your questions one step beyond what you think you can answer. Allow the questions to modify and change as you go along.*

  *—**Relate** the passage to other elements in the work to reveal its interconnectedness or to expose its lack of wholeness. Let the passage lead you to insights as you reflect upon its implications.*

FOCUSED WRITING

We worry about misleading students. Like other instructors, we often divide a discussion of formal papers into various categories. We point to the introduction, body, and conclusion as if writing consisted of an assemblage of parts. *(Attach frame to rim while inserting tab through slot.)* Yet in writing, such divisions are arbitrary and none more so than discussion of form and content. The search for truth is not separate from the search for language to express it in. Thought must be given shape before it has meaning to either writer or reader. Thought without order, without form, is not truly thought at all. And form without thought is empty, like a vase without flowers. That's why we've emphasized the need for keeping a reader's notebook.

Drafting and Form

Exploring your feelings on paper from the beginning of every reading project sets in motion the process of thinking (of giving form, no matter how rough, to initial hunches) which can eventually bear fruit in a formal paper. The best organization, the most natural form is one that grows out of the excitement you feel when you attempt to frame the motions of your heart. After privately exploring in your notebook your initial reactions to what you've read, after discussing ideas and concepts with others, and giving further reflection on what you've heard (further reflection in writing, that is), after investing so much intellectual vitality, the focus for a formal paper should already be emerging. Ideally, the discovery draft should be a continuation of efforts already begun in the notebook.

Drafting should be a continuation of the struggle to sharpen insights that might not have emerged if you had not begun to write. The very act of writing a draft usually initiates an organization you could not have preplanned. Such an organization is called "organic," meaning it grows naturally out of the seed you've planted, as the shape of an oak tree grows naturally from an acorn.

Of course it doesn't always happen that way. And even when it does, certain fundamentals will still be expected of you, certain requirements by your audience. This is especially true in an academic world where professors in almost every discipline (from psychology to chemistry) hold certain expectations about how a paper ought to be organized—and even about how it ought to appear on the page. Yet those needs and expectations are no more nor less arbitrary than those you might encounter in, say, a major corporation where the company president demands that all reports submitted to her be limited to two pages. And students who want to become lawyers will find that legal briefs have highly traditional forms and requirements that an attorney deviates from only at great risk.

Attempting to satisfy audience expectations may at first seem irritating. But in truth, as you shape ideas according to a standard required by your reader, you'll usually find that the thoughts themselves quicken and clarify. Here are some of the fundamentals that are expected of you when writing a formal essay for a college professor.

The Introduction

After days of effort on a paper, it's easy to become so absorbed that you forget others are not equally immersed in the same discoveries. One student recently began an essay for us like this:

> I don't see what he means here when he says that style is unimportant. No matter how many times you read it, the words slip away.

Without an introduction, we were lost. What had the student been reading? Who was the author? What was the context? And why would we want to read further since nothing made sense?

On the most basic level introductions are matters of courtesy. Most conventional introductions in the academic world consist of three components:

(a) the author's name and the title of the work you plan to discuss;
(b) a brief overview of the issue or text you plan to write about;
(c) a focus, direct or implied, that points toward where the paper is going, where these thoughts will lead us, and why it might be important.

Here's an example of how Esther Stein might have organized the introduction to her paper on Sherwood Anderson to include all the basics.

Author's name & title	After a first reading, Sherwood Anderson's "Paper Pills" seems quaint and unrelated to today.
Overview	Anderson tells how a Doctor in a small Ohio town writes fragments of thoughts on scraps of paper, saves them in his pocket until they become hard little "pills," then throws them away while riding in his horse and buggy. When he meets a young girl "in the family way" they fall in love and marry, but she dies within a year. The doctor then

	goes back to writing his thoughts--"terrible truths"--on
Focus	scraps of paper. But the simplicity of Anderson's story is deceptive, and its connection to our lives today is more than might first be apparent.

In only five sentences we have all the basic introductory elements a reader might need. We know who and what the student is going to write about. We know the general outline of events so that as the student goes on to discuss various details, we'll be able to place them in the context of the story. And in the final sentence we have a clear focus for the rest of the paper.

The order of introductory information can vary of course. Here's how Marianne Clampett might have shaped the introduction to her paper on Isak Dinesen's essay:

Overview	If you want something beautiful, you must let it go. The colors of a lizard fade as soon as it is killed. A bracelet taken from the arm of a lovely girl seems
Author's name & title	dull in its own right. Isak Dinesen learns this the hard way in her essay, "The Iguana," a
Focus	selection taken from <u>Out of Africa</u>. And she's right. I have learned the same lesson.

Clearly, it doesn't matter which order the three basics are presented in, only that all three are offered to the reader early in a formal paper. The goal is clarity as well as courtesy. And we have to admit that very often, a simple presentation of author and title, brief overview, and focus—as we've tried to show in these two examples—may work best. If you simply can't find your way into a discovery draft, use the conventions. Let them organize your way into writing.

Yet we feel compelled to say that by limiting yourself to dry conventions you may risk losing liveliness, a sense of personal voice, and an originality of individual perception. Here's our advice then: begin your discovery draft any way you want; use your imagination; plunge into the heart of the matter that has concerned you for so long in your reader's notebook. Make the introduction your own. And then—in the revision process—make an absolutely essential, conscious effort to plug in any of the necessary courtesies you've not already included: author, title, and so on. Adapt the conventions to your own beginning, ease them in, and work them over until they sound natural. But retain the vital liveliness of your own voice, your own emotional commitment to the subject.

Here's how Marianne Clampett actually wrote her introduction to Dinesen's essay. Compare it to the version we constructed above. Both provide necessary requirements for a reader's needs, but instead of writing from a formula, Clampett speaks from the heart.

> I am haunted by the image, and yet it's nothing more than two simple sentences. Not even my sentences. They begin an essay by Isak Dinesen.
>
> > Once I shot an iguana. I thought that I should be able to make some pretty things from his skin.
>
> It all seems so simple, yet it brings back memories I had long forgotten. I was six or seven. A grand uncle of mine, Uncle Fletch Sleuder, took me squirrel hunting in the Smokey Mountains. I thought squirrels were lovely. They danced from branch to branch like tree kittens, fluffing their tails, as if taunting us, daring us to catch them. I thought of them as personal pets. Somehow, I had the impression that "going hunting" for them would make them mine forever. I thought that in shooting one, I would carry it home in my arms and it would purr and lick my face in the warm afternoon light.
>
> But Isak Dinesen describes the reality of shooting to kill. In her essay, "The Iguana," she tells how the brilliant colors of the Iguana faded

> almost instantly after it was shot. And she recalls other instances in Africa where in wanting to claim something beautiful as her own, she destroyed its beauty. The lesson is a simple one. Uncle Fletch Sleuder--a religious old man who never missed reading his Bible--would have told me if I had asked.

How do you know you're listening to a real human being here instead of a robot filling in the blanks? What has Clampett done to speak in her own voice? How does she get away with postponing the overview (the context) of Dinesen's essay until the third paragraph? Should it have been offered sooner? In our fictional introduction, we constructed a clear and simple focus. How does Clampett suggest the same focus without ever coming out and saying it?

Clampett's essay is printed in full starting on page 77. You might also want to look at the actual introduction Esther Stein used in her essay on Sherwood Anderson (page 80). Both students include all the necessary basics for clarity, yet both capture the reader's interest by using their own natural voices. And in this case, both have adapted material from their reader's notebook. At the very least, you must include the conventions. At the very best, you should include your imagination.

The Body of the Essay

We've often wished the traditional term for the major portion of an essay was something other than "body." It sounds so dead, lying there naked and headless. But the central core of an essay can't be dead, or deadening, any more than an introduction can. If we compare an introduction to a camcorder taking a panoramic survey of the whole scene, the body of an essay can be thought of as a zoom lens focusing in on various specific details—on a key passage or on special terms, events, examples, actions, or arguments. Each detail must be seen clearly by the reader. Each must be discussed, analyzed, or compared to another element. And before the camera moves away to focus on something else, the significance of each detail must be made perfectly clear or importance suggested in such a way that the reader knows further observations and insights will be forthcoming. Again, the organization of all this may flow naturally, organically, out of your deep investment in the subject. But certain conventions continue to be expected of you. The most traditional organization has three components, and these stages apply not only to the paper as a whole, but to each subpoint within the body:

> **Tell the reader something.** Make an observation. What's the point? What have you noticed or become aware of? What context does the point occur in? That is, where does it occur in the essay or story or poem? Remember that giving the context not only clarifies for the reader, it affects the way we understand the point itself.

Show it (or demonstrate it). What evidence do you have to support your observation? Summarize specific examples, events, actions, statements. Integrate key quotations from the text.

Share your thoughts and feelings. Why is this point significant? What do we learn by having focused in on it? If you're writing about an essay or factual work, can you analyze the specific idea you're considering for its logic? How sound is the evidence the author provides? How does the author's argument here relate to other arguments later? If you're writing about fiction, poetry, or drama, how does the incident or language or whatever reveal some insight into character? How does the event build toward a particular emotional response? What does it all suggest?

Tell, Show, Share could be phrased with more intellectual pomp: *Make a Statement, Provide Supporting Evidence, Discuss or Assess the Meaning.* However you want to phrase it, the final step in this conventional pattern is the crucial element, the point where your personal response and interpretation take over. Yet without the first two components, the reader is usually lost. All three are needed for clarity.

Consider the following example taken from a paper by freshman Sherman Caulfield. Sherman had read William Kotzwinkle's *Swimmer in the Secret Sea* where he found that sea imagery surrounding the birth of a child was for him an important way into understanding the novella. In this portion of his essay, he begins by focusing on how Laski, an expectant father, participates in his wife's long and agonizing labor. Watch how each movement, from point to point, from paragraph to paragraph, repeats the conventional organization: Sherman makes an observation, supports it with evidence, and then shares his thoughts about it.

Observation	Kotzwinkle illuminates Laski's suffering by using the sea as a metaphor:
Supporting evidence	The wave came again and carried them out into the sea of pain, where he wondered again why life ever came into the world," and "the tide that drew them out into the troubled waters once again spent itself and they floated slowly back, resting for a minute. . . .

Discussion

Perhaps many of us deal with pain, discomfort, in much the same way, floating on it, carried along without resistance. But Kotzwinkle's metaphor goes further because it begins to show in a subtle way a deeper side of Laski's character. Kotzwinkle prepares us for later discovering that Laski's "floating" is actually an escapism into dreams.

Observation

Yet the sea imagery has many more sides to it. Kotzwinkle often uses the sea as suggestive of God. After being

Supporting evidence

sent out of the birthing room by the doctor, Laski paces in the hallway and "gathered himself together in a single prayer without words, offered to the ocean." At first glance, a

Discussion

prayer to an ocean might seem strange, but if we think of ocean as an all-surrounding greatness, something so much larger than ourselves as to be awesome and incomprehensible, then the prayer makes sense.

Observation

Laski also sees ocean and sea imagery as aspects of love,

and of the mystery of life in general. He thinks of the yet unborn baby and his "heart became an ocean of love." In his imagination he even sees the child as a "swimmer in the secret sea." Why so much emphasis on the sea? Is Laski's "ocean" of love referring to the "ideal" of love? When Laski says, "we're not across the ocean yet," is he saying wait a minute, life is not over yet, we still have a long way to go? Does Kotzwinkle feel we are all swimmers subject to possibly being drowned by the unknown? Does Kotzwinkle feel that all of us swim in a secret sea, or secret life? Does he feel we don't know what life holds for us, so it is secret? Kotzwinkle makes me think so. Because Laski does not yet know his child, and in the same way, few people know the "secrets of the sea."

Supporting evidence

Discussion

Sherman's study is complex and detailed. The more difficult an interpretation, the better advised you are to keep the conventions before you. A traditional organization provides clarity. It can help both you and your audience follow an argument. Yet your own vitality should not be drowned in conformity. In the best essays, standard conventions are usually absorbed into the voice and style of the author. Each component is blended until the ingredients make up a whole cake—until no one aspect or ingredient is separate from another.

Here, for example, is how Esther Stein handled a portion of her essay on Anderson's "Paper Pills." Stein has just described how the doctor and the tall dark girl have found a "sweetness" in each other, and then lost it because the girl has died less than a year after marriage.

Observation	The sweetness is momentary, and maybe more sweet because of it. But the doctor already knows all that. He knew it even before he met the girl. He wrote thoughts
Supporting evidence	on scraps of paper, "truths" that "arose gigantic in his mind: The truth clouded the world. It became terrible and then faded away. . . ." These truths were also like the
Second observation	gnarled apples. They were rejects that he knew no one would accept. People only want the
Discussion	bright shiny apples, the pleasant ones that look like all the other apples. No one wants to eat gnarled, twisted little rejects. No one wants to hear the "terrible" truths that don't make us happy. Yet they are truths nonetheless. The bright shiny apples are actually illusions. The truths are harder to find and more random, like apples in a frosted field, and

```
most of us do not want them. We
reject them for something more
comforting.
```

Traditional form should assist you, not dominate you. If you're the kind for whom the best ideas come early—when writing your discovery draft—then ignore form and go for content. Get ideas on the page in your own best way. The revision stage will become the place to double-check. Have you included all necessary requirements for a reader to follow your discussion? If not, make adjustments to your essay without erasing the sense of excitement, the sense of yourself that gives a paper vitality.

On the other hand, if you're the type for whom a discovery draft has no vitality at all, who find your early drafts muddy and stupid, do not despair. The French poet Valery said he had to rewrite dozens of times to give a work a sense of spontaneity, to make it sound as if it had flowed naturally from his pen. All that matters is that you follow your own best way of working. And at the appropriate point, remember your audience. Remember the reader's needs and expectations. Remember the conventions and use them to your best advantage.

Using Quotations

As you read a text, certain details take on importance; specific events, scenes, lines of dialogue, or points of argument become central to your personal response. For a reader to understand and appreciate your "reading" of the text, these same details, these specifics, must be included in your essay. Some details may be paraphrased (rephrased) in your own words. Much will be summarized. But to create a sense of precision and close reading, you will also need to include key quotations. Too many quotations, of course, can overwhelm a reader. Too few, or none, can make a paper seem vague and unconvincing. In some way, you'll need to find a balance, sprinkling quoted phrases or key words here and there, summarizing elsewhere, and sometimes providing a longer, essential quotation in its entirety.

Quotations that stand alone, however, without an introduction, context, or identification of speaker, often confuse the reader. Here's one that begins a paragraph in the middle of a student paper on Kaye Gibbons' novel, *Ellen Foster.*

```
"All I know now is that I want Starletta in my house
and if she tells me to I will lick the glass she
used just to show that I love her . . . just the way
she is." I feel this is an important quote.
```

About all we can say is, "Well, maybe." But who is Starletta? Where in the story does the quotation occur? And why is it important? This student writer presumably knows, but as readers we can't look inside his head. He has failed to consider the needs of his audience.

Integrating quotations into an essay is fairly simple when a few guidelines are kept in mind: quotations almost always need to be introduced; readers usually need to know the author or speaker (if it's not already apparent); and readers need to know the context—when and where or under what circumstances the remark is made.

Student Writer 1

Writing in 1888 about his trip to the Appalachian Mountains of North Carolina, William James remarks that his first impression is one of "unmitigated squalor." He longs for the higher culture of Boston. He wants the makings of "civilization" (par 4). But James will discover that in reality he is blind, that all of us are, to the values of a culture different from our own. "Now the blindness of human beings," he states, "is the blindness with which we all are afflicted. . . ." (par 2).

Student Writer 2

In a crucial scene early in Eva Figes' novel <u>Light</u>, the main character Auguste Monet, a 19th century impressionist painter, leaves the house before dawn. He sets up his canvas on a riverbank. He wants to catch the new light. As the morning grows, Monet becomes immersed in his painting. For the first time he realizes he has painted the light as it really is. "I have broken through the envelope," he thinks, "the opaque surface of things" (9). He feels dazzled by his discovery. It turns out to be more important than painting sunshine or water lilies. Monet has spent his life looking at the world but now he is looking through the "surface to the thing itself" (9).

How have these two students prepared readers to understand key quotations in their papers? What information do they provide so that, even if we haven't read the text the students are analyzing, we could follow the discussion without feeling lost? How have they blended quotations into the flow of their own voice?

We have no need to set up arbitrary rules about all of this. What is necessary is to keep your audience in mind. How much does the reader need to know to follow, step-by-step, the discussion being presented? The best assumption you should make is that your reader is intelligent, but may not recently have read the text you're working with, may not have read it at all, and even if he or she has read it, will not have responded as you have. Don't *assume* your audience remembers all the characters, recalls the sequence of the narrative, or has perceived the argument with the same insights you have.

Finally, we have a great deal of flexibility in how to integrate quotations into our own work, but the truth is we have no choice at all about their accuracy. Quotations must be exact. A word or phrase out of place can change the meaning, and just as we owe certain courtesies to our readers, we owe an absolute courtesy to an author being quoted. In an academic community, to misquote or distort an author's words is an intellectual sin: *Thall shalt not misquote.*

No one will ever praise you for accuracy, of course, while everyone will condemn you for error. Fortunately, virtue is easy to attain. Simply reread every quotation you've copied out. Always double-check for accuracy (including the line, page, or paragraph number) and you'll be on the side of angels.

Conclusions

If the introduction and body of an essay often flow naturally from deep immersion in the subject, a writer never hopes more for that flow than at the conclusion. Nothing else can truly guide you through a final paragraph but the intense inner energy that has carried you through the argument of your essay itself. To be effective, a conclusion must grow out of all the preceding points and details discussed and reflected on. Few if any rules exist. Yet we can offer suggestions.

For example, it's usually best to avoid the trite and commonplace such as, "In conclusion I have proven that. . . ." And if possible, avoid reducing your thoughts to a single, simplistic moral, especially a cliched moral: "Love is forever." Or, "Love is fleeting."

Often, the most effective ending will in some way recall the introduction, recast the title of the paper, or echo some early phrase or image. Marianne Clampett's essay on "The Iguana," for example, includes this sentence at the end of her introduction:

> Uncle Fletch Sleuder, a religious old man who never missed reading his Bible, would have told me if I had asked him.

The final two sentences of her conclusion read like this:

> You cannot capture beauty, not preserve it, not stuff it, not even really seek it, because, as my old Uncle Sleuder would have said, if I had asked him, beauty is like grace, it is given. Even a religious old man living in the woods knows that.

This technique is sometimes called theme and variation, a form of repetition that can occur at any time in an essay—a memory tag, if you will—that psychologically unites ideas or portions of a paper by using similar images or similar language. Coming at the end of an essay, it evokes a sense of completeness by "rounding back" to the beginning. We feel a deeper harmony at play. Beginning, middle, and end seem related because the language literally weaves them together. Here are the complete opening and closing paragraphs of an essay by freshman Richard Lyons.

Introduction

> The clock ticks slowly this particular summer evening. My parents and I watch World News Tonight with Peter Jennings as we eat supper before the television set. A story runs about the AIDS epidemic in San Francisco. My mother looks at my father and says, "Good Lord! I'm glad nothing like that ever happens around here." The mountains of Western North Carolina have always seemed to shield their inhabitants from the surrounding world. Certainly in Fred Chappell's novel, I Am One of You Forever, the family in the story, a ten-year-old Jess, along with his parents, his grandmother, and the "adopted" Johnson Gibbs, feel they are separated from the outside world. However, through a series of events, this family realizes that geographical boundaries are not strong enough to block off the rest of the world.

Conclusion

At the beginning of Fred Chappell's novel, I Am One of You Forever, the family believes it lives in a trouble-free mountain community. But events force them to realize that the rest of the world influences them also. Visits from Uncle Luden, Aunt Samantha Barefoot, and other relatives acquaint Jess's family with people who no longer reside in their small community. The death of Johnson Gibbs proves that a war all the way around the globe in Europe can have influence right at home. We are all in a community and each of our individual actions somehow influences the rest of the planet in some way. This novel succeeds in relating this important message: to be part of the world we cannot allow barriers like mountains or rivers or even imaginary boundaries like state lines to disassociate our community from the rest of humanity. Certainly we cannot turn our backs on the problems of other people, as my mother suggested about the AIDS virus in far away big cities. Eventually, the disease has claimed lives even here in Buncombe and Henderson counties--the heart of Western North Carolina. The mountains do not isolate us. After all, how does one isolate destiny?

Which phrases are repeated literally? Which key words are echoed or repeated with slight variations? How does the image of isolation and responsibility in the conclusion derive from something implied but unstated in the introduction? Richard Lyons has written convincingly in his own voice. The conclusion conveys a sense of personal conviction. And by echoing phrases and images from the introduction, he creates a sense of unity and fullness. This technique is sometimes called *bookends.* It can also be thought of as the *sandwiching* of an argument (the meat) between two tasty pieces of rye bread.

Still, if nothing else works and the blank page stares back defiantly, you might ask yourself a series of questions: *What have I learned from looking at the text in this way? What feelings should my reader have about it now? How do all the points or details I've considered relate? Am I convinced? Will my reader be convinced? Has the author shown something here I've not seen or felt before? Is there a difference between the surface appearance and some more subtle or implied significance? And has it been worth it? How can or should this apply to our lives?* These are surely questions we want answered from any reading experience. Why else do we read if not to broaden our experience and cast new understanding on our vision of the world. You are the one who has spent hours—perhaps days—studying the text from your own point of view. Only by looking inside your own heart, only by probing with total honesty can you hope to negotiate a final assessment, one that brings reward to the efforts of sound intellectual work.

THE FORMAL ESSAY

As a work nears the editing stage, if not earlier, successful writers gradually shift their attention away from larger elements of organization. They begin to focus on the shape and flow of every sentence. Finding the exact word becomes important. They edit out unnecessary words—unnecessary articles, prepositions, and adverbs. To strengthen their prose, the best writers turn to nouns instead of adjectives.

For our purposes, we can divide verbs into two simple classes. The first, called *weak verbs,* appears most frequently in poor writing. They're easy to spot because most use what is called a "passive voice": *am, are, is, was, been, were*—all forms of the verb "to be." Other weak verbs consist of those vague little words like *get, make, put,* and *do* which serve adequately, but fail to add action or imagery to a sentence.

He *was* in his chair.
The President's new policy *is* inadequate.
The examples *were* not exciting to the audience.
I *put* the dog in the bath.

We use weak verbs all the time in everyday speech. It's only natural. They come readily to mind as we write, especially as we struggle with a discovery draft. Our minds are searching for ideas, relationships, insights. We can't slow down to think about verbs. But after ideas take shape on the page, after we begin that shift which involves more and more concern for our audience, and how that audience will respond to what we write, then verbs become essential. When presented passively, even the best idea may seem mediocre. The sharpest insight, buried in a boring sentence, may not even be noticed. A potentially exciting new relationship may seem dull when the words are dull.

Successful writers—and that includes almost all professional writers, from journalists to novelists—turn to *strong verbs.* Strong verbs snap a sentence into action, and action interests readers. A movie without action generates snores from the audience. A sentence without action may not be that destructive, but three, five, or seven sentences in a row without action can cause readers to nod with boredom.

Where passive verbs are limited to a dozen or so in the whole English language, active verbs seem almost unlimited: *slip, crush, soar, shove, pull, tuck, lift, call.* Or how about more intellectual ones: *illuminate, transform, render, summarize, inhabit, provoke, collaborate,* and so on. Strong verbs not only transform a sentence from dull to lively, they render the central idea with greater force, and sometimes with imagery. Strong active verbs surprise the reader and stimulate interest.

Weak

I *put* the dog in his bath.

Strong

I *dropped* the dog in his bath.

I *threw* the dog in his bath.

I *plopped* the dog in his bath.

I *drowned* the dog in his bath.

Weak

The story *is* about death.

Strong

The story *focuses* on death.

The story *reveals* the agony of death.

The story *depicts* the fear of death.

The story *describes* an encounter with death.

The list of strong verbs could go on almost forever. Each one adds a new image or sharpens the focus. Each strong verb creates a unique sentence. Watch how William Least Heat Moon uses strong verbs to evoke strength and imagery in this passage about loading crates of hardshell crabs onto a truck:

> Balford and I *slid* crates to the scales. I *weighed* them, Balford in a slow and uncertain hand *wrote* down the number, and we *hoisted* them to Griggs on the truck. . . . the critters kept hopping out of the overfilled boxes like popcorn in a hot skillet. The floor *crawled* with oblique scuttles for the nearest dark underside. They *scrabbled* and *clacked,* and we *crunched* them into an agony of yellow ooze as we *heaved* on the crates. I *started* shuffling to avoid stepping on them. Balford got mad. "Pull on that drawhook, sport. They's crabs, not custard pies." A jimmy *reached* up and *clamped* onto my pant leg and *slid* back and forth across the floor with me until we *finished.* I had to break its claw to free my cuff.

Sometimes strong active verbs occur naturally in the drafting stage. If they don't, a good writer searches for them during the editing stage. Consider the following paragraph taken from an early draft in Esther Stein's paper.

> "Paper Pills" is about a middle-aged doctor who has been writing "truths" on little bits of paper and putting them away in his pockets. After the paper pills get hard he tosses them away. One day a "tall dark girl" is in his office pregnant and he takes her for a buggy ride. They fall in love and get married. Later the girl has a miscarriage and within a year she is dead of an unidentified disease. The doctor continues to write truths on little pieces of paper which he keeps in his pockets.

Here's how Esther edited the paragraph, inserting strong verbs:

> "Paper Pills" tells of a middle-aged doctor who writes "truths" on bits of paper, stuffs them in his pocket until they become hard little "pills" and then tosses them away. When a "tall dark girl" shows up pregnant, he takes her for a buggy ride, they fall in love, and marry. Later the girl suffers a miscarriage and within a year she dies. The doctor continues to write truths on bits of paper which he stuffs in his pockets.

Read each version aloud, comparing one sentence at a time. What changes do you notice? How has the search for stronger verbs also affected the length of sentences? Why has Esther been able to tighten and unite some sentences simply by changing the verbs? What effect does she achieve by repeating "stuffs" twice? Should she have searched for an alternative instead of repeating?

We can't emphasize enough the value of strong verbs. Shakespeare is said to have used four active verbs for every one that was passive. Most of us can't equal that, but all of us can add concrete imagery, eliminate extra words, make details more precise, and give power and action to our writing, merely by editing for strong verbs.

Both Esther Stein and Marianne Clampett edited their essays for verbs as well as for unnecessary words. Both asked other members of the class to read their work and give advice. Here are their final versions. Perhaps the most important thing we can say about each is that they seem to prove a point: good writing always seems to flow from a deep personal commitment, wanting to say something well, and then working hard to bring it about.

SHOOTING TO KILL
Marianne Clampett

I am haunted by the image, and yet it's nothing more than a single sentence. Not even my sentence. It begins an essay by Isak Dinesen.

> Once I shot an iguana. I thought that I should be able to make some pretty things from his skin.

It seems so simple, yet it brings back memories I had long forgotten. I was six or seven. A grand uncle of mine, Uncle Fletch Sleuder, had offered to take me squirrel hunting in the Smokey Mountains. I thought squirrels were lovely. They danced from branch to branch like tree kittens, fluffing their tails, as if taunting us, daring us to catch them. I thought of them as personal pets. Somehow, I had the impression that "going hunting" for them would make them mine forever. I thought that in shooting one, I would carry it home in my arms and it would purr and lick my face in the warm afternoon light.

But Isak Dinesen describes the reality of shooting to kill. In her essay, "The Iguana," she tells how the brilliant colors of the Iguana faded almost instantly after it was shot. And she recalls other instances in Africa where in wanting to claim something beautiful as her own, she destroyed its beauty. The lesson is a simple one. Uncle Fletch Sleuder, a religious old man who never missed reading his Bible, would have told me if I had asked.

Instead, he let me shoot his rifle several times, I don't know how many. I never hit anything and the squirrels kept fleeing from branch to branch. I was having a wonderful time until my uncle took the rifle from me and in a single shot knocked a squirrel tumbling down through a tree, bumping off limbs, and landing like a sack of dry meal in the brown leaves at the bottom. I was still excited until I ran up and saw it's bloody eye. I don't think I'll ever forget how surprised I was at how dead something dead really is. I don't think I knew what death meant until then. I sure didn't realize it would mean that all the life was gone from something so wonderful.

Dinesen says that after she shot the Iguana, its bright colors faded ("a flash of azure, green and purple") even as she walked up to it. The "flame was put out," she writes, and "the soul had flown." On another occasion she purchased a bracelet from a black native girl, but as soon as it was wrung upon her own wrist, it too lost its color. The beauty of it had come from its contact with the young girl's skin ("quick, sweet, brownish black, like peat and black pottery"). Dinesen gives advice: "For the sake of your own eyes and heart, shoot not the iguana."

For the sake of beauty, she means. Beauty cannot be separated from the object it is part of. I am forty-seven years old now, with two grown daughters, and Dinesen brings back another memory I would rather not recall. I was ten, I believe, living a comfortable life on Lookout Mountain, Tennessee. My family took a driving vacation to the gulf coast in a 1949 Hudson. Somewhere in Mississippi we stopped for lunch at a diner where a white sharecropper family, too poor to buy restaurant food, was eating outside under a tree. I remember only the daughter, my age, with a pink barrette in her hair. I had never seen a face so beautiful, so pure and bright with black eyes. Today, after studying art, I know it was the face of a Renaissance Madonna. Her black hair almost reached her waist. Her dress was thin and patched, yet clean. Her arms and legs were burnished from working in the fields. I was stunned by her and knew in my heart that for all my parent's wealth, I was a poor and homely thing by comparison. While my father put gas in the Hudson, I played by a stream behind the diner with the sharecropper's daughter. She was laughing and bending over the stream. When the pink barrette fell softly from her hair, landing in the grass at the water's edge, I covered it with my hand and stole it.

I kept it for some years, hidden in a bottom drawer. It was a pathetic piece of plastic. Dull and ordinary. There was nothing beautiful about it. I would have been embarrassed to wear it. On that poor sharecropper's daughter, it had glistened with all the grace and loveliness I lacked in life. So here's my advice: do not think you can steal beauty any more than you can buy it.

Yet I believe that Dinesen makes a mistake in her essay. She describes how in a museum she saw a stuffed deep-water fish whose coloring had survived. It makes her wonder how much beauty there must be on the bottom of the sea if a dead fish could retain so much color. Maybe she speaks only in comparison. But I think a stuffed fish, behind a glass, could not possibly have retained the "flame," or "soul" or "quick, sweet" life she saw in the iguana or the bracelet on the African girl's arm.

I saw once, in a fingerprint-covered glass case, the ballgown Jackie Kennedy wore to John F. Kennedy's inauguration as president. The gown was no doubt lovely, but it seemed heavy and tired, dusted by stale air. I'm sure that on the night Jackie Kennedy wore that gown, others must have gasped at its beauty and envied her for it. But it was not the gown. The gown was always a dead thing, like the bracelet, the barrette, the fish behind glass, the iguana on rock. You cannot capture beauty, not preserve it, not stuff it, not even really seek it, because, as my old Uncle Sleuder would have said, if I had asked him, beauty is like grace, it is given. Even a religious old man living in the woods knows that.

And here, for comparison, is Esther's final revised and edited paper:

THIS SWEETNESS WE SELDOM KNOW
Esther Stein

When my high school friend Maria told me she had been to an abortion clinic over the weekend, we stood in front of the lockers and cried. I do not know what we were crying about.

The dead fetus? I don't think so.

Maria's misfortune? Probably not.

Probably we cried because it seemed like some rite of passage, like the first menstrual onset or the first boyfriend or graduation. We cried because something vaguely emotional had happened that we didn't fully understand. But abortion was no more to her or me than it had been a year earlier to another friend, Sandy. In our high school, having an abortion gave you an aura. At first everyone hugged a lot and cried. Then we would surround the girl and walk tight against her as we went down the hall, to show our love and protection. But then she would start sleeping with someone again, some guy who heard about the abortion and treated her tenderly and promised always to use a prophylactic. So everything was OK and we forgot about it.

How strange then to read Sherwood Anderson's story, "Paper Pills." Anderson tells the story of a horse-and-buggy doctor in the early part of this century who helps an unmarried girl "in the family way." The quaint language alone makes the story seem from another world. My high school friends, Maria and Sandy, were both "pregnant." Neither of them would ever have considered themselves to be in a "family way." And no doctor would have married them as Doctor Reefy does in "Paper Pills." Maria saw her abortionist for no more than twenty minutes. He wore a green mask most of the time. The nurse at the clinic was the only person who talked to her. She was kind but busy, Maria said.

Anderson's story would at first seem unrelated. A world past. A gesture no longer meaningful. Yet I think that Anderson speaks to us today, as much or more than he spoke to readers in 1919 when his collection of stories, Winesburg, Ohio, was first published.

"Paper Pills" tells of a middle-aged doctor who writes "truths" on bits of paper, stuffs them in his pocket until they become hard little "pills" and then tosses them away. When a "tall dark girl" shows up pregnant, he takes her for a buggy ride, they fall in love, and marry. Later the girl suffers a miscarriage and within a year she dies. The doctor continues to write truths on bits of paper which he stuffs in his pockets.

The key to this seemingly simple story lies in a single passage in which Anderson describes the beginning of the couple's courtship as "delicious," like "the twisted little apples" found in an orchard after all the round shiny apples are shipped to the city.

> On the trees are only a few gnarled apples that the pickers have rejected. They look like the knuckles of Doctor Reefy's hands. One nibbles them and they are delicious. Into a little round place at the side of the apple has been gathered all of its sweetness. . . . Only the few know the sweetness of the twisted apples.

This is what the story is really about. About rejects, and sweetness, and lost truths. And this is what Maria's and Sandy's story is about, only I didn't know it then.

Because the apples are like the tall dark girl. She too was a reject. She was after all pregnant. In 1919 a pregnant girl could not easily obtain an abortion, although that may have been why she came to see Doctor Reefy in the first place. But he did not see her as others would in those days. He did not see her as shameful. He accepted her as she was and the girl, in turn, accepted him. Because he was also a reject--a forty-five year old man (what would have then been called a "confirmed bachelor") who acted strangely and wore a single suit for ten years, frayed at the sleeves with holes in the knees. Like two rejected apples, they found sweetness in each other.

Yet this sweet union ends as it began, without explanation. Some months after her pregnancy has passed "in an illness," the girl dies. We are told nothing else. No cause, no reason, no emotion. The sweetness is momentary, and perhaps more sweet because of it. But the doctor already knows all that. He knew it even before he met the girl. He wrote thoughts on scraps of paper, "truths" that "arose gigantic in his mind."

> The truth clouded the world. It became terrible and then faded away. . . .

These truths were also like the gnarled apples. They were rejects that he knew no one would accept. People only want the bright shiny apples, the pleasant ones that look like all the other apples. No one wants to eat gnarled, twisted little rejects. No one wants to hear the "terrible" truths that don't make us happy. Yet they are truths none-the-less. The bright shiny apples are actually illusions. The truths are harder to find and more random, apples in a frosted field, and most of us do not want them. We reject them for something more comforting.

Doctor Reefy was a reject because he saw through the illusion. He knew the value of the twisted apples others left behind, like the tall dark girl. But he was also a realist. He knew no one else could understand. The tall dark girl lost her child and later died. Attempting to give reasons or explanations would have been as much an illusion as attempting to explain why she got pregnant in the first place. Or why she happened to arrive in the doctor's office on the day he was pulling an old lady's tooth.

Odd as it may first seem, Anderson's story relates directly to my experience with Maria and Sandy. Not because Maria and Sandy were rejected. After their abortions, they were more popular than ever. And not because they lost their virginity. They offered that up in junior high. But because the abortions were like those paper pills. They contained truths, fragments of truths, beginnings and ends of thoughts that were sweet and then tossed away. The fetuses were rejected. Had to be. There was no place for them. Doctor Reefy knew that rejected things contained truths. "Out of many of them he formed a truth that became gigantic in his mind."

Reminders

Giving shape and focus to the formal essay is not so much a matter of rules and formulas as it is organizing thought itself. The following conventions have helped other writers in the past.

- Introductions usually include the author's name and title of the work, a brief overview of the issue or text, and a focusing sentence.
- As you work your way through the main portion of your paper, keep in mind that for each idea or concept you want to cover, your reader will expect you to

  Tell the Reader Something
  Show It (or Demonstrate It)
  Share Your Thoughts and Feelings

- Quotations are most effective when introduced with a general observation about their importance; both the speaker and the context in which the quotation occurred should be identified.
- Conclusions can be improved by echoing some element of the title or introduction.
- By editing unnecessary words, you strengthen the main ideas. In general, nouns seem more effective than adjectives.
- Strong active verbs create power, add imagery, make sentences more exact, and often eliminate other unnecessary words in a sentence.

The experience of Maria and Sandy was as ignored as the rejected fetuses. We didn't want to sample "the terrible truths." We didn't want to know what it really meant or what loss had come to all of us. We lived without deeper feelings, or rather we held back, pushed down, ignored as best we could, any kind of sensitivity to the shallowness of back-seat sex, sterile clinics, and slippery prophylactics. By ignoring the truths, what we lost was the knowledge of a painful sweetness, a kindness that we ought to have shared. Doctor Reefy could not change the world. He could only reach out and for a moment be tender with someone else who also had to endure the loneliness.

We find both Esther and Marianne writing with great depth of feeling, but also with a sharp discriminating intelligence. In part, that's because they've worked hard to shape their ideas and feelings in forceful ways. Fine hunches and vague emotions are not enough in themselves. An inner voice becomes meaningful only when we find a form in which to express it. Learning how to use repetition, opposition, and conflict, learning how to structure introductions and conclusions, learning how to create strength through verbs—all this suggests how essential integrity of thought and form really are to writing with power. All must be made habits of the mind. Only then can thinking itself become an art.

CHAPTER 4

EXPERIENCING IDEAS

THOUGHTFUL READING AND PRIVATE EXPLORATION

At the beginning of one of his novels, E.M. Forster once used the epigram ". . . only connect." Forster's words echo Aristotle who said that the sign of intelligence is the ability to see relationships.

To connect: to see relationships.

Until now we've been arguing that reading with the heart is essential. Bringing all your experience and all your feelings to bear upon a text, we've said, is the only way to make it yours. An essay, novel, biography, poem—each must be lived wholly if it is to come alive for a reader. And there is a truth to that. Yet surely all of us recognize that seeing the world only through the eye of the heart is incomplete. We have two eyes. We must also see the world through the eye of the mind. A raw emotional reaction does not necessarily lead to sound judgment. Nor, by contrast, does stark objective logic lead to the fullness of human experience. We have two eyes, and we must see through both if we are to see the world wholly.*

The concept of critical thinking can be thought of as the need to bring all our experience and all our reason to bear upon a single inquiry. We must teach ourselves to see ideas with both mind and heart, using each to test the other. Our initial response may often serve only as a starting point for further exploration.

Here's a well-known essay by Virginia Woolf, first delivered as a speech to the Women's Service League in 1931. We asked several of our students to study it and to explore their initial reactions in reading notebooks.

*We are indebted for this image, and much of the following argument, to Parker J. Palmer, *To Know As We Are Known,* Harper & Row, 1983.

The Angel in the House

When your secretary invited me to come here, she told me that your Society is concerned with the employment of women and she suggested that I might tell you something about my own professional experiences. It is true I am a woman; it is true I am employed; but what professional experiences have I had? It is difficult to say. My profession is literature; and in that profession there are fewer experiences for women than in any other, with the exception of the stage—fewer, I mean, that are peculiar to women. For the road was cut many years ago—by Fanny Burney, by Aphra Behn, by Harriet Martineau, by Jane Austen, by George Eliot—many famous women, and many more unknown and forgotten, have been before me, making the path smooth, and regulating my steps. Thus, when I came to write, there were very few material obstacles in my way. Writing was a reputable and harmless occupation. The family peace was not broken by the scratching of a pen. No demand was made upon the family purse. For ten and sixpence one can buy paper enough to write all the plays of Shakespeare—if one has a mind that way. Pianos and models, Paris, Vienna, and Berlin, masters and mistresses, are not needed by a writer. The cheapness of writing paper is, of course, the reason why women have succeeded as writers before they have succeeded in the other professions.

But to tell you my story—it is a simple one. You have only got to figure to yourselves a girl in a bedroom with a pen in her hand. She had only to move that pen from left to right—from ten o'clock to one. Then it occurred to her to do what is simple and cheap enough after all—to slip a few of those pages into an envelope, fix a penny stamp in the corner, and drop the envelope into the red box at the corner. It was thus that I became a journalist; and my effort was rewarded on the first day of the following month—a very glorious day it was for me—by a letter from an editor containing a cheque for one pound ten shillings and sixpence. But to show you how little I deserve to be called a professional woman, how little I know of the struggles and difficulties of such lives, I have to admit that instead of spending that sum upon bread and butter, rent, shoes and stocking, or butcher's bills, I went out and bought a cat—a beautiful cat, a Persian cat, which very soon involved me in bitter disputes with my neighbours.

What could be easier than to write articles and to buy Persian cats with the profits? But wait a moment. Articles have to be about something. Mine, I seem to remember, was about a novel by a famous man. And while I was writing this review, I discovered that if I were going to review books I should need to do battle with a certain phantom. And the phantom was a woman, and when I came to know her better I called her after the heroine of a famous poem. The Angel in the House. It was she who used to come between me and my paper when I was writing reviews. It was she who bothered me and wasted my time and so tormented me that at last I killed her. You who come of a younger and happier generation may not have heard of her—you may not know what I mean by the Angel in the House. I will describe her as shortly as I can. She was intensely sympathetic. She was immensely charming. She was utterly unselfish. She excelled in the difficult arts of family life. She sacrificed herself daily. If there was chicken, she took the leg; if there was a draught she sat in it—in short she was so constituted that she never had a mind or a wish of her own, but preferred to sympathize always with the minds and wishes of others. Above all—I need not say it—she was pure. Her purity was supposed to be her chief beauty—her blushes, her great grace. In those days—the last of Queen Victoria—every house had its Angel. And when I came to write I encountered her with the very first words. The shadow of her wings fell on my page; I heard the rustling of her skirts in the room. Directly, that is to say, I took my pen in hand to review that novel by a famous man, she slipped behind me and whispered: "My dear, you are a young woman. You are writing about a book that has been written by a man. Be sympathetic; be tender; flatter; deceive; use all the arts and wiles of our sex. Never let anybody guess that you have a mind of your own. Above all, be pure." And she made as if to guide my pen. I now record the one act for which I take some credit to myself, though the credit rightly belongs to some excellent ancestors of mine who left me a certain sum of money—shall we say five hundred pounds a year?—so that it was not necessary for me to depend solely on charm for my living. I turned upon her and caught her by the throat. I did my best to kill her. My excuse, if I were to be had up in a court of law, would be that I acted in self-defense. Had I not killed her she would have killed me. She would have plucked the heart out of my writing. For, as I found, directly I put pen to paper, you cannot review even a novel without having a mind of your own, without expressing what you think to be the truth about human relations, morality, sex. And all these questions, according to the Angel in the House, cannot be dealt with freely and openly by women; they must charm, they must conciliate, they must—to put it bluntly—tell lies if they are to succeed. Thus, whenever I felt the shadow of her wing or the radiance of her halo upon my page, I took up the inkpot and flung it at her. She died hard. Her fictitious nature was of great assistance to her. It is far harder to kill a phantom than a reality. She was always creeping back when I thought I had despatched her. Though I flatter myself that I killed her in the end, the struggle was severe; it took much time that had better have been spent upon learning Greek grammar; or in roaming the world in search of adventures. But it was a real experience; it was an experience that was bound to befall all women writers at that time. Killing the Angel in the House was part of the occupation of a woman writer.

But to continue my story. The Angel was dead; what then remained? You may say that what remained was a simple and common object—a young woman in a bedroom with an inkpot. In other words, now that she had rid herself of falsehood, that young woman had only to be herself. Ah, but what is "herself"? I mean, what is a woman? I assure you, I do not know. I do not believe that you know. I do not believe that anybody can know until she has expressed herself in all the arts and professions open to human skill. That indeed is one of the reasons why I have come here—out of respect for you, who are in process of showing us by your experiments what a woman is, who are in process of providing us, by your failures and successes, with that extremely important piece of information.

But to continue the story of my professional experiences. I made one pound ten and six by my first review; and I bought a Persian cat with the proceeds. Then I grew ambitious. A Persian cat is all very well, I said; but a Persian cat is not enough. I must have a motor car. And it was thus that I became a novelist—for it is a very strange thing that people will give you a motor car if you will tell them a story. It is a still stranger thing that there is nothing so delightful in the world as telling stories. It is far pleasanter than writing reviews of famous novels. And yet, if I am to obey your secretary and tell you my professional experiences as a novelist, I must tell you about a very strange experience that befell me as a novelist. And to understand it you must try first to imagine a novelist's state of mind. I hope I am not giving away professional secrets if I say that a novelist's chief desire is to be as unconscious as possible. He has to induce in himself a state of perpetual lethargy. He wants life to proceed with the utmost quiet and regularity. He wants to see the same faces, to read the same books, to do the same things day after day, month after month, while he is writing, so that nothing may break the illusion in which he is living—so that nothing may disturb or disquiet the mysterious nosings about, feelings round, darts, dashes and sudden discoveries of that very shy and illusive spirit, the imagination. I suspect that this state is the same both for men and women. Be that as it may, I want you to imagine me writing a novel in a state of trance. I want you to figure to yourselves a girl sitting with a pen in her hand, which for minutes, and indeed for hours, she never dips into the inkpot. The image that comes to my mind when I think of this girl is the image of a fisherman lying sunk in dreams on the verge of a deep lake with a rod held out over the water. She was letting her imagination sweep unchecked round every rock and cranny of the world that lies submerged in the depths of our unconscious being. Now came the experience, the experience that I believe to be far commoner with women writers than with men. The line raced through the girl's fingers. Her imagination had rushed away. It had sought the pools, the depths, the dark places where the largest fish slumber. And then there was a smash. There was an explosion. There was foam and confusion. The imagination had dashed itself against something hard. The girl was roused from her dream. She was indeed in a state of the most acute and difficult distress. To speak without figure she had thought of something, something about the body, about the passions which it was unfitting for her as a woman to say. Men, her reason told her, would be shocked. The consciousness of what men will say of a woman who speaks the truth about her passions had roused her from her artist's state of unconsciousness. She could write no more. The trance was over. Her imagination could work no longer. This I believe to be a very common experience with women writers—they are impeded by the extreme conventionality of the other sex. For though men sensibly allow themselves great freedom in these respects, I doubt that they realize or can control the extreme severity with which they condemn such freedom in women.

These then were two very genuine experiences of my own. These were two of the adventures of my professional life. The first—killing the Angel in the House—I think I solved. She died. But the second, telling the truth about my own experiences as a body, I do not think I solved. I doubt that any woman has solved it yet. The obstacles against her are still immensely powerful—and yet they are very difficult to define. Outwardly, what is simpler than to write books? Outwardly, what obstacles are there for a woman rather than for a man? Inwardly, I think, the case is very different; she has still many ghosts to fight, many prejudices to overcome. Indeed it will be a long time still, I think, before a woman can sit down to write a book without finding a phantom to be slain, a rock to be dashed against. And if this is so in literature, the freest of all professions for women, how is it in the new professions which you are now for the first time entering?

Those are the questions that I should like, had I time, to ask you. And indeed, if I have laid stress upon these professional experiences of mine, it is because I believe that they are, though in different forms, yours also. Even when the path is nominally open—when there is nothing to prevent a woman from being a doctor, a lawyer, a civil servant—there are many phantoms and obstacles, as I believe, looming in her way. To discuss and define them is I think of great value and importance; for thus only can the labor be shared, the difficulties be solved. But besides this, it is necessary also to discuss the ends and the aims for which we are fighting, for which we are doing battle with these formidable obstacles. Those aims cannot be taken for granted; they must be perpetually questioned and examined. The whole position, as I see it—here in this hall surrounded by women practising for the first time in history I know not how many different professions—is one of extraordinary interest and importance. You have won rooms of your own in the house hitherto exclusively owned by men. You are able, though not without great labor and effort, to pay the rent. You are earning your five hundred pounds a year. But this freedom is only a beginning; the room is your own, but it is still bare. It has to be furnished; it has to be decorated; it has to be shared. How are you going to furnish it, how are you going to decorate it? With whom are you going to share it, and upon what terms? These, I think are questions of the utmost importance and interest. For the first time in history you are able to ask them; for the first time you are able to decide for yourselves what the answers should be. Willingly would I stay and discuss those questions and answers—but not tonight. My time is up; and I must cease.

Addie Gilbert turned in her notebook the same day she read the essay. Addie, a 22-year-old first-year student, had worked several years before deciding to enter college. Usually bouncy and responsive to everything we'd read that term, she found this particular essay dull going. She marked her text and took marginal notes, but when handing in her notebook she said, "I've seen all this before."

> To tell you the truth, I'm sort of tired of reading this kind of thing. Everybody by now knows that women had to fight for their rights, but I think that's mostly behind us now. My mother and grandmother had "Victorian" upbringings and thought a lady's place was in the home, but by the time my sisters and I grew up, that kind of thing was long past. My sister Jennie is in her second year with a public relations firm, and my other sister Sandra is in graduate school studying veterinary medicine. I'm not sure what I plan to do with my life, but after working in everything from food service to a day-care center, I know what I don't want to do. I don't feel any doors are closed to me just because I'm a woman. I don't think there any more "phantoms to be slain."
>
> Even Virginia Woolf herself says that " . . . when I came to write, there were very few material obstacles in my way." If that was true I'm not sure what all the fuss is about for her. To tell you the truth, I'm not very positive about feminists. They're a little too radical for me.
>
> Woolf's essay is easy to read. But don't you think the language gets a little strong? She says she had to "kill" the angel or she would have been killed by it. She uses the term repeatedly. Why so? If it was already ok to become a writer, why do you have to be so radical about killing off the old im-

age. And I'm bothered most by how she interchanges the terms "angel" and "phantom." Phantoms are negative things that haunt you, but angels are good things that protect you. (Maybe this is just my Catholic upbringing coming out.) Somehow, it all seems like a little too heavy for today, a little too shrill and overdone.

Todd Porter turned in a different response. A second-semester student from Atlanta, Todd was one of those bright young men who overwhelms others with eagerness.

Virginia Woolf's "Angel in the House" is powerful stuff. She tells the story of all women. The struggle to find her own way, free of male domination. She writes about overcoming the expectations of men everywhere.

> . . . flatter; deceive, use all the arts and wiles of our sex. Never let anybody guess that you have a mind of your own. Above all, be pure.

It's hard to believe that men still think like this. But over and over again, she struggles against what males want her to be. But what she discovers, and what makes this such a good essay, is that even after she has killed off the imposition of society, she is not free. She's got to struggle again to find out who she really is. Who her inner self is, her imagination and her unconscious. And what she finds is that she has passions, a body. "Men, her reason told her, would be shocked." The struggle never ends. Absolutely nothing has really changed. Women must fight to overcome what men have done to them.

Virginia Woolf is still struggling with "ghosts" and "prejudices" that prevent her from becoming what she wants to be, which is a novelist.

I get angry when I think about the way women are treated. Women have a right to go into any profession they want. They have a right to have the same feelings men do, the same sexual drives. They shouldn't have to disguise who they really are. I think men have an obligation to help them achieve those rights. As the case of Virginia Woolf points out, women can't do it on their own.

Both Addie and Todd have begun, as they should, by relating Virginia Woolf's essay to ideas and values from their own experience. Yet to us both responses seem limited and inadequate. Neither student has yet pursued his or her immediate reaction with any sort of self-reflection. Why, for example, does Addie believe Woolf's views are extreme and out of date? Why does Woolf's language disturb her? Is there a difference between Addie's image of "angel" and Woolf's image of the same term? Why should Addie be disturbed by comparing an angel to a phantom? Is this a case where the writer and the reader have different meanings and different connotations for the same words?

Todd's reaction raises similar concerns. Why does he "get angry"? Is he substituting slogans ("The struggle never ends. Women must fight to overcome . . . ") for more reflective thought? Can he support his initial generalizations: "She tells the story of all women," and "She writes about overcoming the expectations of men everywhere"? Wouldn't Addie's reaction suggest that Woolf does not speak for "all women"? On the surface of it, wouldn't Todd's own position suggest that not all men everywhere expect women to flatter and deceive? Is he correct in saying "Absolutely nothing has really changed?"

Critical Reading

The first requirement of critical reading is to place in perspective our own emotional reactions—the experience we bring to the text. All of us, no matter our age, sex or education, retain prejudices and preoccupations that may cause us to read with a limited perspective. The particular culture we live in shapes our values and our lives through inherent traditions and myths. But simultaneously our cultural background may limit our understanding of other cultural traditions and myths. In a similar way, the historical events of our time contribute to our perception of what we like to think of as "human nature," leading us to make judgments we may consider true of all human beings in all times and cultures. Perhaps most important, our very language affects almost every aspect of our lives, usually in unconscious ways. Unless, through self-scrutiny, we bring to conscious awareness the many assumptions and constraints that shape our lives, we cannot test their validity. Nor can we be aware of how they limit our reading of a new text. Conscious self-reflection may lead to confirmation of our original opinions. Or self-reflection may guide us toward revision and modification of our initial reaction.

Critical reading has a second and equally important requirement. If history, culture, and language affect our reading, they also have affected the author's writing. In addition to searching the text itself (the literal words on the page) for details, patterns, conflicts, and key passages, the strong reader takes into account other forces that may have influenced the construction of the text. This may be especially necessary for works written in an era or culture different from our own. Lacking in such background, both Addie and Todd may have misconstrued certain aspects of Woolf's essay.

Virginia Woolf could have assumed that many in her original audience were fully familiar with cultural and historical pressures on women in the late 19th and early 20th century. Today, more than half a century after Woolf delivered her address, a reader may know of such things only by hearsay or in the most general of ways. Addie and Todd, for example, sometimes seem to judge Woolf in terms of the 1990s. Neither student may appreciate the full dimension of Woolf's struggle with Victorian repression. And even though it can be argued that basic principles raised by Woolf have not changed, the cultural context has changed dramatically. The conditions of struggle may seem different to everyone involved.

Finally, for contemporary readers, some of Woolf's language may carry different emotional connotations, or no connotations at all. For example, the phrase "Angel in the House" seems to have been familiar to women of the last century, yet even by the 1930s, Woolf found it necessary to remind her readers of its significance. As a metaphor in the 1990s, the phrase may be empty of content, failing to convey the powerful negative images it once provoked.

Critical reading, then, involves a consideration of multiple forces, both those which act on us and those which may have acted on the author and the text. We might diagram it like this:*

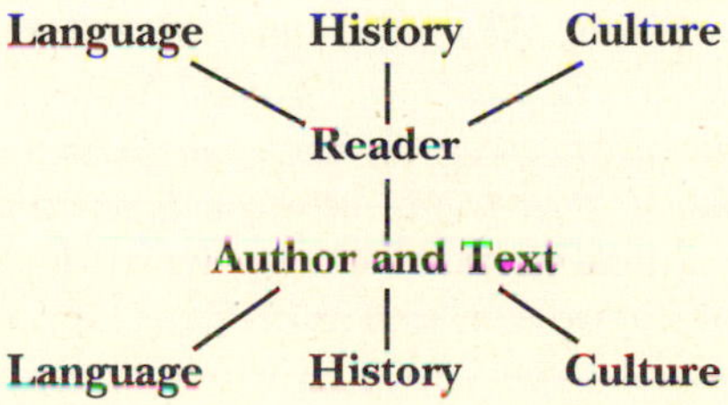

*Our discussion of cultural influences has been directly affected by the work of Kathleen McCormick, Gary Waller, and Linda Flower, in *Reading Texts,* D.C. Heath, 1987.

Without consideration of all these factors, a critical reading may not be complete. The richness, delight, or insight a text can evoke may never be fully opened to you. Critical reading is the interaction of mind and feeling. To respond to a text with raw emotion is not necessarily wrong, merely limiting. The intellectual dimension of the text remains to be negotiated.

PUBLIC EXPLORATION

In earlier chapters we suggested it was important to discuss initial reading responses with colleagues and peers. Testing opinions and attitudes against the views of others helps us broaden perspective and reconsider our initial reactions. In separate groups, both Addie and Todd faced challenges to some of their responses. Addie found a number of students strongly disagreeing that for women there were no more "phantoms to be slain." Todd was surprised when a female student actually questioned his sincerity. How, she demanded, could he claim to present himself as a supporter of female rights but also imply that women, without the help of males, did not have ability or strength to win those rights? Was he biased in unconscious ways? For both Addie and Todd, an open discussion of initial views provoked a great deal of self-reflection.

But group discussions revealed something else. Everyone realized how little they knew about the culture or history that had influenced Woolf's text. The full historical significance of the phrase, "The Angel in the House," escaped everyone. And most first-year students were unclear about when the women's movement in England began or who Virginia Woolf was, the social class in which she lived, or the influences British culture may have had on her childhood in the late 19th century.

Another dimension of the exploratory process, then, may be the search for additional knowledge that can be brought to bear on a text. For that, we may need to turn to other kinds of "public" sources, beyond our peers and colleagues—to essays, articles, books, encyclopedias, and so on—to any source that may open up additional insights. This is sometimes called the "cross-breeding of ideas." Such a process still begins, as we described in Chapters 2 and 3, with asking yourself, *What things do I already know, or what experiences have I already had, that may help me read this text?* At another level, however, we have to ask, *What bodies of knowledge from other disciplines or cultures can I bring to bear on the reading? How do these points interact with or influence each other?* In this advanced stage—the critical thinking stage—the reader explores relationships outside the context of the work as well as inside. The result leads to a text that is connected to personal experience, to other texts, to other worlds. Such reading adds resonance, not only to the work itself, but to our experience with it. Reason, ideas, and feelings all interact to guide judgment.

Here are three important areas you may need to look into: *language, history,* and *culture.*

Language

Few of us recognize how vital language is in shaping our lives. The language we use—the language culture we are born into—determines much about how we perceive the world. Clearly, we see with our eyes, but our vocabulary—the words we have at our command with which we "name" the world—affects what we see. In "From Sight into Insight" (p. 169), Annie Dillard has said, "Seeing is very much a matter of verbalization." This came home to us recently when a friend complained that the game of basketball consisted only of a bunch of people running wildly up and down the court. Each of the plays, each skilled move or technique, remained obscure. Only when such patterns as a *pick and roll* or a *four corners* were named and identified could our friend actually see these plays take shape. In the same way, most of us can see only three or four different kinds of snow: *wet, dry, flaky,* and *deep,* perhaps. But a professional skier may be able to see ten or twelve kinds of snow: *powder, corn, glaze, groomed.* And Eskimos possess more than twenty words for snow. An Eskimo literally sees fine distinctions most of us fail to notice. Does that mean our eyes are different? Obviously not. It means that language brings to consciousness what our senses perceive. The act of naming provokes awareness, it intensifies experience. In some ways language may be said to actually create experience.

The corollary to this is the relationship of language to ideas, for quite simply, without language, we would have no ideas. We might have hunches or urges, but not concepts. The student who says, "I know what I mean but I just can't say it," does not, in reality, *know* what he or she means at all. *The New York Times Book Review* carried an essay recently in which a professional Russian translator observed that the Russian language has no specific word for *individualism.* Without such a word, how can the concept be understood or felt? How can a nation move toward a democratic system of government if something so inherent in democracy as individualism is missing from its vocabulary? We have the same problem in English when we attempt to understand Aristotle's theory of tragedy. Aristotle argued that a tragic hero falls because of *hamartia.* But we have no word in English for such a concept. The term has been translated as "flaw" or "frailty" or sometimes as "pride." But each of these terms is quite different, and none mean the same as *hamartia.* Our understanding of tragedy can never be quite the same as Aristotle's. The thought process of every language culture is both shaped by and limited by its own vocabulary (not to mention syntax and grammar).

Language also directly affects our emotions. Words not only have denotations (dictionary definitions), they carry with them connotations (emotive forces). For most of us, *summertime* may convey a pleasant emotion, whereas *Nazi* calls up negative feelings. The phrase, "I want to make love to you," carries with it a certain tenderness that seems lacking in the phrase "I want to make it with you"—even though both may share the same denotative meaning. In a similar way, the military may call for a *strategic withdrawal* instead of a *retreat.* A businessman may insist that his company produces *Kitty Purr,* not *Ground Fish Heads.* The emotional power of language is so great that words can easily be used to manipulate our attitudes, our actions, and our beliefs.

Politicians take a bold stand for *family values* because the phrase conveys such positive emotional force, even though the denotative meaning may be different for almost everyone. When Soviet armies marched into Afghanistan, the incursion was labeled a *liberation.* When American troops fought in Korea, the administration called it a *police action.* Neither government wanted to use the word war.

In turn, ideas themselves can seldom be limited to an objective precision. Ideas are embedded in emotional connotations. Consider such concepts as *justice, democracy, abortion, school prayer, affirmative action, Marxism, feminism, welfare, minimum wage, human rights, gay rights, smokers' rights,* and so on. Both denotation and connotation interact to create meaning. And because the connotations are often different for each of us (depending on our past experience with language, our life experience, and the era we live in), a single idea can never rightly be said to have a single universal meaning.

Why did Virginia Woolf need to kill the "angel in the house"? Our students weren't sure. We suggested that Addie Gilbert look into the phrase. Could she find its origins? What cultural values lay behind the metaphor? What emotional force did those words have on women of the 19th century? Why was that force so strong that Woolf needed to fight it again and again, even in the privacy of her own study? Was it possible that a younger generation of women, more than half a century later, might read the phrase differently and react with different emotions?

We are like goldfish swimming in the bowl of our own language. We can never fully objectify ourselves from the shaping power of words. Our perceptions, our emotions, our ideas, our culture are all generated to a great extent by the particular language we find ourselves born into. No wonder critical reading requires that we direct special attention to the language a writer uses. No wonder we must scrutinize, as best we can, our subjective responses to that language.

History

Both authors and their works exist in an historical context. Our understanding or acquaintance with that context can often clarify forces that moved the author and shaped the text. We can see this most easily in someone like Shakespeare. Writing in the reign of the House of Tudor, Shakespeare portrays kings from the earlier House of York as far worse than they were, and kings from the Tudor line as far better. Richard III, for example, is characterized as humpbacked, devious, and power hungry. Shakespeare's Richard even orders the murder of two innocent children, both potential heirs to the throne. Yet there is little historical evidence supporting the notion that Richard III was such an evil man. Did Shakespeare distort the original Richard for dramatic purposes? Possibly. But he must surely have been influenced by other factors as well. The histories of his time, which served as Shakespeare's sources for the play, were written by supporters of the House of Tudor, the victors of a civil war. To justify an overthrow of the previous line of kings, Tudor historians portrayed the rebellion as essential to God's plan. The new royal line was characterized as religiously inspired, decent, and honorable men who found it their painful duty to drive out the corruption that had infected England. Shakespeare followed the accepted text of events as the Tudor historians had shaped them. But Shakespeare may have felt certain other pressures. He was, after all, writing in the time of Queen Elizabeth, the then-current reigning member of the Tudor family. He could hardly have portrayed her ancestors as villainous usurpers of the throne. If he wanted to continue to produce plays, support of the governing monarch was essential.

In more recent times, we can see World War I, the first major war on the European continent in one hundred years, as a direct force shaping the early novels of Ernest Hemingway. All the major Western powers entered the war proclaiming it a glorious cause. In August 1914, soldiers marched into battle heeding the call to duty, sacred honor, and sacrifice. But after four years of modern warfare—of machine guns and tanks and poison gas—after four years and the deaths of over six million lives (sometimes at the rate of 50,000 a month), all the old values had lost their meaning. Hemingway and others felt betrayed. They felt they had been lied to.

> I had seen nothing sacred, and the things that were glorious had no glory and the sacrifices were like the stockyards at Chicago. . . . Words such as glory, honor, courage, or hallow were obscene. . . .

Such a strong condemnation of conventional values might not be understood without at least a general understanding of events that brought it about.

An historical awareness then provides reference points; it helps us recognize that a subjective reading of a text may be limited; it prevents us from judging a work solely by the social and cultural values of our own time. Both Addie and Todd admitted they knew little about Virginia Woolf's era or the forces that may have shaped her world. We suggested they might want to look into an encyclopedia for a general background, perhaps under Victorianism or Feminist Movement. And for Todd, who seemed especially interested, we recommended he research several lives of women writers mentioned in Woolf's essay: Fanny Burney, Aphra Behn, Harriet Martineau. What historical roles had they played? Why were they important to Virginia Woolf?

Knowledge of historical conditions does not mean we should abandon our own late 20th century perspective, which would be false to ourselves, if not impossible anyway. Instead, knowledge of the author and his or her times adds dimension to our understanding. It locates our feelings and insights in a broader context. Above all, such background enriches and illuminates the reading of a text.

Culture

The term "culture" includes just about everything that might be considered habit or tradition or "our way of living or thinking or acting" for any group of people. And cultural influence is often overwhelming. Much of who we are for life—our religion, our values, our conduct—may be derived from the community we are born into. Consider such simple things as gestures: in North America we point at something with an extended index finger; in Latin America people often point with their noses. Both groups think each other's conduct strange, if not downright rude. Or consider clothing worn at certain traditional ceremonies. In the Western world, brides usually marry in white, but in the Islamic world, brides marry in black. For most people in the West, black seems more appropriate for a funeral. But for Islamic cultures, white is worn at funerals.

Yet these constitute mere surface examples. Consider how deeper beliefs and values are associated with different cultures. In the essay "Blue Winds Dancing" (p. 184), the author writes that upon returning home he sees the tracks of deer and snowshoe rabbits. We might assume the author is merely offering a physical description of nature because of its beauty. Or we might assume that he calls our attention to rabbits and deer because they are such cuddly animals with such big eyes. Either response could be normal to those of us raised in a culture where nature is something found in state parks on weekends and our perception of forest animals derives from Walt Disney. But for the author, Tom Whitecloud, a native American Indian, a renewed experience with nature reminds him of how all living things are united in our spiritual force. To impose our own cultural background or to be unaware of his, could mean that the special richness of Whitecloud's experience would be missed.

Even within the same culture, different generations can lose touch with one another. In our classes, for example, we often find that when F. Scott Fitzgerald in his 1918 novel, *This Side of Paradise,* describes various young girls as "making love," our students today assume Fitzgerald means they engaged in sexual intercourse. But throughout the late Victorian era and into the early 20th century, "making love" meant to *make verbal love,* that is, to talk sweetly or to flirt. For his heroines to "make love" was in fact a wild and outrageous act for the times, since only men and women with serious intentions (or better, those who were already engaged) should do such things. But to read Fitzgerald's text solely from a late 20th century perspective is to misunderstand the culture, and the culture shift then underway, that Fitzgerald was depicting.

Something similar often happens when our students read Charlotte Bronte's 1848 novel, *Jane Eyre.* One of the key scenes in the story occurs when Mr. Rochester, an "older" man (in his thirties), a member of the gentry with both wealth and bloodline, proposes to Jane, an 18-year-old governess with no family or social connections. Jane, believing Rochester may be making fun of her, becomes angry and asserts he has no right to toy with her emotions because she is, after all, his equal. Many of our students take little notice of this. But in early Victorian culture, Rochester's marriage proposal was scandalous. Readers of the time objected to both disparity of age and rank. A gentleman should not condescend to notice a lowly governess, let alone offer his hand in marriage. The proposal violated a code of conduct and offended proper society. Even worse, Jane Eyre's assertion of equality (which Rochester does not dispute) was astonishing. Not only was Jane of a lower rank, she was a woman. If such a claim were allowed to stand, it could threaten the very fabric of Victorian class and societal structure. A 20th century reader may experience only pleasure in reading about how two lonely people fall in love. But many Victorian readers must have felt a tumult of confused emotions, perhaps enjoying the Cinderella quality of the scene, but simultaneously feeling anger, disgust, and outrage. More than one critic of the time called the book immoral.

When we read something from another culture, then, or from another historical era, we may risk imposing our own cultural assumptions on the text. Critical thinking requires that we approach such works with a degree of caution. The new insights we bring to the text today are valuable. But we need to ask whether our reading would be modified or enriched by broader knowledge.

To better understand Virginia Woolf's essay on "The Angel in the House," we suggested that Todd Porter might want to look into 19th century cultural attitudes toward women, and perhaps into Virginia Woolf's own background. Who was her audience for the original lecture? Did she truly speak for all women (as Todd claimed)? What did she mean by saying there were few "material obstacles" to a woman who wanted to become an author? Why was Woolf able to overcome only one of the two problems confronting her? Why did she find her struggle to express the views of woman's sexuality doomed to failure? Is it true, as Todd had written in his initial exploration of the essay, that "absolutely nothing has changed"?

Without some insight into the cultural values (and related historical forces) that may have shaped a text, we limit our response to the chance circumstances of our own background. A thoughtful reading, and a corresponding critical judgment, usually require broader perspectives.

PRIVATE REFLECTION

Both Addie and Todd investigated Virginia Woolf and her era. Addie looked into such works as *A Madwoman in the Attic* and *A Widening Sphere,* as well as Coventry Patmore's original collection of poems, *The Angel in the House,* dated 1854. Todd found his best information in a work called *Suffer and Be Still,* as well as in a feminist text, *A History of Their Own,* which Addie also looked into. (See the Appendix for advice on locating and evaluating scholarly sources.)

For this project, neither Addie nor Todd read entire books. Instead they focused on specific chapters or portions of works related to their inquiry. They weren't expected to become major scholars in the field, only to broaden the base of their perspective. They did keep rough notes on their findings, however, and after reading Woolf a second time, both modified their responses.

Here are excerpts from Addie Gilbert's second reading:

Why is Woolf so angry? And why does she keep harping on how women should continue to battle against "a certain phantom"? She says, "There are many phantoms and obstacles . . . , many ghosts to fight, many prejudices to overcome," What ghosts? What prejudices? Just what is it she's encouraging women to guard against?

Carol Christ's essay, "Victorian Masculinity and the Angel in the House," was really helpful to me. Ms. Christ says the phrase "angel in the house" was first used as the title of a "domestic epic poem" by Coventry Patmore (NOTE: find this poem). He was supposed to be some kind of famous Victorian poet. He describes the courtship and marriage of Honoria, the so-called perfect lady, the angel. She is unselfish, gentle, simple, and noble. She came to represent the ideal woman (146). The angel in the house existed to protect men from evil, and in order to accomplish that a woman needed to be pure and lovely and unselfish (149). Apparently God made women to please men and knowing how made them angelic.

Reading about the history of the angel in the house, I became more and more aware of how often the word "traditional" appeared. <u>The American Heritage Dictionary</u> defines "traditional" as "the mode of thought or behavior followed by people continuously from one generation to another." For the first time I began to understand Woolf's anger and hostility. I feel angry too. If women follow Coventry Patmore's tradition, if they continue to believe that their role is to be the angel, then they have to give up everything that makes them an individual. Their only role in life is to act out a stereotype someone else created for them. Virginia Woolf's essay is making a lot more sense.

And here's a brief excerpt from Todd's second response, written after beginning his research:

I already knew I was strongly in favor of women's rights, so when I read Woolf's "Angel" my first response was it just confirmed what I already felt. But after I began to think about it I realized where my feelings came from. I think it had to do with my own feelings for my mother after she got divorced. In an essay I found by Peter Cominos found in Martha Vicinus' Suffer and Be Still, he writes that for Victorian men "pure-mindedness . . . was an exalted state of feminine consciousness, a state of unique deficiency or mindlessness in their daughters of that most elementary, but forbidden knowledge of their own sexuality, instincts and desires as well as the knowledge of good and evil." Innocence became a "mechanism of sexual repression" (157). The problem is, after centuries of training, almost all women accepted that they had to be a certain type of creature--innocent. They had to be inferior and submissive to men in all things.

When my mother married I don't think much had really changed. She found the obstacles to work basically gone. With only a year of college, she could never obtain a job at a high level, but she could develop an identity, a sense of pride and self-competence, through her work. Her superiors respected her for the quality of her work as well as her intelligence. But inwardly, my mother had been trained to believe that her relationship with men had to be one of submission and innocence. In a work setting, she could be as strong as any man. After her divorce however she returned to being a piece of fluff. When she dated men her voice became child-like and her own ideas just vanished. It was like her knowledge of the world evaporated. Whatever men she happened to be dating defined her in his own image and my mother went along with it without any awareness of degradation. It was me who felt humiliated.

Both Addie and Todd are moving through similar stages here. Both are extending their base of understanding by researching historical ideas and forces that affected the author of the text and the culture in which the author

Reminders

Critical reading is a process of learning how to discipline a reading response by considering the multiple influences on text, author, and reader.

- Begin with self-scrutiny of your emotional reactions. Clarify assumptions and constraints that may limit or influence initial judgment. Be willing, if necessary, to modify your immediate responses.
- Train yourself to recognize the vital power of language:

  —how it shapes and limits perception of the world,
  —how it both forms and influences ideas and values,
  —how "meaning" is usually an interaction of denotation and connotation.

- Whenever possible, consider how historical forces may have influenced an author or text, and how historical events in your own era may shape a reading response.
- Account for cultural influences that affect the author as well as your own reaction.
- Remember that fullness of judgment involves both heart and mind. Thought and feeling always interact. Critical reading is the ability to explore and discover those relationships.

lived. And both are using their new information to reflect upon their personal responses to the text. The result is a developing sense of critical perspective.

Research of this type is not always possible or necessary. Yet a strong reading, a critical reading, almost always involves placing a text in its cultural and historical context, considering the forces of language at work on both author and reader, and reflecting seriously upon our own emotional reactions. *How* we reach the "meaning" of a text, *how* we try to understand it becomes a key in determining the quality of the significance we finally arrive at.

All of this may seem complex, and in one sense it is. Thought and feeling interact. Critical thinking is both an act of the mind and a disciplining of (or listening to) our emotions. It should seldom involve a total repression of emotion just as it should never involve unlimited subjective indulgence. The trick here is to bring to life the feelings and ideas a text stirs in us, seeking out the patterns and relationships we discover, and connecting them to what we already know—to our life's experiences—as well as to other forces at play in the world around us.

FOCUSED WRITING

The merit of the mind lies not so much in its ability to store information and ideas, but in its potential for being lively and vital, for its ability to move facts and ideas around, to probe them and discover points at which they act upon each other.

To write a critical essay may at first seem forbiddingly complex. You may find yourself juggling emotions and experience (both yours and the author's). You may find ideas, cultural values, and historical forces struggling against each other (both yours and the author's). Where do you begin? How do you narrow your focus? How can you incorporate these different forces into one coherent paper? Your discovery draft may have no more shape and form than an amoeba in love. All the more important at this stage that you allow yourself the right to fail, to explore passages that go nowhere, to cross out and throw away.

Incorporating Research

If you've done research, the temptation may be to cut and paste a series of quotations together, merely to get something on the page. But the essay you're trying to construct must still be yours. A long series of quotations and paraphrases taken from others will not show *your* mind and heart engaged with the text at hand. The secondary sources you may have looked into as part of your study should be used only to support—or to argue against—an interpretation of your own. In some cases, of course, "your own interpretation" may derive from insights you've gained through studying those outside sources. Your reading of a text may be modified or changed dramatically by considering the historical or cultural context. Yet the essay should still be yours.

The solution here is not that difficult. If some portion of your thoughts is derived primarily from information you've found elsewhere, simply be honest and identify the source. Acknowledge your debt. Then use your own words to shape your reading, incorporating that influential source at a few key places.

Here is how a sophomore, David Dawson, writing on values expressed in Renaissance art, handled it:

> I want to acknowledge the influence of John Berger's Ways of Seeing on my own understanding of Hollyforth's pictorial essay on Renaissance art. Until I read Berger, I assumed that when I looked at Leonardo's Virgin of the Rocks, I was looking at it exactly as Leonardo himself looked at it, or as others later in the 18th century had looked at it. But Berger points out that "Today we see the art of the past as nobody saw it before. We actually perceive it in a different way" (16). Why? Because of changes in our understanding of perspective, and, strangely enough, in the development of the camera. These two developments taught us to literally see the world differently. Thus, when Hollyforth writes that. . . .

Dawson makes no attempt here to disguise who has influenced his reading of Caroline Hollyforth's work on Leonardo Da Vinci. And why should he? His initial experience of a painting by Leonardo has been modified by Berger's insight that our way of perceiving art (and the world) is affected by cultural and historical developments. Dawson now has a richer perspective of his own visual and experiential reaction. An instructor reading this essay will be impressed, not only by Dawson's growth—which is after all why students come to college—but also by his honesty in identifying the source of that growth.

Remember, however, that your personal reading of a text should not necessarily be abandoned—and certainly not suppressed—merely because others read it differently. You may recall how Todd Porter, for example, was not interested so much in the women's movement of the 19th century as such, but in why Virginia Woolf's essay made him angry. Why did it have a personal affect on him? Why did he feel so strongly about the cultural conditioning of women in an earlier era? Why was he convinced that "nothing had changed"? For Todd, looking into outside sources became a way of confirming his own response, as much as a way of clarifying Virginia Woolf's essay. For Todd, the difficulty in writing his paper lay more in the technical difficulty of integrating historical facts that reflected on or amplified his initial reading experience.

Identifying Secondary Sources

All ideas and information concerning cultural, social, or historical background, as well as quotations and paraphrases (rephrasings in your own words) taken from other authors must be clearly documented. The formal methods of documentation, such as where to place the page numbers and whether or not to use commas and parentheses are illustrated in the Appendix. But the technicalities are not enough. A well-written essay must not only incorporate secondary materials correctly, it needs to do so with grace and style.

Assuming a quotation fits properly into a clear context, a writer might insert it into an essay like this?

> "Lincoln could argue with lucidity and passion against slavery on moral grounds, while acting cautiously in practical points" (Zinn 183).

All other information about the quote (who wrote it, what source it's taken from, dates of publication, and so on) would have to be listed at the end of the essay on a Works Cited page. (A sample of a Works Cited page can be found on p. 740.)

However, experienced writers know that quotations and paraphrases can be made stronger—and that one's own writing will take on more authority—by including the author of the quotation in the text itself.

> Howard Zinn has observed that "Lincoln could argue with lucidity and passion against slavery on moral grounds, while acting cautiously in practical points" (183).

Authority can be further strengthened by adding information that support Zinn's credentials.

> Historian Howard Zinn has observed that . . .

or

> Social historian Howard Zinn has observed that . . .

or

> Howard Zinn, author of a dozen controversial books that challenge conventional interpretations of history, has observed that . . .

Sometimes, the title of the source might be more meaningful to a reader than the name of the author:

> In *A People's History of the United States,* Lincoln is described as one who "could argue with lucidity and passion against slavery on moral grounds, while acting cautiously in practical points" (Zinn 183).

Usually, some combination of all these techniques, especially the first time a quotation or paraphrase is used, is probably the strongest approach:

> In *A People's History of the United States,* Howard Zinn, an iconoclastic historian, writes that "Lincoln could argue with lucidity and passion against slavery on moral grounds, while acting cautiously in practical points" (183).

Clearly other information may sometimes be needed. The date of publication, in some instances, might affect the reader's judgment. A work published in 1845 opposing the right of women to vote would be perceived differently than the same argument published in 1990. Historical and cultural changes would affect our reading of it.

The point here is to provide your audience with an appropriate amount of data so that those outside sources you find important enough to include can be fairly evaluated in the context of your own paper. Once you've provided such data, however, all further references can be abbreviated.

> Zinn later argues that when Lincoln issued his first Emancipation Proclamation, it was for political, not moral reasons (187).

> Even though the thesis of *A People's History* seems to be that Lincoln was pressured into taking his position (187), the result has to be looked at in different terms . . .

We aren't advocating a formula for any of this. Only common sense. Details that support your sources should be included as appropriate, first to clarify, and second to lend weight and authority to your own writing.

Integrating Secondary Sources

Quotations from outside sources are not something tossed into a paper for decorative effect. Your reader needs to understand why the material was important enough to include, the context it originally occurred in, and how it relates to your argument. Presumably, as the writer, you've seen all these points in your head. But unless it's explained on paper, the reader may only be puzzled.

Here's an example of the problem in an early draft from Todd's paper on Virginia Woolf.

> In the essay, Woolf describes her efforts to become a novelist. She has to overcome her limitations.

> <u>. . . the making of Feather Flowers, Hair Ornaments, Flowers of Fruit in Wax, Shell Work, Porcupine Quill Work, the gilding of Plaster Casts, Bead and Bugle Work, and Seaweed Pictures</u> (Anderson 141).

Although women authors were frowned upon, a long history of women novelists had begun to set a precedent, beginning with Aphra Behn in the 1660s who was the first middle-class woman to openly write for profit. But Woolf is eventually able to overcome the oppressive conditioning imposed on her by her culture.

Todd has provided a correct technical documentation of a quotation from an author named Anderson. Yet on first reading we have a difficult time understanding how the quotation relates to anything. The paragraph seems to suggest that Anderson is writing about Virginia Woolf's "limitations," which include making Feather Flowers, something that strikes us as odd. Nor can we understand how the quotation from Anderson relates to Todd's following sentence on women novelists. No doubt Todd knows how each part connects, but he needs to slow down and provide each step of his thinking process. The context for the essay by Woolf itself needs to be provided; then the context for the quotation by Anderson, as well as its connection to Woolf. And finally, we need to know what Anderson's observation signifies or how it relates, especially to women authors.

Todd rewrote and came back with the following:

Context for Woolf essay now provided

In a 1931 speech to a society devoted to women's right to work, Woolf describes her attempts at becoming a novelist. The effort involved two phases.

Overview of Woolf essay

First, Woolf had to overcome the image of the pure, incompetent, naive, virtuous woman who was, according to the Victorian standards of the 19th century, capable only of looking beautiful and making doilies for sofa arms. In A History of Our Own, Bonnie Anderson and Judith Zinsser report that "lady's work," by definition, was anything lacking in utilitarian value. Appropriate activities included "the making of Feather Flowers, Hair Ornaments, Flowers of Fruit in Wax, Shell Work, Porcupine Quill Work, the gilding of Plaster Casts, Bead and Bugle Work, and Seaweed Pictures" (141). Woolf admits that becoming a writer was probably the easiest way for a woman to break the chains. Although women authors were frowned upon, a long history of women novelists had begun to set a precedent, beginning with Aphra Behn in the 1660s who was the first middle-class woman to openly write for profit (Norton 87). Yet even though Woolf came from a literary family, the image of what a woman was supposed to be--the "angel" who always sacrificed for others, who had no opinions of her own, who needed a man to

Outside source introduced with title, authors, & context

Quotation now part of correct context

Connection to Woolf noted

Explanation & discussion

Paraphrase now documented

Relationship to Woolf's struggle clarified

```
support and protect her--the
angel haunted her. Woolf says
she "encountered her with the
very first words" she ever
wrote. "The shadow of her wings
fell on my page. . . ." But
Woolf was eventually able to
overcome the oppressive condi-
tioning imposed on her by her
culture.
```

Now we can see that Todd's source, Bonnie Anderson, is not writing about Virginia Woolf specifically, but about the limitations imposed on Victorian women in general. And Todd has clarified how Woolf, in an attempt to break away from such meaningless "women's work," attempted to become an author. Thus the context for the quotation is clarified, as well as its relationship to Virginia Woolf. Finally, at the end of the paragraph, by using Woolf's own words from her essay, Todd shows how all points interact: the cultural background, Woolf's method for escaping it, the inner struggle it involved, and the results. The step-by-step reasoning here is now clear and satisfying.

In simple terms, you must aid your reader by including each phase of your thinking process. When you use quotations, paraphrases, ideas, and facts from other sources, locate the material in a context, discuss it, and point to specific connections, the ones that made you decide to use the material in the first place. Then explain the importance of what you've found. Intelligence, according to Aristotle, is essentially an act of perceiving relationships. The writing of a critical essay, then, one that combines both thought and feeling, should reveal, as simply and as clearly as possible, each of those relationships. Your role as writer is to lead us into seeing the interaction and cross-breeding of ideas and emotions that provoke insight and critical judgment.

THE FORMAL ESSAY

The editing stage of writing is the place to listen to your prose—literally "listen" to it. Read it aloud. Listen to the rhythms. The ear often tells you more than the eye. Why is it some writers move us with such power? Why can some writers convince us of their ideas with such force? Perhaps it's because the best writers create a sense of rhythm and pattern that moves us in almost inexplicable ways: we hear the power of their writing with the ear of the imagination.

Listen to Martin Luther King Jr. (We mean it. Read the following passage aloud and listen.)

> How does one determine whether a law is just or unjust? A just law is a man-made code that squares with the moral law or the law of God. An unjust law is a code that is out of harmony with the moral law. . . . Any law that uplifts human personality is just. Any law that degrades human personality is unjust. All segregation statutes are unjust because segregation distorts the soul and damages the personality. . . . Hence segregation is not only politically, economically, and sociologically unsound, it is morally wrong and sinful (507).

Some might argue that the strength of King's prose lies in the strength of his moral argument. Clearly there's some truth to that. But an author might possess all the forces of goodness and still not convince others. In fact, an author might—like Hitler—have all the force of evil in his or her words and convince a whole nation.

Experienced writers know that rhythms and patterns in language, not merely the ideas being expressed, affect both our hearts and our minds. Writing that persuades does so through consciously organized repetitions that can be identified and learned.

Repetition

In the same way that rhythm in music moves us to dance, rhythm in language can move us to believe or consent. Organized patterns of language actually affect our response to content. A patterned, rhythmical sentence clarifies the relationship between ideas, creates a sense of coherence and unity, and suggests to the reader a psychological sense of completeness.

The challenge for the writer is to repeat without seeming to do so. Direct repetition of the same word or sentence pattern can quickly put us to sleep.

> Jose walks to school each day. Jose dusts the black board each day. Jose eats his lunch each day.

Unless the goal is to show a reader the deadly repetition of Jose's life, such repetition is unsatisfying.

But controlled repetition—so-called theme and variation—has always been a key element of prose, as it has for all other art forms. Here's a passage from an essay on laughter by Henri Bergson.

> The first point to which attention should be called is that the comic does not exist outside the pale of what is strictly human. A landscape may be beautiful, charming, and sublime, or insignificant and ugly; it will never be laughable. You may laugh at an animal but only because you have detected it in some human attitude or expression. You may laugh at a hat, but what you are making fun of, in this case, is

> not the piece of felt or straw, but the shape that men have given it—the human caprice whose mold it has assumed. It is strange that so important a fact, and such a simple one, too, has not attracted to a greater degree the attention of philosophers. Several have defined man as "an animal which laughs." They might equally have defined him as an animal which is laughed at; for if any other animal, or some lifeless object, produces the same effect, it is always because of some resemblance to man, of the stamp he gave it or the use he puts it to.

On a first reading, you may have noticed no repetition at all. But try the paragraph again, this time reading aloud using a pencil to mark the text. Circle and underline the repetitions and variations. How many times does the word *human* occur? Look for variations of *men* and *man.* Count the references to *animal,* the variants of *laugh,* and the phrases that incorporate *defined.* Each repetition is interwoven, yet no single one seems particularly obvious. To the ear of the imagination, however, they establish an idea by reinforcing it: *laugh, laughable, laughed at.*

Now go back and read Martin Luther King, Jr.'s passage with a pencil in hand. Mark every repetition, every theme and variation.

You can create the same tight interweaving during the editing phase of your own essay. Read whole paragraphs of your essay aloud. Remove weak substitutes or vague terms like "it" or "things" for the name of the idea you're writing about—*laughter, human, animal.* The repetition of the noun is usually more effective. If the same word annoys the ear, replace it with a variation. But if a key word occurs only once, consider whether the word can be worked into the paragraph at appropriate intervals to reinforce it in the reader's mind.

The Parallel Sentence

Strong rhythms can also be created by a technique called *parallelism,* a method of showing the relationship between two or more ideas by using the same grammatical structure to express both components. What that structure might be is open to the writer's imagination: similar verb forms, similar nouns, similar prepositional phrases, similar introductory clauses. Here's how it works.

Begin with a single idea.

> *Chan Li's father promised to take him for a visit to Hong Kong.*

Add a second idea, one that relates in some way to the first.

> *Chan Li's father promised to take him for a visit to Hong Kong and that he would let him visit graves of his ancestors.*

Now we have two related ideas, but the sentence structure does not show that relationship. The promised idea in the first clause (before the *and*) is expressed differently from the promised idea in the second. Both ideas must be phrased in grammatically similar ways.

> Chan Li's father promised *to take* him for a visit to Hong Kong and *to let* him visit graves of his ancestors.

By making the infinitives (to take, to let) parallel, we have connected the two promises, first with a rhythmical similarity (de dum, de dum) and second with a psychological coherence that develops from the grammatical similarity.

Parallelism can be created with other grammatical structures.

> The director wants an actor *who knows* the part and *who has* an established sense of the stage. (*Adjective clauses are parallel.*)
>
> In his speech the President claimed to believe in *God, flag, and country.* (*Nouns are parallel.*)
>
> There I was, *running down the path, trying to pull up my pants,* and *tripping over my shoe laces.* (*Gerund phrases are parallel.*)

Perhaps the most common form of parallelism repeats an initial phrase before each clause.

> It is about time we realize that women make *better* teachers than mothers, *better* actresses than wives, *better* diplomats than cooks.
>
> —MARYA MANNES

The effectiveness of parallel structure is most obviously revealed when we encounter a passage in which the parallels are not grammatically constructed.

> Ask not what your country can do for you, but instead consider the ways that you might get involved in doing something for your nation if you had the opportunity to do it.

We need to point out, of course, that too much parallel structure can call attention to itself and seem artificial. Politicians and others who make speeches use extensive use of repetition and parallelism to aid the ear in following an argument. On the written page, selected parallelisms are usually more successful. But wherever significant points need to be forcefully related, parallel structure is essential.

Balanced Sentences

Another version of parallelism balances two ideas that may relate but which often show an element of contrast as part of that relationship.

> I come to bury Caesar, not to praise him.
>
> —SHAKESPEARE

> It is a sin to believe evil of others—but it is not a mistake.
>
> —H. L. MENCKEN

> The world will little note, nor long remember what we say here, but it can never forget what they did here.
>
> —ABRAHAM LINCOLN

If we return now to the passage from Martin Luther King, Jr. we can see him using all these variations.

> How does one determine whether a law is just or unjust? A just law is a man-made code that squares with the moral law or the law of God. An unjust law is a code that is out of harmony with the moral law. . . . Any law that uplifts human personality is just. Any law that degrades human personality is unjust. All segregation statutes are unjust because segregation distorts the soul and damages the personality. . . . Hence segregation is not only politically, economically, and sociologically unsound, it is morally wrong and sinful.

How many times is the word *law* repeated? The word *just* or its opposite *unjust?* The word *moral* or its variant? How does King balance one sentence against another? What different variations of parallelisms does he use throughout? How does it all work together to reach a powerful, reasoned, and seemingly inevitable conclusion in the final sentence?

Here is a passage from freshman Addie Gilbert, taken from an early draft of her essay on Virginia Woolf:

> The danger is for men as well as women that these phantoms which are really cultural stereotypes can be so easily accepted as positive models when in truth they are restrictive, reductive, unreal, and unpractical. Who wants to live in a world where half the race is passive and fails to act responsibly? What woman today wants to exist solely to please a man? I find it hard to believe that there are even many men today who want a woman to be passive and inactive. These then are the ghosts Woolf warns against. They justify doing "battle" against them because they "torment" and "kill" us.

The passage is not bad in itself. But we felt Addie missed an opportunity to strengthen it. A number of related points appear throughout which are not connected with parallel structure or with the conscious use of repetition. For example, the initial sentence is long and rambling. Could she tighten it by finding related qualities, then reorganize with similar syntax or similar grammatical patterns?

Here's how the original sentence begins:

```
The danger is that these phantoms for men as well as
women are really cultural stereotypes which can be
so easily accepted as positive models. . . .
```

After some study, Addie felt that "phantoms" and "cultural stereotypes" were clearly related. She wanted readers to see them as identical, but they were separated by a separate clause and unrelated grammatically. Addie rearranged the sentence to unite the linking elements:

```
These phantoms, these cultural stereotypes, may be
as dangerous to men as to women. . . .
```

Addie also begins two sentences with questions that might be extended as a pattern.

```
Who wants to live . . .?
What woman today wants to exist . . .?
```

By rearranging the next sentence, Addie created a third repetition:

```
What man today wants a woman to be passive and in-
active?
```

Because the word "ghost" is a key term throughout Virginia Woolf's essay as well as in Addie's response, Addie rewrote the ending in order to consciously repeat the term.

```
These then are the ghosts Woolf warns against,
ghosts which justify doing "battle" against. . . .
```

The resulting paragraph is now more pleasing to the ear and stronger in its overall effect. The reader can follow each step of the logic with more clarity.

```
These phantoms, these cultural stereotypes, may be
as dangerous to men as to women because they can so
easily be accepted as positive models when in truth
```

> they are restrictive and reductive, unreal and unpractical. Who wants to live in a world where half the race is passive, where half the race fails to act responsibly? What woman today wants to exist solely to please a man? What man today wants a woman to be passive and inactive? These then are the ghosts Woolf warns against, ghosts which justify doing "battle" against, because they "torment" and "kill."

With practice, using parallelism and balanced sentences can become almost intuitive, something you'll find yourself doing as early as the discovery draft. In the meantime, like other arts that must be learned, you'll probably need to make a conscious effort, both to study how successful writers incorporate such techniques and to use them in your own work.

Both Addie and Todd read their papers to members of their class. Both listened well to advice they received and revised again. Perhaps most importantly, they began to care deeply about the ideas they found themselves exploring. Virginia Woolf's original text became a way of clarifying values that were important to their own lives as well as a way of understanding more about the relationship of men and women in their own time.

Here is Addie's final draft.

KILLING THE PHANTOMS
Addie Gilbert

My Victorian grandmother believed that a woman's place was in the home, a myth she passed on to my mother, and one my mother would have liked to pass on to my sisters and me. But by the time we reached adulthood, things had changed. More and more women, married or not, were working outside the home, doing pretty much as they pleased. My sisters and I would never have accepted the restricted life my mother and my grandmother conformed to. We had minds of our own--something my mother continues to blame on our Italian father. Reading Virginia Woolf's speech, "Angel in the House," reminded me of the roles my grandmother and mother accepted without question.

Even after the second reading, I didn't find anything especially insightful or startlingly new about women and work. I'd heard most of it before. Woolf's speech seems to speak to a different generation of women. Surely today most women think for themselves, and surely most feel free to think and write whatever they want. What disturbs me about her speech is the language. Why does Woolf keep repeating the phrase, "kill the angel"? And why is the language so violent: "I killed her," and "Had I not killed her, she would have killed me," and "I did my best to kill her"? If I could be so calm about it all, why is Woolf so heated?

Woolf also disturbs me by using the synonym of "phantom" for "angel," even though for me the connotations are exact opposites. I realize my own resistance to thinking of the word "angel" in anything other than a positive sense. My Catholic upbringing has led me to believe angels are guardians who watch over and protect us, prodding us to make the right decisions. My angel is my protector. Watching Woolf use the words "angel" and "phantom" negatively and interchangeably puzzles me.

Woolf clearly distinguishes her angel as a phantom who "bothered," "wasted," and "tormented" her--all negative words. She defines the angel as sympathetic, charming, and unselfish--all positive adjectives in my mind. But Woolf makes her readers understand that this phantom-angel is dangerous because she refuses to allow a woman to think for herself. The words that accompany Woolf's description are violent: "battle," "fighting," "tormented," and "kill." She repeats the words "kill" and "killing" eight times.

I find myself asking the same questions over and over again: Why is Woolf so angry? And why does she caution us that women must continue to battle against "a certain phantom"? She warns, "There are many phantoms and obstacles . . . , many ghosts to fight, many prejudices to overcome." What ghosts? What prejudices? Just what is it she's encouraging women to guard against? What did Woolf know about the angel that I didn't understand?

I found some helpful background information in Carol Christ's essay, "Victorian Masculinity and the Angel in the House," from <u>A Widening Sphere</u>. The phrase "angel in the house" was first used as a title of a domestic epic poem by Coventry Patmore, a prominent Victorian poet. It describes the courtship and marriage of Honoria, the perfect lady, the angel, who is unselfish, gentle, simple, and noble. During the Victorian period, she came to represent the ideal woman (146). The angel in the house existed to protect men from evil, and in order to accomplish that a woman needed to be pure and lovely and unselfish (149). According to Sandra Gilbert and Susan Garbar in <u>The Madwoman in the Attic</u>, numerous books printed during the period describe the proper conduct for ladies reminding them to be submissive, modest, and selfless (23). Women were meant to please men and knowing how made them angelic (24).

According to Bonnie Anderson and Judith Zinsser in A History of Their Own, it was generally agreed that Victorian women would have a more positive impact if they stayed at home and were good wives and mothers. "If a woman remained traditionally subservient and deferential to men and did not challenge women's traditional behavior," she was not only considered virtuous, but morally superior to men, or in other words, an angel. On the other hand, if she became involved outside the home in political activities, education, and civil rights, she was criticized and condemned (122).

Reading about the history of the angel in the house, I became more and more aware of how often the word "traditional" appeared. The American Heritage Dictionary defines "traditional" as "the mode of thought or behavior followed by people continuously from one generation to another." For the first time I began to understand Woolf's anger and hostility. If women follow the "tradition," if they continue to believe that their role is to be the angel, then they must give up their individuality. They must conform. While the angel in the house suggests the glorification of women, it is actually a cultural stereotype that limits and constrains her. A woman who conforms to the angel status neither thinks nor acts; she is not free to. Several historians perceive this status as a form of slavery (Helsinger et al. 92). Angel and phantom merge to become one thing.

"The certain phantom" Woolf warns us to keep up our guard against then is any cultural stereotype that becomes binding, any model that narrowly restricts what women can do and be. These phantoms, these cultural stereotypes, may be as dangerous to men as to women because they can so easily be accepted as positive models when in truth they are restrictive and reductive, unreal and unpractical. Who wants to live in a world where half the race is passive, where half the race fails to act responsibly? What woman today wants to exist solely to please a man? What man today wants a woman to be passive and inactive? These then are the ghosts Woolf warns against, ghosts which do justify doing "battle" against, because they "torment" and "kill."

If we allow ourselves to conform to a cultural stereotype, then we can easily be prejudged by the model. We are expected to act in a certain way and in failing to do so risk alienation or condemnation. What growth, what change, what possible new alternatives can evolve in a society that condemns original thought and action?

Unfortunately, for some men and women in the nineties, the angel in the house still exists, just as it existed for my grandmother and my mother. For others, the Victorian ideal has been replaced by newer cultural stereotypes for both men and women which are perhaps just as dangerous: the Supermom, the Good Mother, the Yuppie Executive, the Self-Made

Woman. Woolf reminds us to be wary of any stereotype which prevents us from thinking and feeling and acting as individuals. Her warning to be on guard for other phantoms, is a plea to all of us to be cautious of any stereotype we blindly accept without question. Emancipation for women (and men) can exist only when we are free to be true to our hearts and our minds. Killing the phantoms in our houses is a responsible act, and no small deed, even today.

Addie has attempted to relate her discoveries to her own era, finding a connection between Virginia Woolf's argument and the different, yet related, problems of the 1990s. In Todd Porter's final draft, Todd has focused on a more personal exploration, yet he too sees an ultimate connection to the world around him.

EVERYTHING HAS CHANGED, NOTHING HAS CHANGED
by
Todd Porter

I was raised by two different women who claimed to be the same person. My parents were divorced when my sister Sheila was five and I was three. Since then, my mom has eked out a living as a bookkeeper in a small savings and loan. She gets up at six each morning. When we were small, she made our breakfasts and lunches, then caught her own bus on dark winter streets. At work she had a reputation for efficiency. She knew clearly her own sense of responsibilities. She was proud of her abilities. She never wavered. When the washing machine died or Sheila needed braces or the rent went up, my mom took a second job. Sometimes she sold tickets at night at a movie theater. But dinner was always there waiting for us. She had prepared it before she left. Sometimes she worked the midnight shift in a nursing home. But the next morning the clothes we needed for school were always ironed. She was a fortress of strength, except on strange occasions.

When she dated a man something weird happened to her. She reverted to a giddy young girl. She wore too much makeup. She flounced about in frilly dresses. She smiled and giggled and asked questions she already knew the answer to. And always she submitted to whatever her man of the moment thought or said or did. Did he like World Wide Wrestling on late-night TV? Then my mom liked wrestling. Was he a Republican? Then my mom became a Republican. Did he eat sunflower seeds? My mom suddenly adored sunflower seeds.

It struck me as crazy, even when I was very small. By the time I was in high school and my mom was in her late thirties, it embarrassed me. How could she be two people? One person was full of strength and determination. That person was strong, intelligent, committed to her children and her work. And then there was that other person, the one my sister and I rolled our eyes at behind her back, the one that turned to Silly Putty when a man came in the door. Who was that person?

Not until I read Virginia Woolf's "The Angel in the House" did the answer begin to come clear. Woolf, of course, is writing about something totally different. In a 1931 speech to a society devoted to women's right to work, Woolf describes her attempts at becoming a novelist. The effort involved two phases. First, Woolf had to overcome the image of the pure, incompetent, naive, virtuous woman. That Victorian woman, according to standards of the 19th century, was capable only of looking beautiful and making doilies for sofa arms. In A History of Our Own, Bonnie Anderson and Judith Zinsser report that "lady's work," by definition, was anything lacking in utilitarian value. Appropriate activities included "the making of Feather Flowers, Hair Ornaments, Flowers of Fruit in Wax, Shell Work, Porcupine Quill Work, the gilding of Plaster Casts, Bead and Bugle Work, and Seaweed Pictures" (141). Woolf admits that becoming a writer was probably the easiest way for a woman to break the chains.

Although women authors were frowned upon, a long history of women novelists had begun to set a precedent, beginning with Aphra Behn in the 1660s who was the first middle-class woman to openly write for profit (Norton 87). Yet even though Woolf came from a literary family, the image of what a woman was supposed to be--the "angel" who always sacrificed for others, who had no opinions of her own, who needed a man to support and protect her--the angel haunted her. Woolf says she "encountered her with the very first words" she ever wrote. "The shadow of her wings fell on my page. . . . " But Woolf was eventually able to overcome the oppressive conditioning imposed on her by her culture.

Her second struggle proved more difficult. Freeing herself to work and write was one thing.

Being able to write honestly from a woman's point of view was a different kind of problem. I think the problem was that after centuries of training almost all women accepted that they were and must be a certain type of creature: inferior, submissive to men in all things, lacking in physical strength and moral judgment, and most of all, "pure." An essay that seems helpful on this subject is by Peter Cominos, reprinted in Martha Vicinus' <u>Suffer and Be Still</u>. Cominos writes that for Victorian men "pure-mindedness . . . was an exalted state of feminine consciousness, a state of unique deficiency or mindlessness in their daughters of that most elementary, but forbidden knowledge of their own sexuality, instincts and desires as well as the knowledge of good and evil." Innocence, Cominos says, became a "mechanism of sexual repression" (157).

For Woolf, her imagination as a writer was "dashed" against the rocks of such repression. She found she could not write honestly about passion, or about her body. She could never quite overcome the fact that her inner image of self was defined not by her but by men. Outwardly, she says, the obstacles to work had been removed by the time she began writing in the early part of the 20th century. But inwardly, there were "still many ghosts to fight, many prejudices to overcome." Woolf observes, rather sadly it seems to me, that she thinks it will be a long time before that final phantom is slain.

Almost half a century later, when my mom married at age 19 (my age now) little had changed. She found the obstacles to work basically gone. Although with only a year of college, she could never obtain a job at a high level, she did find she could develop an identity, a sense of pride and self-competence, through her work. She found that her superiors, both male and female, respected her for the quality of her work as well as the intelligence she brought to the job. But inwardly, my mom had been trained to believe that her relationship with men must be one of submission and innocence. In a work setting, she could be as strong as any man. On a date, she became a piece of fluff. Her voice became almost child-like, her own ideas vanished, her knowledge of the world evaporated. The man she was with defined her in his own image and my mom submitted to the change without ever feeling degraded.

I have heard people argue that today's 19-year-old woman has overcome that final struggle. Many of the females I've met since coming to college act as sexually free as any male. Unlike Virginia Woolf, they can be honest about their bodies and their passions. But one of the freshmen women I know, a really smart girl who attends this college on an honors scholarship and who proudly claims to be a feminist, is also living with a man who verbally abuses her, privately and in public. He has twice driven her to attempted suicide. In class, she speaks up, argues with male students, and is a leader of at least one group of female students. But in private, with her lover, she allows him to define her as he wishes, as incompetent and submissive.

Reminders

Incorporating research into any essay is always a matter of integrating your own ideas, feelings, and perceptions with those of others. Here are a few suggestions and expectations.

- Identify all sources for cultural, social, or historical information and ideas, whether used as quotations or as paraphrases.
- To add clarity and authority to your own text, introduce outside sources by providing the author, title, and context.
- Discuss the connection to your own material and explain the importance of it. Do not assume your reader will already see the connection as you see it.
- Document all quotations, paraphrases, ideas, information, and patterns of organization with parenthetical (in-text) references, even if you've already identified author or title in your essay.
- If possible, read your draft essay aloud (to others or to yourself) and listen to the rhythms, emphasis, and flow of language.

—Edit for effective repetition to clarify a relationship between ideas and to create coherence and unity.

—Watch for opportunities to use parallel and balanced sentence structures whenever related or opposing ideas might be made stronger.

She represses her own ideas and becomes dependent on him.

How much has changed? A woman in the 1990s can enter almost any profession. She can work as a laborer on a highway crew or as an astronaut. She can have a sexual life as free or as limited as she now chooses, based on her own desires and values. But does that really mean women today have erased the stereotype of their relation to men, as lovers, as friends? How many college-aged women still defer to male egos? How many are still two women pretending to be one? For some at least, everything has changed, and nothing has changed.

The act of critical thinking brings our experience of a text to life, encouraging us to reflect on both thought and feeling. For that reason, we were pleased with Todd and Addie's efforts. They worked in the true spirit of a liberal arts tradition, attempting to find a "liberating knowledge" that would free them from their own limitations. Perhaps what pleased us most was that they found such knowledge by testing emotion and reason against the other. Their personal feelings were not considered sacred or closed to modification, but as starting places for reflection. Nor were ideas treated as abstract information, to be sorted out and placed on a dusty shelf of the mind, but as things integral to living a life. Todd and Addie not only developed insight into a single text by another author, they developed a context for understanding their own culture and for making choices important to their future.

CHAPTER 5

MAKING MEANING

THOUGHTFUL READING

Some evenings our friends Meg and Steve would sit with us on the summer porch. They'd been married about a year then. We would laugh and argue, rocking in the old wicker chairs. After dark we switched on the yellow light, hoping to keep away bugs. One evening we talked about the senior art exhibit we'd all gone to see, and once we ate popcorn and played Trivial Pursuit. The time we remember most, however, happened just before classes began in September. The evenings were chilly and Steve had decided to smoke a cigar. Meg announced she had a riddle for us.

"I'm a riddle in nine syllables," she said. "What am I?"

"You're a parliamentarian," Olivia said.

Steve counted on his fingers. "That's only six syllables."

We tried others: Afganistani, psychobiologist, valetudinarian. Meg had to help us out. "It comes from a poem by Sylvia Plath."

She read the poem to us, turning in her chair so that the yellow light would fall across a book she'd brought with her.

▪ Metaphors ▪

I'm a riddle in nine syllables
An elephant, a ponderous house,
A melon strolling on two tendrils.
A red fruit, ivory, fine timbers!
This loaf's big with its yeasty rising.
Money's new-minted in this fat purse.
I'm a means, a stage, a cow in calf.

I've eaten a bag of green apples,
Boarded the train, there's no getting off.

We asked her to read it a second time and then we began to play with it. Every line contained a new metaphor, sometimes two or three, far more than most poems, it seemed. Steve pointed out that most of the metaphors suggested something swollen, overly large, or ripe: an "elephant," a "melon," a "loaf" rising. But I objected. What about "stage," "means," or "train"? Two kinds of metaphor, then. Those that depicted ripeness, and those that expressed a passage or movement toward something else. But what about "fine timbers"? What on earth were those? Or "ivory"?

Olivia pointed out that both were highly valuable. As was new-minted money in your purse. "It's self-evident," she said. "The poem is about being pregnant."

"Well, yes," Steve agreed, but reluctantly. "There seems more to it. What's really going on here is the joy of pregnancy." Steve pointed to images he associated with pleasure: "melons," "red fruit," "ivory," "yeasty rising," and so on. "The poet," he argued, "is showing us the funny, clumsy, pleasure of a woman ripe with the life of an unborn child. The poem is about the sweet swelling of waiting, knowing that the most special thing in the world is happening to you."

"Now wait a minute," I said. Look at all the negative images: "a ponderous house," "a cow," or eating a "bag of green apples"—something that would make most people sick. And although a melon is an image that usually suggests something sweet, a "melon strolling on two tendrils" is grotesque. Even the over-stuffing of too many metaphors into the poem itself might suggest bloating, an undesirable condition. We noted that seeing oneself only as a "stage" in a process or a "means" to something else could be depressing.

"And what about that train ride?" Meg asked. "She's boarded the train and can't get off. She's a prisoner."

"Not necessarily," Steve said. "A train ride can be an exciting journey, it leads to new places, a new life."

Meg had passed the book around and Olivia was studying the page. "Nine lines," she said, laughing. "And nine syllables in every line."

We all agreed that Plath was counting the months. We had solved the riddle. But of course we hadn't solved the poem. A poem isn't something you solve. It's not a mystery with a right answer. On some points we all agreed, but on others we read the poem quite differently. In fact, we had come at it from opposite attitudes and found opposing qualities in the text. The poet herself may have felt ambivalent. The poem is both playful and serious. It contains a tension that plays two attitudes off against each other. Plath may have been a "riddle in nine syllables," even to herself, pondering and ponderous. Was her pregnancy something she felt happy over, something that made her feel the biological pleasure of ripening and bearing fruit, or was it something she felt trapped with, something that had turned her into a cow and made her sick, physically and emotionally? Was it perhaps both at the same time? No matter which way we read the poem, the poet herself seemed to have found that her life had become a literal metaphor. She was one thing becoming another, a metamorphosis.

Later, after Meg and Steven had left and we were cleaning up the glasses, Olivia said she was glad Meg was expecting a child.

"Is she?" I asked. "When did she say that?"

Olivia only rolled her eyes.

Language and Metaphor

We said in Chapter 4 that without language, we would not have ideas at all. We pointed out how the denotation and connotation of a word combine to create its meaning or significance. The result is that ideas—shaped and formed by language—are complex interactions of mind and feeling. If we add to this Aristotle's observation that intelligence is the ability to see relationships, it then becomes clear that ideas may also be shaped by discovering relationships through words themselves.

In simple terms, metaphor unites unlike or unexpected qualities, usually by applying the name of one thing to another. In doing so we discover a relationship not seen or felt before. When Plath calls herself a "ponderous house," we must rethink and resee the whole nation of her condition, in a way that we would not if she simply announced she was expecting a child.

In a similar way, we can write that "Richard has great courage," but the description lies on the page dull as soap. When we unite Richard with the courage of a powerful beast, however, when we call him "Richard the Lion Hearted," we not only create a mental image (or picture) of Richard's courage, we metaphorically invest Richard with all the emotional and mythical qualities a lion calls up in us—powerful, fearful, ferocious, unflinching, dignified, and so on. Richard becomes something new, something that wasn't there until language created it, or perhaps something that *was* there but could not be fully experienced until metaphor exposed it.

Metaphor works best when it's unexpected, either because the context it occurs in surprises us, or because while the word or image suggests one reference the context points to another.

Consider the following poem by X. J. Kennedy.

▪ Ars Poetica ▪

The goose that laid the golden egg
Died looking up its crotch
To find out how its sphincter worked.
Would you lay well? Don't watch.

Here the metaphor occurs in the final line where the poet turns from describing the goose to addressing "you" the reader. The word "lay" clearly recalls the goose. But because the context has shifted to "you," the term now points to a new reference. To some type of accomplishment? To creativity? To success? Because of the context shift, the first three lines themselves suddenly become more than humorous description. They now take on the quality of a parable—a type of story with metaphorical or symbolic suggestiveness. An unexpected twist has turned a funny rhyme about a goose into a serious (although still tongue-in-cheek) observation about human success and failure.

Poets have traditionally spent much of their effort searching for new metaphors—for an exactness of metaphor—that will open the mind and heart to new insight. How does one convey the qualities of a lover: "Shall I compare thee to a summer's day?" Or the recognition that death comes to us all: "But at my back I always hear/ Time's winged chariot hurrying near." Or the deep feeling of faith: "The Lord is my shepherd." Yet there is an inescapable paradox here. The poet tries for exactness but because words never convey the exact meaning to everyone, and because they suggest different qualities and evoke different emotional responses depending upon a variety of factors, including the context in which they appear and the cultural and historical influences that shape both writer and reader, a metaphor almost always has a multiplicity of meanings, sometimes even for a single reader.

(By permission of John Hart and Field Enterprises, Inc.)

Poets strive for exactness, yet poets know and even love the paradox that language is never fixed and unchanging. Poets love the play, the pleasure of words and images that shift under their very pen. To enjoy poetry, then, even the most serious of poetry, requires you adopt a different reading attitude. A phone book is read for a single purpose: information. A brochure on the assembly of a new lawn mower is read for information and instruction. A news magazine might be read for information plus analysis and explanation, as well as entertainment. And from a novel, we might expect deeper experiences: entertainment and escape, but also insight into human character, society, and perhaps the human condition itself. The problem occurs when we approach all reading experiences with the same attitude or expectations.

A phone book is not intended to give us deep emotional pleasure. We do not expect a novel to instruct us on how to assemble machinery. The first reading of a poem, then, often disappoints or confuses an inexperienced reader. A poem may seem obscure. The words link together in odd ways. Sometimes, the language refers to nothing tangible, or worse, it refers to more than one thing at a time. If we approach the reading of a poem looking for information, or a single meaning, a specific message or theme, we're almost bound to be disappointed. If the poem "does not make sense," we may feel disgusted and decide we just don't like poetry.

The problem lies in expectations. Poetry does require the highest level of mental concentration (which is one reason it develops powers of critical thinking) just as trigonometry requires a higher level of mental attention than simple addition and subtraction (thus developing powers of abstract logic). But poetry is also play. The writer shapes language into new forms, using all the rich powers of connotations, images, rhythms, and sounds, as well as metaphor, to push both mind and heart toward new experience.

Thinking Through Metaphor

Metaphor, as we've been discussing it, is not mere ornamentation limited to poetry. Even though we may be unconscious of it, all of us use metaphor in everyday speech. Most nouns are essentially metaphorical or contain metaphorical roots. When you pay for *board* at college, you're paying for meals that were once literally served on a board—a table. Someone once saw in a *daisy* the image of the sun which in turn was already known metaphorically as the *eye of day*, or *day's eye*. Even a relatively abstract noun such as *reality* derives from Latin roots meaning *property*, leading us to conceive of that which is real as that which is tangible, something that can be possessed and controlled. In most cases, we fail to recognize the metaphors inherent in ordinary language. The insight and excitement of a new relationship has faded from overuse. When we *catch a cold* we don't envision ourselves running across center field with leather mitt in hand, attempting to catch a virus. When we speak of Indianapolis as the *heart of the country* we seldom think of the actual physical heart with ventricles and aortas.

Yet metaphor is so fundamental to language it actually contributes to the way we perceive the world. We tend to understand one thing in terms of another.

> Space is curved.
>
> Time is money.
>
> Politics is war.
>
> God is love.

These are metaphors we may live by, that we may accept without question. We even use whole bodies of related metaphors to express single concepts. For example, how do we get ideas? Where does creative thinking come from? We may find we can discuss such questions—questions that deal with the mind—only in biological terms that seem more familiar.

The original development was *spawned* by discoveries in computer graphics.

His work *gave birth to* the field of hydrolics.

Research on AIDS remains in its *infancy*.

This new book was the *brainchild* of the publisher's wife.

Her philosophy will *live* forever.

His study of depression in monkeys is *moribund*.

Belief in the Great Chain of Being *died* in the 17th century.

It's time to *resurrect* older concepts of honor and courtesy.

These everyday metaphors may subtly, and without our knowing, affect basic values and beliefs. Consider how love, when conceived of in economic metaphors, might influence an understanding of our relationship with others.

Love requires an *investment* of emotions.

Marriage is a *gamble*.

She's a *gold-digger*.

They're involved in a *high-stakes* affair.

He's *shopping* for a new bride.

She's a real *asset* to him.

Such metaphors imply that love is a commodity, that one of the most important experiences in life may be relegated to one of possession, competition, and exchange. In an essay on "The Art of Loving," philosopher Eric Fromm points out how young people who think in such metaphors may feel they are in love when they've found "the best object available on the market." When love is conceived in economic metaphors, it may exclude spiritual values and influence the course of one's life.

And note that our example here comes from an essay, not from poetry. Too often we tend to think of metaphor as a figurative device limited to verse. But metaphor is central to the way human beings use language to make meaning. Understanding metaphor is therefore central to critical thinking in general. Just as our culture, history, personal experience, and background may all have an unconscious affect on our response to reading, so may our language—and the language of the author. Critical thinking requires us to bring all these elements to consciousness.

Interpreting

When we apply any or all of the various aspects of critical thinking to something we read—a novel, poem, play, or a work of science, biography, history and so on—we're engaged in an act of interpretation. To interpret simply means to clarify, elucidate or explain something, as the reader sees it. Interpretation could potentially involve every element of "reading" we've discussed so far: seeking out the details of a text and taking notes in the margins or in

Metaphor

A metaphor, through an implied or suggested comparison, unites two unlike qualities as one, revealing a new or unexpected insight. "The greatest thing by far," Aristotle has said, "is to be a master of metaphor. It is the one thing that cannot be learned from others; and it is also a sign of genius, since a good metaphor implies an intuitive perception of the similarity in dissimilars."

- A dream is a little hidden door in the innermost and most secret recesses of the soul.

  —CARL JUNG

- Every man must walk to the beat of his own drummer.

  —HENRY DAVID THOREAU

- After thousands of years we're still strangers to darkness, fearful aliens in an enemy camp with our arms crossed over our chests.

  —ANNIE DILLARD

Simile

A simile makes a direct comparison between two unlike qualities, often using the terms ***like*** *or* ***as****. Similes are like windows in dark rooms; they let in light and clarify both the familiar and the obscure.*

- Days darted past us like minnows.

  —FRED CHAPPELL

- His hands were like wild birds.

  —JOHN UPDIKE

- The crickets sounded like the slipping each time of three matched links of small chain.

  —JAMES AGEE

Analogy

An analogy, somewhat like a simile, finds similarities in qualities or things otherwise dissimilar. But analogies, as poet Donald Hall has remarked, are usually extended in length, "running through a paragraph like a thread in tweed." Analogies use one point of comparison to explain another more difficult point.

- Injustice is "like a boil that can never be cured so long as it is covered up but must be opened with all its ugliness to the natural medicines of air and light, injustice must be exposed with all the tension its exposure creates, to the light of human conscience and the air of national opinion, before it can be cured."

  —MARTIN LUTHER KING

- Life's but a walking shadow, a poor player that struts and frets his hour upon the stage and then is heard no more.

  —WILLIAM SHAKESPEARE

a notebook; looking for patterns, repetitions, conflict, and contrast; finding key passages; accounting for cultural and historical influences; and considering all the varying powers of language such as connotations, denotations, and metaphor. It would also involve all the various experiences you bring to the text: your own reading background, the culture and family you grew up in, your gender and age, as well as your experience with language.

Interpretation may sound hopelessly complex, but in fact it's doubtful if all of these elements would ever be consciously brought to bear on a single reading experience. They represent options. An act of interpretation is enriched when you have choices and when you've developed the potential for selecting which choice or which blend of choices might be most effective and appropriate for any given reading.

The problem is that for many years the concept of interpretation has excluded all these options in favor of a single approach, one which took its model from the sciences. We have to confess that this so-called "objective" method dominated our own thinking until a few years ago. It was Steve and Meg who first helped us understand the limitations of the older approach.

When we discussed poetry with them, we were surprised that Meg—a chemist—would show such delight in poetry. She obviously enjoyed playing with language, finding multiple readings, and leaving any given poem open to further experiences in the future. We had thought that as a scientist she would approach a poem as if it were a scientific fact that needed proving or disproving. Or that she might scoff at poetry. We assumed she might want to demonstrate that poetry was mere fantasy, that it lacked objective reference. But she countered our biases and false stereotypes.

"Everybody in chemistry tries to be objective all the time," she said. "It's just a stance, an attitude you have to adopt. But it's not real, you know."

We didn't know that and we told her so. "Science is about facts, isn't it? Aren't facts supposed to be objective? Isn't that what you do for a living?"

"Objectivity doesn't really exist," Meg explained. "Unless you're a computer, maybe. In the sciences we pretend to objectify ourselves, to suspend emotion and subjectivity. But we've known for a long time that subject and object interact."

"In quantum physics," Steve said, "they've shown that the presence of an observer actually changes the thing being observed."

"Right," Meg said. "On the everyday level, we still go around pretending to be objective. We couldn't really make scientific method work if we didn't. And let's face it, when it comes to manipulating the physical world, the 'objective' approach has been remarkably successful. But in our hearts, we know that every scientific finding is a mysterious mix of objective and subjective."

"And that 'truths' constantly shift," Steve added.

"But what," asked Olivia, "has all this to do with poetry?"

They both laughed. "Everything. Everything."

Here's how Meg and Steve explained it.

If you treat a poem (or any text) as an object, separate from yourself, as you might treat a study of the circulation of blood, then the "meaning" of the poem would be found inside the poem, as an understanding of the circulation of blood would be found inside the circulatory system. There would be a single meaning and your job, as reader observing the poem from the outside (as if you were reading through a microscope), would be to find the meaning and to publish your findings for others to verify. Who you are, your background or gender, or the era you live in would have nothing to do with it; nor would the culture or history of the author's own era. Even the author's biographical experiences might be excluded. After all, none of those things would affect the truth of how the circulatory system functions. The influence of science in the modern world, then, has caused many to read poetry, to read literature in general, as if we were all "objective" scientists studying an "objective" artifact, as if truth were something external to our inner lives.

But Meg recalled a philospher of science, Gary Zukav, writing about quantum mechanics: "We cannot eliminate ourselves from the picture," Zukov had written. "We are a part of nature, and when we study nature there is no way around the fact that nature is studying itself." The same is true of poetry. Each poem (or almost any text for that matter) is an expression of complex mental, emotional and cultural factors, and each reader is equally complex. An act of interpretation is, therefore, an interactive process, one in which you as reader explore a variety of influences and responses in the text as well as in yourself. The kind of interpretation we're talking about acknowledges that both text and reader are immersed in language, culture, and history.

The reading of a poem (or any text) in this manner locates you and the text in a human world. It makes reading a poem a human activity, one which you can share with others (without fearing you might be "wrong"), one which has a potential for relating to your own values and which may enable you to reflect and better understand the values of a society in which you or the author live. Some scholars have argued that this type of reading should not even be called *Interpretation* because the term has so many of those older negative connotations. But the denotation remains: to clarify or explain as you see it, as you feel it. We understand interpretation as an act of interacting with the implications, suggestions, complexities, and mysteries of a text's specific details, as an act of moving from detail to a body of feeling, to ideas and significance in a larger, human or societal context. Call it what you will.

Here's a poem by John Logan that we offered to our students and asked them to read in this broader sense.

■ The Picnic ■

It is the picnic with Ruth in the spring.
Ruth was third on my list of seven girls
But the first two were gone (Betty) or else
Had someone (Ellen has accepted Doug).
Indian Gully the last day of school;

Girls make the lunches for the boys too.
I wrote a note to Ruth in algebra class
Day before the test. She smiled, and nodded.
We left the cars and walked through the young corn
The shoots green as paint and the leaves like
Tongues trembling. Beyond the fence where we stood
Some wild strawberry flowered by an elm tree
And Jack-in-the-pulpit was olive ripe.
A blackbird fled as I crossed, and showed
A spot of gold or red under its quick wing.
I held the wire for Ruth and watched the whip
Of her long, striped skirt as she followed.
Three freckles blossomed on her thin, white back
Underneath the loop where the blouse buttoned.
We went for our lunch away from the rest,
Stretched in the new grass, our heads close
Over unknown things wrapped up in wax papers.
Ruth tried for the same, I forget what it was,
And our hands were together. She laughed,
And a breeze caught the edge of her little
Collar and the edge of her brown, loose hair
That touched my cheek. I turned my face into
the gentle fall. I saw how sweet it smelled.
She didn't move her head or take her hand.
I felt a soft caving in my stomach
As at the top of the highest slide
When I had been a child, but was not afraid,
And did not know why my eyes moved with wet
As I brushed her cheek with my lips and brushed
Her lips with my own lips. She said to me
Jack, Jack, different than I had ever heard,
Because she wasn't calling me, I think,
Or telling me. She used my name to
Talk in another way I wanted to know.
She laughed again and then she took her hand;
I gave her what we both had touched—can't
Remember what it was, and we ate the lunch.
Afterward we walked in the small, cool creek
Our shoes off, her skirt hitched, and she smiling,
My pants rolled, and then we climbed up the high
Side of Indian Gully and looked
Where we had been, our hands together again.
It was then some bright thing came in my eyes,
Starting at the back of them and flowing
Suddenly through my head and down my arms
And stomach and my bare legs that seemed not

To stop in feet, not to feel the red earth
Of the Gully, as though we hung in a
Touch of birds. There was a word in my throat
With the feeling and I knew the first time
What it meant and I said, it's beautiful.
Yes, she said, and I felt the sound and word
In my hand join the sound and word in hers
As in one name said, or in one cupped hand.
We put back on our shoes and socks and we
Sat in the grass awhile, crosslegged, under
A blowing tree, not saying anything.
And Ruth played with shells she found in the creek,
As I watched. Her small wrist which was so sweet
To me turned by her breast and the shells dropped
Green, white, blue, easily into her lap,
Passing light through themselves. She gave the pale
Shells to me, and got up and touched her hips
With her light hands, and we walked down slowly
To play the school games with the others.

Almost all our students liked this poem, but for different reasons. Here is 19-year-old Raoul Farizzi's response, taken from his notebook after he'd read and marked the poem several times.

Enormous simplicity. Yet deep feelings for the emotions of discovering the first feelings of love. This begins with a simple school picnic, perhaps in the 7th grade. I'm not sure why I think it's still junior high, but the "list of seven girls" suggests a still immature kid. The opening sensory details of corn, strawberries, blackbirds, etc. etc. set up the image of nature, but also it seems to me begin to set up how all that's about to happen is also "natural." Maybe we're being shown how love happens *in* nature and in that sense it's as pure and simple as the cool creek in Indian Gully.

Logan shows too that it's a shared first experience. The boy and girl both reach for "unknown things" in their lunch. I think as goofy as it sounds, the unknown things wrapped in wax paper were metaphorically like the unknown feelings both are reaching for. Maybe metaphor is the wrong word here.

More evidence of how young these kids are. After he kisses her lightly, he is reminded of how his stomach felt at the top of a high slippery slide. His memory takes him back to something still close to him, a childhood experience which is all he has to compare it to. Why are the feelings so simple? Is it because he hasn't got any mature memories to draw on? The images are all drawn from childhood, but the experience is the first entrance into adulthood.

The two kids have known something magical has happened. They have known for the first time what the word "beautiful" really means, a joining of two previously unconnected things (aha--metaphor again)--the joining of their hands, their lips, their physical and emotional experience, like "a touch of birds," meaning, I think, as gently as the brushing of two bird wings in flight, two birds that may just happen to touch for a moment. It makes them aware of their soaring, the air under them. What makes this so good is that the image is as simple as the feelings. No complications here as there will be even a few years later. No jealousy, no claims on each other, no arguments, no power plays. Just the momentary joining of male and female in the first conscious awareness of their likeness and their differences. God do I remember how wonderful that was compared to how complex it all seems to be now.

But it's the scene at the end when Ruth plays with the shells, after it's all over that seems most suggestive to me. I had to read this over and over. The boy watches her turn the shells over, her wrist and hand just inches from her breast as she looks at them. The boy's attention is focused on the shells and on her "sweet wrist" but intentionally or not "her breast" enters the picture. It almost seems as if the words themselves, like her sexuality, slip into the picture unconsciously. This is hard to explain. He is watching the shells and her wrist. But he can no longer keep her physical image separate as they "fall into her lap." And here the metaphor opens up everything for me. When the shells fall, light passes "through" them. Since light cannot literally pass through hard shells, the image has got to be a metaphor for the light the boy himself has reached. Maybe for his first awareness? (This is kind of hard right here.) I think maybe he has passed through an experience that wasn't possible for him only a few days before. He has reached what seems an almost magical consciousness of the wonderful delightful feeling of all the possibilities of sex without knowing of all the difficulties of it. He can't know that yet. He can only know the magic part, like light coming out of nature to reveal what is "beautiful" to him.

I feel elated by the poem. Also sad, because I'm not sure it can be this way anymore. My younger brothers and sister have been exposed to MTV since they were born practically. The open sexuality of it, the hips and breasts and flesh are more part of their lives than fairy tales ever were. My six-year-old step-sister dances to the music, bumping her hips like the sexually charged women on TV. My brothers, nine and fourteen, may not yet have experienced sex, but they can snear about it graphically. Can any of us today discover each other out of the kind of innocence Logan has? I end up regretfully having to feel that this is a poem about a past era when light still passed through shells. If the poem was written today, the more appropriate metaphor would be one of hard shells bumping against each other, like the bones of young hips.

Raoul's response seems to us a good illustration of how one might develop an interpretation of John Logan's poem.

1. First, Raoul has begun with his own feelings. He identifies details in the text that seem to have called up those feelings and he asks questions about why they might be important. In the process, he begins to establish for himself the context in which his experience of the poem has occurred.

2. Next, Raoul summarizes a number of points in the poem, lingering momentarily on details and exploring how certain images—such as "a touch of birds"—open up possible insights, and how those insights please him even though they contrast to his own experiences today.

3. Raoul then discusses what for him seems to be the central metaphor of the text: light passing through shells. Here he slows down and considers how the words create a sequence of events, some of them perhaps unconscious. He probes the metaphoric qualities in the scene, relating them to the young boy's feelings, without claiming that this is the only possible "meaning." In fact, he opens up the image with questions so that it becomes expansive rather than exclusive.

4. In his final paragraph, Raoul steps back and considers his overall experience of the poem, both the feelings it evokes in him, as well as insights generated by the final metaphor. He relates what he has discovered about the text and about his reading of it to society, to his own culture, and to a set of values that might contrast to the values in the poem.

We found this a fine reading of the poem, yet others in Raoul's class had other experiences with the same text and followed a different pattern in exploring it. Here's a notebook response by Tracy Gilbert, a sophomore literature major.

I remember having to read some pretty cheesey love poems in high school. "My love is like a red, red rose," was one of them. And there was another one by Elizabeth Barrett Browning, "How Do I Love Thee." Mrs. Childress read that one aloud. She kept telling us what a great love poem it was. She even wanted us to memorize it. But I only felt embarrassed, disappointed even. I didn't feel anything. But reading "The Picnic" was different. It's the first poem I've read about love that made me feel something.

I didn't feel anything the first time I read it. But the second time one line stood out: "It was then some bright thing came in my eyes," the boy says as he looks back at the place on Indian Gully where he and Ruth had been earlier. I kept wondering about the brightness. When he describes "the bright thing," that began at the back of his eyes and flowed through his body to his feet, I felt something too. The boy doesn't know what the brightness is at first. It has been a slow and gradual recognition for him. As I read the poem the first time, I was aware of other bright things--external things--"the green shoots" of corn, the bright "spot of gold or red under the blackbird's wings." The boy is aware of the brightness around him, but his recognition of Ruth and his feelings for her have been slower. I think it begins when he sees through the loop where her blouse buttons and "three freckles blossomed on her white back." An external brightness. One way to read this would be to see that the two of them have been surrounded by brightness and blossoming, the wild strawberries and the Jack-in-the-Pulpit, external things that can be named. Now it's Ruth's freckles that blossom. Later in the poem, the brightness that flows through the boy is a lot more internal and inexplicable. Now he has to struggle to define it. He can't name what he feels, and he doesn't need to; we know without naming that it's love he feels. His awareness of Ruth and his growing realization of his love for her all flow together in "the bright" sensation.

> There was a word in my throat
> With the feeling and I knew the first time
> What it meant.

We know too, without saying.

Reading this poem I was reminded of all the times I've seen pictures of lovers in advertising and in the movies. You know, the tanned hunk wearing a tuxedo leans over the bare shoulder of a beautiful woman dressed in black velvet. Everything about them seems distant, diffuse, as if the photo was shot through gauze. But its all fake. The people are too beautiful, too perfect, too rich. The lover dangles a diamond bracelet in front of the woman (the diamonds-are-forever-bit) and the diamond shoots out hard bright flashes. All this is supposed to show his love. In the ad, the only bright thing in the lover's eyes is the diamond, as if love is measured in carats. Love is an object not a feeling. There's no physical sensation, no sensual delight, no pleasure and buoyancy of feeling beauty "hung in a touch of birds."

I've seen this all before, even in movies. In "Pretty Woman" Richard Gere plays the handsome rich executive who shows his love by giving the girl a diamond necklace. When he snaps open the velvet case, there it is--hard and bright and flashy. Of course the girl is just thrilled as he clasps the necklace around her neck. Now she has a tangible symbol of his love for her, something she can show off. The love here is culiminated in a material object. It isn't quiet and tender like the love shared in "The Picnic." In the poem the lovers hardly speak, and it's not flashy diamonds that represent their love. Nothing external. It's an internal feeling, the elated brightness of love, as delicate as the shells "Passing light through themselves." Who wouldn't want to know that feeling?

Tracy's exploration of John Logan's poem has some similarities to Raoul Farizzi's, but Tracy has brought to bear on the poem a different background and experience.

1. First, Tracy establishes the context in which she is reading the poem, in this case drawing upon her past reading experience. By comparing the poem to others she's read in high school, she establishes a contrast with earlier assumptions about "love poems."

2. Next, she summarizes and discusses some of the opening images, not merely to retell the poem, but to establish a context for the "story" or argument of the text. In the process, she discovers a pattern in the images that moves from external brightness to internal brightness. This turns out to be a discovery that will guide her toward a possible interpretation of the poem.

3. Finally, Tracy compares the two feelings of "brightness" found in this text to images of brightness in other kinds of texts (advertising and films), resulting in a recognition that such a comparison leads to two different kinds of feelings about love. She discovers that a common version of love in her own culture, one where feelings are found in external objects, is for her less desirable than a more rare and internal feeling of love found in the poem.

Both Tracy and Raoul do something else. By the end of each response, both make use of metaphor in their own writing (in their own thinking) to express conflicting values. Raoul constructs a new metaphor of the shells.

Reminders

The act of interpretation is one of moving from details to generalizations, from the text to your experience of it. But that may include a wide variety of approaches. The following are meant to suggest possibilities.

- Train yourself to become sensitive to an author's use of language: to connotations as well as denotations, but especially to use of metaphor (including similes, analogies, or parables).
- In turn, make yourself conscious of how language affects your own perceptions, of how it may influence your beliefs, values, and understanding.
- Recognizing that language may create multiple experiences and responses, be open to a multiplicity of readings—even from yourself—for any given text.
- Remember that both text and reader are immersed not only in language, but in culture and history, and that the fullest response acknowledges a variety of influences (this may sometimes require research).
- After reading, rereading, and annotating a text, explore the text as an interaction of reader, author, text, culture, and history:

  —Consider any assumptions or cultural conflicts you bring to the text, as well as the feelings it generates in you.

  —Explore individual words, patterns, conflicts, or passages in the text with close attention to both denotation and connotation, as well as to any metaphoric qualities.

  —Summarize or discuss the context of the work, including any relevant cultural or historical influences, especially implicit attitudes that even the author may not have been conscious of.

  —Focus on any aspect that seems to open up the reading experience for you: probe, question, and discuss.

  —Perhaps most important, seek out relationships or connections, both within the text and to external elements, either in your own feelings and assumptions or to cultural and societal situations.

- Use language as part of the discovery of knowledge. Play with words, images, and if possible, explore metaphors (or similes and analogies) to open up new insights.

Tracy incorporates the metaphor of "brightness" into her own analysis. Perhaps as much as anything else, this final touch illustrates the power of metaphor to bring us to new awareness. (In the next section, on *Focused Writing*, we'll discuss how professional writers use metaphors throughout their essays to explore ideas and even to organize their material.)

Finally, if we recall one last time Aristotle's observation that intelligence is the ability to see relationships, we hope it will become clear why in this chapter we've combined a brief discussion of metaphor with a study of the act of interpreting. Both are intricately bound up with the discovery of relationships, and both then would seem to represent some of the highest forms of mental activity. Robert Frost called metaphor "the profoundest thinking that we have." To train oneself in the interpretation of poetry then is not an esoteric specialization for literature majors. It is rather to train the mind in critical thinking. It expands our potential for perceiving relationships as well as for uniting them imaginatively. To become conscious of metaphor, better yet to *make* metaphor, unites yourself with the thing (by interacting with it, mind, feeling, and object) in order to make it truth.

FOCUSED WRITING

Somewhere in the city a bag lady roots through trash without questioning the purpose of her life. In New Mexico an old man sits in the dark heat of his apartment, watching soap operas in the afternoon and waiting for a neighbor to bring his dinner. In an executive board room in Fort Worth a lawyer proposes a method of taking over another company solely for profit: no consideration is given to whether the lives of workers will be improved.

Presumably not all of us seek some higher meaning for our actions. Many of us live moment to moment, sometimes because we have no choice. Others work with awesome dedication toward goals that may contribute little to human happiness. Many of us, in fact, may suffer a separation of our inner and outer lives—or have no inner life at all. There is nothing new here. Yet one purpose of this book has been to suggest that the richest rewards may occur when the wholeness of an inner and outer world are brought together through an interactive process of reading and writing. In America, a life of the mind is sometimes scoffed at or dismissed as "ivory tower." Yet a life of the mind is also the life of the heart and spirit. It is an imaginative quest for some kind of truth, found only momentarily we suppose, and in brief fragments, but all the more valuable because of this. That is why we offered the following poem to our class. We could have given them an essay or an excerpt from biography or history or science. We could have asked them to watch TV or read advertisements in magazines. The act of interpretation is clearly not limited to poetry. Yet a poem offers a condensed world of experience, one that can be transformed and made meaningful by our imaginations.

Consider this one.

The House Was Quiet and the World Was Calm

WALLACE STEVENS

The house was quiet and the world was calm.
The reader became the book; and summer night

Was like the conscious being of the book.
The house was quiet and the world was calm.

The words were spoken as if there was no book,
Except that the reader leaned above the page,

Wanted to lean, wanted much most to be
The scholar to whom his book is true, to whom

The summer night is like a perfection of thought.
The house was quiet because it had to be.

The quiet was part of the meaning, part of the mind.
The access of perfection to the page.

And the world was calm. The truth in a calm world,
In which there is no other meaning, itself

Is calm, itself is summer and night, itself
Is the reader leaning late and reading there.

For us the poem seemed to say so much about how we saw ourselves engaged in learning and in how we hoped our students might also discover the pleasure of learning. We asked them to write about the poem in their notebooks and to discuss it in small groups the next day. But this time we did not organize the small groups. We did not even hold class. This time, we told them, it's up to you. Find the friends you can sit down and share with. Explore and argue and play. Find your own summer porch or its equivalent, under a tree, by a stream, in a smokey bar, on the afternoon steps of your apartment. Live the poem with others and find if you can grow from it.

Afterward we asked them to write an essay on what they had discovered, if anything. And this time we explained the original French meaning of the term essay: "to attempt," or "to try."

Interpretation

Interpretation (or if you wish, "critical response") is always a process of constructing sense from various evolving details, feelings, and contexts. Drafting is a continuation of the exploration begun in your reading, questioning, discussing, and early note-taking, a process of discovering a focus and direction to your thoughts and emotions. But an interpretive essay, from long tradition, also has three or four elements to it that your audience will expect to find. The order or sequence of those elements, and their degree of formality, will always vary depending on the occasion and the purpose for which you're writing.

We are not talking here about external form—introductions, bodies, and conclusions—all of which must be structured in at some time. (See Chapter 3 for that.) Instead, we want to focus now on content, on the "sense" and "meaning" you eventually hope to share, on how those qualities became meaningful to you as you read and reflect on the text, and then on how those same qualities can convincingly demonstrate the act of critical thinking to your audience.

In one way or another, critical thinking always involves identifying relationships, making reasoned inferences about relationships, questioning or considering other possible connections (or omissions), and then judging or evaluating what you've found. An interpretive essay, then, will probably contain all of these components. By the time you've finished, here is what the reader needs to know from you.

1. *What meaning, if any, do you find in your interaction with the text?*

The key here is not to confuse the question with "What meaning is *in* the text?" You cannot set out to find the one true theme. By now you know that the complexities of the reading experience preclude a single right "answer." Yet the audience for your essay will expect you to give the work enough serious attention that you arrive at some understanding, one perhaps that suggests possible insights into the text, or one that decries some weakness in the text, or one that argues against the text, or one that points to both its strengths and weaknesses. This means that merely summarizing what you've read is unacceptable. Although you may often retell incidents or summarize ideas and arguments, the reader expects you to do so only to establish a clear context for the next step: to discover relationships, feelings, or reflections that grow out of those points.

In writing about Wallace Stevens' poem, for example, we might summarize it in a single sentence: the poem describes a scholar reading deeply one quiet summer night. The summary establishes a framework for anything else we now want to say, about how the book and the night and the quiet relate in some mysterious and important way to the scholar's life and values. Our job is to explore those more important connections and to find their significance, if there is any, to ourselves and our society.

2. *How did you arrive at your discoveries?*

This may seem a strange question at first, but when you consider all the many complexities of the reading process, it becomes a key one for the audience. To understand your response to the first question above, we may need to know all (or at least some of) the varying considerations that led to it. What aspects of your personal experience, your reading background, your culture or language may have influenced your approach to the text? Did you bring certain assumptions or biases to the text (to the very act of reading a poem for example?) You need to know all this for yourself if you are to understand your own reading reaction. Clearly the audience cannot evaluate your interpretation without also having some clues. If you tell us you've always hated poetry, always disdained scholars in favor of "men of industry," then we'll read your essay with a somewhat different attitude from the student who says she's written poetry since she was six and plans to continue on in college until she receives her PhD in English literature—but not because either attitude is necessarily better or worse than the other. Indeed, we may learn more from a negative approach, one that challenges, than from one that slavishly adores every word on the page.

Other factors may also shape your reading. Your knowledge of the influencing factors of language, history, and culture on the author or the text could affect your interpretation, and that knowledge must be shared with your audience. Who is Wallace Stevens? A college professor in South Africa? A military commander under Queen Victoria? A struggling poet who starved to death at 30? What influences shaped his life? What assumptions may he have made about his own likely readers? Although the poem can be fully and profitably discussed without necessarily knowing the answer to any of these questions, your audience will need to be informed of the knowledge you discover about the text itself.

3. *What has been left out of your reading? What continues to puzzle you? What alternatives might be considered at some other time?*

Since no single reading of a text may be complete in itself, it's usually wise to be honest with your reader about where your own reading leaves gaps. There seems little reason to pretend your interpretation will be the last word. Thousands and thousands of interpretations have been published on Shakespeare's *Hamlet.* Each adds to the richness of our experience of the work. None is final. Your own audience will only respect you for noting that a particular line of poetry continues to puzzle you, or that because of the length and complexity of the text you've chosen to leave out a certain portion in order to concentrate on another portion, one that at this point in your life seems more central.

Asking questions that have not yet been answered by your own interpretation only engages the audience more. We begin to build on points you've developed, seeing for ourselves new possibilities, and perhaps responding in our minds to the questions you've raised. Your essay begins, as it should, to form a dialogue with others. What could Wallace Stevens mean by "truth"? Is there a special kind of "truth" he's finding in his book, or is he talking about absolute "truth," some kind of higher "truth"? Or both? Here, you say to your audience, is one possibility based on all the variables and patterns you've looked at. But could some element in the text also suggest something else? Perhaps something even the poet was not conscious of? Our response is doubly stimulated. We have your interpretation to reflect on and we have questions you've raised in light of it.

4. *Finally, what larger implications or suggestions arise from your reading of the work?*

Over the years we've discovered this may be the one element most omitted from student papers. Yet it's also the most crucial element. Unless you point out implications of your reading for society, for the culture you live in, you've merely led us down a trail that has no purpose. We may have enjoyed the scenery, but why did we come this way? To what end? You, as author of the interpretation, have an obligation to your audience to explore the final relationship. Has all this mental and emotional effort been worth it? Have we learned anything we didn't already know? Has any light been cast on human experience? Can we now see the context of the poet's life or times, or the context of our own, with more clarity? What is there here to help us grow? Or, if the text leads to none of this, should we say it fails? Is it merely clever or entertaining or escapist? Is it propaganda for a particular ideology or value system for promoting human welfare that in itself may be good or bad?

Surely the purpose of critical thinking is not merely to exercise mental muscle. The purpose is to develop our powers of discrimination. We need to know how to distinguish between that which is worthwhile and that which is not, between that which is of value to our lives (and sometimes, of course, something "merely" entertaining or escapist may be of great value), and that which is superficial, shallow, or even dangerous. We cannot make choices about values at all without the ability to discriminate between that which is worthwhile and that which is not.

Pushing your interpretation through this final stage, then, is central to the act of critical thinking. As reader, turned writer, you move from the details of a text to generalizations about those details in a broader human or societal context. You make judgments. Only then have you brought to closure the circle of relationships expected in any sound interpretive act.

Metaphor as Discovery and Argument

We've already discussed how metaphor functions to clarify relationships, and how metaphor is not limited to poetry but is inherent in language and thought. Metaphor (and its variations, simile and analogy) can therefore be a central device for you to use consciously in your own essays. First, of course, it holds open the potential of making discoveries about whatever text you're working with. The simple act of asking "What is this *like*?" can lead to insights.

Consider how you might apply the question to one of the essays included in this book. Soetsu Yanagi argues in "Seeing and Knowing" (p. 179) that the two activities are different. *Seeing*, Yanagi claims, involves an intuitive act which looks directly into the mystery of beauty. But *knowing* is an intellectual discrimination based on learned facts. In writing about Yanagi's essay you could ask yourself: "What is knowing *like* when it's separated from seeing?"

We asked our class this question and they came up with several immediate responses:

```
Knowing is like trying to appreciate the colors of
flowers by reading a text in braille.
```

<u>Knowing</u> without <u>seeing</u> is like the preacher who rails against sex without ever having experienced temptation.

<u>Knowing</u> is like learning how to dance by following footprints pasted on the floor.

<u>Knowing</u> is going to the lake to set up an instrument to measure the reflection; <u>seeing</u> is like going to the lake to watch sunlight floating on water.

Each of these is a simple simile that for a given individual reader may be the key to shaping a portion if not an entire interpretation. Here is sophomore Patricia Canneda writing about Wallace Stevens' poem. (For the full essay, see p. 158.) Patricia uses a simile to explain her decision to investigate the poet's language in depth.

Sometimes eating breakfast in the cafeteria, I've watched the sun burn through the fog. Gradually the fog shrinks back unveiling lawn and woods and mountains and then it disappears into the valley below. Suddenly I have a clear view and the fog is like a dream I try to remember. At times in Stevens' poem, the words are like the fog, and yet the words are also the very thing which open up and reveal the truth.

The following paragraph from Thoreau's "Civil Disobedience" (p. 496) shows how an author could develop an image into a more extended analogy.

> If . . . injustice is part of the necessary friction of the machine of government, let it go, let it go: perchance it will wear smooth—certainly the machine will wear out. If the injustice has a spring, or a pulley, or a rope, or a crank, exclusively for itself, then perhaps you may consider whether the remedy will not be worse than the evil; but if it is of such a nature that it requires you to be the agent of injustice to another, then, I say, break the law. Let your life be a counter friction to stop the machine. . . .

What analogy is Thoreau using here? How does the analogy illustrate visually the argument Thoreau wants to put across? Why not discuss injustice in abstract terms?

Clearly the effectiveness of metaphor reinforces the concept that we acquire new knowledge by finding a relationship between what we already know and what we want to understand. The conscious use of metaphoric thinking is therefore invaluable for an author. In turn, the use of metaphor influences an audience. Because it almost always involves something concrete (something that affects our senses or calls up a mental image) metaphor contains a persuasive power that often moves us more than abstract language.

> Laws are like cobwebs, which may catch small flies, but let wasps and hornets break through.
>
> —JONATHAN SWIFT

> It is permissible to say this sort of thing about humans. They do resemble, in their most compulsively social behavior, ants at a distance.
>
> —LEWIS THOMAS

> We are not unlike a particularly hardy crustacean. The lobster grows by developing and shedding a series of hard, protective shells. Each time it expands from within, the confining shell must be sloughed off. It is left exposed and vulnerable until, in time, a new covering grows to replace the old. With each passage from one stage of human growth to the next, we, too, must shed a protective structure.
>
> —GAIL SHEEHY

The use of metaphors, similes, and analogies is in fact a traditional argumentative strategy: As they enrich and clarify, they persuade. They expose the heart of an argument and may be the surest way of winning the emotions and concurrence of your reader.

THE FORMAL ESSAY

In this chapter we've been going over ways of thinking about a text during the discovery draft of an interpretation. We've suggested you'll want to consider and write about those aspects of personal experience you may have brought to the text and about how they may have influenced the meaning or significance of your reading experience. We've suggested you may want to write about important elements of language, culture, or history that might have affected the author. We've urged you to consider aspects of the text your reading has omitted and perhaps to suggest alternative readings that might remain to be explored. We've pointed to the essential need for evaluating the implications of your interpretation. And finally, we talked about how using metaphors, similes, or analogies in your writing can clarify and enrich your own argument. Yet none of this falls into any particular order on the page. Where's your focus? How can you organize it all into something cohesive? Which point should come first? How many points should you have?

Development of Focus and Form

The truth is, the reader doesn't care how you organize, only that you do. And the number of options open to you are extensive. One of the most popular in contemporary letters involves moving through a series of small points, seemingly at random but in fact circling or spiraling toward an emerging focus, one that is arrived at only toward the end of the essay. As effective as such a method is for highly sophisticated writers and readers, it probably won't do in college. Most instructors do not have time for a leisurely ramble. Most will expect you to develop a focus in a more traditional manner, and indeed, doing so is probably essential at this stage to developing clear critical thinking. Here are a number of patterns you should be familiar with.

The Thesis

The most conventional organization in academic writing involves making a clear and simple statement of the significance you've found in a text. Traditionally, we've been told that a thesis statement should be provided in the first or last sentence of the opening paragraph, but professional writers usually begin with more imaginative leads and then focus in several paragraphs later. Here are several examples that can be found in essays used in this book.

From Annie Dillard, "Sight into Insight"

> . . . If you cultivate a healthy poverty and simplicity, so that finding a penny will literally make your day, then, since the world is in fact planted in pennies, you have with your poverty bought a lifetime of days. It is that simple. What you see is what you get.

From Lance Morrow, "The Value of Working"

> The work ethic is not dead, but it is weaker now. The psychology of work is much changed in America.

From Bruno Bettelheim, "The Ignored Lesson of Anne Frank"

> What is at issue is the universal and uncritical response to [Anne Frank's] diary and to the play and movie based on it, and what this reaction tells about our attempt to cope with the feelings of her fate—used by us to serve as a symbol of a most human reaction to Nazi terror—arouses in us. I believe that the world-wide acclaim given her story cannot be explained unless we recognize in it our wish to forget the gas chambers, and our effort to do so by glorifying the ability to retreat into an extremely private, gentle, sensitive world. . . .

The point of a thesis statement is to restrict the subject, state or imply a purpose, and provide a sense of direction for the rest of the paper. Certainly nothing is wrong with any of that. The problem in the past has been that students were often left with the impression they had to write a thesis statement *before* they wrote another word of their first draft. This was supposedly to guide them toward a coherent essay that stuck with a main point and provided evidence to support it. But not all of us know what we want to write before we even begin. Those who do are lucky and for them a clear thesis statement on a white sheet of paper may be just the thing. We've always envied such individuals. If you're one of them, gloat in your good fortune. Use a simple thesis early and let it guide your work.

Our own experience has been less happy. We must write, cross out, start over, and suffer a good number of hours before our ideas begin to take on any clarity. For us, a thesis statement comes only when we sit back and say, ok, now what's all this about? Can we sum up in two or three sentences what we've been exploring here? Trying to create a sharp focus, even after completing a discovery draft, may take several more hours. But we have to confess that coming up with a simple, unadorned statement about it all gives one a fine satisfaction and may be an effective way for helping you re-see all you've been trying to say, and then helping you reshape it into an organized essay during the revision stage.

How does it do that? Simple. Now that you've made a bold statement, you've got to prove it. The tradition is to develop (reshape or reorganize) what you've written around several main points, each of which supports the thesis. Each point may, of course, have several subpoints. And by the end, the reader should have the feeling of having read a step-by-step argument, one that leads inevitably back to the thesis.

Magic Numbers

How many points you want to develop in an essay is of course dependent on numerous factors: the length of the essay you plan to write, the complexity of the work you've read, and the depth of interaction between you and the work. One guideline has it that you should have at least three main points. Why three should be an effective number, instead of two or four, is hard to say. Authors tend to create three-act plays. Sonatas usually come in three movements. And even the organization we've selected for this book has three parts. Nothing requires you to work in odd numbers—3, 5, 7—but tradition supports it. Making a single major point in a paper with two examples may suffice perfectly well, but making a single point with three examples could be more convincing. A longer paper with three major points may need only to develop each point fully for the reader to feel satisfied.

Even if you can select from your discovery draft the three components you feel are most important, you'll still need to organize them in some kind of order. Again you have choices: from least to most important, or the reverse, from most to least. Both can be effective depending on the type of argument you're constructing. Beginning with the most important point can grab your reader's attention immediately, but you take a risk of fading away as your points grow less effective. Beginning with the least important point may cause your reader to be more skeptical in the early stages, but can seem more powerful as you lead toward the big climax.

Although we encourage students to explore different forms, we inevitably find that many of them work in patterns of three, even without our instruction.

Perhaps it occurs naturally. Or perhaps Western culture has accepted the pattern for so long as "natural" that our minds tend to think in such ways.

For example, look back at Marianne Clampett's essay, "Shooting to Kill" (p. 77). Clampett is writing about Isak Dinesen's "The Iguana." Her method integrates three of her own memories called up by the text with three points made by Dinesen herself. The result is that each point plays off against the other, clarifying the reading experience through contrasts and similarities.

In Addie Gilbert's paper, "Killing the Phantom" (p. 117), Addie considers a single major point she has found important in Virginia Woolf's "The Angel in the House." Addie focuses in on why Woolf finds it necessary to write in such violent terms about a Victorian convention. Then Addie organizes her essay around three separate discussions, each of which helps her to develop her own answer: first, she considers the historical context Woolf was writing out of, then she looks at the language and metaphor Woolf uses, and finally, she compares Woolf's concerns to contemporary culture. Each of these three components reflects back on Addie's original question and, by the end, the reader senses that although the question itself may have other possible answers, Addie has looked at it with fullness and intelligence.

Obviously, if you don't have three points to make, you shouldn't fake it. Very few instructors today would argue for setting up such narrow restrictions. There are no rules here, only convention. If the convention helps, use it. If your ideas are moving in another direction, find another pattern to organize them around.

Organic Form

Most of the writing we've encouraged throughout this book might fall under the category of "organic form." An oak tree does not take the shape of a wild cherry. A kitten does not grow up attempting to walk like a duck. In nature, things find a shape organic to their own nature. Because the reading experience as we've discussed it consists of an interaction between you and the text, and because so many other variables such as language and culture impinge upon the experience, it hardly seems sensible to suggest the result can or should take only a single traditional form. Clearly it would be wrong to limit your experience to something so inflexible as a "five-paragraph essay." And you may find it stifling to force out a thesis statement with three supporting points. That's why we encourage you to think of the discovery draft as an exploration. To clarify a subject for yourself, you must write out of your own inherent nature. The shape of your reflections must be allowed to extend here and there and everywhere, like blackberry brambles. But in revision, you must take into account that ideas without form are not really ideas at all. Robert Frost once said that writing free verse was like playing tennis with the net down. It just isn't tennis. Form is necessary for the game to have meaning, form is essential for human understanding. The point, however, is that form can evolve naturally out of the content of your explorations. It need not be imposed externally.

The problem here is how to illustrate such a concept. Since each organically organized essay is unique, no single example provides a model that might serve for your own work. Our best advice is to put aside your discovery draft for up to several days if time allows. Come back to it fresh, as if you were the audience rather than the writer. Read as if you had never seen the essay before. Where does it work best for you? Do each of the parts relate? Can some sections be cut or moved to a more coherent location? Can you rearrange elements to relate more effectively? What advice could you give the writer? Usually, your best instincts will reveal the flaws, the inconsistencies, and weaknesses. If that doesn't work, try reading the draft to others, to those who won't lie to you just to remain your best friends. You need honest criticism here, not compassion.

In any case, the responsibility for creating a meaningful organization remains yours and yours alone. It's something you must take seriously. Try to avoid the trap of believing there's anything sacred about the words you've set down, or that vagueness is profound, or that others must try harder to appreciate your genius. Those are usually the first steps toward a poverty of thought.

Metaphor as an Organizational Principle

We've pointed out the values of metaphor for both clarity of idea and effectiveness of persuasion. But metaphor (using the term in its broadest sense to include simile, analogy, and allegory) can help you organize the structure for an essay. Indeed, many of the finest classic and contemporary texts use metaphor as a unifying principle. You'll find several of them collected in this book.

Plato's "Allegory of the Cave" (p. 224), like most allegories, tells a story with two simultaneous levels of meaning. The first level, the literal story of prisoners in a cave, is sometimes called a "camouflage" for the more important abstract level—the supposed nature of humankind's preference for darkness and illusion over the bright light of truth. Allegories give concrete images to abstract ideas, and they have been both highly popular and highly successful. George Orwell's *Animal Farm* remains an important novel in this century because it explores the nature of totalitarianism (an abstraction) in common barnyard imagery. And Albert Camus' "Myth of Sisyphus" (p. 440) remains one of our strongest statements on the contemporary human condition. But allegories are sometimes considered out of fashion today. Contemporary writers usually turn to analogy, a more direct comparison of unlike things extended throughout an essay—that is, an overt comparison that does not pretend to "camouflage" the second level of significance.

Anne Morrow Lindbergh's "Channelled Whelk" (p. 215) comes easily to mind. Holding a shell in her hand, she meditates on how her own life resembles the shell, or perhaps a whelk, the snail-like creature who once inhabited the shell. Like the whelk, Lindbergh says at the beginning, she has shed the shell of her life. And throughout the essay, sometimes paragraph by paragraph, Lindbergh refers back to the shell, its former occupant, or to a variety of similes and images from the sea, each of which keeps the metaphor alive for us, linking numerous related points, and giving the essay as a whole unity and power that might not otherwise have been obtained.

Wendell Berry, in "The Likeness of Atonement" (p. 353) plunges more directly into metaphor itself for his unifying focus: what he calls "the expansive metaphor of farming and marriage and worship." He begins by observing how the metaphors of everyday language create a link for three qualities: a man planting a crop is like a man making love to his wife, a man praying is like a lover, and such a "husbandman" is in turn like God, "the lover of the world." Berry establishes in the first few paragraphs a metaphor—or series of related similes—by which he claims all essential relationships can be comprehended. Like Lindbergh, he recalls elements of the metaphor, almost paragraph by paragraph, drawing all to a concluding "metaphor of atonement" ("at-one-ment") in which our relationships to each other and to a spiritual force unite, or if they fail to unite, leave us alone and empty. The same essay might have been written without use of metaphor and simile, but for both Berry and the reader, it would have lacked its emotional force and freshness.

All this may seem highly sophisticated for a college writer. Yet we need only remember that the act of seeing and of thinking is in fact metaphoric (the discovery of relationship). Making metaphor to shape our world and to construct meaning from it is what we do as human beings. We should not cast aside the possibility that all of us can attempt a conscious use of metaphor in our writing. Metaphor is not limited to poetry. Metaphor is, as scientist Jacob Bronowski has so forcefully observed, "a hand reaching straight into experience and arranging it with new meaning." You may find that you cannot yet organize an entire essay around a single metaphor. But unless you attempt to use metaphor (or its variations, simile, analogy, and allegory) and to use it frequently, you will not be pushing your mind toward your own highest potential. Only by taking risks, only by seeking through constant questioning and reflection the hidden likeness—in nature, in experience, in the text and its context—do you open up for yourself the potential for creative thought.

We said something like this for our students before they began writing about Wallace Stevens' poem, "The House Was Quiet and the World Was Calm." Here is one of the essays that pleased us most. Patricia Canneda was a sophomore from Oregon. Her background with poetry was limited, but she confessed that she loved language and had spent her childhood reading novels while other children played. She also confessed that Stevens' poem "drove her crazy." The following finished draft of her essay required repeated rewriting as she struggled to simplify the complexity of her discoveries.

A QUIET BETROTHAL

Patricia Canneda

In the lights from the dorm, an oak tree outside my window casts a shadow on the lawn. I know it isn't tangible. Reading Wallace Stevens' poem "The House Was Quiet and the World Was Calm" is like that shadow in the dark. Although I can read the words, I cannot grasp the meaning. On the surface, the poem simply describes a scholar studying late at night over his book, until in some way, through the calm quiet of it all, the scholar and the book, or the scholar and the truth of the book, become one.

> <u>The house was quiet and the world was calm.</u>
> <u>The reader became the book; and the summer</u>
>   <u>night</u>
>
> <u>Was like the conscious being of the book.</u>

I think I understand, or do I? Hasn't everyone read a book and become a part of it? When I was eight the book was Laura Ingalls Wilder's <u>Little House in the Big Woods</u>; when I was twelve, <u>A Tree Grows in Brooklyn</u>, and last year, Kate Chopin's <u>The Awakening</u>. As I read those books, I became the book. I lived in a different time and place. I lived the book. The first lines of Wallace Stevens' poem, then, seem to set up the relationship of a reader to a book. Simple. But the stanzas also set up a problem because it's unclear how all this happens, or how the quiet summer night itself enters into becoming part of "the conscious being of the book." The phrase seems so abstract and philosophical, especially in relationship to the concrete image of a summer night, that the reader must slow down and reflect. How can a book be perceived as a "conscious being"?

Although I've always loved reading, the reading of dictionaries has never been a pastime of mine. Yet something tells me that one way into this poem is through the words themselves. According to The Oxford English Dictionary, the word "conscious" means "knowing, or sharing the knowledge of anything together with another." On the one hand, the phrase might suggest that the "being" of the book, the words themselves, come alive, become conscious of sharing their knowledge with the reader. The mind of the reader and the mind of the book become one. On the other hand, Stevens also unites the summer night with that consciousness, maybe suggesting that the knowledge shared is not limited to book and reader, but reaches out and becomes one with the world around it.

The opening lines then are not really simple at all. And I'm not sure that my experience with House in the Big Woods or A Tree Grows in Brooklyn was as simple as I thought. Stevens fills me with curiosity. What exactly does it mean to say, "I became the book"? As if anticipating my question, Stevens goes on in the following lines to describe the scholar and his experience one more time.

> The words were spoken as if there was no book,
> Except that the reader leaned above the page.
>
> Wanted to lean, wanted much most to be
> The scholar to whom his book is true, to whom
>
> The summer night is like a perfection of
> thought.

In one way Stevens has only repeated himself, but in another, he's added a new level to the experience. He has introduced truth, and the strange concept of "a perfection of thought."

I find myself leaning closer. What is truth, and what is a perfection of thought? Whenever I hear these words I want to duck my head and hide. Writers are always searching for truths. So are readers, just as I'm searching now.

Sometimes eating breakfast in the cafeteria, I've watched the sun burn through the fog. Gradually the fog shrinks back unveiling lawn and woods and mountains and then it disappears into the valley below. Suddenly I have a clear view and the fog is like a dream I try to remember. At times in Stevens' poem, the words are like the fog, and yet the words are also the very thing which may open up and reveal the truth.

I go back to my dictionary.

<u>The Oxford English Dictionary</u> tells me that truth is "the quality of being true," which only sends me in circles and doesn't help at all. Another reference does. The word "truth" once meant "to plight one's troth; to enter into an engagement or marriage." "Marriage: a close union." What does all this have to do with Stevens' poem and its truth?

At this point I'm not sure. The poem also begins to circle back on itself. The first two stanzas set up a situation and a problem. The next two stanzas move the problem to a new level: the seeking of truth and a "perfection of thought." And yet we're still in the same situation: a reader leaning over his book. Stevens then adds one more quality.

> The house was quiet because it had to be.
>
> The quiet was part of the meaning, part of the mind.
>
> The access of perfection to the page.

The "quiet" in the house is now more than just an absence of sound and movement, as it seemed to be in the beginning. Now it is "part of the meaning, part of the mind." Two parts. Two parallels. Two relationships that become dependent. The American Heritage Dictionary defines the word "part" as "one's proper or expected share in responsibility, obligation, duty." Maybe Stevens is telling us that the truth any scholar seeks depends on a responsible relationship with the book. Maybe the truth can only be found in the quiet house of the active mind as it looks for a "meaning." Isn't that what is happening here as I search the dictionary for definitions?

It is like a Mobius strip moving from the external world to the internal, from the mind of the reader to the mind of the book, and through the world (the summer, the night, the house) and back again. Both the poem and its reader become more focused, more quiet.

I lean in closer.

Stevens has slipped in one final turn on the Mobius strip. Just what is "The access of perfection of the page"? Access. Perfection. The OED offers this definition: access is the action of coming into contact with. The key insight here may be in the term "action." It implies perfection can only be obtained by effort. The intermingling of a scholar's thoughts with the words on the page form an active relationship.

But wait a minute. What is "perfection"? The <u>OED</u> defines it as the act of completing or consummating. Of course. A perfection of thought is like the perfection of love: it is the access of lover to be loved, it is a consummation, an active bringing to completion. It's only when a scholar acts to unify all the words with himself and the world that some kind of truth can be found.

The final two stanzas now seem to act as a consummation of all the parts: reader, text, meaning.

> <u>And the world was calm. The truth in a calm</u>
> <u>world,</u>
> <u>In which there is no other meaning, itself</u>
>
> <u>Is calm, itself is summer and night, itself</u>
> <u>Is the reader leaning late and reading there</u>.

Stevens unites all the parts metaphorically. The quiet, the summer night, the reader, and the book, all become the meaning and the truth. And suddenly I remember that earlier definition of truth: "to plight one's troth; to enter into an engagement or marriage." The complexity of Stevens' poem seems suddenly clear. Maybe the truth that any scholar seeks from his poem or any printed page depends on a kind of marriage, the active consummation of reader and text in which truth becomes the creation of meaning.

There may be so much more here. I don't know who Wallace Stevens is or even when he lived. Maybe in his world this poem has a different significance. I haven't had time to look into it. But using a dictionary and looking up the words offers one way into the poem. And the poem offers a metaphor for the act of reading anything and everything. Stevens gives an insight into the nature of meaning and truth, and how those things relate to the world--how we read to give the world a meaning and a truth.

Outside my dorm the shadow of the oak tree is almost gone. Most of the lights are turned out. Oak and night and shadow are almost one. Stevens' poem is like that. What at first seemed mysterious and intangible seems simpler now. All the quiet and calm is inside me. I have found the truth. I am the reader. I lean toward the words making meaning. The world is calm. I am "the conscious being of the book" betrothed to the words on the page. It is a perfect union, like summer and night.

Patricia's struggle here to establish an understanding of a particular poem reminds us of our own experience with Steve and Meg and all those delightful evenings on our summer porch. The attempt to read a text, any text, and through writing to make sense of it, is ongoing. We are all students, all struggling—as Patricia says—"to give the world a meaning and a truth." The temptation is to allow others to define experience for us. Only when we actively commit ourselves to exploring and questioning with both heart and mind will we find our own values and have the courage to live by them.

Reminders

An interpretative essay attempts to construct sense from various evolving details, feelings, and contexts. You may want to review the following questions as checkpoints for consideration.

- What meaning or significance, if any, do you find in your interaction with the text?
- How did you arrive at your discoveries (personal experience comparisons to other readings, cultural or historical influences, language)?
- What has been omitted from your reading? What continues to puzzle you? What alternatives might be considered?
- What larger implications or suggestions arise from your interpretation?
- What final assessment or judgment are you led to form?

Photograph by Andreas Feininger

PART 2

Readings on Personal Values

CHAPTER 6

PASSIONATE ATTENTION

The greatest thing a human soul ever does in this world is to see something. . . . To see clearly is poetry, prophecy, and religion—all in one.

—John Ruskin

Late one spring on the beach south of Whalebone, a lacy ripple of tide planted a shell at our feet. We recognized the knobby horn as a whelk, an unusual find on that beach, its smudged edges buffed smooth as eggshell. When we left, we took it home and placed it on a sunny window sill with other finds—a sand dollar and a starfish with four arms.

Years later, on another beach, we stayed at a two-hundred-year-old inn with a saggy veranda overlooking dunes and sea oats and the Atlantic. Early mornings we liked to sit in the bleached rockers and watch the mockingbirds in the barberry bushes. Sometimes we read aloud to each other in the still pink light. One morning we read *Gift from the Sea* by Anne Morrow Lindbergh.

Like us, Lindbergh had spent her vacation on a beach. Her experiences there triggered a series of reflective essays. Like us, one of her gifts from the sea had been a shell.

An ink sketch of the shell first drew our attention to her essay, "The Channelled Whelk." Reading it that morning in the quiet light, Lindbergh reminded us of how limited our awareness of the world had become. The whelk we had found was merely an object to be placed on the shelf, a reminder of our days at the beach. But for Lindbergh, who had held the shell in her hands exploring the details, paying passionate attention to its ridges and curves, its small history, the whelk became the object through which she reflected on her life and her values. Her attention to detail ultimately led to new knowledge, the distinction one writer, Soetsu Yanagi, has made between "seeing and knowing." For Lindbergh, the outer eye had opened to the inner one, while our eyes had remained closed. We had fallen victim to the blinders of bad habit. We had stopped seeing.

"A man is as much as he sees," wrote Henry David Thoreau. "Try to be one of those people on whom nothing is lost," wrote Henry James. Their familiar words came back to us like the rush of the tide. We had heard them before. Like prisoners in Plato's cave, blinded by darkness, we had ignored the light of their wisdom. We had forgotten to listen and to see. We had forgotten the gift of perception, the preliminary value from which so many others may follow.

Sight into Insight

ANNIE DILLARD

When I was six or seven years old, growing up in Pittsburgh, I used to take a precious penny of my own and hide it for someone else to find. It was a curious compulsion; sadly, I've never been seized by it since. For some reason I always "hid" the penny along the same stretch of sidewalk up the street. I would cradle it at the roots of a sycamore, say, or in a hole left by a chipped-off piece of sidewalk. Then I would take a piece of chalk, and, starting at either end of the block, draw huge arrows leading up to the penny from both directions. After I learned to write I labeled the arrows: SURPRISE AHEAD or MONEY THIS WAY. I was greatly excited, during all this arrow-drawing, at the thought of the first lucky passer-by who would receive in this way, regardless of merit, a free gift from the universe. But I never lurked about. I would go straight home and not give the matter another thought, until, some months later, I would be gripped again by the impulse to hide another penny.

I've been thinking about seeing. There are lots of things to see, unwrapped gifts and free surprises. The world is fairly studded and strewn with pennies cast broadside from a generous hand. But—and this is the point—who gets excited by a mere penny? If you follow one arrow, if you crouch motionless on a bank to watch a tremulous ripple thrill on the water and are rewarded by the sight of a muskrat kit paddling from its den, will you count that sight a chip of copper only, and go your rueful way? It is dire poverty indeed when a man is so malnourished and fatigued that he won't stoop to pick up a penny. But if you cultivate a healthy poverty and simplicity, so that finding a penny will literally make your day, then, since the world is in fact planted in pennies, you have with your poverty bought a lifetime of days. It is that simple. What you see is what you get.

Unfortunately, nature is very much a now-you-see-it, now-you-don't affair. A fish flashes, then dissolves in the water before my eyes like so much salt. Deer apparently ascend bodily into heaven; the brightest oriole fades into leaves. These disappearances stun me into stillness and concentration; they say of nature that it conceals with a grand nonchalance, and they say of vision that it is a deliberate gift, the revelation of a dancer who for my eyes only flings away her seven veils. For nature does reveal as well as conceal: now-you-don't-see-it, now-you-do. For a week last September migrating red-winged blackbirds were feeding heavily down by the creek at the back of the house. One day I went out to investigate the racket; I walked up to a tree, an Osage orange, and a hundred birds flew away. They simply materialized out of the tree. I saw a tree, then a whisk of color, then a tree again. I walked closer and another hundred blackbirds took flight. Not a branch, not a twig budged: the birds were apparently weightless as well as invisible. Or, it was as if the leaves of the Osage orange had been freed from a spell in the form of red-winged blackbirds; they flew from the tree, caught my eye in the sky, and vanished. When I looked again at the tree the leaves had reassembled as if nothing had happened. Finally I walked directly to the trunk of the tree and a final hundred, the real diehards, appeared, spread, and vanished. How could so many hide in the tree without my seeing them? The Osage orange, unruffled, looked just as it had looked from the house, when three hundred red-winged blackbirds cried from its crown. I looked downstream where they flew, and they were gone. Searching, I couldn't spot one. I wandered downstream to force them to play their hand, but they'd crossed the creek and scattered. One show to a customer. These appearances catch at my throat; they are the free gifts, the bright coppers at the roots of trees.

It's all a matter of keeping my eyes open. Nature is like one of those line drawings of a tree that are puzzles for children: Can you find hidden in the leaves a duck, a house, a boy, a bucket, a zebra, and a boot? Specialists can find the most incredibly well-hidden things. A book I read when I was young recommended an easy way to find caterpillars to rear: you simply find some fresh caterpillar droppings, look up, and there's your caterpillar. More recently an author advised me to set my mind at ease about those piles of cut stems on the ground in grassy fields. Field mice make them; they cut the grass down by degrees to reach the seeds at the head. It seems that when the grass is tightly packed, as in a field of ripe grain, the blade won't topple at a single cut through the stem; instead, the cut stem simply drops vertically, held in the crush of grain. The mouse severs the bottom again and again, the stem keeps dropping an inch at a time, and finally the head is low enough for the mouse to reach the seeds. Meanwhile, the mouse is positively littering the field with its little piles of cut stems into which, presumably, the author of the book is constantly stumbling.

If I can't see these minutiae, I still try to keep my eyes open. I'm always on the lookout for antlion traps in sandy soil, monarch pupae near milkweed, skipper larvae in locust leaves. These things are utterly common, and I've not seen one. I bang on hollow trees near water, but so far no flying squirrels have appeared. In flat country I watch every sunset in hopes of seeing the green ray. The green ray is a seldom-seen streak of light that rises from the sun like a spurting fountain at the moment of sunset; it throbs into the sky for two seconds and disappears. One more reason to keep my eyes open. A photography professor at the University of Florida just happened to see a bird die in midflight; it jerked, died, dropped, and smashed on the ground. I squint at the wind because I read Stewart Edward White: "I have always maintained that if you looked closely enough you could *see* the wind—the dim, hardly-made-out, fine débris fleeing high in the air." White was an excellent observer, and devoted an entire chapter of *The Mountains* to the subject of seeing deer: "As soon as you can forget the naturally obvious and construct an artificial obvious, then you too will see deer."

But the artificial obvious is hard to see. My eyes account for less than one percent of the weight of my head; I'm bony and dense; I see what I expect. I once spent a full three minutes looking at bullfrog that was so unexpectedly large I couldn't see it even though a dozen enthusiastic campers were shouting directions. Finally I asked, "What color am I looking for?" and a fellow said, "Green." When at last I picked out the frog, I saw what painters are up against: the thing wasn't green at all, but the color of wet hickory bark.

The lover can see, and the knowledgeable. I visited an aunt and uncle at a quarter-horse ranch in Cody, Wyoming. I couldn't do much of anything useful, but I could, I thought, draw. So, as we all sat around the kitchen table after supper, I produced a sheet of paper and drew a horse. "That's one lame horse," my aunt volunteered. The rest of the family joined in: "Only place to saddle that one is his neck"; "Looks like we better shoot the poor thing, on account of those terrible growths." Meekly, I slid the pencil and paper down the table. Everyone in that family, including my three young cousins, could draw a horse. Beautifully. When the paper came back it looked as though five shining, real quarter horses had been corraled by mistake with a papier-mâché moose; the real horses seemed to gaze at the monster with a steady, puzzled air. I stay away from horses now, but I can do a creditable goldfish. The point is that I just don't know what the lover knows; I just can't see the artificial obvious that those in the know construct. The herpetologist asks the native, "Are there snakes in that ravine?" "Nosir." And the herpetologist comes home with, yessir, three bags full. Are there butterflies on that mountain? Are the bluets in bloom, are there arrowheads here, or fossil shells in the shale?

Peeping through my keyhole I see within the range of only about thirty percent of the light that comes from the sun; the rest is infrared and some little ultraviolet, perfectly apparent to many animals, but invisible to me. A nightmare network of ganglia, charged and firing without my knowledge, cuts and splices what I do see, editing it for my brain. Donald E. Carr points out that the sense impressions of one-celled animals are *not* edited for the brain: "This is philosophically interesting in a rather mournful way, since it means that only the simplest animals perceive the universe as it is."

A fog that won't burn away drifts and flows across my field of vision. When you see fog move against a backdrop of deep pines, you don't see the fog itself, but streaks of clearness floating across the air in dark shreds. So I see only tatters of clearness through a pervading obscurity. I can't distinguish the fog from the overcast sky; I can't be sure if the light is direct or reflected. Everywhere darkness and the presence of the unseen appalls. We estimate now that only one atom dances alone in every cubic meter of intergalactic space. I blink and squint. What planet or power yanks Halley's Comet out of orbit? We haven't seen that force yet; it's a question of distance, density, and the pallor of reflected light. We rock, cradled in the swaddling band of darkness. Even the simple darkness of night whispers suggestions to the mind. Last summer, in August, I stayed at the creek too late.

Where Tinker Creek flows under the sycamore log bridge to the tear-shaped island, it is slow and shallow, fringed thinly in cattail marsh. At this spot an astonishing bloom of life supports vast breeding populations of insects, fish, reptiles, birds, and mammals. On windless summer evenings I stalk along the creek bank or straddle the sycamore log in absolute stillness, watching for muskrats. The night I stayed too late I ws hunched on the log staring spellbound at spreading, reflected stains of lilac on the water. A cloud in the sky suddenly lighted as if turned on by a switch; its reflection just as suddenly materialized on the water upstream, flat and floating, so that I couldn't see the creek bottom, or life in the water under the cloud. Downstream, away from the cloud on the water, water turtles smooth as beans were gliding down with the current in a series of easy, weightless push-offs, as men bound on the moon. I didn't know whether to trace the progress of one turtle I was sure of, risking sticking my face in one of the bridge's spider webs made invisible by the gathering dark, or take a chance on seeing the carp, or scan the mudbank in hope of seeing a muskrat, or follow the last of the swallows who caught at my heart and trailed it after them like streamers as they appeared from directly below, under the log, flying upstream with their tails forked, so fast.

But shadows spread, and deepened, and stayed. After thousands of years we're still strangers to darkness, fearful aliens in an enemy camp with our arms crossed over our chests. I stirred. A land turtle on the bank, startled, hissed the air from its lungs and withdrew into its shell. An uneasy pink here, an unfathomable blue there, gave great suggestion of lurking beings. Things were going on. I couldn't see whether that sere rustle I heard was a distant rattlesnake, slit-eyed, or a nearby sparrow kicking in the dry flood debris slung at the foot of a willow. Tremendous action roiled the water everywhere I looked, big action, inexplicable. A tremor welled up beside a gaping muskrat burrow in the bank and I caught my breath, but no muskrat appeared. The ripples continued to fan upstream with a steady, powerful thrust. Night was knitting over my face an eyeless mask, and I still sat transfixed. A distant airplane, a delta wing out of nightmare, made a gliding shadow on the creek's bottom that looked like a stingray cruising upstream. At once a black fin slit the pink cloud on the water, shearing it in two. The two halves merged together and seemed to dissolve before my eyes. Darkness pooled in the cleft of the creek and rose, as water collects in a well. Untamed, dreaming lights flickered over the sky. I saw hints of hulking underwater shadows, two pale splashes out of the water, and round ripples rolling close together from a blackened center.

At last I stared upstream where only the deepest violet remained of the cloud, a cloud so high its underbelly still glowed feeble color reflected from a hidden sky lighted in turn by a sun halfway to China. And out of that violet, a sudden enormous black body arced over the water. I saw only a cylindrical sleekness. Head and tail, if there was a head and tail, were both submerged in cloud. I saw only one ebony fling, a headlong dive to darkness; then the waters closed, and the lights went out.

Sometimes here in Virginia at sunset low clouds on the southern or northern horizon are completely invisible in the lighted sky. I only know one is there because I can see its reflection in still water. The first time I discovered this mystery I looked from cloud to no-cloud in bewilderment, checking my bearings over and over, thinking maybe the ark of the covenant was just passing by south of Dead Man Mountain. Only much later did I read the explanation: polarized light from the sky is very much weakened by reflection, but the light in clouds isn't polarized. So invisible clouds pass among visible clouds, till all slide over the mountains; so a greater light extinguishes a lesser as though it didn't exist.

In the great meteor shower of August, the Perseid, I wail all day for the shooting stars I miss. They're out there showering down, committing hara-kiri in a flame of fatal attraction, and hissing perhaps at last into the ocean. But at dawn what looks like a blue dome clamps down over me like a lid on a pot. The stars and planets could smash and I'd never know. Only a piece of ashen moon occasionally climbs up or down the inside of the dome, and our local star without surcease explodes on our heads. We have really only that one light, one source for all power, and yet we must turn away from it by universal decree. Nobody here on the planet seems aware of this strange, powerful taboo, that we all walk about carefully averting our faces, this way and that, lest our eyes be blasted forever.

Darkness appalls and light dazzles; the scrap of visible light that doesn't hurt my eyes hurts my brain. What I see sets me swaying. Size and distance and the sudden swelling of meanings confuse me, bowl me over. I straddle the sycamore log bridge over Tinker Creek in the summer. I look at the lighted creek bottom: snail tracks tunnel the mud in quavering curves. A crayfish jerks, but by the time I absorb what has happened, he's gone in a billowing smoke-screen of silt. I look at the water: minnows and shiners. If I'm thinking minnows, a carp will fill my brain till I scream. I look at the water's surface: skaters, bubbles, and leaves sliding down. Suddenly, my own face, reflected, startles me witless. Those snails have been tracking my face! Finally, with a shuddering wrench of the will, I see clouds, cirrus clouds. I'm dizzy, I fall in. This looking business is risky.

Once I stood on a humped rock on nearby Purgatory Mountain, watching through binoculars the great autumn hawk migration below, until I discovered that I was in danger of joining the hawks on a vertical migration of my own. I was used to binoculars, but not, apparently, to balancing on humped rocks while looking through them. I staggered. Everything advanced and receded by turns; the world was full of unexplained foreshortenings and depths. A distant huge tan object, a hawk the size of an elephant, turned out to be the browned bough of a nearby loblolly pine. I followed a sharp-shinned hawk against a featureless sky, rotating my head unawares as it flew, and when I lowered the glass a glimpse of my own looming shoulder sent me staggering. What prevents the men on Palomar from falling, voiceless and blinded, from their tiny, vaulted chairs?

I reel in confusion; I don't understand what I see. With the naked eye I can see two million light-years to the Andromeda galaxy. Often I slop some creek water in a jar and when I get home I dump it in a white china bowl. After the silt settles I return and see tracings of minute snails on the bottom, a planarian or two winding round the rim of water, roundworms shimmying frantically, and finally, when my eyes have adjusted to these dimensions, amoebae. At first the amoebae look like muscae volitantes, those curled moving spots you seem to see in your eyes when you stare at a distant wall. Then I see the amoebae as drops of water congealed, bluish, translucent, like chips of sky in the bowl. At length I choose one individual and give myself over to its idea of an evening. I see it dribble a grainy foot before it on its wet, unfathomable way. Do its unedited sense impressions include the fierce focus of my eyes? Shall I take it outside and show it Andromeda, and blow its little endoplasm? I stir the water with a finger, in case it's running out of oxygen. Maybe I should get a tropical aquarium with motorized bubblers and lights, and keep this one for a pet. Yes, it would tell its fissioned descendants, the universe is two feet by five, and if you listen closely you can hear the buzzing music of the spheres.

Oh, it's mysterious lamplit evenings, here in the galaxy, one after the other. It's one of those nights when I wander from window to window, looking for a sign. But I can't see. Terror and a beauty insoluble are a ribband of blue woven into the fringes of garments of things both great and small. No culture explains, no bivouac offers real haven or rest. But it could be that we are not seeing something. Galileo thought comets were an optical illusion. This is fertile ground: since we are certain that they're not, we can look at what our scientists have been saying with fresh hope. What if there are *really* gleaming, castellated cities hung upside-down over the desert sand? What limpid lakes and cool date palms have our caravans always passed untried? Until, one by one, by the blindest of leaps, we light on the road to these places, we must stumble in darkness and hunger. I turn from the window. I'm blind as a bat, sensing only from every direction the echo of my own thin cries.

I chanced on a wonderful book by Marius von Senden, called *Space and Sight.* When Western surgeons discovered how to perform safe cataract operations, they ranged across Europe and America operating on dozens of men and women of all ages who had been blinded by cataracts since birth. Von Senden collected accounts of such cases; the histories are fascinating. Many doctors had tested their patients' sense perceptions and ideas of space both before and after the operations. The vast majority of patients, of both sexes and all ages, had, in von Senden's opinion, no idea of space whatsoever. Form, distance, and size were so many meaningless syllables. A patient "had no idea of depth, confusing it with roundness." Before the operation a doctor would give a blind patient a cube and a sphere; the patient would tongue it or feel it with his hands, and name it correctly. After the operation the doctor would show the same objects to the patient without letting him touch them; now he had no clue whatsoever what he was seeing. One patient called lemonade "square" because it pricked on his tongue as a square shape pricked on the touch of his hands. Of another postoperative patient, the doctor writes, "I have found in her no notion of size, for example, not even within the narrow limits which she might have encompassed with the aid of touch. Thus when I asked her to show me how big her mother was, she did not stretch out her hands, but set her two index-fingers a few inches apart." Other doctors reported their patients' own statements to similar effect. "The room he was in . . . he knew to be but part of the house, yet he could not conceive that the whole house could look bigger"; "Those who are blind from birth . . . have no real conception of height or distance. A house that is a mile away is thought of as nearby, but requiring the taking of a lot of steps. . . . The elevator that whizzes him up and down gives no more sense of vertical distance than does the train of horizontal."

For the newly sighted, vision is pure sensation unencumbered by meaning: "The girl went through the experience that we all go through and forget, the moment we are born. She saw, but it did not mean anything but a lot of different kinds of brightness." Again, "I asked the patient what he could see; he answered that he saw an extensive field of light, in which everything appeared dull, confused, and in motion. He could not distinguish objects." Another patient saw "nothing but a confusion of forms and colours." When a newly sighted girl saw photographs and paintings, she asked, " 'Why do they put those dark marks all over them?' "Those aren't dark marks,' her mother explained, 'those are shadows. That is one of the ways the eye knows that things have shape. If it were not for shadows many things would look flat.' 'Well, that's how things do look,' Joan answered. 'Everything looks flat with dark patches.' "

On the other hand, many newly sighted people speak well of the world, and teach us how dull is our own vision. To one patient, a human hand, unrecognized, is "something bright and then holes." Shown a bunch of grapes, a boy calls out, "It is dark, blue and shiny. . . . It isn't smooth, it has bumps and hollows." A little girl visits a garden. "She is greatly astonished, and can scarcely be persuaded to answer, stands speechless in front of the tree, which she only names on taking hold of it, and then as 'the tree with the lights in it.' "Some delight in their sight and give themselves over to the visual world. Of a patient just after her bandages were removed, her doctor writes, "The first things to attract her attention were her own hands; she looked at them very closely, moved them repeatedly to and fro, bent and stretched the fingers, and seemed greatly astonished at the sight." One girl was eager to tell her blind friend that "men do not really look like trees at all," and astounded to discover that her every visitor had an utterly different face. Finally, a twenty-two-year-old girl was dazzled by the world's brightness and kept her eyes shut for two weeks. When at the end of that time she opened her eyes again, she did not recognize any objects, but, "the more she now directed her gaze upon everything about her, the more it could be seen how an expression of gratification and astonishment overspread her features; she repeatedly exclaimed: 'Oh God! How beautiful!' "

Seeing is of course very much a matter of verbalization. Unless I call my attention to what passes before my eyes, I simply won't see it. I have to say the words, describe what I'm seeing. If Tinker Mountain erupted, I'd be likely to notice. But if I want to notice the lesser cataclysms of valley life, I have to maintain in my head a running description of the present.

When I see this way I analyze and pry. I hurl over logs and roll away stones; I study the bank a square foot at a time, probing and tilting my head. Some days when a mist covers the mountains, when the muskrats won't show and the microscope's mirror shatters, I want to climb up the blank blue dome as a man would storm the inside of a circus tent, wildly, dangling, and with a steel knife claw a rent in the top, peep, and, if I must, fall.

But there is another kind of seeing that involves a letting go. When I see this way I sway transfixed and emptied. The difference between the two ways of seeing is the difference between walking with and without a camera. When I walk with a camera I walk from shot to shot, reading the light on a calibrated meter. When I walk without a camera, my own shutter opens, and the moment's light prints on my own silver gut. When I see this second way I am above all an unscrupulous observer.

It was sunny one evening last summer at Tinker Creek; the sun was low in the sky, upstream. I was sitting on the sycamore log bridge with the sunset at my back, watching the shiners the size of minnows who were feeding over the muddy sand in skittery schools. Again and again, one fish, then another, turned for a split second across the current and flash! the sun shot out from its silver side. I couldn't watch for it. It was always just happening somewhere else, and it drew my vision just as it disappeared: flash, like a sudden dazzle of the thinnest blade, a sparking over a dun and olive ground at chance intervals from every direction. Then I noticed white specks, some sort of pale petals, small, floating from under my feet on the creek's surface, very slow and steady. So I blurred my eyes and gazed towards the brim of my hat and saw a new world. I saw the pale white circles roll up, roll up, like the world's turning, mute and perfect, and I saw the linear flashes, gleaming silver, like stars being born at random down a rolling scroll of time. Something broke and something opened. I filled up like a new wineskin. I breathed an air like light; I saw a light like water. I was the lip of a fountain the creek filled forever; I was ether, the leaf in the zephyr; I was fleshflake, feather, bone.

When I see this way I see truly. As Thoreau says, I return to my senses.

The secret of seeing is, then, the pearl of great price. If I thought he could teach me to find it and keep it forever I would stagger barefoot across a hundred deserts after any lunatic at all. But although the pearl may be found, it may not be sought. The literature of illumination reveals this above all: although it comes to those who wait for it, it is always, even to the most practiced and adept, a gift and a total surprise. I return from one walk knowing where the killdeer nests in the field by the creek and the hour the laurel blooms. I return from the same walk a day later scarcely knowing my own name. Litanies hum in my ears; my tongue flaps in my mouth Ailinon, alleluia! I cannot cause light; the most I can do is try to put myself in the path of its beam. It is possible, in deep space, to sail on solar wind. Light, be it particle or wave, has force: you rig a giant sail and go. The secret of seeing is to sail on solar wind. Hone and spread your spirit till you yourself are a sail, whetted, translucent, broadside to the merest puff.

When her doctor took her bandages off and led her into the garden, the girl who was no longer blind saw "the tree with the lights in it." It was for this tree I searched through the peach orchards of summer, in the forests of fall and down winter and spring for years. Then one day I was walking along Tinker Creek thinking of nothing at all and I saw the tree with the lights in it. I saw the backyard cedar where the mourning doves roost charged and transfigured, each cell buzzing with flame. I stood on the grass with the lights in it, grass that was wholly fire, utterly focused and utterly dreamed. It was less like seeing than like being for the first time seen, knocked breathless by a powerful glance. The flood of fire abated, but I'm still spending the power. Gradually the lights went out in the cedar, the colors died, the cells unflamed and disappeared. I was still ringing. I had been my whole life a bell, and never knew it until at that moment I was lifted and struck. I have since only very rarely seen the tree with the lights in it. The vision comes and goes, mostly goes, but I live for it, for the moment when the mountains open and a new light roars in spate through the crack, and the mountains slam.

Reflections

Private Exploration

1. Which passage in Dillard's essay excites, delights, angers, or bores? Explore the passage in your notebook. Ask questions. Relate it to your own experience or to other readings. In what way might the passage illuminate the essay as a whole?
2. Reading the essay we wondered if such deliberate and concentrated effort at "seeing" could bring as much reward and insight as Dillard claims? Are you convinced? Do you doubt? Try an experiment.
   - **a.** Spend at least 15 minutes in a familiar place with a notebook and pen in hand. Make a deliberate effort to see as much as possible. Allow nothing to escape your eyes. Create a spontaneous list of everything you see. Challenge yourself to come up with a list of 50 or more items, actions, events.
   - **b.** When you've completed the list, move to a quiet location where you can explore in your notebook what you saw. Reflect on how this deliberate attention to details affected you. Or how it might affect you if you gave this much attention to detail all the time. What do you learn about perception? Or about yourself? What did you see that you might not have noticed if you hadn't forced yourself to look? What might be missing in a life when perception of details is not valued?

Public Exploration

Consider the following:

> It is dire poverty indeed when a man is so malnourished and fatigued that he won't stop to pick up a penny. But if you cultivate a healthy poverty and simplicity, so that finding a penny will literally make your day . . . you have with your poverty bought a lifetime of days. What you see is what you get.

Private Reflection

After reading Dillard, writing about Dillard, discussing Dillard, consider her observation that "The secret of seeing, then, is the pearl of great price . . . although the pearl may be found, it may not be sought." What is the secret of seeing?

Seeing and Knowing

SOETSU YANAGI

Seeing and knowing are often separate. Nothing could be more admirable than when they coincide, but only too often they remain estranged. In some fields this does not matter, but in the areas of aesthetics or art history or the like, any gap between perception and knowledge assumes fatal proportions. This is an obvious fact that is too frequently overlooked. Similar cases are common in other fields as well.

The critic of religion, for example, who has no religious feelings has no force in his criticisms. In the same way, the moralist who does not live by his theories carries no weight, however brilliant he may be. I know many famous art critics who have no feeling of beauty, and I cannot therefore respect their knowledge. They may be learned, but it avails nothing. It is the same with philosophy and history. The student of philosophy and the philosopher should be distinguished; a man who knows a great deal about history is not necessarily a historian.

Doubtless many would reply that intuitive perception of beauty is incomplete without learning, that without knowledge one does not see a thing as a whole. Socrates saw the identity of action and knowing. To see and at the same time to comprehend is the ideal, but in practise we are far removed from this unity. The things to be seen and the knowledge to be gained have so vastly increased in this modern age that man's activities have been pushed either into one direction or the other. But of the two, those forced into the field of knowledge are in the worse position as far as beauty is concerned.

To be unable to *see* beauty properly is to lack the basic foundation for any aesthetic understanding. One should refrain from becoming a student of aesthetics just because one has a good brain; to know a lot about beauty is no qualification. Seeing and knowing form an exterior and an interior, not a right and a left. Either way, they are not equal. In understanding beauty, intuition is more of the essence than intellectual perception.

The reversal of these two faculties stultifies vision. To "see" is to go direct to the core; to know the facts about an object of beauty is to go around the periphery. Intellectual discrimination is less essential to an understanding of beauty than the power of intuition that precedes it.

Beauty is a kind of mystery, which is why it cannot be grasped adequately through the intellect. The part of it available to intellection lacks depth. This might seem to be a denial of aesthetics, but it is as Aquinas said: "No one shows such a knowledge of God as he who says that one can know nothing". Aquinas was one of the greatest minds of medieval times and knew well how foolish his own wisdom was in the face of God. No one could rival the wisdom with which he acknowledged the poverty of his own mind. Though he is renowned as a theologian, he was surely still greater as a man of faith; without that fact he would have been a commonplace intellectual.

He who only knows, without seeing, does not understand the mystery. Even should every detail of beauty be accounted for by the intellect, does such a tabulation lead to beauty? Is the beauty that can be neatly reckoned really profound? The scholar of aesthetics tends to base his ideas on knowledge—or rather, he tries to make seeing proceed from knowing. But this is a reversal of the natural order of things.

The eye of knowledge cannot, thereby, see beauty. What is the beauty that a man of erudition sees as he holds a fine pot in his hands? If he picks a wild flower to pieces, petal by petal, and counts them, and tries to put them together again, can he regain the beauty that was there? All the assembly of dead parts cannot bring life back again. It is the same with knowing. One cannot replace the function of seeing by the function of knowing. One may be able to turn intuition into knowledge, but one cannot produce intuition out of knowledge. Thus the basis of aesthetics must not be intellectual concepts. For this purpose all the classification in the world avails nothing, and the scholar does not even become a good student of aesthetics. There are so many whose voices invariably rise round works of art, trying to pin them down in neat categories, always preceding the verification of beauty with such questions as "who made it, when, and where". The recognition of date and school, etc. is a matter of pride for them. They are intensely ashamed of leaving any mystery unaccounted for in their explanations. This is commonly referred to as the "academic conscience". In fact, I suspect it is because they have not better work to do, or cannot do it properly.

The man in the street is hoodwinked, he thinks he is being informed by a man who really does know everything. Should we apply the adjective "good" to such critics and art historians? How their writings on art are flooded with exaggerated and strained expressions. They use words, too, in remarkable numbers. They cannot suggest beauty without great heaps of adjectives.

When the power to see does not accompany the power to know—when the power to see is blunted—art historians, critics, and collectors all fall into the same kind of confusion. Even assuming that they correctly praise beautiful things, they will also, without fail, praise the ugly as well. This shows that, ultimately, they are not even praising the beautiful for the right reasons. Their blurred eyesight is incapable of distinguishing beauty and ugliness. They have not grasped the yardstick of beauty. They study things that have no place in history and cheerfully rank the good and bad side by side. They have no sense of values, when they are right, they are right by luck. Beauty is essentially a matter of values; if values are confused, if there are no standards, if valueless things are admitted among the valued, judgements of beauty lose their basis.

The number of collectors of art in the world is constantly increasing, but there are few whose perceptions are developed enough to gather various types of art together with a uniformity of standard and taste. This is undoubtedly due to the foot-rule approach that I am decrying. As great an importance is placed on secondary issues, for example the idea that because something is expensive it is necessarily good. It may be rare, or unblemished, or be inscribed with the name of a famous artist, but these are all tradesman's arguments or tactics, after all, and have nothing to do with beauty. These good people are deceived in this way because they have not got eyes to see with. If they had, they would not be concerned with rarity, perfect condition, or former ownership. There is no real point in collecting unless for the sake of beauty, nor is it truly possible for those who cannot see, for if they persist, their collections are bound to be a jumble of good and bad. This is the inevitable result of putting a foot-rule between ones eyes and an object.

To look at the question from a different angle, seeing relates to the concrete, knowing to the abstract. Let us say that we have a painting by Tawaraya Sōtatsu in front of us: it is an object that the eyes see and research, and to which one's heart can respond, but the knower with the foot-rule is immediately busy with a dozen questions as to age, authenticity, previous ownership, technique and the like. These secondary and circumferential matters are all very well only if they lead to a better appreciation of Sōtatsu's painting. Without such appreciation all the knowledge in the world will take one nowhere. Thereby it becomes clear that both to see and to know is best, but that in any case seeing comes first. See first and know afterwards.

Seeing is a born faculty, knowledge is acquired. To a point anyone can acquire knowledge, but the potential of seeing is born with us. Although some are more gifted than others, it is generally accepted that the musical or the artistic gifts are born with us and that there is nothing to be done about it if one is not so fortunate. The gift of seeing is of the same order. This leaves the ungifted forlorn. I would like to give them three pieces of advice.

First, put aside the desire to judge immediately; acquire the habit of just looking. Second, do not treat the object as an object for the intellect. Third, just be ready to receive, passively, without interposing yourself. If you can void your mind of all intellectualization, like a clear mirror that simply reflects, all the better. This nonconceptualization—the Zen state of *mushin* ("no mind")—may seem to represent a negative attitude, but from it springs the true ability to contact things directly and positively.

Reflections

Private Exploration

1. Which passage in Yanagi seems important to you? Copy it out in your notebook. Explore why the passage seems to evoke in you a special feeling or question. Does it open up an insight into yourself? Something from your experience? Does it raise questions? Consider how it might illuminate other aspects of Yanagi's essay? Take your time here, ask questions, probe, and dig deep.

2. What do you make of this:

> Beauty is a kind of mystery which is why it cannot be grasped adequately through the intellect.

3. Study the photos of three women on page 183. Each has been considered beautiful. Explore their differences, their similarities. First consider what you see. Write about specific details that might be said to make each woman beautiful. Then consider what you know about each woman, if anything, and how that might affect reactions to their beauty.

Public Exploration

1. Use the following passage from Yanagi to consider how seeing and knowing might affect our concept of values:

> When the power to see does not accompany the power to know—when the power to see is blunted . . . all fall into the same kind of confusion. Even assuming that they correctly praise beautiful things, they will also, without fail, praise the ugly as well. This shows that, ultimately, they are not even praising the beautiful for the right reasons. . . . They study things that have no place in history and cheerfully rank the good and bad side by side. They have no sense of values, when they are right, they are right by luck.

2. Consider the following argument by the 18th century Romantic poet and artist William Blake: "As a man is, so he sees."
3. According to Yanagi, "Beauty is essentially a matter of values." Reflect individually on some object you value. (You might want to take a few minutes and write about it, describing why it is beautiful and what it means to you.) Then in turn, share the object you value with others, noting why it is beautiful. After everyone has spoken, consider as a group how initial responses to individual "objects" changed, if they did, and why. How does knowing affect seeing? How are values formed? Does Yanagi provide us with any new insight into this?

Private Reflection

1. After you've had an opportunity to hear others discuss their views of knowing and seeing, consider the following. Does it relate to what you read in Yanagi? To what you've heard? To yourself?

> The eye is the lamp of the body. So, if your eye is sound, your whole body will be full of light; but if your eye is not sound, your whole body will be full of darkness. If then the light in you is darkness, how great is the darkness!
>
> —MATTHEW 6:19-34

2. Reflect on this:

> . . . all the knowledge in the world will take one nowhere. Thereby it becomes clear that both to see and to know is best, but that in any case seeing comes first. See first, and know afterwards.

Blue Winds Dancing

TOM WHITECLOUD

There is a moon out tonight. Moon and stars and clouds tipped with moonlight. And there is a fall wind blowing in my heart. Ever since this evening, when against a fading sky I saw geese wedge southward. They were going home. . . . Now I try to study, but against the pages I see them again, driving southward. Going home.

Across the valley there are heavy mountains holding up the night sky, and beyond the mountains there is home. Home, and peace, and the beat of drums, and blue winds dancing over snow fields. The Indian lodge will fill with my people, and our gods will come and sit among them. I should be there then. I should be at home.

But home is beyond the mountains, and I am here. Here where fall hides in the valleys, and winter never comes down from the mountains. Here where all the trees grow in rows; the palms stand stiffly by the roadsides, and in the groves of the orange trees line in military rows, and endlessly bear fruit. Beautiful, yes; there is always beauty in order, in rows of growing things! But it is the beauty of captivity. A pine fighting for existence on a windy knoll is much more beautiful.

In my Wisconsin, the leaves change before the snows come. In the air there is the smell of wild rice and venison cooking; and when the winds come whispering through the forests, they carry the smell of rotting leaves. In the evenings, the loon calls, lonely; and birds sing their last songs before leaving. Bears dig roots and eat late fall berries, fattening for their long winter sleep. Later, when the first snows fall, one awakens in the morning to find the world white and beautiful and clean. Then one can look back over his trail and see the tracks following. In the woods there are tracks of deer and snowshoe rabbits, and long streaks where partridges slide to alight. Chipmunks make tiny footprints on the limbs and one can hear squirrels busy in hollow trees, sorting acorns. Soft lake waves wash the shores, and sunsets burst each evening over the lakes, and make them look as if they were afire.

That land which is my home! Beautiful, calm—where there is no hurry to get anywhere, no driving to keep up in a race that knows no ending and no goal. No classes where men talk and talk and then stop now and then to hear their own words come back to them from the students. No constant peering into the maelstrom of one's mind; no worries about grades and honors; no hysterical preparing for life until that life is half over; no anxiety about one's place in the thing they call Society.

I hear again the ring of axes in deep woods, the crunch of snow beneath my feet. I feel again the smooth velvet of ghost-birch bark. I hear the rhythm of the drums. . . . I am tired. I am weary of trying to keep up this bluff of being civilized. Being civilized means trying to do everything you don't want to, never doing anything you want to. It means dancing to the strings of custom and tradition; it means living in houses and never knowing or caring who is next door. These civilized white men want us to be like them—always dissatisfied—getting a hill and wanting a mountain.

Then again, maybe I am not tired. Maybe I'm licked. Maybe I am just not smart enough to grasp these things that go to make up civilization. Maybe I am just too lazy to think hard enough to keep up.

Still, I know my people have many things that civilization has taken from the whites. They know how to give; how to tear one's piece of meat in two and share it with one's brother. They know how to sing—how to make each man his own songs and sing them; for their music they do not have to listen to other men singing over a radio. They know how to make things with their hands, how to shape beads into design and make a thing of beauty from a piece of birch bark.

But we are inferior. It is terrible to have to feel inferior; to have to read reports of intelligence tests, and learn that one's race is behind. It is terrible to sit in classes and hear men tell you that your people worship sticks of wood—that your gods are all false, that the Manitou forgot your people and did not write them a book.

I am tired. I want to walk again among the ghost-birches. I want to see the leaves turn in autumn, the smoke rise from the lodgehouses, and to feel the blue winds. I want to hear the drums; I want to hear the drums and feel the blue whispering winds.

There is a train wailing into the night. The trains go across the mountains. It would be easy to catch a freight. They will say he has gone back to the blanket; I don't care. The dance at Christmas. . . .

A bunch of bums warming at a tiny fire talk politics and women and joke about the Relief and the WPA and smoke cigarettes. These men in caps and overcoats and dirty overalls living on the outskirts of civilization are free, but they pay the price of being free in civilization. They are outcasts. I remember a sociology professor lecturing on adjustment to society; hobos and prostitutes and criminals are individuals who never adjusted, he said. He could learn a lot if he came and listened to a bunch of bums talk. He would learn that work and a woman and a place to hang his hat are all the ordinary man wants. These are all he wants, but other men are not content to let him want only these. He must be taught to want radios and automobiles and a new suit every spring. Progress would stop if he did not want these things. I listen to hear if there is any talk of communism or socialism in the hobo jungles. There is none. At best there is a sort of disgusted philosophy about life. They seem to think there should be a better distribution of wealth, or more work, or something. But they are not rabid about it. The radicals live in the cities.

I find a fellow headed for Albuquerque, and talk road-talk with him. "It is hard to ride fruit cars. Bums break in. Better to wait for a cattle car going back to the Middle West, and ride that." We catch the next east-bound and walk the tops until we find a cattle car. Inside, we crouch near the forward wall, huddle, and try to sleep. I feel peaceful and content at last. I am going home. The cattle car rocks. I sleep.

Morning and the desert. Noon and the Salton Sea, lying more lifeless than a mirage under a somber sun in a pale sky. Skeleton mountains rearing on the skyline, thrusting out of the desert floor, all rock and shadow and edges. Desert. Good country for an Indian reservation. . . .

Yuma and the muddy Colorado. Night again, and I wait shivering for the dawn.

Phoenix. Pima country. Mountains that look like cardboard sets on a forgotten stage. Tucson. Papago country. Giant cacti that look like petrified hitchhikers along the highways. Apache country. At El Paso my road-buddy decides to go on to Houston. I leave him, and head north to the mesa country. Las Cruces and the terrible Organ Mountains, jagged peaks that instill fear and wondering. Albuquerque. Pueblos along the Rio Grande. On the boardwalk there are some Indian women in colored sashes selling bits of pottery. The stone age offering its art to the twentieth century. They hold up a piece and fix the tourist with black eyes until, embarrassed, he buys or turns away. I feel suddenly angry that my people should have to do such things for a living. . . .

Santa Fe trains are fast, and they keep them pretty clean of bums. I decide to hurry and ride passenger coaltenders. Hide in the dark, judge the speed of the train as it leaves, and then dash out, and catch it. I hug the cold steel wall of the tender and think of the roaring fire in the engine ahead, and of the passengers back in the dining car reading their papers over hot coffee. Beneath me there is a blur of rails. Death would come quick if my hands should freeze and I fall. Up over the Sangre De Cristo range, around cliffs and through canyons to Denver. Bitter cold here, and I must watch out for Denver Bob. He is a railroad bull who has thrown bums from fast freights. I miss him. It is too cold, I suppose. On north to the Sioux country.

Small towns lit for the coming Christmas. On the streets of one I see a beam-shouldered young farmer gazing into a window filled with shining silver toasters. He is tall and wears a blue shirt buttoned, with no tie. His young wife by his side looks at him hopefully. He wants decorations for his place to hang his hat to please his woman. . . .

Northward again. Minnesota, and great white fields of snow; frozen lakes, and dawn running into dusk without noon. Long forests wearing white. Bitter cold, and one night the northern lights. I am nearing home.

I reach Woodruff at midnight. Suddenly I am afraid, now that I am but twenty miles from home. Afraid of what my father will say, afraid of being looked on as a stranger by my own people. I sit by a fire and think about myself and all other young Indians. We just don't seem to fit in anywhere—certainly not among the whites, and not among the older people. I think again about the learned sociology professor and his professing. So many things seem to be clear now that I am away from school and do not have to worry about some man's opinion of my ideas. It is easy to think while looking at dancing flames.

Morning. I spend the day cleaning up, and buying some presents for my family with what is left of my money. Nothing much, but a gift is a gift, if a man buys it with his last quarter. I wait until evening, then start up the track toward home.

Christmas Eve comes in on a north wind. Snow clouds hang over the pines, and the night comes early. Walking along the railroad bed, I feel the calm peace of snowbound forests on either side of me. I take my time; I am back in a world where time does not mean so much now. I am alone; alone but not nearly so lonely as I was back on the campus at school. Those are never lonely who love the snow and the pines; never lonely when the pines are wearing white shawls and snow crunches coldly underfoot. In the woods I know there are the tracks of deer and rabbit; I know that if I leave the rails and go into the woods I shall find them. I walk along feeling glad because my legs are light and my feet seem to know that they are home. A deer comes out of the woods ahead of me, and stands silhouetted on the rails. The North, I feel, has welcomed me home. I watch him and am glad that I do not wish for a gun. He goes into the woods quietly, leaving only the design of his tracks in the snow. I walk on. Now and then I pass a field, white under the night sky, with houses at the far end. Smoke comes from the chimneys of the houses, and I try to tell what sort of wood each is burning by the smoke; some burn pine, others aspen, others tamarack. There is one from which comes black coal smoke that rises lazily and drifts out over the tops of the trees. I like to watch houses and try to imagine what might be happening in them.

Just as a light snow begins to fall I cross the reservation boundary; somehow it seems as though I have stepped into another world. Deep woods in a white-and-black winter night. A faint trail leading to the village.

The railroad on which I stand comes from a city sprawled by a lake—a city with a million people who walk around without seeing one another; a city sucking the life from all the country around; a city with stores and police and intellectuals and criminals and movies and apartment houses; a city with its politics and libraries and zoos.

Laughing, I go into the woods. As I cross a frozen lake I begin to hear the drums. Soft in the night the drums beat. It is like the pulse beat of the world. The white line of the lake ends at a black forest, and above the trees the blue winds are dancing.

I come to the outlying houses of the village. Simple box houses, etched black in the night. From one or two windows soft lamplight falls on the snow. Christmas here, too, but it does not mean much; not much in the way of parties and presents. Joe Sky will get drunk. Alex Bodidash will buy his children red mittens and a new sled. Alex is a Carlisle man, and tries to keep his home up to white standards. White standards. Funny that my people should be ever falling farther behind. The more they try to imitate whites the more tragic the result. Yet they want us to be imitation white men. About all we imitate well are their vices.

The village is not a sight to instill pride, yet I am not ashamed; one can never be ashamed of his own people when he knows they have dreams as beautiful as white snow on a tall pine.

Father and my brother and sister are seated around the table as I walk in. Father stares at me for a moment, then I am in his arms, crying on his shoulder. I give them the presents I have brought, and my throat tightens as I watch my sister save carefully bits of red string from the packages. I hide my feelings by wrestling with my brother when he strikes my shoulder in token of affection. Father looks at me, and I know he has many questions, but he seems to know why I have come. He tells me to go alone to the lodge, and he will follow.

I walk along the trail to the lodge, watching the northern lights forming in the heavens. White waving ribbons that seem to pulsate with the rhythm of the drums. Clean snow creaks beneath my feet, and a soft wind sighs through the trees, singing to me. Everything seems to say, "Be happy! You are home now—you are free. You are among friends—we are your friends; we, the trees, and the snow, and the lights." I follow the trail to the lodge. My feet are light, my heart seems to sing to the music, and I hold my head high. Across white snow fields blue winds are dancing.

Before the lodge door I stop, afraid, I wonder if my people will remember me. I wonder—"Am I Indian, or am I white?" I stand before the door a long time. I hear the ice groan on the lake, and remember the story of the old woman who is under the ice, trying to get out, so she can punish some runaway lovers. I think to myself, "If I am white I will not believe that story; If I am Indian, I will know that there is an old woman under the ice." I listen for a while, and I know that there is an old woman under the ice. I look again at the lights, and go in.

Inside the lodge there are many Indians. Some sit on benches around the walls, others dance in the center of the floor around a drum. Nobody seems to notice me. It seems as though I were among a people I have never seen before. Heavy women with long hair. Women with children on their knees—small children that watch with intent black eyes the movements of the dancers, whose small faces are solemn and serene. The faces of the old people are serene, too, and their eyes are merry and bright. I look at the old men. Straight, dressed in dark trousers and beaded velvet vests, wearing soft moccasins. Dark, lined faces intent on the music. I wonder if I am at all like them. They dance on, lifting their feet to the rhythm of the drums swaying lightly, looking upward. I look at their eyes, and am startled at the rapt attention to the rhythm of the music.

The dance stops. The men walk back to the walls, and talk in low tones or with their hands. There is little conversation, yet everyone seems to be sharing some secret. A woman looks at a small boy wandering away, and he comes back to her.

Strange, I think and then remember. These people are not sharing words—they are sharing a mood. Everyone is happy. I am so used to white people that it seems strange so many people could be together without someone talking.

These Indians are happy because they are together, and because the night is beautiful outside, and the music is beautiful. I try hard to forget school and white people, and be one of these—my people. I am trying to forget everything but the night, and it is a part of me that I am one with my people and we are all a part of something universal. I watch eyes, and see now that the old people are speaking to me. They nod slightly, imperceptibly, and their eyes laugh into mine. I look around the room. All the eyes are friendly; they all laugh. No one questions my being here. The drums begin to beat again, and I catch the invitation in the eyes of the old men. My feet begin to lift to the rhythm, and I look out beyond the walls into the night and see the lights. I am happy. It is beautiful. I am home.

Reflections

Private Exploration

1. Explore the title, "Blue Winds Dancing." What does it reveal about the young man? Search through the story to find additional references to wind and dancing. What might the metaphor suggest about the narrator's perception of what he values most? Is there a place for such values in a "civilized world" dedicated to order and technological progress?
2. Identifying key words and phrases repeated throughout a story often leads to insight. What key words and phrases does the author use here? If you have not already annotated "Blue Winds Dancing," read it a second time and mark or circle every major repetition. What new knowledge is gained by becoming aware of these repetitions? How might they point toward a larger significance?

Public Exploration

After living for many years in a white culture, the narrator of "Blue Winds Dancing," returns home to ask, "Am I Indian, or am I white?" What earlier values is the narrator of the story seeking? In college, many of you may be exposed to a culture that differs from the one you've left behind. Some of you will be changed forever. Returning home becomes more and more difficult, even when your parents are proud of you. Why? Using "Blue Winds Dancing" as a starting point, consider what really happens when you are exposed to new cultural experiences. Are the gains worth the losses?

Private Reflection

1. What do you make of this passage?

   > I am alone; alone but not nearly so lonely as I was back on the campus at school.

2. If you've ever been away from home even for a short time, you can probably identify with the narrator's longing to return. You too may recall specific images that stimulate emotions and thoughts when you think about home. You too may have experienced some misgivings about returning, about being accepted. Reflect on any time you've

found yourself away from home and thought about returning. Write about that experience in as much detail as possible and consider what changes you perceived upon return. Was it the home you imagined? Were your relationships with others the same? How were your thoughts and feelings altered? To what do you attribute the changes?

Good Country People

FLANNERY O'CONNOR

Besides the neutral expression that she wore when she was alone, Mrs. Freeman had two others, forward and reverse, that she used for all her human dealings. Her forward expression was steady and driving like the advance of a heavy truck. Her eyes never swerved to left or right but turned as the story turned as if they followed a yellow line down the center of it. She seldom used the other expression because it was not often necessary for her to retract a statement, but when she did, her face came to a complete stop, there was an almost imperceptible movement of her black eyes, during which they seemed to be receding, and then the observer would see that Mrs. Freeman, though she might stand there as real as several grain sacks thrown on top of each other, was no longer there in spirit. As for getting anything across to her when this was the case, Mrs. Hopewell had given it up. She might talk her head off. Mrs. Freeman could never be brought to admit herself wrong on any point. She would stand there and if she could be brought to say anything, it was something like, "Well, I wouldn't of said it was and I wouldn't of said it wasn't," or letting her gaze range over the top kitchen shelf where there was an assortment of dusty bottles, she might remark, "I see you ain't ate many of them figs you put up last summer."

They carried on their most important business in the kitchen at breakfast. Every morning Mrs. Hopewell got up at seven o'clock and lit her gas heater and Joy's. Joy was her daughter, a large blonde girl who had an artificial leg. Mrs. Hopewell thought of her as a child though she was thirty-two years old and highly educated. Joy would get up while her mother was eating and lumber into the bathroom and slam the door, and before long, Mrs. Freeman would arrive at the back door. Joy would hear her mother call, "Come on in," and then they would talk for a while in low voices that were indistinguishable in the bathroom. By the time Joy came in, they had usually finished the weather report and were on one or the other of Mrs. Freeman's daughters, Glynese or Carramae. Joy called them Glycerin and Caramel. Glynese, a redhead, was eighteen and had many admirers; Carramae, a blonde, was only fifteen but already married and pregnant. She could not keep anything on her stomach. Every morning Mrs. Freeman told Mrs. Hopewell how many times she had vomited since the last report.

Mrs. Hopewell liked to tell people that Glynese and Carramae were two of the finest girls she knew and that Mrs. Freeman was a *lady* and that she was never ashamed to take her anywhere or introduce her to anybody they might meet. Then she would tell how she happened to hire the Freemans in the first place and how they were a godsend to her and how she had had them four years. The reason for her keeping them so long was that they were not trash. They were good country people. She had telephoned the man whose name they had given as a reference and he had told her that Mr. Freeman was a good farmer but that his wife was the nosiest woman ever to walk the earth. "She's got to be into everything," the man said. "If she don't get there before the dust settles, you can bet she's dead, that's all. She'll want to know all your business. I can stand him real good," he had said, "but me nor my wife neither could have stood that woman one more minute on this place." That had put Mrs. Hopewell off for a few days.

She had hired them in the end because there were no other applicants but she had made up her mind beforehand exactly how she would handle the woman. Since she was the type who had to be into everything, then, Mrs. Hopewell had decided, she would not only let her be into everything, she would see *to it* that she was into everything—she would give her the responsibility of everything, she would put her in charge. Mrs. Hopewell had no bad qualities of her own but she was able to use other people's in such a constructive way that she never felt the lack. She had hired the Freemans and she had kept them four years.

Nothing is perfect. This was one of Mrs. Hopewell's favorite sayings. Another was: that is life! And still another, the most important, was: well, other people have their opinions too. She would make these statements, usually at the table, in a tone of gentle insistence as if no one held them but her, and the large hulking Joy, whose constant outrage had obliterated every expression from her face, would stare just a little to the side of her, her eyes icy blue, with the look of someone who has achieved blindness by an act of will and means to keep it.

When Mrs. Hopewell said to Mrs. Freeman that life was like that, Mrs. Freeman would say, "I always said so myself." Nothing had been arrived at by anyone that had not first been arrived at by her. She was quicker than Mr. Freeman. When Mrs. Hopewell said to her after they had been on the place a while, "You know, you're the wheel behind the wheel," and winked, Mrs. Freeman had said, "I know it. I've always been quick. It's some that are quicker than others."

"Everybody is different," Mrs. Hopewell said.

"Yes, most people is," Mrs. Freeman said.

"It takes all kinds to make the world."

"I always said it did myself."

The girl was used to this kind of dialogue for breakfast and more of it for dinner; sometimes they had it for supper too. When they had no guest they ate in the kitchen because that was easier. Mrs. Freeman always managed to arrive at some point during the meal and to watch them finish it. She would stand in the doorway if it were summer but in the winter she would stand with one elbow on top of the refrigerator and look down on them, or she would stand by the gas heater, lifting the back of her skirt slightly. Occasionally she would stand against the wall and roll her head from side to side. At no time was she in any hurry to leave. All this was very trying on Mrs. Hopewell but she was a woman of great patience. She realized that nothing is perfect and that in the Freemans she had good country people and that if, in this day and age, you get good country people, you had better hang onto them.

She had had plenty of experience with trash. Before the Freemans she had averaged one tenant family a year. The wives of these farmers were not the kind you would want to be around you for very long. Mrs. Hopewell, who had divorced her husband long ago, needed someone to walk over the fields with her; and when Joy had to be impressed for these services, her remarks were usually so ugly and her face so glum that Mrs. Hopewell would say, "If you can't come pleasantly, I don't want you at all," to which the girl, standing square and rigid-shouldered with her neck thrust slightly forward, would reply, "If you want me, here I am—LIKE I AM."

Mrs. Hopewell excused this attitude because of the leg (which had been shot off in a hunting accident when Joy was ten). It was hard for Mrs. Hopewell to realize that her child was thirty-two now and that for more than twenty years she had had only one leg. She thought of her still as a child because it tore her heart to think instead of the poor stout girl in her thirties who had never danced a step or had any *normal* good times. Her name was really Joy but as soon as she was twenty-one and away from home, she had had it legally changed. Mrs. Hopewell was certain that she had thought and thought until she had hit upon the ugliest name in any language. Then she had gone and had the beautiful name, Joy, changed without telling her mother until after she had done it. Her legal name was Hulga.

When Mrs. Hopewell thought the name, Hulga, she thought of the broad blank hull of a battleship. She would not use it. She continued to call her Joy to which the girl responded but in a purely mechanical way.

Hulga had learned to tolerate Mrs. Freeman who saved her from taking walks with her mother. Even Glynese and Carramae were useful when they occupied attention that might otherwise have been directed at her. At first she had thought she could not stand Mrs. Freeman for she had found that it was not possible to be rude to her. Mrs. Freeman would take on strange resentments and for days together she would be sullen but the source of her displeasure was always obscure; a direct attack, a positive leer, blatant ugliness to her face—these never touched her. And without warning one day, she began calling her Hulga.

She did not call her that in front of Mrs. Hopewell who would have been incensed but when she and the girl happened to be out of the house together, she would say something and add the name Hulga to the end of it, and the big spectacled Joy-Hulga would scowl and redden as if her privacy had been intruded upon. She considered the name her personal affair. She had arrived at it first purely on the basis of its ugly sound and then the full genius of its fitness had struck her. She had a vision of the name working like the ugly sweating Vulcan who stayed in the furnace and to whom, presumably, the goddess had to come when called. She saw it as the name of her highest creative act. One of her major triumphs was that her mother had not been able to turn her dust into Joy, but the greater one was that she had been able to turn it herself into Hulga. However, Mrs. Freeman's relish for using the name only irritated her. It was as if Mrs. Freeman's beady steel-pointed eyes had penetrated far enough behind her face to reach some secret fact. Something about her seemed to fascinate Mrs. Freeman and then one day Hulga realized that it was the artificial leg. Mrs. Freeman had a special fondness for the details of secret infections, hidden deformities, assaults upon children. Of diseases, she preferred the lingering or incurable. Hulga had heard Mrs. Hopewell give her the details of the hunting accident, how the leg had been literally blasted off, how she had never lost consciousness. Mrs. Freeman could listen to it any time as if it had happened an hour ago.

When Hulga stumped into the kitchen in the morning (she could walk without making the awful noise but she made it—Mrs. Hopewell was certain—because it was ugly-sounding), she glanced at them and did not speak. Mrs. Hopewell would be in her red kimono with her hair tied around her head in rags. She would be sitting at the table, finishing her breakfast and Mrs. Freeman would be hanging by her elbow outward from the refrigerator, looking down at the table. Hulga always put her eggs on the stove to boil and then stood over them with her arms folded, and Mrs. Hopewell would look at her—a kind of indirect gaze divided between her and Mrs. Freeman—and would think that if she would only keep herself up a little, she wouldn't be so bad looking. There was nothing wrong with her face that a pleasant expression wouldn't help. Mrs. Hopewell said that people who looked on the bright side of things would be beautiful even if they were not.

Whenever she looked at Joy this way, she could not help but feel that it would have been better if the child had not taken the Ph.D. It had certainly not brought her out any and now that she had it, there was no more excuse for her to go to school again. Mrs. Hopewell thought it was nice for girls to go to school to have a good time but Joy had "gone through." Anyhow, she would not have been strong enough to go again. The doctors had told Mrs. Hopewell that with the best of care, Joy might see forty-five. She had a weak heart. Joy had made it plain that if it had not been for this condition, she would be far from these red hills and good country people. She would be in a university lecturing to people who knew what she was talking about. And Mrs. Hopewell could very well picture her there, looking like a scarecrow and lecturing to more of the same. Here she went about all day in a six-year-old skirt and a yellow sweat shirt with a faded cowboy on a horse embossed on it. She thought this was funny; Mrs. Hopewell thought it was idiotic and showed simply that she was still a child. She was brilliant but she didn't have a grain of sense. It seemed to Mrs. Hopewell that every year she grew less like other people and more like herself—bloated, rude, and squint-eyed. And she said such strange things! To her own mother she had said—without warning, without excuse, standing up in the middle of a meal with her face purple and her mouth half full—"Woman! Do you ever look inside? Do you ever look inside and see what you are *not*? God!" she had cried sinking down again and staring at her plate, "Malebranche was right: we are not our own light. We are not our own light!" Mrs. Hopewell had no idea to this day what brought that on. She had only made the remark, hoping Joy would take it in, that a smile never hurt anyone.

The girl had taken the Ph.D. in philosophy and this left Mrs. Hopewell at a complete loss. You could say, "My daughter is a nurse," or "My daughter is a school teacher," or even, "My daughter is a chemical engineer." You could not say, "My daughter is a philosopher." That was something that had ended with the Greeks and Romans. All day Joy sat on her neck in a deep chair, reading. Sometimes she went for walks but she didn't like dogs or cats or birds or flowers or nature or nice young men. She looked at nice young men as if she could smell their stupidity.

One day Mrs. Hopewell had picked up one of the books the girl had just put down and opening it at random, she read, "Science, on the other hand, has to assert its soberness and seriousness afresh and declare that it is concerned solely with what-is. Nothing—how can it be for science anything but a horror and a phantasm? If science is right, then one thing stands firm: science wishes to know nothing of nothing. Such is after all the strictly scientific approach to Nothing. We know it by wishing to know nothing of Nothing." These words had been underlined with a blue pencil and they worked on Mrs. Hopewell like some evil incantation in gibberish. She shut the book quickly and went out of the room as if she were having a chill.

This morning when the girl came in, Mrs. Freeman was on Carramae. "She thrown up four times after supper," she said, "and was up twict in the night after three o'clock. Yesterday she didn't do nothing but ramble in the bureau drawer. All she did. Stand up there and see what she could run up on."

"She's got to eat," Mrs. Hopewell muttered, sipping her coffee, while she watched Joy's back at the stove. She was wondering what the child had said to the Bible salesman. She could not imagine what kind of a conversation she could possibly have had with him.

He was a tall gaunt hatless youth who had called yesterday to sell them a Bible. He had appeared at the door, carrying a large black suitcase that weighted him so heavily on one side that he had to brace himself against the door facing. He seemed on the point of collapse but he said in a cheerful voice, "Good morning, Mrs. Cedars!" and set the suitcase down on the mat. He was not a bad-looking young man though he had on a bright blue suit and yellow socks that were not pulled up far enough. He had prominent face bones and a streak of sticky-looking brown hair falling across his forehead.

"I'm Mrs. Hopewell," she said.

"Oh!" he said, pretending to look puzzled but with his eyes sparkling, "I saw it said 'The Cedars,' on the mailbox so I thought you was Mrs. Cedars!" and he burst out in a pleasant laugh. He picked up the satchel and under cover of a pant, he fell forward into her hall. It was rather as if the suitcase had moved first, jerking him after it. "Mrs. Hopewell!" he said and grabbed her hand. "I hope you are well!" and he laughed again and then all at once his face sobered completely. He paused and gave her a straight earnest look and said, "Lady, I've come to speak of serious things."

"Well, come in," she muttered, none too pleased because her dinner was almost ready. He came into the parlor and sat down on the edge of a straight chair and put the suitcase between his feet and glanced around the room as if he were sizing her up by it. Her silver gleamed on the two sideboards; she decided he had never been in a room as elegant as this.

"Mrs. Hopewell," he began, using her name in a way that sounded almost intimate, "I know you believe in Chrustian service."

"Well yes," she murmured.

"I know," he said and paused, looking very wise with his head cocked on one side, "that you're a good woman. Friends have told me."

Mrs. Hopewell never liked to be taken for a fool. "What are you selling?" she asked.

"Bibles," the young man said and his eye raced around the room before he added, "I see you have no family Bible in your parlor, I see that is the one lack you got!"

Mrs. Hopewell could not say, "My daughter is an atheist and won't let me keep the Bible in the parlor." She said, stiffening slightly, "I keep my Bible by my bedside." This was not the truth. It was in the attic somewhere.

"Lady," he said, "the word of God ought to be in the parlor."

"Well, I think that's a matter of taste," she began. "I think . . . "

"Lady," he said, "for a Chrustian, the word of God ought to be in every room in the house besides in his heart. I know you're a Chrustian because I can see it in every line of your face."

She stood up and said, "Well, young man, I don't want to buy a Bible and I smell my dinner burning."

He didn't get up. He began to twist his hands and looking down at them, he said softly, "Well lady, I'll tell you the truth—not many people want to buy one nowadays and besides, I know I'm real simple. I don't know how to say a thing but to say it. I'm just a country boy." He glanced up into her unfriendly face. "People like you don't like to fool with country people like me!"

"Why!" she cried, "good country people are the salt of the earth! Besides, we all have different ways of doing, it takes all kinds to make the world go 'round. That's life!"

"You said a mouthful," he said.

"Why, I think there aren't enough good country people in the world!" she said, stirred. "I think that's what's wrong with it!"

His face had brightened. "I didn't inraduce myself," he said. "I'm Manley Pointer from out in the country around Willohobie, not even from a place, just from near a place."

"You wait a minute," she said. "I have to see about my dinner." She went to the kitchen and found Joy standing near the door where she had been listening.

"Get rid of the salt of the earth," she said, "and let's eat."

Mrs. Hopewell gave her a pained look and turned the heat down under the vegetables. "*I* can't be rude to anybody," she murmured and went back into the parlor.

He had opened the suitcase and was sitting with a Bible on each knee.

"You might as well put those up," she told him. "I don't want one."

"I appreciate your honesty," he said. "You don't see any more real honest people unless you go way out in the country."

"I know," she said, "real genuine folks!" Through the crack in the door she heard a groan.

"I guess a lot of boys come telling you they're working their way through college," he said, "but I'm not going to tell you that. Somehow," he said, "I don't want to go to college. I want to devote my life to Chrustian service. See," he said, lowering his voice, "I got this heart condition. I may not live long. When you know it's something wrong with you and you may not live long, well then, lady . . ." He paused, with his mouth open, and stared at her.

He and Joy had the same condition! She knew that her eyes were filling with tears but she collected herself quickly and murmured, "Won't you stay for dinner? We'd love to have you!" and was sorry the instant she heard herself say it.

"Yes mam," he said in an abashed voice, "I would sher love to do that!"

Joy had given him one look on being introduced to him and then throughout the meal had not glanced at him again. He had addressed several remarks to her, which she had pretended not to hear. Mrs. Hopewell could not understand deliberate rudeness, although she lived with it, and she felt she had always to overflow with hospitality to make up for Joy's lack of courtesy. She urged him to talk about himself and he did. He said he was the seventh child of twelve and that his father had been crushed under a tree when he himself was eight year old. He had been crushed very badly, in fact, almost cut in two and was practically not recognizable. His mother had got along the best she could by hard working and she had always seen that her children went to Sunday School and that they read the Bible every evening. He was now nineteen year old and he had been selling Bibles for four months. In that time he had sold seventy-seven Bibles and had the promise of two more sales. He wanted to become a missionary because he thought that was the way you could do most for people. "He who losest his life shall find it," he said simply and he was so sincere, so genuine and earnest that Mrs. Hopewell would not for the world have smiled. He prevented his peas from sliding onto the table by blocking them with a piece of bread which he later cleaned his plate with. She could see Joy observing sidewise how he handled his knife and fork and she saw too that every few minutes, the boy would dart a keen appraising glance at the girl as if he were trying to attract her attention.

After dinner Joy cleared the dishes off the table and disappeared and Mrs. Hopewell was left to talk with him. He told her again about his childhood and his father's accident and about various things that had happened to him. Every five minutes or so she would stifle a yawn. He sat for two hours until finally she told him she must go because she had an appointment in town. He packed his Bibles and thanked her and prepared to leave, but in the doorway he stopped and wrung her hand and said that not on any of his trips had he met a lady as nice as her and he asked if he could come again. She had said she would always be happy to see him.

Joy had been standing in the road, apparently looking at something in the distance, when he came down the steps toward her, bent to the side with his heavy valise. He stopped where she was standing and confronted her directly. Mrs. Hopewell could not hear what he said but she trembled to think what Joy would say to him. She could see that after a minute Joy said something and that then the boy began to speak again, making an excited gesture with his free hand. After a minute Joy said something else at which the boy began to speak once more. Then to her amazement, Mrs. Hopewell saw the two of them walk off together, toward the gate. Joy had walked all the way to the gate with him and Mrs. Hopewell could not imagine what they had said to each other, and she had not yet dared to ask.

Mrs. Freeman was insisting upon her attention. She had moved from the refrigerator to the heater so that Mrs. Hopewell had to turn and face her in order to seem to be listening. "Glynese gone out with Harvey Hill again last night," she said. "She had this sty."

"Hill," Mrs. Hopewell said absently, "is that the one who works in the garage?"

"Nome, he's the one that goes to chiropracter school," Mrs. Freeman said. "She had this sty. Been had it two days. So she says when he brought her in the other night he says, 'Lemme get rid of that sty for you,' and she says, 'How?' and he says, 'You just lay yourself down acrost the seat of that car and I'll show you.' So she done it and he popped her neck. Kept on a-popping it several times until she made him quit. This morning," Mrs. Freeman said, "she ain't got no sty. She ain't got no traces of a sty."

"I never heard of that before," Mrs. Hopewell said.

"He ast her to marry him before the Ordinary," Mrs. Freeman went on, "and she told him she wasn't going to be married in no *office*."

"Well, Glynese is a fine girl," Mrs. Hopewell said, "Glynese and Carramae are both fine girls."

"Carramae said when her and Lyman was married Lyman said it sure felt sacred to him. She said he said he wouldn't take five hundred dollars for being married by a preacher."

"How much would he take?" the girl asked from the stove.

"He said he wouldn't take five hundred dollars," Mrs. Freeman repeated.

"Well we all have to work to do," Mrs. Hopewell said.

"Lyman said it just felt more sacred to him," Mrs. Freeman said. "The doctor wants Carramae to eat prunes. Says instead of medicine. Says them cramps is coming from pressure. You know where I think it is?"

"She'll be better in a few weeks," Mrs. Hopewell said.

"In the tube," Mrs. Freeman said. "Else she wouldn't be as sick as she is."

Hulga had cracked her two eggs into a saucer and was bringing them to the table along with a cup of coffee that she had filled too full. She sat down carefully and began to eat, meaning to keep Mrs. Freeman there by questions if for any reason she showed an inclination to leave. She could perceive her mother's eye on her. The first roundabout question would be about the Bible salesman and she did not wish to bring it on. "How did he pop her neck?" she asked.

Mrs. Freeman went into a description of how he had popped her neck. She said he owned a '55 Mercury but that Glynese said she would rather marry a man with only a '36 Plymouth who would be married by a preacher. The girl asked what if he had a '32 Plymouth and Mrs. Freeman said what Glynese had said was a '36 Plymouth.

Mrs. Hopewell said there were not many girls with Glynese's common sense. She said what she admired in those girls was their common sense. She said that reminded her that they had a nice visitor yesterday, a young man selling Bibles. "Lord," she said, "he bored me to death but he was so sincere and genuine I couldn't be rude to him. He was just good country people, you know," she said, "—just the salt of the earth."

"I seen him walk up," Mrs. Freeman said, "and then later—I seen him walk off," and Hulga could feel the slight shift in her voice, the slight insinuation, that he had not walked off alone, had he? Her face remained expressionless but the color rose into her neck and she seemed to swallow it down with the next spoonful of egg. Mrs. Freeman was looking at her as if they had a secret together.

"Well, it takes all kinds of people to make the world go 'round," Mrs. Hopewell said. "It's very good we aren't all alike."

"Some people are more alike than others," Mrs. Freeman said.

Hulga got up and stumped, with about twice the noise that was necessary, into her room and locked the door. She was to meet the Bible salesman at ten o'clock at the gate. She had thought about it half the night. She had started thinking of it as a great joke and then she had begun to see profound implications in it. She had lain in bed imagining dialogues for them that were insane on the surface but that reached below to depths that no Bible salesman would be aware of. Their conversation yesterday had been of this kind.

He had stopped in front of her and had simply stood there. His face was bony and sweaty and bright, with a little pointed nose in the center of it, and his look was different from what it had been at the dinner table. He was gazing at her with open curiosity, with fascination, like a child watching a new fantastic animal at the zoo, and he was breathing as if he had run a great distance to reach her. His gaze seemed somehow familiar but she could not think where she had been regarded with it before. For almost a minute he didn't say anything. Then on what seemed an insuck of breath, he whispered, "You ever ate a chicken that was two days old?"

The girl looked at him stonily. He might have just put this question up for consideration at the meeting of a philosophical association. "Yes," she presently replied as if she had considered it from all angles.

"It must have been mighty small!" he said triumphantly and shook all over with little nervous giggles, getting very red in the face, and subsiding finally into his gaze of complete admiration, while the girl's expression remained exactly the same.

"How old are you?" he asked softly.

She waited some time before she answered. Then in a flat voice she said, "Seventeen."

His smiles came in succession like waves breaking on the surface of a little lake. "I see you got a wooden leg," he said. "I think you're real brave. I think you're real sweet."

The girl stood blank and solid and silent.

"Walk to the gate with me," he said. "You're a brave sweet little thing and I liked you the minute I seen you walk in the door."

Hulga began to move forward.

"What's your name?" he asked, smiling down on the top of her head.

"Hulga," she said.

"Hulga," he murmured, "Hulga. Hulga. I never heard of anybody name Hulga before. You're shy, aren't you, Hulga?" he asked.

She nodded, watching his large red hand on the handle of the giant valise.

"I like girls that wear glasses," he said. "I think a lot. I'm not like these people that a serious thought don't ever enter their heads. It's because I may die."

"I may die too," she said suddenly and looked up at him. His eyes were very small and brown, glittering feverishly.

"Listen," he said, "don't you think some people was meant to meet on account of what all they got in common and all? Like they both think serious thoughts and all?" He shifted the valise to his other hand so that the hand nearest her was free. He caught hold of her elbow and shook it a little. "I don't work on Saturday," he said. "I like to walk in the woods and see what Mother Nature is wearing. O'er the hills and far away. Pic-nics and things. Couldn't we go on a pic-nic tomorrow? Say yes, Hulga," he said and gave her a dying look as if he felt his insides about to drop out of him. He had even seemed to sway slightly toward her.

During the night she had imagined that she seduced him. She imagined that the two of them walked on the place until they came to the storage barn beyond the two back fields and there, she imagined, that things came to such a pass that she very easily seduced him and that then, of course, she had to reckon with his remorse. True genius can get an idea across even to an inferior mind. She imagined that she took his remorse in hand and changed it into a deeper understanding of life. She took all his shame away and turned it into something useful.

She set off for the gate at exactly ten o'clock, escaping without drawing Mrs. Hopewell's attention. She didn't take anything to eat, forgetting that food is usually taken on a picnic. She wore a pair of slacks and a dirty white shirt, and as an afterthought, she had put some Vapex on the collar of it since she did not own any perfume. When she reached the gate no one was there.

She looked up and down the empty highway and had the furious feeling that she had been tricked, that he had only meant to make her walk to the gate after the idea of him. Then suddenly he stood up, very tall, from behind a bush on the opposite embankment. Smiling, he lifted his hat which was new and wide-brimmed. He had not worn it yesterday and she wondered if he had bought it for the occasion. It was toast-colored with a red and white band around it and was slightly too large for him. He stepped from behind the bush still carrying the black valise. He had on the same suit and the same yellow socks sucked down in his shoes from walking. He crossed the highway and said, "I knew you'd come!"

The girl wondered acidly how he had known this. She pointed to the valise and asked, "Why did you bring your Bibles?"

He took her elbow, smiling down on her as if he could not stop. "You can never tell when you'll need the word of God, Hulga," he said. She had a moment in which she doubted that this was actually happening and then they began to climb the embankment. They went down into the pasture toward the woods. The boy walked lightly by her side, bouncing on his toes. The valise did not seem to be heavy today; he even swung it. They crossed half the pasture without saying anything and then, putting his hand easily on the small of her back, he asked softly, "Where does your wooden leg join on?"

She turned an ugly red and glared at him and for an instant the boy looked abashed. "I didn't mean you no harm," he said. "I only meant you're so brave and all. I guess God takes care of you."

"No," she said, looking forward and walking fast, "I don't even believe in God."

At this he stopped and whistled. "No!" he exclaimed as if he were too astonished to say anything else.

She walked on and in a second he was bouncing at her side, fanning with his hat. "That's very unusual for a girl," he remarked, watching her out of the corner of his eye. When they reached the edge of the wood, he put his hand on her back again and drew her against him without a word and kissed her heavily.

The kiss, which had more pressure than feeling behind it, produced that extra surge of adrenalin in the girl that enables one to carry a packed trunk out of a burning house, but in her, the power went at once to the brain. Even before he released her, her mind, clear and detached and ironic anyway, was regarding him from a great distance, with amusement but with pity. She had never been kissed before and she was pleased to discover that it was an unexceptional experience and all a matter of the mind's control. Some people might enjoy drain water if they were told it was vodka. When the boy, looking expectant but uncertain, pushed her gently away, she turned and walked on, saying nothing as if such business, for her, were common enough.

He came along panting at her side, trying to help her when he saw a root that she might trip over. He caught and held back the long swaying blades of thorn vine until she had passed beyond them. She led the way and he came breathing heavily behind her. Then they came out on a sunlit hillside, sloping softly into another one a little smaller. Beyond, they could see the rusted top of the old barn where the extra hay was stored.

The hill was sprinkled with small pink weeds. "Then you ain't saved?" he asked suddenly, stopping.

The girl smiled. It was the first time she had smiled at him at all. "In my economy,'' she said, ''I'm saved and you are damned but I told you I didn't believe in God.''

Nothing seemed to destroy the boy's look of admiration. He gazed at her now as if the fantastic animal at the zoo had put its paw through the bars and given him a loving poke. She thought he looked as if he wanted to kiss her again and she walked on before he had the chance.

''Ain't there somewheres we can sit down sometimes?'' he murmured, his voice softening toward the end of the sentence.

''In that barn,'' she said.

They made for it rapidly as if it might slide away like a train. It was a large two-story barn, cool and dark inside. The boy pointed up the ladder that led into the loft and said, ''It's too bad we can't go up there.''

''Why can't we?'' she asked.

''Yer leg,'' he said reverently.

The girl gave him a contemptuous look and putting both hands on the ladder, she climbed it while he stood below, apparently awestruck. She pulled herself expertly through the opening and then looked down at him and said, ''Well, come on if you're coming,'' and he began to climb the ladder, awkwardly bringing the suitcase with him.

''We won't need the Bible,'' she observed.

''You never can tell,'' he said, panting. After he had got into the loft, he was a few seconds catching his breath. She had sat down in a pile of straw. A wide sheath of sunlight, filled with dust particles, slanted over her. She lay back against a bale, her face turned away, looking out the front opening of the barn where hay was thrown from a wagon into the loft. The two pink-speckled hillsides lay back against a dark ridge of woods. The sky was cloudless and cold blue. The boy dropped down by her side and put one arm under her and the other over her and began methodically kissing her face, making little noises like a fish. He did not remove his hat but it was pushed far enough back not to interfere. When her glasses got in his way, he took them off of her and slipped them into his pocket.

The girl at first did not return any of the kisses but presently she began to and after she had put several on his cheek, she reached his lips and remained there, kissing him again and again as if she were trying to draw all the breath out of him. His breath was clear and sweet like a child's and the kisses were sticky like a child's. He mumbled about loving her and about knowing when he first seen her that he loved her, but the mumbling was like the sleepy fretting of a child being put to sleep by his mother. Her mind, throughout this, never stopped or lost itself for a second to her feelings. ''You ain't said you loved me none,'' he whispered finally, pulling back from her. ''You got to say that.''

She looked away from him off into the hollow sky and then down at a black ridge and then down farther into what appeared to be two green swelling lakes. She didn't realize he had taken her glasses but this landscape could not seem exceptional to her for she seldom paid any close attention to her surroundings.

"You got to say it," he repeated. "You got to say you love me."

She was always careful how she committed herself. "In a sense," she began, "if you use the word loosely, you might say that. But it's not a word I use. I don't have illusions. I'm one of those people who see *through* to nothing."

The boy was frowning. "You got to say it. I said it and you got to say it," he said.

The girl looked at him almost tenderly. "You poor baby," she murmured. "It's just as well you don't understand," and she pulled him by the neck, face-down, against her. "We are all damned," she said, "but some of us have taken off our blindfolds and see that there's nothing to see. It's a kind of salvation."

The boy's astonished eyes looked blankly through the ends of her hair. "Okay," he almost whined, "but do you love me or don'tcher?"

"Yes," she said and added, "in a sense. But I must tell you something. There mustn't be anything dishonest between us." She lifted his head and looked him in the eye. "I am thirty years old," she said. "I have a number of degrees."

The boy's look was irritated but dogged. "I don't care," he said. "I don't care a thing about what all you done. I just want to know if you love me or don'tcher?" and he caught her to him and wildly planted her face with kisses until she said, "Yes, yes."

"Okay then," he said, letting her go. "Prove it."

She smiled, looking dreamily out on the shifty landscape. She had seduced him without even making up her mind to try. "How?" she asked, feeling that he should be delayed a little.

He leaned over and put his lips to her ear. "Show me where your wooden leg joins on," he whispered.

The girl uttered a sharp little cry and her face instantly drained of color. The obscenity of the suggestion was not what shocked her. As a child she had sometimes been subject to feelings of shame but education had removed the last traces of that as a good surgeon scrapes for cancer; she would no more have felt it over what he was asking than she would have believed in his Bible. But she was as sensitive about the artificial leg as a peacock about his tail. No one ever touched it but her. She took care of it as someone else would his soul, in private and almost with her own eyes turned away. "No," she said.

"I known it," he muttered, sitting up. "You're just playing me for a sucker."

"Oh no no!" she cried. "It joins on at the knee. Only at the knee. Why do you want to see it?"

The boy gave her a long penetrating look. "Because," he said, "it's what makes you different. You ain't like anybody else."

She sat staring at him. There was nothing about her face or her round freezing-blue eyes to indicate that this had moved her; but she felt as if her heart had stopped and left her mind to pump her blood. She decided that for the first time in her life she was face to face with real innocence. This boy, with an instinct that came from beyond wisdom, had touched the truth about her. When after a minute, she said in a hoarse high voice, "All right," it was like surrendering to him completely. It was like losing her own life and finding it again, miraculously, in his.

Very gently he began to roll the slack leg up. The artificial limb, in a white sock and brown flat shoe, was bound in a heavy material like canvas and ended in an ugly jointure where it was attached to the stump. The boy's face and his voice were entirely reverent as he uncovered it and said, "Now show me how to take it off and on."

She took it off for him and put it back on again and then he took it off himself, handling it as tenderly as if it were a real one. "See!" he said with a delighted child's face. "Now I can do it myself!"

"Put it back on," she said. She was thinking that she would run away with him and that every night he would take the leg off and every morning put it back on again. "Put it back on," she said.

"Not yet," he murmured, setting it on its foot out of her reach. "Leave it off for a while. You got me instead."

She gave a little cry of alarm but he pushed her down and began to kiss her again. Without the leg she felt entirely dependent on him. Her brain seemed to have stopped thinking altogether and to be about some other function that it was not very good at. Different expressions raced back and forth over her face. Every now and then the boy, his eyes like two steel spikes, would glance behind him where the leg stood. Finally she pushed him off and said, "Put it back on me now."

"Wait," he said. He leaned the other way and pulled the valise toward him and opened it. It had a pale blue spotted lining and there were only two Bibles in it. He took one of these out and opened the cover of it. It was hollow and contained a pocket flask of whiskey, a pack of cards, and a small blue box with printing on it. He laid these out in front of her one at a time in an evenly spaced row, like one presenting offerings at the shrine of a goddess. He put the blue box in her hand. THIS PRODUCT TO BE USED ONLY FOR THE PREVENTION OF DISEASE, she read, and dropped it. The boy was unscrewing the top of the flask. He stopped and pointed, with a smile, to the deck of cards. It was not an ordinary deck but one with an obscene picture on the back of each card. "Take a swig," he said, offering her the bottle first. He held it in front of her, but like one mesmerized, she did not move.

Her voice when she spoke had an almost pleading sound. "Aren't you," she murmured, "aren't you just good country people?"

The boy cocked his head. He looked as if he were just beginning to understand that she might be trying to insult him. "Yeah," he said, curling his lip slightly, "but it ain't held me back none. I'm as good as you any day in the week."

"Give me my leg," she said.

He pushed it farther away with his foot. "Come on now, let's begin to have us a good time," he said coaxingly. "We ain't got to know one another good yet."

"Give me my leg!" she screamed and tried to lunge for it but he pushed her down easily.

"What's the matter with you all of a sudden?" he asked, frowning as he screwed the top on the flask and put it quickly back inside the Bible. "You just a while ago said you didn't believe in nothing. I thought you was some girl!"

Her face was almost purple. "You're a Christian!" she hissed. "You're a fine Christian! You're just like them all—say one thing and do another. You're a perfect Christian, you're . . ."

The boy's mouth was set angrily. "I hope you don't think," he said in a lofty indignant tone, "that I believe in that crap! I may sell Bibles but I know which end is up and I wasn't born yesterday and I know where I'm going!"

"Give me my leg!" she screeched. He jumped up so quickly that she barely saw him sweep the cards and the blue box back into the Bible and throw the Bible into the valise. She saw him grab the leg and then she saw it for an instant slanted forlornly across the inside of the suitcase with a Bible at either side of its opposite ends. He slammed the lid shut and snatched up the valise and swung it down the hole and then stepped through himself.

When all of him had passed but his head, he turned and regarded her with a look that no longer had any admiration in it. "I've gotten a lot of interesting things," he said. "One time I got a woman's glass eye this way. And you needn't to think you'll catch me because Pointer ain't really my name. I use a different name at every house I call at and don't stay nowhere long. And I'll tell you another thing, Hulga," he said, using the name as if he didn't think much of it, "you ain't so smart. I been believing in nothing ever since I was born!" and then the toast-colored hat disappeared down the hole and the girl was left, sitting on the straw in the dusty sunlight. When she turned her churning face toward the opening, she saw his blue figure struggling successfully over the green speckled lake.

Mrs. Hopewell and Mrs. Freeman, who were in the back pasture, digging up onions, saw him emerge a little later from the woods and head across the meadow toward the highway. "Why, that looks like that nice dull young man that tried to sell me a Bible yesterday," Mrs. Hopewell said, squinting. "He must have been selling them to the Negroes back in there. He was so simple," she said, "but I guess the world would be better off if we were all that simple."

Mrs. Freeman's gaze drove forward and just touched him before he disappeared under the hill. Then she returned her attention to the evil-smelling onion shoot she was lifting from the ground. "Some can't be that simple," she said. "I know I never could."

Reflections

Private Exploration

1. Explore your initial impression of "Good Country People." Begin with whatever disturbed, delighted, or shocked you. Ask yourself questions, lots of them. Probe your emotional reaction. What is O'Connor doing to us as readers? Find a specific passage or events to focus on.

2. It's been said that "Good Country People" offers multi-leveled perceptions and misperceptions, ultimately leading to deception. Consider the perceptions and misperceptions of two different characters and how that affects what they "know" and how they act. Include specific phrases, incidents, and selected dialogue to strengthen your findings.

Public Exploration

1. Once Manley Pointer has led Hulga into the barn, she tells him, "I don't have illusions. I'm one of those people who see through to nothing." Later, as he disappears with Hulga's leg, Pointer responds, "You ain't so smart. I been believing in nothing ever since I was born!" How might these lines open up the story?
2. O'Connor pays particular attention to vision and sight details throughout the story. For example, she describes Mrs. Freeman's eyes as "beady and steel-pointed." Her eyes "never swerved to left or right. . . ." By contrast, Joy wears big spectacles, her eyes are "icy blue, with the look of someone who has achieved blindness by an act of will." And Manley Pointer has a gaze that Joy feels vaguely she's seen somewhere before. Why do you think O'Connor pays so much attention to vision? How might it serve as an opening into the story?

Private Reflection

How does perception affect values? Begin by briefly exploring this question in one of the characters from "Good Country People." Then consider how perception might affect values in someone you know. Write about that person in detail. Finally, consider whether your own perceptions affect your own values. Be honest here. Probe deeply.

Memory's Glass

WILLIAM FOX CONNOR

In my desk drawer I have one of those small daguerreotypes housed in a gilt frame and tucked into a black leather box trimmed inside with red velvet. A young woman stares out from it, but she seems to be receding into a misty background. A chemist friend of mine explained that the image is fleeing from the copper plate and that the process is irreversible.

If I look closely, however, I can make out basic features. Her hair is dark and she has it coiffed back so that ringlets fall around her neck and shoulders. She is wearing a dark dress with what appear to be small white flowers sprinkled over it like snowflakes. Her neck and wrists are wreathed in white lace.

Her eyes are the most appealing features in her countenance. Yet they seem empty and emotionless. They appear that way partly because her image is fading and partly because I do not know who she is. I retrieved the picture a few years ago from the attic of my aunt's house the day the house was being sold at auction, but I have been unable to discover the woman's identity.

Although no memory links me to the young woman, the daguerreotype has been a curiosity to me. I have even tried to write poems about it. But, because I have no emotional tie with the image it houses, a precise meaning and purpose has always eluded me, like a word on the tip of my tongue that I can almost taste and feel but can't quite shape into an utterance.

I grew up on a farm in the southwest corner of the Shenandoah Valley in Virginia, an area rich in history and strewn with artifacts. The ruins of an old plantation house lay in an overgrown lot just across the driveway from our house. It had burned several years before we moved to our farm, and the remains lay in a tangle of honeysuckle, blackberry vines, rambling rose bushes, and clumps of lilac.

I often wandered around the edges of the rubble in the first few months after we moved to the farm, peering into the darkness of the tangled undergrowth. I continued my search during the winter months, and one cold February day I found a sword buried under some bricks through which I had been probing with a long pole. At first the object I struck looked like a flat piece of metal that had fallen, probably when the chimney had collapsed during the fire. When I pried the bricks away from the side of the stone foundation, the blackened hilt of a sword appeared.

The sword was still in its scabbard when I first retrieved it, welded in by the searing heat of the fire and by the rust that had grown in it over the years. It was also slightly bent, and I managed to remove it from its housing only after a struggle. The bare blade was pitted with rust and blackened from the fire. The leather that had once made the grip in the handle had also burned away. But for all its defects the sword fascinated me, and I wondered at it as part of an age usually cloistered in museums or locked away in attics and closets. An element of mystery attached to the sword, the kind of mystery I discovered later in the old cap-and-ball revolver that my great grandmother kept wrapped in a shawl in her bureau drawer.

It must have been about 1948 when Great-grandmother told me about watching her father go off to war when she was still a very young girl. She had watched him wave goodbye as he walked across a stubble field. I was eight then, and she was in her 90s.

She and my grandmother were washing supper dishes when she told me. Her hand moved slowly, mechanically, for a moment across a plate she was drying; then it stopped. She allowed her arm to fall slowly, her hand still clutching the plate, until it hung by her side like a stilled pendulum. The gold in her wire-rimmed glasses glowed faintly in the creamy evening light as she turned to stare out the front door and down across the newly cut hayfield, trying to see back as she spoke.

For that instant she escaped the kitchen, the dishes, and the summer heat to another place and time. I remember that moment and her expression. I followed her part of the way and could see a small gray figure moving through the white mist from an empty field on an autumn morning. He paused at the field's distant edge, turned and waved his arm high above his head, then disappeared into the trees beyond.

He did not come back. Among the few belongings of his that remained I only remember the pistol. Great-grandmother allowed me to see it from time to time. I used to be able to cock it, to pull the trigger and feel the small vibration as the hammer slammed down against the nipples on the cylinder. The pistol still had the musty smell of partly oxidized metal and aged grease.

I always wanted that pistol. I wanted to restore it, not so much as a possession but as part of a past that belonged to me. I thought that I could hold the pistol and think about the figure at the far side of that stubble field, and he wouldn't disappear into the trees. At least that's the way I looked at things as a child.

The sword was like the pistol, except that it was a curiosity from the earth and had passed beyond belonging to anyone. I looked at it and held it up to the sky, imagining that its blade had been shiny once and might have cut the air above a horse's head in a cavalry charge. I tried to imagine it hanging by some soldier's side, an officer maybe, swaying gently to the rhythm of a horse's steady gait as a column of soldiers made its way into the haze of the upper Shenandoah. But nothing like the small, gray figure I saw when Great-grandmother spoke that evening ever appeared when I held the sword.

I have since learned that my best memories have never been housed in things. I haven't seen the pistol or the sword for years. Both of them disappeared when I was still a child, and I doubt that I could now select either of them from an accumulation of old weapons. The pistol may be restored in someone else's collection or tucked away in someone else's bureau drawer. The sword may have been carried off by some other, more avid treasure seeker.

But I still remember that summer evening when my great-grandmother looked down across that hayfield. Her image is a moment of personal history, more indelibly etched on my memory than any image tenuously captured on a copper plate. I can still remember the clear, faraway intensity in her eyes as she looked toward the small, gray figure waving at the far side of that stubble field. I can steal into that moment and wrap it around me until all the parts of it flow together and the three of us are joined, like concatenated images in a long poem.

Reflections

Private Exploration

1. Memories may be said to constitute private values. William Fox Conner writes, "I have since learned that my best memories have never been housed in things." Trace the various "things" he ponders throughout the essays and what they represent to him. How does he reach this conclusion? What could he mean by it? Why would the focus of Conner's essay seem to be on "things?"

2. To describe is to picture, to create a scene in the reader's imagination. We particularly admire Conner's ability to create memorable scenes. Select any passage from Conner's essay that you find striking. Copy that scene in your notebook. What particular words and phrases from the passage stimulate pictures for you? What makes those choices particularly poignant? Are there ways the passage might go beyond description and open up insights? In other words, how might seeing details lead us to more general understanding?

Public Exploration

Consider this observation by poet Marvin Bell:

> . . . both sight and insight derive from fierce consciousness, whether it begins in looking at a small object or in paying attention to all the implications and resonances of an idea or image.

What could he mean by "fierce consciousness"? Could such strong language apply to Conner's essay? Does it explain a process of thinking? What might it suggest about the different ways people come to know something?

Compare Bell's position to a 19th century writer, John Ruskin:

> The greatest thing a human soul ever does in this world is to see something, and tell what he saw in a plain way. . . . To see clearly is poetry, prophecy, and religion—all in one.

Private Reflection

Conner considers the image of his great-grandmother looking across the field as "a moment of personal history" that is more valued than any pictures of her. Reflect on your own "moment of personal history," a remembered image of someone important to you. Tell the story you associate with that image. Use concrete specific details and images that will make your memory visible on paper.

Beauty

When the Other Dancer Is the Self

ALICE WALKER

It is a bright summer day in 1947. My father, a fat, funny man with beautiful eyes and a subversive wit, is trying to decide which of his eight children he will take with him to the county fair. My mother, of course, will not go. She is knocked out from getting most of us ready: I hold my neck stiff against the pressure of her knuckles as she hastily completes the braiding and then beribboning of my hair.

My father is the driver for the rich old white lady up the road. Her name is Miss Mey. She owns all the land for miles around, as well as the house in which we live. All I remember about her is that she once offered to pay my mother thirty-five cents for cleaning her house, raking up piles of her magnolia leaves, and washing her family's clothes, and that my mother—she of no money, eight children, and a chronic earache—refused it. But I do not think of this in 1947. I am two and a half years old. I want to go everywhere my daddy goes. I am excited at the prospect of riding in a car. Someone has told me fairs are fun. That there is room in the car for only three of us doesn't faze me at all. Whirling happily in my starchy frock, showing off my biscuit-polished patent-leather shoes and lavender socks, tossing my head in a way that makes my ribbons bounce, I stand, hands on hips, before my father, "Take me, Daddy," I say with assurance: "I'm the prettiest!"

Later, it does not surprise me to find myself in Miss Mey's shiny black car, sharing the back seat with the other lucky ones. Does not surprise me that I thoroughly enjoy the fair. At home that night I tell the unlucky ones all I can remember about the merry-go-round, the man who eats live chickens, and the teddy bears, until they say: that's enough, baby Alice. Shut up now, and go to sleep.

It is Easter Sunday, 1950. I am dressed in a green, flocked, scalloped-hem dress (handmade by my adoring sister, Ruth) that has its own smooth satin petticoat and tiny hot-pink roses tucked into each scallop. My shoes, new T-strap patent leather, again highly biscuit-polished. I am six years old and have learned one of the longest Easter speeches to be heard that day, totally unlike the speech I said when I was two: "Easter lilies / pure and white / blossom in / the morning light." When I rise to give my speech I do so on a great wave of love and pride and expectation. People in the church stop rustling their new crinolines. They seem to hold their breath. I can tell they admire my dress, but it is my spirit, bordering on sassiness (womanishness), they secretly applaud.

"That girl's a little *mess*," they whisper to each other, pleased.

Naturally I say my speech without stammer or pause, unlike those who stutter, stammer, or, worst of all, forget. This is before the word "beautiful" exists in people's vocabulary, but "Oh, isn't she the *cutest* thing!" frequently floats my way. "And got so much sense!" they gratefully add . . . for which thoughtful addition I thank them to this day.

It was great fun being cute. But then, one day, it ended.

I am eight years old and a tomboy. I have a cowboy hat, cowboy boots, checkered skirt and pants, all red. My playmates are my brothers, two and four years older than I. Their colors are black and green, the only difference in the way we are dressed. On Saturday nights we all go to the picture show, even my mother; Westerns are her favorite kind of movie. Back home, "on the ranch," we pretend we are Tom Mix, Hopalong Cassidy, Lash LaRue (we'eve even named one of our dogs Lash LaRue); we chase each other for hours rustling cattle, being outlaws, delivering damsels from distress. Then my parents decide to buy my brothers guns. These are not "real" guns. They shoot "BBs," copper pellets my brothers say will kill birds. Because I am a girl, I do not get a gun. Instantly I am relegated to the position of Indian. Now there appears a great distance between us. They shoot and shoot at everything with their new guns. I try to keep up with my bow and arrows.

One day while I am standing on top of our makeshift "garage"—pieces of tin nailed across some poles—holding my bow and arrow and looking out toward the fields, I feel an incredible blow in my right eye. I look down just in time to see my brother lower his gun.

Both brothers rush to my side. My eye stings, and I cover it with my hand. "If you tell," they say, "we will get a whipping. You don't want that to happen, do you?" I do not. "Here is a piece of wire," says the older brother, picking it up from the roof; "say you stepped on one end of it and the other flew up and hit you." The pain is beginning to start. "Yes," I say. "Yes, I will say this is what happened." If I do not say this is what happened, I know my brothers will find ways to make me wish I had. But now I will say anything that gets me to my mother.

Confronted by our parents we stick to the lie agreed upon. They place me on a bench on the porch and I close my left eye while they examine the right. There is a tree growing from underneath the porch that climbs past the railing to the roof. It is the last thing my right eye sees. I watch as its trunk, its branches, and then its leaves are blotted out by the rising blood.

I am in shock. First there is intense fever, which my father tries to break using lily leaves bound around my head. Then there are chills: my mother tries to get me to eat soup. Eventually, I do not know how, my parents learn what has happened. A week after the "accident" they take me to see a doctor. "Why did you wait so long to come?" he asks, looking into my eye and shaking his head. "Eyes are sympathetic," he says. "If one is blind, the other will likely become blind too."

This comment of the doctor's terrifies me. But it is really how I look that bothers me most. Where the BB pellet struck there is glob of whitish scar tissue, a hideous cataract, on my eye. Now when I stare at people—a favorite pastime, up to now—they will stare back. Not at the "cute" little girl, but at her scar. For six years I do not stare at anyone, because I do not raise my head.

Years later, in the throes of a mid-life crisis, I ask my mother and sister whether I changed after the "accident." "No," they say, puzzled. "What do you mean?"

What do I mean?

I am eight, and, for the first time, doing poorly in school, where I have been something of a whiz since I was four. We have just moved to the place where the "accident" occurred. We do not know any of the people around us because this is a different county. The only time I see the friends I knew is when we go back to our old church. The new school is the former state penitentiary. It is a large stone building, cold and drafty, crammed to overflowing with boisterous, ill-disciplined children. On the third floor there is a huge circular imprint of some partition that has been torn out.

"What used to be here?" I ask a sullen girl next to me on our way past it to lunch.

"The electric chair," says she.

At night I have nightmares about the electric chair, and about all the people reputedly "fried" in it. I am afraid of the school, where all the students seem to be budding criminals.

"What's the matter with your eye?" they ask, critically.

When I don't answer (I cannot decide whether it was an "accident" or not), they shove me, insist on a fight.

My brother, the one who created the story about the wire, comes to my rescue. But then brags so much about "protecting" me, I become sick.

After months of torture at the school, my parents decide to send me back to our old community, to my old school. I live with my grandparents and the teacher they board. But there is no room for Phoebe, my cat. By the time my grandparents decide there *is* room, and I ask for my cat, she cannot be found. Miss Yarborough, the boarding teacher, takes me under her wing, and begins to teach me to play the piano. But soon she marries an African—a "prince," she says—and is whisked away to his continent.

At my old school there is at least one teacher who loves me. She is the teacher who "knew me before I was born" and bought my first baby clothes. It is she who makes life bearable. It is her presence that finally helps me turn on the one child at the school who continually calls me "one-eyed bitch." One day I simply grab him by his coat and beat him until I am satisfied. It is my teacher who tells me my mother is ill.

My mother is lying in bed in the middle of the day, something I have never seen. She is in too much pain to speak. She has an abscess in her ear. I stand looking down on her, knowing that if she dies, I cannot live. She is being treated with warm oils and hot bricks held against her cheek. Finally a doctor comes. But I must go back to my grandparents' house. The weeks pass but I am hardly aware of it. All I know is that my mother might die, my father is not so jolly, my brothers still have their guns, and I am the one sent away from home.

"You did not change," they say.

Did I imagine the anguish of never looking up?

I am twelve. When relatives come to visit I hide in my room. My cousin Brenda, just my age, whose father works in the post office and whose mother is a nurse, comes to find me. "Hello," she says. And then she asks, looking at my recent school picture, which I did not want taken, and on which the "glob," as I think of it, is clearly visible. "You still can't see out of that eye?"

"No," I say, and flop back on the bed over my book.

That night, as I do almost every night, I abuse my eye. I rant and rave at it, in front of the mirror. I plead with it to clear up before morning. I tell it I hate and despise it. I do not pray for sight. I pray for beauty.

"You did not change," they say.

I am fourteen and baby-sitting for my brother Bill, who lives in Boston. He is my favorite brother and there is a strong bond between us. Understanding my feelings of shame and ugliness he and his wife take me to a local hospital, where the "glob" is removed by a doctor named O. Henry. There is still a small bluish crater where the scar tissue was, but the ugly white stuff is gone. Almost immediately I become a different person from the girl who does not raise her head. Or so I think. Now that I've raised my head I win the boyfriend of my dreams. Now that I've raised my head I have plenty of friends. Now that I've raised my head classwork comes from my lips as faultlessly as Easter speeches did, and I leave high school as valedictorian, most popular student, and *queen*, hardly believing my luck. Ironically, the girl who was voted most beautiful in our class (and was) was later shot twice through the chest by a male companion, using a "real" gun, while she was pregnant. But that's another story in itself. Or is it?

"You did not change," they say.

It is now thirty years since the "accident." A beautiful journalist comes to visit and to interview me. She is going to write a cover story for her magazine that focuses on my latest book. "Decide how you want to look on the cover," she says. "Glamorous, or whatever."

Never mind "glamorous," it is the "whatever" that I hear. Suddenly all I can think of is whether I will get enough sleep the night before the photography session: if I don't, my eye will be tired and wander, as blind eyes will.

At night in bed with my lover I think up reasons why I should not appear on the cover of a magazine. "My meanest critics will say I've sold out," I say. "My family will now realize I write scandalous books."

"But what's the real reason you don't want to do this?" he asks.

"Because in all probability," I say in a rush, "my eye won't be straight."

"It will be straight enough," he says. Then, "Besides, I thought you'd made your peace with that."

And I suddenly remember that I have.

I remember.

I am talking to my brother Jimmy, asking if he remembers anything unusual about the day I was shot. He does not know I consider that day the last time my father, with his sweet home remedy of cool lily leaves, chose me, and that I suffered and raged inside because of this. "Well," he says, "all I remember is standing by the side of the highway with Daddy, trying to flag down a car. A white man stopped, but when Daddy said he needed somebody to take his little girl to the doctor, he drove off."

I remember.

I am in the desert for the first time. I fall totally in love with it. I am so overwhelmed by its beauty, I confront for the first time, consciously, the meaning of the doctor's words years ago: "Eyes are sympathetic. If one is blind, the other will likely become blind too." I realize I have dashed about the world madly, looking at that, storing up images against the fading of the light. *But I might have missed seeing the desert!* The shock of that possibility—and gratitude for over twenty-five years of sight—sends me literally to my knees. Poem after poem comes—which is perhaps how poets pray.

• On Sight •

I am so thankful I have seen
The Desert
And the creatures in the desert
And the desert Itself.

The desert has its own moon
Which I have seen
With my own eye.

There is no flag on it.

Trees of the desert have arms
All of which are always up
That is because the moon is up
The sun is up
Also the sky
The stars
Clouds
None with flags.

If there *were* flags, I doubt
the trees would point.
Would you?

But mostly, I remember this:

I am twenty-seven, and my baby daughter is almost three. Since her birth, I have worried about her discovery that her mother's eyes are different from other people's. Will she be embarrassed? I think. What will she say? Every day she watched a television program called "Big Blue Marble." It begins with a picture of the earth as it appears from the moon. It is bluish, a little battered-looking, but full of light, with whitish clouds swirling around it. Every time I see it I weep with love, as if it is a picture of Grandma's house. One day when I am putting Rebecca down for her nap, she suddenly focuses on my eye. Something inside me cringes, gets ready to try to protect myself. All children are cruel about physical differences, I know from experience, and that they don't always mean to be is another matter. I assume Rebecca will be the same.

But no-o-o-o. She studies my face intently as we stand, her inside and me outside her crib. She even holds my face maternally between her dimpled little hands. Then, looking every bit as serious and lawyerlike as her father, she says, as if it may just possibly have slipped my attention: "Mommy, there's a *world* in your eye." (As in, "Don't be alarmed, or do anything crazy.") And then, gently, but with great interest: "Mommy, where did you *get* that world in your eye?"

For the most part, the pain left then. (So what, if my brothers grew up to buy even more powerful pellet guns for their sons and to carry real guns themselves. So what, if a young "Morehouse man" once nearly fell off the steps of Trevos Arnett Library because he thought my eyes were blue.) Crying and laughing I ran to the bathroom, while Rebecca mumbled and sang herself off to sleep. Yes indeed, I realized, looking into the mirror. There *was* a world in my eye. And I saw that it was possible to love it: that in fact, for all it had taught me of shame and anger and inner vision, I *did* love it. Even to see it drifting out of orbit in boredom, or rolling up out of fatigue, not to mention floating back at attention in excitement (bearing witness, a friend has called it), deeply suitable to my personality, and even characteristic of me.

That night I dream I am dancing to Stevie Wonder's song "Always" (the name of the song is really "As," but I hear it as "Always"). As I dance, whirling and joyous, happier than I've ever been in my life, another brightfaced dancer joins me. We dance and kiss each other and hold each other through the night. The other danger has obviously come through all right, as I have done. She is beautiful, whole and free. And she is also me.

Reflections

Private Exploration

1. At some point in our lives, most of us become aware of some physical difference that sets us apart from others. Whether these differences are real (a blind eye) or imagined (ears suitable only for flight training), they are differences we struggle with. Explore an incident in your life, or a series of related incidents, which involved coming to terms with a physical difference of your own or someone else's. Consider your thoughts and feelings, how they changed, if they did, as well as any individuals who may have affected that change.
2. Consider again the final paragraph of Walker's essay.

> That night I dream I am dancing to Stevie Wonder's song "Always" (the name of the song is really "As," but I hear it as "Always"). As I dance, whirling and joyous, happier than I've ever been in my life, another brightfaced dancer joins me. We dance and kiss each other and hold each other through the night.

> The other dancer has obviously come through all right, as I have done. She is beautiful, whole and free. And she is also me.

Explore the particular change Walker experiences at this point. How does her choice of singer (Stevie Wonder) help clarify our perception of what is happening? Consider how the dream relates to the reality of Walker's life. (To do that, you may have to consider the whole pattern of the essay.)

3. Walker uses numerous repetitions throughout her essay: words, phrases, whole sentences. Repetition is like a drum beat; it establishes a rhythm and pattern that affects our response to a piece, as well as pointing toward a possible significance (by saying look, this is important, that's why I'm repeating it). If you've not already annotated the essay, read it a second time and circle all the repetitions. Can you use any of them as a way into exploring what is really going on in Walker's mind and memory?

Public Exploration

How might the following passage open up an understanding of Walker's essay as a whole? Don't stop with a single explanation. Consider varying relationships and possibilities.

> Eyes are sympathetic. If one is blind, the other will likely be blind too.

Private Reflection

After exploring Walker's essay on your own, and after hearing others discuss it, consider how the following by Edward Lewis Wallant might apply to Walker as well as to yourself.

> . . . in order to illuminate for others, one must obviously first be able to see for himself. Seeing is my key word, seeing with the heart, with the brain, with the eye.

Channelled Whelk

ANNE MORROW LINDBERGH

The shell in my hand is deserted. It once housed a whelk, a snail-like creature, and then temporarily, after the death of the first occupant, a little hermit crab, who has run away, leaving his tracks behind him like a delicate vine on the sand. He ran away, and left me his shell. It was once a protection to him. I turn the shell in my hand, gazing into the wide open door from which he made his exit. Had it become an encumbrance? Why did he run away? Did he hope to find a better home, a better mode of living? I too have run away, I realize, I have shed the shell of my life, for these few weeks of vacation.

But his shell—it is simple; it is bare, it is beautiful. Small, only the size of my thumb, its architecture is perfect, down to the finest detail. Its shape, swelling like a pear in the center, winds in a gentle spiral to the pointed apex. Its color, dull gold, is whitened by a wash of salt from the sea. Each whorl, each faint knob, each criss-cross vein in its egg-shell texture, is as clearly defined as on the day of creation. My eye follows with delight the outer circumstance of that diminutive winding staircase up which this tenant used to travel.

My shell is not like this, I think. How untidy it has become! Blurred with moss, knobby with barnacles, its shape is hardly recognizable any more. Surely, it had a shape once. It has a shape still in my mind. What is the shape of my life?

The shape of my life today starts with a family. I have a husband, five children and a home just beyond the suburbs of New York. I have also a craft, writing, and therefore work I want to pursue. This shape of my life is, of course, determined by many other things; my background and childhood, my mind and its education, my conscience and its pressures, my heart and its desires. I want to give and take from my children and husband, to share with friends and community, to carry out my obligations to man and to the world as a woman, as an artist, as a citizen.

But I want first of all—in fact, as an end to these other desires—to be at peace with myself. I want a singleness of eye, a purity of intention, a central core to my life that will enable me to carry out these obligations and activities as well as I can. I want, in fact—to borrow from the language of the saints—to live "in grace" as much of the time as possible. I am not using this term in a strictly theological sense. By grace I mean an inner harmony, essentially spiritual, which can be translated into outward harmony. I am seeking perhaps what Socrates asked for in the prayer from the *Phaedrus* when he said, "May the outward and inward man be at one." I would like to achieve a state of inner spiritual grace from which I could function and give as I was meant to in the eye of God.

Vague as this definition may be, I believe most people are aware of periods in their lives when they seem to be "in grace" and other periods when they feel "out of grace," even though they may use different words to describe these states. In the first happy condition, one seems to carry all one's tasks before one lightly, as if borne alone on a great tide; and in the opposite state one can hardly tie a shoestring. It is true that a large part of life consists in learning a technique of tying the shoe-string, whether one is in grace or not. But there are techniques of living too; there are even techniques in the search for grace. And techniques can be cultivated. I have learned by some experience, by many examples, and by the writings of countless others before me, also occupied in the search, that certain environments, certain modes of life, certain rules of conduct are more conducive to inner and outer harmony than others. There are, in fact, certain roads that one may follow. Simplification of life is one of them.

I mean to lead a simple life, to choose a simple shell I can carry easily—like a hermit crab. But I do not. I find that my frame of life does not foster simplicity. My husband and five children must make their way in the world. The life I have chosen as wife and mother entrains a whole caravan of complications. It involves a house in the suburbs and either household drudgery or household help which wavers between scarcity and non-existence for most of us. It involves food and shelter; meals, planning, marketing, bills, and making the ends meet in a thousand ways. It involves not only the butcher, the baker, the candlestickmaker but countless other experts to keep my modern house with its modern "simplifications" (electricity, plumbing, refrigerator, gas-stove, oil-burner, dish-washer, radios, car, and numerous other labor-saving devices) functioning properly. It involves health; doctors, dentists, appointments, medicine, cod-liver oil, vitamins, trips to the drugstore. It involves education, spiritual, intellectual, physical; schools, school conferences, car-pools, extra trips for basket-ball or orchestra practice; tutoring; camps, camp equipment and transportation. It involves clothes, shopping, laundry, cleaning, mending, letting skirts down and sewing buttons on, or finding someone else to do it. It involves friends, my husband's, my children's, my own, and endless arrangements to get together; letters, invitations, telephone calls and transportation hither and yon.

For life today in America is based on the premise of everwidening circles of contact and communication. It involves not only family demands, but community demands, national demands, international demands on the good citizen, through social and cultural pressures, through newspapers, magazines, radio programs, political drives, charitable appeals, and so on. My mind reels with it. What a circus act we women perform every day of our lives. It puts the trapeze artist to shame. Look at us. We run a tight rope daily, balancing a pile of books on the head. Baby-carriage, parasol, kitchen chair, still under control. Steady now!

This is not the life of simplicity but the life of multiplicity that the wise men warn us of. It leads not to unification but to fragmentation. It does not bring grace; it destroys the soul. And this is not only true of my life, I am forced to conclude; it is the life of millions of women in America. I stress America, because today, the American woman more than any other has the privilege of choosing such a life. Woman in large parts of the civilized world has been forced back by war, by poverty, by collapse, by the sheer struggle to survive, into a smaller circle of immediate time and space, immediate family life, immediate problems of existence. The American woman is still relatively free to choose the wider life. How long she will hold this enviable and precarious position no one knows. But her particular situation has a significance far above its apparent economic, national or even sex limitations.

For the problems of the multiplicity of life not only confronts the American woman, but also the American man. And it is not merely the concern of the American as such, but of our whole modern civilization, since life in America today is held up as the ideal of a large part of the rest of the world. And finally, it is not limited to our present civilization, though we are faced with it now in an exaggerated form. It has always been one of the pitfalls of mankind. Plotinus was preaching the dangers of multiplicity of the world back in the third century. Yet, the problem is particularly and essentially woman's. Distraction is, always has been, and probably always will be, inherent in woman's life.

For to be a woman is to have interests and duties, raying out in all directions from the central mother-core, like spokes from the hub of a wheel. The pattern of our lives is essentially circular. We must be open to all points of the compass; husband, children, friends, home, community; stretched out, exposed, sensitive like a spider's web to each breeze that blows, to each call that comes. How difficult for us, then, to achieve a balance in the midst of these contradictory tensions, and yet how necessary for the proper functioning of our lives. How much we need, and how arduous of attainment is that steadiness preached in all rules for holy living. How desirable and distant is the ideal of the contemplative, artist, or saint—the inner inviolable core, the single eye.

With a new awareness, both painful and humorous, I begin to understand why the saints were rarely married women. I am convinced it has nothing inherently to do, as I once supposed, with chastity or children. It has to do primarily with distractions. The bearing, rearing, feeding and educating of children; the running of a house with its thousand details; human relationships with their myriad pulls—woman's normal occupations in general run counter to creative life, or contemplative life, or saintly life. The problem is not merely one of *Woman and Career, Woman and the Home, Woman and Independence.* It is more basically: how to remain whole in the midst of the distractions of life; how to remain balanced, no matter what centrifugal forces tend to pull one off center; how to remain strong, no matter what shocks come in at the periphery and tend to crack the hub of the wheel.

What is the answer? There is no easy answer, no complete answer. I have only clues, shells from the sea. The bare beauty of the channelled whelk tells me that one answer, and perhaps a first step, is in simplification of life, in cutting out some of the distractions. But how? Total retirement is not possible. I cannot shed my responsibilities. I cannot permanently inhabit a desert island. I cannot be a nun in the midst of family life. I would not want to be. The solution for me, surely, is neither in total renunciation of the world, nor in total acceptance of it. I must find a balance somewhere, or an alternating rhythm between these two extremes; a swinging of the pendulum between solitude and communion, between retreat and return. In my periods of retreat, perhaps I can learn something to carry back into my worldly life. I can at least practice for these two weeks the simplification of outward life, as a beginning. I can follow this superficial clue, and see where it leads. Here, in beach living, I can try.

One learns first of all in beach living the art of shedding; how little one can get along with, not how much. Physical shedding to begin with, which them mysteriously spreads into other fields. Clothes, first. Of course, one needs less in the sun. But one needs less anyway, one finds suddenly. One needs not need a closet-full, only a small suitcase-full. And what a relief it is! Less taking up and down of hems, less mending, and—best of all—less worry about what to wear. One finds one is shedding not only clothes—but vanity.

Next, shelter. One does not need the airtight shelter one has in winter in the North. Here I live in a bare sea-shell of a cottage. No heat, no telephone, no plumbing to speak of, no hot water, a two-burner oil stove, no gadgets to go wrong. No rugs. There were some, but I rolled them up the first day; it is easier to sweep the sand off a bare floor. But I find I don't bustle about with unnecessary sweeping and cleaning here. I am no longer aware of the dust. I have shed my Puritan conscience about absolute tidiness and cleanliness. Is it possible that, too, is a material burden? No curtains. I do not need them for privacy; the pines around my house are enough protection. I want the windows open all the time, and I don't want to worry about rain. I begin to shed my Martha-like anxiety about many things. Washable slipcovers, faded and old—I hardly see them; I don't worry about the impression they make on other people. I am shedding pride. As little furniture as possible; I shall not need much. I shall ask into my shell only those friends with whom I can be completely honest. I find I am shedding hypocrisy in human relationships. What a rest that will be! The most exhausting thing in life, I have discovered, is being insincere. That is why so much of social life is exhausting; one is wearing a mask. I had shed my mask.

I find I live quite happily without those things I think necessary in winter in the North. And as I write these words, I remember, with some shock at the disparity in our lives, a similar statement made by a friend of mine in France who spent three years in a German prison camp. Of course, he said, qualifying his remark, they did not get enough to eat, they were sometimes atrociously treated, they had little physical freedom. And yet, prison life taught him how little one can get along with, and what extraordinary spiritual freedom and peace such simplification can bring. I remember again, ironically, that today more of us in America than anywhere else in the world have the luxury of choice between simplicity and complication of life. And for the most part, we, who could choose simplicity, choose complication. War, prison, survival periods, enforce a form of simplicity on man. The monk and the nun choose it of their own free will. But if one accidentally finds it, as I have for a few days, one finds also the serenity it brings.

It is not rather ugly, one may ask? One collects material possessions not only for security, comfort or vanity, but for beauty as well. Is your sea-shell house not ugly and bare? No, it is beautiful, my house. It is bare, of course, but the wind, the sun, the smell of the pines blow through its bareness. The unfinished beams in the roof are veiled by cobwebs. They are lovely, I think, gazing up at them with new eyes; they soften the hard lines of the rafters as grey hairs soften the lines on a middle-aged face. I no longer pull out grey hairs or sweep down cobwebs. As for the walls, it is true they looked forbidding at first. I felt cramped and enclosed by their blank faces. I wanted to knock holes in them to give them another dimension with pictures or windows. So I dragged home from the beach grey arms of driftwood, worn satin-smooth by wind and sand. I gathered trailing green vines with floppy red-tipped leaves. I picked up the whitened skeletons of conchshells, their curious hollowed-out shapes faintly reminiscent of abstract sculpture. With these tacked to walls and propped up in corners, I am satisfied. I have a periscope out to the world. I have a window, a view, a point of flight from my sedentary base.

I am content. I sit down at my desk, a bare kitchen table with a blotter, a bottle of ink, a sand dollar to weight down one corner, a clam shell for a pen tray, the broken tip of a conch, pink-tinged, to finger, and a row of shells to set my thoughts spinning.

I love my sea-shell of a house. I wish I could live in it always. I wish I could transport it home. But I cannot. It will not hold a husband, five children and the necessities and trappings of daily life. I can only carry back my little channelled whelk. It will sit on my desk in Connecticut, to remind me of the ideal of a simplified life, to encourage me in the game I played on the beach. To ask how little, not how much, can I get along with. To say—is it necessary?—when I am tempted to add one more accumulation to my life, when I am pulled toward one more contrifugal activity.

Simplification of outward life is not enough. It is merely the outside. But I am starting with the outside. I am looking at the outside of a shell, the outside of my life—the shell. The complete answer is not to be found on the outside, in an outward mode of living. This is only a technique, a road to grace. The final answer, I know, is always inside. But the outside can give a clue, can help one to find the inside answer. One is free, like the hermit crab, to change one's shell.

Channelled whelk, I put you down again, but you have set my mind on a journey, up an inwardly winding spiral staircase of thought.

Reflections

Private Exploration

1. Does any specific passage in "Channelled Whelk" seem important to you personally? Explore it in depth. Consider both your own reasons for writing about it, and how they relate to elements of Lindbergh's experience.
2. Reflect on things that shape Lindbergh's life and what she seems to be seeking, then counter your findings with a reflection of the things that shape your life. What do you want most?
3. What do you make of this passage?

    The pattern of our lives is essentially circular.

Public Exploration

Lindbergh writes that "Distraction is, always has been, and probably always will be, inherent in woman's life." What does she mean? Do you believe her observation is as applicable to women today as it was when the essay was written in 1955? Consider the changes, both technological and sociological, which have affected the role of women during the last forty years. Is the "shape" of their lives still as complex? More so? Less? Are "harmony," "grace," and "simplicity" still desirable values? Or have they been replaced (or even fulfilled) by other, more immediate needs and rewards?

Private Reflection

1. How does Lindbergh's perception of beauty change once she rids herself of material possessions? What is the value of this kind of shedding?

2. Lindbergh speaks of the "extraordinary spiritual freedom and peace simplification can bring." In the 19th century, Thoreau claimed that "A man is rich in proportion to the number of things which he can afford to let alone." Consider whether this might be true of your own life. Be honest. Look around you.
3. Lindbergh uses what is called an analogy when she compares her life to a shell. Writers frequently use something familiar to explain the unfamiliar. For example, a student of ours compared her writing to a sailboat. She saw the huge white sail as the blank sheet of paper she was expected to fill. The spar was her pen. Sometimes her ideas filled the sail and she navigated through the ocean of words quickly, effortlessly. At other times, the sail hung slack as she struggled to keep the boat upright waiting for the right phrase that would propel her forward.

   Here's a chance for you to practice writing an analogy. Think of a concrete object to which you might compare your own writing process. Use the details of that object to explore your own understanding of your working methods. Begin as Lindbergh does. Look closely at the details of the object, then branch out, showing how those details relate (or fail to relate) to your way of writing. Allow yourself to have some fun. Allow yourself to play at creating an analogy without feeling threatened.

• Rattler, Alert •

BREWSTER GHISELIN

Slowly he sways that head that cannot hear,
Two-jeweled cone of horn the yellow of rust,
Pooled on the current of his listening fear.
His length is on the tympanum of earth,
And by his tendril tongue's tasting the air
He sips, perhaps, a secret of his race
Or feels for the known vibrations, heat, or trace
Of smoother satin than the hillwind's thrust
Through grass: the aspirate of my half-held breath,
The crushing of my weight upon the dust,
My foamless heart, the bloodleap at my wrist.

• A Narrow Fellow in the Grass •

EMILY DICKINSON

A narrow Fellow in the Grass
Occasionally rides—
You may have met Him—did you not
His notice sudden is—

The Grass divides as with a Comb—
A spotted shaft is seen—
And then it closes at your feet
And opens further on—

He likes a Boggy Acre
A Floor too cool for Corn—
Yet when a Boy, and Barefoot—
I more than once at Noon

Have passed, I thought, a Whip lash
Unbraiding in the Sun
When stooping to secure it
It wrinkled, and was gone—

Several of Nature's People
I know, and they know me—
I feel for them a transport
Of cordiality—

But never met this Fellow
Attended, or alone
Without a tighter breathing
And Zero at the Bone—

• Snake •

D. H. LAWRENCE

A snake came to my water trough
On a hot, hot day, and I in pajamas for the heat,
To drink there.

In the deep, strange-scented shade of the great dark carob tree
I came down the steps with my pitcher
And must wait, must stand and wait, for there he was at the trough
 before me.
He reached down from a fissure in the earth-wall in the gloom
And trailed his yellow-brown slackness soft-bellied down, over the edge
 of the stone trough
And rested his throat upon the stone bottom,
And where the water had dripped from the tap, in a small clearness,
He sipped with his straight mouth,
Softly drank through his straight gums, into his slack long body,
Silently.

Someone was before me at my water trough,
And I, like a second-comer, waiting.

He lifted his head from his drinking, as cattle do,
And looked at me vaguely, as drinking cattle do,
And flickered his two-forked tongue from his lips, and mused
    a moment,
And stooped and drank a little more,
Being earth-brown, earth-golden from the burning bowls of the earth
On the day of Sicilian July, with Etna smoking.

The voice of my education said to me
He must be killed,
For in Sicily the black black snakes are innocent, the gold are venomous.

And voices in me said, If you were a man
You would take a stick and break him now, and finish him off.

But must I confess how I liked him,
How glad I was he had come like a guest in quiet, to drink at my
    water trough
And depart peaceful, pacified, and thankless
Into the burning bowels of this earth?

Was it cowardice, that I dared not kill him?
Was it perversity, that I longed to talk to him?
Was it humanity, to feel so honored?
I felt so honored.

And yet those voices:
If you were not afraid, you would kill him!
And truly I was afraid, I was most afraid,
But even so, honored still more
That he should seek my hospitality
From out the dark door of the secret earth.

Reflections

Private Exploration

Three poets, three poems, and three perceptions of three very different snakes. Take time to read each one several times. Does your reaction shift with each new reading? Select the poem you react to most strongly and, in your notebook, explore your experience with it. What does it make you feel and think? What images and details work to evoke those thoughts and feelings?

Public Exploration

What is the relationship between our sensory perception of something and the worth we place on it? How do our emotions influence our judgment of worth and value? How, in the three preceding poems, does each poet's perception affect their respective attitudes?

What positive qualities does each poet observe in snakes (if any) and what negative values? Attempt to answer these questions in at least two ways: first, consider the types of actual physical details each poet observes, and how those details (those images) lead toward certain types of feelings; second, consider whether each poet reveals preformed judgments or influences that in turn might affect either their perception or their assessment of value.

Private Reflection

Snakes. Black snakes. Copperheads. Rattlers. Water moccasins. Is your personal reaction to snakes based on actual perception or on preformed attitudes? If you've never been around snakes, never even seen one, except in a zoo perhaps, reflect on where your attitudes and feelings come from. If you've ever had a direct experience with a snake, tell your own slithery tale. Try to capture in your writing as much detail describing the snake and your reaction to it as the poets you've read here. Then explore honestly whether your reaction was based on sensory perception or on preformed judgments.

The Allegory of the Cave

PLATO

And now, I said, let me show in an allegory how far our nature is enlightened or unenlightened: Behold! human beings living in an underground cave, which has a mouth open towards the light and reaching all along the cave; here they have been from their childhood, and have their legs and necks chained so that they cannot move, and can only see before them, being prevented by the chains from turning round their heads. Above and behind them a fire is blazing at a distance, and between the fire and the prisoners there is a raised way; and you will see, if you look, a low wall built along the way, like the screen which marionette players have in front of them, over which they show the puppets.

I see.

And do you see, I said, men passing along the wall carrying all sorts of vessels, and statues and figures of animals made of wood and stone and various materials, which appear over the wall? Some of them are talking, others silent.

You have shown me a strange image, and they are strange prisoners.

Like ourselves, I replied; and they see only their own shadows, or the shadows of one another, which the fire throws on the opposite wall of the cave?

True, he said; how could they see anything but the shadows if they were never allowed to move their heads?

And of the objects which are being carried in like manner they would only see the shadows?

Yes, he said.

And if they were able to converse with one another, would they not suppose that they were naming what was actually before them?

Very true.

And suppose further that the prison had an echo which came from the other side, would they not be sure to fancy when one of the passers-by spoke that the voice which they heard came from the passing shadow?

No question, he replied.

To them, I said, the truth would be literally nothing but the shadows of the images.

That is certain.

And now look again, and see what will naturally follow if the prisoners are released and disabused of their error. At first, when any of them is liberated and compelled suddenly to stand up and turn his neck round and walk and look towards the light, he will suffer sharp pains; the glare will distress him and he will be unable to see the realities of which in his former state he had seen the shadows; and then conceive some one saying to him, that what he saw before was an illusion, but that now, when he is approaching nearer to being and his eye is turned towards more real existence, he has a clearer vision—what will be his reply? And you may further imagine that his instructor is pointing to the objects as they pass and requiring him to name them—will he not be perplexed? Will he not fancy that the shadows which he formerly saw as truer than the objects which are now shown to him?

Far truer.

And if he is compelled to look straight at the light, will he not have a pain in his eyes which will make him turn away to take refuge in the objects of vision which he can see, and which he will conceive to be in reality clearer than the things which are now being shown to him?

True, he said.

And suppose once more, that he is reluctantly dragged up a steep and rugged ascent, and held fast until he is forced into the presence of the sun himself, is he not likely to be pained and irritated? When he approaches the light his eyes will be dazzled and he will not be able to see anything at all of what are now called realities.

Not all in a moment, he said.

He will require to grow accustomed to the sight of the upper world. And first he will see the shadows best, next the reflections of men and other objects in the water, and then the objects themselves; then he will gaze upon the light of the moon and the stars and the spangled heaven; and he will see the sky and the stars by night better than the sun or the light of the sun by day?

Certainly.

Last of all he will be able to see the sun, and not mere reflections of him in the water, but he will see him in his own proper place, and not in another; and he will contemplate him as he is.

Certainly.

He will then proceed to argue that this is he who gives the season and the years, and is the guardian of all that is in the visible world, and in a certain way the cause of all things which he and his fellows have been accustomed to behold?

Clearly, he said, he would first see the sun and then reason about him.

And when he remembered his old habitation, and the wisdom of the den and his fellow-prisoners, do you not suppose that he would felicitate himself on the change, and pity them?

Certainly, he would.

And if they were in the habit of conferring honors among themselves on those who were quickest to observe the passing shadows and to remark which of them went before, and which followed after, and which were together; and who were therefore best able to draw conclusions as to the future, do you think that he would care for such honors and glories, or envy the possessors of them? Would he not say with Homer,

Better to be the poor servant of a poor master, and to endure anything, rather than think as they do and live after their manner?

Yes, he said, I think that he would rather suffer anything than entertain these false notions and live in this miserable manner.

Imagine once more, I said, such an one coming suddenly out of the sun to be replaced in his old situation; would he not be certain to have his eyes full of darkness?

To be sure, he said.

And if there were a contest, and he had to compete in measuring the shadows with the prisoners who had never moved out of the den, while his sight was still weak, and before his eyes had become steady (and the time which would be needed to acquire this new habit of sight might be very considerable) would he not be ridiculous? Men would say of him that up he went and down he came without his eyes; and that it was better not even to think of ascending; and if any one tried to loose another and lead him up to the light, let them only catch the offender, and they would put him to death.

No question, he said.

This entire allegory, I said, you may now append, dear Glaucon, to the previous argument; the prison-house is the world of sight, the light of fire is the sun, and you will not misapprehend me if you interpret the journey upwards to be the ascent of the soul into the intellectual world according to my poor belief, which, at your desire, I have expressed—whether rightly or wrongly God knows. But, whether true or false, my opinion is that in the world of knowledge the idea of good appears last of all, and is seen only with an effort; and, when seen, is also inferred to be the universal author of all things beautiful and right, parent of light and of the lord of light in this visible world, and the immediate source of reason and truth in the intellectual; and that this is the power upon which he who would act rationally either in public or private life must have his eye fixed.

I agree, he said, as far as I am able to understand you.

Moreover, I said, you must not wonder that those who attain to this beatific vision are unwilling to descend to human affairs; for their souls are ever hastening into the upper world where they desire to dwell; which desire of theirs is very natural, if our allegory may be trusted.

Yes, very natural.

And is there anything surprising in one who passes from divine contemplations to the evil state of man, misbehaving himself in a ridiculous manner; if, while his eyes are blinking and before he has become accustomed to the surrounding darkness, he is compelled to fight in courts of law, or in other places, about the images or the shadows of images of justice, and is endeavouring to meet the conceptions of those who have never yet seen absolute justice?

Anything but surprising, he replied.

Any one who has common sense will remember that the bewilderments of the eyes are of two kinds, and arise from two causes, either from coming out of the light or from going into the light, which is true of the mind's eye, quite as much as of the bodily eye; and he who remembers this when he sees any one whose vision is perplexed and weak, will not be too ready to laugh; he will first ask whether that soul of man has come out of the brighter life, and is unable to see because unaccustomed to the dark, or having turned from darkness to the day is puzzled by excess of light. And he will count the one happy in his condition and state of being, and he will pity the other; or, if he have a mind to laugh at the soul which comes from below into the light, there will be more reason in this than in the laugh which greets him who returns from above out of the light into the cave.

That, he said, is a very just distinction.

Reflections

Private Exploration

Socrates' pupil, Glaucon, says that individuals in the cave are "strange prisoners." Socrates replies, "Like ourselves." Explore the allegory, applying it whenever possible to ourselves. You might want to consider some of these questions:

a. Can you think of a contemporary example, anything from your own personal experience or contemporary times, which would serve as a specific illustration of the allegory?

b. When the freed prisoner returns to the cave, Socrates claims he would be laughed at by others who feel he has wasted his time. Why? Why would they want to kill the person attempting to free them? Again, can you think of an actual incident which would parallel the reactions of the prisoners in the cave?

c. Why would the prisoners prefer to stay in the cave rather than ascend? Do you believe most people in this situation would react this way? Can you think of contemporary events that might support Socrates' argument?

Public Exploration

Many other authors in this chapter seem to have placed an emphasis on *seeing* as a primary virtue. Socrates seems to suggest that our senses cannot always be trusted. If your group or class has read Soetsu Yanagi's "Seeing and Knowing," Annie Dillard's "Sight into Insight," or even D. H. Lawrence's poem, "Snake," consider whether a genuine contradiction exists here. How can we reconcile the supposed need for developing our senses to discover the world with the need for higher intellectual powers?

Private Reflection

Consider what Socrates is suggesting about human perception and human knowledge. In what ways do you think he's right? Are there any ways he might possibly be wrong? Relate his argument to your own personal experience, especially during your first year at college.

The Barn and the Bees

KIM STAFFORD

My parents and I were driving along Boone's Ferry Road early one Sunday morning with a ripe load of horse manure in the back of the family station wagon when we saw a hand-lettered sign nailed to a telephone pole: "2 × 4 is 25 cents, 2 × 6 is 50 cents." There was so much fog on the glass we had to open the side window to see an arrow in red crayon pointing up a road to the west. Even the steam from the hot stuff behind us couldn't blunt the chill that went through me. Up that road was a barn I had admired since I was a child, and I knew it had fallen. In the same moment I felt the thrill of honest greed.

Twenty minutes later I stood alone in the jumbled ruin of red boards, straw, and the sweet stink of old dairy. No one was around, except the swallows careening overhead where the eaves had been and their nests hung once. Like me, they clung to the vacancy of the familiar. Blackberry vines had held the barn upright for years, and now that it was down the vines trailed over the tangle, dangling in a veil from the south and east walls that still stood crooked somehow. I scrambled up a slanted timber wedged into the pile to survey the place. The deep litter I stood on had a fragile architecture to it, not quite fallen clear down in a crisscross balance of long sagging rafters propped in chaos, with bent tin roofing over half-collapsed rooms where the side bays had been, the rusted stanchions wrenched into twisted contraptions, and everywhere tangles of baling wire and splintered fir siding. The heap made a ticking sound as it settled in the heat. There seemed to be too much light on it all, the fragrant old mystery bleached away and done. Then I heard a low hum from the dark southeast corner.

Lifting a jagged sheet of tin aside, I clambered into the long tunnel of slanted posts and rafters down the nave, stepping from one nail-studded board to the next, putting my body through a snake's contortions without a snake's grace, every pop and squeak of wood on wood a warning, every ping of corrugated tin in the deadfall. I passed a boat filled with hay, its bow beached on a bale that sprouted green, its keel turned to earth. I passed a wagon with no wheels, split in half where a beam had dropped through its bed to the floor. Mice scattered before me, and a bumblebee struggled out from a ball of wool, its nest that had fallen gently to a new niche in the rusted skull-hollow of a drinking pan. I had to inhabit what was left of this palace before it came all the way down, and the bees were beckoning me from their half-shattered hive now thirty feet ahead.

Others were in church. I was in a trance. In the honey-sweet gloom of the back corner I stepped up onto a patch of floor. This dusty vestibule had the privacy and prayer, the solitude of visible history. The combs hung down from a four-by-four rough-cut brace on the wall, and the bees massed quietly there, working. The small back door opened onto acres of blackberry, and thorned vine held it ajar with a double turn around the knob. Inside, a scatter of oats glittered on the threshold. A wheelbarrow stood mounded with jars. A curry comb worn down to nothing hung from a nail on the wall where each knothole was mended with the rusted lid from a tin can. If I stirred, my boot would crush broken glass, so I held still and watched the bees climb each others' backs to toil, to turn over pollen and flowersap in their mouths in a flurry of wings and touch. The blunt, heavier shapes of a few drones waited among them to be fed—so inept they could not lick their own food from underfoot. The queen must have been on the inner combs, laying like mad at this season for the main summer honeyflow. From one mating flight, one meeting with a drone, she bore children all her life. If I stood in the dark, they would not bother me. It was light and work each gave her custom to, spinning out through the open door on the quickly tightening spiral of her errand.

I crawled out and away, the fragrance of the hive, the quiet of that dark corner filling me. Across a field, in what must originally have been the farmhouse, a neighbor of the barn in a heap gave me its owner's phone number, along with a sad look. "They finally got it," she said through the screen door, as she brushed a wisp of hair aside. "I was hoping they'd forget to." She was going to say more, but a child shouted and she closed the door instead. Back home, I called and asked for Peter. It's best not to talk about money at first.

"Howdy," I said. "I was wondering about your plans for the scrap from that barn off Boone's Ferry Road."

"Yeah? Well I don't want anyone in there, the shape it's in. On account of my liability."

"I can understand that, but I noticed some boards piled out in front, and there *was* a sign about it."

"Sign? I didn't put up any sign. Must have been the guy I hired to tear it down. We're stalled on account of some bees in there."

"I can take care of those bees for you."

"Listen, you take care of those bees, and you can take anything you like. I've got to get everything out of there. Some guys complained to the County about it being a fire hazard, and they gave me a week. But do you really think there's anything worth saving? What do you want it for?"

"I want to build a barn."

In the short light at five a.m. I was there in my bee-gloves and veil, mechanic's coveralls and tall rubber boots, threading my way down the tunnel of boards and tin by memory and luck. I carried a hive-box and a spray bottle of water and a soft brush. Bees never sleep, but they generally don't fly when they're chilled. I found them as they would be at that hour, packed together on the combs with a low, sociable hum. Once the sun hit that wall behind them, they would fly.

I stepped on the wrong board, the architectural balance above me groaned and shifted, a dozen bees lifted off with an altered pitch to their buzz, and the whole hive quickened. In their sudden, ordered turmoil, I was seeing a mood-change inside a friend's brain, something naked and fair. I waited without a word. Bits of straw flickered away as the guard-bees settled back onto the wall and climbed into the mass that quieted with their return. The warm scent of wax and honey came my way. Through the doorway, mist settled over the gray sweep of the blackberry meadow. It was in full blossom, and the bees must have been working it hard. I could see the white wax over capped honey cells whenever the mass of bees parted like a retreating wave from the comb's upper rim. There would be sweet enough to keep them alive once I dampened their wings, carved away the comb entire, and swept the chilled bees into the hive-box I carried. Through my veil I saw them in the cleft they had chosen, their little city compact with purpose in a neglected place.

By dawn I had them boxed, sealed in and humming in the shade beside my car. A few had escaped my work, had followed me, then doubled back with the buzz of anger sinking to a different note. No one is quite sure what stray bees do when the home hive is destroyed and the swarm disappears without them. They might follow other bees to a foreign hive and try to take on its scent and be admitted. Or they might hang around the old vacancy, working the local blossoms and resting under a leaf until their wings are too frayed to hold in the air. Bees die when they sting, or when work finally shatters their wings.

Several days after the wall that had harbored the hive came down, I would still see a few bees hovering precisely where the combs had been. At midafternoon I would turn over a board with the print of wax across its grain—some panel or brace that had boxed in the hive—and find a solitary bee fingering the pattern like a disbelieving relative reading by braille the name new-carved on a tombstone. I shared their nostalgia for a shape in the air. And so did others, in their own ways. As I worked on the lumberpile, neighbors came by in little groups or alone to leave with me some story about the barn, and to seek some scrap of it to carry away.

First came three boys to watch me work, to pick their way around the heap so glorious with its ramps and tunnels, its pedestals of triumph and hollows of secrecy. When the pile shifted under them, they leaped off and skittered away, then came back with their father from across the road. They wanted a treehouse made, and he wanted to see the barn. He was in his yard-work clothes, not in a hurry.

"You know the woman that used to live in that old farmhouse and own this barn was a strange one," he said to me, while the boys scattered again toward the ruin. "She'd show up at our place every fall to trade walnuts for whatever we had to trade. We always took the unshelled ones, her hands were so dirty. Or maybe they were dark from the hulling. She had gunny sacks tied around her feet with baling wire."

"When was this?" I asked.

"Before they were born." He gestured toward the three boys now waltzing along a beam thrust like a bowsprit from the pile. "Looks like I'd best get them home."

The four of them went away carrying the small roof from the ventilator cupola. It had somehow stayed intact, riding the whole structure down as it fell, and ending perched on top of the heap. As they drifted across the road, they looked like four posts under the Parthenon.

Next came a gentleman in pressed yellow slacks and a shirt with a little alligator over his heart. His hands were clean and thin. He watched me labor for a while in silence.

"Hard work for a Sunday," he said. I stood up and let the sweat cool on my face.

"Well, I wanted to save some of these boards," I said. "The barn's gone, but there's some lumber left."

"Eyesore. I'm glad to see it finally come down." I looked at the mouth that had said this. I had nothing to say. Away across the pasture a solitary maple stood dark in its neglected shade.

"But say," he said, "I need a board to repair the rail on my deck—two-by-four, about twelve feet long. . . ."

He skirted carefully around the perimeter of the pile, picking at the ends of likely boards clinched firmly into the weave of collapse, now and then looking my way appealingly. I knew who had called the County about the fire hazard, about the old barn settling too slowly deeper into moss and blackberry, the stack rattling in winter storms and the tin roof pinging through each summer's heat. I pulled an eighteen-foot clear-grained length of fir from the stack I had plucked of nails, and he went off with it at an awkward march, holding the board far out to the side of his body with his fingertips. Soon I paused in my work to hear the whine and ring of his powersaw toiling through the wood. I counted seven cuts, then silence.

The woman who had bought the farmhouse, who had given me the owner's name, came down to offer a glass of lemonade. The cold sweat from the glass ran down my wrist.

"I never let my kids go inside." She squinted into the patches of darkness where walls still leaned together. "They get into enough trouble as it is. But I always felt we owned the barn, along with the house—even though we didn't.

You should have seen the place when we moved in: a car in the back yard filled with apples; a drawer in the kitchen packed with red rubber bands, and another with brown ones; mice in the walls and a possum in the attic. The house had been empty a long time too.''

I set the glass down, and bent to my work, wrestling heroically with a long two-by-six mired deep in the hay.

''Are you going to keep these Mason jars?'' She nodded toward a dozen blued quarts lolling in the grass.

''You'll use them before I do.'' I shook the sweat out of my eyes to watch her cradle eleven of them somehow in her arms, with one clenched tight under her chin. She started out with a crooked smile to walk hunched and slow up the lane toward a yard littered with bright toys.

''I'll come back for the glass,'' she called over her shoulder. Then she turned slowly, like a ship halfway out of harbor. ''Or bring it up to the house for a refill.''

The afternoon was a long season of history, a plunge into the archeological midden of my own midwestern ancestors, a seduction of my hands by wood the flanks of the milkers polished. What was a stall of straw but a nest for stories, even under the naked, open light of the sky? Burlap lace around a jar blue with time held something without a name but kin to pleasure. I had to stop, I had to walk away from it, to visit the outlines of the pasture and the farm, to carry the glass to the farmhouse so I could know the rooms of its people, to walk again and rest from the persistent unity of the ruin, to lie down in purple vetch and listen to bee-women sip and dangle on the small blossoms. When the sun woke me and I stood up, there was a shape of my own dwelling in the grass.

By now I had a stack of white, six-by-six posts that had held the stanchions in a row, a heap of two-by-fours in random lengths dried hard as iron, twenty-four sheets of tin rusted on the bottom side from generations of cattle-steam and piss in hay, a whole raft of two-by-sixes in twenty-foot lengths, each dried and set precisely to the same roof-sag. When I built my barn, I would turn them over so the roof began with a slight swell. Over time, they would sag back flat and right.

I was just admiring my favorite stick—the four-by-eight hay-beam from the gambrel's point, complete with a patch of lichen where it had thrust out into the weather, and a rusted iron ring bolted through that had pulleyed up ton after ton of feed—when a red sports car came creeping along the nail-studded road. I glanced at the clouds reflected in the windshield when it stopped, then lowered the beam to the ground.

The driver waited inside, watching me, or finishing a song on the radio, just long enough to show he was in no hurry, then climbed out slow, slid his hands into his pockets, and looked at the sky.

''Name's Peter. Finding anything good?'' He stood by his car.

I pointed a crowbar at the hay-beam. ''Just what you see: lumber with rot on both ends but some good wood in the middle.''

''What about the bees?''

"Right there." I aimed the crowbar at the hive-box humming quietly in the blackberry shade. "I caught all but a few."

"A few?"

"Five."

He nodded slowly, like a bear with ponderous thoughts. "I think I might want those doors," he said, nodding toward the two big wagon doors slapped face-down where they had fallen. He started gingerly around the heap's perimeter in his rubber running shoes. "My wife likes antique stuff—you found anything like that? It doesn't have to be pretty, so long as it's old. My own idea of old is black-and-white TV, but she sees it different."

"There's a wheelbarrow with the bottom rotted out and one handle gone—something like that?"

"She'd love it. Could you wheel it out and leave it by the doors? The County's given me a week to scrape this down to bare dirt. Anything left after Friday will cost me a fine. And the man I hired to take it all down should be along soon. He may have stuff he wants too." He looked at the sky. A quick rain had begun, and he backed away toward the car. "Try to have everything you want out pretty quick. And don't get hurt."

He paused to say more, looked at the ground, then turned and folded himself carefully into the car. The crowbar was warm in my hand, and slick with sweat. The rain felt good. The lights of the car came on, flickered to high-beam, then died as the windshield wipers started to wag. He backed out the long track across the field, his tires spinning a few times on the wet grass.

A cloud moved and sunlight rippled glistening across the field after him. The lumber around me began to steam. My footing was slick but the air was clean. As I worked with steel-hafted hammer in my right hand and crowbar in my left, swinging each long board through the loving rhythm of lift, pound and tease, roll and balance, flip, shove and drop-slap to the stack of clean lumber, I heard the unique machine of the fallen barn flex in the heat, the rippled ping when tin changes its mind, the shriek of a sixteen-penny nail jerked from the sheath rust wedded it to for seventy years, the see-saw rub and grabble of a rafter waggled from the heap, and in a pause the plop of sweat sliding off my elbow to a stone. Before me loomed the raw, steaming tangle of chaos with a history of order, a flavor of tradition, the stiff, wise fiber of old growth; behind me, stacks of lumber rose with a new barn intrinsic in each board, in the rivet of right work I had yet to do to knit it all together again. My hands were twin apprentices to the wreck, to the knowing fragments of joinery still buried there.

As I curled my spine over the tangle to grasp a clear length of one-by-twelve fir, two causes made my task hard: the persistence of the builder, circa 1910, and the haste of the wrecker, 1980. The builder had known how to make things hold, clinching nails that bound the battens down, and pinning the whole fabric of the walls with extra braces scarfed to the frame wherever it might be vulnerable to the wind's pivot or gravity's drag. The wrecker, on the other hand, was in a hurry.

Maybe he heard the bees when he first drove up, and decided not to go inside at all. Maybe the doors were so woven with thumb-thick ropes of blackberry he didn't take the time to pry them apart and find the mahogany skiff locked together with bronze screws, or the wagon bed, the kerosene lamp, its wick last trimmed before he was born, now crushed flat under a three-hundred pound stick of fir. He never saw the stack of two-by-six spare joists, ten foot long and clear. Those the farmer had set aside for years of so much hay even this cathedral wasn't ample enough. With them he would lay an extra hayfloor over the stanchion alley. Instead, the wrecker threw a grappling hook high over the roof and pulled it all down. That must have brought out the bees to kiss him in the eyes. I found the hook abandoned—it had stabbed into a punky rafter with twenty feet of rope dangling where the wrecker had cut it away and fled. I coiled the rope and hung the hook from a volunteer cherry at the field's edge.

Somewhere way down Boone's Ferry Road I heard the low hum of a big bike coming. I heard it slow for the turn, then accelerate with a roar the last two-hundred yards up the side-road toward me. Then it came popping and growling over the field. A nail came out for the crowbar and flipped past my face. I was listening too hard and not watching what I did. I turned.

My face was small and double in the dark glasses on the upturned face of the Gypsy Joker idling his big Harley ten feet away. On the shoulder of his black jacket were stitched the red names of his friends or victims: *Rick, Joe, Rollo.* When the engine rumbled and faded and coughed dead, the black leather of his gloves creaked as he flexed his right hand free.

"Finding some good stuff, buddy?" My double body was still in his glasses. His beard pointed to the field behind me. "I had a nice stack of boards all pulled out over there, but some bastard went and hauled them away."

"Oh, that was me," I said.

"Was, huh?"

"Peter said I get the bees out, I could take any lumber I wanted."

"You talked to Peter about it? I guess that's okay. But what about those bees? Christ, I blow up my truck trying to pull this wreck down, then these bees come busting out with my number in their tails. I don't mess with them little guys. No way." He looked around, raised his hands to his shades, but left them on. "They gone?"

"They're gone," I said.

"Well, hey, soon as I get my truck fixed I'm gonna start hauling this pile to the super dump, so take everything you can." His head turned toward my Chevy low in the grass, then slowly back to me. "I'm on fixed rate. The less I have to haul, the better. Jesus, take it all for firewood. You ain't never going to get another chance like this." He kicked his smoking bike to life with a roar, and had to shout. "I tell you what: I wreck buildings for my living, and I never see pickings easy as these." With a tight nod he turned the bike and bounced across the field, a shrug and hunch restoring his solitude as he waggled away through the grass.

Wind riffled over the mounds and valleys of the blackberry patch, lifting off a harvest of white petals that skimmed across the swell. The two swallows twittered as they spiraled overhead, and a cricket, undisturbed by catastrophe, began to chant from somewhere near the fallen barn doors.

Along toward dusk, as I began sliding the longest boards onto the roof of my car named The Duchess, I saw a little boy come furtively down from the farmhouse, through the lilac hedge, through the wild hawthorn grove and out to the edge of the barn's debris. From the slow bob and swivel of his head, I could read how his gaze followed the outlines of the building that had stood there—first around the footing-wall perimeter, then down the stanchion bay, out into the central floor where the wagon had been, up some invisible ladder to the loft, then south to the back wall. He looked at me. I was part of the treachery. He was polite and said nothing. I began to wrestle a twenty-foot six-by-six, authentic with manure, onto the car.

"It wasn't dangerous," he said quietly, and I knew it was. I got the beam to the balancing joint and stopped to rest.

"Did you go in there a lot?"

"Just sometimes."

"What was it like?"

"It was always dark, and you had to know where you were going. There was broken glass, too, a whole floor of it. But I put a board across it so I could walk."

"What about the ladder?" I said, once I had the beam all the way up at rest on the car roof.

"I knew the good steps to step on. You just go slow, and hold onto other things at the same time. And there were bees in there. They never hurt you. I came up that close." He held his hand in front of his eyes. His face was a blur against the pale swathe of the hawthorn. "They kept working. They never bothered you. Once I even tasted some of their honey that dropped down on the straw." He looked back at me. "What are you going to build here, mister?"

"I'm not going to build anything here," I said, reaching for another board so he wouldn't go away. "Someone just wanted the barn taken down."

"What happened to the bees?"

"They're right there. Can you hear them?" I pointed to the hive-box that glowed a dull white and hummed. We both stood still.

By dark I unloaded the mossy timbers and curve-cured boards at my home, carried them one at a time around the house through the memorized tunnel of plum arch, apple tree, grape arbor. I stacked them in different ways, season by season, putting them to bed under tin, listening to the rattle of rain and fitting them in mind on my pillow to an old shape that would happen simply by happening slow. Whenever I hefted a timber so heavy I feared for my collarbone, or teased a splinter from my palm, I remembered how these boards stood face-to-face in a forest harvesting nineteenth-century light, how they slid through the saws side by side, how the green-chain grader's crayon marked them with a C for clear or an S for standard.

Clinched together in the first barn-shape, wood had a memory, and the boards in my yard now curved again for sun and water with a tree's wish, with the honest warp of their character, with history visible in every stress-ripple, every seam of bark or pitch, every conk-wither or knot. The tight grain of slow growth held steady long. But the oldest memory was of earth. Where any board had touched down to the damp floor below architecture, rot took root, branching upward into heartwood.

I sawed the rot-softened wood away, planed each curve straight, measured the length of firm timber, and began to build the barn again. My industry was slow. The building inspector told me to hurry.

"One hundred and eighty days without visible progress cancels your original permit," he said. "Better get going." But he forgave me. I kept working, resting, remembering the design in the air where the swallows flew. I started remodeling before it was done. The building inspector forgave me even that. Then he retired. His replacement warned me, and then forgave me.

At five a.m. in 1984, I am in the loft. Dust-colored rafters join in marriage above me. The hay-beam behind my head aims toward sunrise. Soon the blackberry pasture out this window will blossom. Soon the bees, daughters of the daughters of the bees I took care of, will winnow out from their white box beyond the pear tree into sunlight.

Reflections

Private Exploration

1. We find Stafford delightfully honest in his writing, especially when he admits, "I felt the thrill of greed." Many of us may be reminded of having experienced that same feeling. How does Stafford's interest in the barn stimulate greed in others? Consider, for instance, the man "with the alligator on his heart" or Peter, the owner. Explore how their actions might remind us of human nature? What do they reveal about perception?
2. Perception has been defined as the wisdom or intuition gained through the senses. Zero in on a passage from Stafford's essay that you find particularly enriched with sensory detail. Copy the passage in your notebook, then analyze the sensory detail. Point out, for example, which words appeal to our sense of touch, hearing, and so on. Finally, consider for yourself the wisdom or intuition these details lead to in terms of your understanding of the essay.
3. Explore the various perceptions of the barn and its values from the point of view of Peter, the farm woman, the wrecker, the little boy, and Stafford. (As you write, include specific passages or phrases from the essay to strengthen your observations.) What insights are you led toward?

Public Exploration

In "Seeing and Knowing," Soetsu Yanagi writes, "He who only knows, without seeing, does not understand the mystery." Stafford refers to the barn heap as a "fragrant old mystery." Consider what Stafford sees and what he knows as a result of his experience.

Private Reflection

Consider this passage:

> In our own country we are so often unbeautiful. We almost take it for granted, tearing down fine old buildings, and then racing off to Europe to gaze at old fountains, old villas, old this, old that. It may be our worst hurt—one which we inflict on ourselves and on other nations. It is a source of whatever actual devastation we have wrought and comes from our impoverished sense of beauty, our grudge against loveliness.
>
> —PATRICIA HAMPL,
> **A Romantic Education**

CONNECTIONS

Although the best papers usually come directly from your own interests, generated often by notes and insights developed in keeping a reading notebook or journal, the following suggestions may provide additional ideas for writing.

1. In his essay, "Seeing and Knowing," Soetsu Yanagi writes "To see and at the same time to comprehend is the ideal. . . ." How might you go about convincing Yanagi that Alice Walker, writing in "Beauty: When the Other Dancer is the Self," has succeeded or failed in reaching "the ideal"?
2. Consider how the following quotation from John Berger, an art critic, might be used as a way of relating Yanagi's "Seeing and Knowing," with essays by Alice Walker, William Fox Conner, Annie Dillard, or even Plato.

   > Seeing comes before words. The child looks and recognizes before he can speak. But there is also another sense in which seeing comes before words. It is seeing which establishes our place in the surrounding world; we explain that world with words, but words can never undo the fact that we are surrounded by it. The relation between what we see and what we know is never settled.

3. A number of readings included here focus on deception caused by the senses, or in contrast, caused by allowing intellectual knowledge to blind the senses. Obviously Yanagi and Plato address this as a central issue. But you might also consider how such a theme could be explored in works like Flannery O'Connor's "Good Country People," Kim Stafford's "The Barn and the Bees," or D. H. Lawrence's "Snake."
4. Anne Morrow Lindbergh's "Channeled Whelk" and Tom Whitecloud's "Blue Winds Dancing," both represent searches for a way to exist peacefully without being burdened by the demands of society. Both authors find solace in nature and in simplifying their lives. But are they realistic? Why does the romantic world they value appeal to us?
5. The subject of beauty arises again and again in many of the readings collected here. Obviously beauty is an element of perception as well as a value. Consider how the following observation might lead one into seeing relationships among Yanagi, Walker, Conner, Dillard, or Lindbergh.

   > My desire to be beautiful (a woman's desire), to create beauty (as an artist), to live surrounded by beauty (a citizen's sense, which is both aesthetic and, in the entirely public sense, cultural) are connected only by the word. They are in themselves quite different things.
   >
   > —PATRICIA HAMPL

6. Consider how the central idea of Plato's "Allegory of the Cave"—the nature of enlightenment and unenlightenment—might relate to D. H. Lawrence's "Snake."

CHAPTER 7

MAKERS OF MUSIC, DREAMERS OF DREAMS

Imagination is more important than knowledge. For knowledge is limited, whereas imagination embraces the entire world.

—Albert Einstein

In France one summer, we visited the famous caves of Lascaux. Here, primitive man produced fifteen thousand paintings and engravings. Deer, horses, wild cattle, ibexes, and bison cover the walls and ceilings. Surprisingly modern, these animals are not crude stick figures but expressive impressions created with graceful lines and shades of ocher.

Cro-Magnon man not only used imagination to create art, but also to invent tools and methods that made his creations possible. Excavators have uncovered hundreds of flint tools, stone lamps, pallets, bones. Our official guide, a plump art historian with a single gold tooth, informed us that these cave artists used twigs for sketching and pads of moss or fur for daubing. They may even have sprayed pigment through a hollow bone—a kind of primitive air brush technique—all this twenty thousand years ago. Standing in the shadowed recesses of the cave, we found it difficult to reconcile our stereotyped image of primitive man toting a club in one hand while dragging his mate by her hair with the other. A single painting, a sketch of two black bison, startled us for its simplicity and beauty. As we stood in the damp light that morning, we heard voices, envisioned faces bronzed by tallow light, smelled the sweet scent of juniper burning. If only stone could speak. What music might we hear, what dreams, from these our first makers. We realized these paintings formed an ancient link that gives culture coherence. Primitive man thought in images just as we do, and he transferred those images to the stone walls of Lascaux to tell his stories. For a few moments, we shared the primitive vision and recognized some part of ourselves.

Samuel Taylor Coleridge has called the imagination "the Prime agent of all human perception." Anne Berthoff, in *Reclaiming the Imagination,* advises us to think of imagination as the name for the active mind, "the mind in action making meaning."

In the following chapter you'll read essays, stories, and poems that encompass a wide scope of imaginative expression by a broad range of thinkers. Some of these works, like the essays by Jacob Brunowski and Ursula Le Guin, move us toward an understanding of the power and value of the imagination. Others, like the thirteenth century Taoist tale, "How Wang Fo was Saved," immerse us in another century, another culture, another's imagination. Like the art imprinted on the walls and ceilings of Lascaux, these works lead us to question man's need to create and to ponder the value of human imagination. They remind us of an insight offered by biographer A. N. Wilson: "It's only through the exercise of the imagination that one glimpses who we might be, what the universe might be."

Memory and Imagination

PATRICIA HAMPL

When I was seven, my father, who played the violin on Sundays with a nicely tortured flair which we considered artistic, led me by the hand down a long, unlit corridor in St. Luke's School basement, a sort of tunnel that ended in a room full of pianos. There many little girls and a single sad boy were playing truly tortured scales and arpeggios in a mash of troubled sound. My father gave me over to Sister Olive Marie, who did look remarkably like an olive.

Her oily face gleamed as if it had just been rolled out of a can and laid on the white plate of her broad, spotless wimple. She was a small, plump woman; her body and the small window of her face seemed to interpret the entire alphabet of olive: her face was a sallow green olive placed upon the jumbo ripe olive of her black habit. I trusted her instantly and smiled, glad to have my hand placed in the hand of a woman who made sense, who provided the satisfaction of being what she was: an Olive who looked like an olive.

My father left me to discover the piano with Sister Olive Marie so that one day I would join him in mutually tortured piano-violin duets for the edification of my mother and brother who sat at the table meditatively spooning in the last of their pineapple sherbet until their part was called for: they put down their spoons and clapped while we bowed, while the sweet ice in their bowls melted, while the music melted, and we all melted a little into each other for a moment.

But first Sister Olive must do her work. I was shown middle C, which Sister seemed to think terribly important. I stared at middle C and then glanced away for a second. When my eye returned, middle C was gone, its slim finger lost in the complicated grasp of the keyboard. Sister Olive struck it again, finding it with laughable ease. She emphasized the importance of middle C, its central position, a sort of North Star of sound. I remember thinking, "Middle C is the belly button of the piano," an insight whose originality and accuracy stunned me with pride. For the first time in my life I was astonished by metaphor. I hesitated to tell the kindly Olive for some reason; apparently I understood a true metaphor is a risky business, revealing of the self. In fact, I have never, until this moment of writing it down, told my first metaphor to anyone.

Sunlight flooded the room; the pianos, all black, gleamed. Sister Olive, dressed in the colors of the keyboard, gleamed; middle C shimmered with meaning and I resolved never—never—to forget its location: it was the center of the world.

Then Sister Olive, who had had to show me middle C twice but who seemed to have drawn no bad conclusions about me anyway, got up and went to the windows on the opposite wall. She pulled the shades down, one after the other. The sun was too bright, she said. She sneezed as she stood at the windows with the sun shedding its glare over her. She sneezed and sneezed, crazy little convulsive sneezes, one after another, as helpless as if she had the hiccups.

"The sun makes me sneeze," she said when the fit was over and she was back at the piano. This was odd, too odd to grasp in the mind. I associated sneezing with colds, and colds with rain, fog, snow and bad weather. The sun, however, had caused Sister Olive to sneeze in this wild way, Sister Olive who gleamed benignly and who was so certain of the location of the center of the world. The universe wobbled a bit and became unreliable. Things were not, after all, necessarily what they seemed. Appearance deceived: here was the sun acting totally out of character, hurling this woman into sneezes, a woman so mild that she was named, so it seemed, for a bland object on a relish tray.

I was given a red book, the first Thompson book, and told to play the first piece over and over at one of the black pianos where the other children were crashing away. This, I was told, was called practicing. It sounded alluringly adult, practicing. The piece itself consisted mainly of middle C, and I excelled, thrilled by my savvy at being able to locate that central note amidst the cunning camouflage of all the other white keys before me. Thrilled too by the shiny red book that gleamed, as the pianos did, as Sister Olive did, as my eager eyes probably did. I sat at the formidable machine of the piano and got to know middle C intimately, preparing to be as tortured as I could manage one day soon with my father's violin at my side.

But at the moment Mary Katherine Reilly was at my side, playing something at least two or three lessons more sophisticated than my piece. I believe she even struck a chord. I glanced at her from the peasantry of single notes, shy, ready to pay homage. She turned toward me, stopped playing, and sized me up.

Sized me up and found a person ready to be dominated. Without introduction she said, "My grandfather invented the collapsible opera hat."

I nodded, I acquiesced, I was hers. With that little stroke it was decided between us—that she should be the leader, and I the sidekick. My job was admiration. Even when she added, "But he didn't make a penny from it. He didn't have a patent"—even then, I knew and she knew that this was not an admission of powerlessness, but the easy candor of a master, of one who can afford a weakness or two.

With the clairvoyance of all fated relationships based on dominance and submission, it was decided in advance: that when the time came for us to play duets, I should always play second piano, that I should spend my allowance to buy her the Twinkies she craved but was not allowed to have, that finally, I should let her copy from my test paper, and when confronted by our teacher, confess with convincing hysteria that it was I, I who had cheated, who had reached above myself to steal what clearly belonged to the rightful heir of the inventor of the collapsible opera hat. . . .

There must be a reason I remember that little story about my first piano lesson. In fact, it isn't a story, just a moment, the beginning of what could perhaps become a story. For the memoirist, more than for the fiction writer, the story seems already *there,* already accomplished and fully achieved in history ("in reality," as we naively say). For the memoirist, the writing of the story is a matter of transcription.

That, anyway, is the myth. But no memoirist writes for long without experiencing an unsettling disbelief about the reliability of memory, a hunch that memory is not, after all, *just* memory. I don't know why I remembered this fragment about my first piano lesson. I don't, for instance, have a single recollection of my first arithmetic lesson, the first time I studied Latin, the first time my grandmother tried to teach me to knit. Yet these things occurred too, and must have their stories.

It is the piano lesson that has trudged forward, clearing the haze of forgetfulness, showing itself bright with detail more than thirty years after the event. I did not choose to remember the piano lesson. It was simply there, like a book that has always been on the shelf, whether I ever read it or not, the binding and title showing as I skim across the contents of my life. On the day I wrote this fragment I happened to take that memory, not some other, from the shelf and paged through it. I found more detail, more event, perhaps a little more entertainment than I had expected, but the memory itself was there from the start. Waiting for me.

Or was it? When I reread what I had written just after I finished it, I realized that I had told a number of lies. I *think* it was my father who took me the first time for my piano lesson—but maybe he only took me to meet my teacher and there was no actual lesson that day. And did I even know then that he played the violin—didn't he take up his violin again much later, as a result of my piano playing, and not the reverse? And is it even remotely accurate to describe as "tortured" the musicianship of a man who began everyday by belting out "Oh What a Beautiful Morning" as he shaved?

More: Sister Olive Marie did sneeze in the sun, but was her name Olive? As for her skin tone—I would have sworn it was olive-like; I would have been willing to spend the better part of an afternoon trying to write the exact description of imported Italian or Greek olive her face suggested: I wanted to get it right. But now, were I to write that passage over, it is her intense black eyebrows I would see, for suddenly they seem the central fact of that face, some indicative mark of her serious and patient nature. But the truth is, I don't remember the woman at all. She's a sneeze in the sun and a finger touching middle C. That, at least, is steady and clear.

Worse: I didn't have the Thompson book as my piano text. I'm sure of that because I remember envying children who did have this wonderful book with its pictures of children and animals printed on the pages of music.

As for Mary Katherine Reilly. She didn't even go to grade school with me (and her name isn't Mary Katherine Reilly—but I made that change on purpose). I met her in Girl Scouts and only went to school with her later, in high school. Our relationship was not really one of leader and follower; I played first piano most of the time in duets. She certainly never copied anything from a test paper of mine: she was a better student, and cheating just wasn't a possibility with her. Though her grandfather (or someone in her family) did invent the collapsible opera hat and I remember that she was proud of that fact, she didn't tell me this news as a deft move in a childish power play.

So, what was I doing in this brief memoir? Is it simply an example of the curious relation a fiction writer has to the material of her own life? Maybe. That may have some value in itself. But to tell the truth (if anyone still believes me capable of telling the truth), I wasn't writing fiction. I was writing memoir—or was trying to. My desire was to be accurate. I wished to embody the myth of memoir: to write as an act of dutiful transcription.

Yet clearly the work of writing narrative caused me to do something very different from transcription. I am forced to admit that memoir is not a matter of transcription, that memory itself is not a warehouse of finished stories, not a static gallery of framed pictures. I must admit that I invented. But why?

Two whys: why did I invent, and then, if a memoirist must inevitably invent rather than transcribe, why do I—why should anybody—write memoir at all?

I must respond to these impertinent questions because they, like the bumper sticker I saw the other day commanding all who read it to QUESTION AUTHORITY, challenge my authority as a memoirist and as a witness.

It still comes as a shock to realize that I don't write about what I know: I write in order to find out what I know. Is it possible to convey to a reader the enormous degree of blankness, confusion, hunch and uncertainty lurking in the act of writing? When I am the reader, not the writer, I too fall into the lovely illusion that the words before me (in a story by Mavis Gallant, an essay by Carol Bly, a memoir by M. F. K. Fisher), which *read* so inevitably, must also have been *written* exactly as they appear, rhythm and cadence, language and syntax, the powerful waves of the sentences laying themselves on the smooth beach of the page one after another faultlessly.

But here I sit before a yellow legal pad, and the long page of the preceding two paragraphs is a jumble of crossed-out lines, false starts, confused order. A mess. The mess of my mind trying to find out what it wants to say. This is a writer's frantic, grabby mind, not the poised mind of a reader ready to be edified or entertained.

I sometimes think of the reader as a cat, endlessly fastidious, capable, by turns, of mordant indifference and riveted attention, luxurious, recumbent, and ever poised. Whereas the writer is absolutely a dog, panting and moping, too eager for an affectionate scratch behind the ears, lunging frantically after any old stick thrown in the distance.

The blankness of a new page never fails to intrigue and terrify me. Sometimes, in fact, I think my habit of writing on long yellow sheets comes from an atavistic fear of the writer's stereotypic "blank white page." At least when I begin writing, my page isn't utterly blank; at least it has a wash of color on it, even if the absence of words must finally be faced on a yellow sheet as truly as on a blank white one. Well, we all have our ways of whistling in the dark.

If I approach writing from memory with the assumption that I know what I wish to say, I assume that intentionality is running the show. Things are not that simple. Or perhaps writing is even more profoundly simple, more telegraphic and immediate in its choices than the grating wheels and chugging engine of logic and rational intention. The heart, the guardian of intuition with its secret, often fearful intentions, is the boss. Its commands are what a writer obeys—often without knowing it. Or, I do.

That's why I'm a strong adherent of the first draft. And why it's worth pausing for a moment to consider what a first draft really is. By my lights, the piano lesson memoir is a first draft. That doesn't mean it exists here exactly as I first wrote it. I like to think I've cleaned it up from the first time I put it down on paper. I've cut some adjectives here, toned down the hyperbole there, smoothed a transition, cut a repetition—that sort of housekeeperly tidying-up. But the piece remains a first draft because I haven't yet gotten to know it, haven't given it a chance to tell me anything. For me, writing a first draft is a little like meeting someone for the first time. I come away with a wary acquaintanceship, but the real friendship (if any) and genuine intimacy—that's all down the road. Intimacy with a piece of writing, as with a person, comes from paying attention to the revelations it is capable of giving, not by imposing my own preconceived notions, no matter how well-intentioned they might be.

I try to let pretty much anything happen in a first draft. A careful first draft is a failed first draft. That may be why there are so many inaccuracies in the piano lesson memoir: I didn't censor, I didn't judge. I kept moving. But I would not publish this piece as a memoir on its own in its present state. It isn't the "lies" in the piece that give me pause, though a reader has a right to expect a memoir to be as accurate as the writer's memory can make it. No, it isn't the lies themselves that makes the piano lesson memoir a first draft and therefore "unpublishable."

The real trouble: the piece hasn't yet found its subject; it isn't yet about what it wants to be about. Note: what *it* wants, not what I want. The difference has to do with the relation a memoirist—any writer, in fact—has to unconscious or half-known intentions and impulses in composition.

Now that I have the fragment down on paper, I can read this little piece as a mystery which drops clues to the riddle of my feelings, like a culprit who wishes to be apprehended. My narrative self (the culprit who has invented) wishes to be discovered by my reflective self, the self who wants to understand and make sense of a half-remembered story about a nun sneezing in the sun. . . .

We only store in memory images of value. The value may be lost over the passage of time (I was baffled about why I remembered that sneezing nun, for example), but that's the implacable judgment of feeling: *this*, we say somewhere deep within us, is something I'm hanging on to. And of course, often we cleave to things because they possess heavy negative charges. Pain likes to be vivid.

Over time, the value (the feeling) and the stored memory (the image) may become estranged. Memoir seeks a permanent home for feeling and image, a habitation where they can live together in harmony. Naturally, I've had a lot of experiences since I packed away that one from the basement of St.

Luke's School; that piano lesson has been effaced by waves of feeling for other moments and episodes. I persist in believing the event has value—after all, I remember it—but in writing the memoir I did not simply relive the experience. Rather, I explored the mysterious relationship between all the images I could round up and the even more impacted feelings that caused me to store the images safely away in memory. Stalking the relationship, seeking the congruence between stored image and hidden emotion—that's the real job of memoir.

By writing about that first piano lesson, I've come to know things I could not know otherwise. But I only know these things as a result of reading this first draft. While I was writing, I was following the images, letting the details fill the room of the page and use the furniture as they wished. I was their dutiful servant—or thought I was. In fact, I was the faithful retainer of my hidden feelings which were giving the commands.

I really did feel, for instance, that Mary Katherine Reilly was far superior to me. She was smarter, funnier, more wonderful in every way—that's how I saw it. Our friendship (or she herself) did not require that I become her vassal, yet perhaps in my heart that was something I wanted; I wanted a way to express my feeling of admiration. I suppose I waited until this memoir to begin to find the way.

Just as, in the memoir, I finally possess that red Thompson book with the barking dogs and bleating lambs and winsome children. I couldn't (and still can't) remember what my own music book was, so I grabbed the name and image of the one book I could remember. It was only in reviewing the piece after writing it that I saw my inaccuracy. In pondering this "lie," I came to see what I was up to: I was getting what I wanted. At last.

The truth of many circumstances and episodes in the past emerges for the memoirist through details (the red music book, the fascination with a nun's name and gleaming face), but these details are not merely information, not flat facts. Such details are not allowed to lounge. They must work. Their work is the creation of symbol. But it's more accurate to call it the *recognition* of symbol. For meaning is not "attached" to the detail by the memoirist: meaning is revealed. That's why a first draft is important. Just as the first meeting (good or bad) with someone who later becomes the beloved is important and is often reviewed for signals, meanings, omens, and indications.

Now I can look at that music book and see it not only as "a detail," but for what it is, how it *acts.* See it as the small red door leading straight into the dark room of my childhood longing and disappointment. That red book *becomes* the palpable evidence of that longing. In other words, it becomes symbol. There is no symbol, no life-of-the-spirit in the general or the abstract. Yet a writer wishes—indeed all of us wish—to speak about profound matters that are, like it or not, general and abstract. We wish to talk to each other about life and death, about love, despair, loss, and innocence. We sense that in order to live together we must learn to speak of peace, of history, of meaning and values. Those are a few.

We seek a means of exchange, a language which will renew these ancient concerns and make them wholly and pulsingly ours. Instinctively, we go to our store of private images and associations for our authority to speak of these weighty issues. We find, in our details and broken and obscured images, the language of symbol. Here memory impulsively reaches out its arms and embraces imagination. That is the resort to invention. It isn't a lie, but an act of necessity, as the innate urge to locate personal truth always is.

All right. Invention is inevitable. But why write memoir? Why not call it fiction and be done with all the hashing about, wondering where memory stops and imagination begins? And if memoir seeks to talk about "the big issues," about history and peace, death and love—why not leave these reflections to those with expert and scholarly knowledge? Why let the common or garden variety memoirist into the club? I'm thinking again of that bumper sticker: why Question Authority?

My answer, of course, is a memoirist's answer. Memoir must be written because each of us must have a created version of the past. Created: that is, real, tangible, made of the stuff of a life lived in place and in history. And the down side of any created thing as well: we must live with a version that attaches us to our limitations, to the inevitable subjectivity of our points of view. We must acquiesce to our experience and our gift to transform experience into meaning and value. You tell me your story, I'll tell you my story.

If we refuse to do the work of creating this personal version of the past, someone else will do it for us. That is a scary political fact. "The struggle of man against power," a character in Milan Kundera's novel *The Book of Laughter and Forgetting* says, "is the struggle of memory against forgetting." He refers to willful political forgetting, the habit of nations and those in power (Question Authority!) to deny the truth of memory in order to disarm moral and ethical power. It's an efficient way of controlling masses of people. It doesn't even require much bloodshed, as long as people are entirely willing to give over their personal memories. Whole histories can be rewritten. As Czeslaw Milosz said in his 1980 Nobel Prize lecture, the number of books published that seek to deny the existence of the Nazi death camps now exceeds one hundred.

What is remembered is what *becomes* reality. If we "forget" Auschwitz, if we "forget" My Lai, what then do we remember? And what is the purpose of our remembering? If we think of memory naively, as a simple story, logged like a documentary in the archive of the mind, we miss its beauty but also its function. The beauty of memory rests in its talent for rendering detail, for paying homage to the senses, its capacity to love the particles of life, the richness and idiosyncrasy of our existence. The function of memory, on the other hand, is intensely personal and surprisingly political.

Our capacity to move forward as developing beings rests on a healthy relation with the past. Psychotherapy, that widespread method of mental health, relies heavily on memory and on the ability to retrieve and organize images and events from the personal past. We carry our wounds and perhaps even worse, our capacity to wound, forward with us. If we learn not only to tell our stories but to listen to what our stories tell us—to write the first draft and then return for the second draft—we are doing the work of memoir.

Memoir is the intersection of narration and reflection, of story-telling and essay-writing. It can present its story *and* reflect and consider the meaning of the story. It is a peculiarly open form, inviting broken and incomplete images, half-recollected fragments, all the mass (and mess) of detail. It offers to shape this confusion—and in shaping, of course it necessarily creates a work of art, not a legal document. But then, even legal documents are only valiant attempts to consign the truth, the whole truth and nothing but the truth to paper. Even they remain versions.

Locating touchstones—the red music book, the olive Olive, my father's violin playing—is deeply satisfying. Who knows why? Perhaps we all sense that we can't grasp the whole truth and nothing but the truth of our experience. Just can't be done. What can be achieved, however, is a version of its swirling, changing wholeness. A memoirist must acquiesce to selectivity, like any artist. The version we dare to write is the only truth, the only relationship we can have with the past. Refuse to write your life and you have no life. At least, that is the stern view of the memoirist.

Personal history, logged in memory, is a sort of slide projector flashing images on the wall of the mind. And there's precious little order to the slides in the rotating carousel. Beyond that confusion, who knows who is running the projector? A memorist steps into this darkened room of flashing, unorganized images and stands blinking for a while. Maybe for a long while. But eventually, as with any attempt to tell a story, it is necessary to put something first, then something else. And so on, to the end. That's a first draft. Not necessarily the truth, not even *a* truth sometimes, but the first attempt to create a shape.

The first thing I usually notice at this stage of composition is the appalling inaccuracy of the piece. Witness my first piano lesson draft. Invention is screamingly evident in what I intended to be transcription. But here's the further truth: I feel no shame. In fact, it's only now that my interest in the piece truly quickens. For I can see what isn't there, what is shyly hugging the walls, hoping not to be seen. I see the filmy shape of the next draft. I see a more acute version of the episode or—this is more likely—as entirely new piece rising from the ashes of the first attempt.

The next draft of the piece would have to be a true re-vision, a new seeing of the materials of the first draft. Nothing merely cosmetic will do—no rouge buffing up the opening sentence, no glossy adjective to lift a sagging line, nothing to attempt covering a patch of gray writing. None of that. I can't say for sure, but my hunch is the revision would lead me to more writing about my father (why was I so impressed by that ancestral inventor of the collapsible opera hat? Did I feel I had nothing as remarkable in my own background? Did this make me feel inadequate?). I begin to think perhaps Sister Olive is less central to this business than she is in this draft. She is meant to be a moment, not a character.

And so I might proceed, if I were to undertake a new draft of the memoir. I begin to feel a relationship developing between a former self and me.

And, even more compelling, a relationship between an old world and me.

Some people think of autobiographical writing as the precious occupation of a particularly self-absorbed person. Maybe, but I don't buy that. True memoir is written in an attempt to find not only a self but a world.

The self-absorption that seems to be the impetus and embarrassment of autobiography turns into (or perhaps always was) a hunger for the world. Actually, it begins as a hunger for *a* world, one gone or lost, effaced by time or a more sudden brutality. But in the act of remembering, the personal environment expands, resonates beyond itself, beyond its "subject," into the endless and tragic recollection that is history.

We look at old family photographs in which we stand next to black, boxy Fords and are wearing period costumes, and we do not gaze fascinated because there we are young again, or there we are standing, as we never will again in life, next to our mother. We stare and drift because there we are . . . historical. It is the dress, the black car that dazzle us now and draw us beyond our mother's bright arms which once caught us. We reach into the attractive impersonality of something more significant than ourselves. We write memoir, in other words. We accept the humble position of writing a version rather than "the whole truth."

I suppose I write memoir because of the radiance of the past—it draws me back and back to it. Not that the past is beautiful. In our communal memoir, in history, the death camps *are* back there. In intimate life too, the record is usually pretty mixed. "I could tell you stories . . ." people say and drift off, meaning terrible things have happened to them.

But the past is radiant. It has the light of lived life. A memoirist wishes to touch it. No one owns the past, though typically the first act of new political regimes, whether of the left or the right, is to attempt to re-write history, to grab the past and make it over so the end comes out right. So their power looks inevitable.

No one owns the past, but it is a grave error (another age would have said a grave sin) not to inhabit memory. Sometimes I think it is all we really have. But that may be a trifle melodramatic. At any rate, memory possesses authority for the fearful self in a world where it is necessary to have authority in order to Question Authority.

There may be no more pressing intellectual need in our culture than for people to become sophisticated about the function of memory. The political implications of the loss of memory are obvious. The authority of memory is a personal confirmation of self-hood. To write one's life is to live it twice, and the second living is both spiritual and historical, for a memoir reaches deep within the personality as it seeks its narrative form and also grasps the life-of-the-times as no political treatise can.

Our most ancient metaphor says life is a journey. Memoir is travel writing, then, notes taken along the way, telling how things looked and what thoughts occurred. But I cannot think of the memoirist as a tourist. This is the traveller who goes on foot, living the journey, taking on mountains, enduring deserts, marveling at the lush green places. Moving through it all faithfully, not so much a survivor with a harrowing tale to tell as a pilgrim, seeking, wondering.

Reflections

Personal Exploration

1. Hampl believes it can be rewarding to discover those images we value. Create your own spontaneous list of memorable firsts: first piano recital, first loss, first fight, first job. Avoid being judgmental. Accept your memories as they surface and jot them down. Then select the single memory that stands out and write about it in your notebook. Search out the details—the light, smells, sounds—and recreate on the page the image or picture in your mind. When you've finished, reflect on the value of that particular memory. Why were you drawn to it? What discoveries have you made as a result of this writing? Did writing about it help you learn anything you hadn't realized before? Did you tell any lies?
2. What do you make of this passage?

   > Memory possesses authority for the fearful self in a world where it is necessary to have authority to Question Authority.

   Take time to look up "authority" in an unabridged dictionary. Study the various definitions before you respond.

Public Exploration

1. Individually and then with your group, reflect on the following from Hampl:

   > The struggle of man against power is the struggle of memory against forgetting.

   What is the political importance of writing about our own pasts? You may want to consider certain historical events, such as those in Poland, East Germany, Romania, China, Kuwait, or the Soviet Union, to explore this concept.
2. In the opening lines of Charles Dickens's novel *Hard Times*, the teacher Thomas Grandgrind announces his philosophy to the class.

   > "Now, what I want is, Facts. Teach these boys and girls nothing but Facts. Facts alone are wanted in life. Plant nothing else, and root out everything else. You can only form the minds of reasoning animals upon Facts: nothing else will ever be of service to them. This is the principle on which I bring up my own children, and this is the principle on which I bring up these children. Stick to the Facts, sir."

   Take a moment and reflect on Gradgrind's principles in your notebook, then join your group and share what you've written. Do you have differing or similar attitudes? Discuss the elements—historical, cultural, personal—that might create that agreement or disagreement. Does Hampl's essay offer any insights that might be of value here?

Private Reflection

1. After writing about Hampl, and if possible, after discussing her ideas with others, reflect on what you now see as the value of remembering, of writing memoirs? Reflect on those values in terms of your own experience, your own writing.

2. Consider what you think Hampl means by "intimacy" with writing. What's the value of this intimacy?

Why Are Americans Afraid of Dragons?

URSULA K. LE GUIN

This was to be a talk about fantasy. But I have not been feeling very fanciful lately, and could not decide what to say; so I have been going about picking people's brains for ideas. "What about fantasy? Tell me something about fantasy." And one friend of mine said, "All right, I'll tell you something fantastic. Ten years ago, I went to the children's room of the library of such-and-such a city, and asked for *The Hobbit*; and the librarian told me, 'Oh, we keep that only in the adult collection; we don't feel that escapism is good for children.' "

My friend and I had a good laugh and shudder over that, and we agreed that things have changed a great deal in these past ten years. That kind of moralistic censorship of works of fantasy is very uncommon now, in the children's libraries. But the fact that the children's libraries have become oases in the desert doesn't mean that there isn't still a desert. The point of view from which that librarian spoke still exists. She was merely reflecting, in perfect good faith, something that goes very deep in the American character: a moral disapproval of fantasy, a disapproval so intense, and often so aggressive, that I cannot help but see it as arising, fundamentally, from fear.

So: Why are Americans afraid of dragons?

Before I try to answer my question, let me say that it isn't only Americans who are afraid of dragons. I suspect that almost all very highly technological peoples are more or less antifantasy. There are several national literatures which, like ours, have had no tradition of adult fantasy for the past several hundred years: the French, for instance. But then you have the Germans, who have a good deal; and the English, who have it, and love it, and do it better than anyone else. So this fear of dragons is not merely a Western, or a technological, phenomenon. But I do not want to get into these vast historical questions; I will speak of modern Americans, the only people I know well enough to talk about.

In wondering why Americans are afraid of dragons, I began to realize that a great many Americans are not only antifantasy, but altogether antifiction. We tend, as a people, to look upon all works of the imagination either as suspect, or as contemptible.

"My wife reads novels. I haven't got the time."

"I used to read that science fiction stuff when I was a teenager, but of course I don't now."

"Fairy stories are for kids. I live in the real world."

Who speaks so? Who is it that dismisses *War and Peace, The Time Machine,* and *A Midsummer Night's Dream* with this perfect self-assurance? It is, I fear, the man in the street—the hardworking, over-thirty American male—the men who run this country.

Such a rejection of the entire art of fiction is related to several American characteristics: our Puritanism, our work ethic, our profit-mindedness, and even our sexual mores.

To read *War and Peace* or *The Lord of the Rings* plainly is not "work"—you do it for pleasure. And if it cannot be justified as "educational" or as "self-improvement," then, in the Puritan value system, it can only be self-indulgence or escapism. For pleasure is not a value, to the Puritan; on the contrary, it is a sin.

Equally, in the businessman's value system, if an act does not bring in an immediate, tangible profit, it has no justification at all. Thus the only person who has an excuse to read Tolstoy or Tolkien is the English teacher, because he gets paid for it. But our businessman might allow himself to read a best-seller now and then: not because it is a good book, but because it is a best-seller—it is a success, it has made money. To the strangely mystical mind of the money-changer, this justifies its existence; and by reading it he may participate, a little, in the power and mana of its success. If this is not magic, by the way, I don't know what is.

The last element, the sexual one, is more complex. I hope I will not be understood as being sexist if I say that, within our culture, I believe that this antifiction attitude is basically a male one. The American boy and man is very commonly forced to define his maleness by rejecting certain traits, certain human gifts and potentialities, which our culture defines as "womanish" or "childish." And one of these traits or potentialities is, in cold sober fact, the absolutely essential human faculty of imagination.

Having got this far, I went quickly to the dictionary.

The *Shorter Oxford Dictionary* says: "Imagination. 1. The action of imagining, or forming a mental concept of what is not actually present to the senses; 2. The mental consideration of actions or events not yet in existence."

Very well; I certainly can let "absolutely essential human faculty" stand. But I must narrow the definition to fit our present subject. By "imagination," then, I personally mean the free play of the mind, both intellectual and sensory. By "play" I mean recreation, re-creation, the recombination of what is known into what is new. By "free" I mean that the action is done without an immediate object of profit—spontaneously. That does not mean, however, that there may not be a purpose behind the free play of the mind, a goal; and the goal may be a very serious object indeed. Children's imaginative play is clearly a practicing at the acts and emotions of adulthood; a child who did not play would not become mature. As for the free play of an adult mind, its results may be *War and Peace,* or the theory of relativity.

To be free, after all, is not to be undisciplined. I should say that the discipline of the imagination may in fact be the essential method or technique of both art and science. It is our Puritanism, insisting that discipline means repression or punishment, which confuses the subject. To discipline something, in the proper sense of the word, does not mean to repress it, but to train it—to encourage it to grow, and act, and be fruitful, whether it is a peach tree or a human mind.

I think that a great many American men have been taught just the opposite. They have learned to repress their imagination, to reject it as something childish or effeminate, unprofitable, and probably sinful.

They have learned to fear it. But they have never learned to discipline it at all.

Now, I doubt that the imagination can be suppressed. If you truly eradicated it in a child, he would grow up to be an eggplant. Like all our evil propensities, the imagination will win out. But if it is rejected and despised, it will grow into wild and weedy shapes; it will be deformed. At its best, it will be mere ego-centered daydreaming; at its worst, it will be wishful thinking, which is a very dangerous occupation when it is taken seriously. Where literature is concerned, in the old, truly Puritan days, the only permitted reading was the Bible. Nowadays, with our secular Puritanism, the man who refuses to read novels because it's unmanly to do so, or because they aren't true, will most likely end up watching bloody detective thrillers on the television, or reading hack Westerns or sports stories, or going in for pornography, from *Playboy* on down. It is his starved imagination, craving nourishment, that forces him to do so. But he can rationalize such entertainment by saying that it is realistic—after all, sex exists, and there are criminals, and there are baseball players, and there used to be cowboys—and also by saying that it is virile, by which he means that it doesn't interest most women.

That all these genres are sterile, hopelessly sterile, is a reassurance to him, rather than a defect. If they were genuinely realistic, which is to say genuinely imagined and imaginative, he would be afraid of them. Fake realism is the escapist literature of our time. And probably the ultimate escapist reading is that masterpiece of total unreality, the daily stock market report.

Now what about our man's wife? She probably wasn't required to squelch her private imagination in order to play her expected role in life, but she hasn't been trained to discipline it, either. She is allowed to read novels, and even fantasies. But, lacking training and encouragement, her fancy is likely to glom on to very sickly fodder, such things as soap operas, and "true romances," and nursy novels, and historico-sentimental novels, and all the rest of the baloney ground out to replace genuine imaginative works by the artistic sweatshops of a society that is profoundly distrustful of the uses of the imagination.

What, then, are the uses of the imagination?

You see, I think we have a terrible thing here: a hardworking, upright, responsible citizen, a full-grown, educated person, who is afraid of dragons, and afraid of hobbits, and scared to death of fairies. It's funny, but it's also terrible. Something has gone very wrong. I don't know what to do about it but to try and give an honest answer to that person's question, even though he often asks it in an aggressive and contemptuous tone of voice. "What's the good of it all?" he says. "Dragons and hobbits and little green men—what's the *use* of it?"

The truest answer, unfortunately, he won't even listen to. He won't hear it. The truest answer is, "The use of it is to give you pleasure and delight."

"I haven't got the time," he snaps, swallowing a Maalox pill for his ulcer and rushing off to the golf course.

So we try the next-to-truest answer. It probably won't go down much better, but it must be said: "The use of imaginative fiction is to deepen your understanding of your world, and your fellow men, and your own feelings, and your destiny."

To which I fear he will retort, "Look, I got a raise last year, and I'm giving my family the best of everything, we've got two cars and a color TV. I understand enough of the world!"

And he is right, unanswerably right, if that is what he wants, and all he wants.

The kind of thing you learn from reading about the problems of a hobbit who is trying to drop a magic ring into an imaginary volcano has very little to do with your social status, or material success, or income. Indeed, if there is any relationship, it is a negative one. There is an inverse correlation between fantasy and money. That is a law, known to economists as Le Guin's Law. If you want a striking example of Le Guin's Law, just give a lift to one of those people along the roads who own nothing but a backpack, a guitar, a fine head of hair, a smile, and a thumb. Time and again, you will find that these waifs have read *The Lord of the Rings*—some of them can practically recite it. But now take Aristotle Onassis, or J. Paul Getty: could you believe that those men ever had anything to do, at any age, under any circumstances, with a hobbit?

But, to carry my example a little further, and out of the realm of economics, did you ever notice how very gloomy Mr. Onassis and Mr. Getty and all those billionaires look in their photographs? They have this strange, pinched look, as if they were hungry. As if they were hungry for something, as if they had lost something and were trying to think where it could be, or perhaps what it could be, what it was they've lost.

Could it be their childhood?

So I arrive at my personal defense of the uses of the imagination, especially in fiction, and most especially in fairy tale, legend, fantasy, science fiction, and the rest of the lunatic fringe. I believe that maturity is not an outgrowing, but a growing up: that an adult is not a dead child, but a child who survived. I believe that all the best faculties of a mature human being exist in the child, and that if these faculties are encouraged in youth they will act well and wisely in the adult, but if they are repressed and denied in the child they will stunt and cripple the adult personality. And finally, I believe that one of the most deeply human, and humane, of these faculties is the power of imagination: so that it is our pleasant duty, as librarians, or teachers, or parents, or writers, or simply as grownups, to encourage that faculty of imagination in our children, to encourage it to grow freely, to flourish like the green bay tree, by giving it the best, absolutely the best and purest, nourishment that it can absorb. And never, under any circumstances, to squelch it, or sneer at it, or imply that it is childish, or unmanly, or untrue.

For fantasy is true, of course. It isn't factual, but it is true. Children know that. Adults know it too, and that is precisely why many of them are afraid of fantasy. They know that its truth challenges, even threatens, all that is false, all that is phony, unnecessary, and trivial in the life they have let themselves be forced into living. They are afraid of dragons, because they are afraid of freedom.

So I believe that we should trust our children. Normal children do not confuse reality and fantasy—they confuse them much less often than we adults do (as a certain great fantasist pointed out in a story called "The Emperor's New Clothes"). Children know perfectly well that unicorns aren't real, but they also know that books about unicorns, if they are good books, are true books. All too often, that's more than Mummy and Daddy know; for, in denying their childhood, the adults have denied half their knowledge, and are left with the sad, sterile little fact: "Unicorns aren't real." And that fact is one that never got anybody anywhere (except in the story "The Unicorn in the Garden," by another great fantasist, in which it is shown that a devotion to the unreality of unicorns may get you straight into the loony bin). It is by such statements as, "Once upon a time there was a dragon," or "In a hole in the ground there lived a hobbit"—it is by such beautiful non-facts that we fantastic human beings may arrive, in our peculiar fashion, at the truth.

Reflections

Personal Exploration

1. Did hobbits hide in your childhood? Are there stories and books from the past you still value? Consider your attitude toward such works then and your current feelings. Are you afraid of dragons? How valuable does the imagination seem to your own life? Do you repress it or allow it to play a prominent role?
2. Who does Le Guin target as her opponents? What reasons does she consider to explain their attitudes? Consider readers in your own family: male and female, children and adults. Would your observations of them support Le Guin's claims? Are males more likely to reject fantasy and imaginative play?

Public Exploration

1. As a class, or in your group, discuss the following:

   > 'Once upon a time there was a dragon,' or 'In a hole in the ground there lived a hobbit'—it is by such beautiful nonfacts that we fantastic human beings may arrive, in our peculiar fashion, at the truth.

   What kind of truth is Le Guin talking about?

2. As a group, consider the following argument by author Vincent Ruggiero:

> Studies confirm that most people behave unimaginatively not because they lack imagination, but because they fear the reaction their ideas will receive. In time they grow used to suppressing ideas that differ from the norm, ideas that might raise eyebrows. They do themselves a great disservice, because creativity depends on imagination. 'No great discovery is ever made without a bold guess,' observed Sir Isaac Newton.

Make a list of "bold guesses" from the past that might have been considered absurd if you had proposed them to your friends at the time. Make another list of "bold guesses" about the future. Are you willing to stake your reputation and the respect of family and friends on your guesses? If not, how confident are you in your own imagination?

Private Reflection

1. If you're convinced that fantasy and imagination might have some value to human beings, consider Le Guin's claim that it needs to be disciplined. What is she getting at? We can educate the mind in such things as chemistry and bridge building, but how can we educate the imagination?
2. If you're still not convinced of the worth of fantasy in adult lives, reflect on the dangers you find in Le Guin's philosophy.

How Wang-Fo Was Saved

MARGUERITE YOURCENAR

translated from the French by
Alberto Manguel *and* **Marguerite Yourcenar**

The old painter Wang-Fo and his disciple Ling were wandering along the roads of the Kingdom of Han.

They made slow progress because Wang-Fo would stop at night to watch the stars and during the day to observe the dragonflies. They carried hardly any luggage, because Wang-Fo loved the image of things and not the things themselves, and no object in the world seemed to him worth buying, except brushes, pots of lacquer and China ink, and rolls of silk and rice paper. They were poor, because Wang-Fo would exchange his paintings for a ration of boiled millet, and paid no attention to pieces of silver. Ling, his disciple, bent beneath the weight of a sack full of sketches, bowed his back with respect as if he were carrying the heavens' vault, because for Ling the sack was full of snow-covered mountains, torrents in spring, and the face of the summer moon.

Ling had not been born to trot down the roads, following an old man who seized the dawn and captured the dusk. His father had been a banker who dealt in gold, his mother the only child of a jade merchant who had left her all his worldly possessions, cursing her for not being a son. Ling had grown up in a house where wealth made him shy: he was afraid of insects, of thunder and the face of the dead. When Ling was fifteen, his father chose a bride for him, a very beautiful one because the thought of the happiness he was giving his son consoled him for having reached the age in which the night is meant for sleep. Ling's wife was as frail as a reed, childish as milk, sweet as saliva, salty as tears. After the wedding, Ling's parents became discreet to the point of dying, and their son was left alone in a house painted vermilion, in the company of his young wife who never stopped smiling and a plum tree that blossomed every spring with pale-pink flowers. Ling loved this woman of a crystal-clear heart as one loves a mirror that will never tarnish, or a talisman that will protect one forever. He visited the tea-houses to follow the dictates of fashion, and only moderately favored acrobats and dancers.

One night, in the tavern, Wang-Fo shared Ling's table. The old man had been drinking in order to better paint a drunkard, and he cocked his head to one side as if trying to measure the distance between his hand and his bowl. The rice wine undid the tongue of the taciturn craftsman, and that night Wang spoke as if silence were a wall and words the colors with which to cover it. Thanks to him, Ling got to know the beauty of the drunkards' faces blurred by the vapors of hot drink, the brown splendor of the roasts unevenly brushed by tongues of fire, and the exquisite blush of wine stains strewn on the tablecloths like withered petals. A gust of wind broke the window: the downpour entered the room. Wang-Fo leaned out to make Ling admire the livid zebra stripes of lightning, and Ling, spellbound, stopped being afraid of storms.

Ling paid the old painter's bill, and as Wang-Fo was both without money and without lodging, he humbly offered him a resting place. They walked away together; Ling held a lamp whose light projected unexpected fires in the puddles. That evening, Ling discovered with surprise that the walls of his house were not red, as he had always thought, but the color of an almost rotten orange. In the courtyard, Wang-Fo noticed the delicate shape of a bush to which no one had paid any attention until then, and compared it to a young woman letting down her hair to dry. In the passageway, he followed with delight the hesitant trail of an ant along the cracks in the wall, and Ling's horror of these creatures vanished into thin air. Realizing that Wang-Fo had just presented him with the gift of a new soul and a new vision of the world, Ling respectfully offered the old man the room in which the father and mother had died.

For many years now, Wang-Fo had dreamed of painting the portrait of a princess of olden days playing the lute under a willow. No woman was sufficiently unreal to be his model, but Ling would do because he was not a woman. Then Wang-Fo spoke of painting a young prince shooting an arrow at the foot of a large cedar tree. No young man of the present was sufficiently unreal to serve as his model, but Ling got his own wife to pose under the plum tree in the garden. Later on, Wang-Fo painted her in a fairy costume against the clouds of twilight, and the young woman wept because it was an omen of death. As Ling came to prefer the portraits painted by Wang-Fo to the young woman herself, her face began to fade, like a flower exposed to warm winds and summer rains. One morning, they found her hanging from the branches of the pink plum tree: the ends of the scarf that was strangling her floated in the wind, entangled with her hair. She looked even more delicate than usual, and as pure as the beauties celebrated by the poets of days gone by. Wang-Fo painted her one last time, because he loved the green hue that suffuses the face of the dead. His disciple Ling mixed the colors and the task needed such concentration that he forgot to shed tears.

One after the other, Ling sold his slaves, his jades, and the fish in his pond to buy his master pots of purple ink that came from the West. When the house was emptied, they left it, and Ling closed the door of his past behind him. Wang-Fo felt weary of a city where the faces could no longer teach him secrets of ugliness or beauty, and the master and his disciple walked away together down the roads of the Kingdom of Han.

Their reputation preceded them into the villages, to the gateway of fortresses, and into the atrium of temples where restless pilgrims halt at dusk. It was murmured that Wang-Fo had the power to bring his paintings to life by adding a last touch of color to their eyes. Farmers would come and beg him to paint a watchdog, and the lords would ask him for portraits of their best warriors. The priests honored Wang-Fo as a sage; the people feared him as a sorcerer. Wang enjoyed these differences of opinion which gave him the chance to study expressions of gratitude, fear, and veneration.

Ling begged for food, watched over his master's rest, and took advantage of the old man's raptures to massage his feet. With the first rays of the sun, when the old man was still asleep, Ling went in pursuit of timid landscapes hidden behind bunches of reeds. In the evening, when the master, disheartened, threw down his brushes, he would carefully pick them up. When Wang became sad and spoke of his old age, Ling would smile and show him the solid trunk of an old oak; when Wang felt happy and made jokes, Ling would humbly pretend to listen.

One day, at sunset, they reached the outskirts of the Imperial City and Ling sought out and found an inn in which Wang-Fo could spend the night. The old man wrapped himself up in rags, and Ling lay down next to him to keep him warm because spring had only just begun and the floor of beaten earth was still frozen. At dawn, heavy steps echoed in the corridors of the inn; they heard the frightened whispers of the innkeeper and orders shouted in a foreign, barbaric tongue. Ling trembled, remembering that the night before, he had stolen a rice cake for his master's supper. Certain that they would come to take him to prison, he asked himself who would help Wang-Fo ford the next river on the following day.

The soldiers entered carrying lanterns. The flames gleaming through the motley paper cast red and blue lights on their leather helmets. The string of a bow quivered over their shoulders, and the fiercest among them suddenly let out a roar for no reason at all. A heavy hand fell on Wang-Fo's neck, and the painter could not help noticing that the soldiers' sleeves did not match the color of their coats.

Helped by his disciple, Wang-Fo followed the soldiers, stumbling along uneven roads. The passing crowds made fun of these two criminals who were certainly going to be beheaded. The soldiers answered Wang's questions with savage scowls. His bound hands hurt him, and Ling in despair looked smiling at his master, which for him was a gentler way of crying.

They reached the threshold of the Imperial Palace, whose purple walls rose in broad daylight like a sweep of sunset. The soldiers led Wang-Fo through countless square and circular rooms whose shapes symbolized the seasons, the cardinal points, the male and the female, longevity, and the prerogatives of power. The doors swung on their hinges with a musical note, and were placed in such a manner that one followed the entire scale when crossing the palace from east to west. Everything combined to give an impression of superhuman power and subtlety, and one could feel that here the simplest orders were as final and as terrible as the wisdom of the ancients. At last, the air became thin and the silence so deep that not even a man under torture would have dared to scream. A eunuch lifted a tapestry; the soldiers began to tremble like women, and the small troop entered the chamber in which the Son of Heaven sat on a high throne.

It was a room without walls, held up by thick columns of blue stone. A garden spread out on the far side of the marble shafts, and each and every flower blooming in the greenery belonged to a rare species brought here from across the oceans. But none of them had any perfume, so that the Celestial Dragon's meditations would not be troubled by fine smells. Out of respect for the silence in which his thoughts evolved, no bird had been allowed within the enclosure, and even the bees had been driven away. An enormous wall separated the garden from the rest of the world, so that the wind that sweeps over dead dogs and corpses on the battlefield would not dare brush the Emperor's sleeve.

The Celestial Master sat on a throne of jade, and his hands were wrinkled like those of an old man, though he had scarcely reached the age of twenty. His robe was blue to symbolize winter, and green to remind one of spring. His face was beautiful but blank, like a looking glass placed too high, reflecting nothing except the stars and the immutable heavens. To his right stood his Minister of Perfect Pleasures, and to his left his Counselor of Just Torments. Because his courtiers, lined along the base of the columns, always lent a keen ear to the slightest sound from his lips, he had adopted the habit of speaking in a low voice.

"Celestial Dragon," said Wang-Fo, bowing low, "I am old, I am poor, I am weak. You are like summer; I am like winter. You have Ten Thousand Lives; I have but one, and it is near its close. What have I done to you? My hands have been tied, these hands that never harmed you."

"You ask what you have done to me, old Wang-Fo?" said the Emperor.

His voice was so melodious that it made one want to cry. He raised his right hand, to which the reflections from the jade pavement gave a pale sea-green hue like that of an underwater plant, and Wang-Fo marveled at the length of those thin fingers, and hunted among his memories to discover whether he had not at some time painted a mediocre portrait of either the Emperor or one of his ancestors that would now merit a sentence of death. But it seemed unlikely because Wang-Fo had not been an assiduous visitor at the Imperial Court. He preferred the farmers' huts or, in the cities, the courtesans' quarters and the taverns along the harbor where the dockers liked to quarrel.

"You ask me what it is you have done, old Wang-Fo?" repeated the Emperor, inclining his slender neck toward the old man waiting attentively. "I will tell you. But, as another man's poison cannot enter our veins except through our nine openings, in order to show you your offenses I must take you with me down the corridors of my memory and tell you the story of my life. My father had assembled a collection of your work and hidden it in the most secret chamber in the palace, because he judged that the people in your paintings should be concealed from the world since they cannot lower their eyes in the presence of profane viewers. It was in those same rooms that I was brought up, old Wang-Fo, surrounded by solitude. To prevent my innocence from being sullied by other human souls, the restless crowd of my future subjects had been driven away from me, and no one was allowed to pass my threshold, for fear that his or her shadow would stretch out and touch me. The few aged servants that were placed in my service showed themselves as little as possible; the hours turned in circles; the colors of your paintings bloomed in the first hours of the morning and grew pale at dusk. At night, when I was unable to sleep, I gazed at them, and for nearly ten years I gazed at them every night. During the day, sitting on a carpet whose design I knew by heart, I dreamed of the joys the future had in store for me. I imagined the world, with the Kingdom of Han at the center, to be like the flat palm of my hand crossed by the fatal lines of the Five Rivers. Around it lay the sea in which monsters are born, and farther away the mountains that hold up the heavens. And to help me visualize these things I used your paintings. You made me believe that the sea looked like the vast sheet of water spread across your scrolls, so blue that if a stone were to fall into it, it would become a sapphire; that women opened and closed like flowers, like the creatures that come forward, pushed by the wind, along the paths of your painted gardens; and that the young, slim-waisted warriors who mount guard in the fortresses along the frontier were themselves like arrows that could pierce my heart. At sixteen I saw the doors that separated me from the world open once again; I climbed onto the balcony of my palace to look at the clouds, but they were far less beautiful than those in your sunsets. I ordered my litter; bounced along roads on which I had not foreseen either mud or stones, I traveled across the provinces of the Empire without ever finding your gardens full of women like fireflies, or a woman whose body was in itself a garden. The pebbles on the beach spoiled my taste for oceans; the blood of the tortured is less red than the pomegranates in your paintings; the village vermin prevented me from seeing the beauty of the rice fields; the flesh of mortal women disgusted me like the dead meat hanging from the butcher's hook, and the coarse laughter of my soldiers made me sick. You lied, Wang-Fo, you old impostor. The world is nothing but a mass of muddled colors thrown into the void by an insane painter, and smudged by our tears. The Kingdom of Han is not the most beautiful of kingdoms, and I am not the Emperor. The only empire which is worth reigning over is that which you alone can enter, old Wang, by the road of One Thousand Curves and Ten Thousand Colors. You alone reign peacefully over mountains covered in snow that cannot melt, and over fields of daffodils that cannot die. And that is why, Wang-Fo, I have conceived a punishment for you, for you whose enchantment has filled me with disgust at everything I own, and with desire for everything I shall never possess. And in order to lock you up in the only cell from which there is no escape, I have decided to have your eyes burned out, because your eyes, Wang-Fo, are the two magic gates that open onto your kingdom. And as your hands are the two roads of ten forking paths that lead to the heart of your kingdom, I have decided to have your hands cut off. Have you understood, old Wang-Fo?''

Hearing the sentence, Ling, the disciple, tore from his belt an old knife and leaped toward the Emperor. Two guards immediately seized him. The Son of Heaven smiled and added, with a sigh: ''And I also hate you, old Wang-Fo, because you have known how to make yourself beloved. Kill that dog.''

Ling jumped to one side so that his blood would not stain his master's robe. One of the soldiers lifted his sword and Ling's head fell from his neck like a cut flower. The servants carried away the remains, and Wang-Fo, in despair, admired the beautiful scarlet stain that his disciple's blood made on the green stone floor.

The Emperor made a sign and two eunuchs wiped Wang's eyes.

''Listen, old Wang-Fo,'' said the Emperor, ''and dry your tears, because this is not the time to weep. Your eyes must be clear so that the little light that is left to them is not clouded by your weeping. Because it is not only the grudge I bear you that makes me desire your death; it is not only the cruelty in my heart that makes me want to see you suffer. I have other plans, old Wang-Fo. I possess among your works a remarkable painting in which the mountains, the river estuary, and the sea reflect each other, on a very small scale certainly, but with a clarity that surpasses the real landscapes themselves, like objects reflected on the walls of a metal sphere. But that painting is unfinished, Wang-Fo; your masterpiece is but a sketch. No doubt, when you began your work, sitting in a solitary valley, you noticed a passing bird, or a child running after the bird. And the bird's beak or the child's cheeks made you forget the blue eyelids of the sea. You never finished the frills of the water's cloak, or the seaweed hair of the rocks. Wang-Fo, I want you to use the few hours of light that are left to you to finish this painting, which will thus contain the final secrets amassed during your long life. I know that your hands, about to fall, will not tremble on the silken cloth, and infinity will enter your work through those unhappy cuts. I know that your eyes, about to be put out, will discover bearings far beyond all human senses. This is my pain, old Wang-Fo, and I can force you to fulfill it. If you refuse, before blinding you, I will have all your paintings burned, and you will be like a father whose children are slaughtered and all hopes of posterity extinguished. However, believe, if you wish, that this last order stems from nothing but my kindness, because I know that the silken scroll is the only mistress you ever deigned to touch. And to offer you brushes, paints, and inks to occupy your last hours is like offering the favors of a harlot to a man condemned to death."

Upon a sign from the Emperor's little finger, two eunuchs respectfully brought forward the unfinished scroll on which Wang-Fo had outlined the image of the sea and the sky. Wang-Fo dried his tears and smiled, because that small sketch reminded him of his youth. Everything in it spoke of a fresh new spirit which Wang-Fo could no longer claim as his, and yet something was missing from it, because when Wang had painted it he had not yet looked long enough at the mountains or at the rocks bathing their naked flanks in the sea, and he had not yet penetrated deep enough into the sadness of the evening twilight. Wang-Fo selected one of the brushes which a slave held ready for him and began spreading wide strokes of blue into the unfinished sea. A eunuch crouched by his feet, mixing the colors; he carried out his task with little skill, and more than ever Wang-Fo lamented the loss of his disciple Ling.

Wang began by adding a touch of pink to the tip of the wing of a cloud perched on a mountain. Then he painted onto the surface of the sea a few small lines that deepened the perfect feeling of calm. The jade floor became increasingly damp, but Wang-Fo, absorbed in his painting, did not seem to notice that he was working with his feet in water.

The fragile rowboat grew under the strokes of the painter's brush and now occupied the entire foreground of the silken scroll. The rhythmic sound of the oars rose suddenly in the distance, quick and eager like the beating of wings. The sound came nearer, gently filling the whole room, then ceased, and a few trembling drops appeared on the boatman's oars. The red iron intended for Wang's eyes lay extinguished on the executor's coals. The courtiers, motionless as etiquette required, stood in water up to their shoulders, trying to lift themselves onto the tips of their toes. The water finally reached the level of the imperial heart. The silence was so deep one could have heard a tear drop.

It was Ling. He wore his everyday robe, and his right sleeve still had a hole that he had not had time to mend that morning before the soldiers' arrival. But around his neck was tied a strange red scarf.

Wang-Fo said to him softly, while he continued painting, "I thought you were dead."

"You being alive," said Ling respectfully, "how could I have died?"

And he helped his master into the boat. The jade ceiling reflected itself in the water, so that Ling seemed to be inside a cave. The pigtails of submerged courtiers rippled up toward the surface like snakes, and the pale head of the Emperor floated like a lotus.

"Look at them," said Wang-Fo sadly. "These wretches will die, if they are not dead already. I never thought there was enough water in the sea to drown an Emperor. What are we to do?"

"Master, have no fear," murmured the disciple. "They will soon be dry again and will not even remember that their sleeves were ever wet. Only the Emperor will keep in his heart a little of the bitterness of the sea. These people are not the kind to lose themselves inside a painting."

And he added: "The sea is calm, the wind high, the seabirds fly to their nests. Let us leave, Master, and sail to the land beyond the waves."

"Let us leave," said the old painter.

Wang-Fo took hold of the helm, and Ling bent over the oars. The sound of rowing filled the room again, strong and steady like the beating of a heart. The level of the water dropped unnoticed around the large vertical rocks that became columns once more. Soon only a few puddles glistened in the hollows of the jade floor. The courtiers' robes were dry, but a few wisps of foam still clung to the hem of the Emperor's cloak.

The painting finished by Wang-Fo was leaning against a tapestry. A rowboat occupied the entire foreground. It drifted away little by little, leaving behind it a thin wake that smoothed out into the quiet sea. One could no longer make out the faces of the two men sitting in the boat, but one could still see Ling's red scarf and Wang-Fo's beard waving in the breeze.

The beating of the oars grew fainter, then ceased, blotted out by the distance. The Emperor, leaning forward, a hand above his eyes, watched Wang's boat sail away till it was nothing but an imperceptible dot in the paleness of the twilight. A golden mist rose and spread over the water. Finally the boat veered around a rock that stood at the gateway to the ocean; the shadow of a cliff fell across it; its wake disappeared from the deserted surface, and the painter Wang-Fo and his disciple Ling vanished forever on the jade-blue sea that Wang-Fo had just created.

Reflections

Private Exploration

1. What idea or events in Yourcenar's story surprised, confused, angered, or delighted you? Search the text for a key passage, pattern, or repetition that you feel is particularly illuminating. Explore it in your notebook. Use the passage to reflect on the most puzzling or provocative elements of the story.
2. Consider how Wang Fo's values relate to his artist's perception of the world. Or consider the changes his disciple Ling undergoes after learning to see the world differently. In either case, what is ultimately suggested about the relationship between perception and values?
3. We particularly admire the rich language used in this recreation of a 13th century Taoist tale. Metaphor, similes, imagery, and symbols abound. What patterns or repetitions of these various figures of speech become particularly significant in our understanding of the story? You might want to reflect on the use of color, light images, or sound.

Public Exploration

1. "How Wang Fo Was Saved" encourages us to think about the world we actually live in compared to the imaginative world of the artist. What is being suggested about the value of art and imagination? In what ways might art be considered dangerous? Why is art sometimes a threat to government?
2. The Japanese painter, Hokusai, once said, "To paint the bird you must become the bird." And the British poet, Keats, once wrote in a letter that when he looked out a window and saw a sparrow, he became the sparrow; when the sparrow picked up a piece of straw, he became the straw. Reflect on what it is the artist may be doing or feeling that most of us never do. What could we learn from studying the minds and methods of the artist?

   As a group, consider what artists have to teach us about our own limitations, our own potential? For example, are there ways the imagination of the artist might be valuable to a psychologist? A military leader? A scientist? A college student?

Private Reflection

1. What do you make of the Celestial Master here:

   > The Celestial Master sat on a throne of jade, and his hands were wrinkled like those of an old man, though he had scarcely reached the age of twenty. His robe was blue to symbolize winter, and green to remind him of spring. His face was beautiful but blank, like a looking glass too high, reflecting nothing except the stars the immutable heavens.

2. Reflect on how the following might contradict your experience as a college student, or how it might be important to you as a student, or as an individual:

   > Imagination is more important than knowledge. For knowledge is limited, whereas imagination embraces the entire world.
   >
   > —ALBERT EINSTEIN

• THE TYGER •

WILLIAM BLAKE

Tyger! Tyger! burning bright
In the forests of the night,
What immortal hand or eye
Could frame thy fearful symmetry?

In what distant deeps or skies
Burnt the fire of thine eyes?
On what wings dare he aspire?
What the hand dare seize the fire?

And what shoulder, & what art,
Could twist the sinews of thy heart?
And when thy heart began to beat,
What dread hand? & what dread feet?

What the hammer? what the chain?
In what furnace was thy brain?
What the anvil? what dread grasp
Dare its deadly terrors clasp?

When the stars threw down their spears
And water'd heaven with their tears,
Did he smile his work to see?
Did he who made the Lamb make thee?

Tyger! Tyger! burning bright
In the forests of the night,
What immortal hand or eye
Dare frame thy fearful symmetry?

Reflections

Private Exploration

1. Even if you've read Blake's poem before, read it again several times. Read it at least once aloud, listening to rhythms and sounds. Make marginal notes and look up words you might be unfamiliar with. (This is where a major dictionary such as the *Oxford English Dictionary* can be of help, providing historical meanings and usages.) Then write down your response to the poem. Begin with your feelings. Identify details—especially patterns and repetitions—that evoke those feelings. Reflect on how any specific details or images contribute to your experience of the text, and on how any aspect of your personal life or background might also affect your experience of the text.
2. Writer Peter Elbow has said that "to find the metaphor in someone's language is to find the key to how he [she] understands the world." Are there striking metaphors in the poem that help you gain insight into it? Be willing to explore both ideas and feelings freely here.

Public Exploration

After a member of your group has read the poem aloud, take turns reading your notebook responses to the poem. Listen carefully, jotting down any fresh insights or questions you may have. When everyone has read, discuss the reactions and discoveries being made. Consider how the ideas or reactions your group has expressed might relate to society, to culture, or to values. Is there any common thread?

Private Reflection

Reread your first response to the poem, then write an additional response reflecting on any feelings or ideas that may have been modified or solidifed. If possible, relate your experience with the poem, negative or positive, to some aspect of your own culture and values.

The Imaginative Mind in Art

JACOB BRONOWSKI

It is not certain when human beings started to speak, but it was certainly not very long ago, on the time scale of evolution. We believe that human beings became clearly differentiated from the common ape stock about a million generations ago. However, human speech is probably not much older than a hundred thousand years. The whole of human converse as we know it fits into this small fraction of our evolution.

The raw material of literature is not simply words, but words as human beings use them; and human beings do not use language in the limited way that animals do. There is a cardinal difference between human language and animal languages. Let me begin, then, by comparing the two, and specifically by describing an animal language.

Many species of animals have some kind of language. Some of them, for example the insects, have a language which is certainly older than our own. I shall take as my example one of these old insect languages: the language of the bees.

It has been known for two hundred years that when a bee which has found a source of honey returns home, it makes a violent agitated movement which in time is taken up by the whole hive. The beekeepers who first noticed this in the eighteenth century supposed it to express a primitive emotion. They believed that the bee comes home in a state of excitement, and that it simply communicates this excitement to the other bees in the hive. However, they were wrong; the communication between bees is more precise and more remarkable than mere excitement.

It has now been shown by the delicate studies of Karl von Frisch and others that the bee that comes home laden with honey talks to the other bees in the hive in quite specific symbols. The returning bee does a round dance, shaped like a flattened figure of eight, and other bees take up this dance and begin to follow the leader along its figure of eight. This figure of eight has two exact messages for the bees that follow it. The direction in which the main line of the figure points tells the bees in the hive where to go for the source of the honey that they smell on the leader. And the speed at which the figure is run tells the bees how far away the source of honey is.

I apologize for telling this story so briefly and so roughly, because those who already know it will know it more fully, and those who do not know it will scarcely believe it. Yet the story is true and, in its essence, is as simple as this. The dance of the bees is a complete instruction by which one bee tells the others in what direction to fly and how far to fly. The bees that take up the dance learn the instruction by actually following the movements of the first bee in the dance—that is, by going through the same steps as if they themselves had brought the message.

This is characteristic of the language of any animal, even when it utters something as simple as a cry of alarm. What the animal says is very specific: it communicates a piece of information to the other animals. The other animals do not hold a meeting about what they are told, do not discuss it or consider it or even reflect on it. When a group of monkeys hears the cry of alarm of its sentry, it scatters. when a hive of bees observes the dance of the homecomer, it carries out his instructions without argument—at least, so long as there is only one homecomer.

Human beings also have a language of instruction and information. For example, my description of the behavior of bees has been as specific as their own language. True, my description does not instruct you what to do; but that is only because you are not a bee. Essentially, I have given you (or tried to give you) an uncolored piece of information, which in itself makes no demand from you but simple assent. This is the language of communication.

But human beings also use language for quite a different purpose: for personal reflection and elaboration. When you have finished reading this essay, you will go away and think about it; and you will think about it in your personal language, privately. You may begin by thinking about the behavior of bees, and then your thoughts will go off elsewhere, to subjects which have no more to do with bees than the rest of my essay has. You will reflect, you will make analogies and draw conclusions, and all this you will do by manipulating inside your head all the ideas that are touched off by, say, the idea that bees talk. This is the ability that makes you human: the use of words or symbols, not to communicate with others, but to manipulate your own ideas inside your own head.

Let me pause to underline this critical point. I began by saying that the raw material of the art of literature is words. Now I have made a distinction between two kinds of words, or rather, between two uses of words. On the one hand, there are the words of command or communication—words which are mere signals, and tell us, as it were, to stop or to go. The language of bees and monkeys and other animals is made up of these words, and does not go beyond them. On the other hand, human language goes beyond these words of communication, and uses words also in order to formulate ideas inside our minds. We reflect on our own ideas, we change them and enlarge them, and they carry our personal associations for us. It is words in this sense which are the vehicles of our imagination, and the raw material of literature.

How do we know that human beings use words in this way, to recreate the world inside their minds? And how do we know that animals do not? We know it by experiment—by watching the experiment which nature carries out before our eyes every day, of slowly transforming a young animal or child into an adult. We know it, that is, by watching the development of the young, and seeing whether they do or do not ever reach the stage of thinking about something which is not present in front of their eyes or other senses.

We can actually watch and see the stage at which a child learns to use words for objects which are not immediately present to him. Anyone who has had a baby, and who is reasonably perceptive, has seen this moment. There comes a stage in a child's life, before he is twelve months old, when he visibly takes the great step. Before this stage, if you show a child a toy and then put it behind your back, his interest disappears: he is not aware of objects which are not in his actual field of sensation. And then one day there comes a moment when the child is aware that the toy behind your back is still a toy—it is still somewhere, it exists, and it will return.

This is a huge moment of illumination, not only in your child's life, but in the whole evolution of the human race. The ability to conceive of things which are not present to the senses is crucial to the development of man. And this ability requires the existence of a symbol somewhere inside the mind for something that is not there. Of course the young child does not know the word "toy"; but he has in his head some image which says, what was in my field of vision was a toy, it still exists, and it will return.

Probably the images that we use most often in the mind are words themselves. But all our symbols have the same purpose; words are merely the symbols we use most commonly. The function of words in human thought is to stand for things which are not present to the senses, and to allow the mind to manipulate them—things, concepts, ideas, everything which does not have a physical reality in front of us now.

The enlargement of experience which comes from the use of symbols is perhaps most tellingly presented as a numerical account. Consider, then, one of the relatives of man that has been studied—say, the rhesus monkey.

Rhesus monkeys have a fair vocabulary. They can make about twenty sounds and about twenty gestures, so that they have a total of about forty distinct words. Of course these are all command words, such as "come here," "go away," or else words (including gestures) which convey strong emotion.

Now compare the monkey's vocabulary of forty words with a reasonable human vocabulary. In round figures, a man's vocabulary is at least a hundred times as large. That is, four thousand words is a fair vocabulary that a human being can get along with, if he is not going to spend too much time in thinking. And the total store in a good dictionary is more than a hundred times larger again, for a good dictionary contains nearly a million words.

This, then, is a measure of the distance from the language of command to the language of ideas. The language of ideas creates a different universe: a universe which has multiplied the monkey's vocabulary of forty words to the million words in a human dictionary. Moreover, a monkey knows all the words in the monkey dictionary; but a human being, though he knows a hundred times as many words as a monkey, still knows less than a hundredth of the words in a human dictionary.

Let me take one more step in this description of the raw material of one of the arts, of the evolution of language or symbolism. I have described the great step which human beings take as children when they become aware of more than is in front of their senses. When the human species became able to hold absent things in the mind, it took a critical step in its evolution. Why do I think this step is so critical?

The ability to hold absent things in mind gives human beings a freedom inside their environment which no animal has. Animals are environment-bound: that is, they react to outside stimuli in a tightly limited way. They have little choice of response. Much fascinating experimental work shows that an animal which has a strong stimulus in front of it is not able to resist its compulsion. Whether the stimulus is food, or is the affection of a hen for her chicks, the animal is unable to make any response but the obvious one. It rushes straight for the food or the chicks; and if there is some obstacle in the way, the animal is so much dominated by what is in front of its eyes that it cannot remember its way round the obstacle. The animal has no words, no mental images, which allow it to visualize anything but the situation in front of its senses.

By contrast, the language of human beings gives us the ability to see ourselves in a thousand situations which are not present to us, and never may be. Foresight is a characteristically human attribute. Only human beings are capable of projecting themselves into imaginary situations, and considering a week ahead, "If it snows I'll have to wear my galoshes, but if it doesn't snow I'll be able to wear my new shoes." And this we can do only because we have words like "snow" and "galoshes" and "new shoes" all going round inside our heads without any of these things having to be physically in front of us.

I have used the word "imagination" in the title of this essay because it is the right word to describe the most human gift. Imagination simply means the human habit of making images inside one's head. And the ability to make these personal images is the giant step in the evolution of man and in the growth of every child. Human beings can imagine situations which are different from those in front of their eyes; and they can do so because they make and hold in their minds images for absent things.

A child can remember absent things quite early, but he cannot do imaginary actions with them until much later in his development. When the child takes this second step, when he discovers his own imagination, he suddenly walks into a new life. At this moment, the child opens a door into the world beyond his immediate experience, because he is now seeing situations that do not exist. The child treats these imaginary situations in part as fantasy, and in part as a quite rational exploration of future experiences. A child's play does both: it frolics in the fantasy world, and it experiments in the rational world, which are both created by these images. This is why children love to make up fairy stories, and also love to play at marriage and hospitals and all the rituals of adult life. They project themselves into all worlds, possible and impossible, and discover for themselves the knife-edge boundary between them.

The ability to make images for absent things, and to use them to experiment with imaginary situations, gives man a freedom which an animal does not possess. That freedom has two distinct parts. One part is the pleasure that human beings feel in trying out and exploring imaginary situations. A child's play is concerned with this pleasure; and so is much of art, and much of science too. At bottom, pure science itself is a form of play, in this sense.

The second part of the freedom which words and images give us is that they are personal to us. All bees have exactly the same language; when one bee dances, the other bees listen simply by imitating the same dance. The bees have only one vocabulary, with the same words and the same meanings. But human beings, because they manipulate words inside their minds for themselves, change them and develop them and give them their own meanings. No two human beings, not even identical twins, speak quite the same language.

This personal manipulation of language, this gift of recreating for ourselves, in a fresh way, the images which other people present to us, is the foundation of art. When you read a poem you all see the same words, and yet each of you makes the poem something different and personal for himself. You pick out odd points, you hear different overtones, new analogies start up in your mind. And this is individual to you, and forms a complex amalgam which is yours and no one else's—indeed, which in the end is you.

It is time to end this analysis of the raw material of an art, and to turn to the art itself. Let us consider the following poem by Dylan Thomas.

> The force that through the green fuse drives the flower
> Drives my green age; that blasts the roots of trees
> Is my destroyer.
> And I am dumb to tell the crooked rose
> My youth is bent by the same wintry fever.
>
> The force that drives the water through the rocks
> Drives my red blood; that dries the mouthing streams
> Turns mine to wax.
> And I am dumb to mouth unto my veins
> How at the mountain spring the same mouth sucks.
>
> The hand that whirls the water in the pool
> Stirs the quicksand; that ropes the blowing wind
> Hauls my shroud sail.

And I am dumb to tell the hanging man
How of my clay is made the hangman's lime.

The lips of time leech to the fountain head;
Love drips and gathers, but the fallen blood
Shall calm her sores.

And I am dumb to tell a weather's wind
How time has ticked a heaven round the stars.
And I am dumb to tell the lover's tomb
How at my sheet goes the same crooked worm.

As in many of Dylan Thomas's beautiful poems, the central thought here is simple. It consists of the confrontation in each verse of the same two ideas.

One is the idea of the green fuse, the power in nature that drives everything forward; we feel this, we share its activity, and it makes us feel stronger and bolder with each experience, and life and time seem to be on our side. The second idea in each verse is that we are, however, being destroyed by this very same power. We are getting older, life and time are killing us a little with each experience. I suggest reading the first verse again; it shows the contrast of the two meanings clearly—the predicament of all living and growing things.

However, I did not choose this poem in order to discuss its philosophy. I chose it to illustrate the nature of human language. Here the very act of exploring the medium of his art, of exploring the language, is an excitement to the poet. The poet must take pleasure in discovering what language can do; that is his starting point. And this sense of pleasure is obvious in the poem; it is obvious that Dylan Thomas was not merely in love with poetry, he was in love with words.

If we think of the poem as a formal statement, then it is rather repetitive: each verse restates the same simple thought which one could write out in two lines. The same thought is illustrated by images from different fields—in verse one they are trees, in verse two water and rocks, in verse three whirlpools and quicksand, and in verse four inevitably the images relate to love. And yet each of us is aware that when he comes to the end of the poem, my restatement of it only brushes a fringe of what the poem says to him. In some way the imagery which Dylan Thomas runs through his hands so prodigally touches each one of us at one spot or another on the raw.

Whether you are the person on whom the word "hangman" in the third verse strikes like thunder, or whether to you the word "love" in the fourth verse comes like a revelation, it is you individually who has been moved. Something in this lavish imagery reaches each of us, and has the effect of carrying a personal message to each of us. My dry prose statement of the meaning of the poem means much the same to each of us, and that much the same is very little. But the poem itself is rich in meaning because everyone makes his or her own poem out of it. What poem you make out of it depends on which of the images suddenly sets you on fire. I am captured by the word "fuse" in the first line, and its explosive urgency carries me headlong into the poem from the beginning. Ask yourself what image rises from the poem like a rocket for you, and spills a bright rain of light over your understanding.

Everyone of us reads the same poem, and yet each one of us makes his own poem. This is the nature of imagination: that everyone has to reimagine, and to reimagine for himself. Dylan Thomas certainly imagined this poem first, certainly created the poem. And yet, if you want to understand the poem, you have to recreate it for yourself.

This is a strange thought, but it is fundamental. No work of art has been created with such finality that you need contribute nothing to it. You must recreate the work for yourself—it cannot be presented to you ready-made. You cannot look at a picture and find it beautiful by a merely passive act of seeing. The internal relations that make it beautiful to you have to be discovered and in some way have to be put in by you. The artist provides a skeleton; he provides guiding lines; he provides enough to engage your interest and to touch you emotionally. But there is no picture and no poem unless you yourself enter it and fill it out.

I chose Dylan Thomas's poetry as the first example because it illustrates so clearly what the poet can give and what we must add. If this had been a bad and unsuccessful poem, we would all say instantly, "This poet is threshing about; each verse tries a new spurt of imagery; he is trying to blunder his way toward saying the thing right, by mere repetition." And that is true of Dylan Thomas; yet when his poem comes off, you see that it is marvelous. But it is true that this is what Dylan Thomas is trying to do: he is trying by any means to find a way into your personality so that you may reimagine his simple thought for yourself. You must be faced with the thought in your own way, and seize it for yourself.

What thought? The thought that when you are young, growing older is wonderful, but when you are old, growing older is tragic. For that is what the poem says. It does not say it in any single line or in any single image, yet that is what it says somewhere. At least (I beg your pardon) that is what the poem says to me—or better, that is what I say to myself through the poem. And even this expression is not quite right: that is one part of what the poem says to me, or of what I say to myself through the poem.

I have called the metaphorical figures of speech in the poem its imagery, and that is a fair reminder: it is the poet's images that set off our own imagination. The metaphorical images work in our minds, and shape our thought and are the essence of it. The fact that the metaphors in the first verse are of growing things, and in the second verse are of water and rocks—this gives the poem its quality. Each verse draws in a different field of experience, and it might seem that none is essential to the poem. "When you are young, growing older is wonderful, but when you are old, growing older is tragic"—surely it is true that none of the metaphors by which that is conveyed is a necessary part of the statement. But it is also true, and more deeply true, that without the metaphors the statement becomes meaningless. The metaphors link the different fields of our experience and seek out the likeness between them.

When Dylan Thomas says, in his first verse, that the sap which pushes through the branch to burst into leaf and flower is also the force that bursts the roots, he is not merely making my prose statement more vivid. He is joining one area of experience to another, and illuminating and enriching each with each. The images of growth in the first verse, the images of fertilizing water in the second, the mounting death images of the hangman in the third verse, and the ambivalent images of love in the last verse: these join together to make a poem exactly as a man's experiences join together to make a personality. In this sense, all art is metaphor. It takes one part of your experience, and another part of your experience, and it forces you to look at them together. And by this act of looking at them together, the work of art makes you see each experience afresh and differently.

Now, to close my essay, I ought to turn to the other of the two freedoms which I said human language gives us. One is the freedom to be personal, to enjoy the implications of the language for ourselves and to be stimulated by it. That I have displayed in detail in Dylan Thomas's poem, and in the highly personal recreation of the poem which each of us makes for himself. The other is the freedom to imagine different courses of action, and to explore their possibilities in the mind, one against the other.

The ability to foresee several different courses of action and to weigh them in the mind might be thought to be a purely logical and scientific faculty. But in fact, this is the nature of all imagination, in art and science alike. In this simple respect, there is no difference between a great theorem, like that of Pythagoras, and a great poem like Homer's *Iliad*. The difference lies at a deeper level: Pythagoras is deliberately trying to mean the same thing to everybody who listens to him—one thing and one thing only—and Homer is not. Homer is content to say something universal and yet to mean different things to everybody who listens to him. We know this, we have just heard it. We know that Dylan Thomas's thought, because it deals with youth and age, evokes a different poem in a young reader from that which it evokes in an older reader.

But this is not yet deep enough; we must go deeper still to understand the full power of a work of art. A poem does not present a number of alternatives in order to invite you to come down for one or another. The poem asks you to weigh them, but not to judge them: unlike the theorem of Pythagoras, it is not a blueprint for action. On the contrary, the poem or other work of art is so arranged that it positively discourages you from deciding which of its imaginary actions (which of its possible meanings) you like best and should follow.

Turn back to the poem by Dylan Thomas and the two conflicting things that it says in each verse. At the end of the to-and-fro, are you joyful at the thought that growing older is wonderful when you are young? Or are you cast down at the thought that growing older is tragic when you are old? Neither; you cannot make up your mind. And the poem, unlike the theorem of Pythagoras, is not meant to make up your mind for you. On the contrary: fundamentally and literally, the poem is deliberately arranged to prevent you from making up your mind.

I shall illustrate this important point, my final point, with a poem by Robert Frost. It is not a lyrical poem; it has no bright and poetic imagery of evocation; and neither is it one of those milk-and-honey poems into which Frost often lapsed. It is a tough and searching and extraordinary poem, and it is called "Provide, Provide."

> The witch that came (the withered hag)
> To wash the steps with pail and rag
> Was once the beauty Abishag,
>
> The picture pride of Hollywood.
> Too many fall from great and good
> For you to doubt the likelihood.
>
> Die early and avoid the fate.
> Or if predestined to die late,
> Make up your mind to die in state.
>
> Make the whole stock exchange your own!
> If need be occupy a throne,
> Where nobody can call *you* crone.
>
> Some have relied on what they knew,
> Others on being simply true.
> What worked for them might work for you.
>
> No memory of having starred
> Atones for later disregard
> Or keeps the end from being hard.
>
> Better to go down dignified
> With boughten friendship at your side
> Than none at all. Provide, Provide!

The imagery of this poem belongs to our own generation. It uses the verb "to star," for example, not for poetic effect, but simply to describe a Hollywood celebrity. Elsewhere it chooses equally direct phrases of today, such as the command to make the whole stock exchange your own. That is, the poem is deliberately worded to draw in fields of experience which you will feel to be relevant to your own life.

The story in the poem is also clear and contemporary. The poet meets a woman who has been a great star in her past, and now she is nothing. He reflects that people have dealt with the problem of old age in various ways. You can avoid it by dying early; but if you must grow old, then you had better ensure that you keep your dignity at any price—even if you have to buy it. The moral would be (if there were a moral), Do not become a fallen star: provide for your survival, whatever its cost, by any means at all, however mercenary, flamboyant, or tawdry.

But do you really think there is a moral? Do you know whose side you are on, or Robert Frost is on? Do you really believe that Frost meant to tell you that it is better to provide for your old age by buying friends, than to live with the memory of having starred? Of course not; the poet is not giving you this advice—and neither is he giving you the opposite advice.

The poet is not giving you advice at all. He is not asking you to accept a moral, or even to draw one for yourself. The universe of art is one in which there is a suspension of decision, what Samuel Taylor Coleridge called a willing suspension of disbelief: a suspension of the sense of judgment.

There are no morals in a poem; there are no morals in any work of art. There are no specific lessons to be learned and there is no advice to be followed. There are many implications in a poem which enrich our experience of life: but it is a many-sided experience, and we are not supposed to come down on one side or the other. Dylan Thomas confronting two issues for us in each verse, or Robert Frost with a macabre sense of humor pretending to teach a lesson which he does not want us to learn, epitomizes the nature of art. Here the imagination explores the alternatives of human action without ever deciding for one rather than another. And in this tense and happy indecision, and only in this, the work of art is profoundly different from the work of science.

Reflections

Personal Exploration

1. Which key sentence or passage in Bronowski seems to strike you with the most force or to raise the most significant questions for you? Copy that passage in your notebook and explore its many ramifications. Consider especially your own understanding of imagination before and after reading Bronowski's essay.
2. Consider this: "The ability to conceive of things which are not present to the senses is crucial to the development of man."
3. Reread Robert Frost's poem (p. 274). Jot down your first reaction quickly and without reflection. Now, as a way of slowing down the eye to pay more attention to the details of language, copy the poem by hand into your notebook. When you've finished record your impressions. What image, if any, "rises from the poem like a rocket for you, spills a bright rain of light over your understanding?" Zero in on the word or words that seem most important to you.

   Bronowski believes that "if you want to understand the poem, you have to recreate it for yourself." What does this statement mean to you? In writing about Frost's poem, did you in fact recreate it for yourself? Did the poet's use of metaphor contribute to this re-creation?

Public Exploration

1. Reflect on the distinctions Bronowski makes between animals' use of language and man's use of language. Consider how words become the vehicles of our imaginations.

Is this a new concept for you? Does it make sense? Can you find examples that would tend to support it or refute it? What questions does it raise? Is the imagination limited to words?

2. Many people consider things imaginative to be an "illusion." Science, on the other hand, is usually thought to deal with "reality." Consider the relationship between the two. Bronowski is a scientist, but he uses poems to illustrate his argument. Could he have used any examples from his own discipline? Is the imagination limited to literature and the arts—to fantasy—while science is limited to "truth"? Is the imagination essentially false or at least valuable only as entertainment and escapism?

Private Reflection

After discussing Bronowski with others, reflect on how works rich in imagination open up questions about that which makes us human. Is Bronowski's essay itself as rich as the poems by Dylan Thomas or Robert Frost? Is it more or less imaginative? What is the difference between what Bronowski is doing and what the two poets are doing?

Landscape, History, and the Pueblo Imagination

LESLIE MARMON SILKO

From a High Arid Plateau in New Mexico

You see that after a thing is dead, it dries up. It might take weeks or years, but eventually if you touch the thing, it crumbles under your fingers. It goes back to dust. The soul of the thing has long since departed. With the plants and wild game the soul may have already been borne back into bones and blood or thick green stalk and leaves. Nothing is wasted. What cannot be eaten by people or in some way used must then be left where other living creatures may benefit. What domestic animals or wild scavengers can't eat will be fed to the plants. The plants feed on the dust of these few remains.

The ancient Pueblo people buried the dead in vacant rooms or partially collapsed rooms adjacent to the main living quarters. Sand and clay used to construct the roof make layers many inches deep once the roof has collapsed. The layers of sand and clay make for easy gravedigging. The vacant room fills with cast-off objects and debris. When a vacant room has filled deep enough, a shallow but adequate grave can be scooped in a far corner. Archaeologists have remarked over formal burials complete with elaborate funerary objects excavated in trash middens of abandoned rooms. But the rocks and adobe mortar of collapsed walls were valued by the ancient people. Because each rock had been carefully selected for size and shape, then chiseled to an even face. Even the pink clay adobe melting with each rainstorm had to be prayed over, then dug and carried some distance. Corn cobs and husks, the rinds and stalks and animal bones were not regarded by the ancient people as filth or garbage. The remains were merely resting at a midpoint in their journey back to dust. Human remains are not so different. They should rest with the bones and rinds where they all may benefit living creatures—small rodents and insects—until their return is completed. The remains of things—animals and plants, the clay and the stones—were treated with respect. Because for the ancient people all these things had spirit and being.

The antelope merely consents to return home with the hunter. All phases of the hunt are conducted with love. The love the hunter and the people have for the Antelope People. And the love of the antelope who agree to give up their meat and blood so that human beings will not starve. Waste of meat or even the thoughtless handling of bones cooked bare will offend the antelope spirits. Next year the hunters will vainly search the dry plains for antelope. Thus it is necessary to return carefully the bones and hair, and the stalks and leaves to the earth who first created them. The spirits remain close by. They do not leave us.

The dead become dust, and in this becoming they are once more joined with the Mother. The ancient Pueblo people called the earth the Mother Creator of all things in this world. Her sister, the Corn Mother, occasionally merges with her because all succulent green life rises out of the depths of the earth.

Rocks and clay are part of the Mother. They emerge in various forms, but at some time before, they were smaller particles or great boulders. At a later time they may again become what they once were. Dust.

A rock shares this fate with us and with animals and plants as well. A rock has being or spirit, although we may not understand it. The spirit may differ from the spirit we know in animals or plants or in ourselves. In the end we all originate from the depths of the earth. Perhaps this is how all beings share in the spirit of the Creator. We do not know.

From the Emergence Place

Pueblo potters, the creators of petroglyphs and oral narratives, never conceived of removing themselves from the earth and sky. So long as the human consciousness remains *within* the hills, canyons, cliffs, and the plants, clouds, and sky, the term *landscape*, as it has entered the English language, is misleading. "A portion of territory the eye can comprehend in a single view" does not correctly describe the relationship between the human being and his or her surroundings. This assumes the viewer is somehow *outside* or *separate from* the territory he or she surveys. Viewers are as much a part of the landscape as the boulders they stand on. There is no high mesa edge or mountain peak where one can stand and not immediately be part of all that surrounds. Human identity is linked with all the elements of Creation through the clan: you might belong to the Sun Clan or the Lizard Clan or the Corn Clan or the Clay Clan.* Standing deep within the natural world, the ancient Pueblo understood the thing as it was—the squash blossom, grasshopper, or rabbit itself could never be created by the human hand. Ancient Pueblos took the modest view that the thing itself (the landscape) could not be improved upon. The ancients did not presume to tamper with what had already been created. Thus *realism,* as we now recognize it in painting and sculpture, did not catch the imaginations of Pueblo people until recently.

The squash blossom itself is *one thing*: itself. So the ancient Pueblo potter abstracted what she saw to be the key elements of the squash blossom—the four symmetrical petals, with four symmetrical stamens in the center. These key elements, while suggesting the squash flower, also link it with the four cardinal directions. By representing only its intrinsic form, the squash flower is released from a limited meaning or restricted identity. Even in the most sophisticated abstract form, a squash flower or a cloud or a lightning bolt became intricately connected with a complex system of relationships which the ancient Pueblo people maintained with each other, and with the populous natural world they lived within. A bolt of lightning is itself, but at the same time it may mean much more. It may be a messenger of good fortune when summer rains are needed. It may deliver death, perhaps the result of manipulations by the Gunnadeyahs, destructive necromancers. Lightning may strike down an evil-doer. Or lightning may strike a person of good will. If the person survives, lightning endows him or her with heightened power.

Pictographs and petroglyphs of constellations or elk or antelope draw their magic in part from the process wherein the focus of all prayer and concentration is upon the thing itself, which, in its turn, guides the hunter's hand. Connection with the spirit dimensions requires a figure or form which is all-inclusive. A "lifelike" rendering of an elk is too restrictive. Only the elk *is* itself. A *realistic* rendering of an elk would be only one particular elk anyway. The purpose of the hunt rituals and magic is to make contact with *all* the spirits of the Elk.

The land, the sky, and all that is within them—the landscape—includes human beings. Interrelationships in the Pueblo landscape are complex and fragile. The unpredictability of the weather, the aridity and harshness of much of the terrain in the high plateau country explain in large part the relentless attention the ancient Pueblo people gave the sky and the earth around them. Survival depended upon harmony and cooperation not only among human beings, but among all things—the animate and the less animate, since rocks and mountains were known to move, to travel occasionally.

The ancient Pueblos believed the Earth and the Sky were sisters (or sister and brother in the post-Christian version). As long as good family relations

*Clan—A social unit composed of families sharing common ancestors who trace their lineage back to the Emergence where their ancestors allied themselves with certain plants or animals or elements (Silko).

are maintained, then the Sky will continue to bless her sister, the Earth, with rain, and the Earth's children will continue to survive. But the old stories recall incidents in which troublesome spirits or beings threaten the earth. In one story, a malicious ka'tsina, called the Gambler, seizes the Shiwana, or Rainclouds, the Sun's beloved children.* The Shiwana are snared in magical power late one afternoon on a high mountain top. The Gambler takes the Rainclouds to his mountain stronghold where he locks them in the north room of his house. What was his idea? The Shiwana were beyond value. They brought life to all things on earth. The Gambler wanted a big stake to wager in his games of chance. But such greed, even on the part of only one being, had the effect of threatening the survival of all life on earth. Sun Youth, aided by old Grandmother Spider, outsmarts the Gambler and the rigged game, and the Rainclouds are set free. The drought ends, and once more life thrives on earth.

Through the Stories We Hear Who We Are

All summer the people watch the west horizon, scanning the sky from south to north for rain clouds. Corn must have moisture at the time the tassels form. Otherwise pollination will be incomplete, and the ears will be stunted and shriveled. An inadequate harvest may bring disaster. Stories told at Hopi, Zuni, and at Acoma and Laguna describe drought and starvation as recently as 1900. Precipitation in west-central New Mexico averages fourteen inches annually. The western pueblos are located at altitudes over 5,600 feet above sea level, where winter temperatures at night fall below freezing. Yet evidence of their presence in the high desert plateau country goes back ten thousand years. The ancient Pueblo people not only survived in this environment, but many years they thrived. In A.D. 1100 the people at Chaco Canyon had built cities with apartment buildings of stone five stories high. Their sophistication as skywatchers was surpassed only by Mayan and Inca astronomers. Yet this vast complex of knowledge and belief, amassed for thousands of years, was never recorded in writing.

Instead, the ancient Pueblo people depended upon collective memory through successive generations to maintain and transmit an entire culture, a world view complete with proven strategies for survival. The oral narrative, or "story," became the medium in which the complex of Pueblo knowledge and belief was maintained. Whatever the event or the subject, the ancient people perceived the world and themselves within that world as part of an ancient continuous story composed of innumerable bundles of other stories.

The ancient Pueblo vision of the world was inclusive. The impulse was to leave nothing out. Pueblo oral tradition necessarily embraced all levels of human experience. Otherwise, the collective knowledge and beliefs comprising ancient Pueblo culture would have been incomplete. Thus stories about

*Ka'tsina—Ka'tsinas are spirit beings who roam the earth and who inhabit kachina masks worn in Pueblo ceremonial dances (Silko).

the Creation and Emergence of human beings and animals into this World continue to be retold each year for four days and four nights during the winter solstice. The "humma-hah" stories related events from the time long ago when human beings were still able to communicate with animals and other living things. But, beyond these two preceding categories, the Pueblo oral tradition knew no boundaries. Accounts of the appearance of the first Europeans in Pueblo country or of the tragic encounters between Pueblo people and Apache raiders were no more and no less important than stories about the biggest mule deer ever taken or adulterous couples surprised in cornfields and chicken coops. Whatever happened, the ancient people instinctively sorted events and details into a loose narrative structure. Everything became a story.

Traditionally everyone, from the youngest child to the oldest person, was expected to listen and to be able to recall or tell a portion, if only a small detail, from a narrative account or story. Thus the remembering and retelling were a communal process. Even if a key figure, an elder who knew much more than others, were to die unexpectedly, the system would remain intact. Through the efforts of a great many people, the community was able to piece together valuable accounts and crucial information that might otherwise have died with an individual.

Communal storytelling was a self-correcting process in which listeners were encouraged to speak up if they noted an important fact or detail omitted. The people were happy to listen to two or three different versions of the same event or the same humma-hah story. Even conflicting versions of an incident were welcomed for the entertainment they provided. Defenders of each version might joke and tease one another, but seldom were there any direct confrontations. Implicit in the Pueblo oral tradition was the awareness that loyalties, grudges, and kinship must always influence the narrator's choices as she emphasizes to listeners this is the way *she* has always heard the story told. The ancient Pueblo people sought a communal truth, not an absolute. For them this truth lived somewhere within the web of differing versions, disputes over minor points, outright contradictions tangling with old feuds and village rivalries.

A dinner-table conversation, recalling a deer hunt forty years ago when the largest mule deer ever was taken, inevitably stimulates similar memories in listeners. But hunting stories were not merely after-dinner entertainment. These accounts contained information of critical importance about behavior and migration patterns of mule deer. Hunting stories carefully described key landmarks and locations of fresh water. Thus a deer-hunt story might also serve as a "map." Lost travelers, and lost piñon-nut gatherers, have been saved by sighting a rock formation they recognize only because they once heard a hunting story describing this rock formation.

The importance of cliff formations and water holes does not end with hunting stories. As offspring of the Mother Earth, the ancient Pueblo people could not conceive of themselves within a specific landscape. Location, or "place," nearly always plays a central role in the Pueblo oral narratives. Indeed, stories are most frequently recalled as people are passing by a specific geographical feature or the exact place where a story takes place. The precise date of the incident often is less important than the place or location of the happening. "Long, long ago," "a long time ago," "not too long ago," and "recently" are usually how stories are classified in terms of time. But the places where the stories occur are precisely located, and prominent geographical details recalled, even if the landscape is well-known to listeners. Often because the turning point in the narrative involved a peculiarity or special quality of a rock or tree or plant found only at that place. Thus, in the case of many of the Pueblo narratives, it is impossible to determine which came first: the incident or the geographical feature which begs to be brought alive in a story that features some unusual aspect of this location.

There is a giant sandstone boulder about a mile north of Old Laguna, on the road to Paguate. It is ten feet tall and twenty feet in circumference. When I was a child, and we would pass this boulder driving to Paguate village, someone usually made reference to the story about Kochininako, Yellow Woman, and the Estrucuyo, a monstrous giant who nearly ate her. The Twin Hero Brothers saved Kochininako, who had been out hunting rabbits to take home to feed her mother and sisters. The Hero Brothers had heard her cries just in time. The Estrucuyo had cornered her in a cave too small to fit its monstrous head. Kochininako had already thrown to the Estrucuyo all her rabbits, as well as her moccasins and most of her clothing. Still the creature had not been satisfied. After killing the Estrucuyo with their bows and arrows, the Twin Hero Brothers slit open the Estrucuyo and cut out its heart. They threw the heart as far as they could. The monster's heart landed there, beside the old trail to Paguate village, where the sandstone boulder rests now.

It may be argued that the existence of the boulder precipitated the creation of a story to explain it. But sandstone boulders and sandstone formations of strange shapes abound in the Laguna Pueblo area. Yet most of them do not have stories. Often the crucial element in a narrative is the terrain—some specific detail of the setting.

A high dark mesa rises dramatically from a grassy plain fifteen miles southeast of Laguna, in an area known as Swanee. On the grassy plain one hundred and forty years ago, my great-grandmother's uncle and his brother-in-law were grazing their herd of sheep. Because visibility on the plain extends for over twenty miles, it wasn't until the two sheepherders came near the high dark mesa that the Apaches were able to stalk them. Using the mesa to obscure their approach, the raiders swept around from both ends of the mesa. My great-grandmother's relatives were killed, and the herd lost. The high dark mesa played a critical role: the mesa had compromised the safety which the openness of the plains had seemed to assure. Pueblo and Apache alike relied upon the terrain, the very earth herself, to give them protection and aid. Human activities or needs were maneuvered to fit the existing surroundings and conditions. I imagine the last afternoon of my distant ancestors as warm and sunny for late September. They might have been traveling slowly, bringing the sheep closer to Laguna in preparation for the approach of colder weather. The grass was tall and only beginning to change from green to a yellow which matched the late-afternoon sun shining off it. There might have been comfort in the warmth and the sight of the sheep fattening on good pasture which lulled my ancestors into their fatal inattention. They might have had a rifle whereas the Apaches had only bows and arrows. But there would have been four or five Apache raiders, and the surprise attack would have canceled any advantage the rifles gave them.

Survival in any landscape comes down to making the best use of all available resources. On that particular September afternoon, the raiders made better use of the Swanee terrain than my poor ancestors did. Thus the high dark mesa and the story of the two lost Laguna herders became inextricably linked. The memory of them and their story resides in part with the high black mesa. For as long as the mesa stands, people within the family and clan will be reminded of the story of that afternoon long ago. Thus the continuity and accuracy of the oral narratives are reinforced by the landscape—and the Pueblo interpretation of that landscape is *maintained.*

Reflections

Private Exploration

1. We grew up in the West. The Rocky Mountains formed a natural barrier from the Eastern part of the United States, while the great salt desert west of us provided more flatland and space than anyone could possibly perceive. Like the Pueblo people, we grew up conscious of our landscape. Raising trees or flowers or a vegetable garden took effort and care. Only scrub oak and sagebrush grew with a comfortable twisted ease. We learned not to take water, the earth, or the life it struggled to nourish, for granted. And we grew up hearing stories about those rugged mountains and about our ancestors who struggled to settle there generations before.

   Write about your own most familiar landscape. Were you raised in an apartment complex in a major city where factories and office buildings were part of your daily life? Were you raised in a suburb where shopping malls and fast food restaurants prevailed, or on a farm surrounded by acres of flatland? Are there any special landmarks that remain meaningful to you either because of the stories you grew up hearing about them or because of some personal associations? Are myths or legends connected with the landscape where you grew up? Consider how that landscape may have shaped your values.

2. Consider this passage:

   > We consult troops of specialists on the question of how to live when memory alone, heard with common sense and compassion, will tell us most of what we need to know.
   >
   > —ROBERT GRUDIN

Can you relate Grudin's position with Silko's description of the Pueblo people? How might communal story-telling support such an idea. Consider other historical examples where memory has taught us how to live.

Public Exploration

1. In class or in small groups, discuss Silko's statement that "The ancient people sought a communal truth, not an absolute." Does this differ from what we seek today or is it in fact quite similar? What does it say about values?
2. Take a moment to write down what you understand by the Pueblo people's vision of the world as "inclusive," then discuss this concept with your group. How does it compare or contrast to the vision of the world you have brought with you from your own cultural background? What is the importance of story-telling in relationship to this vision? How is a "vision" of the world related to values?

Private Reflection

Reread Silko's essay carefully, paying particular attention to the language. What key words are repeated throughout? What fresh insight into the Pueblo imagination might be gained by identifying key words? Or, as an alternative, consider the Pueblo people's use of metaphor. What affect might it have on us to think of the world in personal references? What feelings or attitudes are evoked? What shape does it give to human values?

• Psalm Concerning the Castle •

DENISE LEVERTOV

Let me be at the place of the castle.
Let the castle be within me.
Let it rise foursquare from the moat's ring.
Let the moat's waters reflect green plumage of ducks, let
the shells of swimming turtles break the surface or be
seen through the rippling depths.
Let horsemen be stationed at the rim of it, and a dog,
always alert on the brink of sleep.
Let the space under the first storey be dark, let the water
lap the stone posts, and vivid green slime glimmer upon
them; let a boat be kept there.
Let the caryatids* of the second storey be bears upheld on
beams that are dragons.
On the parapet of the central room, let there be four
archers, looking off to the four horizons. Within, let
the prince be at home, let him sit in deep thought, at
peace, all the windows open to the loggias.

*Caryatids: pillars carved in the form of human or animal figures.

Let the young queen sit above, in the cool air, her child in
her arms; let her look with joy at the great circle, the
pilgrim shadows, the work of the sun and the play of
the wind. Let her walk to and fro. Let the columns uphold
the roof, let the storeys uphold the columns, let there
be dark space below the lowest floor, let the castle rise
foursquare out of the moat, let the moat be a ring and
the water deep, let the guardians guard it, let there be
wide lands around it, let that country where it stands be
within me, let me be where it is.

• The Creation of the Inaudible •

PATTIANN ROGERS

Maybe no one can distinguish which voice
Is god's voice sounding in a summer dusk
Because he calls with the same rising frequency,
The same rasp and rattling rustle the cicadas use
As they cling to the high leaves in the glowing
Dust of the oaks.

His exclamations might blend so precisely with the final
Crises of the swallows settling before dark
That no one will ever be able to say with certainty,
"That last long cry winging over the rooftop
Came from god."

Breathy and low, the vibrations of his nightly
Incantations could easily be masked by the scarcely
Audible hush of the lakeline dealing with the rocky shore,
And when a thousand dry sheaths of rushes and thistles
Stiffen and shiver in an autumn wind, anyone can imagine
How quickly and irretrievably his whisper might be lost.

Someone faraway must be saying right now:
The only unique sound of his being
Is the spoken postulation of his unheard presence.

Reflections

Private Exploration

The following questions can apply to both of the preceding poems. You might want to consider them together; however, if you feel uncomfortable reading poetry, or if either Levertov's or Roger's poem seems especially difficult for you, or important to you, work with only one poem at a time.

a. Read with careful attention, looking up unfamiliar words and making marginal notations. Pay particular attention to the sensory details, the images that help you experience a poem.
b. Read each poem aloud, listening to the patterns and repetitions. Allow sound alone to involve you, speak to you. Then write freely, jotting down your reaction. Begin with feelings, negative or positive. Or begin with questions that puzzle you. Focus in on specific phrases and details in the poem that evoke your feelings.
c. Use your questions or feelings to open up the reading experience for you. Seek out relationships between your own personal values or experience and what the poem means for you at this point. Or consider how the poem connects for you to some other poem or work you've read in the past.
d. Reflect on what the poem expresses about the value of the imagination and how it might relate to your world or to your own values.

Public Exploration

Ask someone in your class or group to read aloud the poem you've decided to focus on (or both poems if you've attempted both).

a. Share the various responses you've written in your notebooks and let your initial reactions lead your discussion.
b. How do either of these poems deal with the imagination? How do they use metaphors to express spiritual values? *Why* do they use metaphors? Why not just write a brief prose essay and explain the point more clearly?
c. Consider how either poem, or both, might reflect ideas or values in contemporary culture.

Private Reflection

Reread your initial reactions and reflect how your ideas may have changed, if they have, after discussing the poems with your group. What now seems most important to you about either poem?

Portrait of A Drummer at the Edge of Magic

MICKEY HART
(with JAY STEVENS)

They were sisters killed by an epidemic, that's what the dealer said. It's Tibetan, really old.''

My friend pushed the little skull drum across the table, encouraging me to feel how easily the delicate crania fit the palm of my hand. I shook it tentatively.

Binnnggg . . . Gunnngggg.

My friend leaned closer. "It's called a *damaru.* It's a power drum; only the most enlightened lamas have one of these. I just had to buy it for you when I spotted it. I knew you could appreciate its power."

When I had first met my friend, in the cheerful early months of the Haight, everyone had agreed that he was one of the most mystically savvy people in a place that was teeming with mystically savvy people. His rap on the Big Picture was one of the great ones.

I set the skull drum on the table, feeling a kind of creepy fascination.

"Thanks, Bear."

Perhaps a week went by before I remembered the *damaru* and brought it out to play.

Binngggg . . . Gunnnngggg.

The sound was much bigger than I had expected. I examined the drum closely, noticing for the first time that the pieces of cloth that hung from it were decorated with exquisitely embroidered symbols. Someone had devoted a lot of time to the look of this drum.

Binngggg . . . Gunnnngggg.

That big sound again. Who'd have thought our skulls were so resonant?

Unfortunately, big sound seemed to be the extent of this *damaru*'s novelty; rhythmically it was quite boring. I played it for ten or fifteen more minutes before putting it away. It was fun to look at and would be fun to tell stories about, but I never expected to play it again. I set it back on a shelf and then went and threw up.

I had no reason to associate my nausea with the *damaru.* But I soon began bumping into things, falling down when I shouldn't have, injuring myself in minor but annoying ways; it gradually felt as if everything in my life was starting to unravel. It was only after several weeks of such uncharacteristic misfortune that I suddenly remembered the odd little Tibetan drum that Bear had given me. *It's a power drum!* And I remembered my friend's fondness for mystical jokes.

I tried playing the drum again but felt so awful that I telephoned psychologist Stanley Krippner and asked him to examine it. Krippner agreed with me about the *damaru*'s big sound and the unpleasant physical side effects, but he parried my suggestion that he take the drum with him for further study. I wanted the thing out of my house. Finally, I called bandmate Phil Lesh, explained the situation, and suggested that he might find Bear's gift interesting.

Phil took the drum off my hands, but two weeks later, the phone rang. It was Phil. "Mickey! I want you to come over and get this drum right now. I don't want it here another minute."

We sat at his table, drinking coffee and speculating on how we might honorably rid ourselves of this perverse instrument. Suddenly Phil said, "Why don't we give it back to the Tibetans."

Both of us had read in a recent article in the *San Francisco Chronicle* that the Tibetan Buddhists had opened a center in Berkeley, and one of the head lamas, Tarthang Tulku, was in town for the opening ceremonies. We grabbed the *damaru*, jumped into the car, and drove as quickly as we could to Berkeley. A golden-robed attendant ushered us inside, smiling benignly as we babbled on about needing to see his holiness on a matter of some urgency involving a drum.

After a few minutes' consultation among the monks, we were ushered into a room at the end of which Tarthang Tulku, an elegant little man, was sitting in a chair; an attendant was whispering the nature of our business. I walked forward and handed the head lama our *damaru*. He seemed to marvel at how comfortably the delicate crania fit his palm.

"So you've come home at last," he said, looking at the drum. Then he turned to me.

"I hope you have been most careful, Mickey Hart. This is a drum of great, great power. It wakes the dead, you know."

Not long after this, I drove my car over a cliff. It snagged on a tree halfway down, saving my life, but not all my bones.

Over the years I've entertained many interpretations of the lama's warning, the most obvious being that it referred to my impending car accident, to my sudden glimpse of my own mortality—the real Edge. But, as someone once pointed out to me, you could also interpret it as a reference to the Grateful Dead, since it was shortly after this that we returned to the studio and, for the first time in years, spent months just playing together and exploring, an adventure that produced our *Blues for Allah* album.

Lately I've come to focus more on the "waking up" and less on the "dead." It seems to me now that what the lama was telling me was that by playing the *damaru* I might have accidentally brought something back to life, I might have unwittingly opened the door for the spirits, and that is always risky.

But what door, what spirits?

My image of myself during that period is as a sort of human antenna swinging in the breeze, constantly scanning for musical information, completely absorbed in the endless symphony that was always playing in my head, my synethesia intensified by the fact that I was only seconds away from my studio.

Sunsets were an endless variation on a kind of red-gold tone that sounded to me like the tones you get from Tibetan bowls. Sometimes the sunsets were fuzzy, with a lot of humming overtones, and sometimes they had the clarity and serenity of a single ringing tone, very powerful, with a lot of body, lasting a whole orchestral movement. Whenever the rhythmic gurgling of the pump started, I'd hear my grandfather singing "Froggy Went a-Courtin'." Rain on the roof of the Barn became millions of soldiers on the march; it seemed to me that swarms of faces lived in the rain's harmonics, GI Joe types, stopping for smokes, resting awhile, then moving on, always marching, like some mythical army, coming in waves, disappearing in waves.

Everybody at the ranch was an explorer of one sort or another; my territory happened to be sound. I decorated the gardens with sounding objects of metal, glass, and bamboo. I hung wind chimes and metal strips in all the trees. It looked like a strange planet of percussion. Anything that made sound I listened to. I stood in the woods for long periods of time, my ear to the trunk of a tree, listening to its inner voice as it creaked in the wind, trying to push the edges of my sound envelope. I realized that everything must be making sound; the process of photosynthesis must be producing vibrations, if only we had sensitive enough ears. I began hearing the sacred in the noise.

Toward the end of this period I began to crave fire. Perhaps this was Rolling Thunder's influence, but fire filled me with a sense of deep, peaceful power. I started building fires at night and chanting around them, playing bullroarers and gongs. There was something about the outdoors, the night sky, the crackling fire, and the particular voices of these two instruments that cried out to be combined. I didn't know much about ritual then; I was just making it up as I went along.

The bullroarer fascinated me. It's one of the most ancient instruments on the planet, basically a slotted piece of wood with a rope attached that is swung around the head in an arc emitting a sound that ranges—depending on the length of the rope and the shape of the wood—from a slow *whoooo* to a piercing shriek. Swing one over your head for ten or fifteen minutes and a globe of sound will form with you as the vortex. Whenever I did this I caught glimpses of animals and sometimes lost track of time altogether.

All this ended around the time of the *damaru.* Perhaps you've snapped awake in the middle of the night and found yourself sitting in the bed with your body on full alert, all the senses humming, but with nothing—no dream, no stranger rustling at the door—to account for your energized state. What I experienced was a little like that. Suddenly I snapped to attention, though there was nothing immediately apparent to account for my excitement, aside from my growing realization that I had been like a little kid playing with his father's tools, but playtime was over now; the work was about to begin. But what work?

One thing I can definitely date from the moment of that first *Binnngggg . . . Gunnngggg* is my awareness that I was living on a planet that was alive with odd and powerful instruments, many of them in my tradition as a percussionist. And though it was certainly true that no one I knew seemed interested in these instruments, particularly in their powers, that was no longer an excuse for me. It would be overstating things to say that what I felt was like a command; it was more like a hunger to collect and investigate as many of these instruments as I could find, as quickly as possible. Whenever I brought a new one into the Barn I tried to live with it for a while before playing it, making it welcome, quietly observing it. I didn't want any more unpleasant surprises.

This was mostly a private pursuit, though now that I had rejoined the band on stage, some of my experiments occasionally crossed over into my public life as a percussionist. I brought the *balafon* (an African marimba), the talking drum, and steel drums from the Caribbean on stage. I also played gongs, experimenting with all sorts of mallets, and grew very fond of the sound made when a hard rubber ball attached to the end of a chopstick was rubbed across the metal surface of the gong, creating a sound like the song of a humpbacked whale.

The two instruments that turned up most often in my onstage performances were the Beast and the Beam. The Beast—at least in its original form—was a circular stand on which I hung several large bass drums I played standing up, using large mallets. I still use a smaller version of this original conception in concert. The largest of the drums, which I call "home plate," produces the lowest drum sound I can make.

The Beam is an expansion on the idea that underlies the Pythagorean monochord; it illustrates the ancient perception that the divine was contained in certain mathematical relationships that could be turned into sound—the music of the cosmos. My first Beam was made out of driftwood, but almost from the beginning it was an instrument that mutated, assuming numerous forms until it achieved its current manifestation as a ten-foot aluminum girder. Stretching the entire length of the girder are twelve piano strings tuned to very low pitches (30 Hz) in pure unisons, octaves, and fifths. The vibrations are picked up by a magnetic pickup that's a giant version of the one you find on an electric guitar, except this one is fed into a 170,000-watt sound system.

The result is one of the most powerfully ethereal instruments I have ever played. The Beam can be an instrument of war or an instrument of peace. It can purr like a Tibetan choir or it can explode like napalm. I pluck it with my fingers or strike it with a metal pipe. Sometimes I kick it with the heel of my foot. You can get rough with the Beam without hurting its feelings—and it can get rough with you. You can go lower and deeper with the Beam than with anything else I know, descending into vibrations that are perceived less by the ear than felt as shockwaves throughout the body. There is nothing like a long vibrating string.

I usually play these instruments during the Rhythm Devils solo, when the other members of the band disappear, and Billy and I go exploring for fifteen or twenty minutes. The backbeat is one kind of drum groove; it's the essential one for rock and roll, but percussion can live in other grooves, and Kreutzmann and I have gradually evolved in those directions. All a groove is, really, is a rhythmic cycle that gets repeated over and over; it's a foundation you can build on. The stronger the groove, the higher the building you can erect, and the more elaborate the ornamentation. Temperamentally, I'm an ornamenter and Kreutzmann a foundation man, though we have played together enough that we frequently play against temperament.

We start on our drum sets, locking in the groove, and once we've sunk to a deep enough level one of us will usually head for the part of the stage where the Beat and Beam await. I think of it as the zone—once in the zone the point is to go somewhere you've never gone before. That's what we try for; it's what keeps us fresh. It's something the Grateful Dead has always tried to build into its music, but it's become increasingly harder to nurture the more successful we've become. The tension between our obligations to our audience and our obligations to the bond of exploration that first drew us together, between entertainment and art, is one that waxes and wanes but never disappears. Sometimes we dance the dance better than other times; sometimes we stumble: it's all part of the ride.

Reflections

Personal Exploration

1. Every year millions of "Deadheads" flock to just one more Grateful Dead concert. Whether your favorite music is rock, country and western, classical, jazz, or heavy metal; whether your favorite instrument is the drum, the piccolo, or your own voice, the magic of music has touched your life. Perhaps you write your own songs. Perhaps you can recall the magic of the first live concert you attended or your own first recital. Or perhaps you've followed a favorite musician or group yourself. Write about the music in your life you've valued most.
2. Use the *Oxford English Dictionary* to look up the word "noise." List the major definitions, then react to your findings. How did looking up the word alter your initial reaction to this assignment?
3. Mickey Hart recalls "the powerful excitement" of sounds and rhythms he grew up with as a child that influenced his music.

   > Twenty feet from Grandfather's house a trolley kept up an insistent, clattering rhythm. It was the timekeeper, pulsing from every twenty to forty minutes, never diminishing or increasing, rain or shine, summer or winter, dawn or dusk. At the other extreme, humming and atonally melodic, was the constant surge of traffic up and down Nostrand Avenue, flowing into the big artery of Quentin Road. And layered on top was the drone of TVs and radios, exuberant sometimes angry bellowing, and the slap-slap-slap of gangs of kids running the territory. Loud, percussive, industrial urban sound.

   Like Hart, you may recall the extreme sounds of the place you grew up in or you may need to take some time now to become aware of the sounds around you. You choose. Recall as Hart does, the influential sounds of your childhood. Or take your notebook outside and sit for five minutes listening to the sounds you hear. Challenge yourself as Hart did to listen to the trunk of a tree. Afterwards, write a page or so about your experience and the insights gained.
3. Explore your initial impression of Hart's portrait. Begin with whatever surprised, delighted, or bothered you. Probe your emotional reactions as well as your thoughts as you reflect on his involvement with drums, noise, sound, music, magic.

Public Exploration

Why is it that millions of people still value The Grateful Dead? Divide into small groups and decide on some element of The Grateful Dead that you are particularly interested in. You might want to focus on the band's style and performance qualities, on the band's evolution as a group, on any one member of the band and his contribution, or on The Dead culture. Research several articles in the library. Keep carefully documented notes on where you found your information (see the Appendix for guidance). Once you've completed your research, rejoin your group and share your insights. Then, working together, write a brief collaborative paper on your findings.

Private Reflection

What do you make of this sentence:

> Lately I've come to focus more on the 'waking up' and less on the 'dead.'

Reread Hart's portrait carefully and jot down words and phrases or even whole paragraphs that convince you that he is concentrating on waking up. What is the value of this point of concentration?

The Beginning

SHIRLEY ANN GRAU

In the beginning there was just my mother and me.

"You are," my mother would say, "the queen of the world, the jewel of the lotus, the pearl without price, my secret treasure."

She whispered words like that, singsonging them in her soft high voice that had a little tiny crackle in it like a scratched record, to comfort me when I was a baby. Her light high whisper threaded through all my days, linking them tightly together, from the day of my birth, from that first moment when I slid from her body to lie in the softness of her bed, the same bed she slept in now. The one we took with us from place to place. And there were many different places. We were wanderers, my mother and I. I even had a wicker basket for my toys; I would pack and carry them myself.

It mattered little to me where we lived. I did not go outside. I did not go for walks, nor play on park swings. On the one day my mother was home, on Sunday, we worked together, all the while she sang her murmured song to me. Secret treasure. Lotus flower. And in her murmuring way she told me all she knew about my father, a Hindu from Calcutta, a salesman of Worthington pumps. Of all the many men my mother had known, he was the only one she had loved. She told me about his thin face and his large eyes black as oil, and his skin that was only slightly lighter than her own.

"You have his eyes and his skin," she said as, after my bath, she rubbed me with oil. (It was baby oil, its vanilla scent soon lost in her heavier perfume.) "And you have his hair," she said, combing in more oil.

And there is, to be sure, a certain look of India about me. Even now, in the grown woman.

"You are a little queen," my mother would say, turning me around and around. "You are exquisite, a princess of all the world. You must have a lovely new dress."

And so I would. She made all my clothes, made and designed. Summer dresses of handkerchief linen and soft smooth voile, winter dresses of dark rich velvets, and monk's-cloth coats so heavily smocked across the shoulders they were almost waterproof.

Of course we couldn't afford to buy fabrics like that, not in those days. My mother worked as a stock girl for Lambert Brothers Department Store. She had worked there for years, even before I was born. Ever since she'd come out of the country. (That was the way she put it, as if it were the bottom of a well or a deep hole.) And Lambert Brothers provided our material, quite a lot of it over the years. It all began on a city bus when my mother met a clerk from the Perfection Cloth Shoppe. They began talking, casually at first and then with purpose. My mother exchanged a bottle of perfume or a box of dusting powder or some Lancôme lipsticks from Lambert Brothers for small lengths of expensive material from the Perfection Cloth Shoppe.

My mother never told me how she smuggled the cosmetics out of the store. I suppose she'd been there so long and so faithfully that they half-trusted her. She did tell me how she and her friend robbed the Perfection Cloth Shoppe—a simple plan that worked for years.

My mother's friend collected the fabrics over a period of weeks, hiding them among the hundreds of stacked bolts. When she saw her chance, she bundled the pieces tightly and dropped them in a box of trash, making a small red check on the outside. My mother had only to pass along the service drive at the back of the building, look for the mark, remove the package. That evening we spread out the material on our kitchen table (the only table we had) and admired it together. Only once did something go wrong. Once the trash was collected an hour earlier than usual and my beautiful dress went to the city incinerator. My mother and I managed to laugh about that.

During the early years, during the long dull hours checking stock in dusty rooms, my mother began planning a business of her own, as dressmaker. My stolen clothes were the beginning. I was her model, the body on which her work came to life, the living sketchbook. Too small to see above the knees of adults, but perfectly quiet and perfectly composed, I displayed her clothes. My mother did not need to teach me how to walk or to act. Remember your father is an Indian prince and you are his only daughter, she would say to me. And so we made our rounds, peddling our wares, much like my father and his Worthington pumps. If he had traveled farther, half a world, our merchandise was far more beautiful. My mother and I went to talent shows and beauty contests, to church services and choir rehearsals. Wherever ladies gathered and the admission was free, there we were. My mother sold her clothes, as it were, from off my back.

"We are selling very well in the Afro-American community," my mother would say. "Soon I will open a small showroom. The walls will be painted white and the only thing on them will be pictures of you. On every wall, the entire way around."

And eventually she did just that. I remember it very clearly, the white room, quite bare and businesslike and lined with pictures of me. They were color photographs, very expensive for a woman just starting in business, but they showed the details of the clothes beautifully. My face, I remember, was rather blurred, but the light always seemed to catch the smooth line of my long dark hair. When I modeled for the customers (seated in creaking folding chairs and reeking with conflicting perfumes), my hair was always swept forward over one shoulder. My mother ironed it carefully in the dressing room at the very last moment. I remember the glare of the naked light bulbs around the mirror and the smell of singeing as my mother pressed my hair on her ironing board.

I don't remember saying a single word at any time. I have since noticed that people usually speak to a child, but no one spoke to me. Perhaps they did not think I was quite real.

Twice a month, in the evenings, my mother did her books. For years these were my favorite times. I sat, in my nightgown (always ankle length, always with a drawn-lace yoke), in the corner of the sofa, its red velvet worn and prickling on the sides of my arms, and watched my mother with her check-books and her account books and her order books. I watched her pencil picking away at the pages, flicking, stabbing, moving. She was a very good bookkeeper. In different circumstances I suppose she would have gone to college and earned a CPA to put behind her name. But she didn't. She just remained somebody who was very quick with numbers. And there was another strange thing about her, though I didn't notice it until many years later. She was so good with figures, she spoke so very well in soft tones as soothing as a cough lozenge—but she could hardly read at all. She wasn't illiterate, but she read street signs and phone books, business forms and contracts all the same way: carefully, taking a very long time, sounding out the words. As a child, I thought that muttering was the way everyone read. (The nuns at school soon corrected me.) Eventually I just fell asleep on the old sofa with that comforting whispering lullaby in my ears.

When my mother picked me up to carry me to bed, which was next to hers, she would always be smiling. "The figures dance so beautifully for me, my little love. The Afro-American community is contributing devotedly to the treasure of the mahal. The daughters saw her and blessed her, also the queens and the concubines." (Someone had once read the Bible to my mother; bits and pieces kept appearing in her talk.)

In the morning when I woke, she was gone. At first, when I was very small, when I first remember things, like wet diapers and throwing up in my bed, there was someone who stayed with me, an old old woman who sat in a rocker all day long and listened to the radio. Her name was Miss Beauty. I don't remember her ever feeding me, but I suppose she must have. She died one day, in her rocking chair. I thought she was asleep so I went on playing with my doll. My cat—we kept one to kill the mice that played all over the old house—jumped on Miss Beauty's lap, then jumped down again quickly, coming to sit next to me in the window. "You heard her snore," I whispered to the cat, very severely. "Don't wake her, she won't like that at all." At the usual time I heard my mother's key in the lock and the funny little nine-note tune she whistled every evening just inside the door. (It was from *Lucia di Lammermoor,** I discovered years later in a college music appreciation class, and I rose in my seat with the impact of memory.) I put my finger to my lips and pointed silently to Miss Beauty. My mother hesitated, eyes flicking between us, nose wrinkling like an animal. Without moving, she bent forward toward Miss Beauty. Then quickly, so quickly, with a clatter of feet across the linoleum floor, she snatched me up and ran outside.

After Miss Beauty's death, there was no one. I stayed by myself. We moved to a nicer neighborhood, a street with trees and double cottages behind small front gardens. (The landlord had paved over our garden with pale green cement.) I never felt afraid. If I got lonely, I could sit in the big front window and watch the neighborhood children play in the street. I never joined them.

During these years I do not remember my mother having any friends. I remember only one visitor. He was short and wore a plaid coat and a wide-brimmed hat, and the ring on his left hand flashed colored lights. He was waiting for my mother when she came home after work. They talked briefly, standing at the curb next to his big white car, then the two of them came into the house. He smiled at me, saying, "Well, well, now, is that your little girl? Hello there, little girl." My mother went straight to the red sofa, reached inside the top cushion. When she turned around, there was a gun in her hand. She just stood there, her long fingers wrapped around that small dull-blue gun, both hands holding it firm and steady. The man stopped smiling and backed out the door. He never said another word. Nor did my mother.

We moved again then, away from the house with the front yard of green-tinted cement. This time we packed and moved quickly, far away across town. My mother rented a truck and she hired two men to load it for us. She hurried them too. Our beds, the red velvet sofa, the two folding bridge chairs, the refrigerator and the gas stove, the enamel-topped kitchen table, the armoire with the cracked mirrored doors—they fitted neatly into the truck along with the boxes of clothes and dishes and my mother's sewing machine, which was the only new thing we owned.

"Hurry," my mother said, carrying some of the smaller things herself, "we haven't got all day. I am paying you to be quick."

Grumbling and complaining, the men finished the loading and took their money and stood on the sidewalk to watch us leave.

"Get in," my mother said to me. "Be quick."

We drove down highways lined with withered brown palm trees, past endless intersections where traffic lights stabbed out their signals like lighthouses. We waited, part of an impatient horn-blowing crowd, while canal bridges opened to let gravel-filled barges glide past through oily water.

And my mother said nothing at all. When I could wait no longer, when the silence between us seemed more dangerous and frightening than any nightmare, I asked, "Why are we running away?"

**Lucia di Lammermoor:* tragic opera (1835) by Gaetano Donizetti.

"To be safe," she said.

"Is it far?"

"It is far enough to be safe," she said.

When we finally reached the place where we would live, she hired two more neighborhood men to take our things up the stairs. She had moved without leaving a trace behind.

I guessed it had something to do with her visitor, but I did not worry. In all the stories my mother had told me, there were always threats and pursuits and enemies to be avoided. It was the way a princess lived. And my mother was always there, to bring me to safety at last.

When we sat in our new home, in the clutter of boxes and furniture, when we were safely inside, the door locked behind us, my mother smiled at me, a great slow smile that showed square strong teeth in the smooth darkness of her face. "My hidden princess," she said, "my lotus flower . . ."

The accustomed endearments tumbled from her lips, the expected exotic song of love and praise. I, young as I was, noted the change. For the past few days, and on the drive across town, she had spoken rarely, and then only in the crisp blunt language of everyday.

Now, by the smooth soft flow of her words, I knew that we were indeed safe. We had passed through a series of lodgings—I think I remember them all, even the one where I was born, the one with a chinaberry tree outside the window—but we had finally gained our castle, the one we had been searching for. There was even a turret, to command the approaches and to defend against enemies.

The house stood on a corner. Its old clapboard walls rose directly from the sidewalk through two stories of flaking gray paint to a roof decorated with fancy wooden scallops; in the dark spaces under the eaves generations of pigeons nested and fluttered. At the second-floor corner, jutting over the sidewalk, was a small turret or tower, capped with a high pointed roof like a clown's hat.

Inside the tower was a hinged seat of varnished wood entirely covered by scratch drawings: flowers and initials and hearts, dancing stick figures and even a face or two. Here we stored odd bits of things: old shoes, an umbrella with a broken rib, a doll in a pink and blue gingham dress, an Easter bunny of purple and yellow plush, a black patent purse. Roaches lived there too; they ate the stuffing from the doll and the feather from her hat, and they ate spots of fur from the Easter bunny so that it looked burned. I thought they had also nibbled the edge of the patent leather purse, but my mother said no, it was just use-worn.

Day after day, I sat on top that jumble of things, above the secret workings of insects, and I watched through the windows, three panes of glass on the three sides of my tower, which my mother washed every month, so that I might see clearly.

Most of the floor below us was occupied by a drugstore, a small dark place that smelled of disinfectant and sugar candy, of brown paper and cough medicine. On two of the other corners were small houses, one room wide, perched off the ground on low brick foundations and edged by foot-wide runners of grass. On the third corner, directly across from my window was Providence Manor, a home for the old. A tall iron fence enclosed an entire block of grass and trees and even occasional blooming flowers, a wilderness that stretched out of my sight. Just inside the fence was a gravel path where, on good days, the old people walked, some slowly on canes, some with arms flexing rapidly in a military march, some in chairs wheeled by nuns in black habits and white headdresses. They rotated past the spear points of the fence, every good day taking their quota of sun and exhaust-laden air. After dark, on rainy nights, the flashing sign in the drugstore window beat against those railings, broke and ran off down the shiny black street.

Downstairs too, directly below, in our small slice of the old house, were the two rooms that were my mother's workshop and showroom. On our front door—up two wooden steps from the uneven brick sidewalk—was a small neat sign: MODISTE. My mother had lettered that herself; she had always been very clever with her hands. It was the first real shop she had.

I spent my days either at my window or in my mother's workrooms. The rest of the house, the other two rooms, I don't remember at all. I was either a princess in my tower or a mannequin in my mother's clothes.

Not until years later did I realize that all the faces I saw were black. (To me they had no color, no color at all.) The people walking on the street, the old on their therapeutic rounds, the Sisters of the Holy Family, the drivers impatiently threading their way through the heavy street traffic, my mother, and her customers—they all wore black skin.

As did the children in school. Eventually I had to go to school. My mother did not send me when I was six, as the law said she must. For one extra year I dreamed and flaunted my beautiful dresses. I doubt that the authorities would have noticed had I not gone to school at all. I think it was my mother's new friend who finally persuaded her. For my mother at last had a friend, a good friend whose visits were regular and predictable. For him my mother bathed and did her hair and cooked specially and smiled when the doorbell rang.

My mother's friend was a tall, heavy man who came to church with us every Sunday and afterwards held my hand as I walked along the top of the low wall that bordered the churchyard. He owned a small cab company—he drove one himself—whose insignia was a lightning bolt across a bright blue circle. His name was David Clark, and he took me to school and picked me up every day of my first year.

I went to parochial school. Navy skirts and white blouses and black and white saddle oxfords, all of us. All of us, rows of little black raisins, waiting to be taught to read and to count and to love Lord Jesus. But I was the only one picked up by taxi every day at three o'clock. The children stared at me as I rode away, the Indian princess in her palanquin, the treasure of the mahal above Leconte's Drugstore.

On the first day of school my mother went with me. I remember very little about that day—I was nauseated with excitement, gripped with fear—but I remember the dress she wore. She had made it herself of course, just as she had made my school uniform; it was brown linen, a long-sleeved blouse and an eight-gore skirt. I saw the nuns' eyes flick over us in brief appraisal: We passed with honors. (I took it as my due. I wonder now how my mother felt.)

The school smelled of peanuts and garlic bologna. The floor of my classroom was spotted with puddles of slimy liquid. Oddly enough, the other children's panic quieted me. In the reek of their nervousness, my own stomach settled, and when the harried janitor arrived with a bucket of sawdust to sprinkle on the vomit, I helped him by pushing aside the desks.

That first day was the longest I have ever known. And the hottest. It was early September and the afternoon sun burned through the window shades to polish our faces with sweat—all except the teaching sister. Her face remained dry and dull as if coated with a film of dust.

I never grew used to the noise and rush of children leaving class. When the bell sounded, I always waited while the room emptied. Then, in a pause disturbed only by the soft sounds of the teacher gathering her papers, I walked slowly through the door, last and alone. Always alone, except for once, years later when I was at boarding school at St. Mary's, mine the only dark face in a sea of Irish skin. (The other girls simply ignored me, saw through me as if I were invisible or transparent.) By the time I had gathered my books and reached the door, their departing backs were far down the hall. But at St. Mary's I was not alone. My companion was a moonfaced child of my own age who had rheumatoid arthritis, took massive doses of cortisone, and moved with the slow painful dignity of an ancient woman. She died in our second year of high school. I, along with every other girl in the school, wrote a letter of condolence to her parents. Mine was never acknowledged.

But that was in the future, in the time when I was no longer a child, a good many years away.

For first grade, I had two skirts, made by my mother according to the uniform dress code of the parochial school system, and two blouses. Every second day, when I came home, I was expected to wash my blouse carefully, using the kitchen sink and a small scrubbing board that my mother kept underneath, propped against the pipes. I then hung it on the back porch inside the screen, where no bird could soil it. Every so often my mother was dissatisfied with its whiteness and she would wash it again in bleach. The next time I wore that blouse I was certain to have a rash across my neck and shoulders where the fabric rubbed my skin.

Later on, when my growing required new blouses (the skirts had deep hems to let down), my mother made them slightly different. She added small tucks down the front, two tiny rows on each side of the buttons. I noticed the nuns looking at me—they were very strict about uniforms in those days—and they must have written to my mother. My next blouses were perfectly plain. What the nuns couldn't know about were my slips. My mother made my slips too, and they had all the elaborate decorations that my blouses lacked. They were tucked, with drawn lace and wide bands of crochet at the shoulders, and a deep flounce of lace at the hem. Only one nun ever saw them and she wasn't really a nun. She was a novice: very young, shorter even than I was. She was cleaning the bathrooms and I, not noticing her, was fanning myself with my skirt against the heat. She stopped and fingered my slip. "What lovely work, what exquisite work." Then she looked shocked and ashamed—perhaps she had made a vow of silence—and she went hastily back to her pail and mop.

After the first year at school, I took the city bus home. The stop was at our corner. All I had to do was cross the street and open the door. Once inside, I rushed to bathe, to brush my hair, to put on the dresses that my mother would sell. Wearing her clothes and her dreams, I would move carefully among her customers, gracefully, as only a princess can.

The lotus blossom. The treasure of the mahal. In the women's faces I saw greed and covetousness. My mother's order books rustled busily. I myself drew spirit and sustenance from the flickering eyes and the fingers stretched out to touch. In the small crowded room, I had come into my castle and my kingdom.

And so I passed my childhood disguised to myself as a princess. I thrived, grew strong and resilient. When the kingdom at last fell and the castle was conquered, and I lost my crown and my birthright, when I stood naked and revealed as a young black female of illegitimate birth, it hardly mattered. By then the castle and the kingdom were within me and I carried them away.

Reflections

Private Exploration

1. Consider both the positive and negative effects the mother's words have on her daughter in Grau's story. What is the value of imagination in shaping an individual's life?
2. What's really going on here?

   I was either a princess in my tower or a mannequin in my mother's clothes.

3. Consider how the mother's voice and language contribute to the narrator's image of herself. Cite specific words and describe their effect on the narrator. How would it feel to hear such words spoken over and over again? What strengths might they impart to an individual? What concerns do you have as an outside observer?

Public Exploration:

In 1907 Maria Montessori envisioned special educational programs for children who had not yet reached school age in Italy. The program she imagined became a reality and even today thousands of children benefit from programs she initiated. By contrast, Hitler imagined creating the perfect race and six million Jews were systematically killed in order to fulfill his dream. Both examples serve to illustrate the power of imagination. As a group, consider how imagination has been used positively and constructively in our culture to enrich our lives, then reflect on examples where it has gotten out of control and become destructive. Is there any way to determine in advance the value of an imaginative vision?

Private Reflection

For many of us there may be a time in our lives when we become aware of how others see us. We're forced into confronting the image we've created of ourselves and the image we project on others. This awareness that others don't perceive us as we perceive ourselves usually comes as a surprise and seems both mysterious and illuminating. And then the question arises: Whose imagination helped shape the self-image I cling to and why? A teacher, a grandmother, an older brother? Tell your story from the moment you first became aware of others' perceptions of you, then explore your past to discover who and how that image was created. What did you think and feel when you discovered others saw you in a different light?

CONNECTIONS

Although your best writing will usually emerge from insights already under development in your reading notebook, here are some additional possibilities for exploring relationships between and among various works of literature.

1. In "The Imaginative Mind in Art," Jacob Bronowski writes: "The ability to conceive of things which are not present to the senses is crucial to the development of man." Use Bronowski's position to explore a connection between "How Wang Fo was Saved" (p. 256) and "The Beginning" (p. 291).
2. Consider how the following statement might illuminate a connection among Hampl's "Memory and Imagination" (p. 241), Silko's "Landscape, History and Imagination" (p. 276), and Le Guin's "What Americans are Afraid of Dragons" (p. 251).

   > In imagination we rehearse various possibilities of action in a given situation. We go through a process of imaginative trial and error, trying out different modes of behavior and working out their probable effects. When the situation arises in actual life, we are better prepared to act successfully.
   >
   > —LOUISE ROSENBLATT

3. According to author and scholar Vincent Ruggerio, studies have shown that most people are unimaginative not because they lack imagination, but because they are afraid to be ridiculed. Instead of taking risks, they tend to conform, and the urge to conform can paralyze thought. Many of the essays in this chapter touch on the importance of freedom and creativity. For example, Silko writes "The Pueblo oral tradition knew no boundaries," and Bronowski writes, "the ability to make images from absent things, and to use them to experiment with imaginary situations gives man a freedom which an animal does not have." In addition, Ursula Le Guin offers her own concept of freedom: "To be free, after all, is not to be undisciplined. . . . To discipline something [means] to train it—to encourage it to grow, and act, and be fruitful, whether it is a peach tree or a human mind."

   Reflect on the value of freedom and risk-taking as it relates to the creative process in such works as Hart's "Portrait of a Drummer at the Edge of Magic" (p. 285), Hampl's "Memory and Imagination" (p. 241), and Roger's "Creation of the Inaudible" (p. 284)—or to Joyce Carol Oates novella, *Theft* (p. 612).
4. In his essay, "Seven Wonders," physician Lewis Thomas offers this insight:

   > We are not like social insects. They have only one way of doing things and they will do it forever, coded for that way. We are coded differently, not just for binary choices, *go* or *no go*. We can go four ways at once depending on how the air feels: *go*, *no-go*, but also *maybe*, plus *what the hell let's give it a try*. We are in for one surprise after another if we keep at it and keep alive. We can build structures for human society never seen before, music never heard before.

   Develop an essay on your view of Thomas' hope for the future. What does it mean to you to "build structures for human society never seen before, thoughts never thought before, music never heard before"?

5. Write an essay focusing on the relationship of memory and imagination, drawing from writers in this chapter such as Hampl (p. 241), Silko (p. 276), or Hart (p. 285).
6. In a discussion of the importance of story-telling, physician and poet William Carlos Williams made the following comment:

    > Their story, yours, mine, it's what we carry with us on this trip we take, and we owe it to each other to respect our stories and learn from them.

    By contrast, others have argued that stories are not to be "learned from" at all, that they are morally neutral with no specific lessons or advice to follow. Some have said that all works of the imagination are like symphonies or paintings or dance: they move us by their aesthetic beauty, but we should not attempt to find profound meanings in them. Draw from your own experience in reading the works in this chapter to compose an essay on the question of whether we can or should learn anything at all from our readings of stories, poems, or plays.

CHAPTER 8

LOVE AND OTHER DIFFICULTIES

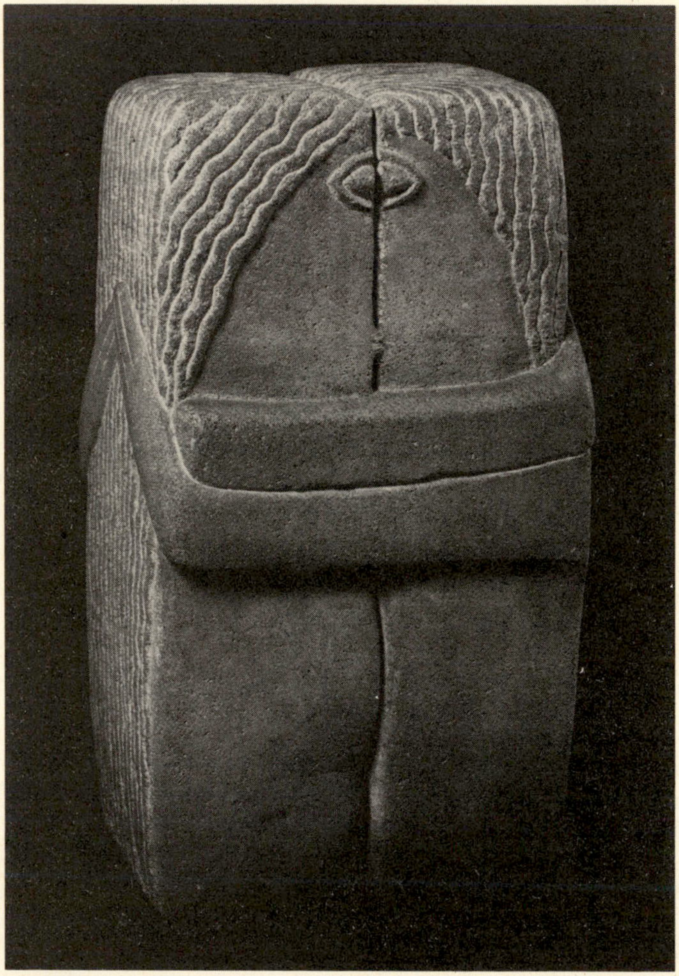

For one human being to love another: that is perhaps the most difficult of all our tasks . . .

—Rainer Maria Rilke

In 1896, Leonardo Gentelini wrote from Wyoming to a village newspaper in Trento, Italy. He needed a wife. Like many immigrants to America, he found himself eager to work and prosper, but he was lonely. Other young men had sent similar requests. Harsh winters in a new country made idealistic men practical before their time. The possibility of love or romance was something left behind in their crumbling villages. A woman who could clean and cook was all he expected.

So perhaps we can understand how Leonardo Gentelini felt seven months later when he received a letter from someone named Isabella Roselli who consented to be his wife. Inside he found a small sepia photograph wrapped in tissue. Leonardo could scarcely believe his good fortune. The delicate young woman who looked out at him turned practicality into dreaming, longing into love. Through a lonely winter he carried the photograph over his heart until the edges were creased and smudged. At night he propped her photo against the base of an oil lamp. He admired her wide intelligent eyes, her trim waist that he could easily encircle with his calloused hands. This would be his wife, a fragile girl with wisps of curls under a straw hat. When the train arrived the next spring, a squat, dull-faced child, scarcely fifteen and carrying a rag bundle tied with rope, stepped down to the platform. Eager to come to America and eager for marriage, Isabella Roselli too had her dreams. She had sent a photograph of an older sister. Perhaps her future husband would overlook the slight differences. Perhaps the long journey would transform her.

Leonardo Gentelini and Isabella Roselli did marry, June 4th, 1897. And although Leonardo never forgave the deception, he learned to make adjustments. He learned to be grateful in a cold winter for small kindnesses, to cope without love as he learned to cope with other difficulties. And Isabella? What did she feel living on for fifty more years with a hard man in a raw country?

Loneliness and longing, dreams and disillusionment texture all our lives. The emotions Leonardo and Isabella experienced a hundred years ago are the same emotions we struggle with today.

In the following chapter you will find essays, stories, and poems that express the complexities of love—from a young girl's infatuation with a pilot, and a father's love for his daughter, to a middle-aged couple's struggle with that ancient question—What exactly are we talking about when we talk about love? You may find more questions than answers. Is love still possible? Is it something we should fear and avoid, or is it the very source of our deepest values? We have taken the title of this chapter from poet Rainer Maria Rilke who tells us to "Live the questions now. Perhaps you will then gradually, without noticing it, live along some distant day into the answer."

The Unromantic Generation

BRUCE WEBER

Here is a contemporary love story.

Twenty-four-year-old Clark Wolfsberger, a native of St. Louis, and Kim Wright, twenty-five, who is from Chicago, live in Dallas. They've been going together since they met as students at Southern Methodist University three years ago. They are an attractive pair, trim and athletic, she dark and lissome, he broad-shouldered and square-jawed. They have jobs they took immediately after graduating—Clark works at Talent Sports International, a sports marketing and management company; Kim is an assistant account executive at Tracy-Locke, a large advertising agency—and they are in love.

"We're very compatible," she says.

"We don't need much time together to confirm our relationship," he says.

When they speak about the future, they hit the two-career family notes that are conventional now in the generation ahead of them. "At thirty, I'll probably be married and planning a family," says Kim. "I'll stay in advertising. I'll be a late parent."

"By thirty, I'll definitely be married; either that or water-skiing naked in Monaco," Clark says, and laughs. "No. I'll be married. Well-established in my line of work. Have the home, have the dog. Maybe not a kid yet, but eventually. I'm definitely in favor of kids."

In the month I spent last winter visiting several cities around the country, interviewing recent college graduates about marriage, relationships, modern romance, I heard a lot of this, life equations already written, doubt banished. I undertook the trip because of the impression so many of us have; that in one wavelike rush to business school and Wall Street, young Americans have succumbed to a culture of immediate gratification and gone deep-down elitist on us. I set out to test the image with an informal survey meant to take the emotional temperature of a generation, not far behind my own, that *seems* so cynical, so full of such "material" girls and boys.

The sixty or so people I interviewed, between the ages of twenty-two and twenty-six, were a diverse group. They spoke in distinct voices, testifying to a range of political and social views. Graduate students, lawyers, teachers, entertainers, business people, they are pursuing a variety of interests. What they have in common is that they graduated from college, are living in or around an urban center, and are heterosexual, mirrors of myself when I graduated from college in 1975. And yet as I moved from place to place, beginning with acquaintances of my friends and then randomly pursuing an expanding network of names and phone numbers, another quality emerged to the degree that I'd call it characteristic: they are planners. It was the one thing that surprised me, this looking ahead with certainty. They have priorities. I'd ask about love; they'd give me a graph.

This isn't how I remember it. Twelve years ago, who knew? I was three years away from my first full-time paycheck, six from anything resembling the job I have now. It was all sort of desultory and hopeful, a time of dabbling and waiting around for some event that would sprout a future. Frankly, I had it in mind that meeting a woman would do it.

My cultural prototype was Benjamin Braddock, the character played by Dustin Hoffman in Mike Nichols's 1967 film *The Graduate*, who, returning home after his college triumphs, finds the prospect of life after campus daunting in the extreme, and so plunges into inertia. His refrain "I'm just a little worried about my future," served me nicely as a sort of wryly understated mantra.

What hauls Benjamin from his torpor is love. Wisely or not, he responds to a force beyond logic and turns the world upside down for Elaine Robinson. And though in the end their future together is undetermined, the message of the movie is that love is meant to triumph, that its passion and promise, however naïve, are its strengths, and that if we are lucky it will seize us and transform our lives.

Today I'm still single and, chastened by that, I suppose, a little more rational about what to expect from love. Setting out on my trip, I felt as if I'd be plumbing a little of my past. But the people I spoke with reminded me more of the way I am now than the way I was then. I returned thinking that young people are older than they used to be, *The Graduate* is out of date, and for young people just out of college today, the belief that love is all you need no longer obtains.

"Kim's a great girl; I love her," Clark Wolfsberger says. "But she's very career-oriented. I am, too, and with our schedules the way they are, we haven't put any restrictions on each other. I think that's healthy."

"He might want to go back to St. Louis," Kim Wright says. "I want to go back to Chicago. If it works out, great. If not, that's fine, too. I can handle it either way."

They are not heartless, soulless, cold, or unimaginative. They *are* self-preoccupied, but that's a quality, it seems to me, for which youthful generations have always been known. What distinguishes this generation from mine, I think, is that they're aware of it. News-conscious, media-smart, they are sophisticated in a way I was not.

They have come of age, of course, at a time when American social traditions barely survive. Since 1975, there have been more than a million divorces annually, and it is well publicized that nearly half of all marriages now end in divorce. Yet the era of condoned casual promiscuity and sexual experimentation—itself once an undermining of the nation's social fabric—now seems to be drawing to a close with the ever-spreading plague of sexually transmitted disease.

The achievements of feminist activism—particularly the infusion of women into the work force—have altered the expectations that the sexes have for each other and themselves.

And finally, the new collage graduates have been weaned on scarifying forecasts of economic gloom. They feel housing problems already; according to *American Demographics* magazine, the proportion of young people living at home with their parents was higher in 1985 than in the last three censuses. They're aware, too, of predictions that however affluent they are themselves, they're probably better off than their children will be.

With all this in mind, today's graduates seem keenly aware that the future is bereft of conventional expectations, that what's ahead is more chaotic than mysterious. I've come to think it ironic that in a youth-minded culture such as ours, one that ostensibly grants greater freedom of choice to young people than it ever has before, those I spoke with seem largely restrained. Concerned with, if not consumed by, narrowing the options down, getting on track, they are aiming already at a distant comfort and security. I spoke, on my travels, with several college counselors and administrators, and they concur that the immediate concerns of today's graduates are more practical than those of their predecessors. "I talk to them about sex," says Gail Short Hanson, dean of students at George Washington University, in Washington. "I talk about careers. And marriage, with women, because of the balancing act they have to perform these days. But love? I can't remember the last conversation I had about love."

Career-minded, fiercely self-reliant, they responded to me, a single man with a good job, with an odd combination of comradeliness and respect. When the interviews were over, I fielded a lot of questions about what it's like to work at *The New York Times.* How did I get my job? Occasionally, someone would ask about my love life. Considering the subject of our discussions, I was surprised it happened so rarely. When it did, I told them I'd come reasonably close to marriage once, but it didn't work out. Nobody asked me why. Nobody asked if I was lonely.

Micah Materre, twenty-five, recently completed an internship at CBS News in Chicago and is looking for a job in broadcast journalism. Like many of the young people I talked to, she is farsighted in her romantic outlook: "I went out with a guy last fall. He had a good job as a stockbroker. He was nice to me. But then he started telling me about his family. And there were problems. And I thought, 'What happens if I fall in love and we get married? What then?' "

It may be a memory lapse, but I don't recall thinking about marriage much at all until I fell in love. I was twenty-nine; late, that's agreed. But the point is that for me (and for my generation as a whole, I believe, though you hate to make a statement like that), marriage loomed only as an outgrowth of happenstance; you met a person. Today's graduates, however, seem uneasy with that kind of serendipity. All of the married couples I spoke with are delighted to be married, but they do say their friends questioned their judgment, "I heard a lot of reasons why I shouldn't do it," one recent bride told me. "Finally, I just said to myself, 'I feel happier than I've ever felt. Why should I give this up just because I'm young?' "

Most of them too young to remember the assassination of *either* Kennedy, they are old enough to have romantic pasts, to have experienced the trauma of failure in love. What surprised me was how easily so many of them accepted it; it seems a little early to be resigned to the idea that things fall apart. In each interview, I asked about past involvements. Were you ever serious about anyone? Any marital close calls? And virtually everyone had a story. But I heard very little about heartbreak or lingering grief. Instead, with an almost uniform equanimity, they spoke of maturity gained, lessons learned. It isn't disillusionment exactly, and they *are* too young to be weary; rather, it sounds like determination.

Twenty-five-year-old Peter Mundy of San Francisco, for example, says that until six months ago he'd had a series of steady girlfriends. "I'm down on romance," he says. "There's too much pain, too much pressure. There are so many variables, and you can't tell until you're in the middle of it whether it'll be positive. It's only in retrospect that you can see how things went wrong. In the meantime, you end up neglecting other things."

The prevalent notion is that chemistry is untrustworthy; partners need to be up to snuff according to pretty rigorous standards. Ellen Lubin, twenty-six, of Los Angeles, for example, has just gotten engaged to the man she has been living with for two years. When she met him, she says: "I wasn't that attracted to him right away. But there were things about him that made me say 'This is what I want in a man.' He's bright. He's a go-getter. He was making tons of money at the age of twenty-five. He's well-connected. He was like my mentor in coming to deal with life in the city."

At the end of *The Graduate*, Benjamin Braddock kidnaps his lady love at the altar, an instant after she has sealed her vows to someone else, and they manage to make their escape because Benjamin bolts the church door from the outside with a cross. That was the 1960s, vehement times. When I graduated, we were less obstreperous. Sacraments we could take or leave. And marriage wasn't much of an issue. If we put it off, it wasn't for the sake of symbolism so much as that it didn't seem necessary. In the last few years, I've been to a number of weddings among my contemporaries, people in their thirties, and that impression of us is still with me. What we did was drift toward marriage, arriving at it eventually, and with some surprise. Some of us are still drifting.

Today's graduates have forged a new attitude entirely. In spite of the high divorce rate, many of those I spoke with have marriage in mind. Overwhelmingly, they see it as not only desirable, but inevitable. Because of the odds, they approach it with wariness and pragmatism. More cautious than their parents (for American men in 1985, the median age at the time of their first marriage was 25.5, the highest since the turn of the century; it was 23.3 for women, a record), they are methodical in comparison with me.

Perhaps that explains why I find the way they speak about marriage so unromantic. Men and women tend to couch their views in different terms, but they seem to share the perception that marriage is necessarily restricting. Nonetheless they trust in its rewards, whatever they are. Overall, it doesn't represent the kind of commitment that seems viable without adequate preparation.

"I've been dating someone for a year and a half," says Tom Grossman, a twenty-four-year-old graduate of the University of Texas. "We don't talk about marriage, and frankly I don't think it'll occur." Currently area sales manager in San Antonio for the John H. Harland Company, a check-printing concern, Grossman says he has professional success in mind first. "I want to be really well-off financially, and I don't want that struggle to interfere with the marriage. There are too many other stress factors involved. I want to be able to enjoy myself right away. And I never want to look back and think that if I hadn't gotten married, I could have accomplished more."

Many young women say they responded with some alarm to last year's *Newsweek* report on the controversial demographic study conducted at Harvard, which concluded that once past thirty, a woman faces rapidly dwindling chances of marrying. At a time when women graduates often feel it incumbent on them to pursue careers, they worry that the possibility of "having it all" is, in fact, remote.

Janie Russell, twenty-five, graduated from the University of North Carolina in 1983, left a serious boyfriend behind, and moved to Los Angeles to pursue a career in the film industry. Working now as a director of production services at New Visions Inc., like many other young women she believes the independence fostered by a career is necessary, not only for her own self-esteem but as a foundation for a future partnership. "I look forward to marriage," she says. "But this is a very selfish time for me. I have to have my career. I have to say to myself, 'I did this on my own.' It makes me feel more interesting than I would otherwise. Of course, what may happen is that I'll look up one day and say, 'O.K., husband, where are you?' And he won't be there."

About halfway through my trip I stopped interviewing married couples because they tended to say similar things. They consider themselves the lucky ones. As twenty-four-year-old Adam Cooper put it, at dinner with his wife, Melanee, also twenty-four, in their Chicago apartment: "The grass is not greener on the other side."

I came away thinking it is as true as ever: all happy families are the same. But the couples I spoke with seemed to me part of a generation other than their own, older even than mine. Calling the Coopers to arrange an interview, I was invited for "a good, home-cooked meal."

The next day, I met Micah Materre, who expressed the prevailing contemporary stance as well as anyone. Outgoing and self-possessed, she gave me a long list of qualities she's looking for in a man: good looks, sense of humor, old-fashioned values, but also professional success, financial promise, and a solid family background. "Why not?" she said. "I deserve the best." But as I was folding up my notebook, she added a plaintive note: "I'll get married, won't I? It's the American way, right?"

Very early on in my sexual experience I was flattered by a woman who told me she ordinarily wouldn't go to bed with men who were under twenty-six.

"Until then," she said, "all they're doing when they're with you is congratulating themselves." For whatever reason, she never returned my calls after that night. Not an untypical encounter, all in all. Congratulations to both of us.

We were a lusty, if callow, bunch, not least because we thought we could afford to be. Encouraged by the expansive social mores spawned by the sexual revolution, fortified by the advent of a widespread availability of birth control, and fundamentally unaware of germs, we interpreted sex, for our convenience, as pure pleasure shared by "consenting parties." If it feels good, do it. Remember that?

It is an attitude that the current generation inherited and put into practice at an early age. Asked about her circle of friends in Los Angeles, Lesley Bracker, twenty-three, puts it nonchalantly: "Oh, yeah, we were all sexually active as teen-agers. When we were younger, it was considered O.K. to sleep around."

Now, however, they are reconsidering. In general, on this topic, I found them shy. They hesitate to speak openly about their sex lives, are prone to euphemism ("I'm not exactly out there, you know, mingling"), and say they worry about promiscuity only because they have friends who still practice it. According to Laura Kavesh and Cheryl Lavin, who write a column about single life, "Tales from the Front," for the *Chicago Tribune* that is syndicated in some sixty other papers around the country, a letter from a reader about the virtues of virginity generated more supportive mail than anything that has appeared in the column in its two years of existence. I'm not about to say there's a new celibacy among the young, but my impression is that even if they're having twice as much sex as they say they're having, it's not as much as you would think.

The AIDS scare, of course, is of primary relevance. "I talk about AIDS on first dates," says Jill Rotenberg, twenty-five, publishing manager of a rare-book company in San Francisco. "I talk about it all the time. I've spoken with the guy I'm dating about taking an AIDS test. Neither one of us is thrilled about condoms. But we use them. The first time we had sex, I was the one who had one in my wallet."

Not everyone is so vehement. But seriously or jokingly, in earnest tête-à-tête or idly at dinner parties, they all talk about it. To some, the new concern is merely a source of disappointment. Several of the young people I spoke with express the sense of having been robbed. It's tough to find sex when you want it, tougher than it used to be, is the lament of many, mostly men. As it was put to me at one point, "I wish I'd been born ten years earlier."

Jill Rotenberg says she feels betrayed: "I've had one long relationship in my life. He was my first lover, and for a long time my only one. So I feel I've had an untainted past. Now I feel I'm being punished anyway, even though I've been a good girl."

"I feel like I'm over the hurdle," says Douglas Ertman, twenty-two, of San Francisco, who got engaged last summer. "I'm really lucky to know that I'll have one sexual partner forever."

Most agree that the solution is monogamy, at least on a temporary basis. "It's a coupled-up society," says Alan Forman, twenty-six, a law student of George Washington University who, for the last several months, has been in a monogamous relationship. "Now more than ever. A lot of people I know are feeling the pressure to get hooked up with somebody."

I ask Forman and his girlfriend, twenty-four-year-old Debra Golden, about their future together. They say they don't know ("I'm too insecure to make a decision like that," she says), and I get the sense they never talk about it. Then she turns to him, genuinely curious. "Say you break up with me and go on to New York next year," she says.

"I don't know," he says. "If I meet someone and I like her, what do I have to do, ask her to take a blood test?"

A decade ago, one of the privileges that my contemporaries and I inferred from our sexual freedom was more or less to deny that there might be, in the sexual act, an innately implied emotional exchange. It's no longer feasible, however, to explain away sex as frivolity, inconsequential gratification. And that has complicated things for all of us, of course, whatever age, single or not.

But for young people, it's an issue, like marriage, that has been raised early: what does sex mean, if it doesn't mean nothing?

It's clearly a struggle for them. In one of my first interviews, twenty-five-year-old Karl Wright of Chicago told me: "Maybe there's a silver lining in all this. Maybe AIDS will bring back romance." The more I think about that, the more chilling it gets.

Beverly Caro, a twenty-five-year-old associate in the Dallas law firm of Gardere & Wynne, graduated from Drake University, in Des Moines, in 1983, and attended law school there as well. Her office high above the street looks out on the city's jungle of futuristic skyscrapers. She had offers from firms in Denver and her hometown of Kansas City, Mo., she says, but chose to come to Dallas because "I see upward mobility here; that's what I was looking for."

Ms. Caro has an attractive, thoughtful manner and a soft voice, but like many of her contemporaries, given the chance to discuss her personal goals, she speaks with a certitude that borders on defiance. Currently, she sees two men "somewhat regularly," she says. "I'd like to have a companion. A friend, I guess. But finding a man is not a top priority. I want to travel. I want to establish myself in the community. I don't see any drastic changes in my life by the time I turn thirty. Except that I'll be a property owner."

During my interviews, the theme of getting on track and staying there surfaced again and again. I came to think of it as the currency of self-definition. As a generation, they are not a particularly well-polled group, but certain figures bear out my impression.

According to annual surveys of 300,000 college freshmen conducted by the Higher Education Research Institute at the Graduate School of Education of the University of California at Los Angeles, young people today, by the time they *enter* college, are more inclined to express concrete life objectives than they've been for many years. Of those surveyed last fall, 73.2 percent cited being "very well off financially" as an essential or very important objective. That's up from 63.3 percent in 1980, 49.5 percent in 1975. Other objectives that the survey shows have risen in importance include "obtain recognition from colleagues for contributions to my special field"; "have administrative responsibility for the work of others"; "be successful in my own business"; and "raise a family." At the same time, the percentage of freshmen who consider it important to "develop a meaningful philosophy of life" has declined from 64.2 percent in 1975 to 40.6 percent last year.

Many of the people I spoke to feel the pressure of peer scrutiny. A status thing has evolved, to which many seem to have regretfully succumbed. Several expressed a weariness with meeting someone new and having to present themselves by their credentials. Yet, overwhelmingly, asked what they're looking for in a romantic partner, they responded first with phrases such as "an educated professional" and "someone with direction." They've conceded, more or less consciously, that unenlightened and exclusionary as it is, it's very uncool not to know what you want and not to be already chasing it.

"Seems like everyone in our generation has to be out there achieving," says Scott Birnbaum, twenty-five, who is the chief accountant for TIC United Corp., a holding company in Dallas.

Birnbaum graduated from the University of Texas in 1984, where, he says, "For me, the whole career-oriented thing kicked in." A native Texan with a broad drawl, he lives in the Greenville section of the city, an area populated largely by young singles. His apartment is comfortably roomy, not terribly well appointed. He shakes his head amiably as he points to the television set propped on a beer cooler. "What do I need furniture for?" he says. "Most of my time is taken up going to work."

Confident in himself professionally, Birnbaum was one of very few interviewees who spoke frankly about the personal cost of career success. Many speculated that they'll be worried if, in their thirties, they haven't begun to settle their love lives; this was more true of women than men. But Birnbaum confesses a desire to marry now. "It's kind of lonely being single," he says. "I'd hate to find myself successful at thirty without a family. Maybe once I'm married and have children, that might make being successful career-wise less important."

The problem, he goes on, is the collective outlook he's part and parcel of. "Here's how we think," he says. "Get to this point, move on. Get to that point, move on. Acquire, acquire. Career, career. We're all afraid to slow down for fear of missing out on something. That extends to your social life as well. You go out on a date and you're thinking, 'Hell, is there someone better for me?' I know how terrible that sounds but it seems to be my problem. Most of my peers are in the same position. Men and women. I tell you, it's tough out there right now."

When I returned to New York, I called Alex de Gramont, whom I'd been saving to interview last. I've known Alex for a long time, since he was a gawky and curious high school student and I was his teacher. Handsome now, gentle-looking, he's a literary sort, prone to attractive gloom and a certain lack of perspective. He once told me that his paradigm of a romantic, his role model, was Heathcliff, the mad, doomed passion-monger from Emily Brontë's *Wuthering Heights*.

A year out of Wesleyan University in Middletown, Conn., Alex has reasons to be hopeful. His book-length senior thesis about Albert Camus has been accepted for publication, and on the strength of it, he has applied to four graduate programs in comparative literature. But he's unenthusiastic, and he has applied to law schools, too. In the meantime, he is living with his parents in New Jersey.

He tells me that last summer he went to West Germany in pursuit of a woman he'd met when he was in college. He expected to live there with her, but he was back in this country in a couple of weeks. "Camus has a line," Alex says, " 'Love can burn or love can last. It can't do both.' " Like Benjamin Braddock, Alex is a little worried about his future.

Dustin Hoffman is forty-nine. I'm thirty-three. Both of us are doing pretty well. Alex, at twenty-three, confesses to considerable unease. "Every minute I'm not accomplishing something, I feel is wasted," he says, sort of miserably. "I feel a lot of pressure to decide what to do with my life. I'm a romantic, but these are very unromantic times."

Reflections

Private Exploration

1. Explore a key statement or passage from Weber's article that you feel is especially true or false—to you personally or to your generation.
2. Do you agree these are unromantic times? If so, what changes have contributed to the decline of romantic love?
3. Weber believes romance is dead. Explore privately and for yourself what you expect from a relationship. Draw from your own experiences. What have you learned from former relationships? How have they shaped your expectations?

Public Exploration

Would your generation still identify with characteristics Weber finds among young people in the 1980s? Consider these lines:

> . . . young Americans have succumbed to a culture of immediate gratification and gone deep-down elitist on us.

Do the goals and objectives of students your age preclude romance? Marriage? Family? Make a list of those values that seem most important to your friends today. In what ways are these values positive and productive? In what ways might such values be negative or even destructive?

Private Reflection

1. Draw from your discussion with others and reflect further on values that seem most dominant in your own generation. Make a list—or use the list composed by those you spoke with. What does the list seem to tell you about yourselves? What kinds of emotions does it evoke in you personally? That is, do you find the list inspiring? Depressing? Where do you place yourself and your own values in comparison or contrast to the list?
2. How do you define romance? Reflect on the influences that have shaped your personal views of love. Consider how books, movies, music, MTV, your friends, the relationship of your parents, or perhaps your religious beliefs, have all influenced your understanding of the term.

• Sex Without Love •

SHARON OLDS

How do they do it, the ones who make love
without love? Beautiful as dancers,
gliding over each other like ice-skaters
over the ice, fingers hooked
inside each other's bodies, faces
red as steak, wine, wet as the
children at birth whose mothers are going to
give them away. How do they come to the
come to the   come to the   God   come to the
still waters, and not love
the one who came there with them, light
rising slowly as steam off their joined
skin? These are the true religious,
the purists, the pros, the ones who will not
accept a false Messiah, love the
priest instead of the God. They do not
mistake the lover for their own pleasure,
they are like great runners: they know they are alone
with the road surface, the cold, the wind,
the fit of their shoes, their over-all cardio-
vascular health—just factors, like the partner
in the bed, and not the truth, which is the
single body alone in the universe
against its own best time.

Reflections

Private Exploration

After you've read Sharon Olds's poem several times and made marginal notes, reflect on the images that are strongest for you, the ones that seem to convey truth or falsity. Do you find yourself disturbed by the poem? Do you find yourself nodding in agreement? Either way, consider especially the following lines:

> . . . These are the true religious,
> the purists, the pros, the ones who will not
> accept a false Messiah, love the
> priest instead of the God. . . .

Public Exploration

1. After a member of your group or class has read the poem aloud, take turns sharing your notebook responses. Feel free to ask each other questions, to probe, or to try on different perspectives.
2. After the poem is read aloud in your group, explore Sharon Olds's claim of "truth" at the end of the poem:

   > . . . which is the
   > single body alone in the universe
   > against its own best time.

Private Reflection

If you've had the opportunity to hear others discuss Olds's poem, reflect on the initial response that you wrote in your notebook. Consider whether those first thoughts and feelings have been altered, strengthened, or modified. What does the poem mean to you now in terms of your own values or expectations?

Love or Marriage?

ERNEST VAN DEN HAAG

If someone asks, "Why do people marry?" he meets indignation or astonishment. The question seems absurd if not immoral: the desirability of marriage is regarded as unquestionable. Divorce, on the other hand, strikes us as a problem worthy of serious and therapeutic attention. Yet marriage precedes divorce as a rule, and frequently causes it.

What explains marriage? People divorce often but they marry still more often. Lately they also marry—and divorce, of course—younger than they used to, particularly in the middle classes (most statistics understate the change by averaging all classes). And the young have a disproportionate share of divorces. However, their hasty exertions to get out of wedlock puzzle me less than their eagerness to rush into it in the first place.

What has happened is that the physical conveniences which reduced the material usefulness of marriage have also loosened the bonds of family life. Many other bonds that sustained us psychologically were weakened as they were extended: beliefs become vague; associations impersonal, discontinuous, and casual. Our contacts are many, our relationships few: our lives, externally crowded, often are internally isolated; we remain but tenuously linked to each other and our ties come easily undone. One feels lonely surrounded by crowds and machines in an unbounded, abstract world that has become morally unintelligible; and we have so much time now to feel lonely in. Thus one longs, perhaps more acutely than in the past, for somebody to be tangibly, individually, and definitely one's own, body and soul.

This is the promise of marriage. Movies, songs, TV, romance magazines, all intensify the belief that love alone makes life worthwhile, is perpetual, conquers the world's evils, and is fulfilled and certified by marriage. "Science" hastens to confirm as much. Doesn't popular psychology, brandishing the banner of Freud with more enthusiasm than knowledge, tell us, in effect, that any male who stays single is selfish or homosexual or mother-dominated and generally neurotic? and any unmarried female frustrated (or worse, not frustrated) and neurotic? A "normal" person, we are told, must love and thereupon marry. Thus love and marriage are identified with each other and with normality, three thousand years of experience notwithstanding. The yearning for love, attended by anxiety to prove oneself well-adjusted and normal, turns into eagerness to get married.

The young may justly say that they merely practice what their parents preached. For, indeed, the idea that "love and marriage go together like a horse and carriage" has been drummed into their heads, so much that it finally has come to seem entirely natural. Yet, nothing could be less so. Love has long delighted and distressed mankind, and marriage has comforted us steadily and well. Both, however, are denatured—paradoxically enough, by their staunchest supporters—when they are expected to "go together." For love is a very unruly horse, far more apt to run away and overturn the carriage than to draw it. That is why, in the past, people seldom thought of harnessing marriage to love. They felt that each has its own motive power: one primed for a lifelong journey; the other for an ardent improvisation, a voyage of discovery.

Though by no means weaker, the marital bond is quite different from the bond of love. If you like, it is a different bond of love—less taut, perhaps, and more durable. By confusing these two related but in many ways dissimilar bonds, we stand to lose the virtues and gain the vices of both: the spontaneous passion of love and the deliberate permanence of marriage are equally endangered as we try to live up to an ideal which bogs down one and unhinges the other.

Marriage is an immemorial institution which, in some form, exists everywhere. Its main purpose always was to unite and to continue the families of bride and groom and to further their economic and social position. The families, therefore, were the main interested parties. Often marriages were arranged (and sometimes they took place) before the future husbands or wives were old enough to talk. Even when they were grown up, they felt, as did their parents, that the major purpose of marriage was to continue the family, to produce children. Certainly women hoped for kind and vigorous providers and men for faithful mothers and good housekeepers; both undoubtedly hoped for affection, too; but love did not strike either of them as indispensable and certainly not as sufficient for marriage.

Unlike marriage, love has only recently come to be generally accepted as something more than a frenzied state of pleasure and pain. It is a welcome innovation—but easily ruined by marriage; which in turn has a hard time surviving confusion with love. Marriage counselors usually recognize this last point, but people in love seldom consult them. Perhaps their limited clientele colors the views of too many marriage counselors: instead of acknowledging that love and marriage are different but equally genuine relationships, they depict love as a kind of dependable wheel horse that can be harnessed to the carriage of married life. For them, any other kind of love must be an "immature" or "neurotic" fantasy, something to be condemned as Hollywood-inspired, "unrealistic" romanticism. It is as though a man opposed to horse racing—for good reasons perhaps—were to argue that race horses are not real, that all real horses are draft horses. Thus marriage counselors often insist that the only "real" and "true" love is "mature"—it is the comfortable workaday relation Mommy and Daddy have. The children find it hard to believe that there is nothing more to it.

They are quite right. And they have on their side the great literature of the world, and philosophers from Plato to Santayana. What is wrong with Hollywood romance surely is not that it is romantic, but that its romances are shoddy clichés. And since Hollywood shuns the true dimensions of conflict, love in the movies is usually confirmed by marriage and marriage by love, in accordance with wishful fantasy, though not with truth.

Was the love Tristan bore Isolde "mature" or "neurotic"? They loved each other before and after Isolde was married—to King Mark. It never occurred to them to marry each other; they even cut short an extramarital idyll together in the forest. (And Tristan too, while protesting love for Isolde, got married to some other girl.) Dante saw, but never actually met, Beatrice until he reached the nether world, which is the place for permanent romance. Of course, he was a married man.

It is foolish to pretend that the passionate romantic longing doesn't exist or is "neurotic," i.e., shouldn't exist; it is as foolish to pretend that romantic love can be made part of a cozy domesticity. The truth is simple enough, though it can make life awfully complicated: there are two things, love and affection (or marital love), not one; they do not usually pull together as a team; they tend to draw us in different directions, if they are present at the same time. God nowhere promised to make this a simple world.

In the West, love came to be socially approved around the twelfth century. It became a fashionable subject of discussion then, and even of disputation, in formal "courts of love" convoked to argue its merits and to elaborate its true characteristics. Poets and singers created the models and images of love. They still do—though mass production has perhaps affected the quality; what else makes the teen-age crooners idols to their followers and what else do they croon about? In medieval times, as now, manuals were written, codifying the behavior recommended to lovers. With a difference though. Today's manuals are produced not by men of letters, but by doctors and therapists, as though love, sex, and marriage were diseases or therapeutic problems—which they promptly become if one reads too many of these guidebooks (any one is one too many). . . . The authors are sure that happiness depends on the sexual mechanics they blueprint. Yet, one doesn't make love better by reading a book any more than one learns to dance, or ride a bicycle, by reading about it.

The sexual engineering (or cook-book) approach is profitable only for the writer: in an enduring relationship, physical gratification is an effect and not a cause. If a person does not acquire sexual skill from experience, he is not ready for it. Wherever basic inhibitions exist, no book can remove them. Where they do not, no book is necessary. I have seen many an unhappy relationship in my psychoanalytic practice, but none ever in which sexual technique or the lack of it was more than a symptom and an effect. The mechanical approach never helps.

The troubadours usually took sex and marriage for granted and dealt with love—the newest and still the most surprising and fascinating of all relationships. And also the most unstable. They conceived love as a longing, a tension between desire and fulfillment. This feeling, of course, had been known before they celebrated it. Plato described love as a desire for something one does not have, implying that it is a longing, not a fulfillment. But in ancient Greece, love was regarded diffidently, as rather undesirable, an intoxication, a bewitchment, a divine punishment—usually for neglecting sex. The troubadours thought differently, although, unlike many moderns, they did not deny that love is a passion, something one suffers. But they thought it a sweet suffering to be cultivated, and they celebrated it in song and story.

The troubadours clearly distinguished love and sex. Love was to them a yearning for a psychic gratification which the lover feels only the beloved can give; sex, an impersonal desire anybody possessing certain fairly common characteristics can gratify by physical actions. Unlike love, sex can thrive without an intense personal relationship and may erode it if it exists. Indeed, the Romans sometimes wondered if love would not blunt and tame their sexual pleasures, whereas the troubadours fretted lest sex abate the fervor of love's longing. They never fully resolved the contest between love and sex; nor has anyone else. (To define it away is, of course, not to solve it.)

Since love is longing, experts in the Middle Ages held that one could not love someone who could not be longed for—for instance, one's wife. Hence, the Comtesse de Champagne told her court in 1174: "Love cannot extend its rights over two married persons." If one were to marry one's love, one would exchange the sweet torment of desire, the yearning, for that which fulfills it. Thus the tension of hope would be replaced by the comfort of certainty. He who longs to long, who wants the tension of desire, surely should not marry. In former times, of course, he married—the better to love someone else's wife.

When sexual objects are easily and guiltlessly accessible, in a society that does not object to promiscuity, romantic love seldom prospers. For example, in imperial Rome it was rare and in Tahiti unknown. And love is unlikely to arouse the heart of someone brought up in a harem, where the idea of uniqueness has a hard time. Love flowers best in a monogamous environment morally opposed to unrestrained sex, and interested in cultivating individual experience. In such an environment, longing may be valued for itself. Thus, love as we know it is a Christian legacy, though Christianity in the main repudiates romantic love where the object is worldly, and accepts passion only when transcendent, when God is the object—or when muted into affection: marital love.

Sexual gratification, of course, diminishes sexual desire for the time being. But it does more. It changes love. The longing may become gratitude; the desire tenderness; love may become affectionate companionship—"After such knowledge, what forgiveness?" Depending on character and circumstance, love may also be replaced by indifference or hostility.

One thing is certain though: if the relationship is stabilized, love is replaced by other emotions. (Marriage thus has often been recommended as the cure for love. But it does not always work.) The only way to keep love is to try to keep up—or re-establish—the distance between lovers that was inevitably shortened by intimacy and possession, and thus, possibly, regain desire and longing. Lovers sometimes do so by quarreling. And some personalities are remote enough, or inexhaustible enough, to be longed for even when possessed. But this has disadvantages as well. And the deliberate and artificial devices counseled by romance magazines and marriage manuals ("surprise your husband . . .")—even when they do not originate with the love of pretense—are unlikely to yield more than the pretense of love.

The sexual act itself may serve as a vehicle for numberless feelings: lust, vanity, and self-assertion, doubt and curiosity, possessiveness, anxiety, hostility, anger, or indifferent release from boredom. Yet, though seldom the only motive, and often absent altogether, love nowadays is given as the one natural and moral reason which authorizes and even ordains sexual relations. What we have done is draw a moral conclusion from a rule of popular psychology: that "it is gratifying and therefore healthy and natural, to make love when you love, and frustrating, and therefore unhealthy and unnatural, not to; we must follow nature; but sex without love is unnatural and therefore immoral."

Now, as a psychological rule, this is surely wrong; it can be as healthy to frustrate as it is to gratify one's desires. Sometimes gratification is very unhealthy; sometimes frustration is. Nor can psychological health be accepted as morally decisive. Sanity, sanitation, and morality are all desirable, but they are not identical; our wanting all of them is the problem, not the solution. It may be quite "healthy" to run away with your neighbor's wife, but not, therefore, right. And there is nothing unhealthy about wishing to kill someone who has injured you—but this does not morally justify doing so. Finally, to say "we must follow nature" is always specious: we follow nature in whatever we do—we can't ever do what nature does not let us do. Why then identify nature only with the nonintellectual, the sensual, or the emotional possibilities? On this view, it would be unnatural to read: literacy is a gift of nature only if we include the intellect and training in nature's realm. If we do, it makes no sense to call a rule unnatural merely because it restrains an urge: the urge is no more natural than the restraint.

The combination of love and sex is no more natural than the separation. Thus, what one decides about restraining or indulging an emotion, or a sexual urge, rests on religious, social, or personal values, none of which can claim to be more natural than any other.

Not that some indulgences and some inhibitions may not be healthier than others. But one cannot flatly say which are good or bad for every man. It depends on their origins and effects in the personalities involved. Without knowing these, more cannot be said—except, perhaps, that we should try not to use others, or even ourselves, merely as a means—at least not habitually and in personal relations. Sex, unalloyed, sometimes leads to this original sin which our moral tradition condemns. Psychologically, too, the continued use of persons merely as instruments ultimately frustrates both the user and the used. This caution, though it justifies no positive action, may help perceive problems; it does not solve them; no general rule can.

What about marriage? In our society, couples usually invite the families to their weddings, although the decision to marry is made exclusively by bride and groom. However, a license must be obtained and the marriage registered; and it can be dissolved only by a court of law. Religious ceremonies state the meaning of marriage clearly. The couple are asked to promise "forsaking all others, [to] keep thee only unto her [him], so long as ye both shall live." The vow does not say, "as long as ye both shall want to," because marriage is a promise to continue even when one no longer wishes to. If marriage were to end when love does, it would be redundant: why solemnly ask two people to promise to be with each other for as long as they want to be with each other?

Marriage was to cement the family by tying people together "till death do us part" in the face of the fickleness of their emotions. The authority of state and church was to see to it that they kept a promise voluntarily made, but binding, and that could not be unmade. Whether it sprang from love did not matter. Marriage differed from a love affair inasmuch as it continued regardless of love. Cupid shoots his arrows without rhyme or reason. But marriage is a deliberate rational act, a public institution making the family independent of Cupid's whims. Once enlisted, the volunteers couldn't quit, even when they didn't like it any longer. That was the point.

The idea that marriage must be synchronous with love or even affection nullifies it altogether. (That affection should coincide with marriage is, of course, desirable, though it does not always happen.) We would have to reword the marriage vow. Instead of saying, "till death do us part," we might say, "till we get bored with each other"; and, instead of "forsaking all others," "till someone better comes along." Clearly, if the couple intend to stay "married" only as long as they want to, they only pretend to be married: they are having an affair with legal trimmings. To marry is to vow fidelity regardless of any future feeling, to vow the most earnest attempt to avoid contrary feelings altogether, but, at any rate, not to give in to them.

Perhaps this sounds grim. But it needn't be if one marries for affection more than for love. For affection, marital love may grow with knowledge and intimacy and shared experience. Thus marriage itself, when accepted as something other than a love affair, may foster affection. Affection differs from love as fulfillment differs from desire. Further, love longs for what desire and imagination make uniquely and perfectly lovable. Possession erodes it. Affection, however,—which is love of a different, of a perhaps more moral and less aesthetic kind—cares deeply also for what is unlovable without transforming it into beauty. It cares for the unvarnished person, not the splendid image. Time can strengthen it. But the husband who wants to remain a splendid image must provide a swan to draw him away, or find a wife who can restrain her curiosity about his real person—something that Lohengrin did not succeed in doing. Whereas love stresses the unique form perfection takes in the lover's mind, affection stresses the uniqueness of the actual person.

One may grow from the other. But not when this other is expected to remain unchanged. And affection probably grows more easily if not preceded by enchantment. For the disenchantment which often follows may turn husband and wife against each other, and send them looking elsewhere for reenchantment—which distance lends so easily. Indeed, nothing else does.

Reflections

Private Exploration

1. Zero in on any one passage from van den Haag's essay to explore more fully. Choose a passage that seems important to you and question why it strikes you as significant. Does this particular passage raise any questions or open up insights into the essay as a whole?
2. Explore the following:

   > Movies, songs, T.V. romance magazines, all intensify the belief that love alone makes life worthwhile, is perpetual, conquers the world's evils, is fulfilled and certified by marriage?

   Consider whether van den Haag might be right or wrong? Is it possible that your own view of love and marriage has been influenced by the popular culture of your time? Be as thoughtful as you can.

3. Are you convinced that love undermines marriage?

Public Exploration

1. Writing more than 30 years ago, van den Haag claims that "the desirability of marriage is regarded as unquestionable." Would most people think so today? What problems might exist that van den Haag could not have anticipated? Why are people still getting married? Is it for the right reasons? Are there such things as right reasons for marriage?
2. Consider this excerpt:

> The combination of love and sex is no more natural than the separation. Thus, what one decides about restraining or indulging an emotion, or a sexual urge, rests on religious, social, or personal values, no one of which can claim to be more natural than any other.

Private Reflection

Van den Haag distinguishes between "love" and "affection." He calls affection a "more moral and less aesthetic" kind of love. What is he getting at? If you want to marry at all, would you be willing to marry for affection rather than love? Be as honest as you can about your own feelings. What do you learn about yourself?

How I Met My Husband

ALICE MUNRO

We heard the plane come over at noon, roaring through the radio news, and we were sure it was going to hit the house, so we all ran out into the yard. We saw it come in over the treetops, all red and silver, the first close-up plane I ever saw. Mrs. Peebles screamed.

"Crash landing," their little boy said. Joey was his name.

"It's okay," said Dr. Peebles. "He knows what he's doing." Dr. Peebles was only an animal doctor, but had a calming way of talking, like any doctor.

This was my first job—working for Dr. and Mrs. Peebles, who had bought an old house out on the Fifth Line, about five miles out of town. It was just when the trend was starting of town people buying up old farms, not to work them but to live on them.

We watched the plane land across the road, where the fairgrounds used to be. It did make a good landing field, nice and level for the old race track, and the barns and display sheds torn down now for scrap lumber so there was nothing in the way. Even the old grandstand bays had burned.

"All right," said Mrs. Peebles, snappy as she always was when she got over her nerves. "Let's go back in the house. Let's not stand here gawking like a set of farmers."

She didn't say that to hurt my feelings. It never occurred to her.

I was just setting the dessert down when Loretta Bird arrived, out of breath, at the screen door.

"I thought it was going to crash into the house and kill youse all!"

She lived on the next place and the Peebleses thought she was a countrywoman, they didn't know the difference. She and her husband didn't farm, he worked on the roads and had a bad name for drinking. They had seven children and couldn't get credit at the HiWay Grocery. The Peebleses made her welcome, not knowing any better, as I say, and offered her dessert.

Dessert was never anything to write home about, at their place. A dish of Jell-O or sliced bananas or fruit out of a tin. "Have a house without a pie, be ashamed until you die," my mother used to say, but Mrs. Peebles operated differently.

Loretta Bird saw me getting the can of peaches.

"Oh, never mind," she said. "I haven't got the right kind of a stomach to trust what comes out of those tins, I can only eat home canning."

I could have slapped her. I bet she never put down fruit in her life.

"I know what he's landed here for," she said. "He's got permission to use the fairgrounds and take people up for rides. It costs a dollar. It's the same fellow who was over at Palmerston last week and was up the lakeshore before that. I wouldn't go up, if you paid me."

"I'd jump at the chance," Dr. Peebles said. "I'd like to see this neighborhood from the air."

Mrs. Peebles said she would just as soon see it from the ground. Joey said he wanted to go and Heather did, too. Joey was nine and Heather was seven.

"Would you, Edie?" Heather said.

I said I didn't know. I was scared, but I never admitted that, especially in front of children I was taking care of.

"People are going to be coming out here in their cars raising dust and trampling your property, if I was you I would complain," Loretta said. She hooked her legs around the chair rung and I knew we were in for a lengthy visit. After Dr. Peebles went back to his office or out on his next call and Mrs. Peebles went for her nap, she would hang around me while I was trying to do the dishes. She would pass remarks about the Peebleses in their own house.

"She wouldn't find time to lay down in the middle of the day, if she had seven kids like I got."

She asked me did they fight and did they keep things in the dresser drawer not to have babies with. She said it was a sin if they did. I pretended I didn't know what she was talking about.

I was fifteen and away from home for the first time. My parents had made the effort and sent me to high school for a year, but I didn't like it. I was shy of strangers and the work was hard, they didn't make it nice for you or explain the way they do now. At the end of the year the averages were published in the paper, and mine came out at the very bottom, 37 percent. My father said that's enough and I didn't blame him. The last thing I wanted, anyway, was to go on and end up teaching school. It happened the very day the paper came out with my disgrace in it, Dr. Peebles was staying at our place for dinner, having just helped one of our cows have twins, and he said I looked smart to him and his wife was looking for a girl to help. He said she felt tied down, with the two children, out in the country. I guess she would, my mother said, being polite, though I could tell from her face she was wondering what on earth it would be like to have only two children and no barn work, and then to be complaining.

When I went home I would describe to them the work I had to do, and it made everybody laugh. Mrs. Peebles had an automatic washer and dryer, the first I ever saw. I have had those in my own home for such a long time now it's hard to remember how much of a miracle it was to me, not having to struggle with the wringer and hang up and haul down. Let alone not having to heat water. Then there was practically no baking. Mrs. Peebles said she couldn't make pie crust, the most amazing thing I ever heard a woman admit. I could, of course, and I could make light biscuits and a white cake and dark cake, but they didn't want it, she said they watched their figures. The only thing I didn't like about working there, in fact, was feeling half hungry a lot of the time. I used to bring back a box of doughnuts made out at home, and hide them under my bed. The children found out, and I didn't mind sharing, but I thought I better bind them to secrecy.

The day after the plane landed Mrs. Peebles put both children in the car and drove over to Chesley, to get their hair cut. There was a good woman then at Chesley for doing hair. She got hers done at the same place, Mrs. Peebles did, and that meant they would be gone a good while. She had to pick a day Dr. Peebles wasn't going out into the country, she didn't have her own car. Cars were still in short supply then, after the war.

I loved being left in the house alone, to do my work at leisure. The kitchen was all white and bright yellow, with fluorescent lights. That was before they ever thought of making the appliances all different colors and doing the cupboards like dark old wood and hiding the lighting. I loved light. I loved the double sink. So would anybody new-come from washing dishes in a dishpan with a rag-plugged hole on an oilcloth-covered table by light of a coal-oil lamp. I kept everything shining.

The bathroom too. I had a bath in there once a week. They wouldn't have minded if I took one oftener, but to me it seemed like asking too much, or maybe risking making it less wonderful. The basin and the tub and the toilet were all pink, and there were glass doors with flamingoes painted on them, to shut off the tub. The light had a rosy cast and the mat sank under your feet like snow, except that it was warm. The mirror was three-way. With the mirror all steamed up and the air like a perfume cloud, from things I was allowed to use, I stood up on the side of the tub and admired myself naked, from three directions. Sometimes I thought about the way we lived out at home and the way we lived here and how one way was so hard to imagine when you were living the other way. But I thought it was still a lot easier, living the way we lived at home, to picture something like this, the painted flamingoes and the warmth and the soft mat, than it was anybody knowing only things like this to picture how it was the other way. And why was that?

I was through my jobs in no time, and had the vegetables peeled for supper and sitting in cold water besides. Then I went into Mrs. Peebles' bedroom. I had been in there plenty of times, cleaning, and I always took a good look in her closet, at the clothes she had hanging there. I wouldn't have looked in her drawers, but a closet is open to anybody. That's a lie. I would have looked in drawers, but I would have felt worse doing it and been more scared she could tell.

Some clothes in her closet she wore all the time, I was quite familiar with them. Others she never put on, they were pushed to the back. I was disappointed to see no wedding dress. But there was one long dress I could just see the skirt of, and I was hungering to see the rest. Now I took note of where it hung and lifted it out. It was satin, a lovely weight on my arm, light bluish-green in color, almost silvery. It had a fitted, pointed waist and a full skirt and an off-the-shoulder fold hiding the little sleeves.

Next thing was easy. I got out of my own things and slipped it on. I was slimmer at fifteen than anybody would believe who knows me now and the fit was beautiful. I didn't of course, have a strapless bra on, which was what it needed, I just had to slide my straps down my arms under the material. Then I tried pinning up my hair, to get the effect. One thing led to another. I put on rouge and lipstick and eyebrow pencil from her dresser. The heat of the day and the weight of the satin and all the excitement made me thirsty, and I went out to the kitchen, got-up as I was, to get a glass of ginger ale with ice cubes from the refrigerator. The Peebleses drank ginger ale, or fruit drinks, all day, like water, and I was getting so I did too. Also there was no limit on ice cubes, which I was so fond of I would even put them in a glass of milk.

I turned from putting the ice tray back and saw a man watching me through the screen. It was the luckiest thing in the world I didn't spill the ginger ale down the front of me then and there.

"I never meant to scare you. I knocked but you were getting the ice out, you didn't hear me."

I couldn't see what he looked like, he was dark the way somebody is pressed up against a screen door with the bright daylight behind them. I only knew he wasn't from around here.

"I'm from the plane over there. My name is Chris Watters and what I was wondering was if I could use that pump."

There was a pump in the yard. That was the way the people used to get their water. Now I noticed he was carrying a pail.

"You're welcome," I said. "I can get it from the tap and save you pumping." I guess I wanted him to know we had piped water, didn't pump ourselves.

"I don't mind the exercise." He didn't move, though, and finally he said, "Were you going to a dance?"

Seeing a stranger there had made me entirely forget how I was dressed.

"Or is that the way ladies around here generally get dressed up in the afternoon?"

I didn't know how to joke back then. I was too embarrassed.

"You live here? Are you the lady of the house?"

"I'm the hired girl."

Some people change when they find that out, their whole way of looking at you and speaking to you changes, but his didn't.

"Well, I just wanted to tell you you look very nice. I was so surprised when I looked in the door and saw you. Just because you looked so nice and beautiful."

I wasn't even old enough then to realize how out of the common it is, for a man to say something like that to a woman, or somebody he is treating like a woman. For a man to say a word like *beautiful.* I wasn't old enough to realize or to say anything back, or in fact to do anything but wish he would go away. Not that I didn't like him, but just that it upset me so, having him look at me, and me trying to think of something to say.

He must have understood. He said good-bye, and thanked me, and went and started filling his pail from the pump. I stood behind the Venetian blinds in the dining room, watching him. When he had gone, I went into the bedroom and took the dress off and put it back in the same place. I dressed in my own clothes and took my hair down and washed my face, wiping it on Kleenex, which I threw in the wastebasket.

The Peebleses asked me what kind of man he was. Young, middle-aged, short, tall? I couldn't say.

"Good-looking?" Dr. Peebles teased me.

I couldn't think a thing but that he would be coming to get his water again, he would be talking to Dr. or Mrs. Peebles, making friends with them, and he would mention seeing me that first afternoon, dressed up. Why not mention it? He would think it was funny. And no idea of the trouble it would get me into.

After supper the Peebleses drove into town to go to a movie. She wanted to go somewhere with her hair fresh done. I sat in my bright kitchen wondering what to do, knowing I would never sleep. Mrs. Peebles might not fire me, when she found out, but it would give her a different feeling about me altogether. This was the first place I ever worked but I already had picked up things about the way people feel when you are working for them. They like to think you aren't curious. Not just that you aren't dishonest, that isn't enough. They like to feel you don't notice things, that you don't think or wonder about anything but what they liked to eat and how they liked things ironed, and so on. I don't mean they weren't kind to me, because they were. They had me eat my meals with them (to tell the truth I expected to, I didn't know there were families who don't) and sometimes they took me along in the car. But all the same.

I went up and checked on the children being asleep and then I went out. I had to do it. I crossed the road and went in the old fairgrounds gate. The plane looked unnatural sitting there, and shining with the moon. Off at the far side of the fairgrounds, where the bush was taking over, I saw his tent.

He was sitting outside it smoking a cigarette. He saw me coming.

"Hello, were you looking for a plane ride? I don't start taking people up till tomorrow." Then he looked again and said, "Oh, it's you. I didn't know you without your long dress on."

My heart was knocking away, my tongue was dried up. I had to say something. But I couldn't. My throat was closed and I was like a deaf-and-dumb.

"Did you want a ride? Sit down. Have a cigarette."

I couldn't even shake my head to say no, so he gave me one.

"Put it in your mouth or I can't light it. It's a good thing I'm used to shy ladies."

I did. It wasn't the first time I had smoked a cigarette, actually. My girl friend out home, Muriel Lower, used to steal them from her brother.

"Look at your hand shaking. Did you just want to have a chat, or what?"

In one burst I said, "I wisht you wouldn't say anything about that dress."

"What dress? Oh, the long dress."

"It's Mrs. Peebles'."

"Whose? Oh, the lady you work for? Is that it? She wasn't home so you got dressed up in her dress, eh? You got dressed up and played queen. I don't blame you. You're not smoking the cigarette right. Don't just puff. Draw it in. Did anybody ever show you how to inhale? Are you scared I'll tell on you? Is that it?"

I was so ashamed at having to ask him to connive this way I couldn't nod. I just looked at him and he saw *yes.*

"Well I won't. I won't in the slightest way mention it or embarrass you. I give you my word of honor."

Then he changed the subject, to help me out, seeing I couldn't even thank him.

"What do you think of this sign?"

It was a board sign lying practically at my feet.

SEE THE WORLD FROM THE SKY. ADULTS $1.00. CHILDREN 50¢. QUALIFIED PILOT.

"My old sign was getting pretty beat up, I thought I'd make a new one. That's what I've been doing with my time today."

The lettering wasn't all that handsome, I thought. I could have done a better one in half an hour.

"I'm not an expert at sign making."

"It's very good," I said.

"I don't need it for publicity, word of mouth is usually enough. I turned away two carloads tonight. I felt like taking it easy. I didn't tell them ladies were dropping in to visit me."

Now I remembered the children and I was scared again, in case one of them had waked up and called me and I wasn't there.

"Do you have to go so soon?"

I remembered some manners. "Thank you for the cigarette."

"Don't forget. You have my word of honor."

I tore off across the fairgrounds, scared I'd see the car heading home from town. My sense of time was mixed up, I didn't know how long I'd been out of the house. But it was all right, it wasn't late, the children were asleep. I got in bed myself and lay thinking what a lucky end to the day, after all, and among things to be grateful for I could be grateful Loretta Bird hadn't been the one who caught me.

The yard and borders didn't get trampled, it wasn't as bad as that. All the same it seemed very public, around the house. The sign was on the fairgrounds gate. People came mostly after supper but a good many in the afternoon, too. The Bird children all came without fifty cents between them and hung on the gate. We got used to the excitement of the plane coming in and taking off, it wasn't excitement anymore. I never went over, after that one time, but would see him when he came to get his water. I would be out on the steps doing sitting-down work, like preparing vegetables, if I could.

"Why don't you come over? I'll take you up in my plane."

"I'm saving my money," I said, because I couldn't think of anything else.

"For what? For getting married?"

I shook my head.

"I'll take you up for free if you come sometime when it's slack. I thought you would come, and have another cigarette."

I made a face to hush him, because you never could tell when the children would be sneaking around the porch, or Mrs. Peebles herself listening in the house. Sometimes she came out and had a conversation with him. He told her things he hadn't bothered to tell me. But then I hadn't thought to ask. He told her he had been in the war, that was where he learned to fly a plane, and now he couldn't settle down to ordinary life, this was what he liked. She said she couldn't imagine anybody liking such a thing. Though sometimes, he said, she was almost bored enough to try anything herself, she wasn't brought up to living in the country. It's all my husband's idea, she said. This was news to me.

"Maybe you ought to give flying lessons," she said.

"Would you take them?"

She just laughed.

Sunday was a busy flying day in spite of it being preached against from two pulpits. We were all sitting out watching. Joey and Heather were over on the fence with the Bird kids. Their father had said they could go, after their mother saying all week they couldn't.

A car came down the road past the parked cars and pulled up right in the drive. It was Loretta Bird who got out, all importance, and on the driver's side another woman got out, more sedately. She was wearing sunglasses.

"This is a lady looking for the man that flies the plane," Loretta Bird said. "I heard her inquire in the hotel coffee shop where I was having a Coke and I brought her out."

"I'm sorry to bother you," the lady said. "I'm Alice Kelling, Mr. Watter's fiancée."

This Alice Kelling had on a pair of brown and white checked slacks and a yellow top. Her bust looked to me rather low and bumpy. She had a worried face. Her hair had had a permanent, but had grown out, and she wore a yellow band to keep it off her face. Nothing in the least pretty or even young-looking about her. But you could tell from how she talked she was from the city, or educated, or both.

Dr. Peebles stood up and introduced himself and his wife and me and asked her to be seated.

"He's up in the air right now, but you're welcome to sit and wait. He gets his water here and he hasn't been yet. He'll probably take his break about five."

"That is him, then?" said Alice Kelling, wrinkling and straining at the sky.

"He's not in the habit of running out on you, taking a different name?" Dr. Peebles laughed. He was the one, not his wife, to offer iced tea. Then she sent me into the kitchen to fix it. She smiled. She was wearing sunglasses too.

"He never mentioned his fiancée," she said.

I loved fixing iced tea with lots of ice and slices of lemon in tall glasses. I ought to have mentioned before, Dr. Peebles was an abstainer, at least around the house, or I wouldn't have been allowed to take the place. I had to fix a glass for Loretta Bird too, though it galled me, and when I went out she had settled in my lawn chair, leaving me the steps.

"I knew you was a nurse when I first heard you in that coffee shop."

"How would you know a thing like that?"

"I get my hunches about people. Was that how you met him, nursing?"

"Chris? Well yes. Yes, it was."

"Oh, were you overseas?" said Mrs. Peebles.

"No, it was before he went overseas. I nursed him when he was stationed at Centralia and had a ruptured appendix. We got engaged and then he went overseas. My, this is refreshing, after a long drive."

"He'll be glad to see you," Dr. Peebles said. "It's a rackety kind of life, isn't it, not staying one place long enough to really make friends."

"Youse've had a long engagement," Loretta Bird said.

Alice Kelling passed that over. "I was going to get a room at the hotel, but when I was offered directions I came on out. Do you think I could phone them?"

"No need," Dr. Peebles said. "You're five miles away from him if you stay at the hotel. Here, you're right across the road. Stay with us. We've got rooms on rooms, look at this big house."

Asking people to stay, just like that, is certainly a country thing, and maybe seemed natural to him now, but not to Mrs. Peebles, from the way she said, oh yes, we have plenty of room. Or to Alice Kelling, who kept protesting, but let herself be worn down. I got the feeling it was a temptation to her, to be that close. I was trying for a look at her ring. Her nails were painted red, her fingers were freckled and wrinkled. It was a tiny stone. Muriel Lowe's cousin had one twice as big.

Chris came to get his water, late in the afternoon just as Dr. Peebles had predicted. He must have recognized the car from a way off. He came smiling.

"Here I am chasing after you to see what you're up to," called Alice Kelling. She got up and went to meet him and they kissed, just touched, in front of us.

"You're going to spend a lot on gas that way," Chris said.

Dr. Peebles invited Chris to stay for supper, since he had already put up the sign that said: NO MORE RIDES TILL 7 P.M. Mrs. Peebles wanted it served in the yard, in spite of the bugs. One thing strange to anybody from the country is this eating outside. I had made a potato salad earlier and she had made a jellied salad, that was one thing she could do, so it was just a matter of getting those out, and some sliced meat and cucumbers and fresh leaf lettuce. Loretta Bird hung around for some time saying, "Oh, well, I guess I better get home to those yappers," and, "It's so nice just sitting here, I sure hate to get up," but nobody invited her, I was relieved to see, and finally she had to go.

That night after rides were finished Alice Kelling and Chris went off somewhere in her car. I lay awake till they got back. When I saw the car lights sweep my ceiling I got up to look down on them through the slats of my blind. I don't know what I thought I was going to see. Muriel Lowe and I used to sleep on her front veranda and watch her sister and her sister's boyfriend saying good night. Afterward we couldn't get to sleep, for longing for somebody to kiss us and rub up against us and we would talk about suppose you were out in a boat with a boy and he wouldn't bring you in to shore unless you did it, or what if somebody got you trapped in a barn, you would have to, wouldn't you, it wouldn't be your fault. Muriel said her two girl cousins used to try with a toilet paper roll that one of them was a boy. We wouldn't do anything like that; just lay and wondered.

All that happened was that Chris got out of the car on one side and she got out on the other and they walked off separately—him toward the fairgrounds and her toward the house. I got back in bed and imagined about me coming home with him, not like that.

Next morning Alice Kelling got up late and I fixed a grapefruit for her the way I had learned and Mrs. Peebles sat down with her to visit and have another cup of coffee. Mrs. Peebles seemed pleased enough now, having company. Alice Kelling said she guessed she better get used to putting in a day just watching Chris take off and come down, and Mrs. Peebles said she didn't know if she should suggest it because Alice Kelling was the one with the car, but the lake was only twenty-five miles away and what a good day for a picnic.

Alice Kelling took her up on the idea and by eleven o'clock they were in the car, with Joey and Heather and a sandwich lunch I had made. The only thing was that Chris hadn't come down, and she wanted to tell him where they were going.

"Edie'll go over and tell him," Mrs. Peebles said. "There's no problem."

Alice Kelling wrinkled her face and agreed.

"Be sure and tell him we'll be back by five!"

I didn't see that he would be concerned about knowing this right away, and I thought of him eating whatever he ate over there, alone, cooking on his camp stove, so I got to work and mixed up a crumb cake and baked it, in between the other work I had to do; then, when it was a bit cooled, wrapped it in a tea towel. I didn't do anything to myself but take off my apron and comb my hair. I would like to have put some makeup on, but I was too afraid it would remind him of the way he first saw me, and that would humiliate me all over again.

He had come and put another sign on the gate: NO RIDES THIS P.M. APOLOGIES. I worried that he wasn't feeling well. No sign of him outside and the tent flap was down. I knocked on the pole.

"Come in," he said, in a voice that would just as soon have said *Stay out.*

I lifted the flap.

"Oh, it's you, I'm sorry. I didn't know it was you."

He had been just sitting on the side of the bed, smoking. Why not at least sit and smoke in the fresh air?

"I brought a cake and hope you're not sick," I said.

"Why would I be sick? Oh—that sign. That's all right. I'm just tired of talking to people. I don't mean you. Have a seat." He pinned back the tent flap. "Get some fresh air in here."

I sat on the edge of the bed, there was no place else. It was one of those fold-up cots, really: I remembered and gave him his fiancée's message.

He ate some of the cake. "Good."

"Put the rest away for when you're hungry later."

"I'll tell you a secret. I won't be around here much longer."

"Are you getting married?"

"Ha ha. What time did you say they'd be back?"

"Five o'clock."

"Well, by that time this place will have seen the last of me. A plane can get further than a car." He unwrapped the cake and ate another piece of it, absent-mindedly.

"Now you'll be thirsty."

"There's some water in the pail."

"It won't be very cold. I could bring some fresh. I could bring some ice from the refrigerator."

"No," he said. "I don't want you to go. I want a nice long time of saying good-bye to you."

He put the cake away carefully and sat beside me and started those little kisses, so soft. I can't ever let myself think about them, such kindness in his face and lovely kisses, all over my eyelids and neck and ears, all over, then me kissing back as well as I could (I had only kissed a boy on a dare before, and kissed my own arms for practice) and we lay back on the cot and pressed together, just gently, and he did some other things, not bad things or not in a bad way. It was lovely in the tent, that smell of grass and hot tent cloth with the sun beating down on it, and he said, "I wouldn't do you any harm for the world." Once, when he had rolled on top of me and we were sort of rocking together on the cot, he said softly, "Oh, no," and freed himself and jumped up and got the water pail. He splashed some of it on his neck and face, and the little bit left, on me lying there.

"That's to cool us off, miss."

When we said good-bye I wasn't at all said, because he held my face and said "I'm going to write you a letter. I'll tell you where I am and maybe you can come and see me. Would you like that? Okay then. You wait." I was really glad I think to get away from him, it was like he was piling presents on me I couldn't get the pleasure of till I considered them alone.

No consternation at first about the plane being gone. They thought he had taken somebody up, and I didn't enlighten them. Dr. Peebles had phoned he had to go to the country, so there was just us having supper, and then Loretta Bird thrusting her head in the door and saying, "I see he's took off."

"What?" said Alice Kelling, and pushed back her chair.

"The kids come and told me this afternoon he was taking down his tent. Did he think he'd run through all the business there was around here? He didn't take off without letting you know, did he?"

"He'll send me word," Alice Kelling said. "He'll probably phone tonight. He's terribly restless, since the war."

"Edie, he didn't mention to you, did he?" Mrs. Peebles said. "When you took over the message?"

"Yes," I said. So far so true.

"Well why didn't you say?" All of them were looking at me. "Did he say where he was going?"

"He said he might try Bayfield," I said. What made me tell such a lie? I didn't intend it.

"Bayfield, how far is that?" said Alice Kelling.

Mrs. Peebles said, "Thirty, thirty-five miles."

"That's not far. Oh, well, that's really not far at all. It's on the lake, isn't it?"

You'd think I'd be ashamed of myself, setting her on the wrong track. I did it to give him more time, whatever time he needed. I lied for him, and also, I have to admit, for me. Women should stick together and not do things like that. I see that now, but didn't then. I never thought of myself as being in any way like her, or coming to the same troubles, ever.

She hadn't taken her eyes off me. I thought she suspected my lie.

"When did he mention this to you?"

"Earlier."

"When you were over at the plane?"

"Yes."

"You must've stayed and had a chat." She smiled at me, not a nice smile. "You must've stayed and had a little visit with him."

"I took a cake," I said, thinking that telling some truth would spare me telling the rest.

"We didn't have a cake," said Mrs. Peebles rather sharply.

"I baked one."

Alice Kelling said, "That was very friendly of you."

"Did you get permission," said Loretta Bird. "You never know what these girls'll do next," she said. "It's not they mean harm so much, as they're ignorant."

"The cake is neither here nor there," Mrs. Peebles broke in. "Edie, I wasn't aware you knew Chris that well."

I didn't know what to say.

"I'm not surprised," Alice Kelling said in a high voice. "I knew by the look of her as soon as I saw her. We get them at the hospital all the time." She looked hard at me with her stretched smile. "Having their babies. We have to put them in a special ward because of their diseases. Little country tramps. Fourteen and fifteen years old. You should see the babies they have, too."

"There was a bad woman here in town had a baby that pus was running out of its eyes," Loretta Bird put in.

"Wait a minute," said Mrs. Peebles. "What is this talk? Edie. What about you and Mr. Watters? Were you intimate with him?"

"Yes," I said. I was thinking of us lying on the cot and kissing, wasn't that intimate? And I would never deny it.

They were all one minute quiet, even Loretta Bird.

"Well," said Mrs. Peebles. "I am surprised. I think I need a cigarette. This is the first of any such tendencies I've seen in her," she said, speaking to Alice Kelling, but Alice Kelling was looking at me.

"Loose little bitch." Tears ran down her face. "Loose little bitch, aren't you? I knew as soon as I saw you. Men despise girls like you. He just made use of you and went off, you know that, don't you? Girls like you are just nothing, they're just public conveniences, just filthy little rags!"

"Oh, now," said Mrs. Peebles.

"Filthy," Alice Kelling sobbed. "Filthy little rags!"

"Don't get yourself upset," Loretta Bird said. She was swollen up with pleasure at being in on this scene. "Men are all the same."

"Edie, I'm very surprised," Mrs. Peebles said. "I thought your parents were so strict. You don't want to have a baby, do you?"

I'm still ashamed of what happened next. I lost control, just like a six-year-old, I started howling. "You don't get a baby from just doing that!"

"You see. Some of them are that ignorant," Loretta Bird said.

But Mrs. Peebles jumped up and caught my arms and shook me.

"Calm down. Don't get hysterical. Calm down. Stop crying. Listen to me. Listen. I'm wondering, if you know what being intimate means. Now tell me. What did you think it meant?"

"Kissing," I howled.

She let go. "Oh, Edie. Stop it. Don't be silly. It's all right. It's all a misunderstanding. Being intimate means a lot more than that. Oh, I *wondered*."

"She's trying to cover up, now," said Alice Kelling. "Yes. She's not so stupid. She sees she got herself in trouble."

"I believe her," Mrs. Peebles said. "This is an awful scene."

"Well there is one way to find out," said Alice Kelling, getting up. "After all, I am a nurse."

Mrs. Peebles drew a breath and said, "No. No. Go to your room, Edie. And stop that noise. This is too disgusting."

I heard the car start in a little while. I tried to stop crying, pulling back each wave as it started over me. Finally I succeeded, and lay heaving on the bed.

Mrs. Peebles came and stood in the doorway.

"She's gone," she said. "That Bird woman too. Of course, you know you should never have gone near that man and that is the cause of all this trouble. I have a headache. As soon as you can, go and wash your face in cold water and get at the dishes and we will not say any more about this."

Nor we didn't. I didn't figure out till years later the extent of what I had been saved from. Mrs. Peebles was not very friendly to me afterward, but she was fair. Not very friendly is the wrong way of describing what she was. She had never been very friendly. It was just that now she had to see me all the time and it got on her nerves, a little.

As for me, I put it all out of my mind like a bad dream and concentrated on waiting for my letter. The mail came every day except Sunday, between one-thirty and two in the afternoon, a good time for me because Mrs. Peebles was always having her nap. I would get the kitchen all cleaned and then go up to the mailbox and sit in the grass, waiting. I was perfectly happy, waiting, I forgot all about Alice Kelling and her misery and awful talk and Mrs. Peebles and her chilliness and the embarrassment of whether she had told Dr. Peebles and the face of Loretta Bird, getting her fill of other people's troubles. I was always smiling when the mailman got there, and continued smiling even after he gave me the mail and I saw today wasn't the day. The mailman was a Carmichael. I knew by his face because there are a lot of Carmichaels living out by us and so many of them have a sort of sticking-out top lip. So I asked his name (he was a young man, shy, but good-humored, anybody could ask him anything) and then I said, "I knew by your face!" He was pleased by that and always glad to see me and got a little less shy. "You've got the smile I've been waiting on all day!" he used to holler out the car window.

It never crossed mind for a long time a letter might not come. I believed in it coming just like I believed the sun would rise in the morning. I just put off my hope from day to day, and there was the goldenrod out around the mailbox and the children gone back to school, and the leaves turning, and I was wearing a sweater when I went to wait. One day walking back with the hydro bill stuck in my hand, that was all, looking across at the fairgrounds with the full-blown milkweed and dark teasels, so much like fall, it just struck me: *No letter was ever going to come.* It was an impossible idea to get used to. No, not impossible. If I thought about Chris's face when he said he was going to write to me, it was impossible, but if I forgot that and thought about the actual tin mailbox, empty, it was plain and true. I kept on going to meet the mail, but my heart was heavy now like a lump of lead. I only smiled because I thought of the mailman counting on it, and he didn't have an easy life, with the winter driving ahead.

Till it came to me one day there were women doing this with their lives, all over. There were women just waiting and waiting by mailboxes for one letter or another. I imagined me making this journey day after day and year after year, and my hair starting to go gray, and I thought, I was never made to go on like that. So I stopped meeting the mail. If there were women all through life waiting, and women busy and not waiting, I knew which I had to be. Even though there might be things the second kind of women have to pass up and never know about, it still is better.

I was surprised when the mailman phoned the Peebleses' place in the evening and asked for me. He said he missed me. He asked if I would like to go to Goderich, where some well-known movie was on, I forget now what. So I said yes, and I went out with him for two years and he asked me to marry him, and we were engaged a year more while I got my things together, and then we did marry. He always tells the children the story of how I went after him by sitting by the mailbox every day, and naturally I laugh and let him, because I like for people to think what pleases them and makes them happy.

Reflections

Private Exploration

1. Edie seems keenly aware of the differences between city women and country women. Consider her perception of each of the three women. What assumptions does she make about them? What assumptions do they make about her? What different sets of values are being expressed?
2. Use the distance of memory to reflect on a time when you became thoroughly infatuated with another person. The infatuation may have been purely imaginary (nothing may have happened except in your mind), or the infatuation may have led to some moment that helped you understand yourself in a way you hadn't expected.

Public Exploration

1. Consider the nature of "love" in Munro's story. What is it for Edie? For Chris Watters (the pilot)? For Alice Kelling (the fiance)? For the mailman? What truth about love may be coming at us here? Or is it true?
2. Is Chris meant to be a stereotype of the romantic hero? If so, then what is the mailman? Explore the possible implications—both within the story and for men and women in general.

Private Reflections

After talking about "How I Met My Husband" with others, use the following lines as a way into further reflection on the possible implications of the story:

> . . . it came to me one day there were women doing this with their lives, all over. There were women just waiting and waiting by mailboxes for one letter or another. . . . So I stopped meeting the mail. If there were women all through life waiting, and women busy and not waiting, I knew which I had to be. Even though there might be things the second kind of women have to pass up and never know about, it still is better.

Where Is the Love?

JUNE JORDAN

The 1978 National Black Writers Conference at Howard University culminated with an extremely intense public seminar entitled *Feminism and the Black Woman Writer.* This was an historic, unprecedented event tantamount to conceding that, under such a heading, there might be something to discuss! Acklyn Lynch, Sonia Sanchez, Barbara Smith, and myself were the panelists chosen to present papers to the standing room only audience. I had been asked, also, to moderate the proceedings and therefore gave the opening statement, *Where Is the Love?* which was later published in *Essence* magazine.

From phone calls and other kinds of gossip, I knew that the very scheduling of this seminar had managed to divide people into camps prepared for war. Folks were so jumpy, in fact, that when I walked into the theater I ran into several Black feminists and then several Black men who, I suppose, just to be safe, had decided not to speak to anyone outside the immediate circle of supportive friends they had brought with them.

The session was going to be hot. Evidently, feminism was being translated into lesbianism, into something interchangeable with lesbianism, and the taboo on feminism, within the Black intellectual community, had long been exceeded in its orthodox severity only by the taboo on the subject of the lesbian. I say within the intellectual Black community, because, minus such terms as *feminist* and *lesbian,* the phenomena of self-directed Black women or the phenomena of Black women loving other women have hardly been uncommon, let alone unbelievable, events to Black people not privy to theoretical strife about correct and incorrect Black experience.

This blurring of issues seemed to me incendiary and obnoxious. Once again, the Black woman writer would be lost to view as issues of her sex life claimed public attention at the expense of intellectual and aesthetic focus upon her work. Compared to the intellectual and literary criticism accorded to James Baldwin and Richard Wright, for example, there is damned little attention paid to their bedroom activities. In any case, I do not believe that feminism is a matter, first or last, of sexuality.

The seminar was going to be a fight. It was not easy to prepare for this one. From my childhood in Brooklyn I knew that your peers would respect you if you could hurt somebody. Much less obvious was how to elicit respect as somebody who felt and who meant love.

I wanted to see if it was possible to say things that people believe they don't want to hear, without having to kick ass and without looking the fool for holding out your hand. Was there some way to say, to insist on, each, perhaps disagreeable, individual orientation and nonetheless leave the union of Black men and Black women, as a people, intact? I felt that there had to be: If the individual cannot exist then who will be the people?

I expected that we, Black panelists and audience, together, would work out a way to deal, even if we didn't want to deal. And that's what happened, at Howard. We did. Nobody walked out. Nobody stopped talking. The session ended because we ran out of time.

As I think about anyone or any thing—whether history or literature or my father or political organizations or a poem or a film—as I seek to evaluate the potentiality, the life-supportive commitment/possibilities of anyone or any thing, the decisive question is, always, *Where is the love?* The energies that flow from hatred, from negative and hateful habits and attitudes and dogma do not promise something good, something I would choose to cherish, to honor with my own life. It is always the love, whether we look to the spirit of Fannie Lou Hamer, or to the spirit of Agostinho Neto, it is always the love that will carry action into positive new places, that will carry your own nights and days beyond demoralization and away from suicide.

I am a feminist, and what that means to me is much the same as the meaning of the fact that I am Black: it means that I must undertake to love myself and to respect myself as though my very life depends upon self-love and self-respect. It means that I must everlastingly seek to cleanse myself of the hatred and the contempt that surrounds and permeates my identity, as a woman, and as a Black human being, in this particular world of ours. It means that the achievement of self-love and self-respect will require inordinate, hourly vigilance, and that I am entering my soul into a struggle that will most certainly transform the experience of all the peoples of the earth, as no other movement can, in fact, hope to claim: because the movement into self-love, self-respect, and self-determination is the movement now galvanizing the true, the unarguable majority of human beings everywhere. This movement explicitly demands the testing of the viability of a moral idea: that the health, the legitimacy of any status quo, any governing force, must be measured according to the experiences of those who are, comparatively, powerless. Virtue is not to be discovered in the conduct of the strong vis-à-vis the powerful, but rather it is to be found in our behavior and policies affecting those who are different, those who are weaker, or smaller than we. How do the strong, the powerful, treat children? How do we treat the aged among us? How do the strong and the powerful treat so-called minority members of the body politic? How do the powerful regard women? How do they treat us?

Easily you can see that, according to this criterion, the overwhelming reality of power and government and tradition is evil, is diseased, is illegitimate, and deserves nothing from us—no loyalty, no accommodation, no patience, no understanding—except a clear-minded resolve to utterly change this total situation and, thereby, to change our own destiny.

As a Black woman, as a Black feminist, I exist, simultaneously, as part of the powerless and as part of the majority peoples of the world in two ways: I am powerless as compared to any man because women, per se, are kept powerless by men/by the powerful; I am powerless as compared to anyone white because Black and Third World peoples are kept powerless by whites/by the powerful. I am the majority because women constitute the majority gender. I am the majority because Black and Third World peoples constitute the majority of life on this planet.

And it is here, in this extreme, inviolable coincidence of my status as a Black feminist, my status as someone twice stigmatized, my status as a Black woman who is twice kin to the despised majority of all the human life that there is, it is here, in that extremity, that I stand in a struggle against suicide. And it is here, in this extremity, that I ask, of myself, and of any one who would call me sister, *Where is the love?*

The love devolving from my quest for self-love and self-respect and self-determination must be, as I see it, something you can verify in the ways that I present myself to others, and in the ways that I approach people different from myself. How do I reach out to the people I would like to call my sisters and my brothers and my children and my lovers and my friends? If I am a Black feminist serious in the undertaking of self-love, then it seems to me that the legitimate, the morally defensible character of that self-love should be such that I gain and gain and gain in the socio-psychic strength needed so that I may, without fear, be able and willing to love and respect women, for example, who are not like me: women who are not feminists, women who are not professionals, women who are not as old or as young as I am, women who have neither job nor income, women who are not Black.

And it seems to me that the socio-psychic strength that should follow from a morally defensible Black feminism will mean that I become able and willing, without fear, to love and respect all men who are willing and able, without fear, to love and respect me. In short, if the acquirement of my self-determination is part of a worldwide, an inevitable, and a righteous movement, then I should become willing and able to embrace more and more of the whole world, without fear, and also without self-sacrifice.

This means that, as a Black feminist, I cannot be expected to respect what somebody else calls self-love if that concept of self-love requires my suicide to any degree. And this will hold true whether that somebody else is male, female, Black, or white. My Black feminism means that you cannot expect me to respect what somebody else identifies as Good of The People, if that so-called Good (often translated into *manhood* or *family* or *nationalism*) requires the deferral or the diminution of my self-fulfillment. We *are* the people. And, as Black women, we are most of the people, any people, you care to talk about. And, therefore, nothing that is Good for The People is good unless it is good for me, as I determine myself.

When I speak of Black feminism, then, I am speaking from an exacerbated consciousness of the truth that we, Black women, huddle together, miserably, on the very lowest levels of the economic pyramid. We, Black women, subsist among the most tenuous and least likely economic conditions for survival.

When I speak of Black feminism, then, I am not speaking of sexuality. I am not speaking of heterosexuality or lesbianism or homosexuality or bisexuality;

whatever sexuality anyone elects for his or her pursuit is not my business, nor the business of the state. And, furthermore, I cannot be persuaded that one kind of sexuality, as against another, will necessarily provide for the greater happiness of the two people involved. I am not talking about sexuality. I am talking about love, about a steady-state deep caring and respect for every other human being, a love that can only derive from a secure and positive self-love.

As a Black woman/feminist, I must look about me, with trembling, and with shocked anger, at the endless waste, the endless suffocation of my sisters: the bitter sufferings of hundreds of thousands of women who are the sole parents, the mothers of hundreds of thousands of children, the desolation and the futility of women trapped by demeaning, lowest-paying occupations, the unemployed, the bullied, the beaten, the battered, the ridiculed, the slandered, the trivialized, the raped, and the sterilized, the lost millions and multimillions of beautiful, creative, and momentous lives turned to ashes on the pyre of gender identity. I must look about me and, as a Black feminist, I must ask myself: *Where is the love?* How is my own lifework serving to end these tyrannies, these corrosions of sacred possibility?

As a Black feminist poet and writer I must look behind me with trembling, and with shocked anger, at the fate of Black women writers until now. From the terrible graves of a traditional conspiracy against my sisters in art, I must exhume the works of women writers and poets such as Georgia Douglas Johnson (who?).

In the early flush of the Harlem Renaissance, Georgia Johnson accomplished an astonishing, illustrious life experience. Married to Henry Lincoln Johnson, U.S. Recorder of Deeds in Washington, D.C., the poet, in her own right, became no less than Commissioner of Conciliation for the U.S. Department of Labor (*who was that again? Who?*). And she, this poet, furthermore enjoyed the intense, promotional attention of Dean Kelley Miller, here at Howard, and W. E. B. Du Bois, and William Stanley Braithwaite, and Alain Locke. And she published three volumes of her own poetry and I found her work in Countee Cullen's anthology, *Caroling Dusk*, where, Countee Cullen reports, she, Georgia Douglas Johnson, thrived as a kind of Gwendolyn Brooks, holding regular Saturday night get-togethers with the young Black writers of the day.

And what did this poet of such acclaim, achievement, connection, and generosity, what did this poet have to say in her poetry, and who among us has ever heard of Georgia Douglas Johnson? And is there anybody in this room who can tell me the name of two or three other women poets from the Harlem Renaissance? And why did she die, and why does the work of all women die with no river carrying forward the record of such grace? How is it the case that whether we have written novels or poetry or whether we have raised our children or cleaned and cooked and washed and ironed, it is all dismissed as "women's work"; it is all, finally, despised as nothing important, and there is no trace, no echo of our days upon the earth?

Why is it not surprising that a Black woman as remarkably capable and gifted and proven as Georgia Douglas Johnson should be the poet of these pathetic, beggarly lines:

> I'm folding up my little dreams
> within my heart tonight
> And praying I may soon forget
> the torture of their sight
> "*My Little Dreams*"

How long, how long will we let the dreams of women serve merely to torture and not to ignite, to enflame, and to ennoble the promise of the years of every lifetime? And here is Georgia Douglas Johnson's poem "The Heart of a Woman":

> The heart of a woman goes forth with the dawn,
> As a lovebird, softwinging, so restlessly on,
> Afar o'er life's turrets and vales does it roam
> In the wake of those echoes the heart calls home.
>
> The heart of a woman falls back with the night
> And enters some alien cage in its plight,
> And tries to forget it has dreamed of the stars,
> While it breaks, breaks, breaks on the sheltering bars.

And it is against such sorrow, and it is against such suicide, and it is against such deliberated strangulation of the possible lives of women, of my sisters, and of powerless peoples—men and children—everywhere, that I work and live, now, as a feminist trusting that I will learn to love myself well enough to love you (whoever you are), well enough so that you will love me well enough so that we will know exactly where is the love: that it is here, between us, and growing stronger and growing stronger.

Reflections

Private Exploration

1. Jordan finds power in her own voice and, for us, her words speak clearly and directly. Select and copy any one passage you find particularly powerful. After you've explained your choice, pay close attention to the writing itself. What do you recognize in Jordan's style of writing that stirs your emotions and makes her argument so convincing? On the other hand, if Jordan's writing does not seem effective to you, select a passage, copy it in your notebook, and explore its flaws. In either case, can you identify how the quality of the writing might influence your response to the ideas?

2. Consider this line:

   If the individual cannot exist then who will be the people?

3. When Amitai Etzioni, a visiting professor from Georgetown University teaching a class in ethics to Harvard Business School students, found that most of his students' values were limited to "money, power, fame and self-interest," he felt discouraged. June Jordan also writes of power and self-interest, but with a different slant. At what point can power and self-interest be considered destructive? In what ways can self-interest and power be perceived as both positive and unselfish?

Public Exploration

Jordan writes:

> The love devolving from my quest for self-love and self-respect and self-determination must be, as I see it, something you can verify in the ways that I present myself to others, and in the ways that I approach people different from myself.

Research several sources in your library on June Jordan. (See the Appendix, pp. 726–740 for suggestions.) What evidence can you find that would prove or disprove that June Jordan is true to herself, that she does indeed "practice what she preaches" in "Where is the Love?" Keep track of your sources and document your information carefully.

With your group, share your findings and by using selections from your notes as well as those provided by other students, write a collaborative paper on June Jordan complete with a Works Cited page. (Again, check the Appendix if you need help.)

Private Reflection

Jordan offers a strong argument that the struggle for self-respect and for self-love is a struggle against "suicide," against the death of the individual. Reflect thoughtfully on your own concept of self-respect and self-love. What do these words mean to you? Consider any experience, any individual, or any institution that helped shape your perceptions here. Finally, place your own sense of values in a cultural or historical perspective if you can. Is it possible that you would have felt and thought differently had you been born a century ago? Or in a different culture?

• Marriage Amulet •

NANCY WILLARD

You are polishing me like old wood.
At night we curl together like two rings
on a dark hand. After many nights,
the rough edges wear down.

If this is aging, it is warm as fleece.
I will gleam like ancient wood.

I will wax smooth, my crags and cowlicks
well-rubbed to show my grain.

Some sage will keep us in his hand for peace.

• Hemispheres •

GRACE SCHULMAN

Our bodies, luminary under bedclothes,
fit tightly like the pieces of a broken
terra cotta vase that is newly mended,
smooth surfaces, no jagged edges visible.

I've read that countries were so interlocked
before the oceans fractured them and splayed
Mexico enfolding Mauritania;
Brazil's round shoulder hoisted to Nigeria;
Italy pressing Libya; Alaska
so linked with Russia in the Bering Straits
that fingers touched, like dead hands on a harp.
Our tremulous hands held fast in sleep at dawn;
legs, arms entwined, one continent, one mass.

Reflections

Private Exploration

Consider the poems of Willard and Schulman together. As always, read each poem several times, looking up words you might be unsure of and taking marginal notes. Then use your notebook to explore the feelings each poem creates for you. Focus especially on details, specific words, or metaphors that evoke your feelings. Finally—and this is most important—consider the perspective each woman offers concerning marriage. Reflect deliberately on how you would evaluate or assess their points of view. Even though both are writing about the bedroom, do their attitudes suggest the bedroom itself is only a metaphor for something else?

Public Exploration

After someone has read both poems aloud to your class or group, share your notebook responses. As a group, consider the similarities or differences between the attitudes being expressed by these women. What do the central metaphors in each reveal about their marriages? Is this only romantic fantasy? If so, why might it be so appealing to us (assuming your group sees the poems in a positive light)? Even if both poems express only an ideal rather than a permanent reality, are they any less meaningful or valuable?

Private Reflection

Using either or both of these poems as starting points, reflect on the ideal relationship you'd like to have in your own marriage. Consider why you might hold these ideals, where they come from, and why they seem important to you?

What We Talk About When We Talk About Love

RAYMOND CARVER

My friend Mel McGinnis was talking. Mel McGinnis is a cardiologist, and sometimes that gives him the right.

The four of us were sitting around his kitchen table drinking gin. Sunlight filled the kitchen from the big window behind the sink. These were Mel and me and his second wife, Teresa—Terri, we called her—and my wife, Laura. We lived in Albuquerque then. But we were all from somewhere else.

There was an ice bucket on the table. The gin and the tonic water kept going around, and we somehow got on the subject of love. Mel thought real love was nothing less than spiritual love. He said he'd spent five years in a seminary before quitting to go to medical school. He said he still looked back on those years in the seminary as the most important years in his life.

Terri said the man she lived with before she lived with Mel loved her so much he tried to kill her. Then Terri said, "He beat me up one night. He dragged me around the living room by my ankles. He kept saying, 'I love you, I love you, you bitch.' He went on dragging me around the living room. My head kept knocking on things." Terri looked around the table. "What do you do with love like that?"

She was a bone-thin woman with a pretty face, dark eyes, and brown hair that hung down her back. She liked necklaces made of turquoise, and long pendant earrings.

"My God, don't be silly. That's not love, and you know it," Mel said. "I don't know what you'd call it, but I sure know you wouldn't call it love."

"Say what you want to, but I know it was," Terri said. "It may sound crazy to you, but it's true just the same. People are different, Mel. Sure, sometimes he may have acted crazy. Okay. But he loved me. In his own way maybe, but he loved me. There was love there, Mel. Don't say there wasn't."

Mel let out his breath. He held his glass and turned to Laura and me. "The man threatened to kill me," Mel said. He finished his drink and reached for the gin bottle. "Terri's a romantic. Terri's of the kick-me-so-I'll-know-you-love-me school. Terri, hon, don't look that way." Mel reached across the table and touched Terri's cheek with his fingers. He grinned at her.

"Now he wants to make up," Terri said.

"Make up what?" Mel said. "What is there to make up? I know what I know. That's all."

"How'd we get started on this subject, anyway?" Terri said. She raised her glass and drank from it. "Mel always has love on his mind," she said. "Don't you, honey?" She smiled, and I thought that was the last of it.

"I just wouldn't call Ed's behavior love. That's all I'm saying, honey," Mel said. "What about you guys?" Mel said to Laura and me. "Does that sound like love to you?"

"I'm the wrong person to ask," I said. "I didn't even know the man. I've only heard his name mentioned in passing. I wouldn't know. You'd have to know the particulars. But I think what you're saying is that love is an absolute."

Mel said, "The kind of love I'm talking about is. The kind of love I'm talking about, you don't try to kill people."

Laura said, "I don't know anything about Ed, or anything about the situation. But who can judge anyone else's situation?"

I touched the back of Laura's hand. She gave me a quick smile. I picked up Laura's hand. It was warm, the nails polished, perfectly manicured. I encircled the broad wrist with my fingers, and I held her.

"When I left, he drank rat poison," Terri said. She clasped her arms with her hands. "They took him to the hospital in Santa Fe. That's where we lived then, about ten miles out. They saved his life. But his gums went crazy from it. I mean they pulled away from his teeth. After that, his teeth stood out like fangs. My God," Terri said. She waited a minute, then let go of her arms and picked up her glass.

"What people won't do!" Laura said.

"He's out of the action now," Mel said. "He's dead."

Mel handed me the saucer of limes. I took a section, squeezed it over my drink, and stirred the ice cubes with my finger.

"It's gets worse," Terri said. "He shot himself in the mouth. But he bungled that too. Poor Ed," she said. Terri shook her head.

"Poor Ed nothing," Mel said. "He was dangerous."

Mel was forty-five years old. He was tall and rangy with curly soft hair. His face and arms were brown from the tennis he played. When he was sober, his gestures, all his movements, were precise, very careful.

"He did love me though, Mel. Grant me that," Terri said. "That's all I'm asking. He didn't love me the way you love me. I'm not saying that. But he loved me. You can grant me that, can't you?"

"What do you mean, he bungled it?" I said.

Laura leaned forward with her glass. She put her elbows on the table and held her glass in both hands. She glanced from Mel to Terri and waited with a look of bewilderment on her open face, as if amazed that such things happened to people you were friendly with.

"How'd he bungle it when he killed himself?" I said.

"I'll tell you what happened," Mel said. "He took this twenty-two pistol he'd bought to threaten Terri and me with. Oh, I'm serious, the man was always threatening. You should have seen the way we lived in those days. Like fugitives. I even bought a gun myself. Can you believe it? A guy like me? But I did. I bought one for self-defense and carried it in the glove compartment. Sometimes I'd have to leave the apartment in the middle of the night. To go to the hospital, you know? Terri and I weren't married then, and my first wife had the house and kids, the dog, everything, and Terri and I were living in this apartment here. Sometimes, as I say, I'd get a call in the middle of the night and have to go in to the hospital at two or three in the morning. It'd be dark out there in the parking lot, and I'd break into a sweat before I could even get to my car. I never knew if he was going to come up out of the shrubbery or from behind a car and start shooting. I mean, the man was crazy. He was capable of wiring a bomb, anything. He used to call my service at all hours and say he needed to talk to the doctor, and when I'd return the call, he'd say, 'Son of a bitch, your days are numbered.' Little things like that. It was scary, I'm telling you."

"I still feel sorry for him," Terri said.

"It sounds like a nightmare," Laura said. "But what exactly happened after he shot himself?"

Laura is a legal secretary. We'd met in a professional capacity. Before we knew it, it was a courtship. She's thirty-five, three years younger than I am. In addition to being in love, we like each other and enjoy one another's company. She's easy to be with.

"What happened?" Laura said.

Mel said, "He shot himself in the mouth in his room. Someone heard the shot and told the manager. They came in with a passkey, saw what had happened, and called an ambulance. I happened to be there when they brought him in, alive but past recall. The man lived for three days. His head swelled up to twice the size of a normal head. I'd never seen anything like it, and I hope I never do again. Terri wanted to go in and sit with him when she found out about it. We had a fight over it. I didn't think she should see him like that. I didn't think she should see him, and I still don't."

"Who won the fight?" Laura said.

"I was in the room with him when he died," Terri said. "He never came up out of it. But I sat with him. He didn't have anyone else."

"He was dangerous," Mel said. "If you call that love, you can have it."

"It was love," Terri said. "Sure, it's abnormal in most people's eyes. But he was willing to die for it. He did die for it."

"I sure as hell wouldn't call it love," Mel said. "I mean, no one knows what he did it for. I've seen a lot of suicides, and I couldn't say anyone ever knew what they did it for."

Mel put his hands behind his neck and tilted his chair back. "I'm not interested in that kind of love," he said. "If that's love, you can have it."

Terri said, "We were afraid. Mel even made a will out and wrote to his brother in California who used to be a Green Beret. Mel told him who to look for if something happened to him."

Terri drank from her glass. She said, "But Mel's right—we lived like fugitives. We were afraid. Mel was, weren't you, honey? I even called the police at one point, but they were no help. They said they couldn't do anything until Ed actually did something. Isn't that a laugh?'' Terri said.

She poured the last of the gin into her glass and waggled the bottle. Mel got up from the table and went to the cupboard. He took down another bottle.

''Well, Nick and I know what love is,'' Laura said. ''For us, I mean,'' Laura said. She bumped my knee with her knee. ''You're supposed to say something now,'' Laura said, and turned her smile on me.

For an answer, I took Laura's hand and raised it to my lips. I made a big production out of kissing her hand. Everyone was amused.

''We're lucky,'' I said.

''You guys,'' Terri said. ''Stop that now. You're making me sick. You're still on the honeymoon, for God's sake. You're still gaga, for crying out loud. Just wait. How long have you been together now? How long has it been? A year? Longer than a year?''

''Going on a year and a half,'' Laura said, flushed and smiling.

''Oh, now,'' Terri said. ''Wait awhile.''

She held her drink and gazed at Laura.

''I'm only kidding,'' Terri said.

Mel opened the gin and went around the table with the bottle.

''Here, you guys,'' he said. ''Let's have a toast. I want to propose a toast. A toast to love. To true love,'' Mel said.

We touched glasses.

''To love,'' we said.

Outside in the backyard, one of the dogs began to bark. The leaves of the aspen that leaned past the window ticked against the glass. The afternoon sun was like a presence in this room, the spacious light of ease and generosity. We could have been anywhere, somewhere enchanted. We raised our glasses again and grinned at each other like children who had agreed on something forbidden.

''I'll tell you what real love is,'' Mel said. ''I mean, I'll give you a good example. And then you can draw your own conclusions.'' He poured more gin into his glass. He added an ice cube and a sliver of lime. We waited and sipped our drinks. Laura and I touched knees again. I put a hand on her warm thigh and left it there.

''What do any of us really know about love?'' Mel said. ''It seems to me we're just beginners at love. We say we love each other and we do, I don't doubt it. I love Terri and Terri loves me, and you guys love each other too. You know the kind of love I'm talking about now. Physical love, that impulse that drives you to someone special, as well as love of the other person's being, his or her essence, as it were. Carnal love and, well, call it sentimental love, the day-to-day caring about the other person. But sometimes I have a hard time accounting for the fact that I must have loved my first wife too. But I did, I know I did. So I suppose I am like Terri in that regard. Terri and Ed.'' He thought about it and then he went on. "There was a time when I thought I loved my first wife more than life itself. But now I hate her guts. I do. How do you explain that? What happened to that love? What happened to it, is what I'd like to know. I wish someone could tell me. Then there's Ed. Okay, we're back to Ed. He loves Terri so much he tries to kill her and he winds up killing himself." Mel stopped talking and swallowed from his glass. "You guys have been together eighteen months and you love each other. It shows all over you. You glow with it. But you both loved other people before you met each other. You've both been married before, just like us. And you probably loved other people before that too, even. Terri and I have been together five years, been married for four. And the terrible thing, the terrible thing is, but the good thing too, the saving grace, you might say, is that if something happened to one of us—excuse me for saying this—but if something happened to one of us tomorrow, I think the other one, the other person, would grieve for a while, you know, but then the surviving party would go out and love again, have someone else soon enough. All this, all of this love we're talking about, it would just be a memory. Maybe not even a memory. Am I wrong? Am I way off base? Because I want you to set me straight if you think I'm wrong. I want to know. I mean, I don't know anything, and I'm the first one to admit it."

"Mel, for God's sake," Terri said. She reached out and took hold of his wrist. "Are you getting drunk? Honey? Are you drunk?"

"Honey, I'm just talking," Mel said. "All right? I don't have to be drunk to say what I think. I mean, we're all just talking, right?" Mel said. He fixed his eyes on her.

"Sweetie, I'm not criticizing," Terri said.

She picked up her glass.

"I'm not on call today," Mel said. "Let me remind you of that. I am not on call," he said.

"Mel, we love you," Laura said.

Mel looked at Laura. He looked at her as if he could not place her, as if she was not the woman she was.

"Love you too, Laura," Mel said. "And you, Nick, love you too. You know something?" Mel said. "You guys are our pals," Mel said.

He picked up his glass.

Mel said, "I was going to tell you about something. I mean, I was going to prove a point. You see, this happened a few months ago, but it's still going on right now, and it ought to make us feel ashamed when we talk like we know what we're talking about when we talk about love."

"Come on now," Terri said. "Don't talk like you're drunk if you're not drunk."

"Just shut up for once in your life," Mel said very quietly. "Will you do me a favor and do that for a minute? So as I was saying, there's this old couple who had this car wreck out on the interstate. A kid hit them and they were all torn to shit and nobody was giving them much chance to pull through."

Terri looked at us and then back at Mel. She seemed anxious, or maybe that's too strong a word.

Mel was handing the bottle around the table.

"I was on call that night," Mel said. "It was May or maybe it was June. Terri and I had just sat down to dinner when the hospital called. There'd been this thing out on the interstate. Drunk kid, teenager, plowed his dad's pickup into this camper with this old couple in it. They were up in their mid-seventies, that couple. The kid—eighteen, nineteen, something—he was DOA. Taken the steering wheel through his sternum. The old couple, they were alive, you understand. I mean, just barely. But they had everything. Multiple fractures, internal injuries, hemorrhaging, contusions, lacerations, the works, and they each of them had themselves concussions. They were in a bad way, believe me. And, of course, their age was two strikes against them. I'd say she was worse off than he was. Ruptured spleen along with everything else. Both kneecaps broken. But they'd been wearing their seatbelts and, God knows, that's what saved them for the time being."

"Folks, this is an advertisement for the National Safety Council," Terri said. "This is your spokesman, Dr. Melvin R. McGinnis, talking." Terri laughed. "Mel," she said, "sometimes you're just too much. But I love you, hon," she said.

"Honey, I love you," Mel said.

He leaned across the table. Terri met him halfway. They kissed.

"Terri's right," Mel said as he settled himself again. "Get those seatbelts on. But seriously, they were in some shape, those oldsters. By the time I got down there, the kid was dead, as I said. He was off in a corner, laid out on a gurney. I took one look at the old couple and told the ER nurse to get me a neurologist and an orthopedic man and a couple of surgeons down there right away."

He drank from his glass. "I'll try to keep this short," he said. "So we took the two of them up to the OR and worked like fuck on them most of the night. They had these incredible reserves, those two. You see that once in a while. So we did everything that could be done, and toward morning we're giving them a fifty-fifty chance, maybe less than that for her. So here they are, still alive the next morning. So, okay, we move them into the ICU, which is where they both kept plugging away at it for two weeks, hitting it better and better on all the scopes. So we transfer them out to their own room."

Mel stopped talking. "Here," he said, "let's drink this cheapo gin the hell up. Then we're going to dinner, right? Terri and I know a new place. That's where we'll go, to this new place we know about. But we're not going until we finish up this cut-rate, lousy gin."

Terri said, "We haven't actually eaten there yet. But it looks good. From the outside, you know."

"I like food," Mel said. "If I had it to do all over again, I'd be a chef, you know? Right, Terri?" Mel said.

He laughed. He fingered the ice in his glass.

"Terri knows," he said. "Terri can tell you. But let me say this. If I could come back again in a different life, a different time and all, you know what? I'd like to come back as a knight. You were pretty safe wearing all that armor. It was all right being a knight until gunpowder and muskets and pistols came along."

"Mel would like to ride a horse and carry a lance," Terri said.

"Carry a woman's scarf with you everywhere," Laura said.

"Or just a woman," Mel said.

"Shame on you," Laura said.

Terri said, "Suppose you came back as a serf. The serfs didn't have it so good in those days," Terri said.

"The serfs never had it good," Mel said. "But I guess even the knights were vessels to someone. Isn't that the way it worked? But then everyone is always a vessel to someone. Isn't that right? Terri? But what I liked about knights, besides their ladies, was that they had that suit of armor, you know, and they couldn't get hurt very easy. No cars in those days, you know? No drunk teenagers to tear into your ass."

"Vassals," Terri said.

"What?" Mel said.

"Vassals," Terri said. "They were called vassals, not vessels."

"Vassals, vessels," Mel said, "what the fuck's the difference? You knew what I meant anyway. All right," Mel said. "So I'm not educated. I learned my stuff. I'm a heart surgeon, sure, but I'm just a mechanic. I go in and I fuck around and I fix things. Shit," Mel said.

"Modesty doesn't become you," Terri said.

"He's just a humble sawbones," I said. "But sometimes they suffocated in all that armor, Mel. They'd even have heart attacks if it got too hot and they were too tired and worn out. I read somewhere that they'd fall off their horses and not be able to get up because they were too tired to stand with all that armor on them. They got trampled by their own horses sometimes."

"That's terrible," Mel said. "That's a terrible thing, Nicky. I guess they'd just lay there and wait until somebody came along and made a shish kebab out of them."

"Some other vessel," Terri said.

"That's right," Mel said. "Some vassal would come along and spear the bastard in the name of love. Or whatever the fuck it was they fought over in those days."

"Same things we fight over these days," Terri said.

Laura said, "Nothing's changed."

The color was still high in Laura's cheeks. Her eyes were bright. She brought her glass to her lips.

Mel poured himself another drink. He looked at the label closely as if studying a long row of numbers. Then he slowly put the bottle down on the table and slowly reached for the tonic water.

"What about the old couple?" Laura said. "You didn't finish that story you started."

Laura was having a hard time lighting her cigarette. Her matches kept going out.

The sunshine inside the room was different now, changing, getting thinner. But the leaves outside the window were still shimmering, and I stared at the pattern they made on the panes and on the Formica counter. They weren't the same patterns, of course.

"What about the old couple?" I said.

"Older but wiser," Terri said.

Mel stared at her.

Terri said, "Go on with your story, hon. I was only kidding. Then what happened?"

"Terri, sometimes," Mel said.

"Please, Mel," Terri said. "Don't always be so serious, sweetie. Can't you take a joke?"

"Where's the joke?" Mel said.

He held his glass and gazed steadily at his wife.

"What happened?" Laura said.

Mel fastened his eyes on Laura. He said, "Laura, if I didn't have Terri and if I didn't love her so much, and if Nick wasn't my best friend, I'd fall in love with you. I'd carry you off, honey," he said.

"Tell your story," Terri said. "Then we'll go to that new place, okay?"

"Okay," Mel said. "Where was I?" he said. He stared at the table and then he began again.

"I dropped in to see each of them every day, sometimes twice a day if I was up doing other calls anyway. Casts and bandages, head to foot, the both of them. You know, you've seen it in the movies. That's just the way they looked, just like in the movies. Little eye-holes and nose-holes and mouth-holes. And she had to have her legs slung up on top of it. Well, the husband was very depressed for the longest while. Even after he found out that his wife was going to pull through, he was still very depressed. Not about the accident, though. I mean, the accident was one thing, but it wasn't everything. I'd get up to his mouth-hole, you know, and he'd say no, it wasn't the accident exactly but it was because he couldn't see her through his eye-holes. He said that was what was making him feel so bad. Can you imagine? I'm telling you, the man's heart was breaking because he couldn't turn his goddamn head and *see* his goddamn wife."

Mel looked around the table and shook his head at what he was going to say.

"I mean, it was killing the old fart just because he couldn't *look* at the fucking woman."

We all looked at Mel.

"Do you see what I'm saying?" he said.

Maybe we were a little drunk by them. I know it was hard keeping things in focus. The light was draining out of the room, going back through the window where it had come from. Yet nobody made a move to get up from the table to turn on the overhead light.

"Listen," Mel said. "Let's finish this fucking gin. There's about enough left here for one shooter all around. Then let's go eat. Let's go to the new place."

"He's depressed," Terri said. "Mel, why don't you take a pill?"

"We all need a pill now and then," I said.

"Some people are born needing them," Terri said.

She was using her finger to rub at something on the table. Then she stopped rubbing.

"I think I want to call my kids," Mel said. "Is that all right with everybody? I'll call my kids," he said.

Terri said, "What if Marjorie answers the phone? You guys, you've heard us on the subject of Marjorie? Honey, you know you don't want to talk to Marjorie. It'll make you feel even worse."

"I don't want to talk to Marjorie," Mel said. "But I want to talk to my kids."

"There isn't a day goes by that Mel doesn't say he wishes she'd get married again. Or else die," Terri said. "For one thing," Terri said, "she's bankrupting us. Mel says it's just to spite him that she won't get married again. She has a boyfriend who lives with her and the kids, so Mel is supporting the boyfriend too."

"She's allergic to bees," Mel said. "If I'm not praying she'll get married again, I'm praying she'll get herself stung to death by a swarm of fucking bees."

"Shame on you," Laura said.

"Bzzzzzzz," Mel said, turning his fingers into bees and buzzing them at Terri's throat. Then he let his hands drop all the way to his sides.

"She's vicious," Mel said. "Sometimes I think I'll go up there dressed like a beekeeper. You know, that hat that's like a helmet with the plate that comes down over your face, the big gloves, and the padded coat? I'll knock on the door and let loose a hive of bees in the house. But first I'd make sure the kids were out, of course."

He crossed one leg over the other. It seemed to take him a lot of time to do it. Then he put both feet on the floor and leaned forward, elbows on the table, his chin cupped in his hands.

"Maybe I won't call the kids, after all. Maybe it isn't such a hot idea. Maybe we'll just go eat. How does that sound?"

"Sounds fine to me," I said. "Eat or not eat. Or keep drinking. I could head right on out into the sunset."

"What does that mean, honey?" Laura said.

"It just means what I said," I said. "It means I could just keep going. That's all it means."

"I could eat something myself," Laura said. "I don't think I've ever been so hungry in my life. Is there anything to nibble on?"

"I'll put out some cheese and crackers," Terri said.

But Terri just sat there. She did not get up to get anything.

Mel turned his glass over. He spilled it out on the table.

"Gin's gone," Mel said.

Terri said, "Now what?"

I could hear my heart beating. I could hear everyone's heart. I could hear the human noise we sat there making, not one of us moving, not even when the room went dark.

Reflections

Private Exploration

1. Writing as spontaneously as possible, explore your most immediate response to Carver's story, your most dominant feeling evolving from the couple's discussion. Try to pinpoint for yourself particulars of the story that prompt your reaction.
2. True love, blind love, puppy love, physical love, sensual love, real love, absolute love—these are just a few of the common expressions we use when we talk about love. As the couples struggle to define it, explore for yourself what love is. You may want to draw from personal experience and observations, as well as from your reading or from films.
3. Zero in on a single line, passage, or incident in the story that disturbs you. What is it that bothers you? Why? (Make sure you place your selection within a context.)

Public Exploration

What are these people talking about? Consider what love is to each of them, what they are struggling to say to each other. Is this what we mean when we talk about love? What is love in reality? (Sex? Commitment? Sharing? Affection? Spiritual connections? Or mere rationalizations about our emotions, our loneliness, our desire for power over others? What?)

Private Reflection

1. After discussing Carver's story with others, use the following passage for a final reflection on love. Dig deep and write from your own heart.

> You guys have been together eighteen months and you love each other. It shows all over you. You glow with it. But you loved other people before you met each other. You've both been married before, just like us. And you probably loved other people before that too, even. Terri and I have been together five years, been married four. And the terrible thing, the terrible thing is, but the good thing too, the saving grace, you might say, is that if something happened to one of us tomorrow, I think the other one, the other person, would grieve for a while, you know, but then the surviving party would go out and love again, have someone else soon enough. All this, all of this love we're talking about, it would just be a memory.

2. Carver ends with a particularly haunting last line.

> I could hear my heart beating. I could hear everyone's heart. I could hear the human noise we sat there making, not one of us moving, not even when the room went dark.

Consider the significance to ourselves in Mel's final words. Consider too their implications for developing a sense of values. Where do we go from here?

• To His Coy Mistress •

ANDREW MARVELL

Had we but world enough, and time,
This coyness, lady, were no crime.
We would sit down, and think which way
To walk, and pass our long love's day.
Though by the Indian Ganges' side
Should'st rubies find: I by the tide
Of Humber would complain. I would
Love you ten years before the Flood,
And you should, if you please, refuse
Till the conversion of the Jews.
My vegetable love should grow
Vaster than empires, and more slow.
An hundred years should go to praise
Thine eyes, and on thy forehead gaze:
Two hundred to adore each breast:
But thirty thousand to the rest.
An age at least to every part,
And the last age should show your heart.
For, lady, you deserve this state,
Nor would I love at lower rate.

But at my back I always hear
Time's wingèd chariot hurrying near;
And yonder all before us lie
Deserts of vast eternity.
Thy beauty shall no more be found,
Nor in thy marble vault shall sound
My echoing song; then worms shall try
That long preserved virginity,
And your quaint honor turn to dust,
And into ashes all my lust.
The grave's a fine and private place,
But none, I think, do there embrace.

Now therefore, while the youthful hue
Sits on thy skin like morning dew,
And while thy willing soul transpires
At every pore with instant fires,
Now let us sport us while we may;
And now, like am'rous birds of prey,
Rather at once our time devour,
Than languish in his slow-chapt power
Let us roll all our strength, and all
Our sweetness, up into one ball;
And tear our pleasures with rough strife

Thorough the iron gates of life.
Thus, though we cannot make our sun
Stand still, yet we will make him run.

Reflections

Personal Exploration

Although you may not understand all of Marvell's images or allusions, you can probably still catch the basic drift of this 17th century poem. Assume you are the young woman Marvell is addressing. How would you paraphrase his argument to you? What rationale does he offer to sway you with? How would you characterize the values that underlie such an argument? Are you convinced?

Public Exploration

After someone in your class or group reads the poem aloud, share your notebook responses. Is this a poem about a dude scamming some chick? Is the speaker being serious or playful? And what do you make of the woman? Is there any irony here? Does the poem suggest the type of culture or world view that Marvell must have lived in during the 17th century? How do the possible values implicit here compare or contrast to the 20th century?

Private Reflection

After listening to others share their insights and feelings, has your own sense of the poem been modified? Reflect on what you now feel is the central idea of the poem in terms of your own life and values.

The Likenesses of Atonement (At-one-ment)

WENDELL BERRY

Living in our speech, though no longer in our consciousness, is an ancient system of analogies that clarifies a series of mutually defining and sustaining unities: of farmer and field, of husband and wife, of the world and God. The language both of our literature and of our everyday speech is full of references and allusions to this expansive metaphor of farming and marriage and worship. A man planting a crop is like a man making love to his wife, and vice versa: he is a husband or a husbandman. A man praying is like a lover, or he is like a plant in a field waiting for rain. As husbandman, a man is both the steward and the likeness of God, the greater husbandman. God is the lover of the world and its faithful husband. Jesus is a bridegroom. And he is a planter; his words are seeds. God is a shepherd and we are his sheep. And so on.

All the essential relationships are comprehended in this metaphor. A farmer's relation to his land is the basic and central connection in the relation of humanity to the creation; the agricultural relation *stands for* the larger relation. Similarly, marriage is the basic and central community tie; it begins and stands for the relation we have to family and to the larger circles of human association. And these relationships to the creation and to the human community are in turn basic to, and may stand for, our relationship to God—or to the sustaining mysteries and powers of the creation.

(These three relationships are dependent—and even intent—upon renewals of various sorts: of season, of fertility, of sexual energy, of love, of faith. And these concepts of renewal are always accompanied by concepts of loss or death; in order for the renewal to take place, the old must be not forgotten but relinquished; in order to become what we may be, we must cease to be as we are; in order to leave life we must lose it. Our language bears abundant testimony to these deaths: the year's death that precedes spring; the burial of the seed before germination; sexual death, as in the Elizabethan metaphor, death as the definitive term of marriage; the spiritual death that must precede rebirth; the death of the body that must precede resurrection.)

As the metaphor comprehends all the essential relationships, so too it comprehends all the essential moralities. The moralities are ultimately emulative. For the metaphor does not merely perceive the likeness of these relationships. It perceives also that they are understandable only in terms of each other. They are the closed system of our experience; no instructions come from outside. A man finally cannot act upon the basis of absolute law, for the law is more fragmentary than his own experience; finally, he must emulate in one relationship what he knows of another. Thus, if the metaphor of atonement is alive in his consciousness, he will see that he should love and care for his land as for his wife, that his relation to his place in the world is as solemn and demanding, and as blessed, as marriage; and he will see that he should respect his marriage as he respects the mysteries and transcendent powers—that is, as a sacrament. Or—to move in the opposite direction through the changes of the metaphor—in order to care properly for his land he will see that he must emulate the Creator: to learn to use and preserve the open fields, as Sir Albert Howard said, he must look into the woods; he must study and follow natural process; he must understand the *husbanding* that, in nature, always accompanies providing.

Like any interlinking system, this one fails in the failure of any one of its parts. When we obscure or corrupt our understanding of any one of the basic unities, we begin to misunderstand all of them. The vital knowledge dies out of our consciousness and becomes fossilized in our speech and our culture. This is our condition now. We have severed the vital links of the atonement metaphor, and we did this initially, I think, by degrading and obscuring our connection to the land, by looking upon the land as merchandise and ourselves as its traveling salesmen.

I do not know how exact a case might be made, but it seems to me that there is a historical parallel, in white American history, between the treatment of the land and the treatment of women. The frontier, for instance, was notoriously exploitive of both, and I believe for largely the same reasons. Many of the early farmers seem to have worn out farms and wives with equal regardlessness, interested in both mainly for what they would produce, crops and dollars, labor and sons; they clambered upon their fields and upon their wives, struggling for an economic foothold, the having and holding that cannot come until both fields and wives are properly cherished. And today there seems to me a distinct connection between our nomadism (our "social mobility") and the nearly universal disintegration of our marriages and families.

The prevalent assumption appears to be that marriage problems are problems strictly of "human relations": if the husband and wife will only assent to a number of truisms about "respect for the other person," "giving and taking," et cetera, and if they will only "understand" each other, then it is believed that their problems will be solved. The difficulty is that marriage is only partly a matter of "human relations," and only partly a circumstance of the emotions. It is also, and as much as anything, a practical circumstance. It is very much under the influence of things and people outside itself; that is, it must make a household, it must make a place for itself in the world and in the community. But with us, getting someplace always involves going somewhere. Every professional advance leads to a new place, a new house, a new neighborhood. Our marriages are always been cut off from what they have made; their substance is always disappearing into the thin air of human relations.

I think there is a limit to the portability of human relationships. Tribal nomads, when they moved, moved as a tribe; their personal and cultural identity—their household and community—accompanied them as they went. But our modern urban nomads are always moving away from the particulars by which they know themselves, and moving into abstraction (*a* house, *a* neighborhood, *a* job) in which they can only feel threatened by new particulars. The marriage becomes a sort of assembly-line product, made partly here and partly there, the whole of it never quite coming into view. Provided they stay married (which is unlikely) until the children leave (which is usually soon), the nomadic husband and wife who look to see what their marriage has been—that is to say, what it *is*—are apt to see only the lines in each other's face.

The carelessness of place that must accompany our sort of nomadism makes a vagueness in marriage that is its antithesis. And vagueness in marriage, the most sacred human bond and perhaps the basic metaphor of our moral and religious tradition, cannot help but produce a diminishment of reverence, and of the care for the earth that must accompany reverence.

When the metaphor of atonement ceases to be a live function of our consciousness, we lose the means of relationship. We become isolated in our-

selves, and our behavior becomes the erratic destructive behavior of people who have no bonds and no limits.

Reflections

Private Exploration

1. We find Berry's insights rich and thought-provoking. Almost every sentence triggers ideas and emotions, yet the essay is not particularly easy to grasp. After a quick reading, jot down in your reader's notebook whatever questions you have, then read the essay a second time. (Forming questions about your reading may seem irritating at times, but thoughtful reading always involves reading with a sense of a question in the back of your mind.) On your second reading, be sure to mark and annotate the text closely. Use a dictionary for emphasized words such as "atonement" and "analogy."

   Select a key passage and copy it out word for word. Explore possible directions it might take you in. Here are two you might consider:

   > Living in our speech, though no longer in our consciousness, is an ancient system of analogies that clarifies a series of mutually defining and sustaining unities: of farmer and field, of husband and wife, of the world and God.

   > Like any interlinking system, this one fails in the failure of any one of its parts. When we obscure or corrupt our understanding of any one of the basic unities, we begin to misunderstand all of them. The vital knowledge dies out of our consciousness and becomes fossilized in our speech and culture. This is our condition now.

2. Berry seems to suggest that a meaningful marriage is directly tied to other factors: place (the land), and faith (God, prayer, spiritual values). Does this seem reasonable? Exaggerated? Too reliant on an "old fashioned" morality? Test Berry's ideas against the world you live in. (Is someone who lives in a twenty-story apartment building or who is transferred from New York to Fort Worth to Minneapolis every two years condemned to an empty marriage? Are those who have no "spiritual" feelings also lacking in the emotions of love?)

Public Exploration

1. Consider this excerpt:

   > When the metaphor of atonement ceases to be a live function of our consciousness, we lose the means of relationship. We become isolated in ourselves, and our behavior becomes the erratic destructive behavior of people who have no bonds and no limits.

2. If we admit that Berry's vision (a unity of land-faith-marriage) is both inspiring and profound, should we also consider it so idealistic as to be naive? Is it a vision more suitable for the 19th century than the late 20th? Or is it still possible to achieve

atonement? Can a man's or woman's work (an absorption in one's craft, a personal investment in quality) substitute for attachment to the land? Can spiritual values include a commitment to protecting the environment or a devotion to a particular cause? Are there other ways to achieve the trinity of values Berry promotes?

3. Consider the role of women in Berry's metaphor. What assumptions are being made?

Private Reflections

After discussing Berry's essay with other's, reread it. If possible, consider how ideas in it might compare or contrast to other works you've read. Consider how your parents or grandparents might have responded to the concepts of land-faith-marriage. Let your notebook serve as a place where you can quietly, deliberately, search out the values you now feel may be taking shape for you.

Bridging

MAX APPLE

At the Astrodome, Nolan Ryan is shaving the corners. He's going through the Giants in order. The radio announcer is not even mentioning that by the sixth the Giants haven't had a hit. The K's mount on the scoreboard. Tonight Nolan passes the Big Train and is now the all-time strikeout king. He's almost as old as I am and he still throws nothing but smoke. His fastball is an aspirin; batters tear their tendons lunging for his curve. Jessica and I have season tickets, but tonight she's home listening and I'm in the basement of St. Anne's Church watching Kay Randall's fingertips. Kay is holding her hands out from her chest, her fingertips on each other. Her fingers move a little as she talks and I can hear her nails click when they meet. That's how close I'm sitting.

Kay is talking about "bridging"; that's what her arched fingers represent.

"Bridging," she says, "is the way Brownies become Girl Scouts. It's a slow steady process. It's not easy, but we allow a whole year for bridging."

Eleven girls in brown shirts with red bandannas at their neck are imitating Kay as she talks. They hold their stumpy chewed fingertips out and bridge them. So do I.

I brought the paste tonight and the stick-on gold stars and the thread for sewing buttonholes.

"I feel a little awkward," Kay Randall said on the phone, "asking a man to do these errands . . . but that's my problem, not yours. Just bring the supplies and try to be at the church meeting room a few minutes before seven."

I arrive a half hour early.

"You're off your rocker," Jessica says. She begs me to drop her at the

Astrodome on my way to the Girl Scout meeting. "After the game, I'll meet you at the main souvenir stand on the first level. They stay open an hour after the game. I'll be all right. There are cops and ushers every five yards."

She can't believe that I am missing this game to perform my functions as an assistant Girl Scout leader. Our Girl Scout battle has been going on for two months.

"Girl Scouts is stupid," Jessica says. "Who wants to sell cookies and sew buttons and walk around wearing stupid old badges?"

When she agreed to go to the first meeting, I was so happy I volunteered to become an assistant leader. After the meeting, Jessica went directly to the car the way she does after school, after a birthday party, after a ball game, after anything. A straight line to the car. No jabbering with girlfriends, no smiles, no dallying, just right to the car. She slides into the back seat, belts in, and braces herself for destruction. It has already happened once.

I swoop past five thousand years of stereotypes and accept my assistant leader's packet and credentials.

"I'm sure there have been other men in the movement," Kay says, "we just haven't had any in our district. It will be good for the girls."

Not for my Jessica. She won't bridge, she won't budge.

"I know why you're doing this," she says. "You think that because I don't have a mother, Kay Randall and the Girl Scouts will help me. That's crazy. And I know that Sharon is supposed to be like a mother too. Why don't you just leave me alone."

Sharon is Jessica's therapist. Jessica sees her twice a week. Sharon and I have a meeting once a month.

"We have a lot of shy girls," Kay Randall tells me. "Scouting brings them out. Believe me, it's hard to stay shy when you're nine years old and you're sharing a tent with six other girls. You have to count on each other, you have to communicate."

I imagine Jessica zipping up in her sleeping bag, mumbling good night to anyone who first says it to her, then closing her eyes and hating me for sending her our among the happy.

"She likes all sports, especially baseball," I tell my leader.

"There's room for baseball in scouting," Kay says. "Once a year the whole district goes to a game. They mention us on the big scoreboard."

"Jessica and I go to all the home games. We're real fans."

Kay smiles.

"That's why I want her in Girl Scouts. You know, I want her to go to things with her girlfriends instead of always hanging around with me at ball games."

"I understand," Kay says. "It's part of bridging."

With Sharon the term is "separation anxiety." That's the fastball, "bridging" is the curve. Amid all their magic words I feel as if Jessica and I are standing at home plate blindfolded.

While I await Kay and the members of Troop 111, District 6, I eye St. Anne in her grotto and St. Gregory and St. Thomas. Their hands are folded as if they started out bridging, ended up praying.

In October the principal sent Jessica home from school because Mrs. Simmons caught her in spelling class listening to the World Series through an earphone.

"It's against the school policy," Mrs. Simmons said. "Jessica understands school policy. We confiscate radios and send the child home."

"I'm glad," Jessica said. "It was a cheap-o radio. Now I can watch the TV with you."

They sent her home in the middle of the sixth game. I let her stay home for the seventh too.

The Brewers are her favorite American League team. She likes Rollie Fingers, and especially Robin Yount.

"Does Yount go in the hole better than Harvey Kuenn used to?"

"You bet," I tell her. "Kuenn was never a great fielder but he could hit three hundred with his eyes closed."

Kuenn is the Brewers' manager. He has an artificial leg and can barely make it up the dugout steps, but when I was Jessica's age and the Tigers were my team, Kuenn used to stand at the plate, tap the corners with his bat, spit some tobacco juice, and knock liners up the alley.

She took the Brewers' loss hard.

"If Fingers wasn't hurt they would have squashed the Cards, wouldn't they?"

I agreed.

"But I'm glad for Andujar."

We had Andujar's autograph. Once we met him at a McDonald's he was a relief pitcher then, an erratic right-hander. In St. Louis he improved. I was happy to get his name on a napkin. Jessica shook his hand.

One night after I read her a story, she said, "Daddy, if we were rich could we go to the away games too? I mean, if you didn't have to be at work every day."

"Probably we could," I said, "but wouldn't it get boring? We'd have to stay at hotels and eat in restaurants. Even the players get sick of it."

"Are you kidding?" she said. "I'd never get sick of it."

"Jessica has fantasies of being with you forever, following baseball or whatever," Sharon says. "All she's trying to do is please you. Since she lost her mother she feels that you and she are alone in the world. She doesn't want to let anyone or anything else into that unit, the two of you. She's afraid of any more losses. And, of course, her greatest worry is about losing you."

"You know," I tell Sharon, "that's pretty much how I feel too."

"Of course it is," she says. "I'm glad to hear you say it."

Sharon is glad to hear me say almost anything. When I complain that her $100-a-week fee would buy a lot of peanut butter sandwiches, she says she is "glad to hear me expressing my anger."

"Sharon's not fooling me," Jessica says. "I know that she thinks drawing those pictures is supposed to make me feel better or something. You're just wasting your money. There's nothing wrong with me."

"It's a long, difficult, expensive process," Sharon says. "You and Jessica have lost a lot. Jessica is going to have to learn to trust the world again. It would help if you could do it too."

So I decide to trust Girl Scouts. First Girl Scouts, then the world. I make my stand at the meeting of Kay Randall's fingertips. While Nolan Ryan breaks Walter Johnson's strikeout record and pitches a two-hit shutout, I pass out paste and thread to nine-year-olds who are sticking and sewing their lives together in ways Jessica and I can't.

II

Scouting is not altogether new to me. I was a Cub Scout. I owned a blue beanie and I remember very well my den mother, Mrs. Clark. A den mother made perfect sense to me then and still does. Maybe that's why I don't feel uncomfortable being a Girl Scout assistant leader.

We had no den father. Mr. Clark was only a photograph on the living room wall, the tiny living room where we held our monthly meetings. Mr. Clark was killed in the Korean War. His son John was in the troop. John was stocky but Mrs. Clark was huge. She couldn't sit on a regular chair, only on a couch or a stool without sides. She was the cashier in the convenience store beneath their apartment. The story we heard was that Walt, the old man who owned the store, felt sorry for her and gave her the job. He was her landlord too. She sat on a swivel stool and rang up the purchases.

We met at the store and watched while she locked the door; then we followed her up the steep staircase to her three-room apartment. She carried two wet glass bottles of milk. Her body took up the entire width of the staircase. She passed the banisters the way semi trucks pass each other on a narrow highway.

We were ten years old, a time when everything is funny, especially fat people. But I don't remember anyone ever laughing about Mrs. Clark. She had great dignity and character. So did John. I didn't know what to call it then, but I knew John was someone you could always trust.

She passed out milk and cookies, then John collected the cups and washed them. They didn't even have a television set. The only decoration in the room that barely held all of us was Mr. Clark's picture on the wall. We saw him in his uniform and we knew he died in Korea defending his country. We were little boys in blue beanies drinking milk in the apartment of a hero. Through that aura I came to scouting. I wanted Kay Randall to have all of Mrs. Clark's dignity.

When she took a deep breath and then bridged, Kay Randall had noticeable armpits. Her wide shoulders slithered into a tiny rib cage. Her armpits were like bridges. She said "bridging" like a mantra, holding her hands before her for about thirty seconds at the start of each meeting.

"A promise is a promise," I told Jessica. "I signed up to be a leader, and I'm going to do it with you or without you."

"But you didn't even ask me if I liked it. You just signed up without talking it over."

"That's true; that's why I'm not going to force you to go along. It was my choice."

"What can you like about it? I hate Melissa Randall. She always has a cold."

"Her mother is a good leader."

"How do you know?"

"She's my boss. I've got to like her, don't I?" I hugged Jessica. "C'mon, honey, give it a chance. What do you have to lose?"

"If you make me go I'll do it, but if I have a choice I won't."

Every other Tuesday, Karen, the fifteen-year-old Greek girl who lives on the corner, babysits Jessica while I go to the Scout meetings. We talk about field trips and how to earn merit badges. The girls giggle when Kay pins a promptness badge on me, my first.

Jessica thinks it's hilarious. She tells me to wear it to work.

Sometimes when I watch Jessica brush her hair and tie her ponytail and make up her lunch kit I start to think that maybe I should just relax and stop the therapy and the scouting and all my not-so-subtle attempts to get her to invite friends over. I start to think that, in spite of everything, she's a good student and she's got a sense of humor. She's barely nine years old. She'll grow up like everyone else does. John Clark did it without a father; she'll do it without a mother. I start to wonder if Jessica seems to the girls in her class the way John Clark seemed to me: dignified, serious, almost an adult even while we were playing. I admired him. Maybe the girls in her class admire her. But John had that hero on the wall, his father in a uniform, dead for reasons John and all the rest of us understood.

My Jessica had to explain a neurologic disease she couldn't even pronounce. "I hate it when people ask me about Mom," she says. "I just tell them she fell off the Empire State Building."

III

Before our first field trip I go to Kay's house for a planning session. We're going to collect wildflowers in East Texas. It's a one-day trip. I arranged to rent the school bus.

I told Jessica that she could go on the trip even though she wasn't a troop member, but she refused.

We sit on colonial furniture in Kay's den. She brings in coffee and we go over the supply list. Another troop is joining ours so there will be twenty-two girls, three women, and me, a busload among the bluebonnets.

"We have to be sure the girls understand that the bluebonnets they pick are on private land and that we have permission to pick them. Otherwise they might pick them along the roadside, which is against the law."

I imagine all twenty-two of them behind bars for picking bluebonnets and Jessica laughing while I scramble for bail money.

I keep noticing Kay's hands. I notice them as she pours coffee, as she checks off the items on the list, as she gestures. I keep expecting her to bridge. She has large, solid, confident hands. When she finishes bridging I sometimes feel like clapping the way people do after the national anthem.

"I admire you," she tells me. "I admire you for going ahead with Scouts even though your daughter rejects it. She'll get a lot out of it indirectly from you."

Kay Randall is thirty-three, divorced, and has a Bluebird too. Her older daughter is one of the stubby-fingered girls, Melissa. Jessica is right; Melissa always has a cold.

Kay teaches fifth grade and has been divorced for three years. I am the first assistant she's ever had.

"My husband, Bill, never helped with Scouts," Kay says. "He was pretty much turned off to everything except his business and drinking. When we separated I can't honestly say I missed him; he'd never been there. I don't think the girls miss him either. He only sees them about once a month. He has girlfriends, and his business is doing very well. I guess he has what he wants."

"And you?"

She uses one of those wonderful hands to move the hair away from her eyes, a gesture that makes her seem very young.

"I guess I do too. I've got the girls and my job. I'm lonesome, though. It's not exactly what I wanted."

We both think about what might have been as we sit beside her glass coffeepot with our lists of sachet supplies. If she was Barbara Streisand and I Robert Redford and the music started playing in the background to give us a clue and there was a long close-up of our lips, we might just fade into middle age together. But Melissa called for Mom because her mosquito bite was bleeding where she scratched it. And I had an angry daughter waiting for me. And all Kay and I had in common was Girl Scouts. We were both smart enough to know it. When Kay looked at me before going to put alcohol on the mosquito bite, our mutual sadness dripped from us like the last drops of coffee through the grinds.

"You really missed something tonight," Jessica tells me. "The Astros did a double steal. I've never seen one before. In the fourth they sent Thon and Moreno together, and Moreno stole home."

She knows batting averages and won-lost percentages too, just like the older boys, only they go to play. Jessica stays in and waits for me.

During the field trip, while the girls pick flowers to dry and then manufacture into sachets, I think about Jessica at home, probably beside the radio. Juana, our once-a-week cleaning lady, agreed to work on Saturday so she could stay with Jessica while I took the all-day field trip.

It was no small event. In the eight months since Vicki died I had not gone away for an entire day.

I made waffles in the waffle iron for her before I left, but she hardly ate.

"If you want anything, just ask Juana."

"Juana doesn't speak English."

"She understands, that's enough."

"Maybe for you it's enough."

"Honey, I told you, you can come; there's plenty of room on the bus. It's not too late for you to change your mind."

"It's not too late for you either. There's going to be plenty of other leaders there. You don't have to go. You're just doing this to be mean to me."

I'm ready for this. I spent an hour with Sharon steeling myself. "Before she can leave you," Sharon said, "you'll have to show her that you can leave. Nothing's going to happen to her. And don't let her be sick that day either."

Jessica is too smart to pull the "I don't feel good" routine. Instead she becomes more silent, more unhappy looking than usual. She stays in her pajamas while I wash the dishes and get ready to leave.

I didn't notice the sadness as it was coming upon Jessica. It must have happened gradually in the years of Vicki's decline, the years in which I paid so little attention to my daughter. There were times when Jessica seemed to recognize the truth more than I did.

As my Scouts picked their wildflowers, I remembered the last outing I had planned for us. It was going to be a Fourth of July picnic with some friends in Austin. I stopped at the bank and got $200 in cash for the long weekend. But when I came home Vicki was too sick to move and the air conditioner had broken. I called our friends to cancel the picnic; then I took Jessica to the mall with me to buy a fan. I bought the biggest one they had, a 58-inch oscillating model that sounded like a hurricane. It could cool 10,000 square feet, but it wasn't enough.

Vicki was home sitting blankly in front of the TV set. The fan could move eight tons of air an hour, but I wanted it to save my wife. I wanted a fan that would blow the whole earth out of its orbit.

I had $50 left. I gave it to Jessica and told her to buy anything she wanted.

"Whenever you're sad, Daddy, you want to buy me things." She put the money back in my pocket. "It won't help." She was seven years old, holding my hand tightly in the appliance department at J. C. Penney's.

I watched Melissa sniffle even more among the wildflowers, and I pointed out the names of various flowers to Carol and JoAnne and Sue and Linda and Rebecca, who were by now used to me and treated me pretty much as they treated Kay. I noticed that the Girl Scout flower book had very accurate photographs that made it easy to identify the bluebonnets and buttercups and poppies. There were also several varieties of wild grasses.

We were only 70 miles from home on some land a wealthy rancher long ago donated to the Girl Scouts. The girls bending among the flowers seemed to have been quickly transformed by the colorful meadow. The gigglers and monotonous singers on the bus were now, like the bees, sucking strength from the beauty around them. Kay was in the midst of them and so, I realized, was I, not watching and keeping score and admiring from the distance but a participant, a player.

JoAnne and Carol sneaked up from behind me and dropped some dandelions down my back. I chased them; then I helped the other leaders pour the Kool-Aid and distribute the Baggies and the name tags for each girl's flowers.

My daughter is home listening to a ball game, I thought, and I'm out here having fun with nine-year-olds. It's upside down.

When I came home with dandelion fragments still on my back, Juana had cleaned the house and I could smell the taco sauce in the kitchen. Jessica was in her room. I suspected that she had spent the day listless and tearful, although I had asked her to invite a friend over.

"I had a lot of fun, honey, but I missed you."

She hugged me and cried against my shoulder. I felt like holding her the way I used to when she was an infant, the way I rocked her to sleep. But she was a big girl now and needed not sleep but wakefulness.

"I heard on the news that the Rockets signed Ralph Sampson," she sobbed, "and you hardly ever take me to any pro basketball games."

"But if they have a new center things will be different. With Sampson we'll be contenders. Sure I'll take you."

"Promise?"

"Promise." I promise to take you everywhere, my lovely child, and then to leave you. I'm learning to be a leader.

Reflections

Private Exploration

1. What is being expressed here?

    > I felt like holding her the way I used to when she was an infant, the way I rocked her to sleep. But she was a big girl now and needed not sleep but wakefulness.

    Even though you may not have been a parent, can you associate with this emotion? Have you felt it in yourself, or from someone else? Explore the feeling as deeply as you can.

2. Consider this passage:

    > With Sharon the term is 'separation anxiety.' That's the fastball, 'bridging' is the curve. Amid all their magic words I feel as if Jessica and I are standing at home plate blindfolded.

Public Exploration

What do you make of the final lines: "I promise to take you everywhere, my lovely child, and then to leave you. I'm learning to be a leader." What kind of love is going on here? Explore how love between parent and child, or between others in a family grouping, seems to be different from romantic love. It might help to draw up a list on each side. Where do they seem similar, where overlap, where diverge totally? What can we learn about love, if anything, from such a list?

Private Reflection

Reflect one more time on the emotions involved in the love between parent and child. "Bridging" involves a struggle, not a solution. Is this kind of love any easier (more difficult?) than love between male and female? Can you get at the root of it all?

• (Untitled) •

PETER MEINKE

this is a poem to my son Peter
whom I have hurt a thousand times
whose large and vulnerable eyes
have glazed in pain at my ragings
thin wrists and fingers hung
boneless in despair, pale freckled back
bent in defeat, pillow soaked
by my failure to understand.
I have scarred through weakness
and impatience your frail confidence forever
because when I needed to strike
you were there to be hurt and because
I thought you knew
you were beautiful and fair
your bright eyes and hair
but now I see that no one knows that
about himself, but must be told
and retold until it takes hold
because I think anything can be killed
after a while, especially beauty
so I write this for life, for love, for
you, my oldest son Peter, age 10,
going on 11.

Reflections

Private Exploration

Read the poem at least twice, and then as a way of getting closer to the details, copy it word for word by hand, paying attention to the images and how they change from the beginning of the poem to the end. When you have finished, write a quick summary of what you feel is happening in the poem. Reflect on conflicting emotions that surface as you read and the impact, if any, they make on you.

Public Exploration

After a member of your class or group has read the poem aloud, take turns sharing your notebook responses. What do you make of these lines:

> . . . I think anything can be killed after a while, especially beauty

Do you feel the writing of this poem can make a difference in the relationship between Peter and his father? What does it reveal about the father's values?

Private Reflection

Someone once said that we all carry with us the scars our parents gave us as children. Perhaps the reverse is also true. Reflect now privately on a time when either of your parents "scarred your confidence." Try to recall the event, the words spoken, the actions taken, your remembered feelings and thoughts. If you were to write a poem to your father or mother now, focusing on that painful moment, what would you say? How has your perspective of the event changed over the months or years? Is there any value to you in writing about it now?

A Prologue to Parallel Lives

PHYLLIS ROSE

I believe, first of all, that living is an act of creativity and that, at certain moments of our lives, our creative imaginations are more conspicuously demanded than at others. At certain moments, the need to decide upon the story of our own lives becomes particularly pressing—when we choose a mate, for example, or embark upon a career. Decisions like that make sense, retroactively, of the past and project a meaning onto the future, knit past and future together, and create, suspended between the two, the present. Questions we have all asked of ourselves, such as Why am I doing this? or the even more basic What am I doing? suggest the way in which living forces us to look for and forces us to find a design within the primal stew of data which is our daily experience. There is a kind of arranging and telling and choosing of detail—of narration, in short—which we must do so that one day will prepare for the next day, one week prepare for the next week. In some way we all decide when we have grown up and what event will symbolize for us that state of maturity—leaving home, getting married, becoming a parent, losing our parents, making a million, writing a book. To the extent that we impose some narrative form onto our lives, each of us in the ordinary process of living is a fitful novelist, and the biographer is a literary critic.

Marriages, or parallel lives as I have chosen to call them, hold a particular fascination for the biographer-critic because they set two imaginations to work constructing narratives about experience presumed to be the same for both. In using the word *parallel*, however, I hope to call attention to the gap between the narrative lines as well as to their similarity.

An older school of literary biography was concerned to show "life" had influenced an author's work. My own assumption is that certain imaginative patterns—call them mythologies or ideologies—determine the shape of a writer's life as well as his or her work. I therefore look for connection between the two without assuming that reality is the template for fiction—assuming, if anything, the reverse. In first approaching this material, I looked for evidence that what people read helped form their views of their own experience. Some emerged. Jane Welsh, for example, being courted by Thomas Carlyle, derived her view of their relationship from reading *La Nouvelle Héloïse.* Dickens's management of his separation from his wife seemed influenced by the melodramas in which he was fond of acting. But what came to interest me more was the way in which every marriage was a narrative construct—or two narrative constructs. In unhappy marriages, for example, I see two versions of reality rather than two people in conflict. I see a struggle for imaginative dominance going on. Happy marriages seem to me those in which the two partners agree on the scenario they are enacting, even if, as was the case with Mr. and Mrs. Mill, their own idea of their relationship is totally at variance with the facts. I speak with great trepidation about "facts" in such matters, but, speaking loosely, the facts in the Mills' case—that a woman of strong and uncomplicated will dominated a guilt-ridden man—were less important than their shared imaginative view of the facts, that their marriage fitted their shared ideal of a marriage of equals. I assume, then, as little objective truth as possible about these parallel lives, for every marriage seems to me a subjective fiction with two points of view often deeply in conflict, sometimes fortuitously congruent.

That, sketchily, is the ground of my literary interest in parallel lives, but there is a political dimension as well. On the basis of family life, we form our expectations about power and powerlessness, about authority and obedience in other spheres, and in that sense the family is, as has so often been insisted, the building block of society. The idea of the family as a school for civil life goes back to the ancient Romans, and feminist criticism of the family as such a school—the charge that it is a school for despots and slaves—goes back at least to John Stuart Mill. I cite this tradition to locate, in part, my own position: like Mill, I believe marriage to be the primary political experience in which most of us engage as adults, and so I am interested in the management of power between men and women in that microcosmic relationship. Whatever the balance, every marriage is based upon some understanding, articulated or not, about the relative importance, the priority of desires, between its two partners. Marriages go bad not when love fades—love can modulate into affection without driving two people apart—but when this understanding about the balance of power breaks down, when the weaker member feels exploited or the stronger feels unrewarded for his or her strength.

People who find this a chilling way to talk about one of our most treasured human bonds will object that "power struggle" is a flawed circumstance into which relationships fall when love fails. (For some people it is impossible to discuss power without adding the word *struggle.*) I would counter by pointing out the human tendency to invoke love at moments when we want to disguise transactions involving power. Like the aged Lear handing over his kingdom to his daughters, when we resign power, or assume new power, we insist it is not happening and demand to be talked to about love. Perhaps that is what love is—the momentary or prolonged refusal to think of another person in terms of power. Like an enzyme which blocks momentarily a normal biological process, what we call love may inhibit the process of power negotiation—from which inhibition comes the illusion of equality so characteristic of lovers. If the impulse to abjure measurement and negotiation comes from within, unbidden, it is one of life's graces and blessings. But if it is culturally induced, and more particularly desired of one segment of humanity than another, then we may perhaps find it repugnant and call it a mask for exploitation. Surely, in regard to marriage, love has received its fair share of attention, power less than its share. For every social scientist discussing the family as a psychopolitical structure, for every John Stuart Mill talking about "subjection" in marriage, how many pieties are daily uttered about love? Who can resist the thought that love is the ideological bone thrown to women to distract their attention from the powerlessness of their lives? Only millions of romantics can resist it—and other millions who might see it as the bone thrown to men to distract them from the bondage of *their* lives.

In unconscious states, as we know from Freud, the mind is astonishingly fertile and inventive in its fiction-making, but in conscious states this is not so. The plots we choose to impose on our own lives are limited and limiting. And in no area are they so banal and sterile as in this of love and marriage. Nothing else being available to our imaginations, we will filter our experience through the romantic clichés with which popular culture bombards us. And because the callowness and conventionality of the plots we impose on ourselves are a betrayal of our inner richness and complexity, we feel anxious and unhappy. We may turn to therapy for help, but the plots *it* evokes, if done less than expertly, are also fairly limiting.

Easy stories drive out hard ones. Simple paradigms prevail over complicated ones. If, within marriage, power is the ability to impose one's imaginative vision and make it prevail, then power is more easily obtained if one has a simple and widely accepted paradigm at hand. The patriarchal paradigm has long enforced men's power within marriage: a man works hard to make himself worthy of a woman; they marry; he heads the family; she serves him, working to please him and care for him, getting protection in return. This plot regularly generates its opposite, the plot of female power through weakness: the woman, somehow wounded by family life, needs to be cared for and requires an offering of guilt. Mrs. Rochester, the madwoman in the attic in *Jane Eyre*, is a fairly spectacular example. The suffering female demanding care has often proved stronger than the conquering male deserving care—a dialectic of imaginative visions of which the Carlyles provide a good example—but neither side of the patriarchal paradigm seems to bring out the best in humanity. In regard to marriage, we need more and more complex plots. I reveal my literary bias in saying I believe we need literature, which, by allowing us to experience more fully, to imagine more fully, enables us to live more freely. In a pragmatic way, we can profit from an immersion in the nineteenth-century novel which took the various stages of marriage as its central subject.

Before the Matrimonial Causes Act of 1857, divorce was possible in England only by Act of Parliament, a process so expensive and unusual as to place it virtually out of reach of the middle class, although, in special cases such as non-consummation, annulments were possible through the ecclesiastical courts. Even after 1857, when secular courts were established to grant divorces, relatively few people could bring themselves to submit to the scandalous procedure: adultery had invariably to be one of the grounds. So these unions, however haphazardly undertaken, were intended to last for life. Comparatively, our easy recourse to divorce seems—to adopt Robert Frost's image—like playing tennis without the net. John Stuart Mill, who advocated divorce, nevertheless believed that re-marriage was an inefficient remedy for certain kinds of marital distress, those caused by the human tendency to grow unhappy in the course of years and to blame this unhappiness on one's spouse. The sufferer, after the initial elation brought by change, would reach the same point eventually with a second mate, said Mill, and at what a cost of disrupted life! It has become a story familiar enough today. But the Victorians, with no easy escape from difficult domestic situations, were forced to be more inventive.

Few were more inventive than Mill's eventual wife, Harriet Taylor, who, for twenty years, arranged to live in a virtual *ménage à trois* with her husband and Mill, a companion to both, lover to neither. Her inventiveness depended on a de-emphasis of sexual fulfillment which it requires effort to perceive as useful rather than merely pinched. But I think the effort must be made.

In fact, scholars in our own post-liberated age who interest themselves in innovative living arrangements are beginning to discover that people a hundred years ago may have had *more* flexibility than we do now. Lillian Faderman, for example, has described with great sympathy the nineteenth-century American practice of the ''Boston marriage,'' a long-term monogamous relationship between two women who are otherwise unmarried. The emotional and even financial advantages of such a relationship are immediately evident, whether or not—and this is something we shall never know—sex was involved. The important point is that such relationships were seen as healthy and useful. Henry James, for one, was delighted that his sister Alice had some joy in her life, in the form of her Boston marriage to Katherine Loring. But what seemed healthy and useful to the nineteenth century suddenly became ''abnormal'' after the impact, in the early twentieth century, of popular Freudianism. With all experience sexualized, living arrangements such as those Boston marriages could not be so easily entered upon or easily discussed; they became outlaw, suppressed, matters to hide. By the mid-1920s, it was no longer possible to mention a Boston marriage without embarrassment. By sexualizing experience, popular Freudianism had the moralistic result of limiting possibilities.

I prefer to see sexless marriages as examples of flexibility rather than of abnormality. Some people might say they are not really marriages because they are sexless; it's a point I'd want to argue. There must be other models of marriage—of long-term association between two people—than the very narrow one we are all familiar with, beginning with a white wedding gown, leading to children, and ending in death, or, these days increasingly often, in divorce.

Many cultural circumstances worked against the likelihood of sexual satisfaction with Victorian marriages. The inflexible taboo on pre-marital sex for middle-class women meant, among other things, that it was impossible to determine sexual compatibility before marriage. The law then made the wife absolute property of her husband and sexual performance one of her duties. Imagine a young woman married to a man she finds physically repulsive. She is in the position of being raped nightly—and with the law's consent. The legendary Victorian advice about sex, "Lie back and think of England," may be seen as not entirely comical if we realize that in many cases a distaste for sex developed from a distaste for the first sexual partner and from sexual performance which was essentially forced. In addition, the absence of birth control made it impossible to separate sex from its reproductive function, so that to be sexually active meant also the discomforts of pregnancy, the pain of childbirth, and the burden of children. For men, the middle-class taboo on premarital sex meant sexual experience could be obtained only with prostitutes or working-class women, an early conditioning which Freud said breeds dangers in the erotic life, by encouraging a split between objects of desire and objects of respect.

We would seem to have a greater chance of happiness now. Theoretically, men and women can get to know each other in casual, relaxed circumstances before marrying. More young people feel free to sleep together, to live together before marriage. They do not have to wait until they are irrevocably joined to discover they are incompatible. Nor are they so irrevocably joined. If we discover, as we seem to, early and late, that despite all our opportunity to test compatibility, we have married someone with whom we are not compatible, we can disconnect ourselves and try again. Perhaps most important, women can hold jobs, earn a living, own property, thereby gaining a chance for some status in the family. Birth control is reliable and available, so women needn't be, quite so much as formerly, the slaves of children. Nor need men be so oppressed by the obligation of supporting large and expensive families. We can separate sex from reproduction; it can be purely a source of pleasure. If all this does not ensure that, cumulatively, we are happier in our domesticity than the Victorians, then perhaps we expect even more of our marriages than the Victorians did—perhaps we place too much of a burden on our personal relationships, as Christopher Lasch, among others, has suggested. Or perhaps the deep tendency of human nature to unhappiness is even harder to reach by legislation and technology than one might have thought.

Neither in novels nor in biographical material can I find much evidence that people of the last century placed less emphasis on their personal relationships than we do. Romantic expectations seem to know no season, except the season of life. Dickens and Carlyle offer examples of one connubial dream: that an idealized woman will reward the young man for his professional labors. The Mills and the Leweses, for various reasons, expected less out of marriage and found greater satisfaction in it than the others. Temperament and ideological bent seem more important in determining happiness than whether one lived in the nineteenth or the twentieth century.

We should remind ourselves, I think, of the romantic bias in Anglo-American attitudes toward marriage, whether of the nineteenth or the twentieth century. Effie Ruskin, travelling in Italy, discovered how much more comfortable Continental ways of being married were than English. For the English assumed you loved your husband and were loved by him and wanted to be with him as much as possible, whereas the Europeans made no such extraordinary assumption. They knew they were making the best of a difficult situation often arranged by people other than the participants and for reasons quite apart from love, and so they gave each other considerable latitude. One hardly knows whether the Victorians suffered more from their lack of easy recourse to divorce or from the disappearance of the brisk assumptions of arranged marriages. At least when marriages were frankly arrangements of property, no one expected them to float on an unceasing love-tide, whereas we and the Victorians have been in the same boat on that romantic flood.

In general, the similarities between marriages then and now seem to me greater than the differences. Then as now certain problems of adjustment, focussing usually on sex or relatives, seem typical of early stages of marriage, and others, for example absence of excitement, seem typical of later stages. In good marriages then as now shared experience forms a bond increasingly important with time, making discontents seem minor. And then as now, love also tends to walk out the door when poverty flies in the window. Conditions I would have thought unreproducible today—Ruskin's total innocence of the female nude and consequent shock when confronted by one—turn out to have been reproduced in the lives of people I know. I have been reminded continually in these Victorian marriages of marriages of friends: strong women still adopt a protective coloring of weakness as George Eliot did; earnest men with strongly egalitarian politics are still subject to domination by shrews, as John Mill was; men like Dickens still divorce in middle age the wives they have used up and outdistanced; clever women like Jane Carlyle still solace themselves for their powerlessness by mocking their husbands. Moreover, attitudes towards marriage which I would have thought outdated prove not to be. Apparently it is still possible to assume that the man is without question the more important partner in a marriage. That is, the patriarchal paradigm still prevails. Indeed, as fundamentalist religion and morality revive in contemporary America's ethical vacuum, we are likely to find ourselves fighting the nineteenth-century wars of personal morality all over again. Since we have not come so far as some of us fear and some of us hope we have, people who want to legislate morality back to an imagined ideal should, at the least, learn some humility in the face of the conservatism of human nature.

Reflections

Private Exploration

1. According to Rose, "We all decide when we have grown up and what event will symbolize that state of maturity—leaving home, getting married, becoming a parent, losing our parents, making a million, writing a book." Recall an event which has

come to symbolize your own realization of maturity. Consider how that realization has affected your goals and your values in terms of personal relationships. Then, if possible, reflect on how Rose's concept of the importance of power might be involved in your step toward maturity.

2. Reread "A Prologue to Parallel Lives." This time read more slowly. Look up words you don't know and make marginal notations. Pay particular attention to key words that are repeated throughout. Afterwards select one of the key words you have discovered and use it as a starting point to explore the "meaning" this essay has for you. Use the same key word to explore your own thoughts concerning marriage. Feel free to draw on any of your previous readings or from personal experience as you write.

Public Exploration

1. Before dividing into small groups, reflect on Rose's statement that "We . . . filter our experience through romantic cliches with which culture bombards us." Make a personal list of cliches regarding love and romance that surface in films, television, popular fiction, and advertising. Then with your group, explore the cultural impact of those cliches. Consider how cliches shape our expectations and values. What evidence can you find that would prove or disprove Rose's notion that these cliches are or are not responsible for raising the very expectations that she believes contributes to the failure of marriages?
2. Today, we have more personal freedom than ever before. Individually, then with your group, consider the personal freedoms you became aware of during your first year at college. Have those freedoms guaranteed a happier life, better choices, more enduring relationships? Is there a point where personal responsibility seems to overpower reason? As a group, do you agree or disagree with writer John Ehle's comment that freedom is "the worst form of slavery"?

Private Reflection

Explore the "imagined pattern" of your own life. Consider how that pattern has been influenced by your parents and others. How might you convince Rose that the fictionalized plot you have created is or is not limited or limiting.

The Necessary Enemy

KATHERINE ANNE PORTER

She is a frank, charming, fresh-hearted young woman who married for love. She and her husband are one of those gay, good-looking young pairs who ornament this modern scene rather more in profusion perhaps than ever before in our history. They are handsome, with a talent for finding their way in their world, they work at things that interest them, their tastes agree and their hopes. They intend in all good faith to spend their lives together, to have children and do well by them and each other—to be happy, in fact, which for them is the whole point of their marriage. And all in stride, keeping their wits about them. Nothing romantic, mind you; their feet are on the ground.

Unless they were this sort of person, there would be not much point to what I wish to say; for they would seem to be an example of the high-spirited, right-minded young whom the critics are always invoking to come forth and do their duty and practice all those sterling old-fashioned virtues which in every generation seem to be falling into disrepair. As for virtues, these young people are more or less on their own, like most of their kind; they get very little moral or other aid from their society; but after three years of marriage this very contemporary young woman finds herself facing the oldest and ugliest dilemma of marriage.

She is dismayed, horrified, full of guilt and forebodings because she is finding out little by little that she is capable of hating her husband, whom she loves faithfully. She can hate him at times as fiercely and mysteriously, indeed in terribly much the same way, as often she hated her parents, her brothers and sisters, whom she loves, when she was a child. Even then it had seemed to her a kind of black treacherousness in her, her private wickedness that, just the same, gave her her only private life. That was one thing her parents never knew about her, never seemed to suspect. For it was never given a name. They did and said hateful things to her and to each other as if by right, as if in them it was a kind of virtue. But when they said to her, "Control your feelings," it was never when she was amiable and obedient, only in the black times of her hate. So it was her secret, a shameful one. When they punished her, sometimes for the strangest reasons, it was, they said, only because they loved her—it was for her good. She did not believe this, but she thought herself guilty of something worse than ever they had punished her for. None of this really frightened her: the real fright came when she discovered that at times her father and mother hated each other; this was like standing on the doorsill of a familiar room and seeing in a lightning flash that the floor was gone, you were on the edge of a bottomless pit. Sometimes she felt that both of them hated her, but that passed, it was simply not a thing to be thought of, much less believed. She thought she had outgrown all this, but here it was again, an element in her own nature she could not control, or feared she could not. She would have to hide from her husband, if she could, the same spot in her feelings she had hidden from her parents, and for the same no doubt disreputable, selfish reason: she wants to keep his love.

Above all, she wants him to be absolutely confident that she loves him, for that is the real truth, no matter how unreasonable it sounds, and no matter how her own feelings betray them both at times. She depends recklessly on his love; yet while she is hating him, he might very well be hating her as much or even more, and it would serve her right. But she does not want to be served right, she wants to be loved and forgiven—that is, to be sure he would forgive her anything, if he had any notion of what she had done. But best of all she would like not to have anything in her love that should ask for forgiveness. She doesn't mean about their quarrels—they are not so bad. Her feelings are out of proportion, perhaps. She knows it is perfectly natural for people to disagree, have fits of temper, fight it out; they learn quite a lot about each other that way, and not all of it disappointing either. When it passes, her hatred seems quite unreal. It always did.

Love. We are early taught to say it. I love you. We are trained to the thought of it as if there were nothing else, or nothing else worth having without it, or nothing worth having which it could not bring with it. Love is taught, always by precept, sometimes by example. Then hate, which no one meant to teach us, comes of itself. It is true that if we say I love you, it may be received without doubt, for there are times when it is hard to believe. Say I hate you, and the one spoken to believes it instantly, once for all.

Say I love you a thousand times to that person afterward and mean it every time, and still it does not change the fact that once we said I hate you, and meant that too. It leaves a mark on that surface love had worn so smooth with its eternal caresses. Love must be learned, and learned again and again; there is no end to it. Hate needs no instruction, but waits only to be provoked . . . hate, the unspoken word, the unacknowledged presence in the house, that faint smell of brimstone among the roses, that invisible tongue-tripper, that unkempt finger in every pie, that sudden oh-so-curiously *chilling* look—could it be boredom?—on your dear one's features, making them quite ugly. Be careful: love, perfect love, is in danger.

If it is not perfect, it is not love, and if it is not love, it is bound to be hate sooner or later. This is perhaps a not too exaggerated statement of the extreme position of Romantic Love, more especially in America, where we are all brought up on it, whether we know it or not. Romantic Love is changeless, faithful, passionate, and its sole end is to render the two lovers happy. It has no obstacles save those provided by the hazards of fate (that is to say, society), and such sufferings as the lovers may cause each other are only another word for delight: exciting jealousies, thrilling uncertainties, the ritual dance of courtship within the charmed closed circle of their secret alliance; all *real* troubles come from without, they face them unitedly in perfect confidence. Marriage is not the end but only the beginning of true happiness, cloudless, changeless to the end. That the candidates for this blissful condition have never seen an example of it, nor ever knew anyone who had, makes no difference. That is the ideal and they will achieve it.

How did Romantic Love manage to get into marriage at last, where it was most certainly never intended to be? At its highest it was tragic; the love of Héloise and Abélard.* At its most graceful, it was the homage of the trouvère for his lady. In its most popular form, the adulterous strayings of solidly married couples who meant to stray for their own good reasons, but at the same time do nothing to upset the property settlements or the line of legitimacy; at its most trivial, the pretty trifling of shepherd and shepherdess.

*Pierre Abélard (1079–1142), philosopher and theologian, fell in love with his student Héloise (1101?–1164?), who became his mistress and later, after a secret marriage, his wife. When Héloise's powerful uncle had Abelard emasculated as punishment, he became a monk. Héloise then became a nun. [Porter]

This was generally condemned by church and state and a word of fear to honest wives whose mortal enemy it was. Love within the sober, sacred realities of marriage was a matter of personal luck, but in any case, private feelings were strictly a private affair having, at least in theory, no bearing whatever on the fixed practice of the rules of an institution never intended as a recreation ground for either sex. If the couple discharged their religious and social obligations, furnished forth a copious progeny, kept their troubles to themselves, maintained public civility and died under the same roof, even if not always on speaking terms, it was rightly regarded as a successful marriage. Apparently this testing ground was too severe for all but the stoutest spirits; it too was based on an ideal, as impossible in its way as the ideal Romantic Love. One good thing to be said for it is that society took responsibility for the conditions of marriage, and the sufferers within its bonds could always blame the system, not themselves. But Romantic Love crept into the marriage bed, very stealthily, by centuries, bringing its absurd notions about love as eternal springtime and marriage as a personal adventure meant to provide personal happiness. To a Western romantic such as I, though my views have been much modified by painful experience, it still seems to me a charming work of the human imagination, and it is a pity its central notion has been taken too literally and has hardened into a convention as cramping and enslaving as the older one. The refusal to acknowledge the evils in ourselves which therefore are implicit in any human situation is as extreme and unworkable a proposition as the doctrine of total depravity; but somewhere between them, or maybe beyond them, there does exist a possibility for reconciliation between our desires for impossible satisfactions and the simple unalterable fact that we also desire to be unhappy and that we create our own sufferings; and out of these sufferings we salvage our fragments of happiness.

Our young woman who has been taught that an important part of her human nature is not real because it makes trouble and interferes with her peace of mind and shakes her self-love, has been very badly taught; but she has arrived at a most important stage of her re-education. She is afraid her marriage is going to fail because she has not love enough to face its difficulties; and this because at times she feels a painful hostility toward her husband, and cannot admit its reality because such an admission would damage in her own eyes her view of what love should be, an absurd view, based on her vanity of power. Her hatred is real as her love is real, but her hatred has the advantage at present because it works on a blind instinctual level, it is lawless; and her love is subjected to a code of ideal conditions, impossible by their very nature of fulfillment, which prevents its free growth and deprives it of its right to recognize its human limitations and come to grips with them. Hatred is natural in a sense that love, as she conceives it, a young person brought up in the tradition of Romantic Love, is not natural at all. Yet it did not come by hazard, it is the very imperfect expression of the need of the human imagination to create beauty and harmony out of chaos, no matter how mistaken its notion of these things may be, nor how clumsy its methods. It has conjured love out of the air, and seeks to preserve it by incantations; when she spoke a vow to love and honor her husband until death, she did a very reckless thing, for it is not possible by an act of the will to fulfill such an engagement. But it was the necessary act of faith performed in defense of a mode of feeling, the statement of honorable intention to practice as well as she is able the noble, acquired faculty of love, that very mysterious overtone to sex which is the best thing in it. Her hatred is part of it, the necessary enemy and ally.

Reflections

Private Exploration

1. Explore the following:

   Love must be learned, and learned again and again; there is no end to it. Hate needs no instruction, but waits only to be provoked.

2. Zero in on any key passage in Porter that piques your interest or strikes you as a curious insight you may never have considered before. How does the passage open up insights into the essay as a whole? How does it open up insights into your own feelings?

Public Exploration

Porter argues that it is not possible by an act of will to "love and honor a mate until death." Consider the truth or falsity of her position, and whatever implications it may have about the nature of love or the permanency of marriage.

Private Reflection

Have you ever loved and hated at the same time (a boyfriend, girlfriend, spouse, or parent)? Was guilt a part of your experience? Porter suggests that at least within marital love, hatred is a natural and perhaps even necessary ally. Was it for you? How did you finally resolve your own conflict? Or have you?

On Love

RAINER MARIA RILKE

translated by **John J. L. Mood**

There is scarcely anything more difficult than to love one another. That it is work, day labor, day labor, God knows there is no other word for it. And look, added to this is the fact that young people are not prepared for such difficult loving; for convention has tried to make this most complicated and ultimate relationship into something easy and frivolous, has given it the appearance of everyone's being able to do it. It is not so. Love is something difficult and it is more difficult than other things because in other conflicts nature herself enjoins men to collect themselves, to take themselves firmly in hand with all their strength, while in the heightening of love the impulse is to give oneself wholly away. But just think, can that be anything beautiful, to give oneself away not as something whole and ordered, but haphazard rather, bit by bit, as it comes? Can such giving away, that looks so like a throwing away and dismemberment, be anything good, can it be happiness, joy, progress? No, it cannot. . . . When you give someone flowers, you arrange them beforehand, don't you? But young people who love each other fling themselves to each other in the impatience and haste of their passion, and they don't notice at all what a lack of mutual esteem lies in this disordered giving of themselves; they notice it with astonishment and indignation only from the dissension that arises between them out of all this disorder. And once there is disunity between them, the confusion grows with every day; neither of the two has anything unbroken, pure, and unspoiled about him any longer, and amid the disconsolateness of a break they try to hold fast to the semblance of their happiness (for all that was really supposed to be for the sake of happiness). Alas, they are scarcely able to recall any more what they meant by happiness. In his uncertainty each becomes more and more unjust toward the other; they who wanted to do each other good are now handling one another in an imperious and intolerant manner, and in the struggle somehow to get out of their untenable and unbearable state of confusion, they commit the greatest fault that can happen to human relationships: they become impatient. They hurry to a conclusion; to come, as they believe, to a final decision, they try once and for all to establish their relationship, whose surprising changes have frightened them, in order to remain the same now and *forever* (as they say). That is only the last error in this long chain of errings linked fast to one another. What is dead cannot even be clung to (for it crumbles and changes its character); how much less can what is living and alive be treated definitely, once and for all. Self-transformation is precisely what life is, and human relationships, which are an extract of life, are the most changeable of all, rising and falling from minute to minute, and lovers are those in whose relationship and contact no one moment resembles another. People between whom nothing accustomed, nothing that has already been present before ever takes place, but many new, unexpected, unprecedented things. There are such relationships which must be a very great, almost unbearable happiness, but they can occur only between very rich natures and between those who, each for himself, are richly ordered and composed; they can unite only two wide, deep, individual worlds.—Young people—it is obvious—cannot achieve such a relationship, but they can, if they understand their life properly, grow up slowly to such happiness and prepare themselves for it. They must not forget, when they love, that they are beginners, bunglers of life, apprentices in love,—must *learn* love, and that (like *all* learning) wants peace, patience, and composure!

To take love seriously and to bear and to learn it like a task, this it is that young people need.—Like so much else, people have also misunderstood the place of love in life, they have made it into play and pleasure because they thought that play and pleasure were more blissful than work; but there is nothing happier than work, and love, just because it is the extreme happiness, can be nothing else but work.—So whoever loves must try to act as if he had a great work: he must be much alone and go into himself and collect himself and hold fast to himself; he must work; he must become something!

For believe me, the more one is, the richer is all that one experiences. And whoever wants to have a deep love in his life must collect and save for it and gather honey.

Reflections

Private Exploration

1. Explore your initial impression of Rilke's essay. Select a key passage and copy it into your notebook. In what ways might this passage illuminate the essay as a whole? Does it relate to your own experience or to other readings in this chapter?
2. Jot down your own definition of "labor," then check an unabridged dictionary for as many definitions of "labor" and "work" as you can find. Consider how one's understanding of Rilke's lead sentences are enhanced as a result of this new knowledge.
3. If you have not already read Jane Jordan's "Where is the Love?" (p. 335), read it now and consider the similarities and differences between her essay and Rilke's.

Public Exploration

Rilke argues that love grows out of patience, labor, effort. In your group, consider Rilke's observation that young people are not prepared for that kind of labor; that they are, indeed, impatient. If you agree with Rilke, what are the consequences for human relationships?

Private Reflection

1. What do you make of this excerpt:

   > Self-transformation is precisely what life is, and human relationships, which are an extract of life are the most changeable of all, rising and falling from minute to minute.

2. Reflect on the following statement. What is it you think Rilke is truly saying? Does it have any connection to your own life? Is it realistic in the last decade of the 20th century to think of love in these terms?

   > For believe me, the more one is, the richer is all that one experiences. And whoever wants to have a deep love in his life must collect and save for it and gather honey.

CONNECTIONS

Although your best writing will usually emerge from insights already under development in your reading notebook, here are some additional possibilities for exploring relationships between and among various works of literature.

1. Lawrence Stone has written, "We are in a unique position today in that our culture is dominated by romantic notions of passionate love as the only socially admissible reason for marriage." Consider the contrast here with the results of Bruce Weber's study in which a younger generation seems to marry for financial security and appearances. Or consider the contrast to Wendell Berry's position in which marriage would seem valid only if it has a spiritual foundation. Why do we marry?
2. Write an essay focusing on the relationship of power and love. Draw your ideas from various sources: Jordan's "Where Is the Love?" (p. 335), Roses' "Parallel Lives" (p. 366), Berry's "Likeness of Atonement" (p. 353).
3. In "On Love," Rainer Maria Rilke writes: "There is scarcely anything more difficult than to love one another. That it is work, day labor, day labor, God knows there is no other word for it." Use this as the starting point for a paper in which you show connections among Porter's "The Necessary Enemy," and such works of fiction as "Bridging" (p. 357), or "What We Talk About When We Talk About Love," (p. 342).
4. Consider possible relationships between Andrew Marvell's "To His Coy Mistress," (p. 352) and Sharon Olds' "Sex Without Love" (p. 313). When does sex as playfulness turn into sex as destruction? And why?
5. Consider the nature of love in its most ideal forms: for example, the poems of Nancy Willard and Grace Schulman (pp. 340 and 341). What do our "ideals" tell us about our highest values? And what does that reveal about our humanness?
6. Like the couples in Carver's story, "What We Talk About When We Talk About Love," the more we attempt to define love, the more confused and frustrated we become. The Greeks, however, may have been wiser. Instead of one definition, they had two. Consult several sources in your library on the meaning of the Greek words "eros" and "agape." Explore the contrasting meanings, using material from any readings in this chapter, or from personal experience, as examples. Then consider whether we have, in our own culture, created unnecessary difficulties by confusing two kinds of love?
7. One idea that surfaces in many essays and stories in this chapter is that we seek love as a result of loneliness. Ernest van den Haag writes:

   > Our contacts are many, our relationships few: our lives, externally crowded, often are internally isolated; we remain but tenuously linked to each other and our ties come easily undone. One feels lonely surrounded by crowds and machines in an unbounded, abstract world that has become morally unintelligible; and we have so much time now to feel lonely in. Thus one longs perhaps more acutely than in the past for somebody to be tangibly, individually, and definitely one's own, body and soul.

   Consider whether van den Haag's argument might offer insight into Carver's "What We Talk About When We Talk About Love" (p. 342).

8. Because our perception of love seems to change from era to era, you might find it valuable to research one or more of the following:

Courtly love	Biblical love
Victorian love	Love in Greek mythology
"Modern" love	Love in the 60s
Romance	Mariolatry
Platonic love	

In addition to gaining an understanding of how others in the past thought of love, you might want to consider whether those past concepts continue to influence us today. How might some of them be reflected in the readings in this chapter?

CHAPTER 9

SOWERS AND REAPERS

Without work that fulfills the inner self, there can be no dignity.

—Bertrand Russell

"What are you going to be when you grow up?" At the age of seven, the question seemed as simple as the answer: I want to be a fireman. I want to be a nurse. I want to be a teacher. Somehow the question so simple to answer at seven becomes more ponderous at eighteen and twenty.

Fortunately we live in a democracy that insures freedom of choice. But when it comes to selecting a career, the values of society may dictate our decision without our conscious awareness. In the Western world ambition, getting ahead, comfort, and success are associated with work. Unfortunately, these objectives may become obstacles. Too often, it is not the quality of our work or the pleasure it gives us, but the money we earn that becomes the measure of our lives. What our culture often neglects is the recognition of that fragile thread that attaches the outer life to the inner one. The work we do, the value we attribute to it, are also connected with our sense of self-esteem, respect, and happiness. Philosopher Bertrand Russell reminds us that "without self-respect, genuine happiness is scarcely possible . . . And the man [or woman] who is ashamed of his [or her] work can hardly achieve self-respect."

Some of the most valuable work goes unnoticed. Barbara McClintock, a geneticist, began her pioneering studies in the mechanisms of genetic inheritance alone in 1941, eventually discovering that those portions of DNA which control other genes can move between chromosomes and change the future generation of plants. Although she published her discovery in 1951, scientists mocked her work. Undaunted, she continued on alone for thirty-two more years. Later, after accepting the Nobel Prize in 1983 at the age of eighty-one, McClintock offered this statement to reporters: "The prize is such an extraordinary honor. It might seem unfair, however, to reward a person for having so much pleasure over the years. . . ."

In Arthur Miller's play *Death of a Salesman*, the character Willie Loman finds his greatest pleasure in carpentry and gardening, but Loman measures his success by the number of people he knows, the number of sales he makes. As a businessman he's a failure. He struggles for the recognition of those around him—his business associates, his brother, his wife and children—never allowing himself to recognize the work successfully accomplished with his own hands.

In the chapter which follows you will read essays, stories, and poems about the value of work and how it shapes our lives. You'll contemplate the absurdity of Sisyphus' labor and perhaps begin to question the concept of work as both liberator and creator. Some of the questions you have regarding your future may be answered as you read about the relationship between work and happiness, between success and satisfaction—the golden thread that links the outer world to the inner one. And the answer to the question, "What do you want to be?" may seem more ponderous than ever.

I Stand Here Ironing

TILLIE OLSEN

I stand here ironing, and what you asked me moves tormented back and forth with the iron.

"I wish you would manage the time to come in and talk with me about your daughter. I'm sure you can help me understand her. She's a youngster who needs help and whom I'm deeply interested in helping."

"Who needs help." . . . Even if I came, what good would it do? You think because I am her mother I have a key, or that in some way you could use me as a key? She has lived for nineteen years. There is all that life that has happened outside of me, beyond me.

And when is there time to remember, to sift, to weigh, to estimate, to total? I will start and there will be an interruption and I will have to gather it all together again. Or I will become engulfed with all I did or did not do, with what should have been and what cannot be helped.

She was a beautiful baby. The first and only one of our five that was beautiful at birth. You do not guess how new and uneasy her tenancy in her now-loveliness. You did not know her all those years she was thought homely, or see her poring over her baby pictures, making me tell her over and over how beautiful she had been—and would be, I would tell her—and was now, to the seeing eye. But the seeing eyes were few or nonexistent. Including mine.

I nursed her. They feel that's important nowadays. I nursed all the children, but with her, with all the fierce rigidity of first motherhood, I did like the books then said. Though her cries battered me to trembling and my breasts ached with swollenness, I waited till the clock decreed.

Why do I put that first? I do not even know if it matters, or if it explains anything.

She was a beautiful baby. She blew shining bubbles of sound. She loved motion, loved light, loved color and music and textures. She would lie on the floor in her blue overalls patting the surface so hard in ecstasy her hands and feet would blur. She was a miracle to me, but when she was eight months old I had to leave her daytimes with the woman downstairs to whom she was no miracle at all, for I worked or looked for work and for Emily's father, who "could no longer endure" (he wrote in his good-bye note) "sharing want with us."

I was nineteen. It was the pre-relief, pre-WPA world of the depression. I would start running as soon as I got off the streetcar, running up the stairs, the place smelling sour, and awake or asleep to startle awake, when she saw me she would break into a clogged weeping that could not be comforted, a weeping I can hear yet.

After a while I found a job hashing at night so I could be with her days, and it was better. But it came to where I had to bring her to his family and leave her.

It took a long time to raise the money for her fare back. Then she got chicken pox and I had to wait longer. When she finally came, I hardly knew her, walking quick and nervous like her father, looking like her father, thin, and dressed in a shoddy red that yellowed her skin and glared at the pockmarks. All the baby loveliness gone.

She was two. Old enough for nursery school they said, and I did not know then what I know now—the fatigue of the long day, and the lacerations of group life in the kinds of nurseries that are only parking places for children.

Except that it would have made no difference if I had known. It was the only place there was. It was the only way we could be together, the only way I could hold a job.

And even without knowing, I knew. I knew the teacher that was evil because all these years it has curdled into my memory, the little boy hunched in the corner, her rasp, "why aren't you outside, because Alvin hits you? that's no reason, go out, scaredy." I knew Emily hated it even if she did not clutch and implore "don't go Mommy" like the other children, mornings.

She always had a reason why we should stay home. Momma, you look sick. Momma, I feel sick. Momma, the teachers aren't there today, they're sick. Momma, we can't go, there was a fire there last night. Momma, it's a holiday today, no school, they told me.

But never a direct protest, never rebellion. I think of our others in their three-, four-year-oldness—the explosions, the tempers, the denunciations, the demands—and I feel suddenly ill. I put the iron down. What in me demanded that goodness in her? And what was the cost, the cost to her of such goodness?

The old man living in the back once said in his gentle way: "You should smile at Emily more when you look at her." What *was* in my face when I looked at her? I loved her. There were all the acts of love.

It was only with the others I remembered what he said, and it was the face of joy, and not of care or tightness or worry I turned to them—too late for Emily. She does not smile easily, let alone almost always as her brothers and sisters do. Her face is closed and sombre, but when she wants, how fluid. You must have seen it in her pantomimes, you spoke of her rare gift for comedy on the stage that rouses a laughter out of the audience so dear they applaud and applaud and do not want to let her go.

Where does it come from, that comedy? There was none of it in her when she came back to me that second time, after I had had to send her away again. She had a new daddy now to learn to love, and I think perhaps it was a better time.

Except when we left her alone nights, telling ourselves she was old enough.

"Can't you go some other time, Mommy, like tomorrow?" she would ask. "Will it be just a little while you'll be gone? Do you promise?"

The time we came back, the front door open, the clock on the floor in the hall. She rigid awake. "It wasn't just a little while. I didn't cry. Three times I called you, just three times, and then I ran downstairs to open the door so you could come faster. The clock talked loud. I threw it away, it scared me what it talked."

She said the clock talked loud again that night I went to the hospital to have Susan. She was delirious with the fever that comes before red measles, but she was fully conscious all the week I was gone and the week after we were home when she could not come near the new baby or me.

She did not get well. She stayed skeleton thin, not wanting to eat, and night after night she had nightmares. She would call for me, and I would rouse from exhaustion to sleepily call back: "You're all right, darling, go to sleep, it's just a dream," and if she still called, in a sterner voice, "now go to sleep, Emily, there's nothing to hurt you." Twice, only twice, when I had to get up for Susan anyhow, I went in to sit with her.

Now when it is too late (as if she would let me hold and comfort her like I do the others) I get up and go to her at once at her moan or restless stirring. "Are you awake, Emily? Can I get you something?" And the answer is always the same: "No, I'm all right, go back to sleep, Mother."

They persuaded me at the clinic to send her away to a convalescent home in the country where "she can have the kind of food and care you can't manage for her, and you'll be free to concentrate on the new baby." They still send children to that place. I see pictures on the society page of sleek young women planning affairs to raise money for it, or dancing at the affairs, or decorating Easter eggs or filling Christmas stockings for the children.

They never have a picture of the children so I do not know if the girls still wear those gigantic red bows and the ravaged looks on the every other Sunday when parents can come to visit "unless otherwise notified"—as we were notified the first six weeks.

Oh it is a handsome place, green lawns and tall trees and fluted flower beds. High up on the balconies of each cottage the children stand, the girls in their red bows and white dresses, the boys in white suits and giant red ties. The parents stand below shrieking up to be heard and the children shriek down to be heard, and between them the invisible wall "Not To Be Contaminated by Parental Germs or Physical Affection."

There was a tiny girl who always stood hand in hand with Emily. Her parents never came. One visit she was gone. "They moved her to Rose Cottage" Emily shouted in explanation. "They don't like you to love anybody here."

She wrote once a week, the labored writing of a seven-year-old. "I am fine. How is the baby. If I write my leter nicly I will have a star. Love." There never was a star. We wrote every other day, letters she could never hold or keep but only hear read—once. "We simply do not have room for children to keep any personal possessions," they patiently explained when we pieced one Sunday's shrieking together to plead how much it would mean to Emily, who loved so to keep things, to be allowed to keep her letters and cards.

Each visit she looked frailer. "She isn't eating," they told us.

(They had runny eggs for breakfast or mush with lumps, Emily said later. I'd hold it in my mouth and not swallow. Nothing ever tasted good, just when they had chicken.)

It took us eight months to get her released home, and only the fact that she gained back so little of her seven lost pounds convinced the social worker.

I used to try to hold and love her after she came back, but her body would stay stiff, and after a while she'd push away. She ate little. Food sickened her, and I think much of life too. Oh she had physical lightness and brightness, twinkling by on skates, bouncing like a ball up and down up and down over the jump rope, skimming over the hill; but these were momentary.

She fretted about her appearance, thin and dark and foreign-looking at a time when every little girl was supposed to look or thought she should look a chubby blonde replica of Shirley Temple. The doorbell sometimes rang for her, but no one seemed to come and play in the house or be a best friend. Maybe because we moved so much.

There was a boy she loved painfully through two school semesters. Months later she told me how she had taken pennies from my purse to buy him candy. "Licorice was his favorite and I brought him some every day, but he still liked Jennifer better'n me. Why, Mommy?" The kind of question for which there is no answer.

School was a worry to her. She was not glib or quick in a world where glibness and quickness were easily confused with ability to learn. To her overworked and exasperated teachers she was an overconscientious "slow learner" who kept trying to catch up and was absent entirely too often.

I let her be absent, though sometimes the illness was imaginary. How different from my now-strictness about attendance with the others. I wasn't working. We had a new baby, I was home anyhow. Sometimes, after Susan grew old enough, I would keep her home from school, too, to have them all together.

Mostly Emily had asthma, and her breathing, harsh and labored, would fill the house with a curiously tranquil sound. I would bring the two old dresser mirrors and her boxes of collections to her bed. She would select beads and single earrings, bottle tops and shells, dried flowers and pebbles, old postcards and scraps, all sorts of oddments; then she and Susan would play kingdom, setting up landscapes and furniture, peopling them with action.

Those were the only times of peaceful companionship between her and Susan. I have edged away from it, that poisonous feeling between them, that terrible balancing of hurts and needs I had to do between the two, and did so badly, those earlier years.

Oh there are conflicts between the others too, each one human, needing, demanding, hurting, taking—but only between Emily and Suan, no, Emily toward Susan that corroding resentment. It seems so obvious on the surface, yet it is not obvious. Susan, the second child, Susan, golden- and curly-haired and chubby, quick and articulate and assured, everything in appearance and manner Emily was not; Susan, not able to resist Emily's precious things, losing or sometimes clumsily breaking them; Susan telling jokes and riddles to company for applause while Emily sat silent (to say to me later: that was *my* riddle, Mother, I told it to Susan); Susan, who for all the five years' difference in age was just a year behind Emily in developing physically.

I am glad for that slow physical development that widened the difference between her and her contemporaries, though she suffered over it. She was too vulnerable for that terrible world of youthful competition, of preening and parading, of constant measuring of yourself against every other, of envy. "If I had that copper hair," "If I had that skin. . . ." She tormented herself enough about not looking like the others, there was enough of the unsureness, the having to be conscious of words before you speak, the constant caring—what are they thinking of me? without having it all magnified by the merciless physical drives.

Ronnie is calling. He is wet and I change him. It is rare there is such a cry now. That time of motherhood is almost behind me when the ear is not one's own but must always be racked and listening for the child cry, the child call. We sit for a while and I hold him, looking out over the city spread in charcoal with its soft aisles of light. "*Shoogily*," he breathes and curls closer. I carry him back to bed, asleep. *Shoogily*. A funny word, a family word, inherited from Emily, invented by her to say: *comfort*.

In this and other ways she leaves her seal, I say aloud. And startle at my saying it. What do I mean? What did I start to gather together, to try and make coherent? I was at the terrible, growing years. War years. I do not remember them well. I was working, there were four smaller ones now, there was not time for her. She had to help be a mother, a housekeeper, and shopper. She had to set her seal. Mornings of crisis and near hysteria trying to get lunches packed, hair combed, coats and shoes found, everyone to school or Child Care on time, the baby ready for transportation. And always the paper scribbled on by a smaller one, the book looked at by Susan then mislaid, the homework not done. Running out to that huge school where she was one, she was lost, she was a drop; suffering over the unpreparedness, stammering and unsure in her classes.

There was so little time left at night after the kids were bedded down. She would struggle over books, always eating (it was in those years she developed her enormous appetite that is legendary in our family) and I would be ironing, or preparing food for the next day, or writing V-mail to Bill, or tending the baby. Sometimes, to make me laugh, or out of her despair, she would imitate happenings or types at school.

I think I said once: "Why don't you do something like this in the school amateur show?" One morning she phoned me at work, hardly understandable through the weeping: "Mother, I did it. I won, I won; they gave me first prize; they clapped and clapped and wouldn't let me go."

Now suddenly she was Somebody, and as imprisoned in her difference as she had been in anonymity.

She began to be asked to perform at other high schools, even in colleges, then at city and statewide affairs. The first one we went to, I only recognized her that first moment when thin, shy, she almost drowned herself into the curtains. Then: Was this Emily? The control, the command, the convulsing and deadly clowning, the spell, then the roaring, stamping audience, unwilling to let this rare and precious laughter out of their lives.

Afterwards: You ought to do something about her with a gift like that—but without money or knowing how, what does one do? We have left it all to her, and the gift has as often eddied inside, clogged and clotted, as been used and growing.

She is coming. She runs up the stairs two at a time with her light graceful step, and I know she is happy tonight. Whatever it was that occasioned your call did not happen today.

"Aren't you ever going to finish the ironing, Mother? Whistler painted his mother in a rocker. I'd have to paint mine standing over an ironing board." This is one of her communicative nights and she tells me everything and nothing as she fixes herself a plate of food out of the icebox.

She is so lovely. Why did you want me to come in at all? Why were you concerned? She will find her way.

She starts up the stairs to bed. "Don't get me up with the rest in the morning." "But I thought you were having midterms." "Oh, those," she comes back in, kisses me, and says quite lightly, "in a couple of years when we'll all be atom-dead they won't matter a bit."

She has said it before. She *believes* it. But because I have been dredging the past, and all that compounds a human being is so heavy and meaningful in me, I cannot endure it tonight.

I will never total it all. I will never come in to say: She was a child seldom smiled at. Her father left me before she was a year old. I had to work her first six years when there was work, or I sent her home and to his relatives. There were years she had care she hated. She was dark and thin and foreign-looking in a world where the prestige went to blondeness and curly hair and dimples, she was slow where glibness was prized. She was a child of anxious, not proud, love. We were poor and could not afford for her the soil of easy growth. I was a young mother, I was a distracted mother. There were the other children pushing up, demanding. Her younger sister seemed all that she was not. There were years she did not want me to touch her. She kept too much in herself, her life was such she had to keep too much in herself. My wisdom came too late. She had much to her and probably little will come of it. She is a child of her age, of depression, of war, of fear.

Let her be. So all that is in her will not bloom—but in how many does it? There is still enough left to live by. Only help her to know—help make it so there is cause for her to know—that she is more than this dress on the ironing board, helpless before the iron.

Reflections

Private Exploration

1. Focus on and explore the most important feeling that emerges from Tillie Olsen's story. Focus on specific passages from the text and describe the feelings they give you as fully as possible, or copy a key passage in its entirety and show how the emotion it evokes relates to the whole. Consider how feelings contribute to your understanding of Emily and her mother's relationship.
2. What do you make of this passage?

Let her be. So all that is in her will not bloom—but in how many does it? There is still enough left to live by. Only help her to know—help make it so there is cause for her to know—that she is more than this dress on the ironing board, helpless before the iron.

Public Exploration

Tillie Olsen has indicated that "I Stand Here Ironing" takes place during the 1930s. Child care as we know it today was unavailable. There were few preschools or nurseries, placing an added burden on single mothers who were forced to work in order to survive. Sixty years later, the problem of quality child-care and support for working parents is still an issue. Should mothers of young children stay home to care for them? Should churches, employers, or government assume a responsibility here? How can a nurturing environment be provided for children of working parents or for single parents who cannot afford child care? The responses you develop will all have underlying values. Consider both elements: the answers proposed as well as the values implicit in them.

Personal Reflection

1. Look back on how the essential needs and demands of work affected your own family experience. Was your father gone all the time? Did your mother seem torn between all her duties? Or did your parents somehow balance work and family? How has this dichotomy affected your own life? How has it affected your own perception about work, family, and children?
2. At the conclusion of "I Stand Here Ironing," Emily's mother admits her "wisdom came too late." Consider what she had learned as a result of her daughter's experiences. What does she mean when she says she "will never total it all"? Can any of us?

The Value of Working

LANCE MORROW

During the 19th century industrialization of America, the idea of work's inherent virtue may have seemed temporarily implausible to generations who labored in the mines and mills and sweatshops. The century's huge machinery of production punished and stunned those who ran it.

And yet for generations of immigrants, work *was* ultimately available: the numb toil of an illiterate grandfather got the father a foothold and a high school education, and the son wound up in college or even law school. A woman who died in the Triangle Shirtwaist Co. fire in lower Manhattan had a niece who made it to the halcyon Bronx and another generation on, the family went to Westchester County. So for millions of Americans, as they labored through the complexities of generations, work worked, and the immigrant work ethic came at last to merge with the Protestant work ethic.

The motive of work was all. To work for mere survival is desperate. To work for a better life for one's children and grandchildren lends the labor a fierce dignity. That dignity, an unconquerably hopeful energy and aspiration—driving, persisting like a life force—is the American quality that many find missing now.

The work ethic is not dead, but it is weaker now. The psychology of work is much changed in America. The acute, painful memory of the Great Depression used to enforce a disciplined and occasionally docile approach to work—in much the way that older citizens in the Soviet Union do not complain about scarce food and overpopulated apartments, because they remember how much more horrible everything was during the war. But the generation of the Depression is retiring and dying off, and today's younger workers, though sometimes laid off and kicked around by recessions and inflation, still do not keep in dark storage that residual apocalyptic memory of Hoovervilles and the Dust Bowl and banks capsizing.

Today elaborate financial cushions—unemployment insurance, union benefits, welfare payments, food stamps and so on—have made it less catastrophic to be out of a job for a while. Work is still a profoundly respectable thing in America. Most Americans suffer a sense of loss, of diminution, even of worthlessness if they are thrown out on the street. But the blow seldom carries the life-and-death implications it once had, the sense of personal ruin. Besides, the wild and notorious behavior of the economy takes a certain amount of personal shame out of joblessness; if Ford closes down a plant in New Jersey and throws 3,700 workers into the unemployment lines, the guilt falls less on individuals than on Japanese imports or American car design or an extortionate OPEC.

Because today's workers are better educated than those in the past, their expectations are higher. Many younger Americans have rearranged their ideas about what they want to get out of life. While their fathers and grandfathers and great-grandfathers, concentrated hard upon plow and drill press and pressure gauge and tort, some younger workers now ask previously unimaginable questions about the point of knocking themselves out. For the first time in the history of the world, masses of people in industrially advanced countries no longer have to focus their mind upon work as the central concern of their existence.

In the formulation of Psychologist Abraham Maslow, work functions in a hierarchy of needs: first, work provides food and shelter, basic human maintenance. After that, it can address the need for security and then for friendship and "belongingness." Next, the demands of the ego arise, the need for respect. Finally, men and women assert a larger desire for "self-actualization." That seems a harmless and even worthy enterprise but sometimes degenerates into self-infatuation, a vaporously selfish discontent that dead-ends in isolation, the empty face that gazes back from the mirror.

Of course in patchwork, pluralistic America, different classes and ethnic groups are perched at different stages in the work hierarchy. The immigrants—legal and illegal—who still flock densely to America are fighting for the foothold that the jogging tribes of self-actualizers achieved three generations ago. The zealously ambitious Koreans who run New York City's best vegetable markets, or boat people trying to open a restaurant, or Chicanos who struggle to start a small business in the *barrio* are still years away from est and the Sierra Club. Working women, to the extent that they are new at it, now form a powerful source of ambition and energy. Feminism—and financial need—have made them, in effect, a sophisticated-immigrant wave upon the economy.

Having to work to stay alive, to build a future, gives one's exertions a tough moral simplicity. The point of work in that case is so obvious that it need not be discussed. But apart from the sheer necessity of sustaining life, is there some inherent worth in work? Carlyle believed that "all work, even cotton spinning, is noble; work is alone noble." Was he right?

It is seigneurial cant to romanticize work that is truly detestable and destructive to workers. But misery and drudgery are always comparative. Despite the sometimes nostalgic haze around their images, the preindustrial peasant and the 19th century American farmer did brutish work far harder than the assembly line. The untouchable who sweeps excrement in the streets of Bombay would react with blank incomprehension to the malaise of some $17-an-hour workers on a Chrysler assembly line. The Indian, after all, has passed from "alienation" into a degradation that is almost mystical. In Nicaragua, the average 19-year-old peasant has worked longer and harder than most Americans of middle age. Americans prone to restlessness about the spiritual disappointments of work should consult unemployed young men and women in their own ghettos: they know with painful clarity the importance of the personal dignity that a job brings.

Americans often fall into fallacies of misplaced sympathy. Psychologist Maslow, for example, once wrote that he found it difficult "to conceive of feeling proud of myself, self-loving and self-respecting, if I were working, for example, in some chewing-gum factory . . ." Well, two weeks ago, Warner-Lambert announced that it would close down its gum-manufacturing American Chicle factory in Long Island City, N.Y.: the workers who had spent years there making Dentyne and Chiclets were distraught. "It's a beautiful place to work," one feeder-catcher-packer of chewing gum said sadly. "It's just like home." There is a peculiar elitist arrogance in those who discourse on the brutalizations of work simply because they cannot imagine themselves performing the job. Certainly workers often feel abstracted out, reduced sometimes to dreary robotic functions. But almost everyone commands endlessly subtle systems of adaptation; people can make the work their own and even cherish it against all academic expectations. Such adaptations are often more important than the famous but theoretical alienation from the process and product of labor.

Work is still the complicated and crucial core of most lives, the occupation melded inseparably to the identity; Freud said that the successful psyche is one capable of love and of work. Work is the most thorough and profound organizing principle in American life. If mobility has weakened old blood ties, our co-workers often form our new family, our tribe, our social world; we become almost citizens of our companies, living under the protection of salaries, pensions and health insurance. Sociologist Robert Schrank believes that people like jobs mainly because they need other people; they need to gossip with them, hang out with them, to schmooze. Says Schrank: "The workplace performs the function of community."

Unless it is dishonest or destructive—the labor of a pimp or a hit man, say—all work is intrinsically honorable in ways that are rarely understood as they once were. Only the fortunate toil in ways that express them directly. There is a Renaissance splendor in Leonardo's effusion: "The works that the eye orders the hands to make are infinite." But most of us labor closer to the ground. Even there, all work expresses the laborer in a deeper sense: all life must be worked at, protected, planted, replanted, fashioned, cooked for, coaxed, diapered, formed, sustained. Work is the way that we tend the world, the way that people connect. It is the most vigorous, vivid sign of life—in individuals and in civilizations.

Reflections

Private Exploration

1. Select a key passage from Morrow's essay that you find particularly stimulating or troublesome. Use it as a starting point to explore and amplify your own thoughts and feelings about the values of work. Draw from experience or observations you've made within your family or community.
2. Most of us will never forget our first real job, whether it was mowing someone's lawn, baby-sitting, selling popcorn, or washing cars. Try to recall your thoughts and feelings about that job. What were your expectations, your disappointments. In retrospect, what did you learn that may have shaped your attitude toward work or future goals?
3. Recreate your own family's work history beginning with your grandfather or grandmother down to your own generation. Ponder the attitudes of these family members toward their jobs. Did they find them honorable, demeaning, dignified? In retrospect, do you? How has your family's work history changed and how have these changes affected your expectations and goals?

Public Exploration

1. Morrow claims that our attitude toward work and the American "work ethic" have changed. We need only ponder the attitudes of our great grandparents, grandparents, and parents to discover these changes. Reflect on what the value of work is now in the 1990s. How does the current generation look upon work? Consider your own expectations and needs. Is Morrow correct? And if so, are the changes for the better?
2. Consider this passage:

> Work is the most thorough and profound organizing principle in American life.

3. Strip-tease dancer, stockbroker, politician, used car salesman, college professor, drug dealer, taxi driver, dentist, shoe repairman, bar tender, farmer, real estate developer, street cleaner, garbage collector, doorman, spy, dock worker, trucker, secretary, day-care aid, television evangelist. Explore the following:

   All work is intrinsically honorable in ways that are rarely understood as they once were.

Private Reflection

1. If you had total freedom of choice, and if you could be paid a decent livable salary to do anything personally rewarding to you—to do that which would satisfy the inner life—what would it be? Describe the work and the life you would envision. Then consider a second element. What if absolutely no one respected your choice? Your parents, your friends, your society? Would you still do it? Consider as honestly as possible how external forces might influence you. Are you free to make the choices you want? How might you, or how will you, attempt to balance external with internal values in selecting a career?
2. If you are a woman you may feel extra pressure when it comes to career choices. Consider how you look on the sometimes conflicting values of marriage, motherhood, profession. How do you think now, at this point in your life, that you might balance them? Who or what may be influencing your choices, your concerns? If you could fantasize a perfect life for yourself, with no external influences, what would it be? Are your inner values in conflict with outer values?

The Importance of Work

GLORIA STEINEM

Toward the end of the 1970s, *The Wall Street Journal* devoted an eight-part, front-page series to "the working woman"—that is, the influx of women into the paid-labor force—as the greatest change in American life since the Industrial Revolution.

Many women readers greeted both the news and the definition with cynicism. After all, women have always worked. If all the productive work of human maintenance that women do in the home were valued at its replacement cost, the gross national product of the United States would go up by 26 percent. It's just that we are now more likely than ever before to leave our poorly rewarded, low-security, high-risk job of homemaking (though we're still trying to explain that it's a perfectly good one and that the problem is male society's refusal both to do it and to give it an economic value) for more secure, independent, and better-paid jobs outside the home.

Obviously, the real work revolution won't come until all productive work is rewarded—including child rearing and other jobs done in the home—and men are integrated into so-called women's work as well as vice versa. But the radical change being touted by the *Journal* and other media is one part of that long integration process: the unprecedented flood of women into salaried jobs, that is, into the labor force as it has been male-defined and previously occupied by men. We are already more than 41 percent of it—the highest proportion in history. Given the fact that women also make up a whopping 69 percent of the "discouraged labor force" (that is, people who need jobs but don't get counted in the unemployment statistics because they've given up looking), plus an official female unemployment rate that is substantially higher than men's, it's clear that we could expand to become fully half of the national work force by 1990.

Faced with this determination of women to find a little independence and to be paid and honored for our work, experts have rushed to ask: "Why?" It's a question rarely directed at male workers. Their basic motivations of survival and personal satisfaction are taken for granted. Indeed, men are regarded as "odd" and therefore subjects for sociological study and journalistic reports only when they *don't* have work, even if they are rich and don't need jobs or are poor and can't find them. Nonetheless, pollsters and sociologists have gone to great expense to prove that women work outside the home because of dire financial need, or if we persist despite the presence of a wage-earning male, out of some desire to buy "little extras" for our families, or even out of good old-fashioned penis envy."

Job interviewers and even our own families may still ask salaried women the big "Why?" If we have small children at home or are in some job regarded as "men's work," the incidence of such questions increases. Condescending or accusatory versions of "What's a nice girl like you doing in a place like this?" have not disappeared from the workplace.

How do we answer these assumptions that we are "working" out of some pressing or peculiar need? Do we feel okay about arguing that it's a natural for us to have salaried jobs as for our husbands—whether or not we have young children at home? Can we enjoy strong career ambitions without worrying about being thought "unfeminine"? When we confront men's growing resentment of women competing in the work force (often in the form of such guilt-producing accusations as "You're taking men's jobs away" or "You're damaging your children"), do we simply state that a decent job is a basic human right for everybody?

I'm afraid the answer is often no. As individuals and as a movement, we tend to retreat into some version of a tactically questionable defense: "Womenworkbecausewehaveto." The phrase has become one word, one key on the typewriter—an economic form of the socially "feminine" stance of passivity and self-sacrifice. Under attack, we still tend to present ourselves as creatures of economic necessity and familial devotion. "Womenworkbecausewehaveto" has become the easiest thing to say.

Like most truisms, this one is easy to prove with statistics. Economic need *is* the most consistent work motive—for women as well as men. In 1976, for instance, 43 percent of all women in the paid-labor force were single, widowed, separated, or divorced, and working to support themselves and their dependents. An additional 21 percent were married to men who had earned less than ten thousand dollars in the previous year, the minimum then required to support a family of four. In fact, if you take men's pensions, stocks, real estate, and various forms of accumulated wealth into account, a good statistical case can be made that there are more women who "have" to work (that is, who have neither the accumulated wealth, nor husbands whose work or wealth can support them for the rest of their lives) than there are men with the same need. If we were going to ask one group "Do you really need this job?" we should ask men.

But the first weakness of the whole "have to work" defense is its deceptiveness. Anyone who has ever experienced dehumanized life on welfare or any other confidence-shaking dependency knows that a paid job may be preferable to the dole, even when the handout is coming from a family member. Yet the will and self-confidence to work on one's own can diminish as dependency and fear increase. That may explain why—contrary to the "have to" rationale—wives of men who earn less than three thousand dollars a year are actually *less* likely to be employed than wives whose husbands make ten thousand dollars a year or more.

Furthermore, the greatest proportion of employed wives is found among families with a total household income of twenty-five to fifty thousand dollars a year. This is the statistical underpinning used by some sociologists to prove that women's work is mainly important for boosting families into the middle or upper middle class. Thus, women's incomes are largely used for buying "luxuries" and "little extras": a neat double-whammy that renders us secondary within our families, and makes our jobs expendable in hard times. We may even go along with this interpretation (at least, up to the point of getting fired so a male can have our job). It preserves a husbandly ego-need to be seen as the primary breadwinner, and still allows us a safe "feminine" excuse for working.

But there are often rewards that we're not confessing. As noted in *The Two-Career Couple*, by Francine and Douglas Hall: "Women who hold jobs by choice, even blue-collar routine jobs, are more satisfied with their lives than are the full-time housewives."

In addition to personal satisfaction, there is also society's need for all its members' talents. Suppose that jobs were given out on only a "have to work" basis to both women and men—one job per household. It would be unthinkable to lose the unique abilities of, for instance, Eleanor Holmes Norton, the distinguished chair of the Equal Employment Opportunity Commission. But would we then be forced to question the important work of her husband, Edward Norton, who is also a distinguished lawyer? Since men earn more than twice as much as women on the average, the wife in most households would be more likely to give up her job. Does that mean the nation could do as well without millions of its nurses, teachers, and secretaries? Or that the rare man who earns less than his wife should give up his job?

It was this kind of waste of human talents on a society-wide scale that traumatized millions of unemployed or underemployed Americans during the Depression. Then, a one-job-per-household rule seemed somewhat justified, yet the concept was used to displace women workers only, create intolerable dependencies, and waste female talent that the country needed. That Depression experience, plus the energy and example of women who were finally allowed to work during the manpower shortage created by World War II, led Congress to reinterpret the meaning of the country's full-employment goal in its Economic Act of 1946. Full employment was officially defined as "the employment of those who want to work, without regard to whether their employment is, by some definition, necessary. This goal applies equally to men and to women." Since bad economic times are again creating a resentment of employed women—as well as creating more need for women to be employed—we need such a goal more than ever. Women age again being caught in a tragic double bind: We are required to be strong and then punished for our strength.

Clearly, anything less than government and popular commitment to this 1946 definition of full employment will leave the less powerful groups, whoever they may be, in danger. Almost as important as the financial penalty paid by the powerless is the suffering that comes from being shut out of paid and recognized work. Without it, we lose much of our self-respect and our ability to prove that we are alive by making some difference in the world. That's just as true for the suburban woman as it is for the unemployed steel worker.

But it won't be easy to give up the passive defense of "weworkbecausewehaveto."

When a woman who is struggling to support her children and grandchildren on welfare sees her neighbor working as a waitress, even though that neighbor's husband has a job, she may feel resentful; and the waitress (of course, not the waitress's husband) may feel guilty. Yet unless we establish the obligation to provide a job for everyone who is willing and able to work, that welfare woman may herself be penalized by policies that give out only one public-service job per household. She and her daughter will have to make a painful and divisive decision about which of them gets that precious job, and the whole household will have to survive on only one salary.

A job as a human right is a principle that applies to men as well as women. But women have more cause to fight for it. The phenomenon of the "working woman" has been held responsible for everything from an increase in male impotence (which turned out, incidentally, to be attributable to medication for high blood pressure) to the rising cost of steak (which was due to high energy costs and beef import restrictions, not women's refusal to prepare the cheaper, slower-cooking cuts). Unless we see a job as part of every citizen's right to autonomy and personal fulfillment, we will continue to be vulnerable to someone else's idea of what "need" is, and whose "need" counts the most.

In many ways, women who do not have to work for simple survival, but who choose to do so nonetheless, are on the frontier of asserting this right for all women. Those with well-to-do-husbands are dangerously easy for us to resent and put down. It's easier still to resent women from families of inherited wealth, even though men generally control and benefit from that wealth. (There is no Rockefeller Sisters Fund, no J. P. Morgan & Daughters, and sons-in-law may be the ones who really sleep their way to power.) But to prevent a woman whose husband or father is wealthy from earning her own living, and from gaining the self-confidence that comes with that ability, is to keep her needful of that unearned power and less willing to disperse it. Moreover, it is to lose forever her unique talents.

Perhaps modern feminists have been guilty of a kind of reverse snobbism that keeps us from reaching out to the wives and daughters of wealthy men; yet it was exactly such women who refused the restrictions of class and financed the first wave of feminist revolution.

For most of us, however, "womenworkbecausewehaveto" is just true enough to be seductive as a personal defense.

If we use it without also staking out the larger human right to a job, however, we will never achieve that right. And we will always be subject to the false argument that independence for women is a luxury affordable only in good economic times. Alternatives to layoffs will not be explored, acceptable unemployment will always be used to frighten those with jobs into accepting low wages, and we will never remedy the real cost, both to families and to the country, of dependent women and a massive loss of talent.

Worst of all, we may never learn to find productive, honored work as a natural part of ourselves and as one of life's basic pleasures.

Reflections

Private Exploration

1. What do you make of the following observation from Gloria Steinem? Reflect on and integrate examples for your own observations and experience as you respond.

   > The will and self-confidence to work on one's own can diminish as dependency and fear increase.

2. Steinem argues that a job is a human right for both men and women. Consider the implications. Does every human being have the right to work in the same way that we have a right to freedom of speech or freedom of religion? If so, does government have an obligation to provide a job? If not, how can the right be maintained?

Public Exploration

1. Sociologists tell us that the American family of the past no longer exists. Parents work, children are left to raise themselves. Yet Steinem argues that society benefits from the full employment of men and women. Make a list of the benefits and disadvantages to society and to families of both sexes being employed. Use your own experience as a starting point. What values are at issue here? Can they be reconciled?
2. In an essay titled "Are Women Human?" Dorothy Sayers records a list of jobs that belonged to women in the Medieval era: the entire spinning and dyeing industry; the weaving, catering, brewing, and distilling industries; all the preserving, pickling, bottling, and dairy industries; not to mention the management of many landed estates. Sayers writes that "modern civilization has taken all these pleasant and profitable activities out of the home, where the women looked after them, and handed them over to big industry, to be directed and organized by men at the head of large factories."

   Consider further Sayers's argument that "it is perfectly idiotic to take away women's traditional occupations and then complain because she looks for new ones."

Private Reflection

If your mother worked outside the home, was it by choice or out of economic necessity? How did her work affect your family? Consider the gains and losses of having a working or stay-at-home mother. Given a chance to cast your vote for or against working mothers, what vote would you cast and how would you defend that vote?

Work in an Alienated Society

ERICH FROMM

Unless man exploits others, he has to work in order to live. However primitive and simple his method of work may be, by the very fact of production, he has risen above the animal kingdom; rightly has he been defined as "the animal that produces." But work is not only an inescapable necessity for man. Work is also his liberator from nature, his creator as a social and independent being. *In the process of work, that is, the molding and changing of nature outside of himself, man molds and changes himself.* He emerges from nature by mastering her; he develops his powers of cooperation, of reason, his sense of beauty. He separates himself from nature, from the original unity with her, but at the same time unites himself with her again as her master and builder. The more his work develops, the more his individuality develops. In molding nature and re-creating her, he learns to make use of his powers, increasing his skill and creativeness. Whether we think of the beautiful paintings in the caves of Southern France, the ornaments on weapons among primitive people, the statues and temples of Greece, the cathedrals of the Middle Ages, the chairs and tables made by skilled craftsmen, or the cultivation of flowers, trees or corn by peasants—all are expressions of the creative transformation of nature by man's reason and skill.

In Western history, craftsmanship, especially as it developed in the thirteenth and fourteenth centuries, constitutes one of the peaks in the evolution of creative work. Work was not only a useful activity, but one which carried with it a profound satisfaction. The main features of craftsmanship have been very lucidly expressed by C. W. Mills. "There is no ulterior motive in work other than the product being made and the processes of its creation. The details of daily work are meaningful because they are not detached in the worker's mind from the product of the work. The worker is free to control his own working action. The craftsman is thus able to learn from his work; and to use and develop his capacities and skills in its prosecution. There is no split of work and play, or work and culture. The craftsman's way of livelihood determines and infuses his entire mode of living."

With the collapse of the medieval structure, and the beginning of the modern mode of production, the meaning and function of work changed fundamentally, especially in the Protestant countries. Man, being afraid of his newly won freedom, was obsessed by the need to subdue his doubts and fears by developing a feverish activity. The outcome of this activity, success or failure, decided his salvation, indicating whether he was among the saved or the lost souls. *Work, instead of being an activity satisfying in itself and pleasurable, became a duty and an obsession.* The more it was possible to gain riches by work, the more it became a pure means to the aim of wealth and success. Work became, in Max Weber's terms, the chief factor in a system of "inner-worldly asceticism," an answer to man's sense of aloneness and isolation.

However, work in this sense existed only for the upper and middle classes, those who could amass some capital and employ the work of others. For the vast majority of those who had only their physical energy to sell, work became nothing but forced labor. The worker in the eighteenth or nineteenth century who had to work sixteen hours if he did not want to starve was not doing it because he served the Lord in this way, nor because his success would show that he was among the "chosen" ones, but because he was forced to sell his energy to those who had the means of exploiting it. The first centuries of the modern era find the meaning of work divided into that of *duty* among the middle class, and that of *forced labor* among those without property.

The religious attitude toward work as a duty, which was still so prevalent in the nineteenth century, has been changing considerably in the last decades. Modern man does not know what to do with himself, how to spend his lifetime meaningfully, and he is driven to work in order to avoid an unbearable boredom. But work has ceased to be a moral and religious obligation in the sense of the middle-class attitude of the eighteenth and nineteenth centuries. Something new has emerged. Ever-increasing production, the drive to make bigger and better things, have become aims in themselves, new ideals. Work has become alienated from the working person.

What happens to the industrial worker? He spends his best energy for seven or eight hours a day in producing "something." He needs his work in order to make a living, but his role is essentially a passive one. He fulfills a small isolated function in a complicated and highly organized process of production, and is never confronted with "his" product as a whole, at least not as a producer, but only as a consumer, provided he has the money to buy "his" product in a store. He is concerned neither with the whole product in its physical aspects nor with its wider economic and social aspects. He is put in a certain place, has to carry out a certain task, but does not participate in the organization or management of the work. He is not interested, nor does he know why one produces this, instead of another commodity—what relation it has to the needs of society as a whole. The shoes, the cars, the electric bulbs, are produced by "the enterprise," using the machines. He is a part of the machine, rather than its master as an active agent. The machine, instead of being in his service to do work for him which once had to be performed by sheer physical energy, has become his master. Instead of the machine being the substitute for human energy, man has become a substitute for the machine. *His work can be defined as the performance of acts which cannot yet be performed by machines.*

Work is a means of getting money, not in itself a meaningful human activity. P. Drucker, observing workers in the automobile industry, expresses this idea very succinctly: "For the great majority of automobile workers, the only meaning of the job is in the pay check, not in anything connected with the work or the product. Work appears as something unnatural, a disagreeable, meaningless and stultifying condition of getting the pay check, devoid of dignity as well as of importance. No wonder that this puts a premium on slovenly work, on slowdowns, and on other tricks to get the same pay check with less work. No wonder that this results in an unhappy and discontented worker—because a pay check is not enough to base one's self-respect on."

This relationship of the worker to his work is an outcome of the whole social organization of which he is a part. Being "employed," he is not an active agent, has no responsibility except the proper performance of the isolated piece of work he is doing, and has little interest except the one of bringing home enough money to support himself and his family. Nothing more is expected of him, or wanted from him. He is part of the equipment hired by capital, and his role and function are determined by this quality of being a piece of equipment. In recent decades, increasing attention has been paid to the psychology of the worker, and to his attitude toward his work, to the "human problem of industry"; but this very formulation is indicative of the underlying attitude; there is a human being spending most of his lifetime at work, and what should be discussed is the "*industrial problem of human beings,*" *rather than* "*the human problem of industry.*"

Most investigations in the field of industrial psychology are concerned with the question of how the productivity of the individual worker can be increased, and how he can be made to work with less friction; psychology has lent its services to "human engineering," an attempt to treat the worker and employee like a machine which runs better when it is well oiled. While Taylor was primarily concerned with a better organization of the technical use of the worker's physical powers, most industrial psychologists are mainly concerned with the manipulation of the worker's psyche. The underlying idea can be formulated like this: if he works better when he is happy, then let us make him happy, secure, satisfied, or anything else, provided it raises his output and diminishes friction. In the name of "human relations," the worker is treated with all devices which suit a completely alienated person; even happiness and human values are recommended in the interest of better relations with the public. Thus, for instance, according to *Time* magazine, one of the best-known American psychiatrists said to a group of fifteen hundred supermarket executives: "It's going to be an increased satisfaction to our customers if we are happy. . . . It is going to pay off in cold dollars and cents to management, if we could put some of these general principles of values, human relationships, really into practice." One speaks of "human relations" and one means the most inhuman relations, those between alienated automatons; one speaks of happiness and means the perfect routinization which has driven out the last doubt and all spontaneity.

The alienated and profoundly unsatisfactory character of work results in two reactions: one, the ideal of complete *laziness*; the other a deep-seated, though often unconscious *hostility* toward work and everything and everybody connected with it.

It is not difficult to recognize the widespread longing for the state of complete laziness and passivity. Our advertising appeals to it even more than to sex. There are, of course, many useful and labor saving gadgets. But this usefulness often serves only as a rationalization for the appeal to complete passivity and receptivity. A package of breakfast cereal is being advertised as "*new—easier to eat.*" An electric toaster is advertised with the words: ". . . the most distinctly different toaster in the world! Everything is done *for* you with this new toaster. You need not even bother to lower the bread. Power-action, through a unique electric motor, *gently takes the bread right out of your fingers*!" How many courses in languages, or other subjects, are announced with the slogan "effortless learning, no more of the old drudgery." Everybody knows the picture of the elderly couple in the advertisement of a life insurance company, who have retired at the age of sixty, and spend their life in the complete bliss of having nothing to do except just travel.

Radio and television exhibit another element of this yearning for laziness: the idea of "push-button power"; by pushing a button, or turning a knob on my machine, I have the power to produce music, speeches, ball games, and on the television set, to command events of the world to appear before my eyes. The pleasure of driving cars certainly rests partly upon this same satisfaction of the wish for push-button power. By the effortless pushing of a button, a powerful machine is set in motion; little skill and effort is needed to make the driver feel that he is the ruler of space.

But there is far more serious and deep-seated reaction to the meaninglessness and boredom of work. It is a hostility toward work which is much less conscious than our craving for laziness and inactivity. Many a businessman feels himself the prisoner of his business and the commodities he sells; he has a feeling of fraudulency about his product and a secret contempt for it. He hates his customers, who force him to put up a show in order to sell. He hates his customers because they are a threat; his employees as well as his superiors, because he is in a constant competitive fight with them. Most important of all, he hates himself, because he sees his life passing by, without making any sense beyond the momentary intoxication of success. Of course, this hate and contempt for others and for oneself, and for the very things one produces, is mainly unconscious, and only occasionally comes up to awareness in a fleeting thought, which is sufficiently disturbing to be set aside as quickly as possible.

Reflections

Private Exploration

1. Erich Fromm traces the changing values and expectations of workers, from the Medieval era to the industrial period. Explore a key passage you identify with or one that disturbs or offends you.
2. Consider what it is that makes the difference between a job that is a "duty and an obsession" and one that is a "liberator" and "creator."
3. Reflect on Fromm's statement that "work has become alienated from the working person." Can you compare his observation to your own experience in school? Has education become alienated from the student?

Public Exploration

1. Erich Fromm's argument concerning the alienation of work for the modern worker is drawn from classic Marxism. How does knowing that affect your own response to his argument? Are you more or less inclined to consider the rationale and logic behind it? Should you be affected at all by knowing the historical or cultural context out of which Fromm created his essay? Explore how the values of your own culture might affect your personal attitude toward work, as well as toward a Marxist interpretation of work. Are there ways to sort through the various conflicts and influences? Is it possible the insights of Marx could be of value in a capitalist society?
2. Those who argue that modern workers, especially factory workers, are alienated, are usually intellectuals who do not work in factories. A recent study has shown that many workers find other kinds of rewards in their work (in spite of the repetitious drudgery). For example, many enjoy the social aspect, the gossip, the friendships. When a chewing gum factory closed in New Jersey, a man whose sole job for twenty years was to operate a "wrapping" machine was quoted as saying he would miss the factory because "it was just like home" to him. Are such workers deluded? Could Fromm's argument merely be an elitist stance?

Personal Reflection

Even if you have not yet chosen the kind of career you want to enter, consider the type of life-long work that would nurture self-respect and happiness for you. What elements are needed? Something that allows you to contribute to society? Something that challenges you? Something that allows you to work alone? Or with others? Something outdoors? Something artistic? Consider, too, the personal qualities you have to offer. After you've finished, draw a line on the page, look back over what you've written, and if possible, characterize the value or values that are showing forth there.

How Much Land Does a Man Need?

LEO TOLSTOY

I

An elder sister came to visit her younger sister in the country. The elder was married to a tradesman in town, the younger to a peasant in the village. As the sisters sat over their tea talking, the elder began to boast of the advantages of town life: saying how comfortably they lived there, how well they dressed, what fine clothes her children wore, what good things they ate and drank, and how she went to the theater, promenades, and entertainments.

The younger sister was piqued, and in turn disparaged the life of a tradesman, and stood up for that of a peasant.

"I would not change my way of life for yours," said she. "We may live roughly, but at least we are free from anxiety. You live in better style than we do, but though you often earn more than you need, you're very likely to lose all you have. We know the proverb, 'Loss and gain are brothers twain.' It often happens that people who are wealthy one day are begging their bread the next. Our way is safer. Though a peasant's life is not a fat one, it is long. We shall never grow rich, but we shall always have enough to eat."

The elder sister said sneeringly:

"Enough? Yes, if you like to share with the pigs and the calves! What do you know of elegance or manners! However much your good man may slave, you will die as you are living—on a dung heap—and your children the same."

"Well, what of that?" replied the younger. "Of course our work is rough and coarse. But, on the other hand, it is sure; and we need not bow to anyone. But you, in your towns, are surrounded by temptations; today all may be right, but tomorrow the Evil One may tempt your husband with cards, wine, or women, and all will go to ruin. Don't such things happen often enough?"

Pahom, the master of the house, was lying on the top of the oven, and he listened to the women's chatter.

"It is perfectly true," thought he. "Busy as we are from childhood tilling mother earth, we peasants have no time to let any nonsense settle in our heads. Our only trouble is that we haven't land enough. If I had plenty of land, I shouldn't fear the Devil himself!"

The women finished their tea, chatted a while about dress, and then cleared away the tea things and lay down to sleep.

But the Devil had been sitting behind the oven, and had heard all that had been said. He was pleased that the peasant's wife had led her husband into boasting, and that he had said that if he had plenty of land he would not fear the Devil himself.

"All right," thought the Devil. "We will have a tussle. I'll give you land enough; and by means of that land I will get you into my power."

II

Close to the village there lived a lady, a small landowner who had an estate of about three hundred acres or 120 *desyatins.* The *desyatina* is properly 2.7 acres; but in this story round numbers are used. She had always lived on good terms with the peasants until she engaged as her steward an old soldier, who took to burdening the people with fines. However careful Pahom tried to be, it happened again and again that now a horse of his got among the lady's oats, now a cow strayed into her garden, now his calves found their way into her meadows—and he always had to pay a fine.

Pahom paid up, but grumbled, and, going home in a temper, was rough with his family. All through that summer Pahom had much trouble because of this steward; and he was even glad when winter came and the cattle had to be stabled. Though he grudged the fodder when they could no longer graze on the pasture land, at least he was free from anxiety about them.

In the winter the news got about that the lady was going to sell her land and that the keeper of the inn on the high road was bargaining for it. When the peasants heard this they were very much alarmed.

"Well," thought they, "if the innkeeper gets the land, he will worry us with fines worse than the lady's steward. We all depend on that estate."

So the peasants went on behalf of their Commune, and asked the lady not to sell the land to the innkeeper, offering her a better price for it themselves. The lady agreed to let them have it. Then the peasants tried to arrange for the Commune to buy the whole estate, so that it might be held by them all in common. They met twice to discuss it, but could not settle the matter; the Evil One sowed discord among them and they could not agree. So they decided to buy the land individually, each according to his means; and the lady agreed to this plan as she had to the other.

Presently Pahom heard that a neighbor of his was buying fifty acres, and that the lady had consented to accept one half in cash and to wait a year for the other half. Pahom felt envious.

"Look at that," thought he, "the land is all being sold, and I'll get none of it." So he spoke to his wife.

"Other people are buying," said he, "and we must also buy twenty acres or so. Life is becoming impossible. That steward is simply crushing us with his fines."

So they put their heads together and considered how they could manage to buy it. They had one hundred rubles laid by. They sold a colt and one half of their bees; hired out one of their sons as a laborer, and took his wages in advance; borrowed the rest from a brother-in-law, and so scraped together half the purchase money.

Having done this, Pahom chose a farm of forty acres, some of it wooded, and went to the lady to bargain for it. They came to an agreement, and he shook hands with her upon it and paid her a deposit in advance. Then they went to town and signed the deeds; he paying half the price down, and undertaking to pay the remainder within two years.

So now Pahom had land of his own. He borrowed seed, and sowed it on the land he had bought. The harvest was a good one, and within a year he had managed to pay off his debts both to the lady and to his brother-in-law. So he became a landowner, plowing and sowing his own land, making hay on his own land, cutting his own trees, and feeding his cattle on his own pasture. When he went out to plow his fields, or to look at his growing corn, or at his grass-meadows, his heart would fill with joy. The grass that grew and the flowers that bloomed there seemed to him unlike any that grew elsewhere. Formerly, when he had passed by that land, it had appeared the same as any other land, but now it seemed quite different.

III

So Pahom was well-contented, and everything would have been right if the neighboring peasants would only not have trespassed on his cornfields and meadows. He appealed to them most civilly, but they still went on; now the Communal herdsmen would let the village cows stray into his meadows; then horses from the night pasture would get among his corn. Pahom turned them out again and again, and forgave their owners, and for a long time he forbore to prosecute anyone. But at last he lost patience and complained to the District Court. He knew it was the peasants' want of land, and no evil intent on their part, that caused the trouble, but he thought:

"I can't go on overlooking it, or they will destroy all I have. They must be taught a lesson."

So he had them up, gave them one lesson, and then another, and two or three of the peasants were fined. After a time Pahom's neighbors began to bear him a grudge for this, and would now and then let their cattle on to his land on purpose. One peasant even got into Pahom's wood at night and cut down five young lime trees for their bark. Pahom, passing through the wood one day, noticed something white. He came nearer and saw the stripped trunks lying on the ground, and close by stood the stumps where the trees had been. Pahom was furious.

"If he'd only cut one here and there it would have been bad enough," thought Pahom, "but the rascal has actually cut down a whole clump. If I could only find out who did this, I would pay him out."

He racked his brains as to who it could be. Finally he decided: "It must be Simon—no one else could have done it." So he went to Simon's homestead to have a look around, but he found nothing, and only had an angry scene. However, he now felt more certain than ever that Simon had done it, and he lodged a complaint. Simon was summoned. The case was tried, and retried, and at the end of it all Simon was acquitted, there being no evidence against him. Pahom felt still more aggrieved, and let his anger loose upon the Elder and the Judges.

"You let thieves grease your palms," said he. "If you were honest folk yourselves you would not let a thief go free."

So Pahom quarrelled with the judges and with his neighbors. Threats to burn his building began to be uttered. So though Pahom had more land, his place in the Commune was much worse than before.

About this time a rumor got about that many people were moving to new parts.

"There's no need for me to leave my land," thought Pahom. "But some of the others might leave our village and then there would be more room for us. I would take over their land myself and make my estate a bit bigger. I could then live more at ease. As it is, I'm still too cramped to be comfortable."

One day Pahom was sitting at home, when a peasant, passing through the village, happened to call in. He was allowed to stay the night, and supper was given him. Pahom had a talk with this peasant and asked him where he came from. The stranger answered that he came from beyond the Volga, where he had been working. One word led to another, and the man went on to say that many people were settling in those parts. He told how some people from his village had settled there. They had joined the Commune there and had had twenty-five acres per man granted them. The land was so good, he said, that the rye sown on it grew as high as a horse, and so thick that five cuts of a sickle made a sheaf. One peasant, he said, had brought nothing with him but his bare hands, and now he had six horses and two cows of his own.

Pahom's heart kindled with desire. He thought:

"Why should I suffer in this narrow hole, if one can live so well elsewhere? I will sell my land and my homestead here, and with the money I will start afresh over there and get everything new. In this crowded place one is always having trouble. But I must first go and find out all about it myself."

Toward summer he got ready and started. He went down the Volga on a steamer to Samara, then walked another three hundred miles on foot, and at last reached the place. It was just as the stranger had said. The peasants had plenty of land: every man had twenty-five acres of Communal land given him for his use, and anyone who had money could buy, besides, at two shillings an acre (three rubles per *desyatina*) as much good freehold land as he wanted.

Having found out all he wished to know, Pahom returned home as autumn came on, and began selling off his belongings. He sold his land at a profit, sold his homestead and all his cattle, and withdrew from membership of the Commune. He only waited till the spring, and then started with his family for the new settlement.

IV

As soon as Pahom and his family arrived at their new abode, he applied for admission into the Commune of a large village. He stood treat to the Elders and obtained the necessary documents. Five shares of Communal land were given him for his own and his sons' use: that is to say—125 acres (not all together, but in different fields) besides the use of the Communal pasture. Pahom put up the buildings he needed and bought cattle. Of the Communal land alone he had three times as much as at his former home, and the land was good corn land. He was ten times better off than he had been. He had plenty of arable land and pasturage, and could keep as many head of cattle as he liked.

At first, in the bustle of building and settling down, Pahom was pleased with it all, but when he got used to it he began to think that even here he had not enough land. The first year he sowed wheat on his share of the Communal land and had a good crop. He wanted to go on sowing wheat, but had not enough Communal land for the purpose, and what he had already used was not available; for in those parts wheat is sown only on virgin soil or on fallow land. It is sown for one or two years, and then the land lies fallow till it is again overgrown with prairie grass. There were many who wanted such land, and there was not enough for all; so that people quarreled about it. Those who were better off wanted it for growing wheat, and those who were poor wanted it to let to dealers, so that they might raise money to pay their taxes. Pahom wanted to sow more wheat, so he rented land from a dealer for a year. He sowed much wheat and had a fine crop, but the land was too far from the village—the wheat had to be carted more than ten miles. After a time Pahom noticed that some peasant dealers were living on separate farms and were growing wealthy; and he thought:

"If I were to buy some freehold land and have a homestead on it, it would be a different thing altogether. Then it would all be nice and compact."

The question of buying freehold land recurred to him again and again.

He went on in the same way for three years, renting land and sowing wheat. The seasons turned out well and the crops were good, so that he began to lay money by. He might have gone on living contentedly, but he grew tired of having to rent other people's land every year, and having to scramble for it. Wherever there was good land to be had, the peasants would rush for it and it was taken up at once, so that unless you were sharp about it you got none. It happened in the third year that he and a dealer together rented a piece of pasture land from some peasants; and they had already plowed it up, when there was some dispute and the peasants went to law about it, and things fell out so that the labor was all lost.

"If it were my own land," thought Pahom, "I should be independent, and there would not be all this unpleasantness."

So Pahom began looking out for land which he could buy; he came across a peasant who had bought thirteen hundred acres, but having got into difficulties was willing to sell again cheap. Pahom bargained and haggled with him, and at last they settled the price at 1,500 rubles, part in cash and part to be paid later. They had all but clinched the matter when a passing dealer happened to stop at Pahom's one day to get a feed for his horses. He drank tea with Pahom, and they had a talk. The dealer said that he was just returning home from the land of the Bashkirs, far away, where he had bought thirteen thousand acres of land, all for 1,000 rubles. Pahom questioned him further, and the tradesman said:

"All one need do is to make friends with the chiefs. I gave away about one hundred rubles' worth of dressing gowns and carpets, besides a case of tea, and I gave wine to those who would drink it; and I got the land for less than twopence an acre (five *kapeks* for a *desyatina*)." And he showed Pahom the title-deeds, saying:

"The land lies near a river, and the whole prairie is virgin soil."

Pahom plied him with questions, and the tradesman said:

"There is more land there than you could cover if you walked a year, and it all belongs to the Bashkirs. They are as simple as sheep, and land can be got almost for nothing."

"There now," thought Pahom, "with my one thousand rubles, why should I get only thirteen hundred acres, and saddle myself with a debt besides. If I take it out there, I can get more than ten times as much for the money."

V

Pahom inquired how to get to the place, and as soon as the tradesman had left him, he prepared to go there himself. He left his wife to look after the homestead, and started on his journey taking his hired man with him. They stopped at a town on their way, and bought a case of tea, some wine, and other presents, as the tradesman had advised. On and on they went until they had gone more than three hundred miles, and on the seventh day they came to a place where the Bashkirs had pitched their tents. It was all just as the tradesman had said. The people lived on the steppes, by a river, in felt-covered tents. They neither tilled the ground nor ate bread. Their cattle and horses grazed in herds on the steppe. The colts were tethered behind the tents, and the mares were driven to them twice a day. The mares were milked, and from the milk kumiss was made. It was the women who prepared kumiss, and they also made cheese. As far as the men were concerned, drinking kumiss and tea, eating mutton, and playing on their pipes was all they cared about. They were all stout and merry, and all the summer long they never thought of doing any work. They were quite ignorant, and knew no Russian, but were good-natured enough.

As soon as they saw Pahom, they came out of their tents and gathered round their visitor. An interpreter was found, and Pahom told them he had come about some land. The Bashkirs seemed very glad; they took Pahom and led him into one of the best tents, where they made him sit on some down cushions placed on a carpet, while they sat round him. They gave him some tea and kumiss, and had a sheep killed, and gave him mutton to eat. Pahom took presents out of his cart and distributed them among the Bashkirs, and divided amongst them the tea. The Bashkirs were delighted. They talked a great deal among themselves, and then told the interpreter to translate.

"They wish to tell you," said the interpreter, "that they like you, and that it is our custom to do all we can to please a guest and to repay him for his gifts. You have given us presents, now tell us which of the things we possess please you best, that we may present them to you."

"What pleases me best here," answered Pahom, "is your land. Our land is crowded and the soil is exhausted; but you have plenty of land, and it is good land. I never saw the like of it."

The interpreter translated. The Bashkirs talked among themselves for a while. Pahom could not understand what they were saying, but saw that they were much amused, and that they shouted and laughed. Then they were silent and looked at Pahom while the interpreter said:

"They wish me to tell you that in return for your presents they will gladly give you as much land as you want. You have only to point it out with your hand and it is yours."

The Bashkirs talked again for a while and began to dispute. Pahom asked what they were disputing about, and the interpreter told him that some of them thought they ought to ask their Chief about the land and not act in his absence, while others thought there was no need to wait for his return.

VI

While the Bashkirs were disputing, a man in a large fox fur cap appeared on the scene. They all became silent and rose to their feet. The interpreter said, "This is our Chief himself."

Pahom immediately fetched the best dressing gown and five pounds of tea, and offered these to the Chief. The Chief accepted them, and seated himself in the place of honor. The Bashkirs at once began telling him something. The Chief listened for a while, then made a sign with his head for them to be silent, and addressing himself to Pahom, said in Russian:

"Well, let it be so. Choose whatever piece of land you like; we have plenty of it."

"How can I take as much as I like?" thought Pahom. "I must get a deed to make it secure, or else they may say, 'It is yours,' and afterwards may take it away again."

"Thank you for your kind words," he said aloud. "You have much land, and I only want a little. But I should like to be sure which bit is mine. Could it not be measured and made over to me? Life and death are in God's hands.

You good people give it to me, but your children might wish to take it away again."

"You are quite right," said the Chief. "We will make it over to you."

"I heard that a dealer had been here," continued Pahom, "and that you gave him a little land, too, and signed title deeds to that effect. I should like to have it done in the same way."

The Chief understood.

"Yes," replied he, "that can be done quite easily. We have a scribe, and we will go to town with you and have the deed properly sealed."

"And what will be the price?" asked Pahom.

"Our price is always the same: one thousand rubles a day."

Pahom did not understand.

"A day? What measure is that? How many acres would that be?"

"We do not know how to reckon it out," said the Chief. "We sell it by the day. As much as you can go round on your feet in a day is yours, and the price is one thousand rubles a day."

Pahom was surprised.

"But in a day you can get around a large tract of land," he said.

The Chief laughed.

"It will all be yours!" said he. "But there is one condition: If you don't return on the same day to the spot whence you started, your money is lost."

"But how am I to mark the way that I have gone?"

"Why, we shall go to any spot you like, and stay there. You must start from that spot and make your round, taking a spade with you. Wherever you think necessary, make a mark. At every turning, dig a hole and pile up the turf; then afterwards we will go round with a plow from hole to hole. You may make as large a circuit as you please, but before the sun sets you must return to the place you started from. All the land you cover will be yours."

Pahom was delighted. It was decided to start early next morning. They talked a while, and after drinking some more kumiss and eating some more mutton, they had tea again, and then the night came on. They gave Pahom a feather bed to sleep on, and the Bashkirs dispersed for the night, promising to assemble the next morning at daybreak and ride out before sunrise to the appointed spot.

VII

Pahom lay on the feather bed, but could not sleep. He kept thinking about the land.

"What a large tract I'll mark off!" thought he. "I can easily do thirty-five miles in a day. the days are long now, and within a circuit of thirty-five miles what a lot of land there will be! I'll sell the poorer land, or let it to peasants, but I'll pick out the best and farm it. I will buy two ox teams and hire two more laborers. About a hundred and fifty acres shall be plow land, and I will pasture cattle on the rest."

Pahom lay awake all night, and dozed off only just before dawn. Hardly were his eyes closed when he had a dream. He thought he was lying in that same tent and heard somebody chuckling outside. He wondered who it could be, and rose and went out, and he saw the Bashkir Chief sitting in front of the tent holding his sides and rolling about with laughter. Going nearer to the Chief, Pahom asked: "What are you laughing at?" But he saw that it was no longer the Chief, but the dealer who had recently stopped at his house and had told him about the land. Just as Pahom was going to ask, "Have you been here long?" he saw that it was not the dealer, but the peasant who had come up from the Volga, long ago, to Pahom's old home. Then he saw that it was not the peasant either, but the Devil himself with hoofs and horns, sitting there and chuckling, and before him lay a man barefoot, prostrate on the ground, with only trousers and a shirt on. And Pahom dreamt that he looked more attentively to see what sort of a man it was that was lying there, and he saw that the man was dead, and that it was himself! He awoke horror struck.

"What things one does dream," thought he.

Looking round he saw through the open door that the dawn was breaking.

"It's time to wake them up," thought he. "We ought to be starting."

He got up, roused his man (who was sleeping in his cart), bade him harness; and went to call the Bashkirs.

"It's time to go to the steppe to measure the land," he said.

The Bashkirs rose and assembled, and the Chief came too. Then they began drinking kumiss again, and offered Pahom some tea, but he would not wait.

"If we are to go, let us go. It is high time," said he.

VIII

The Bashkirs got ready and they all started: some mounted on horses and some in carts. Pahom drove in his own small cart with his servant and took a spade with him. When they reached the steppe, the morning red was beginning to kindle. They ascended a hillock (called by the Bashkirs a *shikhan*) and, dismounting from their carts and their horses, gathered in one spot. The Chief came up to Pahom and stretching out his arm towards the plain:

"See," said he, "all this, as far as your eye can reach, is ours. You may have any part of it you like."

Pahom's eyes glistened: it was all virgin soil, as flat as the palm of your hand, as black as the seed of a poppy, and in the hollows different kinds of grasses grew breast high.

The Chief took off his fox fur cap, placed it on the ground, and said:

"This will be the mark. Start from here, and return here again. All the land you go round shall be yours."

Pahom took out his money and put it on the cap. Then he took off his outer coat, remaining in his sleeveless undercoat. He unfastened his girdle and tied it tight below his stomach, put a little bag of bread into the breast of his coat, and tying a flask of water to his girdle, he drew up the tops of his boots, took the spade from his man, and stood ready to start. He considered for some moments which way he had better go—it was tempting everywhere.

"No matter," he concluded, "I'll go towards the rising sun."

He turned his face to the east, stretched himself, and waited for the sun to appear above the rim.

"I must lose no time," he thought, "and it is easier walking while it is still cool."

The sun's rays had hardly flashed above the horizon before Pahom, carrying the spade over his shoulder, went down into the steppe.

Pahom started walking neither slowly nor quickly. After having gone a thousand yards he stopped, dug a hole, and placed pieces of turf one on another to make it more visible. Then he went on; and now that he had walked off his stiffness he quickened his pace. After a while he dug another hole.

Pahom looked back. The hillock could be distinctly seen in the sunlight, with the people on it, and the glittering tires of the cartwheels. At a rough guess Pahom concluded that he had walked three miles. It was growing warmer; he took off his undercoat, flung it across his shoulder, and went on again. It had grown quite warm now; he looked at the sun, it was time to think of breakfast.

"The first shift is done, but there are four in a day, and it is too soon yet to turn. But I will just take off my boots," said he to himself.

He sat down, took off his boots, stuck them into his girdle, and went on. It was easy walking now.

"I will go on for another three miles," thought he, "and then turn to the left. This spot is so fine that it would be a pity to lose it. The further one goes, the better the land seems."

He went straight on for a while, and when he looked round, the hillock was scarcely visible and the people on it looked like black ants, and he could just see something glistening there in the sun.

"Ah," thought Pahom, "I have gone far enough in this direction, it is time to turn. Besides, I am in a regular sweat, and very thirsty."

He stopped, dug a large hole, and heaped up pieces of turf. Next he untied his flask, had a drink, and then turned sharply to the left. He went on and on; the grass was high, and it was very hot.

Pahom began to grow tired: he looked at the sun and saw that it was noon.

"Well," he thought, "I must have a rest."

He sat down, and ate some bread and drank some water; but he did not lie down, thinking that if he did he might fall asleep. After sitting a little while, he went on again. At first he walked easily: the food had strengthened him; but it had become terribly hot and he felt sleepy. Still he went on, thinking: "An hour to suffer, a lifetime to live."

He went a long way in this direction also, and was about to turn the left again, when he perceived a damp hollow: "It would be a pity to leave that out," he thought, "flax would do well there." So he went on past the hollow and dug a hole on the other side of it before he turned the corner. Pahom looked towards the hillock. The heat made the air hazy: it seemed to be quivering, and through the haze the people on the hillock could scarcely be seen.

"Ah," thought Pahom, "I have made the sides too long; I must make this one shorter." And he went along the third side, stepping faster. He looked at the sun: it was nearly half way to the horizon, and he had not yet done two miles of the third side of the square. He was still ten miles from the goal.

"No," he thought, "though it will make my land lopsided, I must hurry back in a straight line now. I might go too far, and as it is I have a great deal of land."

So Pahom hurriedly dug a hole and turned straight towards the hillock.

IX

Pahom went straight towards the hillock, but he now walked with difficulty. He was done up with the heat, his bare feet were cut and bruised, and his legs began to fail. He longed to rest, but it was impossible if he meant to get back before sunset. The sun waits for no man, and it was sinking lower and lower.

"Oh dear," he thought, "if only I have not blundered trying for too much! What if I am too late?"

He looked towards the hillock and at the sun. He was still far from his goal, and the sun was already near the rim.

Pahom walked on and on; it was very hard walking, but he went quicker and quicker. He pressed on, but was still far from the place. He began running, threw away his coat, his boots, his flask, and his cap, and kept only the spade which he used as a support.

"What shall I do?" he thought again. "I have grasped too much, and ruined the whole affair. I can't get there before the sun sets."

And this fear made him still more breathless. Pahom went on running, his soaking shirt and trousers stuck to him, and his mouth was parched. His breast was working like a blacksmith's bellows, his heart was beating like a hammer, and his legs were giving way as if they did not belong to him. Pahom was seized with terror lest he should die of the strain.

Though afraid of death, he could not stop.

"After having run all that way they will call me a fool if I stop now," thought he. And he ran on and on, and drew near and heard the Bashkirs yelling and shouting to him, and their cries inflamed his heart still more. He gathered his last strength and ran on.

The sun was close to the rim, and cloaked in mist, looked large, and red as blood. Now, yes now, it was about to set! The sun was quite low, but he was also quite near his aim. Pahom could already see the people on the hillock waving their arms to hurry him up. He could see the fox fur cap on the ground and the money in it, and the Chief sitting on the ground holding his sides. And Pahom remembered his dream.

"There is plenty of land," thought he, "but will God let me live on it? I have lost my life. I have lost my life! I shall never reach that spot!"

Pahom looked at the sun, which had reached the earth: one side of it had already disappeared. With all his remaining strength he rushed on, bending his body forward so that his legs could hardly follow fast enough to keep him from falling. Just as he reached the hillock it suddenly grew dark. He looked up—the sun had already set!

He gave a cry: "All my labor has been in vain," thought he, and was about to stop, but he heard the Bashkirs still shouting, and remembered that though to him, from below, the sun seemed to have set, they on the hillock could still see it. He took a long breath and ran up the hillock. It was still light there. He reached the top and saw the cap. Before it sat the Chief laughing and holding his sides. Again Pahom remembered his dream, and he uttered a cry: his legs gave way beneath him, he fell forward and reached the cap with his hands.

"Ah, that's a fine fellow!" exclaimed the Chief. "He has gained much land!"

Pahom's servant came running up and tried to raise him, but he saw that blood was flowing from his mouth. Pahom was dead.

The Bashkirs clicked their tongues to show their pity.

His servant picked up the spade and dug a grave long enough for Pahom to lie in, and buried him in it.

Six feet from his head to his heels was all he needed.

Reflections

Private Exploration

1. A parable is a concrete story on one level and an expression of abstract moral truths on another. Explore Tolstoy's story as a parable. Does any element of the story, written over one-hundred years ago, connect to something in your experience or to contemporary culture? Could you turn your answer into a more modern parable?
2. Consider this passage:

> Human consciousness begins with suffering.
>
> —DOSTOEVSKY

Public Exploration

In Tolstoy's story, two sisters argue the virtues of the peasant's and the trademan's life. Each tries to convince the other that one is better than the other. As a starting point for discussion in class or in your group, briefly summarize the evidence given on each side. Then consider the merits of the life of today's blue-collar laborer vs. the white-collar worker. Reflect on both the positive and negative stereotypes or myths associated with each. How do these images affect the values of each group?

Private Reflection

"How Much Land Does a Man Need?" A more contemporary question might be, "How Much Money Does a Man [or Woman] Need?" Explore your own deepest answer. Look into your heart and your experience. Be as honest as possible with yourself. When you're finished, draw a line under your response and ask a second question: What might be gained and what might be lost as a result of what you've discovered about yourself?

The Inheritance of Tools

SCOTT RUSSELL SANDERS

At just about the hour when my father died, soon after dawn one February morning when ice coated the windows like cataracts, I banged my thumb with a hammer. Naturally I swore at the hammer, the reckless thing, and in the moment of swearing I thought of what my father would say: "If you'd try hitting the nail it would go in a whole lot faster. Don't you know your thumb's not as hard as that hammer?" We both were doing carpentry that day, but far apart. He was building cupboards at my brother's place in Oklahoma; I was at home in Indiana putting up a wall in the basement to make a bedroom for my daughter. By the time my mother called with news of his death—the long distance wires whittling her voice until it seemed too thin to bear the weight of what she had to say—my thumb was swollen. A week or so later a white scar in the shape of a crescent moon began to show above the cuticle, and month by month it rose across the pink sky of my thumbnail. It took the better part of a year for the scar to disappear, and every time I noticed it I thought of my father.

The hammer had belonged to him, and to his father before him. The three of us have used it to build houses and barns and chicken coops, to upholster chairs and crack walnuts, to make doll furniture and book shelves and jewelry boxes. The head is scratched and pockmarked, like an old plowshare that has been working rocky fields, and it gives off the sort of dull sheen you see on fast creek water in the shade. It is a finishing hammer, about the weight of a bread loaf, too light, really, for framing walls, too heavy for cabinetwork, with a curved claw for pulling nails, a rounded head for pounding, a fluted neck for looks, and a hickory handle for strength.

The present handle is my third one, bought from a lumberyard in Tennessee down the road from where my brother and I were helping my father build his retirement house. I broke the previous one by trying to pull sixteen-penny nails out of floor joists—a foolish thing to do with a finishing hammer, as my father pointed out. "You ever hear of a crowbar?" he said. No telling how many handles he and my grandfather had gone through before me. My grandfather used to cut down hickory trees on his farm, saw them into slabs, cure the planks in his hayloft, and carve handles with a drawknife. The grain in hickory is crooked and knotty, and therefore rough, hard to split, like the grain in the two men who owned this hammer before me.

After proposing marriage to a neighbor girl, my grandfather used this hammer to build a house for his bride on a stretch of river bottom in northern Mississippi. The lumber for the place, like the hickory for the handle, was cut on his own land. By the day of the wedding he had not quite finished the house, and so right after the ceremony he took his wife home and put her to work. My grandmother had worn her Sunday dress for the wedding, with a fringe of lace tacked on around the hem in honor of the occasion. She removed this lace and folded it away before going out to help my grandfather nail siding on the house. "There she was in her good dress," he told me some fifty-odd years after that wedding day, "holding up them long pieces of clapboard while I hammered, and together we got the place covered up before dark." As the family grew to four, six, eight, and eventually thirteen, my grandfather used this hammer to enlarge his house room by room, like a chambered nautilus expanding his shell.

By and by the hammer was passed along to my father. One day he was up on the roof of our pony barn nailing shingles with it, when I stepped out the kitchen door to call him for supper. Before I could yell, something about the sight of him straddling the spine of that roof and swinging the hammer caught my eye and made me hold my tongue. I was five or six years old, and the world's commonplaces were still news to me. He would pull a nail from the pouch at his waist, bring the hammer down, and a moment later the *thunk* of the blow would reach my ears. And that is what had stopped me in my tracks and stilled my tongue, that momentary gap between seeing and hearing the blow. Instead of yelling from the kitchen door, I ran to the barn and climbed two rungs up the ladder—as far as I was allowed to go—and spoke quietly to my father. On our walk to the house he explained that sound takes time to make its way through air. Suddenly the world seemed larger, the air more dense, if sound could be held back like any ordinary traveler.

By the time I started using this hammer, at about the age when I discovered the speed of sound, it already contained houses and mysteries for me. The smooth handle was one my grandfather had made. In those days I needed both hands to swing it. My father would start a nail in a scrap of wood, and I would pound away until I bent it over.

"Looks like you got a hold of some of those rubber nails," he would tell me. "Here, let me see if I can find you some stiff ones." And he would rummage in a drawer until he came up with a fistful of more cooperative nails. "Look at the head," he would tell me. "Don't look at your hands, don't look at the hammer. Just look at the head of that nail and pretty soon you'll learn to hit it square."

Pretty soon I did learn. While he worked in the garage cutting dovetail joints for a drawer or skinning a deer or tuning an engine, I would hammer nails. I made innocent blocks of wood look like porcupines. He did not talk much in the midst of his tools, but he kept up a nearly ceaseless humming, slipping in and out of a dozen tunes in an afternoon, often running back over the same stretch of melody again and again, as if searching for a way out. When the humming did cease, I knew he was faced with a task requiring great delicacy or concentration, and I took care not to distract him.

He kept scraps of wood in a cardboard box—the ends of two-by-fours, slabs of shelving and plywood, odd pieces of molding—and everything in it was fair game. I nailed scraps together to fashion what I called boats or houses, but the results usually bore only faint resemblance to the visions I carried in my head. I would hold up these constructions to show my father, and he would turn them over in his hands admiringly, speculating about what they might be. My cobbled-together guitars might have been alien spaceships, my barns might have been models of Aztec temples, each wooden contraption might have been anything but what I had set out to make.

Now and again I would feel the need to have a chunk of wood shaped or shortened before I riddled it with nails, and I would clamp it in a vise and scrape at it with a handsaw. My father would let me lacerate the board until my arm gave out, and then he would wrap his hand around mine and help me finish the cut, showing me how to use my thumb to guide the blade, how to pull back on the saw to keep it from binding, how to let my shoulder do the work.

"Don't force it," he would say, "Just drag it easy and give the teeth a chance to bite."

As the saw teeth bit down, the wood released its smell, each kind with its own fragrance, oak or walnut or cherry or pine—usually pine because it was the softest, easiest for a child to work. No matter how weathered and gray the board, no matter how warped and cracked, inside there was this smell waiting, as of something freshly baked. I gathered every smidgen of sawdust and stored it away in coffee cans, which I kept in a drawer of the workbench. When I did not feel like hammering nails I would dump my sawdust on the concrete floor of the garage and landscape it into highways and farms and towns, running miniature cars and trucks along miniature roads. Looming as huge as a colossus, my father worked over and around me, now and again bending down to inspect my work, careful not to trample my creations. It was a landscape that smelled dizzyingly of wood. Even after a bath my skin would carry the smell, and so would my father's hair, when he lifted me for a bedtime hug.

I tell these things not only from memory but also from recent observation, because my own son now turns blocks of wood into nailed porcupines, dumps cans full of sawdust at my feet and sculpts highways on the floor. He learns how to swing a hammer from the elbow instead of the wrist, how to lay his thumb beside the blade to guide a saw, how to tap a chisel with a wooden mallet, how to mark a hole with an awl before starting a drill bit. My daughter did the same before him, and even now, on the brink of teenage aloofness, she will occasionally drag out my box of wood scraps and carpenter something. So I have seen my apprenticeship to wood and tools reenacted in each of my children, as my father saw his own apprenticeship renewed in me.

The saw I use belonged to him, as did my level and both of my squares, and all four tools had belonged to his father. The blade of the saw is the bluish color of gun barrels, and the maple handle, dark from the sweat of hands, is inscribed with curving leaf designs. The level is a shaft of walnut two feet long, edged with brass and pierced by three round windows in which air bubbles float in oil-filled tubes of glass. The middle window serves for testing if a surface is horizontal, the others for testing if a surface is plumb or vertical. My grandfather used to carry this level on the gun-rack behind the seat in his pickup, and when I rode with him I would turn around to watch the bubbles dance. The larger of the two squares is called a framing square, a flat steel elbow, so beat up and tarnished you can barely make out the rows of numbers that show how to figure the cuts on rafters. The smaller one is called a try square, for marking right angles, with a blued steel blade for the shank and a brass-faced block of cherry for the head.

I was taught early on that a saw is not to be used apart from a square: "If you're going to cut a piece of wood," my father insisted, "you owe it to the tree to cut it straight."

Long before studying geometry, I learned there is a mystical virtue in right angles. There is an unspoken morality in seeking the level and the plumb. A house will stand, a table will bear weight, the sides of a box will hold together only if the joints are square and the members upright. When the bubble is lined up between two marks etched in the glass tube of a level, you have aligned yourself with the forces that hold the universe together. When you miter the corners of a picture frame, each angle must be exactly forty-five degrees, as they are in the perfect triangles of Pythagoras, not a degree more or less. Otherwise the frame will hang crookedly, as if ashamed of itself and of its maker. No matter if the joints you are cutting do not show. Even if you are butting two pieces of wood together inside a cabinet, where no one except a wrecking crew will ever see them, you must take pains to insure that the ends are square and the studs are plumb.

I took pains over the wall I was building on the day my father died. Not long after that wall was finished—paneled with tongue-and-groove boards of yellow pine, the nail holes filled with putty and the wood all stained and sealed—I came close to wrecking it one afternoon when my daughter ran howling up the stairs to announce that her gerbils had escaped from their cage and were hiding in my brand new wall. She could hear them scratching and squeaking behind her bed. Impossible! I said. How on earth could they get inside my drum-tight wall? Through the heating vent, she answered. I went downstairs, pressed my ear to the honey-colored wood, and heard the *scritch scritch* of tiny feet.

"What can we do?" my daughter wailed. "They'll starve to death, they'll die of thirst, they'll suffocate."

"Hold on," I shouted, "I'll think of something."

While I thought and she fretted, the radio on her bedside table delivered us the headlines. Several thousand people had died in a city in India from a poisonous cloud that had leaked overnight from a chemical plant. A nuclear-powered submarine had been launched. Rioting continued in South Africa. An airplane had been hijacked in the Mediterranean. Authorities calculated that several thousand homeless people slept on the streets within sight of the Washington Monument. I felt my usual helplessness in face of all these calamities. But here was my daughter weeping because her gerbils were holed up in a wall. This calamity I could handle.

"Don't worry," I told her. "We'll set food and water by the hearting vent and lure them out. And if that doesn't do the trick, I'll tear the wall apart until we find them."

She stopped crying and gazed at me. "You'd really tear it apart? Just for my gerbils? The *wall?*" Astonishment slowed her down only for a second, however, before she ran to the workbench and began tugging at drawers, saying, "Let's see, what'll we need? Crowbar. Hammer. Chisels. I hope we don't have to use them—but just in case."

We didn't need the wrecking tools. I never had to assault my handsome wall, because the gerbils eventually came out to nibble at a dish of popcorn. But for several hours I studied the tongue-and-groove skin I had nailed up on the day of my father's death, considering where to begin prying. There were no gaps in that wall, no crooked joints.

I had botched a great many pieces of wood before I mastered the right angle with a saw, botched even more before I learned to miter a joint. The knowledge of these things resides in my hands and eyes and the webwork of muscles, not in the tools. There are machines for sale—powered miter boxes and radial-arm saws, for instance—that will enable any casual soul to cut proper angles in boards. The skill is invested in the gadget instead of the person who uses it, and this is what distinguishes a machine from a tool. If I had to earn my keep by making furniture or building houses, I suppose I would buy powered saws and pneumatic nailers; the need for speed would drive me to it. But since I carpenter only for my own pleasure or to help neighbors or to remake the house around the ears of my family, I stick with hand tools. Most of the ones I own were given to me by my father, who also taught me how to wield them. The tools in my workbench are a double inheritance, for each hammer and level and saw is wrapped in a cloud of knowing.

All of these tools are a pleasure to look at and to hold. Merchants would never paste NEW NEW NEW! signs on them in stores. Their designs are old because they work, because they serve their purpose well. Like folksongs and aphorisms and the grainy bits of language, these tools have been pared down to essentials. I look at my claw hammer, the distillation of a hundred generations of carpenters, and consider that it holds up well beside those other classics—Greek vases, Gregorian chants, *Don Quixote,* barbed fish hooks, candles, spoons. Knowledge of hammering stretches back to the earliest humans who squatted beside fires chipping flints. Anthropologists have a lovely name for those unworked rocks that served as the earliest hammers. *Dawn stones,* they are called. Their only qualification for the work, aside from hardness, is that they fit the hand. Our ancestors used them for grinding corn, tapping awls, smashing bones. From dawn stones to this claw hammer is a great leap in time, but no great distance in design or imagination.

On that iced-over February morning when I smashed my thumb with the hammer, I was down in the basement framing the wall that my daughter's gerbils would later hide in. I was thinking of my father, as I always did whenever I built anything, thinking how he would have gone about the work, hearing in memory what he would have said about the wisdom of hitting the nail instead of my thumb. I had the studs and plates nailed together all square and trim, and was lifting the wall into place when the phone rang upstairs. My wife answered, and in a moment she came to the basement door and called down softly to me. The stillness in her voice made me drop the framed wall and hurry upstairs. She told me my father was dead. Then I heard the details over the phone from my mother. Building a set of cupboards for my brother in Oklahoma, he had knocked off work early the previous afternoon because of cramps in his stomach. Early this morning, on his way into the kitchen of my brother's trailer, maybe going for a glass of water, so early that no one else was awake, he slumped down on the linoleum and his heart quit.

For several hours I paced around inside my house, upstairs and down, in and out of every room, looking for the right door to open and knowing there was no such door. My wife and children followed me and wrapped me in arms and backed away again, circling and staring as if I were on fire. Where was the door, the door, the door? I kept wondering. My smashed thumb turned purple and throbbed, making me furious. I wanted to cut it off and rush outside and scrape away the snow and hack a hole in the frozen earth and bury the shameful thing.

I went down into the basement, opened a drawer in my workbench, and stared at the ranks of chisels and knives. Oiled and sharp, as my father would have kept them, they gleamed at me like teeth. I took up a clasp knife, pried out the longest blade and tested the edge on the hair of my forearm. A tuft came away cleanly, and I saw my father testing the sharpness of tools on his own skin, the blades of axes and knives and gouges and hoes, saw the red hair shaved off in patches from his arms and the backs of his hands. "That will cut bear," he would say. He never cut a bear with his blades, now my blades, but he cut deer, dirt, wood. I closed the knife and put it away. Then I took up the hammer and went back to work on my daughter's wall, snugging the bottom plate against a chalkline on the floor, shimming the top plate against the joists overhead, plumbing the studs with my level, making sure before I drove the first nail that every line was square and true.

Reflections

Private Exploration

1. If possible, explore as Sanders does, the memories of being taught a skill. Recall the slow motion details, the actions, and the words that have become indelibly etched in your mind as you reflect on the person who taught you that skill. Like Sanders, attempt to find metaphors and similes that evoke feelings about your experience. Consider how the skill itself, or the learning of it, has affected your values and attitude toward work.
2. Trace the history of some tool or object you are proud to have inherited. Recollect the memories you associate with the object in as much detail as possible using sensory details, images, and dialogue. Whose words do you hear, what thoughts and feelings surface as you hold the tool in your hand? Show us why you value this inheritance.
3. What do you make of this passage:

> The tools in my workbench are a double inheritance, for each hammer and level and saw is wrapped in a cloud of knowing.

Public Exploration

1. Man has to work to live. Work is a necessity for survival. Yet Sanders seems to be looking at work as something altogether different. Use your understanding of Sander's feelings to explore other values that might come from work. Do not stop with one or two. Begin with the individual, enlarge to the family, then to community and nation.
2. Consider this passage:

> There are only two essentials in life: work and love. If you have love and no work, your life will eventually become boring and shallow. Love itself will turn bitter on the tongue. But as long as you have work, you may live without love. Better yet, you may live well and full if your work and love are one thing.
>
> —IGNACIO MARQUEZ

Private Reflection

After writing about and discussing some of the deeper and unexpected values that may emerge from work, focus in on an idea or emotion that seems to relate most to your own future. Can you connect it to, or contrast it with, Erich Fromm's argument (p. 398) that work is both "liberator" and "creator"?

• Digging •

SEAMUS HEANEY

Between my finger and my thumb
The squat pen rests; snug as a gun.

Under my window, a clean rasping sound
When the spade sinks into gravelly ground.
My father, digging. I look down

Till his straining rump among the flowerbeds
Bends low, comes up twenty years away
Stooping in rhythm through potato drills
Where he was digging.

The coarse boot nestled on the lug, the shaft
Against the inside knee was levered firmly.
He rooted out tall tops, buried the bright edge deep
To scatter new potatoes that we picked
Loving their cool hardness in our hands.

By God, the old man could handle a spade.
Just like his old man.

My grandfather cut more turf in a day
Than any other man on Toner's bog.
Once I carried him milk in a bottle
Corked sloppily with paper. He straightened up
To drink it, then fell to right away

Nicking and slicing neatly, heaving sods
Over his shoulder, going down and down
For the good turf. Digging.

The cold smell of potato mould, the squelch and slap
Of soggy peat, the curt cuts of an edge
Through living roots awaken in my head.
But I've no spade to follow men like them.

Between my finger and my thumb
The squat pen rests.
I'll dig with it.

Reflections

Private Exploration

1. "Digging" begs to be read aloud. After reading it silently and making marginal notes, read it out loud, listening to the sounds, feeling the rhythms. What do you hear? What do you feel? What words in particular pull you into the experience?
2. Explore your most immediate reaction to the poem as a whole. Do you relate to it? If so, how?
3. Explore the metaphor the speaker uses as he compares his work with the work of his forefathers. How does the metaphor change? How does the new comparison illuminate the speaker's thoughts and feelings?

Public Exploration

In "Digging," the speaker moves back through two generations of workers before returning to himself. Consider the different kinds of images here, the physical labor of the diggers, the mental labor of the writer. How does our society value these two images? Do we react to certain kinds of work (perhaps all kinds) with preformed value judgments? Are you proud or ashamed that your own father or mother works in a factory? Or is Chairman of the board of the factory? Or dances on stage? Or sells shoes? Or does scientific research on genetic splicing? Do your own values concerning work come from family or from society? And how do such values shape your future choices?

Private Reflection

As a child, Heaney was encouraged to get an education "because 'learning's easily carried' and 'the pen is lighter than the spade.' " Reflect on the work of past generations in your own family (male or female). Did their work instill certain values in you? Or did it perhaps have an opposite effect, causing you to seek new values?

Maintenance

NAOMI SHIHAB NYE

The only maid I ever had left messages throughout our house: *Lady as I was cleaning your room I heard a mouse and all the clothes in your closet fell down to the floor there is too many dresses in there take a few off. Your friend Marta Alejandro.* Sometimes I'd find notes stuck into the couch with straight pins. *I cannot do this room today bec. St. Jude came to me in a dream and say it is not safe.* Our darkroom was never safe because the devil liked dark places and also the enlarger had an eye that picked up light and threw it on Marta. She got sick and had to go to a doctor who gave her green medicine that tasted like leaves.

Sometimes I'd come home to find her lounging in the bamboo chair on the back porch, eating melon, or lying on the couch with a bowl of half-melted ice cream balanced on her chest. She seemed depressed by my house. She didn't like the noise the vacuum made. Once she waxed the bathtub with floor wax. I think she was experimenting.

Each Wednesday I paid Marta ten dollars—that's what she asked for. When I raised it to eleven, then thirteen, she held the single dollars away from the ten as if they might contaminate it. She did not seem happy to get raises, and my friends (who paid her ten dollars each for the other days of the week) were clearly unhappy to hear about it. After a while I had less work of my own and less need for help, so I found her a position with two gay men who lived in the neighborhood. She called once to say she liked them very much because mostly what they wanted her to do was shine. Shine?

"You know, silver. They have a lot of bowls. They have real beautiful spoons not like your spoons. They have a big circle tray that shines like the moon."

My friend Kathy had no maid and wanted none. She ran ten miles a day and lived an organized life. Once I brought her a gift—a blue weaving from Guatemala, diagonal patterns of thread on sticks—and she looked at it dubiously. "Give it to someone else," she said. "I really appreciate your thinking of me, but I try not to keep things around here." Then I realized how bare her mantel was. Who among us would fail to place *something* on a mantel? A few shelves in her kitchen also stood empty, and not the highest ones either.

Kathy had very definite methods of housekeeping. When we'd eat dinner with her she'd rise quickly, before dessert, to scrape each plate and place it in one side of her sink to soak. She had Tupperware containers already lined up for leftovers and a soup pan with suds ready for the silverware. If I tried to help she'd slap at my hand. "Take care of your own kitchen," she'd say, not at all harshly. After dessert she'd fold up the card table we'd just eaten on and place it against the wall. Dining rooms needed to be swept after meals, and a stationary table just made sweeping more difficult.

Kathy could listen to any conversation and ask meaningful questions. She always seemed to remember what anybody said—maybe because she'd left space for it. One day she described having grown up in west Texas in a house of twelve children, the air jammed with voices, crosscurrents, the floors piled with grocery bags, mountains of tossed-off clothes, toys, blankets, the clutter of her sisters' shoes. That's when she decided to have only one pair of shoes at any time, running shoes, though she later revised this to include a pair of sandals.

Somehow I understood her better then, her tank tops and wiry arms . . . She ran to shake off dust. She ran to leave it all behind.

Another friend, Barbara, lived in an apartment but wanted to live in a house. Secretly I loved her spacious domain, perched high above the city with a wide sweep of view, but I could understand the wish to plant one's feet more firmly on the ground. Barbara has the best taste of any person I've ever known—the best khaki-colored linen clothing, the best books, the name of the best masseuse. When I'm with her I feel uplifted, excited by life; there's so much to know about that I haven't heard of yet, and Barbara probably has. So I agreed to help her look.

We saw one house where walls and windows had been sheathed in various patterns of gloomy brocade. We visited another where the kitchen had been removed because the owners only ate in restaurants. They had a tiny office refrigerator next to their bed which I peeked into after they'd left the room: orange juice in a carton, coffee beans. A Krups coffee maker on the sink in their bathroom. They seemed unashamed, shrugging, "You could put a new kitchen wherever you like."

Then we entered a house that felt unusually vivid, airy, and hard-to-define until the realtor mentioned, "Have you noticed there's not a stick of wood anywhere in this place? No wood furniture, not even a wooden salad bowl, I'd bet. These people, very hip, you'd like them, want wood to stay in forests. The man says wood makes him feel heavy."

Barbara and her husband bought that house—complete with pear-shaped swimming pool, terraces of pansies, plum trees, white limestone rock gardens lush with succulents—but they brought wood into it. Never before had I been so conscious of things like wooden cutting boards. I helped them unpack and stroked the sanded ebony backs of African animals.

Then, after about a year and a half, Barbara called to tell me they were selling the house. "You won't believe this," she said, "but we've decided. It's the maintenance—the yardmen, little things always breaking—I'm so busy assigning chores I hardly have time for my own work anymore. A house really seems ridiculous to me now. If I want earth I can go walk in a park."

I had a new baby at the time and everything surprised me. My mouth dropped open, oh yes. I was living between a mound of fresh cloth diapers and a bucket of soiled ones, but I agreed to participate in the huge garage sale Barbara was having.

"That day," Barbara said later, "humanity sank to a new lowest level." We had made signs declaring the sale would start at nine A.M.—but by eight, middle-aged women and men were already ripping our boxes open, lunging into the back of my loaded pickup truck to see what I had. Two women argued in front of me over my stained dish-drainer. I sold a kerosene heater which we'd never lit and a stack of my great-uncle's rumpled tablecloths, so large they completely engulfed an ironing board. One woman flashed a charm with my initial on it under my nose, saying, "I'd think twice about selling this, sweetheart—don't you realize it's ten carat?"

Afterwards we counted our wads of small bills and felt drained, diluted. We had spent the whole day bartering in a driveway, releasing ourselves from the burden of things we did not need. We even felt disgusted by the thought of eating—yet another means of accumulation—and would derive no pleasure from shopping, or catalogs, for at least a month.

While their new apartment was being refurbished, Barbara and her husband lived in a grand hotel downtown. She said it felt marvelous to use all the towels and have fresh ones appear on the racks within hours. Life seemed to regain its old recklessness. Soon they moved back to the same wind-swept apartment building they'd left, but to a higher floor. Sometimes I stood in their living room staring out at the horizon, which always seemed flawlessly clean.

My mother liked to sing along to records while she did housework—Mahalia Jackson, the Hallelujah Chorus. Sometimes we would sing duets, "Tell Me Why" and "Nobody Knows the Trouble I've Seen." I felt lucky my mother was such a clear soprano. We also sang while preparing for the big dinners my parents often gave, while folding the napkins or decorating little plates of hummus with olives and radishes.

I hungrily savored the tales told by the guests, the wild immigrant fables and metaphysical links. My mother's favorite friend, a rail-thin vegetarian who had once been secretary to Aldous Huxley, conversed passionately with a Syrian who was translating the Bible from Aramaic, then scolded me for leaving a mound of carrots on my plate.

"I'm not going to waste them!" I said. "I always save carrots for last because I love them best."

I thought this would please her, but she frowned. "Never save what you love, dear. You know what might happen? You may lose it while you are waiting."

It was difficult to imagine losing the carrots—what were they going to do, leap off my plate?—but she continued.

"Long ago I loved a man very much. He had gone on a far journey—our relationship had been delicate—and I waited anxiously for word from him. Finally a letter arrived and I stuffed it into my bag, trembling, thinking I would read it later on the train. Would rejoice in every word, was what I thought, but you know what happened? My purse was snatched away from me—stolen!—before I boarded the train. Things like that didn't even happen much in those days. I never saw the letter again—and I never saw my friend again either."

A pause swallowed the room. My mother rose to clear the dishes. Meaningful glances passed. I knew this woman had never married. When I asked why she hadn't written him to say she lost the letter, she said, "Don't you see, I also lost the only address I had for him."

I thought about this for days. Couldn't she have tracked him down? Didn't she know anyone else who might have known him and forwarded a message? I asked my mother, who replied that love was not easy.

Later my mother told me about a man who had carried a briefcase of important papers on a hike because he was afraid they might get stolen from the car. The trail wove high up the side of a mountain, between stands of majestic piñon. As he leaned over a rocky gorge to breathe the fragrant air, his fingers slipped and the briefcase dropped down into a narrow crevasse. They heard it far below, clunking into a deep underground pool. My mother said the man fell to the ground and sobbed.

The forest ranger whistled when they brought him up to the spot. "Hell of an aim!" He said there were some lost things you just had to say goodbye to, "like a wedding ring down a commode." My parents took the man to Western Union so he could telegraph about the lost papers, and the clerk said, "Don't feel bad, every woman drops an earring down a drain once in her life." The man glared. "This was not an earring—I AM NOT A WOMAN."

I thought of the carrots, and the letter, when I heard his story. And of my American grandmother's vintage furniture, sold to indifferent buyers when I was still a child, too young even to think of antique wardrobes or bed frames. And I also thought of another friend of my parents, Peace Pilgrim, who walked across America for years, lecturing about inner peace and world peace. A single, broad pocket in her tunic contained all her worldly possessions: a toothbrush, a few postage stamps, a ballpoint pen. She had no bank account behind her and nothing in storage. Her motto was, "I walk till given shelter, I fast till given food." My father used to call her a freeloader behind her back, but my mother recognized a prophet when she saw one. I grappled with the details. How would it help humanity if I slept in a cardboard box under a bridge?

Peace Pilgrim told a story about a woman who worked hard so she could afford a certain style of furniture—French Provincial, I think. She struggled to pay for insurance to protect it and rooms large enough to house it. She worked so much she hardly ever got to sit on it. "Then her life was over. And what kind of a life was that?"

Peace Pilgrim lived so deliberately she didn't even have colds. Shortly before her death in a car accident—for years she hadn't even ridden in cars—she sat on the fold-out bed in our living room, hugging her knees. I was grown by then, but all our furniture was still from thrift stores. She invited me to play the piano and sing for her, which I did, as she stared calmly around the room. "I loved to sing as a child," she said. "It is nice to have a piano."

In my grandmother's Palestinian village, the family has accumulated vast mounds and heaps of woolly comforters, stacking them in great wooden cupboards along the walls. The blankets smell pleasantly like sheep and wear coverings of cheerful gingham, but no family—not even our huge one on the coldest night—could possibly use that many blankets. My grandmother smiled when I asked her about them. She said people should have many blankets and head scarves to feel secure.

I took a photograph of her modern refrigerator, bought by one of the emigrant sons on a visit home from America, unplugged in a corner and stuffed with extra yardages of cloth and old magazines. I felt like one of those governmental watchdogs who asks how do you feel knowing your money is being used this way? My grandmother seemed nervous whenever we sat near the refrigerator, as if a stranger who refused to say his name had entered the room.

I never felt women were more doomed to housework than men; I thought women were lucky. Men had to maintain questionably pleasurable associations with less tangible elements—mortgage payments, fan belts and alternators, the IRS. I preferred sinks, and the way people who washed dishes immediately became exempt from after-dinner conversation. I loved to plunge my hands into tubs of scalding bubbles. Once my father reached in to retrieve something and reeled back, yelling, "Do you always make it this hot?" My parents got a dishwasher as soon as they could, but luckily I was out of college by then and never had to touch it. To me it only seemed to extend the task. You rinse, you bend and arrange, you measure soap—and it hasn't even started yet. How many other gratifications were as instant as the old method of washing dishes?

But it's hard to determine how much pleasure someone else gets from an addiction to a task. The neighbor woman who spends hours pinching off dead roses and browned lilies, wearing her housecoat and dragging a hose, may be as close as she comes to bliss, or she may be feeling utterly miserable. I weigh her sighs, her monosyllables about weather. Endlessly I compliment her yard. She shakes her head—"It's a lot of work." For more than a year she tries to get her husband to dig out an old stump at one corner but finally gives up and plants bougainvillea in it. The vibrant splash of pink seems to make her happier than anything else has in a long time.

Certain bylaws: If you have it, you will have to clean it. Nothing stays clean long. No one else notices your messy house as much as you do; they don't know where things are supposed to go anyway. It takes much longer to clean a house than to mess it up. Be suspicious of any cleaning agent (often designated with a single alphabetical letter, like *C* or *M*) that claims to clean everything from floors to dogs. Never install white floor tiles in the bathroom if your family members have brown hair. Cloth diapers eventually make the best rags—another reason beyond ecology. Other people's homes have charisma, charm, because you don't have to know them inside out. If you want high ceilings you may have to give up closets. (Still, as a neighbor once insisted to me, "High ceilings make you a better person.") Be wary of vacuums with headlights; they burn out in a month. A broom, as one of my starry-eyed newlywed sisters-in-law once said, *does a lot.* So does a dustpan. Whatever you haven't touched, worn, or eaten off of in a year should be passed on; something will pop up immediately to take its place.

I can't help thinking about these things—I live in the same town where Heloise lives. And down the street, in a shed behind his house, a man produces orange-scented wood moisturizer containing beeswax. You rub it on three times, let it sit, then buff it off. Your house smells like a hive in an orchard for twenty-four hours.

I'd like to say a word, just a short one, for the background hum of lesser, unexpected maintenances that can devour a day or days—or a life, if one is not careful. The scrubbing of the little ledge above the doorway belongs in this category, along with the thin lines of dust that quietly gather on bookshelves in front of the books. It took me an hour working with a bent wire to unplug the birdfeeder, which had become clogged with fuzzy damp seed—no dove could get a beak in. And who would ever notice? The doves would notice. I am reminded of Buddhism whenever I undertake one of these invisible tasks: one acts, without any thought of reward or foolish notion of glory.

Perhaps all cleaning products should be labeled with additional warnings, as some natural-soap companies have taken to philosophizing right above the price tag. Bottles of guitar polish might read: "If you polish your guitar, it will not play any better. People who close their eyes to listen to your song will not see the gleaming wood. But you may feel more intimate with the instrument you are holding."

Sometimes I like the preparation for maintenance, the motions of preface, better than the developed story. I like to move all the chairs off the back porch many hours before I sweep it. I drag the mop and bucket into the house in the morning even if I don't intend to mop until dusk. This is related to addressing envelopes months before I write the letters to go inside.

Such extended prefacing drives my husband wild. He comes home and can read the house like a mystery story—small half-baked clues in every room. I get out the bowl for the birthday cake two days early. I like the sense of house as still life, on the road to becoming. Why rush to finish? You will only have to do it over again, sooner. I keep a proverb from Thailand above my towel rack: *"Life is so short / we must move very slowly."* I believe what it says.

My Palestinian father was furious with me when, as a teenager, I impulsively answered a newspaper ad and took a job as a maid. A woman, bedfast with a difficult pregnancy, ordered me to scrub, rearrange, and cook—for a dollar an hour. She sat propped on pillows, clicking her remote control, glaring suspiciously whenever I passed her doorway. She said her husband liked green jello with fresh fruit. I was slicing peaches when the oven next to me exploded, filling the house with heavy black smoke. My meat loaf was only half baked. She shrieked and cried, blaming it on me, but how was I responsible for her oven?

It took me a long time to get over my negative feelings about pregnant women. I found a job scooping ice cream and had to wrap my swollen wrists in heavy elastic bands because they hurt so much. I had never considered what ice cream servers went through.

These days I wake up with good intentions. I pretend to be my own maid. I know the secret of travelers: each time you leave your home with a few suitcases, books, and note pads, your maintenance shrinks to a lovely tiny size. All you need to take care of is your own body and a few changes of clothes. Now and then, if you're driving, you brush the pistachio shells off the seat. I love ice chests and miniature bottles of shampoo. Note the expansive breath veteran travelers take when they feel the road spinning open beneath them again.

Somewhere close behind me the outline of Thoreau's small cabin plods along, a ghost set on haunting. It even has the same rueful eyes Henry David had in the portrait in his book. A wealthy woman with a floral breakfast nook once told me I would "get over him" but I have not—documented here, I have not.

Marta Alejandro, my former maid, now lives in a green outbuilding at the corner of Beauregard and Madison. I saw her recently, walking a skinny wisp of dog, and wearing a bandanna twisted and tied around her waist. I called to her from my car. Maybe I only imagined she approached me reluctantly. Maybe she couldn't see who I was.

But then she started talking as if we had paused only a second ago. "Oh hi I was very sick were you? The doctor said it has to come to everybody. Don't think you can escape! Is your house still as big as it used to be?"

Reflections

Private Exploration

1. Select a key passage from Nye's essay and explore it in your notebook. How might the passage open up insights into the essay as a whole? Does it open up insight into yourself? Something from your experience? Does it raise any questions about your own values?
2. Boats, cars, VCRs, camcorders, microwaves, answering machines, and car phones are among a few of the things Americans work long and hard for. We've been dubbed a culture of excess. "*More* is what America is about." At the same time, Americans have also been labeled "the throw-away society." We buy, accumulate, save, and gradually end up either throwing items away or passing them on to others through a yard sale. Think back to a time when you felt compelled to work long and hard for something. Try to recall what motivated you to make the purchase in the first place. What expectations did you have? How did you feel about the purchase several months after you made it? Where is it now? And finally, consider how your life itself

was or was not affected. How much life did you have to give up to earn the money to make the purchase? What kinds of values are at work in all this?

Public Exploration

1. Consider this statement:

> Our society has delivered us—most of us—from the bond of necessity, so that we no longer struggle to find food to keep from starving, clothing and shelter to keep from freezing; yet if the ends for which we work and of which we dream are only clothes and restaurants and houses, possessions, consumption, how have we escaped?—we have exchanged man's old bondage for a new voluntary one.
>
> —RANDALL JARRELL

2. Peace Pilgrim claimed she walked "till given shelter" and fasted "till given food." As a contrast to her own values she tells the story about a woman who worked to buy French Provincial furniture only to struggle again to insure it and find a place to house it.

   Before working with your class or group, jot down your perspectives on these two women's values. Are Peace Pilgrim's values superior to the other woman's or is she a freeloader? Is the woman who bought furniture greedy or is she in love with beauty? Consider the implication of Peace Pilgrim's comment: "I loved to sing as a child. . . . It's nice to have a piano."

   After you've written your response, share it with others. Consider how your perceptions shift and change or harden and rigidify as you listen to other views. Then write an additional paragraph or so recording any fresh perspectives generated by the group.

Private Reflection

Consider the conflicting attitudes the women in Nye's essay reveal toward possession and work. Do you identify with either? Like Kathy, do you run to leave work behind, or like Nye, are you gratified by doing common household things "without any thought of reward or foolish notion of glory"?

Exploring the Managed Heart

ARLIE RUSSELL HOCHSCHILD

> *The one area of her occupational life in which she might be "free to act," the area of her own personality, must now also be managed, must become the alert yet obsequious instrument by which goods are distributed.* —C. Wright Mills

In a section in *Das Kapital* entitled "The Working Day," Karl Marx examines depositions submitted in 1863 to the Children's Employment Commission in England. One deposition was given by the mother of a child laborer in a wallpaper factory: "When he was seven years old I used to carry him [to work] on my back to and fro through the snow, and he used to work 16 hours a day. . . . I have often knelt down to feed him, as he stood by the machine, for he could not leave it or stop." Fed meals as he worked, as a steam engine is fed coal and water, this child was "an instrument of labor."[1] Marx questioned how many hours a day it was fair to use a human being as an instrument, and how much pay for being an instrument was fair, considering the profits that factory owners made. But he was also concerned with something he thought more fundamental: the human cost of becoming an "instrument of labor" at all.

On another continent 117 years later, a twenty-year-old flight attendant trainee sat with 122 others listening to a pilot speak in the auditorium of the Delta Airlines Stewardess Training Center. Even by modern American standards, and certainly by standards for women's work, she had landed an excellent job. The 1980 pay scale began at $850 a month for the first six months and would increase within seven years to about $20,000 a year. Health and accident insurance is provided, and the hours are good.*

The young trainee sitting next to me wrote on her notepad, "Important to smile. Don't forget smile." The admonition came from the speaker in the front of the room, a crew-cut pilot in his early fifties, speaking in a Southern drawl: "Now girls, I want you to go out there and really *smile.* Your smile is your biggest *asset.* I want you to go out there and use it. Smile. *Really* smile. Really *lay it on.*"

The pilot spoke of the smile as the *flight attendant's* asset. But as novices like the one next to me move through training, the value of a personal smile is groomed to reflect the company's disposition—its confidence that its planes

*For stylistic convenience, I shall use the pronoun "she" when referring to a flight attendant, except when a specific male flight attendant is being discussed. Otherwise I shall try to avoid verbally excluding either gender. (Hochschild)

will not crash, its reassurance that departures and arrivals will be on time, its welcome and its invitation to return. Trainers take it as their job to attach to the trainee's smile an attitude, a viewpoint, a rhythm of feeling that is, as they often say, "professional." This deeper extension of the professional smile is not always easy to retract at the end of the workday, as one worker in her first year at World Airways noted: "Sometimes I come off a long trip in a state of utter exhaustion, but I find I can't relax. I giggle a lot, I chatter, I call friends. It's as if I can't release myself from an artificially created elation that kept me 'up' on the trip. I hope to be able to come down from it better as I get better at the job."

As the PSA jingle says, "Our smiles are not just painted on." Our flight attendants' smiles, the company emphasizes, will be more human than the phony smiles you're resigned to seeing on people who are paid to smile. There is a smile-like strip of paint on the nose of each PSA plane. Indeed, the plane and the flight attendant advertise each other. The radio advertisement goes on to promise not just smiles and service but a travel experience of real happiness and calm. Seen in one way, this is no more than delivering a service. Seen in another, it estranges workers from their own smiles and convinces customers that on-the-job behavior is calculated. Now that advertisements, training, notions of professionalism, and dollar bills have intervened between the smiler and the smiled upon, it takes an extra effort to imagine that spontaneous warmth can exist in uniform—because companies now advertise spontaneous warmth, too.

At first glance, it might seem that the circumstances of the nineteenth-century factory child and the twentieth-century flight attendant could not be more different. To the boy's mother, to Marx, to the members of the Children's Employment Commission, perhaps to the manager of the wallpaper factory, and almost certainly to the contemporary reader, the boy was a victim, even a symbol, of the brutalizing conditions of his time. We might imagine that he had an emotional half-life, conscious of little more than fatigue, hunger, and boredom. On the other hand, the flight attendant enjoys the upper-class freedom to travel, and she participates in the glamour she creates for others. She is the envy of clerks in duller, less well-paid jobs.

But a close examination of the differences between the two can lead us to some unexpected common ground. On the surface there is a difference in how we know what labor actually produces. How could the worker in the wallpaper factory tell when his job was done? Count the rolls of wallpaper; a good has been produced. How can the flight attendant tell when her job is done? A service has been produced; the customer seems content. In the case of the flight attendant, the *emotional style of offering the service is part of the service itself,* in a way that loving or hating wallpaper is not a part of producing wallpaper. Seeming to "love the job" becomes part of the job; and actually trying to love it, and to enjoy the customers, helps the worker in this effort.

In processing people, the product is a state of mind. Like firms in other industries, airline companies are ranked according to the quality of service their personnel offer. Egon Ronay's yearly *Lucas Guide* offers such a ranking; besides being sold in airports and drugstores and reported in newspapers, it is cited in management memoranda and passed down to those who train and supervise flight attendants. Because it influences consumers, airline companies use it in setting their criteria for successful job performance by a flight attendant. In 1980 the *Lucas Guide* ranked Delta Airlines first in service out of fourteen airlines that fly regularly between the United States and both Canada and the British Isles. Its report on Delta included passages like this:

> [Drinks were served] not only with a smile but with concerned enquiry such as, "Anything else I can get you, madam?" The atmosphere was that of a civilized party—with the passengers, in response, behaving like civilized guests. . . . Once or twice our inspectors tested stewardesses by being deliberately exacting, but they were never roused, and at the end of the flight they lined up to say farewell with undiminished brightness. . . .
>
> [Passengers are] quick to detect strained or forced smiles, and they come aboard wanting to *enjoy* the flight. One of us looked forward to his next trip on Delta "because it's fun." Surely that is how passengers ought to feel.

The work done by the boy in the wallpaper factory called for a coordination of mind and arm, mind and finger, and mind and shoulder. We refer to it simply as physical labor. The flight attendant does physical labor when she pushes heavy meal carts through the aisles, and she does mental work when she prepares for and actually organizes emergency landings and evacuations. But in the course of doing this physical and mental labor, she is also doing something more, something I define as *emotional labor*.* This labor requires one to induce or suppress feeling in order to sustain the outward countenance that produces the proper state of mind in others—in this case, the sense of being cared for in a convivial and safe place. This kind of labor calls for a coordination of mind and feeling, and it sometimes draws on a source of self that we honor as deep and integral to our individuality.

Beneath the difference between physical and emotional labor their lies a similarity in the possible cost of doing the work: the worker can become estranged or alienated from an aspect of self—either the body or the margins of the soul—that is *used* to do the work. The factory boy's arm functioned like a piece of machinery used to produce wallpaper. His employer, regarding that arm as an instrument, claimed control over its speed and motions. In this

*I use the term *emotional labor* to mean the management of feeling to create a publicly observable facial and bodily display; emotional labor is sold for a wage and therefore has *exchange value*. I use the synonymous terms *emotion work* or *emotion management* to refer to these same acts done in a private context where they have *use value*. (Hochschild)

situation, what was the relation between the boy's arm and his mind? Was his arm in any meaningful sense his *own*?

This is an old issue, but as the comparison with airline attendants suggests, it is still very much alive. If we can become alienated from goods in a goods-producing society, we can become alienated from service in a service-producing society. This is what C. Wright Mills, one of our keenest social observers, meant when he wrote in 1956, "We need to characterize American society of the mid-twentieth century in more psychological terms, for now the problems that concern us most border on the psychiatric."

When she came off the job, what relation had the flight attendant to the "artificial elation" she had induced on the job? In what sense was it her *own* elation on the job? The company lays claim not simply to her physical motions—how she handles food trays—but to her emotional actions and the way they show in the ease of a smile. The workers I talked to often spoke of their smiles as being *on* them but not *of* them. They were seen as an extension of the make-up, the uniform, the recorded music, the soothing pastel colors of the airplane decor, and the daytime drinks, which taken together orchestrate the mood of the passengers. The final commodity is not a certain number of smiles to be counted like rolls of wallpaper. For the flight attendant, the smiles are a *part of her work*, a part that requires her to coordinate self and feeling so that the work seems to be effortless. To show that the enjoyment takes effort is to do the job poorly. Similarly, part of the job is to disguise fatigue and irritation, for otherwise the labor would show in an unseemly way, and the product—passenger contentment—would be damaged.* Because it is easier to disguise fatigue and irritation if they can be banished altogether, at least for brief periods, this feat calls for emotional labor.

The reason for comparing these dissimilar jobs is that the modern assembly-line worker has for some time been an outmoded symbol of modern industrial labor; fewer than 6 percent of workers now work on assembly lines. Another kind of labor has now come into symbolic prominence—the voice-to-voice or face-to-face delivery of service—and the flight attendant is an appropriate model for it. There have always been public-service jobs, of course; what is new is that they are now socially engineered and thoroughly organized from the top. Though the flight attendant's job is no worse and in many ways better than other service jobs, it makes the worker more vulnerable to the social engineering of her emotional labor and reduces her control over that labor. Her problems, therefore, may be a sign of what is to come in other such jobs.

*Like a commodity, service that calls for emotional labor is subject to the laws of supply and demand. Recently the demand for this labor has increased and the supply of it drastically decreased. The airline industry speed-up since the 1970s has been followed by a worker slowdown. The slowdown reveals how much emotional labor the job required all along. It suggests what costs even happy workers under normal conditions pay for this labor without a name. The speed-up has sharpened the ambivalence many workers feel about how much of oneself to give over to the role and how much of oneself to protect from it. (Hochschild)

Emotional labor is potentially good. No customer wants to deal with a surly waitress, a crabby bank clerk, or a flight attendant who avoids eye contact in order to avoid getting a request. Lapses in courtesy by those paid to be courteous are very real and fairly common. What they show us is how fragile public civility really is. We are brought back to the question of what the social carpet actually consists of and what it requires of those who are supposed to keep it beautiful. The laggards and sluff-offs of emotional labor return us to the basic questions. What is emotional labor? What do we do when we manage emotion? What, in fact, is emotion? What are the costs and benefits of managing emotion, in private life and at work?

A nineteenth-century child working in a brutalizing English wallpaper factory and a well-paid twentieth-century American flight attendant have something in common: in order to survive in their jobs, they must mentally detach themselves—the factory worker from his own body and physical labor, and the flight attendant from her own feelings and emotional labor. Marx and many others have told us the factory worker's story. I am interested in telling the flight attendant's story in order to promote a fuller appreciation of the costs of what she does. And I want to base this appreciation on a prior demonstration of what can happen to any of us when we become estranged from our feelings and the management of them.

We feel. But what is a feeling? I would define feeling, like emotion, as a sense, like the sense of hearing or sight. In a general way, we experience it when bodily sensations are joined with what we see or imagine. Like the sense of hearing, emotion communicates information. It has, as Freud said of anxiety, a "signal function." From feeling we discover our own viewpoint on the world.

We often say that we *try* to feel. But how can we do this? Feelings, I suggest, are not stored "inside" us, and they are not independent of acts of management. Both the act of "getting in touch with" feeling and the act of "trying to" feel may become part of the process that makes the thing we get in touch with, or the thing we manage, *into* a feeling or emotion. In managing feeling, we contribute to the creation of it.

If this is so, what we think of as intrinsic to feeling or emotion may have always been shaped to social form and put to civic use. Consider what happens when young men roused to anger go willingly to war, or when followers rally enthusiastically around their king, or mullah, or football team. Private social life may always have called for the management of feeling. The party guest summons up a gaiety owed to the host, the mourner summons up a proper sadness for a funeral. Each offers up feeling as a momentary contribution to the collective good. In the absence of an English-language name for feelings-as-contribution-to-the-group (which the more group-centered Hopi culture called *arofa*), I shall offer the concept of a gift exchange. Muted anger, conjured gratitude, and suppressed envy are offerings back and forth from parent to child, wife to husband, friend to friend, and lover to lover. I shall try to illustrate the intricate designs of these offerings, to point out their shapes, and to study how they are made and exchanged.

What gives social pattern to our acts of emotion management? I believe that when we try to feel, we apply latent feeling rules. . . . We say, "I shouldn't feel so angry at what she did," or "given our agreement, I have no right to feel jealous." Acts of emotion management are not simply private acts; they are used in exchanges under the guidance of feeling rules. Feeling rules are standards used in emotional conversation to determine what is rightly owed and owing in the currency of feeling. Through them, we tell what is "due" in each relation, each role. We pay tribute to each other in the currency of the managing act. In interaction we pay, overpay, underpay, play with paying, acknowledge our dues, pretend to pay, or acknowledge what is emotionally due another person. In these ways . . . we make our try at sincere civility.

Because the distribution of power and authority is unequal in some of the relations of private life, the managing acts can also be unequal. The myriad momentary acts of management compose part of what we summarize in the terms *relation* and *role.* Like the tiny dots of a Seurat painting, the microacts of emotion management compose, through repetition and change over time, a movement of form. Some forms express inequality, others equality.

Now what happens when the managing of emotion comes to be sold as labor? What happens when feeling rules, like rules of behavioral display, are established not through private negotiation but by company manuals? What happens when social exchanges are not, as they are in private life, subject to change or termination but ritually sealed and almost inescapable?

What happens when the emotional display that one person owes another reflects a certain inherent inequality? The airline passenger may choose not to smile, but the flight attendant is obliged not only to smile but to try to work up some warmth behind it. What happens, in other words, when there is a *transmutation* of the private ways we use feeling?

One sometimes needs a grand word to point out a coherent pattern between occurrences that would otherwise seem totally unconnected. My word is "transmutation." When I speak of the transmutation of an emotional system, I mean to point out a link between a private act, such as attempting to enjoy a party, and a public act, such as summoning up good feeling for a customer. I mean to expose the relation between the private act of trying to dampen liking for a person—which overcommitted lovers sometimes attempt—and the public act of a bill collector who suppresses empathy for a debtor. By the grand phrase "transmutation of an emotional system" I mean to convey what it is that we do privately, often unconsciously, to feelings that nowadays often fall under the sway of large organizations, social engineering, and the profit motive.

Trying to feel what one wants, expects, or thinks one ought to feel is probably no newer than emotion itself. Conforming to or deviating from feeling rules is also hardly new. In organized society, rules have probably never been applied only to observable behavior. "Crimes of the heart" have long been recognized because proscriptions have long guarded the "preactions" of the heart; the Bible says not to covet your neighbor's wife, not simply to avoid acting on that feeling. What is new in our time is an increasingly prevalent *instrumental stance* toward our native capacity to play, wittingly and actively, upon a range of feelings for a private purpose and the way in which that stance is engineered and administered by large organizations.

This transmutation of the private use of feeling affects the two sexes and the various social classes in distinctly different ways. . . . As a matter of tradition, emotion management has been better understood and more often used by women as one of the offerings they trade for economic support. Especially among dependent women of the middle and upper classes, women have the job (or think they ought to) of creating the emotional tone of social encounters: expressing joy at the Christmas presents others open, creating the sense of surprise at birthdays, or displaying alarm at the mouse in the kitchen. Gender is not the only determinant of skill in such managed expression and in the emotion work needed to do it well. But men who do this work well have slightly less in common with other men than women who do it well have with other women. When the "womanly" art of living up to *private* emotional conventions goes public, it attaches itself to a different profit-and-loss statement.

Similarly, emotional labor affects the various social classes differently. If it is women, members of the less advantaged gender, who specialize in emotional labor, it is the middle and upper reaches of the class system that seem to call most for it. And parents who do emotional labor on the job will convey the importance of emotion management to their children and will prepare them to learn the skills they will probably need for the jobs they will probably get.

In general, lower-class and working-class people tend to work more with things, and middle-class and upper-class people tend to work more with people. More working women than men deal with people as a job. Thus, there are both gender patterns and class patterns to the civic and commercial use of human feeling. That is the social point.

But there is a personal point, too. There is a cost to emotion work: it affects the degree to which we listen to feeling and sometimes our very capacity to feel. Managing feeling is an art fundamental to civilized living, and I assume that in broad terms the cost is usually worth the fundamental benefit. Freud, in *Civilization and Its Discontents*, argued analogously about the sexual instinct: enjoyable as that instinct is, we are wise in the long run to give up some gratification of it. But when the transmutation of the private use of feeling is successfully accomplished—when we succeed in lending our feelings to the organizational engineers of worker-customer relations—we may pay a cost in how we hear our feelings and a cost in what, for better or worse, they tell us about ourselves. When a speed-up of the human assembly line makes "genuine" personal service harder to deliver, the worker may withdraw emotional labor and offer instead a thin crust of display. Then the cost shifts: the penalty becomes a sense of being phony or insincere. In short, when the transmutation works, the worker risks losing the signal function of feeling. When it does not work, the risk is losing the signal function of display.

Certain social conditions have increased the cost of feeling management. One is an overall unpredictability about our social world. Ordinary people nowadays move through many social worlds and get the gist of dozens of social roles. Compare this with the life of the fourteenth-century baker's apprentice described in Peter Laslett's *The World We Have Lost* (1968): it is a life that begins and ends in one locale, in one occupation, in one household, within one world view, and according to one set of rules. It has become much less common that given circumstances seem to dictate the proper interpretation of them or that they indicate in a plainly visible way what feeling is owed to whom, and when, and how. As a result, we moderns spend more mental time on the question "What, in this situation, should I be feeling?" Oddly enough, a second condition more appropriate to Laslett's baker's apprentice has survived into more modern and fluid times. We still, it seems, ask of ourselves, "Who am I?" as if the question permitted a single neat answer. We still search for a solid, predictable core of self even though the conditions for the existence of such a self have long since vanished.

In the face of these two conditions, people turn to feelings in order to locate themselves or at least to see what their own reactions are to a given event. That is, in the absence of unquestioned external guidelines, the signal function of emotion becomes more important, and the commercial distortion of the managed heart becomes all the more important as a human cost.

We may well be seeing a response to all this in the rising approval of the unmanaged heart, the greater virtue now attached to what is "natural" or spontaneous. Ironically, the person like Rousseau's Noble Savage, who only smiles "naturally," without ulterior purpose, is a poor prospect for the job of waiter, hotel manager, or flight attendant. The high regard for "natural feeling," then, may coincide with the culturally imposed need to develop the precise opposite—an instrumental stance toward feeling. We treat spontaneous feeling, for this reason, as if it were scarce and precious; we raise it up as a virtue. It may not be too much to suggest that we are witnessing a call for the conversation of "inner resources," a call to save another wilderness from corporate use and keep it "forever wild."

With the growing celebration of spontaneity have come the robot jokes. Robot humor plays with the tension between being human—that is to say, having feeling—and being a cog in a socioeconomic machine. The charm of the little robot R2–D2, in the film *Star Wars,* is that he seems so human. Films like this bring us the familiar in reverse: every day, outside the movie house, we see human beings whose show of feeling has a robot quality. The ambiguities are funny now.

Both the growing celebration of spontaneity and the jokes we tell about being robots suggest that in the realm of feeling, Orwell's 1984 came in disguise several years ago, leaving behind a laugh and perhaps the idea of a private way out.

Reflections

Private Exploration

1. Consider this passage:

> Now girls, I want you to go out there and really *smile*. Your smile is your biggest *asset*. I want you to go out there and use it. Smile. *Really smile*. Really *lay it on*.

2. Hochschild sees both differences and similarities between the 19th century factory boy and the 20th century flight attendant. Review her argument and explore the human cost of becoming an "instrument of labor." Consider the losses an employee might suffer when managing personality becomes part of the job.

Public Exploration

1. When we asked our students to talk about their jobs, here are some of the things we heard.

   - A young woman who worked in a bar was required to wear a skirt split to the thigh and to act "perky."
   - A male student was given instruction on how to shake hands "like a man" to impress his clients.
   - A student who worked in a bank complained that her employer hired unidentified "customers" who rated bank employees regularly on whether they smiled enough. She considered it a form of emotional blackmail.
   - Another young woman was instructed to smile before answering the telephone, on the theory that her voice would project a more positive tone to the perspective customer.

Are these students merely griping? Is the business world justified in expecting certain emotional standards from its employees? In your class or group, consider your own collective work experience. Did the job involve emotional labor as well as mental or physical labor? Were you free to be true to yourself, or were you required to manage your personality for the benefit of the company? How, in each instance, did your freedom or lack of it affect your attitude, your performance, your interest in the job?

2. Consider this passage:

> In general, our society is becoming one of giant enterprises directed by a bureaucracy in which man becomes a small, well-oiled cog in the machinery. The oiling is done with higher wages, fringe benefits, well-ventilated factories and piped music, and by psychologists and "human relations experts," yet all this oiling does not alter the fact that [workers] do not wholeheartedly participate in [their] work and that [they] are bored with it.
>
> —C. Wright Mills

Personal Reflection

What do you make of this sentence:

> In managing feeling, we contribute to the creation of it.

The Myth of Sisyphus

ALBERT CAMUS

The gods had condemned Sisyphus to ceaselessly rolling a rock to the top of a mountain, whence the stone would fall back of its own weight. They had thought with some reason that there is no more dreadful punishment than futile and hopeless labor.

If one believes Homer, Sisyphus was the wisest and most prudent of mortals. According to another tradition, however, he was disposed to practice the profession of highwayman. I see no contradiction in this. Opinions differ as to the reasons why he became the futile laborer of the underworld. To begin with, he is accused of a certain levity in regard to the gods. He stole their secrets. Aegina, the daughter of Aesopus, was carried off by Jupiter. The father was shocked by that disappearance and complained to Sisyphus. He, who knew of the abduction, offered to tell about it on condition that Aesopus would give water to the citadel of Corinth. To the celestial thunderbolts he preferred the benediction of water. He was punished for this in the underworld. Homer tells us also that Sisyphus had put Death in chains. Pluto could not endure the sight of his deserted, silent empire. He dispatched the god of war, who liberated Death from the hands of her conqueror.

It is said also that Sisyphus, being near to death, rashly wanted to test his wife's love. He ordered her to cast his unburied body into the middle of the public square. Sisyphus woke up in the underworld. And there, annoyed by an obedience so contrary to human love, he obtained from Pluto permission to return to earth in order to chastise his wife. But when he had seen again the face of this world, enjoyed water and sun, warm stones and the sea, he no longer wanted to go back to the infernal darkness. Recalls, signs of anger, warnings were of no avail. Many years more he lived facing the curve of the gulf, the sparkling sea, and the smiles of earth. A decree of the gods was necessary. Mercury came and seized the impudent man by the collar and, snatching him from his joys, led him forcibly back to the underworld, where his rock was ready for him.

You have already grasped that Sisyphus is the absurd hero. He *is*, as much through his passions as through his torture. His scorn of the gods, his hatred of death, and his passion for life won him that unspeakable penalty in which the whole being is exerted toward accomplishing nothing. This is the price that must be paid for the passions of this earth. Nothing is told us about Sisyphus in the underworld. Myths are made for the imagination to breathe life into them. As for this myth, one sees merely the whole effort of a body straining to raise the huge stone, to roll it and push it up a slope a hundred times over; one sees the face screwed up, the cheek tight against the stone, the shoulder bracing the clay-covered mass, the foot wedging it, the fresh start with arms outstretched, the wholly human security of two earth-clotted hands.

At the very end of his long effort measured by skyless space and time without depth, the purpose is achieved. Then Sisyphus watches the stone rush down in a few moments toward that lower world whence he will have to push it up again toward the summit. He goes back down to the plain.

It is during that return, that pause, that Sisyphus interests me. A face that toils so close to stones is already stone itself! I see that man going back down with a heavy yet measured step toward the torment of which he will never know the end. That hour like a breathing-space which returns as surely as his suffering, that is the hour of consciousness. At each of those moments when he leaves the heights and gradually sinks toward the lairs of the gods, he is superior to his fate. He is stronger than his rock.

If this myth is tragic, that is because its hero is conscious. Where would his torture be, indeed, if at every step the hope of succeeding upheld him? The workman of today works every day in his life at the same tasks, and this fate is no less absurd. But it is tragic only at the rare moments when it becomes conscious. Sisyphus, proletarian of the gods, powerless and rebellious, knows the whole extent of this wretched condition: it is what he thinks of during his descent. The lucidity that was to constitute his torture at the same time crowns his victory. There is no fate that cannot be surmounted by scorn.

If the descent is thus sometimes performed in sorrow, it can also take place in joy. This word is not too much. Again I fancy Sisyphus returning toward his rock, and the sorrow was in the beginning. When the images of each cling too tightly to memory, when the call of happiness becomes too insistent, it happens that melancholy rises in man's heart: this is the rock's victory, this is the rock itself. The boundless grief is too heavy to bear. These are our nights of Gethsemane. But crushing truths perish from being acknowledged. Thus, Oedipus at the outset obeys fate without knowing it. But from the moment he knows, his tragedy begins. Yet at the same moment, blind and desperate, he realizes that the only bond linking him to the world is the cool hand of a girl. Then a tremendous remark rings out: "Despite so many ordeals, my advanced age and the nobility of my soul make me conclude that all is well." Sophocles' Oedipus, like Dostoevsky's Kirilov, thus gives the recipe for the absurd victory. Ancient wisdom confirms modern heroism.

One does not discover the absurd without being tempted to write a manual of happiness. "What! by such narrow ways—?" There is but one world, however. Happiness and the absurd are two sons of the same earth. They are inseparable. It would be a mistake to say that happiness necessarily springs from the absurd discovery. It happens as well as that the feeling of the absurd springs from happiness. "I conclude that all is well," says Oedipus, and that remark is sacred. It echoes in the wild and limited universe of man. It teaches that all is not, has not been, exhausted. It drives out of this world a god who had come into it with dissatisfaction and a preference for futile sufferings. It makes of fate a human matter, which must be settled among men.

All Sisyphus' silent joy is contained therein. His fate belongs to him. His rock is his thing. Likewise, the absurd man, when he contemplates his torment, silences all the idols. In the universe suddenly restored to its silence, the myriad wondering little voices of the earth rise up. Unconscious, secret calls, invitations from all the faces, they are the necessary reverse and price of victory. There is no sun without shadow, and it is essential to know the night. The absurd man says yes and his effort will henceforth be unceasing. If there is a personal fate, there is no higher destiny, or at least there is but one which he concludes is inevitable and despicable. For the rest, he knows himself to be the master of his days. At that subtle moment when man glances backward over his life, Sisyphus returning toward his rock, in that slight pivoting he contemplates that series of unrelated actions which becomes his fate, created by him, combined under his memory's eye and soon sealed by his death. Thus, convinced of the wholly human origin of all that is human, a blind man eager to see who knows that the night has no end, he is still on the go. The rock is still rolling.

I leave Sisyphus at the foot of the mountain! One always finds one's burden again. But Sisyphus teaches the higher fidelity that negates the gods and raises rocks. He too concludes that all is well. This universe henceforth without a master seems to him neither sterile nor futile. Each atom of that stone, each mineral flake of that night-filled mountain, in itself forms a world. The struggle itself toward the heights is enough to fill a man's heart. One must imagine Sisyphus happy.

Reflections

Private Exploration

1. Focus on a key passage from Camus' essay that seems most important to you. If possible, relate some aspect of it to your own personal encounter to struggle and succeed, or explore a single experience that clearly parallels, contradicts or expands on Camus.
2. Camus sees Sisyphus as a metaphor for the human condition. What do you make of the metaphor? Consider how it applies to work, success, and happiness.
3. Camus believes that when Sisyphus descends from the heights he is "superior to his fate" and "stronger than his rock." What could he mean?

Public Exploration

1. Consider this quote:

> We're so engaged in doing things to achieve purpose of outer values that we forget that the inner values, the rapture that is associated with being alive, is what it's all about.
>
> —JOSEPH CAMPBELL

Does Campbell's observation relate to "The Myth of Sisyphus"? What, if anything, does either suggest about the relationship between happiness and work.

2. Camus tells us that myths "are made for the imagination to breath life into them." But the term "myth" in our culture is usually taken to mean a lie, something false. How can reading a myth have any value to us?

Personal Reflection

Camus writes that "The struggle itself toward the heights is enough to fill man's [or a woman's] heart." Consider the significance of this statement in terms of your own life. Ponder how your own struggle has contributed to the formation of your inner and outer values.

• Ox Cart Man •

DONALD HALL

In October of the year,
he counts potatoes dug from the brown field,
counting the seed, counting
the cellar's portion out,
and bags the rest on the cart's floor.

He packs wool sheared in April, honey
in combs, linen, leather
tanned from deerhide,
and vinegar in a barrel
hooped by hand at the forge's fire.

He walks by ox's head, ten days
to Portsmouth Market, and sells potatoes,
and the bag that carried potatoes,
flaxseed, birch brooms, maple sugar, goose
feathers, yarn.

When the cart is empty he sells the cart.
When the cart is sold he sells the ox,
harness and yoke, and walks
home, his pockets heavy
with the year's coin for salt and taxes.

and at home by fire's light in November cold
stitches new harness
for next year's ox in the barn,
and carves the yoke, and saws planks
building the cart again.

Reflections

Private Exploration

1. Reflect on the ox-cart man's attitude toward work, paying particular attention to the concrete details which reveal his philosophy. Consider the central metaphor that unifies his life.
2. Copy the first five lines of the poem. Can this stanza provide an insight into the poem as a whole?

Public Exploration

As students, you too work in cycles. Terms begin and end, vacations follow in the summer, a new term begins in the fall. Consider the difference in feelings and satisfaction, if any, between work that precedes in a cyclic pattern, and work that moves regularly in a linear pattern, without significant change or variation. Which would seem to contribute most to human fulfillment, and why?

Private Reflection

The ox cart man's life is regular and predictable. Yet one interpretation of the poem suggests that his life is full and rich, even though it presumably lacks social prestige and any significant financial return. Consider your own plans, your own dreams. Would you be willing to work at something with such regularity, year after year, if it provided you with inner satisfaction but failed to seem glamorous or respectable to society, and brought you little financial reward. Be as honest as you can.

CONNECTIONS

Although the best papers usually come directly from your own interests, generated often by notes and insights developed in keeping a reading notebook or journal, the following suggestions may provide additional ideas for writing.

1. In "The Value of Working" (p. 389), Lance Morrow suggests that today's generation has a different attitude toward work. Consider how the following two quotations might amplify his observation:

   > One of the great ironies of our time: The country that achieved preeminence in considerable part through an almost religious dedication to work has become the land where leisure and fun are enthroned as the new gods.
   >
   > —HARVEY SWADOS

   > Without a total investment of spirit in your work, without a commitment to it that makes it part of your very self, the world eventually becomes a wasteland. You will find that all things seem empty and you will attempt to fill that emptiness with "happiness" derived from being entertained by others, or with a more desperate attempt at "having fun." And for a while such distractions may substitute for deeper values. But in the end—ah, there's the problem. You will never find the self-respect, the sense of pure grace that fills one's soul when a task, no matter how small, has been accomplished with skill and imagination. I am saying nothing new. Ecclesiastes said it 4000 years ago: "Wherefore I perceive that here is nothing better, than that a man should rejoice in his own works; for that is his portion."
   >
   > —KATRINA STAMM-HAUGHT

2. Consider how certain implicit values expressed in Donald Halls' poem "The Ox Cart Man" (p. 443) might relate to key passages found in Lance Morrow's "The Value of Working," (p. 389) or to Albert Camus' "The Myth of Sisyphus" (p. 440).
3. In "The Importance of Work," Gloria Steinem (p. 393) believes that women have a right to a job and that work for women brings the same inner rewards as it does for men. After its founding in 1917, the Soviet Union guaranteed all individuals, regardless of sex, the right to work. Yet here is an excerpt from a journal by Russian immigrant Nina Markovna who would seem to offer a counter argument to Steinem.

   > I now live in a small town in Florida, where we have a comfortable home only a few hundred steps from the ocean. My husband is a pianist . . . . My son, the same child whom I carried within me while hurrying to reach America, is a lieutenant in the U.S. Navy. I have personally led an "uneventful," calm life since reaching America, enjoying to the utmost my newly found liberties and freedoms, including the freedom to be a housewife. To this very day in the Soviet Union every able-bodied citizen is guaranteed the right to work, but not one citizen is guaranteed the right not to work. I cherish the fact that I [can] cook, wash, mend, garden, housebreak my pet dogs, needlepoint to my heart's

> content, and walk four miles daily on the shores of the Atlantic while almost shouting aloud my thanks to the Almighty for such blessings.

Consider how you might use this quotation as a different way of looking at Steinem's position.

4. Explore how Erich Fromm's concern for the workman (p. 398), or Arlie Russell Hochschild's (p. 431) insights into the sacrifices of employees to demands of their employer, might be amplified by the following.

   > The value of your jobs . . . is determined by the spirit and the inner order that you invest in them and in yourselves as you carry them out.
   >
   > —JEAN GUITTON

5. For Erich Fromm (p. 398), the rewards of work have been genuinely reduced by the coming of industrialism and capitalism. Workers have been turned into cogs in a giant machine. One implication from this might be the need for a radical change in society itself. But is Fromm assuming that humankind can achieve happiness only when external conditions promote it? By contrast, in "The Myth of Sisyphus" (p. 440), Camus seems to suggest that one can take charge of one's fate by an inner shift in attitude, that happiness is possible even under the worst conditions. Is Camus merely being a Romantic? Where are the strengths and weakness of these two contrasting arguments?
6. Consider this passage:

   > Without self-respect genuine happiness is scarcely possible. And the man who is ashamed of his work can hardly achieve self-respect.
   >
   > —BERTRAND RUSSELL

7. Henry David Thoreau observed that "men [and women] have become the tools of their tools." Using Thoreau as a starting point, write an essay in which you trace connections from any of the following readings: Tolstoy's "How Much Land Does a Man Need?" (p. 415); Sanders, "The Inheritance of Tools" (p. 403); Nye's "Maintenance" (p. 423); and Hall's poem "The Ox Cart Man" (p. 443).

CHAPTER 10

COUNTRY OF CONSCIENCE

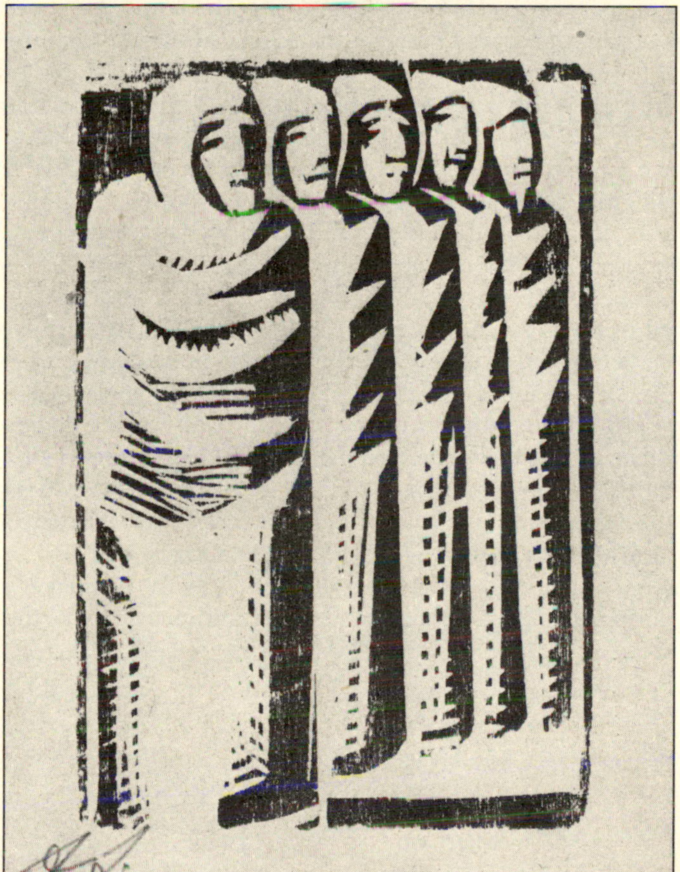

Paul Nash, *The Sun and Moon*, 1924.

The salvation of this human world lies nowhere else than in the human heart, in the human power to reflect, in human meekness and in human responsibility.

—Vaclav Havel

Over the past ten years, we've probably driven cross country a half-dozen times. If you've ever traveled that distance—east to west—you've known the lonely stretches of highway. Interstate 80 cuts through miles of Indiana corn and Nebraska wheat to the far-reaching colonies of Wyoming sage. The journey offers a landscape of surprises. As the evenness of the plains becomes predictable, a lavender smudge swells against the horizon. You think ocean, then ponder the limits of earth. It's easy to envision that peripheral edge as the demarcation where West meets East—a kind of consciousness-rising you could easily lose yourself in. The highway dips and climbs into a brilliant expanse; salt sage pickles the air. The lavender swale in the distance quietly becomes a defined ridge thickening into mountains: Teton, Beartooth, Wind River. If we agree with poet Seamus Heaney that the landscape should be read as text, we get the message: These are the Rocky Mountains, nature's rebels.

The country of conscience is like this—a wide unpredictable plain we've come to consider. We've adopted the title for this chapter from contemporary American poet Jim Wayne Miller, but the Greek philosophers first made us aware of man's conscience. Socrates died for what he believed just, and Plato's famous Dialogues with his teacher continue to encourage us to question and evaluate inner thoughts in conflict. Over and over we're encouraged to be true to ourselves, to allow our conscience to guide us, and like the ancient Rockies, to rebel if necessary.

Clustered in the following pages, you'll find readings that involve the individual struggle to come to terms with conscience. In each case, whether reading Dick Gregory's painful reflection of a childhood experience, or Nadine Gordimer's remarkable story involving the clash of two ideologies in South Africa, you'll be prompted to question the role conscience plays in determining human dignity. At times you'll be forced to reexamine your values and to reconsider those that contradict your own. In each case, you'll be encouraged to develop a sensitivity to others' needs, to ponder what is just and what is fair. Those who have had the courage to follow their sense of what is right—for themselves and for others—have given us the confidence to make that journey.

A Summons at Buchenwald

ELIE WIESEL

At the gate of the camp, SS officers were waiting for us. They counted us. Then we were directed to the assembly place. Orders were given us through loudspeakers:

"Form fives!" "Form groups of a hundred!" "Five paces forward!"

I held onto my father's hand—the old, familiar fear: not to lose him.

Right next to us the high chimney of the crematory oven rose up. It no longer made any impression on us. It scarcely attracted our attention.

An established inmate of Buchenwald told us that we should have a shower and then we could go into the blocks. The idea of having a hot bath fascinated me. My father was silent. He was breathing heavily beside me.

"Father," I said. "Only another moment more. Soon we can lie down—in a bed. You can rest. . . ."

He did not answer. I was so exhausted myself that his silence left me indifferent. My only wish was to take a bath as quickly as possible and lie down in a bed.

But it was not easy to reach the showers. Hundreds of prisoners were crowding there. The guards were unable to keep any order. They struck out right and left with no apparent result. Others, without the strength to push or even to stand up, had sat down in the snow. My father wanted to do the same. He groaned.

"I can't go on. . . . This is the end. . . . I'm going to die here. . . ."

He dragged me toward a hillock of snow from which emerged human shapes and ragged pieces of blanket.

"Leave me," he said to me. "I can't go on. . . . Have mercy on me. . . . I'll wait here until we can get into the baths. . . . You can come and find me."

I could have wept with rage. Having lived through so much, suffered so much, could I leave my father to die now? Now, when we could have a good hot bath and lie down?

"Father!" I screamed. "Father! Get up from here! Immediately! You're killing yourself. . . ."

I seized him by the arm. He continued to groan.

"Don't shout, son. . . . Take pity on your old father. . . . Leave me to rest here. . . . Just for a bit, I'm so tired . . . at the end of my strength. . . ."

He had become like a child, weak, timid, vulnerable.

"Father," I said. "You can't stay here."

I showed him the corpses all around him; they too had wanted to rest here.

"I can see them, son. I can see them all right. Let them sleep. It's so long since they closed their eyes. . . . They are exhausted . . . exhausted. . . ."

His voice was tender.

I yelled against the wind.

"They'll never wake again! Never! Don't you understand?"

For a long time this argument went on. I felt that I was not arguing with him, but with death itself, with the death that he had already chosen.

The sirens began to wail. An alert. The lights went out throughout the camp. The guards drove us toward the blocks. In a flash, there was no one left on the assembly place. We were only too glad not to have had to stay outside longer in the icy wind. We let ourselves sink down onto the planks. The beds were in several tiers. The cauldrons of soup at the entrance attracted no one. To sleep, that was all that mattered.

It was daytime when I awoke. And then I remembered that I had a father. Since the alert, I had followed the crowd without troubling about him. I had known that he was at the end, on the brink of death, and yet I had abandoned him.

I went to look for him.

But at the same moment this thought came into my mind: "Don't let me find him! If only I could get rid of this dead weight, so that I could use all my strength to struggle for my own survival, and only worry about myself." Immediately I felt ashamed of myself, ashamed forever.

I walked for hours without finding him. Then I came to the block where they were giving out black "coffee." The men were lining up and fighting.

A plaintive, beseeching voice caught me in the spine:

"Eliezer . . . my son . . . bring me . . . a drop of coffee. . . ."

I ran to him.

"Father! I've been looking for you so long. . . . Where were you? Did you sleep? . . . How do you feel?"

He was burning with fever. Like a wild beast, I cleared a way for myself to the coffee cauldron. And I managed to carry back a cupful. I had a sip. The rest was for him. I can't forget the light of thankfulness in his eyes while he gulped it down—an animal gratitude. With those few gulps of hot water, I probably brought him more satisfaction than I had done during my whole childhood.

He was lying on a plank, livid, his lips pale and dried up, shaken by tremors. I could not stay by him for long. Orders had been given to clear the place for cleaning. Only the sick could stay.

We stayed outside for five hours. Soup was given out. As soon as we were allowed to go back to the blocks, I ran to my father.

"Have you had anything to eat?"

"No."

"Why not?"

"They didn't give us anything . . . they said that if we were ill we should die soon anyway and it would be a pity to waste the food. I can't go on any more. . . ."

I gave him what was left of my soup. But it was with a heavy heart. I felt that I was giving it up to him against my will. No better than Rabbi Eliahou's son had I withstood the test.

He grew weaker day by day, his gaze veiled, his face the color of dead leaves. On the third day after our arrival at Buchenwald, everyone had to go to the showers. Even the sick, who had to go through last.

On the way back from the baths, we had to wait outside for a long time. They had not yet finished cleaning the blocks.

Seeing my father in the distance, I ran to meet him. He went by me like a ghost, passed me without stopping, without looking at me. I called to him. He did not come back. I ran after him:

"Father, where are you running to?"

He looked at me for a moment, and his gaze was distant, visionary; it was the face of someone else. A moment only and on he ran again.

Struck down with dysentery, my father lay in his bunk, five other invalids with him. I sat by his side, watching him, not daring to believe that he could escape death again. Nevertheless, I did all I could to give him hope.

Suddenly, he raised himself on his bunk and put his feverish lips to my ear:

"Eliezer . . . I must tell you where to find the gold and the money I buried . . . in the cellar. . . . You know. . . ."

He began to talk faster and faster, as though he were afraid he would not have time to tell me. I tried to explain to him that this was not the end, that we would go back to the house together, but he would not listen to me. He could no longer listen to me. He was exhausted. A trickle of saliva, mingled with blood, was running from between his lips. He had closed his eyes. His breath was coming in gasps.

For a ration of bread, I managed to change beds with a prisoner in my father's bunk. In the afternoon the doctor came. I went and told him that my father was very ill.

"Bring him here!"

I explained that he could not stand up. But the doctor refused to listen to anything. Somehow, I brought my father to him. He stared at him, then questioned him in a clipped voice:

"What do you want?"

"My father's ill," I answered for him. "Dysentery. . ."

"Dysentery? That's not my business. I'm a surgeon. Go on! Make room for the others."

Protests did no good.

"I can't go on, son. . . . Take me back to my bunk. . . ."

I took him back and helped him to lie down. He was shivering.

"Try and sleep a bit, father. Try to go to sleep. . . ."

His breathing was labored, thick. He kept his eyes shut. Yet I was convinced that he could see everything, that now he could see the truth in all things.

Another doctor came to the block. But my father would not get up. He knew that it was useless.

Besides, this doctor had only come to finish off the sick. I could hear him shouting at them that they were lazy and just wanted to stay in bed. I felt like leaping at his throat, strangling him. But I no longer had the courage or the strength. I was riveted to my father's deathbed. My hands hurt, I was clenching them so hard. Oh, to strangle the doctor and the others! To burn the whole world! My father's murderers! But the cry stayed in my throat.

When I came back from the bread distribution, I found my father weeping like a child:

"Son, they keep hitting me!"

"Who?"

I thought he was delirious.

"Him, the Frenchman . . . and the Pole . . . they were hitting me."

Another wound to the heart, another hate, another reason for living lost.

"Eliezer . . . Eliezer . . . tell them not to hit me. . . . I haven't done anything. . . . Why do they keep hitting me?"

I began to abuse his neighbors. They laughed at me. I promised them bread, soup. They laughed. Then they got angry; they could not stand my father any longer, they said, because he was now unable to drag himself outside to relieve himself.

The following day he complained that they had taken his ration of bread.

"While you were asleep?"

"No. I wasn't asleep. They jumped on top of me. They snatched my bread . . . and they hit me . . . again. . . . I can't stand any more, son . . . a drop of water . . . ."

I knew that he must not drink. But he pleaded with me for so long that I gave in. Water was the worst poison he could have, but what else could I do for him? With water, without water, it would all be over soon anyway. . . .

"You, at least, have some mercy on me. . . ."

Have mercy on him! I, his only son!

A week went by like this.

"This is your father, isn't it?" asked the head of the block.

"Yes."

"He's very ill."

"The doctor won't do anything for him."

"The doctor *can't* do anything for him, now. And neither can you."

He put his great hairy hand on my shoulder and added:

"Listen to me, boy. Don't forget that you're in a concentration camp. Here, every man has to fight for himself and not think of anyone else. Even of his father. Here, there are no fathers, no brothers, no friends. Everyone lives and dies for himself alone. I'll give you a sound piece of advice—don't give your ration of bread and soup to your old father. There's nothing you can do for him. And you're killing yourself. Instead, you ought to be having his ration."

I listened to him without interrupting. He was right, I thought in the most secret region of my heart, but I dared not admit it. It's too late to save your old father, I said to myself. You ought to be having two rations of bread, two rations of soup. . . .

Only a fraction of a second, but I felt guilty. I ran to find a little soup to give my father. But he did not want it. All he wanted was water.

"Don't drink water . . . have some soup. . . ."

"I'm burning . . . why are you being so unkind to me, my son? Some water. . . ."

I brought him some water. Then I left the block for roll call. But I turned around and came back again. I lay down on the top bunk. Invalids were allowed to stay in the block. So I would be an invalid myself. I would not leave my father.

There was silence all round now, broken only by groans. In front of the block, the SS were giving orders. An officer passed by the beds. My father begged me:

"My son, some water. . . . I'm burning. . . . My stomach. . . ."

"Quiet, over there!" yelled the officer.

"Eliezer," went on my father, "some water. . . ."

The officer came up to him and shouted at him to be quiet. But my father did not hear him. He went on calling me. The officer dealt him a violent blow on the head with his truncheon.

I did not move. I was afraid. My body was afraid of also receiving a blow.

Then my father made a rattling noise and it was my name: "Eliezer."

I could see that he was still breathing—spasmodically.

I did not move.

When I got down after roll call, I could see his lips trembling as he murmured something. Bending over him, I stayed gazing at him for over an hour, engraving into myself the picture of his blood-stained face, his shattered skull.

Then I had to go to bed. I climbed into my bunk, above my father, who was still alive. It was January 28, 1945.

I awoke on January 29 at dawn. In my father's place lay another invalid. They must have taken him away before dawn and carried him to the crematory. He may still have been breathing.

There were no prayers at his grave. No candles were lit to his memory. His last word was my name. A summons, to which I did not respond.

I did not weep, and it pained me that I could not weep. But I had no more tears. And, in the depths of my being, in the recesses of my weakened conscience, could I have searched it, I might perhaps have found something like—free at last!

Reflections

Private Exploration

1. In your reading notebook explore any aspect of Wiesel's autobiography you consider particularly moving or significant.
2. Following his father's death, Wiesel writes: "I could not weep. . . . And, in the depths of my being, in the recesses of my weakened conscience, could I have searched it, I might perhaps have found something like—free at last!" What do you make of those final words? Consider them in all their many ramifications.

3. Write about the following passage: "Here, every man has to fight for himself and not think of anyone else. Even his father. Here, there are not fathers, no brothers, no friends. Everyone lives and dies for himself alone."

Public Exploration

Share your notebook response with other students. Answer questions, clarify statements, or expand on your thoughts. In turn, listen and respond as others read.

Private Reflection

Reflect on insights that may have arisen from your discussion with others. What now seems to you the most important aspect of Wiesel's essay?

Leningrad Cemetery, Winter of 1941

SHARON OLDS

That winter, the dead could not be buried.
The ground was frozen, the gravediggers weak from hunger,
the coffin wood used for fuel. So they were covered with something
and taken on a child's sled to the cemetery
in the sub-zero air. They lay on the soil,
some of them wrapped in dark cloth
bound with rope like the tree's ball of roots
when it waits to be planted; others wound in sheets,
their pale, gauze, tapered shapes
stiff as cocoons that will split down the center
when the new life inside is prepared;
but most lay like corpses, their coverings
coming undone, naked calves
hard as corded wood spilling
from under a cloak, a hand reaching out
with no sign of peace, wanting to come back
even to the bread made of glue and sawdust,
even to the icy winter, and the siege.

Reflections

Private Exploration

1. After reading Olds's poem several times, respond to whatever struck you as most powerful or moving. What do you see as the important ideas or feelings here?
2. What was going on in Leningrad in 1941? What was "the siege" referred to in the last line? If you're not sure, look up these historical references in the library. What new insights into the poem are acquired with this additional knowledge?

3. What do you make of these lines?

   . . . a hand reaching out
   with no sign of peace, wanting to come back
   even to the bread made of glue and sawdust,
   even to the icy winter, and the siege.

Public Exploration

After someone in your class or group has read Olds's poem aloud, take turns sharing your responses to any one of the questions above. As a group, consider how your attitude toward war is affected by the poem, if indeed it is. How can a historical event that took place thousands of miles away in 1941 have any effect on our values today?

Private Reflection

Quietly ponder your original response to the poem. Consider how our attitudes toward war are shaped by history, by family, by culture, and by friends. Can it be shaped by literature or other art forms as well? Has yours been?

Shame

DICK GREGORY

I never learned hate at home, or shame. I had to go to school for that. I was about seven years old when I got my first big lesson. I was in love with a little girl named Helene Tucker, a light-complected little girl with pigtails and nice manners. She was always clean and she was smart in school. I think I went to school then mostly to look at her. I brushed my hair and even got me a little old handkerchief. It was a lady's handkerchief, but I didn't want Helene to see me wipe my nose on my hand. The pipes were frozen again, there was no water in the house, but I washed my socks and shirt every night. I'd get a pot, and go over to Mister Ben's grocery store, and stick my pot down into his soda machine. Scoop out some chopped ice. By evening the ice melted to water for washing. I got sick a lot that winter because the fire would go out at night before the clothes were dry. In the morning I'd put them on, wet or dry, because they were the only clothes I had.

Everybody's got a Helene Tucker, a symbol of everything you want. I loved her for her goodness, her cleanness, her popularity. She'd walk down my street and my brothers and sisters would yell, "Here comes Helene," and I'd rub my tennis sneakers on the back of my pants and wish my hair wasn't so nappy and the white folks' shirt fit me better. I'd run out on the street. If I knew my place and didn't come too close, she'd wink at me and say hello. That was a good feeling. Sometimes I'd follow her all the way home, and shovel the snow off her walk and try to make friends with her Momma and her aunts. I'd drop money on her stoop late at night on my way back home from shining shoes in the taverns. And she had a Daddy, and he had a good job. He was a paper hanger.

I guess I would have gotten over Helene by summertime, but something happened in that classroom that made her face hang in front of me for the next twenty-two years. When I played the drums in high school it was for Helene and when I broke track records in college it was for Helene and when I started standing behind microphones and heard applause I wished Helene could hear it, too. It wasn't until I was twenty-nine years old and married and making money that I finally got her out of my system. Helene was sitting in that classroom when I learned to be ashamed of myself.

It was on a Thursday. I was sitting in the back of the room, in a seat with a chalk circle drawn around it. The idiot's seat, the troublemaker's seat.

The teacher thought I was stupid. Couldn't spell, couldn't read, couldn't do arithmetic. Just stupid. Teachers were never interested in finding out that you couldn't concentrate because you were so hungry, because you hadn't had any breakfast. All you could think about was noontime, would it ever come? Maybe you could sneak into the cloakroom and steal a bite of some kid's lunch out of a coat pocket. A bite of something. Paste. You can't really make a meal of paste, or put it on bread for a sandwich, but sometimes I'd scoop a few spoonfuls out of the big paste jar in the back of the room. Pregnant people get strange tastes. I was pregnant with poverty. Pregnant with dirt and pregnant with smells that made people turn away, pregnant with cold and pregnant with shoes that were never bought for me, pregnant with five other people in my bed and no Daddy in the next room, and pregnant with hunger. Paste doesn't taste too bad when you're hungry.

The teacher thought I was a troublemaker. All she saw from the front of the room was a little black boy who squirmed in his idiot's seat and made noises and poked the kids around him. I guess she couldn't see a kid who made noises because he wanted someone to know he was there.

It was on a Thursday, the day before the Negro payday. The eagle always flew on Friday. The teacher was asking each student how much his father would give to the Community Chest. On Friday night, each kid would get the money from his father, and on Monday he would bring it to the school. I decided I was going to buy a Daddy right then. I had money in my pocket from shining shoes and selling papers, and whatever Helene Tucker pledged for her Daddy I was going to top it. And I'd hand the money right in. I wasn't going to wait until Monday to buy me a Daddy.

I was shaking, scared to death. The teacher opened her book and started calling out names alphabetically.

"Helene Tucker?"

"My Daddy said he'd give two dollars and fifty cents."

"That's very nice, Helene. Very, very nice indeed."

That made me feel pretty good. It wouldn't take too much to top that. I had almost three dollars in dimes and quarters in my pocket. I stuck my hand in my pocket and held onto the money, waiting for her to call my name. But the teacher closed her book after she called everybody else in the class.

I stood up and raised my hand.

"What is it now?"

"You forgot me?"

She turned toward the blackboard. "I don't have time to be playing with you, Richard."

"My Daddy said he'd . . ."

"Sit down, Richard, you're disturbing the class."

"My Daddy said he'd give . . . fifteen dollars."

She turned around and looked mad. "We are collecting this money for you and your kind, Richard Gregory. If your Daddy can give fifteen dollars you have no business being on relief."

"I got it right now, I got it right now, my Daddy gave it to me to turn in today, my Daddy said . . ."

"And furthermore," she said, looking right at me, her nostrils getting big and her lips getting thin and her eyes opening wide. "We know you don't have a Daddy."

Helene Tucker turned around, her eyes full of tears. She felt sorry for me. Then I couldn't see her too well because I was crying, too.

"Sit down, Richard."

And I always thought the teacher kind of liked me. She always picked me to wash the blackboard on Friday, after school. That was a big thrill, it made me feel important. If I didn't wash it, come Monday the school might not function right.

"Where are you going, Richard?"

I walked out of school that day, and for a long time I didn't go back very often. There was shame there.

Now there was shame everywhere. It seemed like the whole world had been inside that classroom, everyone had heard what the teacher had said, everyone had turned around and felt sorry for me. There was shame in going to the Worthy Boys Annual Christmas Dinner for you and your kind, because everybody knew what a worthy boy was. Why couldn't they just call it the Boys Annual Dinner, why'd they have to give it a name? There was shame in wearing the brown and orange and white plaid mackinaw the welfare gave to 3,000 boys. Why'd it have to be the same for everybody so when you walked down the street the people could see you were on relief? It was a nice warm mackinaw and it had a hood, and my Momma beat me and called me a little rat when she found out I stuffed it in the bottom of a pail full of garbage way over on Cottage Street. There was shame in running over to Mister Ben's at the end of the day and asking for his rotten peaches, there was shame in asking Mrs. Simmons for a spoonful of sugar, there was shame in running out to meet the relief truck. I hated that truck, full of food for you and your kind. I ran into the house and hid when it came. And then I started to sneak through alleys, to take the long way home so the people going into White's Eat Shop wouldn't see me. Yeah, the whole world heard the teacher that day, we all know you don't have a Daddy.

It lasted for a while, this kind of numbness. I spent a lot of time feeling sorry for myself. And then one day I met this wino in a restaurant. I'd been out hustling all day, shining shoes, selling newspapers, and I had googobs of money in my pocket. Bought me a bowl of chili for fifteen cents, and a cheeseburger for fifteen cents, and a Pepsi for five cents, and a piece of chocolate cake for ten cents. That was a good meal. I was eating when this old wino came in. I love winos because they never hurt anyone but themselves.

The old wino sat down at the counter and ordered twenty-six cents worth of food. He ate it like he really enjoyed it. When the owner, Mister Williams, asked him to pay the check, the old wino didn't lie or go through his pocket like he suddenly found a hole.

He just said: "Don't have no money."

The owner yelled: "Why in hell you come in here and eat my food if you don't have no money? That food cost me money."

Mister Williams jumped over the counter and knocked the wino off his stool and beat him over the head with a pop bottle. Then he stepped back and watched the wino bleed. Then he kicked him. And he kicked him again.

I looked at the wino with blood all over his face and I went over. "Leave him alone, Mister Williams. I'll pay the twenty-six cents."

The wino got up, slowly, pulling himself up to the stool, then up to the counter, holding on for a minute until his legs stopped shaking so bad. He looked at me with pure hate. "Keep your twenty-six cents. You don't have to pay, not now. I just finished paying for it."

He started to walk out, and as he passed me, he reached down and touched my shoulder. "Thanks, sonny, but it's too late now. Why didn't you pay it before?"

I was pretty sick about that. I waited too long to help another man.

Reflections

Private Exploration

1. Select a key sentence or passage from Dick Gregory's essay and write about how you see it as meaningful to the work as a whole. Begin by placing your selection within a context—what is going on and when? Then explore how the sentence or passage explains or relates to other events and feelings. By looking in extended detail at a single passage, what do you learn about the whole essay?
2. It has been said that "Innocence ends when one is stripped of the delusion that one likes oneself." Does this explain what happened to Gregory? Consider several different events in the story, as well as the shifting emotions. Does it relate to your personal experience?
3. Good writers convince. Gregory convinces us of his shame and the lingering impact of those key incidences in his life by repeating key words. Find such a paragraph. Copy the whole of it as a way of learning the effectiveness of repetition. Now, drawing from your own experience, imitate the passage you selected. The experience you write about should be your own, but the pattern of your sentences and their rhythms should imitate Gregory's.

Public Exploration

How do you define self-respect? How is it acquired? How is it lost? What are its limitations?

Private Reflection

After you've explored any of the above questions and talked about Gregory's essay with others, expand upon any one idea that seems especially important to you. It could be a single point in the essay or it could be a personal feeling that grows out of reading and discussion. What have you learned here? Where does it take you?

Three Thousand Dollar Death Song

WENDY ROSE

Nineteen American Indian Skeletons from Nevada . . . valued at $3000 . . . —Museum invoice, 1975

Is it in cold hard cash? the kind
that dusts the insides of men's pockets
lying silver-polished surface along the cloth.
Or in bills? papering the wallets of they
who thread the night with dark words. Or
checks? paper promises weighing the same
as words spoken once on the other side
of the grown grass and dammed rivers
of history. However it goes, it goes
through my body it goes
assessing each nerve, running its edges
along my arteries, planning ahead
for whose hands will rip me
into pieces of dusty red paper,
whose hands will smooth or smatter me
into traces of rubble. Invoiced now,
it's official how our bones are valued
that stretch out pointing to sunrise
or are flexed into one last foetal bend,
that are removed and tossed about,
catalogued, numbered with black ink
on newly-white foreheads.

As we were formed to the white soldier's voice,
so we explode under white students' hands.
Death is a long trail of days
in our fleshless prison.

From this distant point we watch our bones
auctioned with our careful beadwork,
our quilled medicine bundles, even the bridles
of our shot-down horses. You: who have
priced us, you who have removed us: at what cost?
What price the pits where our bones share
a single bit of memory, how one century
turns our dead into specimens, our history
into dust, our survivors into clowns.
Our memory might be catching, you know;
picture the mortars, the arrowheads, the labrets
shaking off their labels like bears
suddenly awake to find the seasons have ended
while they slept. Watch them touch each other,
measure reality, march out the museum door!
Watch as they lift their faces
and smell about for us; watch our bones rise
to meet them and mount the horses once again!
The cost, then, will be paid
for our sweetgrass-smelling having-been
in clam shell beads and steatite,
dentalia and woodpecker scalp, turquoise
and copper, blood and oil, coal
and uranium, children, a universe
of stolen things.

Reflections

Private Exploration

1. Jot down your most immediate response to the epigraph.
2. You will probably need to reread this poem several times before responding to it. Make sure you check a dictionary for words you might be unfamiliar with: *steatite, dentalia, labrets.*
3. Write a brief prose paraphrase of the first twenty-five lines and then reflect on the speaker's attitude. What is she protesting? Point out specific phrases or metaphors that help illuminate her thoughts and feelings. Then write a brief paraphrase of the final twenty-five lines beginning with "From this distant point . . . ." Now reflect on the shift that occurs in terms of time and place. How does the voice change? Are your thoughts and feelings altered?

Public Exploration

Consider the speaker's protest. What's bothering her? Does the poem change your attitude toward museum collections of Indian artifacts? How can a purchase of skeletons be defended? Does the speaker succeed in tugging at your conscience?

Private Reflection

Consider how Rose's poem might speak to your own heritage. How would you feel if you discovered your ancestors were being unearthed, catalogued, and placed in museums? Would anything be stolen from you? Would you pay a price mentally or emotionally? If you are not particularly moved by such events, consider how your own cultural background might have created a different set of values from those of native Americans.

Six Feet of the Country

NADINE GORDIMER

My wife and I are not real farmers—not even Lerice, really. We bought our place, ten miles out of Johannesburg on one of the main roads, to change something in ourselves, I suppose; you seem to rattle about so much within a marriage like ours. You long to hear nothing but a deep satisfying silence when you sound a marriage. The farm hasn't managed that for us, of course, but it has done other things, unexpected, illogical. Lerice, who I thought would retire there in Chekhovian sadness for a month or two, and then leave the place to the servants while she tried yet again to get a part she wanted and become the actress she would like to be, has sunk into the business of running the farm with all the serious intensity with which she once imbued the shadows in a playwright's mind. I should have given it up long ago if it had not been for her. Her hands, once small and plain and well-kept—she was not the sort of actress who wears red paint and diamond rings—are hard as a dog's pads.

I, of course, am there only in the evenings and at weekends. I am a partner in a travel agency which is flourishing—needs to be, as I tell Lerice, in order to carry the farm. Still, though I know we can't afford it, and though the sweetish smell of the fowls Lerice breeds sickens me, so that I avoid going past their runs, the farm is beautiful in a way I had almost forgotten—especially on a Sunday morning when I get up and go out into the paddock and see not the palm trees and fishpond and imitation-stone bird bath of the suburbs but white ducks on the dam, the lucerne field brilliant as window-dresser's grass, and the little, stocky, mean-eyed bull, lustful but bored, having his face tenderly licked by one of his ladies. Lerice comes out with her hair uncombed, in her hand a stick dripping with cattle dip. She will stand and look dreamily for a moment, the way she would pretend to look sometimes in those plays. "They'll mate tomorrow," she will say. "This is their second day. Look how she loves him, my little Napoleon." So that when people come to see us on Sunday afternoon, I am likely to hear myself saying as I pour out the drinks, "When I drive back home from the city every day past those rows of suburban houses, I wonder how the devil we ever did stand it . . . Would you care to look around?" And there I am, taking some pretty girl and her young husband stumbling down to our riverbank, the girl catching her stockings on the mealie-stooks and stepping over cow turds humming with jewel-green flies while she says, ". . . the *tensions* of the damned city. And you're near enough to get into town to a show, too! I think it's wonderful. Why, you've got it both ways!"

And for a moment I accept the triumph as if I *had* managed it—the impossibility that I've been trying for all my life: just as if the truth was that you could get it "both ways," instead of finding yourself with not even one way or the other but a third, one you had not provided for at all.

But even in our saner moments, when I find Lerice's earthly enthusiasms just as irritating as I once found her histrionical ones, and she finds what she calls my "jealousy" of her capacity for enthusiasm as big a proof of my inadequacy for her as a mate as ever it was, we do believe that we have at least honestly escaped those tensions peculiar to the city about which our visitors speak. When Johannesburg people speak of "tension," they don't mean hurrying people in crowded streets, the struggle for money, or the general competitive character of city life. They mean the guns under the white men's pillows and the burglar bars on the white men's windows. They mean those strange moments on city pavements when a black man won't stand aside for a white man.

Out in the country, even ten miles out, life is better than that. In the country, there is a lingering remnant of the pretransitional stage; our relationship with the blacks is almost feudal. Wrong, I suppose, obsolete, but more comfortable all around. We have no burglar bars, no gun. Lerice's farm boys have their wives and their piccanins living with them on the land. They brew their sour beer without the fear of police raids. In fact, we've always rather prided ourselves that the poor devils have nothing much to fear, being with us; Lerice even keeps an eye on their children, with all the competence of a woman who has never had a child of her own, and she certainly doctors them all—children and adults—like babies whenever they happen to be sick.

It was because of this that we were not particularly startled one night last winter when the boy Albert came knocking at our window long after we had gone to bed. I wasn't in our bed but sleeping in the little dressing-room-cum-linen-room next door, because Lerice had annoyed me and I didn't want to find myself softening towards her simply because of the sweet smell of the talcum powder on her flesh after her bath. She came and woke me up. "Albert says one of the boys is very sick," she said. "I think you'd better go down and see. He wouldn't get us up at this hour for nothing."

"What time is it?"

"What does it matter?" Lerice is maddeningly logical.

I got up awkwardly as she watched me—how is it I always feel a fool when I have deserted her bed? After all, I know from the way she never looks at me when she talks to me at breakfast next day that she is hurt and humiliated at my not wanting her—and I went out, clumsy with sleep.

"Which of the boys is it?" I asked Albert as we followed the dance of my torch.

"He's too sick. Very sick," he said.

"But who? Franz?" I remembered Franz had had a bad cough for the past week.

Albert did not answer; he had given me the path, and was walking along beside me in the tall dead grass. When the light of the torch caught his face, I saw that he looked acutely embarrassed. "What's this all about?" I said.

He lowered his head under the glance of the light. "It's not me, baas. I don't know. Petrus he send me."

Irritated, I hurried him along to the huts. And there, on Petrus's iron bedstead, with its brick stilts, was a young man, dead. On his forehead there was still a light, cold sweat; his body was warm. The boys stood around as they do in the kitchen when it is discovered that someone has broken a dish—uncooperative, silent. Somebody's wife hung about in the shadows, her hands wrung together under her apron.

I had not seen a dead man since the war. This was very different. I felt like the others—extraneous, useless. "What was the matter?" I asked.

The woman patted at her chest and shook her head to indicate the painful impossibility of breathing.

He must have died of pneumonia.

I turned to Petrus. "Who was this boy? What was he doing here?" The light of a candle on the floor showed that Petrus was weeping. He followed me out the door.

When we were outside, in the dark, I waited for him to speak. But he didn't. "Now, come on, Petrus, you must tell me who this boy was. Was he a friend of yours?"

"He's my brother, baas. He came from Rhodesia to look for work."

The story startled Lerice and me a little. The young boy had walked down from Rhodesia to look for work in Johannesburg, had caught a chill from sleeping out along the way and had lain ill in his brother Petrus's hut since his arrival three days before. Our boys had been frightened to ask us for help for him because we had never been intended to know of his presence. Rhodesian natives are barred from entering the Union unless they have a permit; the young man was an illegal immigrant. No doubt our boys had managed the whole thing successfully several times before; a number of relatives must have walked the seven or eight hundred miles from poverty to the paradise of zoot suits, police raids and black slum townships that is their *Egoli*, City of Gold—the African name for Johannesburg. It was merely a matter of getting such a man to lie low on our farm until a job could be found with someone who would be glad to take the risk of prosecution for employing an illegal immigrant in exchange for the services of someone as yet untainted by the city.

Well, this was one who would never get up again.

"You would think they would have felt they could tell *us*," said Lerice next morning. "Once the man was ill. You would have thought at least—" When she is getting intense over something, she has a way of standing in the middle of a room as people do when they are shortly to leave on a journey, looking searchingly about her at the most familiar objects as if she had never seen them before. I had noticed that in Petrus's presence in the kitchen, earlier, she had had the air of being almost offended with him, almost hurt.

In any case, I really haven't the time or inclination anymore to go into everything in our life that I know Lerice, from those alarmed and pressing eyes of hers, would like us to go into. She is the kind of woman who doesn't mind if she looks plain, or odd; I don't suppose she would even care if she knew how strange she looks when her whole face is out of proportion with urgent uncertainty. I said, "Now I'm the one who'll have to do all the dirty work, I suppose."

She was still staring at me, trying me out with those eyes—wasting her time, if she only knew.

"I'll have to notify the health authorities," I said calmly. "They can't just cart him off and bury him. After all, we don't really know what he died of."

She simply stood there, as if she had given up—simply ceased to see me at all.

I don't know when I've been so irritated. "It might have been something contagious," I said. "God knows." There was no answer.

I am not enamoured of holding conversations with myself. I went out to shout to one of the boys to open the garage and get the car ready for my morning drive to town.

As I had expected, it turned out to be quite a business. I had to notify the police as well as the health authorities, and answer a lot of tedious questions: How was it I was ignorant of the boy's presence? If I did not supervise my native quarters, how did I know that that sort of thing didn't go on all the time? And when I flared up and told them that so long as my natives did their work, I didn't think it my right or concern to poke my nose into their private lives, I got from the coarse, dull-witted police sergeant one of those looks that come not from any thinking process going on in the brain but from that faculty common to all who are possessed by the master-race theory—a look of insanely inane certainty. He grinned at me with a mixture of scorn and delight at my stupidity.

Then I had to explain to Petrus why the health authorities had to take away the body for a post-mortem—and, in fact, what a post-mortem was. When I telephoned the health department some days later to find out the result, I was told that the cause of death was, as we had thought, pneumonia, and that the body had been suitably disposed of. I went out to where Petrus was mixing a mash for the fowls and told him that it was all right, there would be no trouble; his brother had died from that pain in his chest. Petrus put down the paraffin tin and said, "When can we go to fetch him, baas?"

"To fetch him?"

"Will the baas please ask them when we must come?"

I went back inside and called Lerice, all over the house. She came down the stairs from the spare bedrooms, and I said, "*Now* what am I going to do?" When I told Petrus, he just asked calmly when they could go and fetch the body. They think they're going to bury him themselves."

"Well, go back and tell him," said Lerice. "You must tell him. Why didn't you tell him then?"

When I found Petrus again, he looked up politely. "Look, Petrus," I said. "You can't go fetch your brother. They've done it already—they've *buried* him, you understand?"

"Where?" he said slowly, dully, as if he thought that perhaps he was getting this wrong.

"You see, he was a stranger. They knew he wasn't from here, and they didn't know he had some of his people here so they thought they must bury him." It was difficult to make a pauper's grave sound like a privilege.

"Please, baas, the baas must ask them." But he did not mean that he wanted to know the burial place. He simply ignored the incomprehensible machinery I told him had set to work on his dead brother; he wanted the brother back.

"But, Petrus," I said, "how can I? Your brother is buried already. I can't ask them now."

"Oh, baas!" he said. He stood with his bran-smeared hands uncurled at his sides, one corner of his mouth twitching.

"Good God, Petrus, they won't listen to me! They can't, anyway. I'm sorry, but I can't do it. You understand?"

He just kept on looking at me, out of his knowledge that white men have everything, can do anything; if they don't, it is because they won't.

And then, at dinner, Lerice started. "You could at least phone," she said.

"Christ, what d'you think I am? Am I supposed to bring the dead back to life?"

But I could not exaggerate my way out of this ridiculous responsibility that had been thrust on me. "Phone them up," she went on. "And at least you'll be able to tell him you've done it and they've explained that it's impossible."

She disappeared somewhere into the kitchen quarters after coffee. A little later she came back to tell me, "The old father's coming down from Rhodesia to be at the funeral. He's got a permit and he's already on his way."

Unfortunately, it was not impossible to get the body back. The authorities said that it was somewhat irregular, but that since the hygiene conditions had been fulfilled, they could not refuse permission for exhumation. I found out that, with the undertaker's charges, it would cost twenty pounds. Ah, I thought, that settles it. On five pounds a month, Petrus won't have twenty pounds—and just as well, since it couldn't do the dead any good. Certainly I should not offer it to him myself. Twenty pounds—or anything else within reason, for that matter—I would have spent without grudging it on doctors or medicines that might have helped the boy when he was alive. Once he was dead, I had no intention of encouraging Petrus to throw away, on a gesture, more then he spent to clothe his whole family in a year.

When I told him, in the kitchen that night, he said, "Twenty pounds?"

I said, "Yes, that's right, twenty pounds."

For a moment, I had the feeling, from the look on his face, that he was calculating. But when he spoke again I thought I must have imagined it. "We must pay twenty pounds!" he said in the faraway voice in which a person speaks of something so unattainable it does not bear thinking about.

"All right, Petrus," I said, and went back to the living room.

The next morning before I went to town, Petrus asked to see me. "Please, baas," he said, awkwardly, handing me a bundle of notes. They're so seldom on the giving rather than the receiving side, poor devils, they don't really know how to hand money to a white man. There it was, the twenty pounds, in ones and halves, some creased and folded until they were soft as dirty rags, others smooth and fairly new—Franz's money, I suppose, and Albert's, and Dora the cook's, and Jacob the gardener's, and God knows who else's besides, from all the farms and small holdings round about. I took it in irritation more than in astonishment, really—irritation at the waste, the uselessness of this sacrifice by people so poor. Just like the poor everywhere, I thought, who stint themselves the decencies of life in order to ensure themselves the decencies of death. So incomprehensible to people like Lerice and me, who regard life as something to be spent extravagantly and, if we think about death at all, regard it as the final bankruptcy.

The farm hands don't work on Saturday afternoon anyway, so it was a good day for the funeral. Petrus and his father had borrowed our donkey-cart to fetch the coffin from the city, where, Petrus told Lerice on their return, everything was "nice"—the coffin waiting for them, already sealed up to save them from what must have been a rather unpleasant sight after two weeks' interment. (It had taken all that time for the authorities and the undertaker to make the final arrangements for moving the body.) All morning, the coffin lay in Petrus's hut, awaiting the trip to the little old burial ground, just outside the eastern boundary of our farm, that was a relic of the days when this was a real farming district rather than a fashionable rural estate. It was pure chance that I happened to be down there near the fence when the procession came past; once again Lerice had forgotten her promise to me and had made the house uninhabitable on a Saturday afternoon. I had come home and been infuriated to find her in a pair of filthy old slacks and with her hair uncombed since the night before, having all the varnish scraped from the living-room floor, if you please. So I had taken my No. 8 iron and gone off to practise my approach shots. In my annoyance, I had forgotten about the funeral, and was reminded only when I saw the procession coming up the path along the outside of the fence towards me; from where I was standing, you can see the graves quite clearly, and that day the sun glinted on bits of broken pottery, a lopsided homemade cross, and jam-jars brown with rainwater and dead flowers.

I felt a little awkward, and did not know whether to go on hitting my golf ball or stop at least until the whole gathering was decently past. The donkey-cart creaks and screeches with every revolution of the wheels, and it came along in a slow, halting fashion somehow peculiarly suited to the two donkeys who drew it, their little potbellies rubbed and rough, their heads sunk between the shafts, and their ears flattened back with an air submissive and downcast; peculiarly suited, too, to the group of men and women who came along slowly behind. The patient ass. Watching, I thought, you can see now why the creature became a Biblical symbol. Then the procession drew level with me and stopped, so I had to put down my club. The coffin was taken down off the cart—it was a shiny, yellow-varnished wood, like cheap furniture—and the donkeys twitched their ears against the flies. Petrus, Franz, Albert and the old father from Rhodesia hoisted it on their shoulders and the procession moved on, on foot. It was really a very awkward moment. I stood there rather foolishly at the fence, quite still, and slowly they filed past, not looking up, the four men bent beneath the shiny wooden box, and the straggling troop of mourners. All of them were servants or neighbours' servants whom I knew as casual easygoing gossipers about our lands or kitchen. I heard the old man's breathing.

I had just bent to pick up my club again when there was a sort of jar in the flowing solemnity of their processional mood; I felt it at once, like a wave of heat along the air, or one of those sudden currents of cold catching at your legs in a placid stream. The old man's voice was muttering something; the people had stopped, confused, and they bumped into one another, some pressing to go on, others hissing them to be still. I could see that they were embarrassed, but they could not ignore the voice; it was much the way that the mumblings of a prophet, though not clear at first, arrest the mind. The corner of the coffin the old man carried was sagging at an angle; he seemed to be trying to get out from under the weight of it. Now Petrus expostulated with him.

The little boy who had been left to watch the donkeys dropped the reins and ran to see. I don't know why—unless it was for the same reason people crowd around someone who has fainted in a cinema—but I parted the wires of the fence and went through, after him.

Petrus lifted his eyes to me—to anybody—with distress and horror. The old man from Rhodesia had let go of the coffin entirely, and the three others, unable to support it on their own, had laid it on the ground, in the pathway. Already there was a film of dust lightly wavering up its shiny sides. I did not understand what the old man was saying; I hesitated to interfere. But now the whole seething group turned on my silence. The old man himself came over to me, with his hands outspread and shaking, and spoke directly to me, saying something that I could tell from the tone, without understanding the words, was shocking and extraordinary.

"What is it, Petrus? What's wrong?" I appealed.

Petrus threw up his hands, bowed his head in a series of hysterical shakes, then thrust his face up at me suddenly. "He says, 'My son was not so heavy.' "

Silence. I could hear the old man breathing; he kept his mouth a little open, as old people do.

"My son was young and thin," he said at last, in English.

Again silence. Then babble broke out. The old man thundered against everybody; his teeth were yellowed and few, and he had one of those fine, grizzled, sweeping moustaches one doesn't often see nowadays, which must have been grown in emulation of early Empire-builders. It seemed to frame all his utterances with a special validity. He shocked the assembly; they thought he was mad, but they had to listen to him. With his own hands he began to prise the lid off the coffin and three of the men came forward to help him. Then he sat down on the ground; very old, very weak and unable to speak, he merely lifted a trembling hand towards what was there. He abdicated, he handed it over to them; he was no good any more.

They crowded round to look (and so did I), and now they forgot the nature of this surprise and the occasion of grief to which it belonged, and for a few minutes were carried up in the astonishment of the surprise itself. They gasped and flared noisily with excitement. I even noticed the little boy who had held the donkeys jumping up and down, almost weeping with rage because the backs of the grownups crowded him out of his view.

In the coffin was someone no one had seen before; a heavily built, rather light-skinned native with a neatly stitched scar on his forehead—perhaps from a blow in a brawl that had also dealt him some other, slower-working injury that had killed him.

I wrangled with the authorities for a week over that body. I had the feeling that they were shocked, in a laconic fashion, by their own mistake, but that in the confusion of their anonymous dead they were helpless to put it right. They said to me, "We are trying to find out," and "We are still making inquiries." It was as if at any moment they might conduct me into their mortuary and say, "There! Lift up the sheets; look for him—your poultry boy's brother. There are so many black faces—surely one will do?"

And every evening when I got home, Petrus was waiting in the kitchen. "Well, they're trying. They're still looking. The baas is seeing to it for you, Petrus," I would tell him. "God, half the time I should be in the office I'm driving around the back end of the town chasing after this affair," I added aside, to Lerice, one night.

She and Petrus both kept their eyes turned on me as I spoke, and, oddly, for those moments they looked exactly alike, though it sounds impossible: my wife, with her high, white forehead and her attenuated Englishwoman's body, and the poultry boy, with his horny bare feet below khaki trousers tied at the knee with string and the peculiar rankness of his nervous sweat coming from his skin.

"What makes you so indignant, so determined about this now?" said Lerice suddenly.

I stared at her. "It's a matter of principle. Why should they get away with a swindle? It's time these officials had a jolt from someone who'll bother to take the trouble."

She said, "Oh." And as Petrus slowly opened the kitchen door to leave, sensing that the talk had gone beyond him, she turned away, too.

I continued to pass on assurances to Petrus every evening, but although what I said was the same and the voice in which I said it was the same, every evening it sounded weaker. At last, it became clear that we would never get Petrus's brother back, because nobody really knew where he was. Somewhere in a graveyard as uniform as a housing scheme, somewhere under a number that didn't belong to him, or in the medical school, perhaps, laboriously reduced to layers of muscle and strings of nerve? Goodness knows. He had no identity in this world anyway.

It was only then, and in a voice of shame, that Petrus asked me to try and get the money back.

"From the way he asks, you'd think he was robbing his dead brother," I said to Lerice later. But as I've said, Lerice had got so intense about this business that she couldn't even appreciate a little ironic smile.

I tried to get the money; Lerice tried. We both telephoned and wrote and argued, but nothing came of it. It appeared that the main expense had been the undertaker, and after all he had done his job. So the whole thing was a complete waste, even more of a waste for the poor devils than I had thought it would be.

The old man from Rhodesia was about Lerice's father's size, so she gave him one of her father's old suits, and he went back home rather better off, for the winter, than he had come.

Reflections

Private Exploration

1. Focus on one of the feelings evoked by Gordimer's story, an emotion that disturbs or moves you. Explore the feeling. Copy out specific passages that seem particularly powerful or important. Consider how emotions you feel may lead you to identify values you hold. Consider why those values seem important to you. What is the relationship between feelings and values?
2. Consider the following passage. How might it illuminate our understanding of the work as a whole?

> She and Petrus both kept their eyes turned on me as I spoke, and, oddly, for those moments they looked exactly alike, though it sounds impossible: my wife with her high, white forehead and her attenuated Englishwoman's body, and the poultry boy, with his horny bare feet below khaki trousers tied at the knees with a string and the peculiar rankness of his nervous sweat coming from his skin.

Public Exploration

Explore this observation by James Baldwin: "It is a terrible and inexorable law that one cannot deny the humanity of another without diminishing one's own: in the face of one's victim, one sees oneself." In addition to Gordimer's story, can you relate this to any of your other readings in "Country of Conscience" or to your own personal experience?

Private Reflection

After discussing the above quotation from Baldwin, or any aspect of "Six Feet of the Country," summarize the views you've heard and how they compare or differ with yours. Has anything changed your insight into the story? Confirmed and made stronger your feelings? Challenged or made you less confident in your initial views?

The Quiet Girl

MAXINE HONG KINGSTON

Most of us eventually found some voice, however faltering. We invented an American-feminine speaking personality, except for that one girl who could not speak up even in Chinese school.

She was a year older than I and was in my class for twelve years. During all those years she read aloud but would not talk. Her older sister was usually beside her; their parents kept the older daughter back to protect the younger one. They were six and seven years old when they began school. Although I had flunked kindergarten, I was the same age as most other students in our class; my parents had probably lied about my age, so I had had a head start and came out even. My younger sister was in the class below me; we were normal ages and normally separated. The parents of the quiet girl, on the other hand, protected both daughters. When is sprinkled, they kept them home from school. The girls did not work for a living the way we did. But in other ways we were the same.

We were similar in sports. We held the bat on our shoulders until we walked to first base. (You got a strike only when you actually struck at the ball.) Sometimes the pitcher wouldn't bother to throw to us. ''Automatic walk,'' the other children would call, sending us on our way. By fourth or fifth grade, though, some of us would try to hit the ball. ''Easy out,'' the other kids would say. I hit the ball a couple of times. Baseball was nice in that there was a definite spot to run to after hitting the ball. Basketball confused me because when I caught the ball I didn't know whom to throw it to. ''Me. Me,'' the kids would be yelling. ''Over here.'' Suddenly it would occur to me I hadn't memorized which ghosts were on my team and which were on the other. When the kids said ''Automatic walk,'' the girl who was quieter than I kneeled with one end of the bat in each hand and placed it carefully on the plate. Then she dusted her hands as she walked to first base, where she rubbed her hands softly, fingers spread. She always got tagged out before second base. She would whisper-read but not talk. Her whisper was as soft as if she had no muscles. She seemed to be breathing from a distance. I heard no anger or tension.

I joined in at lunchtime when the other students, the Chinese too, talked about whether or not she was mute, although obviously she was not if she could read aloud. People told how *they* had tried *their* best to be friendly. *They* said hello, but if she refused to answer, well, they didn't see why they had to say hello anymore. She had no friends of her own but followed her sister everywhere, although people and she herself probably thought I was her friend. I also followed her sister about, who was fairly normal. She was almost two years older and read more than anyone else.

I hated the younger sister, the quiet one. I hated her when she was the last chosen for her team and I, the last chosen for my team. I hated her for her China doll hair cut. I hated her at music time for the wheezes that came out of her plastic flute.

One afternoon in the sixth grade (that year I was arrogant with talk, not knowing there were going to be high school dances and college seminars to set me back), I and my little sister and the quiet girl and her big sister stayed late after school for some reason. The cement was cooling, and the tetherball poles made shadows across the gravel. The hooks at the rope ends were clinking against the poles. We shouldn't have been so late; there was laundry work to do and Chinese school to get to by 5:00. The last time we had stayed late, my mother had phoned the police and told them we had been kidnapped by bandits. The radio stations broadcast our descriptions. I had to get home before she did that again. But sometimes if you loitered long enough in the schoolyard, the other children would have gone home and you could play with the equipment before the office took it away. We were chasing one another through the playground and in and out of the basement, where the playroom and lavatory were. During air raid drills (it was during the Korean War, which you knew about because every day the front page of the newspaper printed a map of Korea with the top part red and going up and down like a window shade), we curled up in this basement. Now everyone was gone. The playroom was army green and had nothing in it but a long trough with drinking spigots in rows. Pipes across the ceiling led to the drinking fountains and to the toilets in the next room. When someone flushed you could hear the water and other matter, which the children named, running inside the big pipe above the drinking spigots. There was one playroom for girls next to the girls' lavatory and one playroom for boys next to the boys' lavatory. The stalls were open and the toilets had no lids, by which we knew that ghosts have no sense of shame or privacy.

Inside the playroom the lightbulbs in cages had already been turned off. Daylight came in x-patterns through the caging at the windows. I looked out and, seeing no one in the schoolyard, ran outside to climb the fire escape upside down, hanging on to the metal stairs with fingers and toes.

I did a flip off the fire escape and ran across the schoolyard. The day was a great eye, and it was not paying much attention to me now. I could disappear with the sun; I could turn quickly sideways and slip into a different world. It seemed I could run faster at this time, and by evening I would be able to fly. As the afternoon wore on we could run into the forbidden places—the boys' big yard, the boys' playroom. We could go into the boys' lavatory and look at the urinals. The only time during school hours I had crossed the boys' yard was when a flatbed truck with a giant thing covered with canvas and tied down with ropes had parked across the street. The children had told one another that it was a gorilla in captivity; we couldn't decide whether the sign said "Trail of the Gorilla" or "Trial of the Gorilla." The thing was as big as a house. The teachers couldn't stop us from hysterically rushing to the fence and clinging to the wire mesh. Now I ran across the boys' yard clear to the Cyclone fence and thought about the hair that I had seen sticking out of the canvas. It was going to be summer soon, so you could feel that freedom coming on too.

I ran back into the girls' yard, and there was the quiet sister all by herself. I ran past her, and she followed me into the girls' lavatory. My footsteps rang hard against cement and tile because of the taps I had nailed into my shoes. Her footsteps were soft, padding after me. There was no one in the lavatory but the two of us. I ran all around the rows of twenty-five open stalls to make sure of that. No sisters. I think we must have been playing hide-and-go-seek. She was not good at hiding by herself and usually followed her sister; they'd hide in the same place. They must have gotten separated. In this growing twilight, a child could hide and never be found.

I stopped abruptly in front of the sinks, and she came running toward me before she could stop herself, so that she almost collided with me. I walked closer. She backed away, puzzlement, then alarm in her eyes.

"You're going to talk," I said, my voice steady and normal, as it is when talking to the familiar, the weak, and the small. "I am going to make you talk, you sissy-girl." She stopped backing away and stood fixed.

I looked into her face so I could hate it close up. She wore black bangs, and her cheeks were pink and white. She was baby-soft. I thought that I could put my thumb on her nose and push it bonelessly in, indent her face. I could poke dimples into her cheeks. I could work her face around like dough. She stood still, and I did not want to look at her face anymore; I hated fragility. I walked around her, looked her up and down the way the Mexican and Negro girls did when they fought, so tough. I hated her weak neck, the way it did not support her head but let it droop; her head would fall backward. I stared at the curve of her nape. I wished I was able to see what my own neck looked like from the back and sides. I hoped it did not look like hers; I wanted a stout neck. I grew my hair long to hide it in case it was a flower-stem neck. I walked around to the front of her to hate her face some more.

I reached up and took the fatty part of her cheek, not dough, but meat, between my thumb and finger. This close, and I saw no pores. "Talk," I said. "Are you going to talk?" Her skin was fleshy, like squid out of which the glassy blades of bones had been pulled. I wanted tough skin, hard brown skin. I had callused my hands; I had scratched dirt to blacken the nails, which I cut straight across to make stubby fingers. I gave her face a squeeze. "Talk." When I let go, the pink rushed back into my white thumbprint on her skin. I walked around to her side. "Talk!" I shouted into the side of her head. Her straight hair hung, the same all these years, no ringlets or braids or permanents. I squeezed her other cheek. "Are you? Huh? Are you going to talk?" She tried to shake her head, but I had hold of her face. She had no muscles to jerk away. Her skin seemed to stretch. I let go in horror. What if it came away in my hand? "No, huh?" I said, rubbing the touch of her off my fingers. "Say 'No,' then," I said. I gave her another pinch and a twist. "Say 'No.' " She shook her head, her straight hair turning with her head, not swinging side to side like the pretty girls'. She was so neat. Her neatness bothered me. I hated the way she folded the wax paper from her lunch; she did not wad her brown paper bag and her school papers. I hated her clothes—the blue pastel cardigan, the white blouse with the collar that lay flat over the cardigan, the home-made flat, cotton skirt she wore when everybody else was wearing flared skirts. I hated pastels; I would wear black always. I squeezed again, harder even though her cheek had a weak rubbery feeling I did not like. I squeezed one cheek, then the other, back and forth until the tears ran out of her eyes as if I had pulled them out. "Stop crying," I said, but although she habitually followed me around, she did not obey. Her eyes dripped; her nose dripped. She wiped her eyes with her papery fingers. The skin on her hands and arms seemed powdery-dry, like tracing paper, onion paper. I hated her fingers. I could snap them like breadsticks. I pushed her hands down. "Say 'Hi,' " I said. " 'Hi'. Like that. Say your name. Go ahead. Say it. Or are you stupid? You're so stupid, you don't know your own name, is that it? When I say, 'What's your name?' you just blurt it out, O.K.? What's your name?" Last year the whole class had laughed at a boy who couldn't fill out a form because he didn't know his father's name. The teacher sighed, exasperated and was very sarcastic, "Don't you notice things? What does your mother call him?" she said. The class laughed at how dumb he was not to notice things. "She calls him father of me," he said. Even we laughed although we knew that his mother did not call his father by name, and a son does not know his father's name. We laughed and were relieved that our parents had had the foresight to tell us some names we could give the teachers. "If you're not stupid," I said to the quiet girl, "what's your name?" She shook her head, and some hair caught in the tears; wet black hair stuck to the side of the pink and white face. I reached up (she was taller than I) and took a strand of hair. I pulled it. "Well, then, let's honk your hair," I said. "Honk. Honk." Then I pulled the other side—"ho-o-n-nk"—a long pull; "ho-o-n-n-nk"—a longer pull. I could see her little white ears, like white cutworms curled underneath the hair. "Talk!" I yelled into each cutworm.

I looked right at her. "I know you talk," I said. "I've heard you." Her eyebrows flew up. Something in those black eyes was startled, and I pursued it. "I was walking past your house when you didn't know I was there. I heard you yell in English and in Chinese. You weren't just talking. You were shouting.

I heard you shout. You were saying, 'Where are you?' Say that again. Go ahead, just the way you did at home." I yanked harder on the hair, but steadily, not jerking. I did not want to pull it out. "Go ahead. Say, 'Where are you?' Say it loud enough for your sister to come. Call her. Make her come help you. Call her name. I'll stop if she comes. So call. Go ahead."

She shook her head, her mouth curved down, crying. I could see her tiny white teeth, baby teeth. I wanted to grow big strong yellow teeth. "You do have a tongue," I said. "So use it." I pulled the hair at her temples, pulled the tears out of her eyes. "Say, 'Ow' " I said. "Just 'Ow.' Say, 'Let go.' Go ahead. Say it. I'll honk you again if you don't say, 'Let me alone.' Say, 'Leave me alone,' and I'll let you go. I will. I'll let go if you say it. You can stop this anytime you want to, you know. All you have to do is tell me to stop. Just say, 'Stop.' You're just asking for it, aren't you? You're just asking for another honk. Well then, I'll have to give you another honk. Say, 'Stop.' " But she didn't. I had to pull again and again.

Sounds did come out of her mouth, sobs, chokes, noises that were almost words. Snot ran out of her nose. She tried to wipe it on her hands, but there was too much of it. She used her sleeve. "You're disgusting," I told her. "Look at you, snot streaming down your nose, and you won't say a word to stop it. You're such a nothing." I moved behind her and pulled the hair growing out of her weak neck. I let go. I stood silent for a long time. Then I screamed, "Talk!" I would scare the words out of her. If she had had little bound feet, the toes twisted under the balls, I would have jumped up and landed on them—crunch!—stomped on them with my iron shoes. She cried hard, sobbing aloud. "Cry, 'Mama,' " I said. "Come on. Cry, 'Mama.' Say, 'Stop it.' "

I put my finger on her pointed chin. "I don't like you. I don't like the weak little toots you make on your flute. Wheeze. Wheeze. I don't like the way you don't swing at the ball. I don't like the way you're the last one chosen. I don't like the way you can't make a fist for tetherball. Why don't you make a fist? Come on. Get tough. Come on. Throw fists." I pushed at her long hands; they swung limply at her sides. Her fingers were so long, I thought maybe they had an extra joint. They couldn't possibly make fists like other people's. "Make a fist," I said. "Come on. Just fold those fingers up; fingers on the inside, thumbs on the outside. Say something. Honk me back. You're so tall, and you let me pick on you.

"Would you like a hanky? I can't get you one with embroidery on it or crocheting along the edges, but I'll get you some toilet paper if you tell me to. Go ahead. Ask me. I'll get it for you if you ask." She did not stop crying. "Why don't you scream, 'Help'?" I suggested. "Say, 'Help.' Go ahead." She cried on. "O.K. O.K. Don't talk. Just scream, and I'll let you go. Won't that feel good? Go ahead. Like this." I screamed not too loudly. My voice hit the tile and rang it as if I had thrown a rock at it. The stalls opened wider and the toilets wider and darker. Shadows leaned at angles I had not seen before. I was very late. Maybe a janitor had locked me in with this girl for the night. Her black eyes blinked and stared, blinked and stared. I felt dizzy from hunger. We had been in this lavatory together forever. My mother would call the police again if I didn't bring my sister home soon. "I'll let you go if you say just one word," I said. "You can even say 'a' or 'the,' and I'll let you go. Come on. Please." She didn't shake her head anymore, only cried steadily, so much water coming out of her. I could see the two duct holes where the tears welled out. Quarts of tears but no words. I grabbed her by the shoulder. I could feel bones. The light was coming in queerly through the frosted glass with the chicken wire embedded in it. Her crying was like an animal's—a seal's—and it echoed around the basement. "Do you want to stay here all night?" I asked. "Your mother is wondering what happened to her baby. You wouldn't want to have her mad at you. You'd better say something." I shook her shoulder. I pulled her hair again. I squeezed her face. "Come on! Talk! Talk! Talk!" She didn't seem to feel it anymore when I pulled her hair. "There's nobody here but you and me. This isn't a classroom or a playground or a crowd. I'm just one person. You can talk in front of one person. Don't make me pull harder and harder until you talk." But her hair seemed to stretch; she did not say a word. "I'm going to pull harder. Don't make me pull anymore, or your hair will come out and you're going to be bald. Do you want to be bald? You don't want to be bald, do you?"

Far away, coming from the edge of town, I heard whistles blow. The cannery was changing shifts, letting out the afternoon people, and still we were here at school. It was a sad sound—work done. The air was lonelier after the sound died.

"Why won't you talk?" I started to cry. What if I couldn't stop, and everyone would want to know what happened? "Now look what you've done," I scolded. "You're going to pay for this. I want to know why. And you're going to tell me why. You don't see I'm trying to help you out, do you? Do you want to be like this, dumb (do you know what dumb means?), your whole life? Don't you ever want to be a cheerleader? Or a pompon girl? What are you going to do for a living? Yeah, you're going to have to work because you can't be a housewife. Somebody has to marry you before you can be a housewife. And you, you are a plant. Do you know that? That's all you are if you don't talk. If you don't talk, you can't have a personality. You'll have no personality and no hair. You've got to let people know you have a personality and a brain. You think somebody is going to take care of you all your stupid life? You think you'll always have your big sister? You think somebody's going to marry you, is that it? Well, you're not the type that gets dates, let alone gets married. Nobody's going to notice you. And you have to talk for interviews, speak right up in front of the boss. Don't you know that? You're so dumb. Why do I waste my time on you?" Sniffling and snorting, I couldn't stop crying and talking at the same time. I kept wiping my nose on my arm, my sweater lost somewhere (probably not worn because my mother said to wear a sweater). It seemed as if I had spent my life in that basement, doing the worst thing I had yet done to another person. "I'm doing this for your own good," I said. "Don't you dare tell anyone I've been bad to you. Talk. Please talk."

I was getting dizzy from the air I was gulping. Her sobs and my sobs were bounding wildly off the tile, sometimes together, sometimes alternating. "I don't understand why you won't say just one word," I cried, clenching my teeth. My knees were shaking, and I hung on to her hair to stand up. Another time I'd stayed too late, I had had to walk around two Negro kids who were bonking each other's head on the concrete. I went back later to see if the concrete had cracks in it. "Look. I'll give you something if you talk. I'll give you my pencil box. I'll buy you some candy. O.K.? What do you want? Tell me. Just say it, and I'll give it to you. Just say, 'yes,' or, 'O.K.,' or, 'Baby Ruth.' " But she didn't want anything.

I had stopped pinching her cheek because I did not like the feel of her skin. I would go crazy if it came away in my hands. "I skinned her," I would have to confess.

Suddenly I heard footsteps hurrying through the basement, and her sister ran into the lavatory calling her name. "Oh, there you are," I said. "We've been waiting for you. I was only trying to teach her to talk. She wouldn't cooperate, though." Her sister went into one of the stalls and got handfuls of toilet paper and wiped her off. Then we found my sister, and we walked home together. "Your family really ought to force her to speak," I advised all the way home. "You mustn't pamper her."

The world is sometimes just, and I spent the next eighteen months sick in bed with a mysterious illness. There was no pain and no symptoms, though the middle line in my left palm broke in two. Instead of starting junior high school, I lived like the Victorian recluses I read about. I had a rented hospital bed in the living room, where I watched soap operas on TV, and my family cranked me up and down. I saw no one but my family, who took good care of me. I could have no visitors, no other relatives, no villagers. My bed was against the west window, and I watched the seasons change the peach tree. I had a bell to ring for help. I used a bedpan. It was the best year and a half of my life. Nothing happened.

But one day my mother, the doctor, said, "You're ready to get up today. It's time to get up and go to school." I walked about outside to get my legs working, leaning on a staff I cut from the peach tree. The sky and trees, the sun were immense—no longer framed by a window, no longer grayed with a fly screen. I sat down on the sidewalk in amazement—the night, the stars. But at school I had to figure out again how to talk. I met again the poor girl I had tormented. She had not changed. She wore the same clothes, hair cut, and manner as when we were in elementary school, no make-up on the pink and white face, while the other Asian girls were starting to tape their eyelids. She continued to be able to read aloud. But there was hardly any reading aloud anymore, less and less as we got into high school.

I was wrong about nobody taking care of her. Her sister became a clerk-typist and stayed unmarried. They lived with their mother and father. She did not have to leave the house except to go to the movies. She was supported. She was protected by her family, as they would normally have done in China if they could have afforded it, not sent off to school with strangers, ghosts, boys.

Reflections

Private Exploration

1. After your first reading of "The Quiet Girl," explore as quickly and spontaneously as possible your initial impressions. Then reread the essay, this time more slowly. When you've completed your second reading, begin writing again. Did you gain new insights on the second reading? What new questions came to mind? Has your perception of the work changed?
2. Kingston writes about the worst thing she ever did to another person. Reflect on your own past. Write on a single incident telling the story of the worst thing you ever did to another person (or that another person did to you). Share the details and images, the actions and dialogue, just as Kingston does. Consider your motivation for acting as you did, the effect of the incident, and what you learned about yourself and others.

Public Exploration

What is needed to trigger the power of conscience? Explore how the urge toward conformity can control us, even force us to hide what we are inside or to act in ways unauthentic to who we really are? How can we become aware of our true selves vs. the self imposed on us?

Private Reflection

Use your notebook explorations to build upon any ideas that may have arisen out of discussing this essay or the above question with others. Push ideas as far as you can take them. Do not accept cliches or easy answers. Every time you come to a point where you seem unable to continue, ask another question: What else is going on here? What can I learn from this? What does this tell me about my own sense of values?

The Greatest Man in the World

JAMES THURBER

Looking back on it now, from the vantage point of 1950, one can only marvel that it hadn't happened long before it did. The United States of America had been, ever since Kitty Hawk, blindly constructing the elaborate petard by which, sooner or later, it must be hoist. It was inevitable that some day there would come roaring out of the skies a national hero of insufficient intelligence, background, and character successfully to endure the mounting orgies of glory prepared for aviators who stayed up a long time or flew a great distance. Both Lindbergh and Byrd, fortunately for national decorum and international amity, had been gentlemen; so had our other famous aviators. They wore their laurels gracefully, withstood the awful weather of publicity, married excellent women, usually of fine family, and quietly retired to private life and the enjoyment of their varying fortunes. No untoward incidents, on a worldwide scale, marred the perfection of their conduct on the perilous heights of fame. The exception to the rule was, however, bound to occur and it did, in July, 1937, when Jack ("Pal") Smurch, erstwhile mechanics' helper in a small garage in Westfield, Iowa, flew a second-hand, single-motored Bresthaven Dragon-Fly III monoplane all the way around the world, without stopping.

Never before in the history of aviation had such a flight as Smurch's ever been dreamed of. No one had even taken seriously the weird floating auxiliary gas tanks, invention of the mad New Hampshire professor of astronomy, Dr. Charles Lewis Gresham, upon which Smurch placed full reliance. When the garage worker, a slightly built, surly, unprepossessing young man of twenty-two appeared at Roosevelt Field in early July, 1937, slowly chewing a great quid of scrap tobacco, and announced "Nobody ain't seen no flyin' yet," the newspapers touched briefly and satirically upon his projected twenty-five-thousand-mild flight. Aeronautical and automotive experts dismissed the idea curtly, implying that it was a hoax, a publicity stunt. The rusty, battered, second-hand plane wouldn't go. The Gresham auxiliary tanks wouldn't work. It was simply a cheap joke.

Smurch, however, after calling on a girl in Brooklyn who worked in the flap-folding department of a large paper-box factory, a girl whom he later described as his "sweet patootie," climbed nonchalantly into his ridiculous plane at dawn of the memorable seventh of July, 1937, spat a curve of tobacco juice into the still air, and took off, carrying with him only a gallon of bootleg gin and six pounds of salami.

When the garage boy thundered out over the ocean the papers were forced to record, in all seriousness, that a mad, unknown young man—his name was variously misspelled—had actually set out upon a preposterous attempt to span the world in a rickety, one-engined contraption, trusting to the long-distance refueling device of a crazy schoolmaster. When, nine days later, without having stopped once, the tiny plane appeared above San Francisco Bay, headed for New York, spluttering and choking, to be sure, but still magnificently and miraculously aloft, the headlines, which long since had crowded everything else off the front page—even the shooting of the Governor of Illinois by the Vileti gang—swelled to unprecedented size, and the news stories began to run to twenty-five and thirty columns. It was noticeable, however, that the accounts of the epoch-making flight touched rather lightly upon the aviator himself. This was not because facts about the hero as a man were too meagre, but because they were too complete.

Reporters, who had been rushed out to Iowa when Smurch's plane was first sighted over the little French coast town of Serly-le-Mar, to dig up the story of the great man's life, had promptly discovered that the story of his life could not be printed. His mother, a sullen short-order cook in a shack restaurant on the edge of a tourists' camping ground near Westfield, met all enquiries as to her son with an angry, "Ah, the hell with him; I hope he drowns." His father appeared to be in jail somewhere for stealing spotlights and laprobes from tourists' automobiles; his younger brother, a weak-minded lad, had but recently escaped from the Preston, Iowa Reformatory and was already wanted in several Western towns for the theft of money-order blanks from post offices. These alarming discoveries were still piling up at the very time that Pal Smurch, the greatest hero of the twentieth century, blear-eyed, dead for sleep, half-starved, was piloting his crazy junk-heap high above the region in which the lamentable story of his private life was being unearthed, headed for New York under greater glory than any man of his time had ever known.

The necessity for printing some account in the papers of the young man's career and personality had led to a remarkable predicament. It was of course impossible to reveal the facts, for a tremendous popular feeling in favor of the young hero had sprung up, like a grass fire, when he was halfway across Europe on his flight around the globe. He was, therefore, described as a modest chap, taciturn, blond, popular with his friends, popular with girls. The only available snapshot of Smurch, taken at the wheel of a phony automobile in a cheap photo studio at an amusement park, was touched up so that the little vulgarian looked quite handsome. His twisted leer was smoothed into a pleasant smile. The truth was, in this way, kept from the youth's ecstatic compatriots; they did not dream that the Smurch family was despised and feared by its neighbors in the obscure Iowa town, nor that the hero himself, because of numerous unsavory exploits, had come to be regarded in Westfield as a nuisance and a menace. He had, the reporters discovered, once knifed the principal of his high school—not mortally, to be sure, but he had knifed him; and on another occasion, surprised in the act of stealing an altar-cloth from a church, he had bashed the sacristan over the head with a pot of Easter lilies; for each of these offences he had served a sentence in the reformatory.

Inwardly, the authorities, both in New York and in Washington, prayed that an understanding Providence might, however awful such a thing seemed, bring disaster to the rusty, battered plane and its illustrious pilot, whose unheard-of flight had aroused the civilized world to hosannas of hysterical praise. The authorities were convinced that the character of the renowned aviator was such that the limelight of adulation was bound to reveal him to all the world, as a congenital hooligan mentally and morally unequipped to cope with his own prodigious fame. "I trust," said the Secretary of State, at one of many secret Cabinet meetings called to consider the national dilemma, "I trust that his mother's prayer will be answered," by which he referred to Mrs. Emma Smurch's wish that her son might be drowned. It was, however, too late for that—Smurch had leaped the Atlantic and then the Pacific as if they were millponds. At three minutes after two o'clock in the afternoon of 17 July, 1937, the garage boy brought his idiotic plane into Roosevelt Field for a perfect three-point landing.

It had, of course, been out of the question to arrange a modest little reception for the greatest flier in the history of the world. He was received at

Roosevelt Field with such elaborate and pretentious ceremonies as rocked the world. Fortunately, however, the worn and spent hero promptly swooned, had to be removed bodily from his plane, and was spirited from the field without having opened his mouth once. Thus he did not jeopardize the dignity of this first reception, a reception illumined by the presence of the Secretaries of War and the Navy, Mayor Michael J. Moriarity of New York, the Premier of Canada, Governors Fanniman, Groves, McFeely, and Critchfield, and a brilliant array of European diplomats. Smurch did not, in fact, come to in time to take part in the gigantic hullabaloo arranged at City Hall for the next day. He was rushed to a secluded nursing home and confined to bed. It was nine days before he was able to get up, or to be more exact, before he was permitted to get up. Meanwhile the greatest minds in the country, in solemn assembly, had arranged a secret conference of city, state and government officials, which Smurch was to attend for the purpose of being instructed in the ethics and behavior of heroism.

On the day that the little mechanic was finally allowed to get up and dress and, for the first time in two weeks, took a great chew of tobacco, he was permitted to receive the newspapermen—this by way of testing him out. Smurch did not wait for questions. "Youse guys," he said—and the *Times* man winced—"youse guys can tell the cock-eyed world dat I put it over on Lindbergh, see? Yeh—an' made an ass o' them two frogs." The "two frogs" was a reference to a pair of gallant French fliers who, in attempting a flight only halfway round the world, had, two weeks before, unhappily been lost at sea. The *Times* man was bold enough, at this point, to sketch out for Smurch the accepted formula for interviews in cases of this kind; he explained that there should be no arrogant statements belittling the achievements of other heroes, particularly heroes of foreign nations. "Ah, the hell with that," said Smurch. "I did it, see? I did it, an' I'm talkin' about it." And he did talk about it.

None of this extraordinary interview was, of course, printed. On the contrary, the newspapers, already under the disciplined direction of a secret directorate created for the occasion and composed of statesmen and editors, gave out to a panting and restless world that "Jacky," as he had been arbitrarily nicknamed, would consent to say only that he was very happy and that anyone could have done what he did. "My achievement has been, I fear, slightly exaggerated," the *Times* man's article had him protest, with a modest smile. These newspaper stories were kept from the hero, a restriction which did not serve to abate the rising malevolence of his temper. The situation was, indeed, extremely grave, for Pal Smurch was, as he kept insisting, "rarin' to go." He could not much longer be kept from a nation clamorous to lionize him. It was the most desperate crisis the United States of America had faced since the sinking of the *Lusitania.*

On the afternoon of the twenty-seventh of July, Smurch was spirited away to a conference-room in which were gathered mayors, governors, government officials, behaviorist psychologists, and editors. He gave them each a limp, moist paw and a brief unlovely grin. "Hah ya?" he said. When Smurch was seated, the Mayor of New York arose and, with obvious pessimism, attempted to explain what he must say and how he must act when presented to the world, ending his talk with a high tribute to the hero's courage and integrity. The Mayor was followed by Governor Fanniman of New York, who, after a touching declaration of faith, introduced Cameron Spottiswood, Second Secretary of the American Embassy in Paris, the gentlemen selected to coach Smurch in the amenities of public ceremonies. Sitting in a chair, with a soiled yellow tie in his hand and his shirt open at the throat, unshaved, smoking a rolled cigarette, Jack Smurch listened with a leer on his lips. "I get ya, I get ya," he cut in nastily. "Ya want me to act like a softy, huh? Ya want me to ack like that—baby-faced Lindbergh, huh? Well, nuts to that, see?" Everyone took in his breath sharply; it was a sigh and a hiss. "Mr. Lindbergh," began a United States Senator, purple with rage, "and Mr. Byrd—" Smurch, who was paring his nails with a jacknife, cut in again, "Byrd!" he exclaimed. "Aw fa God's sake, dat big—" Somebody shut off his blasphemies with a sharp word. A newcomer had entered the room. Everyone stood up, except Smurch, who, still busy with his nails, did not even glance up. "Mr. Smurch," said someone sternly, the President of the United States!" It had been thought that the presence of the Chief Executive might have a chastening effect upon the young hero, and the former had been, thanks to the remarkable co-operation of the press, secretly brought to the obscure conference-room.

A great, painful silence fell. Smurch looked up, waved a hand at the President. "How ya comin'?" he asked, and began rolling a fresh cigarette. The silence deepened. Someone coughed in a strained way. "Geez, it's hot, ain't it?" said Smurch. He loosened two more shirt buttons, revealing a hairy chest and the tattooed word "Sadie" enclosed in a stenciled heart. The great and important men in the room, faced by the most serious crisis in recent American history, exchanged worried frowns. Nobody seemed to know how to proceed. "Come awn, come awn," said Smurch. "Let's get the hell out of here! When do I start cuttin' in on de parties, huh? And what's they goin' to be *in* it?" He rubbed a thumb and a forefinger together meaningly. "Money!" exclaimed a state senator, shocked, pale. "Yeh, money," said Pal, flipping his cigarette out of a window, "an' big money." He began rolling a fresh cigarette. "Big money," he repeated, frowning over the rice paper. He tilted back in his chair, and leered at each gentleman, separately, the leer of an animal that knows its power, the leer of a leopard loose in a bird-and-dog shop. "Aw, fa God's sake, let's get some place where it's cooler," he said. "I been cooped up plenty for three weeks!"

Smurch stood up and walked over to an open window, where he stood staring down into the street, nine floors below. The faint shouting of newsboys floated up to him. He made out his name. "Hot dog!" he cried, grinning, ecstatic. He leaned out over the sill. "You tell 'em, babies!" he shouted down. "Hot diggity dog!" In the tense little knot of men standing behind him, a quick, mad impulse flared up. An unspoken word of appeal, of command, seemed to ring through the room. Yet it was deadly silent. Charles K. L. Brand, secretary to the Mayor of New York City, happened to be standing nearest Smurch; he looked inquiringly at the President of the United States. The

President, pale, grim, nodded shortly. Brand, a tall, powerfully built man, once a tackle at Rutgers, stepped forward, seized the greatest man in the world by his left shoulder and the seat of his pants, and pushed him out of the window.

"My God, he's fallen out the window!" cried a quick-witted editor.

"Get me out of here!" cried the President. Several men sprang to his side and he was hurriedly escorted out of a door toward a side-entrance of the building. The editor of the Associated Press took charge, being used to such things. Crisply he ordered certain men to leave, others to stay; quickly he outlined a story which all the papers were to agree on, sent two men to the street to handle that end of the tragedy, commanded a Senator to sob and two Congressmen to go to pieces nervously. In a word, he skillfully set the stage for the gigantic task that was to follow, the task of breaking to a grief-stricken world the sad story of the untimely, accidental death of its most illustrious and spectacular figure.

The funeral was, as you know, the most elaborate, the finest, the solemnest, and the saddest ever held in the United States of America. The monument in Arlington Cemetery, with its clean white shaft of marble and the simple device of a tiny plane on its base, is a place for pilgrims, in deep reverence, to visit. The nations of the world paid lofty tributes to little Jacky Smurch, America's greatest hero. At a given hour there were two minutes of silence throughout the nation. Even the inhabitants of the small, bewildered town of Westfield, Iowa, observed this touching ceremony; agents of the Department of Justice saw to that. One of them was especially assigned to stand grimly in the doorway of a little shack restaurant on the edge of the tourists' camping ground just outside the town. There, under his stern scrutiny, Mrs. Emma Smurch bowed her head above two hamburger steaks sizzling on her grill—bowed her head and turned away, so that the Secret Service man could not see the twisted, strangely familiar, leer on her lips.

Reflections

Private Exploration

1. Jack Smurch—"the greatest hero of the twentieth century." Consider the man as he actually is in comparison to the man created by newspaper accounts. Why do the journalists refuse to print the facts? What is really going on here?
2. What happens to individuals who refuse to conform to public standards of "the hero"? Can you relate this to any of your previous readings in "The Country of Conscience"?

Public Exploration

Heroes represent the values of our society. The individuals we elevate to be our heroes change constantly. For many, John F. Kennedy, Robert Kennedy, and Martin Luther King shaped the vision of the 60s. In the 1970s Neil Armstrong stepped on the moon and became a national hero, although others might have chosen Sister Teresa as the more important model for life on earth. In the 80s, some in America found heroes in Ronald Reagan and Ollie North.

Consider your own contemporary heroes and heroines. As a group, zero in on two or three people who in your view qualify as heroes. Consider what you respect most about them, their accomplishments, or contributions. What common qualities, if any, do they share? What values do they represent? If you feel heroes do not exist today, consider why, and what that might indicate about our values or our vision of ourselves.

Private Reflection

If you've had an opportunity to discuss the above question with others, write further in your notebook about the concept of the hero. Consider specifically the values we want from heroes, whether such values can be found today, and what it all says about ourselves.

• Ulysses •

ALFRED, LORD TENNYSON

It little profits that an idle king,
By this still hearth, among these barren crags,
Matched with an aged wife, I mete and dole
Unequal laws unto a savage race,
That hoard, and sleep, and feed, and know not me.
I cannot rest from travel; I will drink
Life to the lees. All times I have enjoyed
Greatly, have suffered greatly, both with those
That loved me, and alone; on shore, and when
Thro' scudding drifts the rainy Hyades
Vext the dim sea. I am become a name;
For always roaming with a hungry heart
Much have I seen and known,—cities of men
And manners, climates, councils, governments,
Myself not least, but honored of them all,—
And drunk delight of battle with my peers,
Far on the ringing plains of windy Troy.
I am a part of all that I have met;
Yet all experience is an arch wherethro'
Gleams that untravelled world whose margin fades
For ever and for ever when I move.
How dull it is to pause, to make an end,
To rust unburnished, not to shine in use!
As tho' to breathe were life! Life piled on life
Were all too little, and of one to me
Little remains; but every hour is saved

From that eternal silence, something more,
A bringer of new things; and vile it were
For some three suns to store and hoard myself,
And this gray spirit yearning in desire
To follow knowledge like a sinking star,
Beyond the utmost bound of human thought.

This is my son, mine own Telemachus,
To whom I leave the scepter and the isle,—
Well-loved of me, discerning to fulfill
This labor, by slow prudence to make mild
A rugged people, and thro' soft degrees
Subdue them to the useful and the good.
Most blameless is he, centered in the sphere
Of common duties, decent not to fail
In offices of tenderness, and pay
Meet adoration to my household gods,
When I am gone. He works his work, I mine.

There lies the port; the vessel puffs her sail;
There gloom the dark, broad seas. My mariners,
Souls that have toiled, and wrought, and thought with me,—
That ever with a frolic welcome took
The thunder and the sunshine, and opposed
Free hearts, free foreheads—you and I are old;
Old age hath yet his honor and his toil.
Death closes all; but something ere the end,
Some work of noble note, may yet be done,
Not unbecoming men that strove with Gods.
The lights begin to twinkle from the rocks;
The long day wanes; the slow moon climbs; the deep
Moans round with many voices. Come, my friends.
'Tis not too late to seek a newer world.
Push off, and sitting well in order smite
The sounding furrows; for my purpose holds
To sail beyond the sunset, and the baths
Of all the western stars, until I die.
It may be that the gulfs will wash us down;
It may be we shall touch the Happy Isles,
And see the great Achilles, whom we knew.
Tho' much is taken, much abides; and tho'
We are not now that strength which in old days
Moved earth and heaven, that which we are, we are.
One equal temper of heroic hearts,
Made weak by time and fate, but strong in will
To strive, to seek, to find, and not to yield.

Reflections

Private Exploration

1. Select five or six lines of "Ulysses" that seem important to you and copy them word for word. Explore how those lines, images, or metaphors have meaning for you. How do they open up an understanding into the poem as a whole?
2. Compare Thurber's "The Greatest Hero in the World" to Tennyson's "Ulysses." Are there not in fact some distinct similarities? Are there also crucial differences? What is it that makes one character a hero, the other character a jerk?

Public Exploration

Although Ulysses may see himself as a hero "made weak by time and fate," yet "strong in will," setting off "to sail beyond the sunset"—all of which sounds courageous and noble—discuss his attitude toward those he plans to leave behind: his wife, his son, and the people of his kingdom. What can be learned by focusing on how this hero perceives himself in relation to others? As a group, draw up a list of his "noble" qualities and his less-than-noble qualities. Does this fuller perspective make him more or less heroic? More or less honorable? Could the same list be made up for more recent, real-life heroes (John F. Kennedy, Martin Luther King, Mikhail Gorbachev, Vaclav Havel)?

Private Reflection

Reflect on how or why the following attitude could ever be considered heroic? Would it still be thought so in America by your generation? Would you have the courage, if that's what it is, to follow such a path?

> To follow knowledge like a sinking star,
> Beyond the utmost bound of human thought.

Crito

PLATO

Translated by **Benjamin Jowett**, *revised by* **Peter White**

Socrates: Why have you come at this hour, Crito? It must be quite early?

Crito: Yes, certainly.

Soc: What is the exact time?

Cr: The dawn is breaking.

Soc: I wonder that the keeper of the prison would let you in.

Cr: He knows me, because I often come, Socrates; moreover, I have done him a kindness.

Soc: And are you only just arrived?

Cr: I came some time ago.

Soc: Then why did you sit and say nothing instead of at once awakening me?

Cr: That I could never have done, Socrates. I only wish I were not so sleepless and distressed myself. I have been looking at you, wondering how you can sleep so comfortably, and I didn't wake you on purpose, so that you could go on sleeping in perfect comfort. All through your life, I have often thought you were favored with a good disposition, but I have never been so impressed as in the present misfortune, seeing how easily and tranquilly you bear it.

Soc: Why, Crito, when a man has reached my age he ought not to be repining at the approach of death.

Cr: And yet other old men find themselves in similar misfortunes, and age does not prevent them from repining.

Soc: That is true. But you have not told me why you come at this early hour.

Cr: I come with a message which is painful—not, I expect, to you, but painful and oppressive for me and all your friends, and I think it weighs most heavily of all on me.

Soc: What? Has the ship come from Delos, on the arrival of which I am to die?

Cr: No, the ship has not actually arrived, but she will probably be here today, as persons who have come from Sunium tell me that they left her there; and therefore tomorrow, Socrates, will be the last day of your life.

Soc: Very well, Crito; if such is the will of the gods, I am willing; but my belief is that there will be a day's delay.

Cr: Why do you think so?

Soc: I will tell you. I am to die on the day after the arrival of the ship.

Cr: Yes; that is what the authorities say.

Soc: But I do not think that the ship will be here until tomorrow; this I infer from a vision which I had last night, or rather only just now, when you fortunately allowed me to sleep.

Cr: And what was the nature of the vision?

Soc: There appeared to me the likeness of a woman, fair and comely, clothed in bright raiment, who called to me and said: O Socrates.

> "The third day hence to fertile Phthia shalt thou come."

Cr: What a singular dream, Socrates!

Soc: There can be no doubt about the meaning, Crito, I think.

Cr: Yes; the meaning is only too clear. But, oh! my beloved Socrates, let me entreat you once more to take my advice and escape. For if you die, I shall not only lose a friend who can never be replaced, but there is another evil: people who do not know you and me will believe that I might have saved you if I had been willing to give money but that I did not care. Now, can there be a worse disgrace than this—that I should be thought to value money more than the life of a friend? For the many will not be persuaded that I wanted you to escape and that you refused.

Soc: But why, my dear Crito, should we care about the opinion of the many? Good men, and they are the only persons who are worth considering, will think of these things truly as they occurred.

Cr: But you see, Socrates, that the opinion of the many must be regarded, for what is now happening shows that they can do the greatest evil to anyone who has lost their good opinion.

Soc: I only wish it were so, Crito, and that the many could do the greatest evil; for then they would also be able to do the greatest good—and what a fine thing this would be! But in reality they can do neither; for they cannot make a man either wise or foolish, and whatever result they produce is the result of chance.

Cr: Well, I will not dispute with you; but please tell me, Socrates, whether you are not acting out of regard to me and your other friends: Are you not afraid that, if you escape from prison, we may get into trouble with the informers for having stolen you away and lose either the whole or a great part of our property—or that even a worse evil may happen to us? Now, if you fear on our account, be at ease; for in order to save you, we ought surely to run this or even a greater risk; be persuaded, then, and do as I say.

Soc: Yes, Crito, that is one fear which you mention, but by no means the only one.

Cr: Fear not—there are persons who are willing to get you out of prison at no great cost; and as for the informers, they are far from being exorbitant in their demands—a little money will satisfy them. My means, which are certainly ample, are at your service; and if, out of solicitude about me, you hesitate to use mine, there are non-Athenians here who will give you the use of theirs, and one of them, Simmias the Theban, has brought a large sum of money for this very purpose; and Cebes and many others are prepared to spend their money in helping you to escape. Therefore do not hesitate to save yourself because you are worried about this, and do not say, as you did in the court, that you will have difficulty in knowing what to do with yourself anywhere else. For men will love you in other places to which you may go, and not in Athens only; there are friends of mine in Thessaly, if you would like to go to them, who will value and protect you, and no Thessalian will give you any trouble. Nor can I think that you are at all justified, Socrates, in betraying your own life when you might be saved. You are only working to bring about what your enemies, who want to destroy you, would and did in fact work to accomplish. And further, I should say that you are deserting your own children; for you might bring them up and educate them, instead of which you go away and leave them, and they will have to take their chances; and if they do not meet with the usual fate of orphans, there will be small thanks to you. No man should bring children into the world who is unwilling to persevere to the end in their nurture and education. But you appear to be choosing the easier part, not the better and manlier, which would have been more becoming in one who has professed a life-long concern for virtue, like yourself. And indeed, I am ashamed not only of you but of us, who are your friends, when I reflect that the whole business will be attributed entirely to our want of courage. The trial need never have come on or might have been managed differently. And now it may seem that we have made a ridiculous bungle of this last chance, thanks to our lack of toughness and courage, since we failed to save you and you failed to save yourself, even though it was possible and practicable if we were good for anything at all. So, Socrates, you must not let this turn into a disgrace as well as a tragedy for yourself and us. Make up your mind then, or rather have your mind already made up; for the time of deliberation is over, and there is only one thing to be done, which must be done this very night, and, if we delay at all, it will be no longer practicable or possible; I beseech you therefore, Socrates, be persuaded by me, and do not be contrary.

Soc: My dear Crito, your solicitude is invaluable if it is rightly directed, but otherwise, the more intense, the more difficult it is to deal with. And so we should consider whether I ought to follow this course or not. You know it has always been true that I paid no heed to any consideration I was aware of except that argument which, on reflection, seemed best to me. I cannot throw over the arguments I used to make in times past just because this situation has arisen: they look the same to me as before, and I respect and honor them as much as ever. You must therefore understand that if, on the present occasion, we cannot make better arguments, I will not yield to you—not even if the power of the people conjures up the bugaboos of imprisonment and death and confiscation, as though we could be scared like little children. What will be the fairest way of considering the question? Shall I return to your old argument about the opinions of men? We were saying that some of them are to be regarded, and others not. Now were we right in maintaining this before I was condemned? And has the argument which was once good now proved to be talk for the sake of talking—mere childish nonsense? That is what I want to consider with your help, Crito: whether, under my present circumstances, the argument will appear to be in any way different or not, and whether we shall subscribe to it or let it go. That argument, which, as I believe, is maintained by many persons of authority, was to the effect, as I was saying, that the opinions of some men are to be regarded, and of other men not to be regarded. Now you, Crito, are not going to die tomorrow—at least, there is no human probability of this—and therefore you are disinterested and not liable to be deceived by the circumstances in which you are placed. Tell me, then, whether I am right in saying that some opinions, and the opinions of some men only, are to be valued and that other opinions, and the opinions of other men, are not to be valued. I ask you whether I was right in maintaining this?

Cr: Certainly.

Soc: The good opinions are to be regarded, and not the bad?

Cr: Yes.

Soc: And the opinions of the wise are good, and the opinions of the unwise are bad?

Cr: Certainly.

Soc: Now what was the argument about this: does the serious athlete attend to the praise and blame and opinion of every man or of one man only—his physician or trainer, whoever he may be?

Cr: Of one man only.

Soc: And he ought to fear the censure and welcome the praise of that one only, and not of the many?

Cr: Clearly so.

Soc: And he ought to act and train and eat and drink in the way which seems good to his single master, who has understanding, rather than according to the opinion of all other men put together?

Cr: True.

Soc: And if he disobeys and disregards the opinion and approval of the one, and regards the opinion of the many who have no understanding, will he not suffer harm?

Cr: Certainly he will.

Soc: And what will the harm be: where will it be localized, and what part of the disobedient person will it affect?

Cr: Clearly, it will affect the body, that is what is destroyed.

Soc: Very good, and is not this true, Crito, of other things, which we need not separately enumerate? In questions of just and unjust, fair and foul, good and evil, which are the subjects of our present consultation, ought we to follow the opinion of the many, and to fear them, or the opinion of the one man who has understanding? Ought we not to fear and reverence him more than all the rest of the world, and, if we desert him, shall we not ruin and mutilate that principle in us which is improved by justice and deteriorated by injustice—there is such a principle?

Cr: Certainly there is, Socrates.

Soc: Take a parallel instance: if, ignoring the advice of those who have understanding, we destroy that which is improved by health and is deteriorated by disease, would life be worth having? and that which has been destroyed is—the body?

Cr: Yes.

Soc: Would life be worth living with an evil and corrupted body?

Cr: Certainly not.

Soc: And will life be worth living if that faculty which injustice damages and justice improves is ruined? Do we suppose that principle—whatever it may be in man which has to do with justice and injustice—to be inferior to the body?

Cr: Certainly not.

Soc: More honorable than the body?

Cr: Far more.

Soc: Then, my friend, we must not regard what the many say of us but what he, the one man who has understanding of just and unjust, will say and what the truth will say. And therefore you begin in error when you advise that we should regard the opinion of the many about just and unjust, good and evil, honorable and dishonorable. "Well," someone will say, "but the many can kill us."

Cr: That is plain, and a person might well say so. You are right, Socrates.

Soc: But dear Crito, the argument which we have gone over still seems as valid as before. And I should like to know whether I may say the same of another proposition—that not life, but a good life, is to be chiefly valued?

Cr: Yes, that also remains unshaken.

Soc: And a good life is equivalent to an honorable and just one—that holds also?

Cr: Yes, it does.

Soc: From these premises I proceed to argue the question whether I am justified in trying to escape without the consent of the Athenians; and if I am clearly right in escaping, then I will make the attempt, but, if not, I will abstain. The other considerations which you mention—of money and loss of character and the duty of educating one's children—are, I fear, only the doctrines of the multitude, who, if they could, would restore people to life as readily as they put them to death—and with as little reason. But since we have been forced this far by the logic of our argument, the only question which remains to be considered is whether we shall do right in giving money and thanks to those who will rescue me, and in taking a direct role in the rescue ourselves, or whether in fact we will be doing wrong. And if it appears that we will be doing wrong, then neither death nor any other calamity that follows from staying and doing nothing must be judged more important than that.

Cr: I think that you are right, Socrates. How then shall we proceed?

Soc: Let us consider the matter together, and you, either refute me if you can, and I will be convinced, or else cease, my dear friend, from repeating to me that I ought to escape against the wishes of the Athenians. It is most important to me that I act with your assent and not against your will. And now please consider whether my starting point is adequately stated, and also try to answer my questions as you think best.

Cr: I will.

Soc: Are we to say that we are never intentionally to do wrong, or that in one way we ought and in another we ought not to do wrong? Or is doing wrong always evil and dishonorable, as we often concluded in times past? Or have all those past conclusions been thrown overboard during the last few days? And have we, at our age, been earnestly discouraging with one another all our life long only to discover that we are no better than children? Or, in spite of the opinion of the many, and in spite of consequences, whether better or worse, shall we insist on the truth of what was then said, that injustice is always an evil and a dishonor to him who acts unjustly? Shall we say so or not?

Cr: Yes.

Soc: Then we must do no wrong?

Cr: Certainly not.

Soc: Nor, when injured, injure in return, as the many imagine; for we must injure no one at all?

Cr: Clearly not.

Soc: Again, Crito, may we do evil?

Cr: Surely not, Socrates.

Soc: And what of doing evil in return for evil, which is the morality of the many—is that just or not?

Cr: Not just.

Soc: For doing evil to another is the same as injuring him?

Cr: Very true.

Soc: Then we ought not to retaliate or render evil for evil to anyone, whatever evil we may have suffered from him. But I would have you consider, Crito, whether you really mean what you are saying. For this opinion has never been held, and never will be held, by any considerable number of persons; and those who are agreed and those who are not agreed upon this point have no common ground and can only despise one another when they see how widely they differ. Tell me, then, whether you agree with and assent to my first principle, that neither injury nor retaliation nor warding off evil by evil is ever right. And shall that be the premise of our argument? Or do you decline and dissent from this? For so I have ever thought, and continue to think; but, if you are of another opinion, let me hear what you have to say. If, however, you remain of the same mind as formerly, I will proceed to the next step.

Cr: You may proceed, for I have not changed my mind.

Soc: The next thing I have to say, or, rather, my next question, is this: Ought a man to do what he admits to be right, or ought he to betray the right?

Cr: He ought to do what he things right.

Soc: In light of that, tell me whether or not there is some victim—a particularly undeserving victim—who is hurt if I go away without persuading the city. And do we abide by what we agree was just or not?

Cr: I cannot answer your question, Socrates, because I do not see what you are getting at.

Soc: Then consider the matter in this way: imagine that I am about to run away (you may call the proceeding by any name which you like), and the laws and the government come and interrogate me: "Tell us, Socrates," they say; "what are you up to? are you not going by an act of yours to destroy us—the laws, and the whole state—as far as in you lies? Do you imagine that a state can subsist and not be overthrown in which the decisions of law have no power but are set aside and trampled upon by individuals?" What will be our answer, Crito, to questions like these? Anyone, and especially a rhetorician, would have a good deal to say against abrogation of the law that requires a sentence to be carried out. He will argue that this law should not be set aside. Or shall we retort, "Yes; but the state has injured us and given an unjust sentence." Suppose I say that?

Cr: Very good, Socrates.

Soc: "And was that our agreement with you?" the laws would answer; "or were you to abide by the sentence of the state?" And if I were to express my astonishment at their talking this way, they would probably add: "Take control of your astonishment and answer, Socrates—you are in the habit of asking and answering questions. Tell us: What complaint have you to make against us which justifies you in attempting to destroy us and the state? In the first place, did we not bring you into existence? Your father married your mother by our aid and brought you into the world. Say whether you have any objection to urge against those of us who regulate marriage.'' None, I should reply. ''Or against those of us who after birth regulate the nurture and education of children, in which you also were trained? Were not the laws, which have the charge of education, right in commanding your father to train you in music and athletics?'' Right, I should reply. ''Well then, since you were brought into the world and nurtured and educated by us, can you deny in the first place that you are our child and slave, as your fathers were before you? And if this is true, do you really think you have the same rights as we do and that you are entitled to do to us whatever we do to you? Would you have any right to strike or revile or do any other evil to your father or your master, if you had one, because you had been struck or reviled by him or received some other evil at his hands?—you would not say this? And because we think it right to destroy you, do you think that you have any right to destroy us in return, and your country, as far as in you lies? Will you, o professor of true virtue, pretend that you are justified in this? Has a philosopher like you failed to discover that our country is more to be valued and higher and holier far than mother or father or any ancestor, and more to be regarded in the eyes of the gods and of men of understanding? Also to be soothed and gently and reverently entreated when angry, even more than a father, and either to be persuaded or, if not persuaded, to be obeyed? And when we are punished by her, whether with imprisonment or beatings, the punishment is to be endured in silence; and if she leads us to wounds or death in battle, there we follow as is right; neither may anyone yield or retreat or leave his rank, but whether in battle, or in a court of law, or in any other place, he must do what his city and his country order him, or he must change their view of what is just; and if he may do no violence to his father or mother, much less may he do violence to his country.'' What answer shall we make to this, Crito? Do the laws speak truly, or do they not?

Cr: I think that they do.

Soc: Then the laws will say, ''Consider, Socrates, if we are speaking truly that in your present attempt you are going to do us an injury. For, having brought you into the world, and nurtured and educated you, and given you and every other citizen a share in every good which we had to give, we further proclaim to any Athenian, by the liberty which we allow him, that if he does not like us when he has come of age and has seen the ways of the city and made our acquaintance, he may go where he pleases and take his goods with him. None of us laws will stand in the way if any of you who are dissatisfied with us and the city want to go to a colony or to move anywhere else. None of us forbids anyone to go where he likes, taking his property with him. But he who has experience of the manner in which we order justice and administer the state, and still remains, has entered into an implied contract that he will do as we command him. And he who disobeys us is, as we maintain, thrice wrong: first, because in disobeying us he is disobeying his parents; secondly, because we are the authors of his education; thirdly, because he has made an agreement with us that he will duly obey our commands, but he neither obeys them nor convinces us that our commands are unjust. We show flexibility. We do not brutally demand his compliance but offer him the choice of obeying or persuading us; yet he does neither.

"These are the sorts of accusations to which, as we were saying, you, Socrates, will be exposed if you accomplish your intentions; you, above all other Athenians." Suppose now I ask, why I rather than anybody else? They might reasonably take me to task because I above all other men have acknowledged the agreement. "There is clear proof," they will say, "Socrates, that we and the city were not displeasing to you. Of all Athenians you have been the most constant resident in the city, which, as you never leave it, you may be supposed to love. For you never went out of the city either to see the games, except once, when you went to the Isthmus, or to any other place unless when you were on military service; nor did you travel as other men do. Nor had you any curiosity to know other states or their laws: your affections did not go beyond us and our state; we were your special favorites, and you acquiesced in our government of you; and here in this city you had your children, which is a proof of your satisfaction. Moreover, you might in the course of the trial, if you had liked, have fixed the penalty at banishment, and then you could have done with the city's consent what you now attempt against its will. But you pretended that you preferred death to exile and that you were not unwilling to die. And now you do not blush at the thought of your old arguments and pay no respect to us, the laws, of whom you are the destroyer, and are doing what only a miserable slave would do, running away and turning your back on the compacts and agreements by which you agreed to act as a citizen. And, first of all, answer this very question: Are we right in saying that by your actions if not in words you agreed to our terms of citizenship? Is that true or not?" How shall we answer, Crito? Must we not assent?

Cr: We cannot help it, Socrates.

Soc: Then will they not say: "You, Socrates, are breaking the covenants and agreements which you made with us. You were not compelled to agree, or tricked, or forced to make up your mind in a moment, but had a period of seventy years during which you were free to depart if you were dissatisfied with us and the agreements did not seem fair. You did not pick Sparta or Crete, whose fine government you take every opportunity to praise, or any other state of the Greek or non-Greek world. You spent less time out of Athens than men who are crippled or blind or otherwise handicapped. That shows how much more than other Athenians you valued the city and us too, its laws (for who would value a city without laws?). And will you not now abide by your agreements? You will if you listen to us, Socrates, and you will not make yourself ridiculous by leaving the city.

"For just consider: if you transgress and err in this sort of way, what good will you do either to yourself or to your friends? That your friends will be driven into exile and deprived of citizenship or will lose their property is tolerably certain. And you yourself, if you go to one of the neighboring cities, like Thebes or Megara (both being well-ordered states, of course), will come as an enemy of their government, and all patriotic citizens will eye you suspiciously as a subverter of the laws, and you will confirm in the minds of the judges the justice of their own condemnation of you. For he who is a corrupter of the laws is more than likely to be a corrupter of the young and foolish portion of mankind. Will you then flee from well-ordered cities and law-abiding men? And will life be worth living if you do that? Or will you approach them and discourse unashamedly about—about what, Socrates? Will you discourse as you did here, about how virtue and justice and institutions and laws are the best things among men? Don't you think that such behavior coming from Socrates will seem disgusting? Surely one must think so. But if you go away from well-governed states to Crito's friends in Thessaly, where there is great disorder and license, they will be charmed to hear the tale of your escape from prison, set off with ludicrous particulars of the manner in which you were wrapped in a goatskin or some other disguise and metamorphosed in the usual manner of runaways. But will there be no one to comment that in your old age, when in all probability you had only a little time left to live, you were not ashamed to violate the most sacred laws from the greedy desire of a little more life? Perhaps not, if you keep them in good temper; but if they are out of temper, you will hear many degrading things. You will live as the flatterer and slave of all men, achieving what else but the chance to feast in Thessaly, as though you had gone abroad in order to get a meal? And where will the old arguments be, about justice and virtue? Say that you wish to live for the sake of your children—you want to bring them up and educate them—will you take them into Thessaly and deprive them of Athenian citizenship? Is this the benefit which you will confer upon them? Or are you under the impression that they will be better cared for and educated here if you are still alive, although absent from them; for your friends will take care of them? Do you fancy that, if you move to Thessaly, they will take care of them but that, if you move into the other world, they will not take care of them? No, if those who call themselves friends are good for anything, they will—to be sure, they will.

"Listen, then, Socrates, to us who have brought you up. Think not of life and children first and of justice afterwards but of justice first, so that you may defend your conduct to the rulers of the world below. For neither will you nor any that belong to you be happier or holier or juster in this life, or happier in another, if you do as Crito bids. Now you depart in innocence, a sufferer and not a doer of evil; a victim, not of the laws but of men. But if you escape, returning evil for evil and injury for injury, breaking the convenants and agreements which you have made with us and wronging those you ought least of all to wrong—that is to say, yourself, your friends, your country, and us—we shall be angry with you while you live, and our brethren, the laws in the world below, will receive you in no kindly spirit; for they will know that you have done your best to destroy us. Listen, then, to us and not to Crito."

This, dear Crito, is the voice I seem to hear murmuring in my ears, like the sound of the flute in the ears of the mystic; that voice, I say, is humming in my ears and prevents me from hearing any other. You must realize that you will be wasting your time if you speak against the convictions I hold at the moment. But if you think you will get anywhere, go ahead.

Cr: No, Socrates, I have nothing to say.

Soc: Then be resigned, Crito, and let us follow this course, since this is the way the god points out.

Reflections

Private Exploration

1. a. After first reading "Crito," make a list of any questions you have.
   b. Read the dialogue a second time, slowly. Hold your questions in the back of your mind as you read. Mark the text carefully. Look for patterns, repetitions, relationships. Jot notes in the margins.
   c. In your notebook, copy out lines or passages from the text that still raise problems or that now seem significant.
   d. Before exploring any specific aspect of the dialogue, write out a summary (in your own words) outlining Socrates' general argument as you understand it. Be patient with yourself. If you don't feel you've grasped everything, remember that works of literature, like complex problems in geometry, often require study and repeated reconsideration.
2. Should one save one's life, even if it means doing wrong? Are one's principles and right actions more valuable than life itself? Consider Socrates' proposition "that not life, but a good life, is to be chiefly valued."
3. Explore Socrates question: "And what of doing evil in return for evil, which is the morality of the many—is that just or not?"

Public Exploration

1. Socrates presents a long and detailed description of why laws of the state should be supreme and why—even if the state has condemned him unjustly—he has no right to disobey the law since that would thereby harm the state. He who accepts the benefit and protection of the state, Socrates argues, has an "implied contract" to obey the laws of the state. Consider the implications of his argument.
2. If you've read Thoreau's "On the Duty of Civil Disobedience," or King's "Letter from Birmingham Jail," consider the differences between their views and those of Socrates. Is one position right and the other wrong? What values are at stake in both cases? Can such questions as this be resolved at all? If yes, how? If no, then how are we to guide our lives?

Private Reflection

After discussing Socrates' argument with others, use your notebook to reflect further on it. Frame the issue in terms of what aspects of it you see as most important. On something this complex, you may need to return to your notebook several times. Let the act of writing help you think it all through.

On the Duty of Civil Disobedience

HENRY DAVID THOREAU

I heartily accept the motto, "That government is best which governs least;" and I should like to see it acted up to more rapidly and systematically. Carried out, it finally amounts to this, which also I believe—"That government is best which governs not at all;" and when men are prepared for it, that will be the kind of government which they will have. Government is at best but an expedient; but most governments are usually, and all governments are sometimes, inexpedient. The objections which have been brought against a standing army, and they are many and weighty, and deserve to prevail, may also at last be brought against a standing government. The standing army is only an arm of the standing government. The government itself, which is only the mode which the people have chosen to execute their will, is equally liable to be abused and perverted before the people can act through it. Witness the present Mexican war, the work of comparatively a few individuals using the standing government as their tool; for, in the outset, the people would not have consented to this measure.

This American government—what is it but a tradition, though a recent one, endeavoring to transmit itself unimpaired to posterity, but each instant losing some of its integrity? It has not the vitality and force of a single living man; for a single man can bend it to his will. It is a sort of wooden gun to the people themselves. But it is not the less necessary for this; for the people must have some complicated machinery or other, and hear its din, to satisfy that idea of government which they have. Governments show us how successfully men can be imposed on, even impose on themselves, for their own advantage. It is excellent, we must all allow. Yet this government never of itself furthered any enterprise, but by the alacrity with which it got out of its way. *It* does not keep the country free. *It* does not settle the West. *It* does not educate. The character inherent in the American people has done all that has been accomplished; and it would have done somewhat more, if the government had not sometimes got in its way. For government is an expedient by which men would fain succeed in letting one another alone; and, as has been said, when it is most expedient, the governed are most let alone by it. Trade and commerce, if they were not made of india-rubber, would never manage to bounce over the obstacles which legislators are continually putting in their way; and, if one were to judge these men wholly by the effects of their actions and not partly by their intentions, they would deserve to be classed and punished with those mischievous persons who put obstructions on the railroads.

But, to speak practically and as a citizen, unlike those who call themselves no-government men, I ask for, not at once no government, but *at once* a better government. Let every man make known what kind of government would command his respect, and that will be one step toward obtaining it.

After all, the practical reason why, when the power is once in the hands of the people, a majority are permitted, and for a long period continue, to rule is not because they are most likely to be in the right, nor because this seems fairest to the minority, but because they are physically the strongest. But a government in which the majority rule in all cases cannot be based on justice, even as far as men understand it. Can there not be a government in which majorities do not virtually decide right and wrong, but conscience?—in which majorities decide only those questions to which the rule of expediency is applicable? Must the citizen ever for a moment, or in the least degree, resign his conscience to the legislator? Why has every man a conscience, then? I think that we should be men first, and subjects afterwards. It is not desirable to cultivate a respect for the law, so much as for the right. The only obligation which I have a right to assume is to do at any time what I think right. It is truly enough said that a corporation has no conscience; but a corporation of conscientious men is a corporation *with* a conscience. Law never made men a whit more just; and, by means of their respect for it, even the well-disposed are daily made the agents of injustice.

The mass of men serve the state thus, not as men mainly, but as machines, with their bodies. They are the standing army, and the militia, jailers, constables, *posse comitatus,* etc. In most cases there is no free exercise whatever of the judgment or of the moral sense; but they put themselves on a level with wood and earth and stones; and wooden men can perhaps be manufactured that will serve the purpose as well. Such command no more respect than men of straw or a lump of dirt. They have the same sort of worth only as horses and dogs. Yet such as these even are commonly esteemed good citizens. Others—as most legislators, politicians, lawyers, ministers, and office-holders—serve the state chiefly with their heads; and, as they rarely make any moral distinctions, they are as likely to serve the devil, without *intending* it, as God.

How does it become a man to behave toward this American government today? I answer, that he cannot without disgrace be associated with it. I cannot for an instant recognize that political organization as *my* government which is the *slave's* government also.

All men recognize the right of revolution; that is, the right to refuse allegiance to, and to resist, the government, when its tyranny or its inefficiency are great and unendurable. But almost all say that such is not the case now.

But such was the case, they think, in the Revolution of '75. If one were to tell me that this was a bad government because it taxed certain foreign commodities brought to its ports, it is most probable that I should not make an ado about it, for I can do without them. All machines have their friction; and possibly this does enough good to counter-balance the evil. At any rate, it is a great evil to make a stir about it. But when the friction comes to have its machine, and oppression and robbery are organized, I say, let us not have such a machine any longer. In other words, when a sixth of the population of a nation which has undertaken to be the refuge of liberty are slaves, and a whole country is unjustly overrun and conquered by a foreign army, and subjected to military law, I think that it is not too soon for honest men to rebel and revolutionize. What makes this duty the more urgent is the fact that the country so overrun is not our own, but ours is the invading army.

Paley, a common authority with many on moral questions, in his chapter on the "Duty of Submission to Civil Government," resolves all civil obligation into expediency; and he proceeds to say that "so long as the interest of the whole society requires it, that is, so long as the established government cannot be resisted or changed without public inconveniency, it is the will of God . . . that the established government be obeyed—and no longer. This principle being admitted, the justice of every particular case of resistance is reduced to a computation of the quantity of the danger and grievance on the one side, and of the probability and expense of redressing it on the other." Of this, he says, every man shall judge for himself. But Paley appears never to have contemplated those cases to which the rule of expediency does not apply, in which a people, as well as an individual, must do justice, cost what it may. If I have unjustly wrested a plank from a drowning man, I must restore it to him though I drown myself. This, according to Paley, would be inconvenient. But he that would save his life, in such a case, shall lose it. This people must cease to hold slaves, and to make war on Mexico, though it cost them their existence as a people.

It is not so important that many should be as good as you, as that there be some absolute goodness somewhere; for that will leaven the whole lump. There are thousands who are *in opinion* opposed to slavery and to the war, who yet in effect do nothing to put an end to them; who, esteeming themselves children of Washington and Franklin, sit down with their hands in their pockets, and say that they know not what to do, and do nothing; who even postpone the question of freedom to the question of free trade, and quietly read the prices-current along with the latest advices from Mexico, after dinner, and, it may be, fall asleep over them both. What is the price-current of an honest man and patriot today? They hesitate, and they regret, and sometimes they petition; but they do nothing in earnest and with effect. They will wait, well disposed, for others to remedy the evil, that they may no longer have it to regret. At most, they give only a cheap vote, and a feeble countenance and God-speed, to the right, as it goes by them. There are nine hundred and ninety-nine patrons of virtue to one virtuous man. But it is easier to deal with the real possessor of a thing than with the temporary guardian of it.

All voting is a sort of gaming, like checkers or backgammon, with a slight moral tinge to it, a playing with right and wrong, with moral questions; and betting naturally accompanies it. The character of the voters is not staked. I cast my vote, perchance, as I think right; but I am not vitally concerned that that right should prevail. I am willing to leave it to the majority. Its obligation, therefore, never exceeds that of expediency. Even voting *for the right* is *doing* nothing for it. It is only expressing to men feebly your desire that it should prevail. A wise man will not leave the right to the mercy of chance, nor wish it to prevail through the power of the majority. There is but little virtue in the action of masses of men. When the majority shall at length vote for the abolition of slavery, it will be because they are indifferent to slavery, or because there is but little slavery left to be abolished by their vote. *They* will then be the only slaves. Only *his* vote can hasten the abolition of slavery who asserts his own freedom by his vote.

It is not a man's duty, as a matter of course, to devote himself to the eradication of any, even the most enormous, wrong; he may still properly have other concerns to engage him; but it is his duty, at least, to wash his hands of it, and, if he gives it no thought longer, not to give it practically his support. If I devote myself to other pursuits and contemplations, I must first see, at least, that I do not pursue them sitting upon another man's shoulders. I must get off him first, that he may pursue his contemplations too. See what gross inconsistency is tolerated. I have heard some of my townsmen say, "I should like to have them order me out to help put down an insurrection of the slaves, or to march to Mexico;— see if I would go"; and yet these very men have each, directly by their allegiance, and so indirectly, at least, by their money, furnished a substitute. The soldier is applauded who refuses to serve in an unjust war by those who do not refuse to sustain the unjust government which makes the war; is applauded by those own act and authority he disregards and sets at naught; as if the state were penitent to that degree that it hired one to scourge it while it sinned, but not to that degree that it left off sinning for a moment. Thus, under the name of Order and Civil Government, we are all made at last to pay homage to and support our own meanness. After the first blush of sin comes its indifference; and from immoral it becomes, as it were, *un*moral, and not quite unnecessary to that life which we have made.

How can a man be satisfied to entertain an opinion merely, and enjoy *it?* Is there any enjoyment in it, if his opinion is that he is aggrieved? If you are cheated out of a single dollar by your neighbor, you do not rest satisfied with knowing that you are cheated, or with saying that you are cheated, or even with petitioning him to pay you your due; but you take effectual steps at once to obtain the full amount, and see that you are never cheated again. Action from principle, the perception and the performance of right, changes things and relations; it is essentially revolutionary, and does not consist wholly with anything which was. It not only divides States and churches, it divides families; ay, it divides the *individual,* separating the diabolical in him from the divine.

Unjust laws exist: shall we be content to obey them, or shall we endeavor to amend them, and obey them until we have succeeded, or shall we transgress them at once? Men generally, under such a government as this, think that they ought to wait until they have persuaded the majority to alter them. They think that, if they should resist, the remedy would be worse than the evil. But it is the fault of the government itself that the remedy *is* worse than the evil. *It* makes it worse. Why is it not more apt to anticipate and provide for reform? Why does it not cherish its wise minority? Why does it cry and resist before it is hurt? Why does it not encourage its citizens to be on the alert to point out its faults, and *do* better than it would have them? Why does it always crucify Christ, and excommunicate Copernicus and Luther, and pronounce Washington and Franklin rebels?

One would think, that a deliberate and practical denial of its authority was the only offence never contemplated by government; else, why has it not assigned its definite, its suitable and proportionate, penalty? If a man who has no property refuses but once to earn nine shillings for the State, he is put in prison for a period unlimited by any law that I know, and determined only by the discretion of those who placed him there; but if he should steal ninety times nine shillings from the State, he is soon permitted to go at large again.

If the injustice is part of the necessary friction of the machine of government, let it go, let it go: perchance it will wear smooth—certainly the machine will wear out. If the injustice has a spring, or a pulley, or a rope, or a crank, exclusively for itself, then perhaps you may consider whether the remedy will not be worse than the evil; but if it is of such a nature that it requires you to be the agent of injustice to another, then, I say, break the law. Let your life be a counter friction to stop the machine. What I have to do is to see, at any rate, that I do not lend myself to the wrong which I condemn.

As for adopting the ways which the State has provided for remedying the evil, I know not of such ways. They take too much time, and a man's life will be gone. I have other affairs to attend to. I came into this world, not chiefly to make this a good place to live in, but to live in it, be it good or bad. A man has not everything to do, but something; and because he cannot do *everything,* it is not necessary that he should do *something* wrong. It is not my business to be petitioning the Governor or the Legislature any more than it is theirs to petition me; and if they should not hear my petition, what should I do then? But in this case the State has provided no way: its very Constitution is the evil. This may seem to be harsh and stubborn and unconciliatory; but it is to treat with the utmost kindness and consideration the only spirit that can appreciate or deserves it. So is all change for the better, like birth and death, which convulse the body.

I do not hesitate to say, that those who call themselves Abolitionists should at once effectually withdraw their support, both in person and property, from the government of Massachusetts, and not wait till they constitute a majority of one, before they suffer the right to prevail through them. I think that it is enough if they have God on their side, without waiting for that other one. Moreover, any man more right than his neighbors constitutes a majority of one already.

I meet the American government, or its representative, the State government, directly, and face to face, once a year—no more—in the person of its tax-gatherer; this is the only mode in which a man situated as I am necessarily meets it; and it then says distinctly, Recognize me; and the simplest, the most effectual, and, in the present posture of affairs, the indispensablest mode of treating with it on his head, of expressing your little satisfaction with and love for it, is to deny it then. My civil neighbor, the tax-gatherer, is the very man I have to deal with—for it is, after all, with men and not with parchment that I quarrel—and he has voluntarily chosen to be an agent of the government. How shall he ever know well what he is and does as an officer of the government, or as a man, until he is obliged to consider whether he shall treat me, his neighbor, for whom he has respect, as a neighbor and well-disposed man, or as a maniac and disturber of the peace, and see if he can get over this obstruction to his neighborliness without a ruder and more impetuous thought or speech corresponding with his action. I know this well, that if one thousand, if one hundred, if ten men whom I could name—if ten *honest* men only—ay, if *one* HONEST man, in this State of Massachusetts, *ceasing to hold slaves,* were actually to withdraw from this copartnership, and be locked up in the county jail therefor, it would be the abolition of slavery in America. For it matters not how small the beginning may seem to be: what is once well done is done forever. But we love better to talk about it: that we say is our mission. Reform keeps many scores of newspapers in its service, but not one man. If my esteemed neighbor, the State's ambassador, who will devote his days to the settlement of the question of human rights in the Council Chamber, instead of being threatened with the prisons of Carolina, were to sit down the prisoner of Massachusetts, that State which is so anxious to foist the sin of slavery upon her sister—though at present she can discover only an act of inhospitality to be the ground of a quarrel with her—the Legislature would not wholly waive the subject the following winter.

Under a government which imprisons any unjustly, the true place for a just man is also a prison. The proper place to-day, the only place which Massachusetts has provided for her freer and less desponding spirits, is in her prisons, to be put out and locked out of the State by her own act, as they have already put themselves out by their principles. It is there that the fugitive slave, and the Mexican prisoner on parole, and the Indian come to plead the wrongs of his race should find them; on that separate, but more free and honorable, ground, where the State places those who are not *with* her, but *against* her—the only house in a slave State in which a free man can abide with honor. If any think that their influence would be lost there, and their voices no longer afflict the ear of the State, that they would not be as an enemy within its walls, they do not know by how much truth is stronger than error, nor how much more eloquently and effectively he can combat injustice who has experienced a little in his own person. Cast your whole vote, not a strip of paper merely, but your whole influence. A minority is powerless while it conforms to the majority; it is not even a minority then; but it is irresistible when it clogs by its whole weight. If the alternative is to keep all just men in prison, or give up war and slavery, the State will not hesitate which to choose. If a thousand men were not to pay their tax-bills this year, that would not be a violent and bloody measure, as it would be to pay them, and enable the State to commit violence and shed innocent blood. This is, in fact, the definition of a peaceable revolution, if any such is possible. If the tax-gatherer, or any public officer, asks me, as one has done, "But what shall I do?" my answer is, "If you really wish to do anything, resign your office." When the subject has refused allegiance, and the officer has resigned his office, then the revolution is accomplished. But even suppose blood should flow. Is there not a sort of blood shed when the conscience is wounded? Through this wound a man's real manhood and immortality flow out, and he bleeds to an everlasting death. I see this blood flowing now.

But the rich man—not to make any invidious comparison—is always sold to the institution which makes him rich. Absolutely speaking, the more money, the less virtue; for money comes between a man and his objects, and obtains them for him; and it was certainly no great virtue to obtain it. It puts to rest many questions which he would otherwise be taxed to answer; while the only new question which it puts is the hard but superfluous one, how to spend it. Thus his moral ground is taken from under his feet. The opportunities of living are diminished in proportion as what are called the "means" are increased. The best thing a man can do for his culture when he is rich is to endeavor to carry out those schemes which he entertained when he was poor. Christ answered the Herodians according to their condition. "Show me the tribute-money," said he;—and one took a penny out of his pocket;—if you use money which has the image of Caesar on it, and which he has made current and valuable, that is, *if you are men of the State,* and gladly enjoy the advantages of Caesar's government, then pay him back some of his own when he demands it. "Render therefore to Caesar that which is Caesar's, and to God those things which are God's"—leaving them no wiser than as to which was which; for they did not wish to know.

Some years ago, the State met me in behalf of the Church, and commanded me to pay a certain sum toward the support of a clergyman whose preaching my father attended, but never I myself. "Pay," it said, "or be locked up in the jail." I declined to pay. But, unfortunately, another man saw fit to pay it. I did not see why the schoolmaster should be taxed to support the priest, and not the priest the schoolmaster; for I was not the State's schoolmaster, but I supported myself by voluntary subscription. I did not see why the lyceum should not present its tax-bill, and have the State to back its demand, as well as the Church. However, at the request of the selectmen, I condescended to make some such statement as this in writing:—"Know all men by these presents, that I, Henry Thoreau, do not wish to be regarded as a member of any incorporated society which I have not joined." This I gave to the town clerk; and he has it. The State, having thus learned that I did not wish to be regarded as a member of that church, has never made a like demand on me since; though it said that it must adhere to its original presumption that time. If I had known how to name them, I should then have signed off in detail from all the societies which I never signed on to; but I did not know where to find a complete list.

I have paid no poll-tax for six years. I was put into a jail once on this account, for one night; and, as I stood considering the walls of solid stone, two or three feet thick, the door of wood and iron, a foot thick, and the iron grating which strained the light, I could not help being struck with the foolishness of that institution which treated me as if I were mere flesh and blood and bones to be locked up. I wondered that it should have concluded at length that this was the best use it could put me to, and had never thought to avail itself of my services in some way. I saw that, if there was a wall of stone between me and my townsmen, there was a still more difficult one to climb or break through before they could get to be as free as I was. I did not for a moment feel confined, and the walls seemed a great waste of stone and mortar. I felt as if I alone of all my townsmen had paid my tax. They plainly did not know how to treat me, but behaved like persons who are underbred. In every threat and in every compliment there was a blunder; for they thought that my chief desire was to stand the other side of that stone wall. I could not but smile to see how industriously they locked the door on my meditations, which followed them out again without let or hindrance, and *they* were really all that was dangerous. As they could not reach me, they had resolved to punish my body; just as boys, if they cannot come at some person against whom they have a spite, will abuse his dog. I saw that the State was half-witted, that it was timid as a lone woman with her silver spoons, and that it did not know its friends from its foes, and I lost all my remaining respect for it, and pitied it.

Thus the State never intentionally confronts a man's sense, intellectual or moral, but only his body, his senses. It is not armed with superior wit or honesty, but with superior physical strength. I was not born to be forced. I will breathe after my own fashion. Let us see who is the strongest. What force has a multitude? They only can force me who obey a higher law than I. They force me to become like themselves. I do not hear of *men* being *forced* to live this way or that by masses of men. What sort of life were that to live? When I meet a government which says to me, "Your money or your life," why should I be in haste to give it my money? It may be in a great strait, and not know what to do: I cannot help that. It must help itself; do as I do. It is not worth the while to snivel about it. I am not responsible for the successful working of the machinery of society. I am not the son of the engineer. I perceive that, when an acorn and a chestnut fall side by side, the one does not remain inert to make way for the other, but both obey their own laws, and spring and grow and flourish as best they can, till one, perchance, overshadows and destroys the other. If a plant cannot live according to its nature, it dies; and so a man.

I do not wish to quarrel with any man or nation. I do not wish to split hairs, to make fine distinctions, or set myself up as better than my neighbors. I seek rather, I may say, even an excuse for conforming the laws of the land. I am but too ready to conform to them. Indeed, I have reason to suspect myself on this head; and each year, as the tax-gatherer comes round, I find myself disposed to review the acts and positions of the general and State governments, and the spirit of the people, to discover a pretext for conformity.

> We must affect our country as our parents,
> And if at any time we alienate
> Our love or industry from doing it honor,
> We must respect effects and teach the soul
> Matter of conscience and religion,
> And not desire of rule or benefit.

I believe that the State will soon be able to take all my work of this sort out of my hands, and then I shall be no better a patriot than my fellow-countrymen. Seen from a a lower point of view, the Constitution, with all its faults, is very good; the law and the courts are very respectable; even this State and this American government are, in many respects, very admirable, and rare things, to be thankful for, such as a great many have described them; but seen from a point of view a little higher, they are what I have described them; seen from a higher still, and the highest, who shall say what they are, or that they are worth looking at or thinking of at all?

However, the government does not concern me much, and I shall bestow the fewest possible thoughts on it. It is not many moments that I live under a government, even in this world. If a man is thought-free, fancy-free, imagination-free, that which *is not* never for a long time appearing *to be* to him, unwise rulers or reformers cannot fatally interrupt him.

I know that most men think differently from myself; but those whose lives are by profession devoted to the study of these or kindred subjects content me as little as any. Statesmen and legislators, standing so completely within the institution, never distinctly and nakedly behold it. They speak of moving society, but have no resting-place without it. They may be men of a certain experience and discrimination, and have no doubt invented ingenious and even useful systems, for which we sincerely thank them; but all their wit and usefulness lie within certain not very wide limits. They are wont to forget that the world is not governed by policy and expediency.

No man with a genius for legislation has appeared in America. They are rare in the history of the world. There are orators, politicians, and eloquent men, by the thousand; but the speaker has not yet opened his mouth to speak who is capable of settling the much-vexed questions of the day. We love eloquence for its own sake, and not for any truth which it may utter, or any heroism it may inspire. Our legislators have not yet learned the comparative value of free trade and of freedom, of union, and of rectitude, to a nation. They have no genius or talent for comparatively humble questions of taxation and finance, commerce and manufactures and agriculture. If we were left solely to the wordy wit of legislators in Congress for our guidance, uncorrected by the seasonable experience and the effectual complaints of the people, America would not long retain her rank among the nations. For eighteen hundred years, though perchance I have no right to say it, the New Testament has been written; yet where is the legislator who has wisdom and practical talent enough to avail himself of the light which it sheds on the science of legislation?

The authority of government, even such as I am willing to submit to—for I will cheerfully obey those who know and can do better than I, and in many things even those who neither know nor can do so well—is still an impure one: to be strictly just, it must have the sanction and consent of the governed. It can have no pure right over my person and property but what I concede to it. The progress from an absolute to a limited monarchy, from a limited monarchy, from a limited monarchy to a democracy, is a progress toward a true respect for the individual. Even the Chinese philosopher was wise enough to regard the individual as the basis of the empire. Is a democracy, such as we know it, the last improvement possible in government? Is it not possible to take a step further towards recognizing and organizing the rights of man? There will never be a really free and enlightened State until the State comes to recognize the individual as a higher and independent power, from which all its own power and authority are derived, and treats him accordingly. I please myself with imagining a State at least which can afford to be just to all men, and to treat the individual with respect as a neighbor; which even would not think it inconsistent with its own repose if a few were to live aloof from it, not meddling with it, nor embraced by it, who fulfilled all the duties of neighbors and fellow-men. A State which bore this kind of fruit, and suffered it to drop off as fast as it ripened, would prepare the way for a still more perfect and glorious State, which also I have imagined, but not yet anywhere seen.

Reflections

Private Exploration

1. Thoreau's essay contains ideas that may excite, disturb, confuse, or require quiet reflection. Choose a single point that seems important to you and write about it in detail. Don't hesitate to argue, question, or draw from personal experience to explore the concept. And don't hesitate to change your mind—or to be of two minds—as your own ideas push forward.
2. Consider Thoreau's position:

   > . . . the practical reason why . . . a majority are permitted . . . to rule is not because they are most likely to be in the right, nor because this seems the fairest to the minority, but because they are physically stronger.

   Can you think of specific instances you've observed when majority rule conflicted with what you believed just or fair? Draw from personal examples close to you and explore both their implications and your feelings regarding them.
3. According to Thoreau, "Under a government which imprisons any unjustly, the true place for a just man is also a prison." Many just men, including Socrates, Ghandi, and Martin Luther King, Jr., were imprisoned for causes they considered unjust.

After Thoreau was jailed for refusing to pay taxes that might support the Mexican war, the story goes that Thoreau's friend Ralph Waldo Emerson passed by the jail and asked, "Henry, what are you doing in there?" Thoreau replied, "Ralph, what are you doing out there?" Explore Thoreau's concept of freedom and justice.

Public Exploration

If people find laws unjust, what should they do? What are their options? Consider this:

> The only obligation which I have a right to assume is to do at any time what I think right.

Private Reflection

Everything Thoreau writes in "Civil Disobedience" appeals to individual conscience. Look one more time at your own position. If you support Thoreau in principle, consider circumstances under which you might have the courage to act as a "majority of one." Be as honest as you can.

If you disagree with Thoreau, explore the question of whether you can foresee any time in your life when you would be forced to act in opposition to your friends, family, or country. Search deeply.

• When the Great Reason •

LAOTZE

When the Great Reason is obliterated,
We have benevolence and justice.
When wisdom and sagacity appear,
We have much hypocrisy.
When family relations are no longer harmonious,
We have filial piety and paternal love.
When a nation is in disorder,
We have loyalty and allegiance.

Reflections

Private Exploration

Laotze's poem is organized around contrasting pairs of lines. Select any two lines that contrast or seem to contradict each other. Copy them in your notebook, then explore what they seem to mean. If you are not familiar with the word "paradox," look it up in a good dictionary. Does the concept of paradox contribute to understanding the poem?

Public Exploration

In your group, work your way through Laotze's poem and find historical or current events that might support each of his arguments. (For example, how might the Vietnam war relate to "When a nation is in disorder/We have loyalty and allegiance.") When you've finished, share your examples with the class as a whole.

Private Reflection

When it comes to politics, are we better off adhering to a certain degree of cynicism? Or were we more fortunate in the past when we tended to believe in our heroes and our Presidents were seen as honorable men? Or did that kind of past ever exist?

Letter From Birmingham Jail

MARTIN LUTHER KING, JR.

My Dear Fellow Clergymen:

While confined here in the Birmingham city jail, I came across your recent statement calling my present activities "unwise and untimely." Seldom do I pause to answer criticism of my work and ideas. If I sought to answer all the criticisms that cross my desk, my secretaries would have little time for anything other than such correspondence in the course of the day, and I would have no time for constructive work. But since I feel that you are men of genuine good will and that your criticisms are sincerely set fourth, I want to try to answer your statement in what I hope will be patient and reasonable terms.

I think I should indicate why I am here in Birmingham, since you have been influenced by the view which argues against "outsiders coming in." I have the honor of serving as president of the Southern Christian Leadership Conference, an organization operating in every southern state, with headquarters in Atlanta, Georgia. We have some eighty-five affiliated organizations across the South, and one of them is the Alabama Christian Movement for Human Rights. Frequently we share staff, educational, and financial resources with our affiliates. Several months ago the affiliate here in Birmingham asked us to be on call to engage in a nonviolent direct-action program if such were deemed necessary. We readily consented, and when the hour came we lived up to our promise. So I, along with several members of my staff, am here because I was invited here. I am here because I have organizational ties here.

But more basically, I am in Birmingham because injustice is here. Just as the prophets of the eighth century B.C. left their villages and carried their "thus saith the Lord" far beyond the boundaries of their home towns, and just as the Apostle Paul left his village of Tarsus and carried the gospel of Jesus

Christ to the far corners of the Greco-Roman world, so am I compelled to carry the gospel of freedom beyond my own home town. Like Paul, I must constantly respond to the Macedonian call for aid.

Moreover, I am cognizant of the interrelatedness of all communities and states. I cannot sit idly by in Atlanta and not be concerned about what happens in Birmingham. Injustice anywhere is a threat to justice everywhere. We are caught in an inescapable network of mutuality, tied in a single garment of destiny. Whatever affects one directly, affects all indirectly. Never again can we afford to live with the narrow, provincial "outside agitator" idea. Anyone who lives inside the United States can never be considered an outsider anywhere within its bounds.

You deplore the demonstrations taking place in Birmingham. But your statement, I am sorry to say, fails to express a similar concern for the conditions that brought about the demonstrations. I am sure that none of you would want to rest content with the superficial kind of social analysis that deals merely with effects and does not grapple with underlying causes. It is unfortunate that demonstrations are taking place in Birmingham, but it is even more unfortunate that the city's white power structure left the Negro community with no alternative.

In any nonviolent campaign there are four basic steps: collection of the facts to determine whether injustices exist; negotiation; self-purification; and direct action. We have gone through all these steps in Birmingham. There can be no gainsaying the fact that racial injustice engulfs this community. Birmingham is probably the most thoroughly segregated city in the United States. Its ugly record of brutality is widely known. Negroes have experienced grossly unjust treatment in the courts. There have been more unsolved bombings of Negro homes and churches in Birmingham than in any other city in the nation. These are the hard, brutal facts of the case. On the basis of these conditions, Negro leaders sought to negotiate with the city fathers. But the latter consistently refused to engage in good-faith negotiation.

Then, last September, came the opportunity to talk with leaders of Birmingham's economic community. In the course of the negotiations, certain promises were made by the merchants—for example, to remove the stores' humiliating racial signs. On the basis of these promises, the Reverend Fred Shuttlesworth and the leaders of the Alabama Christian Movement for Human Rights agreed to a moratorium on all demonstrations. As the weeks and months went by, we realized that we were the victims of a broken promise. A few signs, briefly removed, returned; the others remained.

As in so many past experiences, our hopes had been blasted, and the shadow of deep disappointment settled upon us. We had no alternative except to prepare for direct action, whereby we would present our very bodies as a means of laying our case before the conscience of the local and the national community. Mindful of the difficulties involved, we decided to undertake a process of self-purification. We began a series of workshops on nonviolence, and we repeatedly asked ourselves: "Are you able to accept blows without retaliating?" "Are you able to endure the ordeal of jail?" We decided to schedule our direct-action program for the Easter season, realizing that except for Christmas, this is the main shopping period of the year. Knowing that a strong economic-withdrawal program would be the by-product of direct action, we felt that this would be the best time to bring pressure to bear on the merchants for the needed change.

Then it occurred to us that Birmingham's mayoral election was coming up in March, and we speedily decided to postpone action until after election-day. When we discovered that the Commissioner of Public Safety, Eugene "Bull" Connor, had piled up enough votes to be in the run-off, we decided again to postpone action until the day after the run-off so that the demonstrations could not be used to cloud the issues. Like many others, we waited to see Mr. Connor defeated, and to this end we endured postponement after postponement. Having aided in this community need, we felt that our direct-action program could be delayed no longer.

You may well ask, "Why direct action? Why sit-ins, marches, and so forth? Isn't negotiation a better path?" You are quite right in calling for negotiation. Indeed, this is the very purpose of direct action. Nonviolent direct action seeks to create such a crisis and foster such a tension that a community which has constantly refused to negotiate is forced to confront the issue. It seeks so to dramatize the issue that it can no longer be ignored. My citing the creation of tension as part of the work of the nonviolent-resister may sound rather shocking. But I must confess that I am not afraid of the word "tension." I have earnestly opposed violent tension, but there is a type of constructive, nonviolent tension which is necessary for growth. Just as Socrates felt that it was necessary to create a tension in the mind so that individuals could rise from the bondage of myths and half-truths to the unfettered realm of creative analysis and objective appraisal, so must we see the need for nonviolent gadflies to create the kind of tension in society that will help men rise from the dark depths of prejudice and racism to the majestic heights of understanding and brotherhood.

The purpose of our direct-action program is to create a situation so crisis-packed that it will inevitably open the door to negotiation. I therefore concur with you in your call for negotiation. Too long has our beloved Southland been bogged down in a tragic effort to live in monologue rather than dialogue.

One of the basic points in your statement is that the action that I and my associates have taken in Birmingham is untimely. Some have asked: "Why didn't you give the new city administration time to act?" The only answer that I can give to this query is that the new Birmingham administration must be prodded about as much as the outgoing one, before it will act. We are sadly mistaken if we feel that the election of Albert Boutwell as mayor will bring the millennium to Birmingham. While Mr. Boutwell is a much more gentle person than Mr. Connor, they are both segregationists, dedicated to maintenance of the status quo. I have hoped that Mr. Boutwell will be reasonable enough to see the futility of massive resistance to desegregation. But he will not see this without pressure from devotees of civil rights. My friends, I must say to you that we have not made a single gain in civil rights without determined legal and nonviolent pressure. Lamentably, it is an historical fact that privileged groups seldom give up their privileges voluntarily. Individuals may see the moral light and voluntarily give up their unjust posture; but, as Reinhold Niebuhr has reminded us, groups tend to be more immoral than individuals.

We know through painful experience that freedom is never voluntarily given by the oppressor; it must be demanded by the oppressed. Frankly, I have yet to engage in a direct-action campaign that was "well timed" in the view of those who have not suffered unduly from the disease of segregation. For years now I have heard the word "Wait!" It rings in the ear of every Negro with piercing familiarity. This "Wait!" has almost always meant "Never." We must come to see, with one of our distinguished jurists, that "justice too long delayed is justice denied."

We have waited for more than 340 years for our constitutional and God-given rights. The nations of Asia and Africa are moving with jetlike speed toward gaining political independence, but we still creep at horse-and-buggy pace toward gaining a cup of coffee at a lunch counter. Perhaps it is easy for those who have never felt the stinging darts of segregation to say, "Wait." But when you have seen vicious mobs lynch your mothers and fathers at will and drown your sisters and brothers at whim; when you have seen hate-filled policemen curse, kick, and even kill your black brothers and sisters; when you see that vast majority of your twenty million Negro brothers smothering in an airtight cage of poverty in the midst of an affluent society; when you suddenly find your tongue twisted and your speech stammering as you seek to explain to your six-year-old daughter why she can't go to the public amusement park that has just been advertised on television, and see tears welling up in her eyes when she is told that Funtown is closed to colored children, and see ominous clouds of inferiority beginning to form in her little mental sky, and see her beginning to distort her personality by developing an unconscious bitterness toward white people; when you have to concoct an answer for a five-year-old son who is asking, "Daddy, why do white people treat colored people so mean?"; when you take a cross-country drive and find it necessary to sleep night after night in the uncomfortable corners of your automobile because no motel will accept you; when you are humiliated day in and day out by nagging signs reading "white" and "colored"; when your first name becomes "nigger," your middle name becomes "boy" (however old you are) and your last name becomes "John," and your wife and mother are never given the respected title "Mrs."; when you are harried by day and haunted by night by the fact that you are a Negro, living constantly at tiptoe stance, never quite knowing what to expect next, and are plagued with inner fears and outer resentments; when you are forever fighting a degenerating sense of "nobodiness"—then you will understand why we find it difficult to wait. There comes a time when the cup of endurance runs over, and men are no longer willing to be plunged into the abyss of despair. I hope, sirs, you can understand our legitimate and unavoidable impatience.

You express a great deal of anxiety over our willingness to break laws. This is certainly a legitimate concern. Since we so diligently urge people to obey the Supreme Court's decision of 1954 outlawing segregation in the public schools, at first glance it may seem rather paradoxical for us consciously to break laws. One may well ask: "How can you advocate breaking some laws and obeying others?" The answer lies in the fact that there are two types of laws: just and unjust. I would be the first to advocate obeying just laws. One has not only a legal but a moral responsibility to obey just laws. Conversely, one has a moral responsibility to disobey unjust laws. I would agree with St. Augustine that "an unjust law is no law at all."

Now, what is the difference between the two? How does one determine whether a law is just or unjust? A just law is a man-made code that squares with the moral law or the law of God. An unjust law is a code that is out of harmony with the moral law. To put it in the terms of St. Thomas Aquinas: An unjust law is a human law that is not rooted in eternal law and natural law. Any law that uplifts human personality is just. Any law that degrades human personality is unjust. All segregation statutes are unjust because segregation distorts the soul and damages the personality. It gives the segregator a false sense of superiority and the segregated a false sense of inferiority. Segregation, to use the terminology of the Jewish philosopher Martin Buber, substitutes an "I–it" relationship for an "I–thou" relationship and ends up relegating persons to the status of things. Hence segregation is not only politically, economically, and sociologically unsound, it is morally wrong and sinful. Paul Tillich has said that sin is separation. Is not segregation an existential expression of man's tragic separation, his awful estrangement, his terrible sinfulness? Thus it is that I can urge men to obey the 1954 decision of the Supreme Court, for it is morally right; and I can urge them to disobey segregation ordinances, for they are morally wrong.

Let us consider a more concrete example of just and unjust laws. An unjust law is a code that a numerical or power majority group compels a minority group to obey but does not make binding on itself. This is *difference* made legal. By the same token, a just law is a code that a majority compels a minority to follow and that it is willing to follow itself. This is *sameness* made legal.

Let me give another explanation. A law is unjust if it is inflicted on a minority that, as a result of being denied the right to vote, had no part in enacting or devising the law. Who can say that the legislature of Alabama which set up that state's segregation laws was democratically elected? Throughout Alabama all sorts of devious methods are used to prevent Negroes from becoming registered voters, and there are some counties in which, even though Negroes constitute a majority of the population, not a single Negro is registered. Can any law enacted under such circumstances be considered democratically structured?

Sometimes a law is just on its face and unjust in its application. For instance, I have been arrested on a charge of parading without a permit. Now, there is nothing wrong in having an ordinance which requires a permit for a parade. But such an ordinance becomes unjust when it is used to maintain segregation and to deny citizens the First-Amendment privilege of peaceful assembly and protest.

I hope you are able to see the distinction I am trying to point out. In no sense do I advocate evading or defying the law, as would the rabid segregationist. That would lead to anarchy. One who breaks an unjust law must do so openly, lovingly, and with a willingness to accept the penalty. I submit that an individual who breaks a law that conscience tells him is unjust, and who willingly accepts the penalty of imprisonment in order to arouse the conscience of the community over its injustice, is in reality expressing the highest respect for law.

Of course, there is nothing new about this kind of civil disobedience. It was evidenced sublimely in the refusal of Shadrach, Meshach, and Abednego to obey the laws of Nebuchadnezzar, on the ground that a higher moral law was at stake. It was practiced superbly by the early Christians, who were willing to face hungry lions and the excruciating pain of chopping blocks rather than submit to certain unjust laws of the Roman Empire. To a degree, academic freedom is a reality today because Socrates practiced civil disobedience. In our own nation, the Boston Tea Party represented a massive act of civil disobedience.

We should never forget that everything Adolf Hitler did in Germany was "legal" and everything the Hungarian freedom fighters did in Hungary was "illegal." It was "illegal" to aid and comfort a Jew in Hitler's Germany. Even so, I am sure that, had I lived in Germany at the time, I would have aided and comforted my Jewish brothers. If today I lived in a Communist country where certain principles dear to the Christian faith are suppressed, I would openly advocate disobeying that country's anti-religious laws.

I must make two honest confessions to you, my Christian and Jewish brothers. First, I must confess that over the past few years I have been gravely disappointed with the white moderate. I have almost reached the regrettable conclusion that the Negro's great stumbling block in his stride toward freedom is not the white Citizen's Counciler or the Ku Klux Klanner, but the white moderate, who is more devoted to "order" than to justice; who prefers a negative peace which is the absence of tension to a positive peace which is the presence of justice; who constantly says, "I agree with you in the goal you seek, but I cannot agree with your methods of direct action"; who paternalistically believes he can set the timetable for another man's freedom; who lives by a mythical concept of time and who constantly advises the Negro to wait for a "more convenient season." Shallow understanding from people of good will is more frustrating than absolute misunderstanding from people of ill will. Lukewarm acceptance is much more bewildering than outright rejection.

I had hoped that the white moderate would understand that law and order exist for the purpose of establishing justice and that when they fail in this purpose they become the dangerously structured dams that block the flow of social progress. I had hoped that the white moderate would understand that the present tension in the South is a necessary phase of the transition from an obnoxious negative peace, in which the Negro passively accepted his unjust plight, to a substantive and positive peace, in which all men will respect the dignity and worth of human personality. Actually, we who engage in nonviolent direct action are not the creators of tension. We merely bring to the surface the hidden tension that is already alive. We bring it out in the open, where it can be seen and dealt with. Like a boil that can never be cured so long as it is covered up but must be opened with all its ugliness to the natural medicines of air and light, injustice must be exposed, with all the tension its exposure creates, to the light of human conscience and the air of national opinion, before it can be cured.

In your statement you assert that our actions, even though peaceful, must be condemned because they precipitate violence. But is this a logical assertion? Isn't this like condemning a robbed man because his possession of money precipitated the evil act of robbery? Isn't this like condemning Socrates because his unswerving commitment to truth and his philosophical inquiries precipitated the act by the misguided populace in which they made him drink hemlock? Isn't this like condemning Jesus because his unique God-consciousness and never-ceasing devotion to God's will precipitated the evil act of crucifixion? We must come to see that, as the federal courts have consistently affirmed, it is wrong to urge an individual to cease his efforts to gain his basic constitutional rights because the quest may precipitate violence. Society must protect the robbed and punish the robber.

I had also hoped that the white moderate would reject the myth concerning time in relation to the struggle for freedom. I have just received a letter from a white brother in Texas. He writes: "All Christians know that the colored people will receive equal rights eventually, but it is possible that you are in too great a religious hurry. It has taken Christianity almost two thousand years to accomplish what it has. The teachings of Christ take time to come to earth." Such an attitude stems from a tragic misconception of time, from the strangely irrational notion that there is something in the very flow of time that will inevitably cure all ills. Actually, time itself is neutral; it can be used either destructively or constructively. More and more I feel that the people of ill will have used time much more effectively than have the people of good will. We will have to repent in this generation not merely for the hateful words and actions of the bad people, but for the appalling silence of the good people. Human progress never rolls in on wheels of inevitability; it comes through the tireless efforts of men willing to be co-workers with God, and without this hard work, time itself becomes an ally of the forces of social stagnation. We must use time creatively, in the knowledge that the time is always ripe to do right. Now is the time to make real the promise of democracy and transform our pending national clergy into a creative psalm of brotherhood. Now is the time to lift our national policy from the quicksand of racial injustice to the solid rock of human dignity.

You speak of our activity in Birmingham as extreme. At first I was rather disappointed that fellow clergymen would see my nonviolent efforts as those of an extremist. I began thinking about the fact that I stand in the middle of two opposing forces in the Negro community. One is a force of complacency, made up in part of Negroes who, as a result of long years of oppression, are so drained of self-respect and a sense of "somebodiness" that they have adjusted to segregation; and in part of a few middle-class Negroes who, because of a degree of academic and economic security and because in some ways they profit by segregation, have become insensitive to the problems of the masses. The other force is one of bitterness and hatred, and it comes perilously close to advocating violence. It is expressed in the various black nationalist groups that are springing up across the nation, the largest and best-known being Elijah Muhammad's Muslim movement. Nourished by the Negro's frustration over the continued existence of racial discrimination, this movement is made up of people who have lost faith in America, who have absolutely repudiated Christianity, and who have concluded that the white man is an incorrigible "devil."

I have tried to stand between these two forces, saying that we need emulate neither the "do-nothingism" of the complacent nor the hatred and despair of the black nationalist. For there is the more excellent way of love and nonviolent protest. I am grateful to God that, through the influence of the Negro church, the way of nonviolence became an integral part of our struggle.

If this philosophy had not emerged, by now many streets of the South would, I am convinced, be flowing with blood. And I am further convinced that if our white brothers dismiss as "rabble-rousers" and "outside agitators" those of us who employ nonviolent direct action, and if they refuse to support our nonviolent efforts, millions of Negroes will, out of frustration and despair, seek solace and security in black-nationalist ideologies—a development that would inevitably lead to a frightening racial nightmare.

Oppressed people cannot remain oppressed forever. The yearning for freedom eventually manifests itself, and that is what has happened to the American Negro. Something within has reminded him of his birthright of freedom, and something without has reminded him that it can be gained. Consciously or unconsciously, he has been caught up by the *Zeitgeist*, and with his black brothers of Africa and his brown and yellow brothers of Asia, South America, and the Caribbean, the United States Negro is moving with a sense of great urgency toward the promised land of racial justice. If one recognizes this vital urge that has engulfed the Negro community, one should readily understand why public demonstrations are taking place. The Negro has many pent-up resentments and latent frustrations, and he must release them. So let him march; let him make prayer pilgrimages to the city hall; let him go on freedom rides—and try to understand why he must do so. If his repressed emotions are not released in nonviolent ways, they will seek expression through violence; this is not a threat but a fact of history. So I have not said to my people, "Get rid of your discontent." Rather, I have tried to say that this normal and healthy discontent can be channeled into the creative outlet of nonviolent direct action. And now this approach is being termed extremist.

But though I was initially disappointed at being categorized as an extremist, as I continued to think about the matter I gradually gained a measure of satisfaction from the label. Was not Jesus an extremist for love: "Love your enemies, bless them that curse you, do good to them that hate you, and pray for them which despitefully use you, and persecute you." Was not Amos an extremist for justice: "Let justice roll down like waters and righteousness like an ever-flowing stream." Was not Paul an extremist for the Christian gospel:

"I bear in my body the marks of the Lord Jesus." Was not Martin Luther an extremist: "Here I stand; I cannot do otherwise, so help me God." And John Bunyan: "I will stay in jail to the end of my days before I make a butchery of my conscience." And Abraham Lincoln: "This nation cannot survive half slave and half free." And Thomas Jefferson: "We hold these truths to be self-evident, that all men are created equal. . . ." So the question is not whether we will be extremists, but what kind of extremists we will be. Will we be extremists for hate or for love? Will we be extremists for the preservation of injustice or for the extension of justice? In that dramatic scene on Calvary's hill three men were crucified. We must never forget that all three were crucified for the same crime—the crime of extremism. Two were extremists for immorality, and thus fell below their environment. The other, Jesus Christ, was an extremist for love, truth, and goodness, and thereby rose above his environment. Perhaps the South, the nation, and the world are in dire need of creative extremists.

I had hoped that the white moderate would see this need. Perhaps I was too optimistic; perhaps I expected too much. I suppose I should have realized that few members of the oppressor race can understand the deep groans and passionate yearnings of the oppressed race, and still fewer have the vision to see that injustice must be rooted out by strong, persistent, and determined action. I am thankful, however, that some of our white brothers in the South have grasped the meaning of this social revolution and committed themselves to it. They are still all too few in quantity, but they are big in quality. Some—such as Ralph McGill, Lillian Smith, Harry Golden, James McBride Dabbs, Ann Braden, and Sarah Patton Boyle—have written about our struggle in eloquent and prophetic terms. Others have marched with us down nameless streets of the South. They have languished in filthy, roach-infested jails, suffering the abuse and brutality and policemen who view them as "dirty nigger-lovers." Unlike so many of their moderate brothers and sisters, they have recognized the urgency of the moment and sensed the need for powerful "action" antidotes to combat the disease of segregation.

Let me take note of my other major disappointment. I have been so greatly disappointed with the white church and its leadership. Of course, there are some notable exceptions. I am not unmindful of the fact that each of you has taken some significant stands on this issue. I commend you, Reverend Stallings, for your Christian stand on this past Sunday, in welcoming Negroes to your worship service on a nonsegregated basis. I commend the Catholic leaders of this state for integrating Spring Hill College several years ago.

But despite these notable exceptions, I must honestly reiterate that I have been disappointed with the church. I do not say this as one of those negative critics who can always find something wrong with the church. I say this as a minister of the gospel, who loves the church; who was nurtured in its bosom; who has been sustained by its spiritual blessings and who will remain true to it as long as the cord of life shall lengthen.

When I was suddenly catapulted into the leadership of the bus protest in Montgomery, Alabama, a few years ago, I felt we would be supported by the white church. I felt that the white ministers, priests, and rabbis of the South would be among our strongest allies. Instead, some have been outright opponents, refusing to understand the freedom movement and misrepresenting its leaders; all too many others have been more cautious than courageous and have remained silent behind the anesthetizing security of stained-glass windows.

In spite of my shattered dreams. I came to Birmingham with the hope that the white religious leadership of this community would see the justice of our cause and, with deep moral concern, would serve as the channel through which our just grievances could reach the power structure. I had hoped that each of you would understand. But again I have been disappointed.

I have heard numerous southern religious leaders admonish their worshipers to comply with a desegregation decision because it is the law, but I have longed to hear white ministers declare: "Follow this decree because integration is morally right and because the Negro is your brother." In the midst of blatant injustices inflicted upon the Negro, I have watched white churchmen stand on the sideline and mouth pious irrelevancies and sanctimonious trivialities. In the midst of a mighty struggle to rid our nation of racial and economic injustice, I have heard many ministers say: "Those are social issues, with which the gospel has no real concern." And I have watched many churches commit themselves to a completely otherworldly religion which makes a strange, unBiblical distinction between body and soul, between the sacred and the secular.

I have traveled the length and breadth of Alabama, Mississippi, and all the other southern states. On sweltering summer days and crisp autumn mornings I have looked at the South's beautiful churches with their lofty spires pointing heavenward. I have beheld the impressive outlines of her massive religious-education buildings. Over and over I have found myself asking: "What kind of people worship here? Who is their God? Where were their voices when the lips of Governor Barnett dripped with words of interposition and nullification? Where were they when Governor Wallace gave a clarion call for defiance and hatred? Where were their voices of support when bruised and weary Negro men and women decided to rise from the dark dungeons of complacency to the bright hills of creative protest?"

Yes, these questions are still in mind. In deep disappointment I have wept over the laxity of the church. But be assured that my tears have been tears of love. There can be no deep disappointment where there is not deep love. Yes, I love the church. How could I do otherwise? I am in the rather unique position of being the son, the grandson, and the great-grandson of preachers. Yes, I see the church as the body of Christ. But, oh! How we have blemished and scarred that body through social neglect and through fear of being nonconformists.

There was a time when the church was very powerful—in the time when the early Christians rejoiced at being deemed worthy to suffer for what they believed. In those days the church was not merely a thermometer that recorded the ideas and principles of popular opinion; it was a thermostat that transformed the mores of society. Whenever the early Christians entered a town, the people in power became disturbed and immediately sought to convict the Christians for being "disturbers of the peace" and "outside agitators." But the Christians pressed on, in the conviction that they were "a colony of heaven," called to obey God rather than man. Small in number, they were big in commitment. They were too God-intoxicated to be "astronomically intimidated." By their effort and example they brought an end to such ancient evils as infanticide and gladiatorial contests.

Things are different now. So often the contemporary church is a weak, ineffectual voice with an uncertain sound. So often it is an arch defender of the status quo. Far from being disturbed by the presence of the church, the power structure of the average community is consoled by the church's silent—and often even vocal—sanction of things as they are.

But the judgment of God is upon the church as never before. If today's church does not recapture the sacrificial spirit of the early church, it will lose its authenticity, forfeit the loyalty of millions, and be dismissed as an irrelevant social club with no meaning for the twentieth century. Every day I meet young people whose disappointment with the church has turned into outright disgust.

Perhaps I have once again been too optimistic. Is organized religion too inextricably bound to the status quo to save our nation and the world? Perhaps I must turn my faith to the inner spiritual church, the church within the church, as the true *ekklesia* and the hope of the world. But again I am thankful to God that some noble souls from the ranks of organized religion have broken loose from the paralyzing chains of conformity and joined us as active partners in the struggle for freedom. They have left their secure congregations and walked the streets of Albany, Georgia, with us. They have gone down the highways of the South on tortuous rides for freedom. Yes, they have gone to jail with us. Some have been dismissed from their churches, have lost the support of their bishops and fellow ministers. But they have acted in the faith that right defeated is stronger than evil triumphant. Their witness has been the spiritual salt that has preserved the true meaning of the gospel in these troubled times. They have carved a tunnel of hope through the dark mountain of disappointment.

I hope the church as a whole will meet the challenge of this decisive hour. But even if the church does not come to the aid of justice, I have no despair about the future. I have no fear about the outcome of our struggle in Birmingham, even if our motives are at present misunderstood. We will reach the goal of freedom in Birmingham and all over the nation, because the goal of America is freedom. Abused and scorned though we may be, our destiny is tied up with America's destiny. Before the pilgrims landed at Plymouth, we were here. Before the pen of Jefferson etched the majestic words of the Declaration of Independence across the pages of history, we were here. For more than two centuries our forebears labored in this country without wages; they made cotton king; they built the homes of their masters while suffering gross injustice and shameful humiliation—and yet out of a bottomless vitality they continued to thrive and develop. If the inexpressible cruelties of slavery could not stop us, the opposition we now face will surely fail. We will win our freedom because the sacred heritage of our nation and the eternal will of God are embodied in our echoing demands.

Before closing I feel impelled to mention one other point in your statement that has troubled me profoundly. You warmly commended the Birmingham police force for keeping "order" and "preventing violence." I doubt that you would have so warmly commended the police force if you had seen its dogs sinking their teeth into unarmed, nonviolent Negroes. I doubt that you would so quickly commend the policemen if you were to observe their ugly and inhumane treatment of Negroes here in the city jail; if you were to watch them push and curse old Negro women and young Negro girls; if you were to see them slap and kick old Negro men and young boys; if you were to observe them, as they did on two occasions, refuse to give us food because we wanted to sing our grace together. I cannot join you in your praise of the Birmingham police department.

It is true that the police have exercised a degree of discipline in handling the demonstrators. In this sense they have conducted themselves rather "nonviolently" in public. But for what purpose? To preserve the evil system of segregation. Over the past few years I have consistently preached that nonviolence demands that the means we use must be as pure as the ends we seek. I have tried to make clear that it is wrong to use immoral means to attain moral ends. But now I must affirm that it is just as wrong, or perhaps even more so, to use moral means to preserve immoral ends. Perhaps Mr. Connor and his policemen have been rather nonviolent in public, as was Chief Pritchett in Albany, Georgia, but they have used the moral means of nonviolence to maintain the immoral end of racial injustice. As T. S. Eliot has said. "The last temptation is the greatest treason: To do the right deed for the wrong reason."

I wish you had commended the Negro sit-inners and demonstrators of Birmingham for their sublime courage, their willingness to suffer, and their amazing discipline in the midst of great provocation. One day the South will recognize its real heroes. They will be the James Merediths, with the noble sense of purpose that enables them to face jeering and hostile mobs, and with the agonizing loneliness that characterizes the life of the pioneer. They will be old, oppressed, battered Negro women, symbolized in a seventy-two-year-old woman in Montgomery, Alabama, who rose up with a sense of dignity and with her people decided not to ride segregated buses, and who responded with ungrammatical profundity to one who inquired about her weariness: "My feets is tired, but my soul is at rest." They will be the young high school and college students, the young ministers of the gospel and a host of their elders, courageously and nonviolently sitting in at lunch counters and willingly going to jail for conscience' sake. One day the South will know that when these disinherited children of God sat down at lunch counters, they were in reality standing up for what is best in the American dream and for the most sacred values in our Judaeo-Christian heritage, thereby bringing our nation back to those great wells of democracy which were dug deep by the founding fathers in their formulation of the Constitution and the Declaration of Independence.

Never before have I written so long a letter. I'm afraid it is much too long to take your precious time. I can assure you that it would have been much shorter if I had been writing from a comfortable desk, but what else can one do when he is alone in a narrow jail cell, other than write long letters, think long thoughts, and pray long prayers?

If I have said anything in this letter that overstates the truth and indicates an unreasonable impatience, I beg you to forgive me. If I have said anything that understates the truth and indicates my having a patience that allows me to settle for anything less than brotherhood, I beg God to forgive me.

I hope this letter finds you strong in the faith. I hope that circumstances will soon make it possible for me to meet each of you, not as an integrationist or a civil-rights leader but as a fellow clergyman and a Christian brother. Let us all hope that the dark clouds of a racial prejudice will soon pass away and the deep fog of misunderstanding will be lifted from our fear-drenched communities, and in some not too distant tomorrow the radiant stars of love and brotherhood will shine over our great nation with all their scintillating beauty.

Yours for the cause of Peace and Brotherhood,
MARTIN LUTHER KING, JR.

Reflections

Private Exploration

1. Does any part of King's letter stimulate emotions in you? Sympathy, shame, anger, disagreement? Zero in on a key statement that seems to provoke that emotion. Clarify its context and explain why the statement seems important. Feel free to argue, agree, or disagree in part or totally. As King does so well throughout the letter, use examples drawn from history or personal experience to develop your response.
2. King provides an extended definition of the word "extremist" (pp. 513–515). Why does King's attitude toward being labeled an extremist shift from negative to positive. Who in present day society would you label a creative extremist? An immoral extremist? Why? Explore the concept in all its possibilities.

Public Exploration

1. A few years ago, when deaf students at Gallaudet University objected to the appointment of a president who was not hearing impaired, they protested using the same nonviolent approach King advocates in his letter. As a result of their protest the president was replaced. During the spring of 1989, students in Bejing, China, initiated a nonviolent campaign seeking democratic reform against the government. After a month of protest, the government acted. Thousands of lives were lost. In the past students have protested for or against apartheid, women's rights, experimentation with laboratory animals, nuclear warfare, gay rights, and various environmen-

tal issues. Martin Luther King defends such civil disobedience as "standing up for what is best in the American dream and for the most sacred values in our Judaeo-Christian heritage."

But there are those who disagree. Lewis H. Van Duesen, Jr., a Rhodes Scholar and a Philadelphia lawyer, believes:

> There is no man who is above the law, and there is no man who has a right to break the law. Civil disobedience is not above the law, but against the law. When the civil disobedient says that he is above the law, he is saying that democracy is beneath him. His disobedience shows a distrust for the democratic system.

Consider the strengths and weaknesses of both views. What kinds of values does each position imply?

2. Discuss King's argument that "Groups are more immoral than individuals."

Private Reflection

After listening to your class or group discuss some aspect of Martin Luther King's letter, quickly outline the conflicts or varying points of view that arose. Select one key difference with your own views and expand upon it. Ultimately you should attempt to move toward an understanding of what your position may express about your personal beliefs and values.

The New Year's Day Address

Prague, Czechoslovakia, January 1990

VACLAV HAVEL

For 40 years you have heard on this day from the mouths of my predecessors, in a number of variations, the same thing: how our country is flourishing, how many more millions of tons of steel we have produced, how we are all happy, how we believe in our Government and what beautiful prospects are opening ahead of us. I assume you have not named me to this office so that I, too, should lie to you.

Our country is not flourishing. The great creative and spiritual potential of our nation is not being applied meaningfully. Entire branches of industry are producing things for which there is no demand while we are short of things we need.

The state, which calls itself a state of workers, is humiliating and exploiting them instead. Our outmoded economy wastes energy, which we have in short supply. The country, which could once be proud of the education of its people, is spending so little on education that today, in that respect, we rank 72d in the world. We have spoiled our land, rivers and forests, inherited from our ancestors, and we have, today, the worst environment in the whole of Europe. Adults die here earlier than in the majority of European countries.

The worst of it is that we live in a spoiled moral environment. We have become morally ill because we are used to saying one thing and thinking another. We have learned not to believe in anything, not to care about each other, to worry only about ourselves. The concepts of love, friendship, mercy, humility or forgiveness have lost their depths and dimension, and for many of us they represent only some sort of psychological curiosity or they appear as long-lost wanderers from faraway times, somewhat ludicrous in the era of computers and space ships. . . .

The previous regime, armed with a proud and intolerant ideology, reduced people into the means of production, and nature into its tools. So it attacked their very essence, and their mutual relations. . . . Out of talented and responsible people, ingeniously husbanding their land, it made cogs of some sort of great, monstrous, thudding, smelly machine, with an unclear purpose. All it can do is, slowly but irresistibly, wear itself out, with all its cogs.

If I speak about a spoiled moral atmosphere I don't refer only to our masters. . . . I'm speaking about all of us. For all of us have grown used to the totalitarian system and accepted it as an immutable fact, and thereby actually helped keep it going. None of us are only its victims; we are all also responsible for it.

It would be very unwise to think of the sad heritage of the last 40 years only as something foreign, something inherited from a distant relative. On the contrary, we must accept this heritage as something we have inflicted on ourselves. If we accept it in such a way, we shall come to understand it is up to all of us to do something about it.

Let us make no mistake: even the best Government, the best Parliament and the best President cannot do much by themselves. Freedom and democracy, after all, mean joint participation and shared responsibility. If we realize this, then all the horrors that the new Czechoslovak democracy inherited cease to be so horrific. If we realize this, then hope will return to our hearts.

Everywhere in the world, people were surprised how these malleable, humiliated, cynical citizens of Czechoslovakia, who seemingly believed in nothing, found the tremendous strength within a few weeks to cast off the totalitarian system, in an entirely peaceful and dignified manner. We ourselves are surprised at it.

And we ask: Where did young people who had never known another system get their longing for truth, their love of freedom, their political imagination, their civic courage and civic responsibility? How did their parents, precisely the generation thought to have been lost, join them? How is it possible that so many people immediately understood what to do and that none of them needed any advice or instructions? . . .

Naturally we too had to pay for our present-day freedom. Many of our citizens died in prison in the 1950's. Many were executed. Thousands of human lives were destroyed. Hundreds of thousands of talented people were driven abroad. . . . Those who fought against totalitarianism during the war were also persecuted. . . . Nobody who paid in one way or another for our freedom could be forgotten.

Independent courts should justly evaluate the possible guilt of those responsible, so that the full truth about our recent past should be exposed.

But we should also not forget that other nations paid an even harsher price for their present freedom, and paid indirectly for ours as well. All human suffering concerns each human being. . . . Without changes in the Soviet Union, Poland, Hungary and the German Democratic Republic, what happened here could hardly have taken place, and certainly not in such a calm and peaceful way.

Now it depends only on us whether this hope will be fulfilled, whether our civic, national and political self-respect will be revived. Only a man or nation with self-respect, in the best sense of the word, is capable of listening to the voices of others, while accepting them as equals, of forgiving enemies and of expiating sins.

Perhaps you are asking what kind of republic I am dreaming about. I will answer you: a republic that is independent, free, democratic, a republic with economic prosperity and also social justice, a humane republic that serves man and that for that reason also has the hope that man will serve it.

My most important predecessor started his first speech by quoting from Comenius. Permit me to end my own first speech by my own paraphrase. Your Government, my people, has returned to you.

Reflections

Private Exploration

1. Explore your most immediate responses to Havel's speech to the Czechoslovakian parliament. What did you think about as you read it? What did you feel? Does it convince you, and if so, why? (Consider here your own cultural and personal background as part of your answer.)
2. Reread the speech closely, watching for key words and phrases. What insight is gained by becoming aware of these repetitions? What do they reveal about Havel's values and expectations?
3. Havel has been dubbed "the velvet prince." Check several sources in the library to find out more about him. Focus on discovering Havel's beliefs and values, his moral reputation, and why he was elected president of Czechoslovakia. What evidence can you find to demonstrate that he has the very self-respect he claims is "necessary to listen to the voices of others"? Are you more or less swayed by his address after finding out who he is?

Public Exploration

Havel points to a "spoiled moral environment" in Czechoslovakia. What do you understand him to mean by that phrase? What kind of morals is he addressing?

Some have remarked that Havel's accusation might well be directed at the United States. As a class or group, consider in what ways our own country might be considered "morally ill." What do we believe in? What is it we value? What hope do we have that our "moral environment" might change? What do you see as your responsibility to bring about change, assuming it is needed?

Private Reflection

Consider this statement:

> All human suffering concerns each human being.

Gooseberries

ANTON CHEKHOV

Translated from the Russian by **Ivy Litvinov**

The sky had been covered with rain-clouds ever since the early morning; it was a still day, cool and dull, one of those misty days when the clouds have long been lowering overhead and you keep thinking it is just going to rain, and the rain holds off. Ivan Ivanich, the veterinary surgeon, and Burkin, the high-school teacher, had walked till they were tired, and the way over the fields seemed endless to them. Far ahead they could just make out the windmill of the village of Mironositskoye, and what looked like a range of low hills at the right extending well beyond the village, and they both knew that this range was really the bank of the river, and that further on were meadows, green willow trees, country-estates; if they were on top of these hills, they knew they would see the same boundless fields and telegraph-posts, and the train, like a crawling caterpillar in the distance, while in fine weather even the town would be visible. On this still day, when the whole of nature seemed kindly and pensive, Ivan Ivanich and Burkin felt a surge of love for this plain, and thought how vast and beautiful their country was.

"The last time we stayed in Elder Prokofy's hut," said Burkin, "you said you had a story to tell me."

"Yes. I wanted to tell you the story of my brother."

Ivan Ivanich took a deep breath and lighted his pipe as a preliminary to his narrative, but just then the rain came. Five minutes later it was coming down in torrents and nobody could say when it would stop. Ivan Ivanich and

Burkin stood still lost in thought. The dogs, already soaked, stood with drooping tails, gazing at them wistfully.

"We must try and find shelter," said Burkin. "Let's go to Alekhin's. It's quite near."

"Come on, then."

They turned aside and walked straight across the newly reaped field, veering to the right till they came to a road. Very soon poplars, an orchard, and the red roofs of barns came into sight. The surface of a river gleamed, and they had a view of an extensive reach of water, a windmill and a whitewashed bathing-shed. This was Sofyino, where Alekhin lived.

The mill was working, and the noise made by its sails drowned the sound of the rain; the whole dam trembled. Horses, soaking wet, were standing near some carts, their heads drooping, and people were moving about with sacks over their heads and shoulders. It was wet, muddy, bleak, and the water looked cold and sinister. Ivan Ivanich and Burkin were already experiencing the misery of dampness, dirt, physical discomfort, their boots were caked with mud, and when, having passed the mill-dam, they took the upward path to the landowner's barns, they fell silent, as if vexed with one another.

The sound of winnowing came from one of the barns; the door was open, and clouds of dust issued from it. Standing in the door-way was Alekhin himself, a stout man of some forty years, with longish hair, looking more like a professor or an artist than a landed proprietor. He was wearing a white shirt, greatly in need of washing, belted with a piece of string, and long drawers with no trousers over them. His boots, too, were caked with mud and straw. His eyes and nose were ringed with dust. He recognized Ivan Ivanich and Burkin, and seemed glad to see them.

"Go up to the house, gentlemen," he said, smiling. "I'll be with you in a minute."

It was a large two-storey house. Alekhin occupied the ground floor, two rooms with vaulted ceilings and tiny windows, where the stewards had lived formerly. They were poorly furnished, and smelled of rye-bread, cheap vodka, and harness. He hardly ever went into the upstairs rooms, excepting when he had guests. Ivan Ivanich and Burkin were met by a maid-servant, a young woman of such beauty that they stood still involuntarily and exchanged glances.

"You have no idea how glad I am to see you here, dear friends," said Alekhin, overtaking them in the hall. "It's quite a surprise! Pelageya," he said, turning to the maid, "find the gentlemen a change of clothes. And I might as well change, myself. But I must have a wash first, for I don't believe I've had a bath since the spring. Wouldn't you like to go and have a bathe while they get things ready here?"

The beauteous Pelageya, looking very soft and delicate, brought them towels and soap, and Alekhin and his guests set off for the bathing-house.

"Yes, it's a long time since I had a wash," he said, taking off his clothes. "As you see I have a nice bathing place, my father had it built, but somehow I never seem to get time to wash."

He sat on the step, soaping his long locks and his neck, and all round him the water was brown.

"Yes, you certainly . . ." remarked Ivan Ivanich, with a significant glance at his host's head.

"It's a long time since I had a wash . . ." repeated Alekhin, somewhat abashed, and he soaped himself again, and now the water was dark-blue, like ink.

Ivan Ivanich emerged from the shed, splashed noisily into the water, and began swimming beneath the rain, spreading his arms wide, making waves all round him, and the while water-lilies rocked on the waves he made. He swam into the very middle of the river and then dived, a moment later came up at another place and swam further, diving constantly, and trying to touch the bottom. "Ah, my God," he kept exclaiming in his enjoyment. "Ah, my God. . . ." He swam up to the mill, had a little talk with some peasants there and turned back, but when he got to the middle of the river, he floated, holding his face up to the rain. Burkin and Alekhin were dressed and ready to go, but he went on swimming and diving.

"God! God!" he kept exclaiming. "Dear God!"

"Come out!" Burkin shouted to him.

They went back to the house. And only after the lamp was lit in the great drawing-room on the upper floor, and Burkin and Ivan Ivanich, in silk dressing-gowns and warm slippers, were seated in arm-chairs, while Alekhin, washed and combed, paced the room in his new frock-coat, enjoying the warmth, the cleanliness, his dry clothes and comfortable slippers, while the fair Pelageya, smiling benevolently, stepped noislessly over the carpet with her tray of tea and preserves, did Ivan Ivanich embark upon his yarn, the ancient dames, young ladies, and military gentlemen looking down at them severely from the gilded fames, as if they, too, were listening.

"There were two of us brothers," he began. "Ivan Ivanich (me), and my brother Nikolai Ivanich, two years younger than myself. I went in for learning and became a veterinary surgeon, but Nikolai started working in a government office when he was only nineteen. Our father, Chimsha-Himalaisky, was educated in a school for the sons of private soldiers, but was later promoted to officer's rank, and was made a hereditary nobleman and given a small estate. After his death the estate had to be sold for debts, but at least our childhood was passed in the freedom of the countryside, where we roamed the fields and the woods like peasant children, taking the horses to graze, peeling bark from the trunks of lime-trees, fishing, and all that sort of thing. And anyone who has once in his life fished for perch, or watched the thrushes fly south in the autumn, rising high over the village on clear, cool days, is spoilt for town life, and will long for the country-side for the rest of his days. My brother pined in his government office. The years passed and he sat in the same place every day, writing out the same documents and thinking all the time of the same thing—how to get back to the country. And these longings of his gradually turned into a definite desire, into a dream of purchasing a little estate somewhere on the bank of a river or the shore of a lake.

"He was a meek, good-natured chap, I was fond of him, but could feel no sympathy with the desire to lock oneself up for life in an estate of one's own. They say man only needs six feet of earth. But it is a corpse, and not man, which needs these six feet. And now people are actually saying that it is a good sign for our intellectuals to yearn for the land and try to obtain country-dwellings. And yet these estates are nothing but those same six feet of earth. To escape from the town, from the struggle, from the noise of life, to escape and hide one's head on a country-estate, is not life, but egoism, idleness, it is a sort of renunciation, but renunciation without faith. It is not six feet of earth, not a country-estate, that man needs, but the whole globe, the whole of nature, room to display his qualities and the individual characteristics of his soul.

"My brother Nikolai sat at his office-desk, dreaming of eating soup made from his own cabbages, which would spread a delicious smell all over his own yard, of eating out of doors, on the green grass, of sleeping in the sun, sitting for hours on a bench outside his gate, and gazing at the fields and woods. Books on agriculture, and all those hints printed on the calendars were his delight, his favourite spiritual nourishment. He was fond of reading newspapers, too, but all he read in them was advertisements of the sale of so many acres of arable and meadowland, with residence attached, a river, an orchard, a mill, and ponds fed by springs. His head was full of visions of garden paths, flowers, fruit, nesting-boxes, carp-ponds, and all that sort of thing. These visions differed according to the advertisements he came across, but for some reason gooseberry bushes invariably figured in them. He could not picture to himself a single estate or picturesque nook that did not have gooseberry bushes in it.

" 'Country life has its conveniences,' he would say: 'You sit on the verandah, drinking tea, with your own ducks floating on the pond, and everything smells so nice, and . . . and the gooseberries ripen on the bushes.'

"He drew up plans for his estate, and every plan showed the same features: a) the main residence, b) the servant's wing, c) the kitchen-garden, d) gooseberry bushes. He lived thriftily, never ate or drank his fill, dressed anyhow, like a beggar, and saved up all his money in the bank. He became terribly stingy. I could hardly bear to look at him, and whenever I gave him a little money, or sent him a present on some holiday, he put that away, too. Once a man gets an idea into his head, there's no doing anything with him.

"The years passed, he was sent to another gubernia, he was over forty, and was still reading advertisements in the papers, and saving up. At last I heard he had married. All for the same purpose, to buy himself an estate with gooseberry bushes on it, he married an ugly elderly widow, for whom he had not the slightest affection, just because she had some money. After his marriage he went on living as thriftily as ever, half-starving his wife, and putting her money in his own bank account. Her first husband had been a postmaster, and she was used to pies and cordials, but with her second husband she did not even get enough black bread to eat. She began to languish under such a regime, and three years later yielded up her soul to God. Of course my brother did not for a moment consider himself guilty of her death. Money, like vodka, makes a man eccentric. There was a merchant in our town who asked for a plate of honey on his deathbed and ate up all his bank-notes and lottery tickets with the honey, so that no one else should get it. And one day when I was examining a consignment of cattle at a railway station, a drover fell under the engine and his leg was severed from his body. We carried him all bloody into the waiting-room, a terrible sight, and he did nothing but beg us to look for his leg, worrying all the time—there were twenty rubles in the boot, and he was afraid they would be lost.''

''You're losing the thread,'' put in Burkin.

Ivan Ivanich paused for a moment, and went on: ''After his wife's death my brother began to look about for an estate. You can search for five years, of course, and in the end make a mistake, and buy something quite different from what you dreamed of. My brother Nikolai bought three hundred acres, complete with gentleman's house, servants' quarters, and a park, as well as a mortgage to be paid through an agent, but there were neither an orchard, gooseberry bushes, nor a pond with ducks on it. There was a river, but it was as dark as coffee, owing to the fact that there was a brick-works on one side of the estate, and bone-kilns on the other. Nothing daunted, however, my brother Nikolai Ivanich ordered two dozen gooseberry bushes and settled down as a landed proprietor.

''Last year I paid him a visit. I thought I would go and see how he was getting on there. In his letters my brother gave his address as Chumbaroklova Pustosh or Himalaiskoye. I arrived at Himalaiskoye in the afternoon. It was very hot. Everywhere were ditches, fences, hedges, rows of fir-trees, and it was hard to drive into the yard and find a place to leave one's carriage. As I went a fat ginger-coloured dog, remarkably like a pig, came out to meet me. It looked as if it would have barked if it were not so lazy. The cook, who was also fat and like a pig, came out of the kitchen, barefoot, and said her master was having his after-dinner rest. I made my way to my brother's room, and found him sitting up in bed, his knees covered by a blanket. He had aged, and grown stout and flabby. His cheeks, nose and lips protruded—I almost expected him to grunt into the blanket.

''We embraced and wept—tears of joy, mingled with melancholy—because we had once been young and were now both grey-haired and approaching the grave. He put on his clothes and went out to show me over his estate.

'' 'Well, how are you getting on here?' I asked.

'' 'All right, thanks be, I'm enjoying myself.'

''He was no longer the poor, timid clerk, but a true proprietor, a gentleman. He had settled down, and was entering with zest into country life. He ate a lot, washed in the bathhouse, and put on flesh. He had already got into litigation with the village commune, the brick-works and the bone-kilns, and took offence if the peasants failed to call him 'Your Honour.' He went in for religion in a solid, gentlemanly way, and there was nothing casual about his pretentious good works. And what were these good works? He treated all the diseases of the peasants with bicarbonate of soda and castor-oil, and had a special thanksgiving service held on his name-day, after which he provided half a pail of vodka, supposing that this was the right thing to do. Oh, those terrible half pails! Today the fat landlord hauls the peasants before the

Zemstvo representative for letting their sheep graze on his land, tomorrow, on the day of rejoicing, he treats them to half a pail of vodka, and they drink and sing and shout hurrah, prostrating themselves before him when they are drunk. Any improvement in his conditions, anything like satiety or idleness, develops the most insolent complacency in a Russian. Nikolai Ivanich, who had been afraid of having an opinion of his own when he was in the government service, was now continually coming out with axioms, in the most ministerial manner: 'Education is essential, but the people are not ready for it yet,' 'corporal punishment is an evil, but in certain cases it is beneficial and indispensable.'

" 'I know the people and I know how to treat them,' he said. 'The people love me. I only have to lift my little finger, and the people will do whatever I want.'

"And all this, mark you, with a wise, indulgent smile. Over and over again he repeated: 'We the gentry,' or 'speaking as a gentleman,' and seemed to have quite forgotten that our grandfather was a peasant, and our father a common soldier. Our very surname—Chimsha-Himalaisky—in reality so absurd, now seemed to him a resounding, distinguished, and euphonious name.

"But it is of myself, and not of him, that I wish to speak. I should like to describe to you the change which came over me in those few hours I spent on my brother's estate. As we were drinking tea in the evening, the cook brought us a full plate of gooseberries. These were not gooseberries bought for money, they came from his own garden, and were the first fruits of the bushes he had planted. Nikolai Ivanich broke into a laugh and gazed at the gooseberries, in tearful silence for at least five minutes. Speechless with emotion, he popped a single gooseberry into his mouth, darted at me the triumphant glance of a child who has at last gained possession of a longed-for toy, and said:

" 'Delicious!'

'And he ate them greedily, repeating over and over again:

" 'Simply delicious! You try them.'

"They were hard and sour, but, as Pushkin says: "The lie which elates us is dearer than a thousand sober truths.' I saw before me a really happy man, whose dearest wish had come true, who had achieved his aim in life, got what he wanted, and was content with his lot and with himself. There had always been a tinge of melancholy in my conception of human happiness, and now, confronted by a happy man, I was overcome by a feeling of sadness bordering on desperation. This feeling grew strongest of all in the night. A bed was made up for me in the room next to my brother's bedroom, and I could hear him moving about restlessly, every now and then getting up to take a gooseberry from a plate. How many happy, satisfied people there are, after all, I said to myself! What an overwhelming force! Just consider this life—the insolence and idleness of the strong, the ignorance and bestiality of the weak, all around intolerable poverty, cramped dwellings, degeneracy, drunkenness, hypocrisy, lying. . . . And yet peace and order apparently prevail in all those homes and in the streets. Of the fifty thousand inhabitants of a town, not one will be found to cry out, to proclaim his indignation aloud. We see those who go to the market to buy food, who eat in the day-time and sleep at night, who prattle away, marry, grow old, carry their dead to the cemeteries. But we neither hear nor see those who suffer, and the terrible things in life are played out behind the scenes. All is calm and quiet, only statistics, which are dumb, protest: so many have gone mad, so many barrels of drink have been consumed, so many children died of malnutrition. . . . And apparently this is as it should be. Apparently those who are happy can only enjoy themselves because the unhappy bear their burdens in silence, and but for this silence happiness would be impossible. It is a kind of universal hypnosis. There ought to be a man with a hammer behind the door of every happy man, to remind him by his constant knocks that there are unhappy people, and that happy as he himself may be, life will sooner or later show him its claws, catastrophe will overtake him—sickness, poverty, loss—and nobody will see it, just as he now neither sees nor hears the misfortunes of others. But there is no man with a hammer, the happy man goes on living and the petty vicissitudes of life touch him lightly, like the wind in an aspen-tree, and all is well.

"That night I understood that I, too, was happy and content," continued Ivan Ivanich, getting up. "I, too, while out hunting, or at the dinner table, have held forth on the right way to live, to worship, to manage the people. I, too, have declared that without knowledge there can be no light, that education is essential, but that bare literacy is sufficient for the common people. Freedom is a blessing, I have said, one can't get on without it, any more than without air, but we must wait. Yes, that is what I said, and now I ask: In the name of what must we wait?" Here Ivan Ivanich looked angrily at Burkin. "In the name of what must we wait, I ask you. What is there to be considered? Don't be in such a hurry, they tell me, every idea materializes gradually, in its own time. But who are they who say this? What is the proof that it is just? You refer to the natural order of things, to the logic of facts, but according to what order, what logic do I, a living, thinking individual, stand on the edge of a ditch and wait for it to be gradually filled up, or choked with silt, when I might leap across it or build a bridge over it? And again, in the name of what must we wait? Wait, when we have not the strength to live, though live we must and to live we desire!

"I left my brother early the next morning, and ever since I have found town life intolerable. The peace and order weigh on my spirits, and I am afraid to look into windows, because there is now no sadder spectacle for me than a happy family seated around the tea-table. I am old and unfit for the struggle, I am even incapable of feeling hatred. I can only suffer inwardly, and give way to irritation and annoyance, at night my head burns from the rush of thoughts, and I am unable to sleep. . . . Oh, if only I were young!"

Ivan Ivanich began pacing backwards and forwards, repeating:

"If only I were young still!"

Suddenly he went up to Alekhin and began pressing first one of his hands, and then the other.

"Pavel Konstantinich," he said in imploring accents. "Don't *you* fall into apathy, don't *you* let your conscience be lulled to sleep! While you are still young, strong, active, do not be weary of well-doing. There is no such thing as happiness, nor ought there to be, but if there is any sense or purpose in life, this sense and purpose are to be found not in our own happiness, but in something greater and more rational. Do good!"

Ivan Ivanich said all this with a piteous, imploring smile, as if he were asking for something for himself.

Then they all three sat in their arm-chairs a long way apart from one another, and said nothing. Ivan Ivanich's story satisfied neither Burkin or Alekhin. It was not interesting to listen to the story of a poor clerk who ate gooseberries, when from the walls generals and fine ladies, who seemed to come to life in the dark, were looking down from their gilded frames. It would have been much more interesting to hear about elegant people, lovely women. And the fact that they were sitting in a drawing-room in which everything—the swathed chandeliers, the arm-chairs, the carpet on the floor, proved that the people now looking out of the frames had once moved about here, sat in the chairs, drunk tea, where the fair Pelageya was now going noiselessly to and fro, was better than any story.

Alekhin was desperately sleepy. He had got up early, at three o'clock in the morning, to go about his work on the estate, and could now hardly keep his eyes open. But he would not go to bed, for fear one of his guests would relate something interesting after he was gone. He could not be sure whether what Ivan Ivanich had just told them was wise or just, but his visitors talked of other things besides grain, hay, or tar, of things which had no direct bearing on his daily life, and he liked this, and wanted them to go on. . . .

"Well, time to go to bed," said Burkin, getting up. "Allow me to wish you a good night."

Alekhin said good night and went downstairs to his own room, the visitors remaining on the upper floor. They were allotted a big room for the night, in which were two ancient bedsteads of carved wood, and an ivory crucifix in one corner. There was a pleasant smell of freshly laundered sheets from the wide, cool beds which the fair Pelageya made up for them.

Ivan Ivanich undressed in silence and lay down.

"Lord have mercy on us, sinners," he said, and covered his head with the sheet.

There was a strong smell of stale tobacco from his pipe, which he put on the table, and Burkin lay awake a long time, wondering where the stifling smell came from.

The rain tapped on the window-panes all night.

Reflections

Private Exploration

1. Reflect on your own dreams and longings, your own view of happiness. Ponder the source of these dreams as well as the price you have to pay in order to fulfill them. Once you have accomplished those dreams, how will you be sure you will be happy?

2. Focus on a key passage and explore your response. Ask yourself questions, lots of them. Why did you choose that particular passage? What entrance do you gain into the story as a whole?
3. Chekhov once stated that the business of the artist is that of "stating the problem correctly," not that of solving it. Ponder the problem Chekhov's story brings to light and consider its relevance today, drawing on specific examples. Is there a solution? Does the responsibility for solving this problem rest with the young?

Public Exploration

1. Take a few minutes and explore the following questions in your notebook privately before meeting with your class or group to discuss them.

   What do you think about Ivanich's ideas concerning happiness and goodness? Do you accept them? Why? Are you convinced that Ivanich would act differently if he were younger? And what of young people today? Have they grown apathetic, "weary of doing for others"? Has their conscience been "lulled to sleep"? Has yours?

Private Reflection

Consider the relevance of the following quotation from Pushkin:

> The lie which elates us is dearer than a thousand sober truths.

What are the lies, what are the truths being avoided in the story? In contemporary culture? In your life?

• Those Winter Sundays •

ROBERT HAYDEN

Sundays too my father got up early
and put his clothes on in the blueblack cold,
then with cracked hands that ached
from labor in the weekday weather made
banked fires blaze. No one ever thanked him.

I'd wake and hear the cold splintering, breaking.
When the rooms were warm, he'd call,
and slowly I would rise and dress,
fearing the chronic angers of that house,

Speaking indifferently to him,
who had driven out the cold
and polished my good shoes as well.
What did I know, what did I know
of love's austere and lonely offices?

Reflections

Private Exploration

After reading the poem several times, write a prose paraphrase of each of the three stanzas. Look up any words you're unsure of and consider how they may add additional insight into the poem. Consider how this act of slowing down and rewriting the poem in other language affects your perception of the work. Is it enhanced or lessened?

Public Exploration

In your class or group, consider the final lines:

> What did I know, what did I know
> of love's austere and lonely offices?

Use these lines to initiate a discussion of the poem and of the choices some people must often make. Who makes these choices? Why? What kind of values underlie such choices?

Private Reflection

Reflect on your own relationship with a parent or someone who raised you but from whom you feel distant. Tell about your relationship, the details and images you recall as you remember that person. What thoughts come to mind as you ponder the value of that relationship?

CONNECTIONS

Although your best writing will usually emerge from insights already under development in your reading notebook, here are some additional possibilities for exploring relationships between and among various works of literature.

1. Compare Nadine Gordimer's "Six Feet of the Country" with Anouilh's *Antigone* (p. 461). Consider how each work counterposes the conflicting demands of government or the power of authority with individual conscience.
2. In "Self Reliance," Emerson writes: "Who so would be a man must be a nonconformist." Consider how this concept might offer insight into such disparate works as Alfred Lord Tennyson's "Ulysses" (p. 483) and James Thurber's "The Greatest Man in the World" (p. 477).
3. You may at first be puzzled by the Chinese poem, "When the Great Reason," by Laotze (p. 506). Consider it in light of either Martin Luther King's "Letter from Birmingham Jail" (p. 507) or Thoreau's "Civil Disobedience" (p. 496). Why, when "reason is obliterated," do benevolence and justice appear?
4. Reinhold Niebuhr's observation that "Groups are more immoral than individuals," may provide a connection between Elie Wiesel's "A Summons at Buchenwald" (p. 449) and Sharon Olds's poem "Leningrad Cemetery" (p. 454). Consider the historical context of both works.
5. Emerson writes in "Self Reliance" that "Nothing is at last sacred but the integrity of your own mind." Consider how this idea might relate to any of the readings in "Country of Conscience." You might look especially at Plato's "Crito" (p. 485), Maxine Hong Kingston's "The Quiet Girl" (p. 470), Tennyson's "Ulysses" (p. 483), or Wendy Rose's "Three Thousand Dollar Death Song" (p. 459).
6. Write an essay focusing on the concepts of power and conscience, drawing from Phyllis Rose's "Parallel Lives," (p. 366), and June Jordan's "Where is the Love?" (p. 335), or *Antigone* (p. 658).
7. Explore the parallels between King's "Letter from Birmingham Jail" (p. 507) and Thoreau's "On the Duty of Civil Disobedience" (p. 496).
8. Consider the role of conscience and personal integrity in Joyce Carol Oates' *Theft*, (p. 612) or *Antigone* (p. 658).
9. Use any of the following as a starting point for an essay that compares or contrasts the values found in Tolstoy's "How Much Land Does a Man Need?" (p. 403) and Chekhov's "Gooseberries" (p. 523).

   - *Once a man gets an idea into his head, there's no stopping him.* —Chekhov
   - *Money, like vodka, makes a man eccentric.* —Chekhov
   - *The lie which elates us is dearer than a thousand sober truths.* —Pushkin

CHAPTER 11

OUT OF DARKNESS

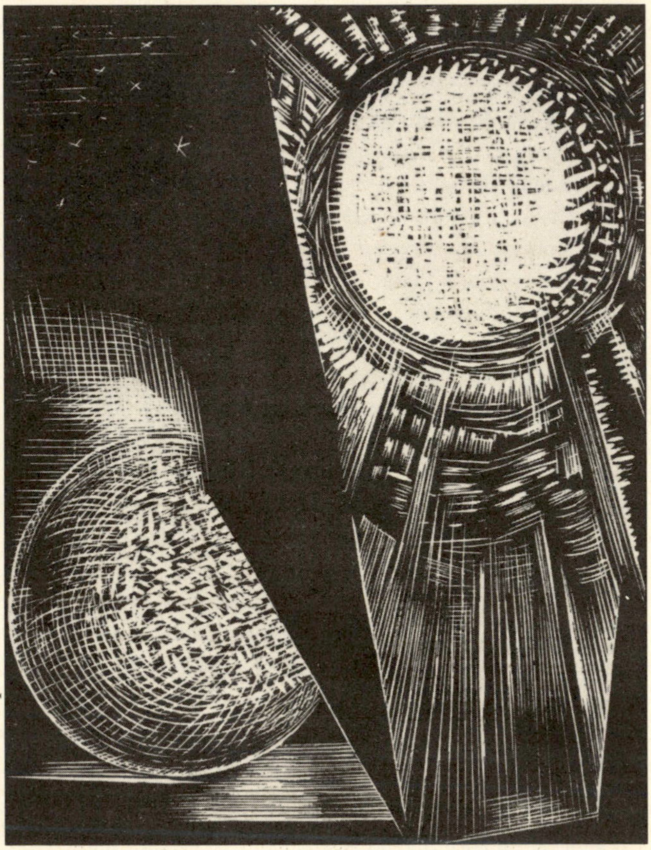

David Alfaro Siqueiros, from *13 Grabados*, 1931.

The values by which we are to survive are not rules for just and unjust conduct, but are those deeper illuminations in whose light justice and injustice, good and evil, means and ends are seen in fearful sharpness. . . .

—Jacob Bronowski

Houdini did it. Time and again the master escape artist risked his life in death-defying acts. Locked in a glass coffin so air-tight that even a candle extinguished after a few moments, he escaped. Padlocked in a forty-quart milk can filled with water, he escaped. Placed in a straightjacket, attached by the ankles to a steel cable, and hoisted halfway up the side of the New York Times building, Houdini escaped.

Yet all this was illusion. Those individuals who struggle to overcome physical, ethnic, social, or cultural barriers, are our true survivors. The obstacles they confront are not illusions easily resolved by a quick trick of hand. Nor are their triumphs always noted or applauded.

Who are these individuals? A few stand out: Nelsen Mandela, Mother Teresa, Christopher Nolan, Helen Keller, Maya Angelou, Shen Tong, and others.

We think of Carolina Maria de Jesus who lived in the slums of Saõ Paulo with her three children. Their only shelter, a rat-infested shack with a cardboard roof, collapsed when it rained. She hunted through trash for paper and scraps of metal that could be sold for rice to keep her family alive. The only thing that kept her from despair was writing. With only two years of schooling, Carolina de Jesus filled twenty-six notebooks describing the violence and hunger she confronted every day. When her notebook was published, it became an instant best seller. Because she had a sense of self-worth, because she refused to lower her own standards, because she chose to resist and somehow change her world by the writing she believed in, de Jesus created a new life for herself and her children outside the slums.

Yet another name comes to mind as we think of individuals who have struggled to resist and achieve: Stephen Hawking. Widely regarded as the most brilliant theoretical physicist since Einstein, Hawking was afflicted with Lou Gehrig's disease while studying for his Ph.D. in 1963. Nevertheless, he completed is degree, became a professor at Cambridge, and married. Although confined to a wheelchair, he has continued his work. Because he cannot hold a pen, he composes and revises in his head and then dictates his polished work to a secretary—one of a few people who can understand his faltering speech. In spite of his declining health, Hawking has continued to publish and edit books that probe the origins of the universe. According to his wife, Jane, he "hasn't wasted any of his talents at all. In fact, he has intensified them."

Finally, we think of Vaclav Havel. For almost five years, Havel, a Czechoslovakian poet, essayist, and playwright, was imprisoned for his resistance to Communist rule. Yet even from his cell, he continued his fight for political freedom. He founded the human-rights group Charter 77 and continued to resist by writing plays that eloquently depict the quiet desperation of life under totalitarianism. Released from prison during the 1989 revolutions, Vaclav Havel became the first democratically elected president of Czechoslovakia since 1946. In an address delivered to a joint session of the United States Congress, February 21, 1990, he shared this light: "Consciousness precedes being. . . . [T]he salvation of this human world lives nowhere else than in the human heart, in the human power to reflect, in human meekness and in human responsibility. . . ."

At the turn of the century when Harry Houdini, a Hungarian, immigrated to America, he made a decision. Rather than resist and confront the discrimination that denied him his civil rights, he chose to survive through a life of illusion. Few lives, if any, were altered by his staged triumphs. By contrast, the individuals who have so courageously confronted and overcome barriers are those who inspire and guide us. The triumphs of people like de Jesus, Hawking, Havel—and those you will read about in this chapter, from Richard Wright to the fictional Norma Jean Moffitt—do make a difference. These individuals have been true to themselves and their values.

"Something radiates from their lives," according to Bertrand Russell, "some light that shows the way to their friends, their neighbors—perhaps to long future ages. . . . the individual, if he [or she] is filled with love of mankind, with the breadth of vision, with courage and endurance, can do a great deal."

The Library Card

RICHARD WRIGHT

One morning I arrived early at work and went into the bank lobby where the Negro porter was mopping. I stood at a counter and picked up the Memphis *Commercial Appeal* and began my free reading of the press. I came finally to the editorial page and saw an article dealing with one H. L. Mencken. I knew by hearsay that he was the editor of the *American Mercury*, but aside from that I knew nothing about him. The article was a furious denunciation of Mencken, concluding with one, hot, short sentence: Mencken is a fool.

I wondered what on earth this Mencken had done to call down upon him the scorn of the South. The only people I had ever heard denounced in the South were Negroes, and this man was not a Negro. Then what ideas did Mencken hold that made a newspaper like the *Commercial Appeal* castigate him publicly? Undoubtedly he must be advocating ideas that the South did not like. Were there, then, people other than Negroes who criticized the South? I knew that during the Civil War the South had hated northern whites, but I had not encountered such hate during my life. Knowing no more of Mencken than I did at that moment, I felt a vague sympathy for him. Had not the South, which had assigned me the role of a non-man, cast at him its hardest words?

Now, how could I find out about this Mencken? There was a huge library near the riverfront, but I knew that Negroes were not allowed to patronize its shelves any more than they were the parks and playgrounds of the city. I had gone into the library several times to get books for the white men on the job.

Which of them would now help me to get books? And how could I read them without causing concern to the white men with whom I worked? I had so far been successful in hiding my thoughts and feelings from them, but I knew that I would create hostility if I went about this business of reading in a clumsy way.

I weighed the personalities of the men on the job. There was a Don, a Jew; but I distrusted him. His position was not much better than mine and I knew that he was uneasy and insecure; he had always treated me in an offhand, bantering way that barely concealed his contempt. I was afraid to ask him to help me to get books; his frantic desire to demonstrate a racial solidarity with the whites against Negroes might make him betray me.

Then how about the boss? No, he was a Baptist and I had the suspicion that he would not be quite able to comprehend why a black boy would want to read Mencken. There were other white men on the job whose attitudes showed clearly that they were Kluxers or sympathizers, and they were out of the question.

There remained only one man whose attitude did not fit into an anti-Negro category, for I had heard the white men refer to him as a "Pope lover." He was an Irish Catholic and was hated by the white Southerners. I knew that he read books, because I had got him volumes from the library several times. Since he, too, was an object of hatred, I felt that he might refuse me but would hardly betray me. I hesitated, weighing and balancing the imponderable realities.

One morning I paused before the Catholic fellow's desk.

"I want to ask you a favor," I whispered to him.

"What is it?"

"I want to read. I can't get books from the library. I wonder if you'd let me use your card?"

He looked at me suspiciously.

"My card is full most of the time," he said.

"I see," I said and waited, posing my question silently.

"You're not trying to get me into trouble, are you, boy?" he asked, staring at me.

"Oh, no, sir."

"What book do you want?"

"A book by H. L. Mencken."

"Which one?"

"I don't know. Has he written more than one?"

"He has written several."

"I didn't know that."

"What makes you want to read Mencken?"

"Oh, I just saw his name in the newspaper," I said.

"It's good of you to want to read," he said. "But you ought to read the right things."

I said nothing. Would he want to supervise my reading?

"Let me think," he said. "I'll figure out something."

I turned from him and he called me back. He stared at me quizzically.

"Richard, don't mention this to the other white men," he said.

"I understand," I said. "I won't say a word."

A few days later he called me to him.

"I've got a card in my wife's name," he said. "Here's mine."

"Thank you, sir."

"Do you think you can manage it?"

"I'll manage fine," I said.

"If they suspect you, you'll get in trouble," he said.

"I'll write the same kind of notes to the library that you wrote when you sent me for books," I told him. "I'll sign your name."

He laughed.

"Go ahead. Let me see what you get," he said.

That afternoon I addressed myself to forging a note. Now, what were the names of books written by H. L. Mencken? I did not know any of them. I finally wrote what I thought would be a foolproof note: *Dear Madam: Will you please let this nigger boy*—I used the word "nigger" to make the librarian feel that I could not possibly be the author of the note—*have some books by H. L. Mencken*? I forged the white man's name.

I entered the library as I had always done when on errands for whites, but I felt that I would somehow slip up and betray myself. I doffed my hat, stood a respectful distance from the desk, looked as unbookish as possible, and waited for the white patrons to be taken care of. When the desk was clear of people, I still waited. The white librarian looked at me.

"What do you want, boy?"

As though I did not possess the power of speech, I stepped forward and simply handed her the forged note, not parting my lips.

"What books by Mencken does he want?" she asked.

"I don't know, ma'am," I said, avoiding her eyes.

"Who gave you this card?"

"Mr. Falk," I said.

"Where is he?"

"He's at work, at M——— Optical Company," I said. "I've been in here for him before."

"I remember," the woman said. "But he never wrote notes like this."

Oh, God, she's suspicious. Perhaps she would not let me have the books? If she had turned her back at that moment, I would have ducked out the door and never gone back. Then I thought of a bold idea.

"You can call him up, ma'am," I said, my heart pounding.

"You're not using these books, are you?" she asked pointedly.

"Oh, no, ma'am. I can't read."

"I don't know what he wants by Mencken," she said under her breath.

I knew now that I had won; she was thinking of other things and the race question had gone out of her mind. She went to the shelves. Once or twice she looked over her shoulder at me, as though she was still doubtful. Finally she came forward with books in her hand.

"I'm sending him two books," she said. "But tell Mr. Falk to come in next time, or send me the names of the books he wants. I don't know what he wants to read."

I said nothing. She stamped the card and handed me the books. Not daring to glance at them, I went out of the library, fearing that the woman would call me back for further questioning. A block away from the library I opened one of the books and read a title: *A Book of Prefaces.* I was nearing my nineteenth birthday and I did not know how to pronounce the word "preface." I thumbed the pages and saw strange words and strange names. I shook my head, disappointed. I looked at the other book; it was called *Prejudices.* I knew what that word meant; I had heard it all my life. And right off I was on guard against Mencken's books. Why would a man want to call a book *Prejudices*? The word was so stained with all my memories of racial hate that I could not conceive of anybody using it for a title. Perhaps I had made a mistake about Mencken? A man who had prejudices must be wrong.

When I showed the books to Mr. Falk, he looked at me and frowned.

"That librarian might telephone you," I warned him.

"That's all right," he said. "But when you're through reading those books, I want you to tell me what you get out of them."

That night in my rented room, while letting the hot water run over my can of pork and beans in the sink, I opened *A Book of Prefaces* and began to read. I was jarred and shocked by the style, the clear, clean, sweeping sentences. Why did he write like that? And how did one write like that? I pictured the man as a raging demon, slashing with his pen, consumed with hate, denouncing everything American, extolling everything European or German, laughing at the weaknesses of people, mocking God, authority. What was this? I stood up, trying to realize what reality lay behind the meaning of the words . . . Yes, this man was fighting, fighting with words. He was using words as a weapon, using them as one would use a club. Could words be weapons? Well, yes, for here they were. Then, maybe, perhaps, I could use them as a weapon? No. It frightened me. I read on and what amazed me was not what he said, but how on earth anybody had the courage to say it.

Occasionally I glanced up to reassure myself that I was alone in the room. Who were these men about whom Mencken was talking so passionately? Who was Anatole France? Joseph Conrad? Sinclair Lewis, Sherwood Anderson, Dostoevski, George Moore, Gustave Flaubert, Maupassant, Tolstoy, Frank Harris, Mark Twain, Thomas Hardy, Arnold Bennett, Stephen Crane, Zola, Norris, Gorky, Bergson, Ibsen, Balzac, Bernard Shaw, Dumas, Poe, Thomas Mann, O. Henry, Dreiser, H. G. Wells, Gogol, T. S. Eliot, Gide, Baudelaire, Edgar Lee Masters, Stendhal, Turgenev, Huneker, Nietzsche, and scores of others? Were these men real? Did they exist or had they existed? And how did one pronounce their names?

I ran across many words whose meanings I did not know, and I either looked them up in a dictionary or, before I had a chance to do that, encountered the word in a context that made its meaning clear. But what strange world was this? I concluded the book with the conviction that I had somehow overlooked something terribly important in life. I had once tried to write, had once reveled in feeling, had let my crude imagination roam, but the impulse to dream had been slowly beaten out of me by experience. Now it surged up again and I hungered for books, new ways of looking and seeing. It was not a matter of believing or disbelieving what I read, but of feeling something new, of being affected by something that made the look of the world different.

As dawn broke I ate my pork and beans, feeling dopey, sleepy. I went to work, but the mood of the book would not die; it lingered, coloring everything I saw, heard, did. I now felt that I knew what the white men were feeling. Merely because I had read a book that had spoken of how they lived and thought, I identified myself with that book. I felt vaguely guilty. Would I, filled with bookish notions, act in a manner that would make the whites dislike me?

I forged more notes and my trips to the library became frequent. Reading grew into a passion. My first serious novel was Sinclair Lewis's *Main Street.* It made me see my boss, Mr. Gerald, and identify him as an American type. I would smile when I saw him lugging his golf bags into the office. I had always felt a vast distance separating me from the boss, and now I felt closer to him, though still distant. I felt now that I knew him, that I could feel the very limits of his narrow life. And this had happened because I had read a novel about a mythical man called George F. Babbitt.

The plots and stories in the novels did not interest me so much as the point of view revealed. I gave myself over to each novel without reserve, without trying to criticize it; it was enough for me to see and feel something different. And for me, everything was something different. Reading was like a drug, a dope. The novels created moods in which I lived for days. But I could not conquer my sense of guilt, my feeling that the white men around me knew that I was changing, that I had begun to regard them differently.

Whenever I brought a book to the job, I wrapped it in newspaper—a habit that was to persist for years in other cities and under other circumstances. But some of the white men pried into my packages when I was absent and they questioned me.

"Boy, what are you reading those books for?"

"Oh, I don't know, sir."

"That's deep stuff you're reading, boy."

"I'm just killing time, sir."

"You'll addle your brains if you don't watch out."

I read Dreiser's *Jennie Gerhardt* and *Sister Carrie* and they revived in me a vivid sense of my mother's suffering; I was overwhelmed. I grew silent, wondering about the life around me. It would have been impossible for me to have told anyone what I derived from these novels, for it was nothing less than a sense of life itself. All my life had shaped me for the realism, the naturalism of the modern novel, and I could not read enough of them.

Steeped in new moods and ideas, I bought a ream of paper and tried to write; but nothing would come, or what did come was flat beyond telling. I discovered that more than desire and feeling were necessary to write and I dropped the idea. Yet I still wondered how it was possible to know people sufficiently to write about them? Could I ever learn about life and people? To me, with my vast ignorance, my Jim Crow station in life, it seemed a task impossible of achievement. I now knew what being a Negro meant. I could endure the hunger. I had learned to live with hate. But to feel that there were feelings denied me, that the very breath of life itself was beyond my reach, that more than anything else hurt, wounded me. I had a new hunger.

In buoying me up, reading also cast me down, made me see what was possible, what I had missed. My tension returned, new, terrible, bitter, surging, almost too great to be contained. I no longer *felt* that the world about me was hostile, killing; I *knew* it. A million times I asked myself what I could do to save myself, and there were no answers. I seemed forever condemned, ringed by walls.

I did not discuss my reading with Mr. Falk, who had lent me his library card; it would have meant talking about myself and that would have been too painful. I smiled each day, fighting desperately to maintain my old behavior, to keep my disposition seemingly sunny. But some of the white men discerned that I had begun to brood.

"Wake up there, boy!" Mr. Olin said one day.

"Sir!" I answered for the lack of a better word.

"You act like you've stolen something," he said.

I laughed in the way I knew he expected me to laugh, but I resolved to be more conscious of myself, to watch my every act, to guard and hide the new knowledge that was dawning within me.

If I went north, would it be possible for me to build a new life then? But how could a man build a life upon vague, unformed yearnings? I wanted to write and I did not even know the English language. I bought English grammars and found them dull. I felt that I was getting a better sense of the language from novels than from grammars. I read hard, discarding a writer as soon as I felt that I had grasped his point of view. At night the printed page stood before my eyes in sleep.

Mrs. Moss, my landlady, asked me one Sunday morning:

"Son, what is this you keep on reading?"

"Oh, nothing. Just novels."

"What you get out of 'em?"

"I'm just killing time," I said.

"I hope you know your own mind," she said in a tone which implied that she doubted if I had a mind.

I knew of no Negroes who read the books I liked and I wondered if any Negroes ever thought of them. I knew that there were Negro doctors, lawyers, newspapermen, but I never saw any of them. When I read a Negro newspaper I never caught the faintest echo of my preoccupation in its pages. I felt trapped and occasionally, for a few days, I would stop reading. But a vague hunger would come over me for books, books that opened up new avenues of feeling and seeing, and again I would forge another note to the white librarian. Again I would read and wonder as only the naive and unlettered can read and wonder, feeling that I carried a secret, criminal burden about with me each day.

That winter my mother and brother came and we set up housekeeping, buying furniture on the installment plan, being cheated and yet knowing no way to avoid it. I began to eat warm food and to my surprise found that regular meals enabled me to read faster. I may have lived through many illnesses and survived them, never suspecting that I was ill. My brother obtained a job and we began to save toward the trip north, plotting our time, setting tentative dates for departure. I told none of the white men on the job that I was planning to go north; I knew that the moment they felt I was thinking of the North they would change toward me. It would have made them feel that I did not like the life I was living, and because my life was completely conditioned by what they said or did, it would have been tantamount to challenging them.

I could calculate my chances for life in the South as a Negro fairly clearly now.

I could fight the southern whites by organizing with other Negroes, as my grandfather had done. But I knew that I could never win that way; there were many whites and there were but few blacks. They were strong and we were weak. Outright black rebellion could never win. If I fought openly I would die and I did not want to die. News of lynchings were frequent.

I could submit and live the life of a genial slave, but that was impossible. All of my life had shaped me to live by my own feelings and thoughts. I could make up to Bess and marry her and inherit the house. But that, too, would be the life of a slave; if I did that, I would crush to death something within me, and I would hate myself as much as I knew the whites already hated those who had submitted. Neither could I ever willingly present myself to be kicked, as Shorty had done. I would rather have died than do that.

I could drain off my restlessness by fighting with Shorty and Harrison. I had seen many Negroes solve the problem of being black by transferring their hatred of themselves to others with a black skin and fighting them. I would have to be cold to do that, and I was not cold and I could never be.

I could, of course, forget what I had read, thrust the whites out of my mind, forget them; and find release from anxiety and longing in sex and alcohol. But the memory of how my father had conducted himself made that course repugnant. If I did not want others to violate my life, how could I voluntarily violate it myself?

I had no hope whatever of being a professional man. Not only had I been so conditioned that I did not desire it, but the fulfillment of such an ambition was beyond my capabilities. Well-to-do Negroes lived in a world that was almost as alien to me as the world inhabited by whites.

What, then, was there? I held my life in my mind, in my consciousness each day, feeling at times that I would stumble and drop it, spill it forever. My reading had created a vast sense of distance between me and the world in which I lived and tried to make a living, and that sense of distance was increasing each day. My days and nights were one long, quiet, continuously contained dream of terror, tension, and anxiety. I wondered how long I could bear it.

Reflections

Private Exploration

1. What's going on here:

   > I now knew what being a Negro meant. I could endure the hunger. I had learned to live with hate. But to feel that there were feelings denied me, that the very breath of life itself was beyond my reach, that more than anything else, wounded me.

2. Focus on any one of the feelings in "The Library Card" that strikes you as worth thinking about. Where in the essay does the feeling become strong? Cite specific passages and describe the feelings as fully as possible. Why are the feelings here important? Why do they speak to you? How do they open up the essay for you?
3. Reflect on any obstacle you have struggled to overcome and survived through your own volition. Share your story by describing the obstacle and tracing the problems and changes you experienced. Was there a single element—a book, an author, some individual or incident—that was instrumental in helping you confront the obstacle and change? In what ways has that experience reshaped your thoughts and feelings, your values?

Public Exploration

1. If you've written about Richard Wright's essay in your notebook, share what you've written with your group or in class as a starting point for discussing the kinds of values Wright is focusing on. After two or three of you in your group have read, consider the differences and similarities. What seems to be most important?
2. Richard Rodriguez has said, "Reading alters life." Consider how such a statement might be true of Richard Wright, of other individuals, of yourself, as well as whole societies.
3. Wright admits, "A million times I asked myself what I could do to save myself, and there were no answers." Yet the essay reveals that he did take action. Discuss the risks and decisions he makes to save himself. What qualities of character might be identified as those which help an individual survive and triumph over prejudice? Are they the same qualities that would help any of us survive and triumph over other obstacles in life?

Private Reflection

After having written about and discussed Wright's essay, consider this statement:

> Life is the sum of all your choices.
>
> —ALBERT CAMUS

Shiloh

BOBBIE ANN MASON

Leroy Moffitt's wife, Norma Jean, is working on her pectorals. She lifts three-pound dumbbells to warm up, then progresses to a twenty-pound barbell. Standing with her legs apart, she reminds Leroy of Wonder Woman.

"I'd give anything if I could just get these muscles to where they're real hard," says Norma Jean. "Feel this arm. It's not as hard as the other one."

"That's 'cause you're right-handed," says Leroy, dodging as she swings the barbell in an arc.

"Do you think so?"

"Sure."

Leroy is a truckdriver. He injured his leg in a highway accident four months ago, and his physical therapy, which involves weights and a pully, prompted Norma Jean to try building herself up. Now she is attending a body-building class. Leroy has been collecting temporary disability since his tractor-trailer jackknifed in Missouri, badly twisting his left leg in its socket. He has a steel pin in his hip. He will probably not be able to drive his rig again. It sits in the backyard, like a gigantic bird that has flown home to roost. Leroy has been home in Kentucky for three months, and his leg is almost healed, but the accident frightened him and he does not want to drive any more long hauls. He is not sure what to do next. In the meantime, he makes things from craft kits. He started by building a miniature log cabin from notched Popsicle sticks. He varnished it and placed it on the TV set, where it remains. It reminds him of a rustic Nativity scene. Then he tried string art (sailing ships on black velvet), a macramé owl kit, a snap-together B-17 Flying Fortress, and a lamp made out of a model truck, with a light fixture screwed in the top of the cab. At first the kits were diversions, something to kill time, but now he is thinking about building a full-scale log house from a kit. It would be considerably cheaper than building a regular house, and besides, Leroy has grown to appreciate how things are put together. He has begun to realize that in all the years he was on the road he never took time to examine anything. He was always flying past scenery.

"They won't let you build a log cabin in any of the new subdivisions," Norma Jean tells him.

"They will if I tell them it's for you," he says, teasing her. Ever since they were married, he has promised Norma Jean he would build her a new home one day. They have always rented, and the house they live in is small and nondescript. It does not even feel like a home, Leroy realizes now.

Norma Jean works at the Rexall drugstore, and she has acquired an amazing amount of information about cosmetics. When she explains to Leroy the three stages of complexion care, involving creams, toners, and moisturizers, he thinks happily of other petroleum products—axle grease, diesel fuel. This is a connection between him and Norma Jean. Since he has been home, he has felt unusually tender about his wife and guilty over his long absences. But he can't tell what she feels about him. Norma Jean has never complained about his traveling; she has never made hurt remarks, like calling his truck a "widow-maker." He is reasonably certain she has been faithful to him, but he wishes she would celebrate his permanent home-coming more happily. Norma Jean is often startled to find Leroy at home, and he thinks she seems a little disappointed about it. Perhaps he reminds her too much of the early days of their marriage, before he went on the road. They had a child who died as an infant, years ago. They never speak about their memories of Randy, which have almost faded, but now that Leroy is home all the time, they sometimes feel awkward around each other, and Leroy wonders if one of them should mention the child. He has the feeling that they are waking up out of a dream together—that they must create a new marriage, start afresh. They are lucky they are still married. Leroy has read that for most people losing a child destroys the marriage—or else he heard this on *Donahue.* He can't always remember where he learns things anymore.

At Christmas, Leroy bought an electric organ for Norma Jean. She used to play the piano when she was in high school. "It don't leave you," she told him once. "It's like riding a bicycle."

The new instrument had so many keys and buttons that she was bewildered by it at first. She touched the keys tentatively, pushed some buttons, then pecked out "Chopsticks." It came out in an amplified fox-trot rhythm, with marimba sounds.

"It's an orchestra!" she cried.

The organ had a pecan-look finish and eighteen preset chords, with optional flute, violin, trumpet, clarinet, and banjo accompaniments. Norma Jean mastered the organ almost immediately. At first she played Christmas songs. Then she bought *The Sixties Songbook* and learned every tune in it, adding variations to each with the rows of brightly colored buttons.

"I didn't like these old songs back then," she said. "But I have this crazy feeling I missed something."

"You didn't miss a thing," said Leroy.

Leroy likes to lie on the couch and smoke a joint and listen to Norma Jean play "Can't Take My Eyes Off You" and "I'll Be Back." He is back again. After fifteen years on the road, he is finally settling down with the woman he loves. She is still pretty. Her skin is flawless. Her frosted curls resemble pencil trimmings.

Now that Leroy has come home to stay, he notices how much the town has changed. Subdivisions are spreading across western Kentucky like an oil slick. The sign at the edge of town says "Pop: 11,500"—only seven hundred more than it said twenty years before. Leroy can't figure out who is living in all the new houses. The farmers who used to gather around the courthouse square on Saturday afternoons to play checkers and spit tobacco juice have gone. It has been years since Leroy has thought about the farmers, and they have disappeared without his noticing.

Leroy meets a kid named Stevie Hamilton in the parking lot at the new shopping center. While they pretend to be strangers meeting over a stalled car, Stevie tosses an ounce of marijuana under the front seat of Leroy's car. Stevie is wearing orange jogging shoes and a T-shirt that says CHATTAHOOCHEE SUPER-RAT. His father is a prominent doctor who lives in one of the expensive subdivisions in a new white-columned brick house that looks like a funeral parlor. In the phone book under his name there is a separate number, with the listing "Teenagers."

"Where do you get this stuff?" asks Leroy. "From your pappy?"

"That's for me to know and you to find out," Stevie says. He is slit-eyed and skinny.

"What else you got?"

"What you interested in?"

"Nothing special. Just wondered."

Leroy used to take speed on the road. Now he has to go slowly. He needs to be mellow. He leans back against the car and says, "I'm aiming to build me a log house, soon as I get time. My wife, though, I don't think she likes the idea."

"Well, let me know when you want me again," Stevie says. He has a cigarette in his cupped palm, as though sheltering it from the wind. He takes a long drag, then stomps it on the asphalt and slouches away.

Stevie's father was two years ahead of Leroy in high school. Leroy is thirty-four. He married Norma Jean when they were both eighteen, and their child Randy was born a few months later, but he died at the age of four months and three days. He would be about Stevie's age now. Norma Jean and Leroy were at the drive-in, watching a double feature (*Dr. Strangelove* and *Lover Come Back*), and the baby was sleeping in the back seat. When the first movie ended, the baby was dead. It was the sudden infant death syndrome. Leroy remembers handing Randy to a nurse at the emergency room, as though he were offering her a large doll as a present. A dead baby feels like a sack of flour. "It just happens sometimes," said the doctor, in what Leroy always recalls as a nonchalant tone. Leroy can hardly remember the child anymore, but he still sees vividly a scene from *Dr. Strangelove* in which the President of the United States was talking in a folksy voice on the hot line to the Soviet premier about the bomber accidentally headed toward Russia. He was in the War Room, and the world map was lit up. Leroy remembers Norma Jean standing catatonically beside him in the hospital and himself thinking: Who is this strange girl? He had forgotten who she was. Now scientists are saying that crib death is caused by a virus. Nobody knows anything, Leroy thinks. The answers are always changing.

When Leroy gets home from the shopping center, Norma Jean's mother, Mabel Beasley, is there. Until this year, Leroy has not realized how much time she spends with Norma Jean. When she visits, she inspects the closets and then the plants, informing Norma Jean when a plant is droopy or yellow. Mabel calls the plants "flowers," although there are never any blooms. She always notices if Norma Jean's laundry is piling up. Mabel is a short, overweight woman whose tight, brown-dyed curls look more like a wig than the actual wig she sometimes wears. Today she has brought Norma Jean an off-white dust ruffle she made for the bed; Mabel works in a custom-upholstery shop.

"This is the tenth one I made this year," Mabel says. "I got started and couldn't stop."

"It's real pretty," says Norma Jean.

"Now we can hide things under the bed," says Leroy, who gets along with his mother-in-law primarily by joking with her. Mabel has never really forgiven him for disgracing her by getting Norma Jean pregnant. When the baby died, she said that fate was mocking her.

"What's that thing?" Mabel says to Leroy in a loud voice, pointing to a tangle of yarn on a piece of canvas.

Leroy holds it up for Mabel to see. "It's my needlepoint," he explains. "This is a *Star Trek* pillow cover."

"That's what a woman would do," says Mabel. "Great day in the morning!"

"All the big football players on TV do it," he says.

"Why, Leroy, you're always trying to fool me. I don't believe you for one minute. You don't know what to do with yourself—that's the whole trouble. Sewing!"

"I'm aiming to build us a log house," says Leroy. "Soon as my plans come."

"Like *heck* you are," says Norma Jean. She takes Leroy's needlepoint and shoves it into a drawer. "You have to find a job first. Nobody can afford to build now anyway."

Mabel straightens her girdle and says, "I still think before you get tied down y'all ought to take a little run to Shiloh."

"One of these days, Mama," Norma Jean says impatiently.

Mabel is talking about Shiloh, Tennessee. For the past few years, she has been urging Leroy and Norma Jean to visit the Civil War battleground there. Mabel went there on her honeymoon—the only real trip she ever took. Her husband died of a perforated ulcer when Norma Jean was ten, but Mabel, who was accepted into the United Daughters of the Confederacy in 1975, is still preoccupied with going back to Shiloh.

"I've been to kingdom come and back in that truck out yonder," Leroy says to Mabel, "but we never yet set foot in that battleground. Ain't that something? How did I miss it?"

"It's not even that far," Mabel says.

After Mabel leaves, Norma Jean reads to Leroy from a list she has made. "Things you could do," she announces. "You could get a job as a guard at Union Carbide, where they'd let you set on a stool. You could get on at the lumberyard. You could do a little carpenter work, if you want to build so bad. You could—"

"I can't do something where I'd have to stand up all day."

"You ought to try standing up all day behind a cosmetics counter. It's amazing that I have strong feet, coming from two parents that never had strong feet at all.'' At the moment Norma Jean is holding on to the kitchen counter, raising her knees one at a time as she talks. She is wearing two-pound ankle weights.

''Don't worry,'' says Leroy. ''I'll do something.''

''You could truck calves to slaughter for somebody. You wouldn't have to drive any big old truck for that.''

''I'm going to build you this house,'' says Leroy. ''I want to make you a real home.''

''I don't want to live in any log cabin.''

''It's not a cabin. It's a house.''

''I don't care. It looks like a cabin.''

''You and me together could lift those logs. It's just like lifting weights.''

Norma Jean doesn't answer. Under her breath, she is counting. Now she is marching through the kitchen. She is doing goose steps.

Before his accident, when Leroy came home he used to stay in the house with Norma Jean, watching TV in bed and playing cards. She would cook fried chicken, picnic ham, chocolate pie—all his favorites. Now he is home alone much of the time. In the mornings, Norma Jean disappears, leaving a cooling place in the bed. She eats a cereal called Body Buddies, and she leaves the bowl on the table, with the soggy tan balls floating in a milk puddle. He sees things about Norma Jean that he never realized before. When she chops onions, she stares off into a corner, as if she can't bear to look. She puts on her house slippers almost precisely at nine o'clock every evening and nudges her jogging shoes under the couch. She saves bread heels for the birds. Leroy watches the birds at the feeder. He notices the peculiar way goldfinches fly past the window. They close their wings, then fall, then spread their wings to catch and lift themselves. He wonders if they close their eyes when they fall. Norma Jean closes her eyes when they are in bed. She wants the lights turned out. Even then, he is sure she closes her eyes.

He goes for long drives around town. He tends to drive a car rather carelessly. Power steering and an automatic shift make a car feel so small and inconsequential that his body is hardly involved in the driving process. His injured leg stretches out comfortably. Once or twice he has almost hit something, but even the prospect of an accident seems minor in a car. He cruises the new subdivisions, feeling like a criminal rehearsing for a robbery. Norma Jean is probably right about a log house being inappropriate here in the new subdivisions. All the houses look grand and complicated. They depress him.

One day when Leroy comes home from a drive he finds Norma Jean in tears. She is in the kitchen making a potato and mushroom-soup casserole, with grated-cheese topping. She is crying because her mother caught her smoking.

''I didn't hear her coming. I was standing here puffing away pretty as you please,'' Norma Jean says, wiping her eyes.

''I knew it would happen sooner or later,'' says Leroy, putting his arm around her.

"She don't know the meaning of the word 'knock,' " says Norma Jean. "It's a wonder she hadn't caught me years ago."

"Think of it this way," Leroy says. "What if she caught me with a joint?"

"You better not let her!" Norma Jean shrieks. "I'm warning you, Leroy Moffitt!"

"I'm just kidding. Here, play me a tune. That'll help you relax."

Norma Jean puts the casserole in the oven and sets the timer. Then she plays a ragtime tune, with horns and banjo, as Leroy lights up a joint and lies on the couch, laughing to himself about Mabel's catching him at it. He thinks of Stevie Hamilton—a doctor's son pushing grass. Everything is funny. The whole town seems crazy and small. He is reminded of Virgil Mathis, a boastful policeman Leroy used to shoot pool with. Virgil recently led a drug bust in a back room at a bowling alley, where he seized ten thousand dollars' worth of marijuana. The newspaper had a picture of him holding up the bags of grass and grinning widely. Right now, Leroy can imagine Virgil breaking down the door and arresting him with a lungful of smoke. Virgil would probably have been alerted to the scene because of all the racket Norma Jean is making. Now she sounds like a hard-rock band. Norma Jean is terrific. When she switches to a Latin-rhythm version of "Sunshine Superman," Leroy hums along. Norma Jean's foot goes up and down, up and down.

"Well, what do you think?" Leroy says, when Norma Jean pauses to search through her music.

"What do I think about what?"

His mind had gone blank. Then he says, "I'll sell my rig and build us a house." That wasn't what he wanted to say. He wanted to know what she thought—what she *really* thought—about them.

"Don't start in on that again," says Norma Jean. She begins playing "Who'll Be the Next in Line?"

Leroy used to tell hitchhikers his whole life story—about his travels, his hometown, the baby. He would end with a question: "Well, what do you think?" It was just a rhetorical question. In time, he had the feeling that he'd been telling the same story over and over to the same hitchhikers. He quit talking to hitchhikers when he realized how his voice sounded—whining and self-pitying, like some teenage-tragedy song. Now Leroy has the sudden impulse to tell Norma Jean about himself, as if he had just met her. They have known each other so long they have forgotten a lot about each other. They could become reacquainted. But when the oven timer goes off and she runs to the kitchen, he forgets why he wants to do this.

The next day, Mabel drops by. It is Saturday and Norma Jean is cleaning. Leroy is studying the plans of his log house, which have finally come in the mail. He has them spread out on the table—big sheets of stiff blue paper, with diagrams and numbers printed in white. While Norma Jean runs the vacuum, Mabel drinks coffee. She sets her coffee cup on a blueprint.

"I'm just waiting for time to pass," she says to Leroy, drumming her fingers on the table.

As soon as Norma Jean switches off the vacuum, Mabel says in a loud voice, "Did you hear about the datsun dog that killed the baby?"

Norma Jean says, "The word is 'dachshund.' "

"They put the dog on trial. It chewed the baby's legs off. The mother was in the next room all the time." She raises her voice. "They thought it was neglect."

Norma Jean is holding her ears. Leroy manages to open the refrigerator and get some Diet Pepsi to offer Mabel. Mabel still has some coffee and she waves away the Pepsi.

"Datsuns are like that," Mabel says. "They're jealous dogs. They'll tear a place to pieces if you don't keep an eye on them."

"You better watch out what you're saying, Mabel," says Leroy.

"Well, facts is facts."

Leroy looks out the window at his rig. It is like a huge piece of furniture gathering dust in the backyard. Pretty soon it will be an antique. He hears the vacuum cleaner. Norma Jean seems to be cleaning the living room rug again.

Later, she says to Leroy, "She just said that about the baby because she caught me smoking. She's trying to pay me back."

"What are you talking about?" Leroy says, nervously shuffling blueprints.

"You know good and well," Norma Jean says. She is sitting in a kitchen chair with her feet up and her arms wrapped around her knees. She looks small and helpless. She says, "The very idea, her bringing up a subject like that! Saying it was neglect."

"She didn't mean that," Leroy says.

"She might not have *thought* she meant it. She always says things like that. You don't know how she goes on."

"But she didn't really mean it. She was just talking."

Leroy opens a king-sized bottle of beer and pours it into two glasses, dividing it carefully. He hands a glass to Norma Jean and she takes it from him mechanically. For a long time, they sit by the kitchen window watching the birds at the feeder.

Something is happening. Norma Jean is going to night school. She has graduated from her six-week body-building course and now she is taking an adult-education course in composition at Paducah Community College. She spends her evenings outlining paragraphs.

"First you have a topic sentence," she explains to Leroy. "Then you divide it up. Your secondary topic has to be connected to your primary topic."

To Leroy, this sounds intimidating. "I never was any good in English," he says.

"It makes a lot of sense."

"What are you doing this for, anyhow?"

She shrugs. "It's something to do." She stands up and lifts her dumbbells a few times.

"Driving a rig, nobody cared about my English."

"I'm not criticizing your English."

Norma Jean used to say, "If I lose ten minutes' sleep, I just drag all day."

Now she stays up late, writing compositions. She got a B on her first paper—a how-to-theme on soup-based casseroles. Recently Norma Jean has been cooking unusual foods—tacos, lasagna, Bombay chicken. She doesn't play the organ anymore, though her second paper was called "Why Music Is Important to Me." She sits at the kitchen table, concentrating on her outlines, while Leroy plays with his log house plans, practicing with a set of Lincoln Logs. The thought of getting a truckload of notched, numbered logs scares him, and he wants to be prepared. As he and Norma Jean work together at the kitchen table, Leroy has the hopeful thought that they are sharing something, but he knows he is a fool to think this. Norma Jean is miles away. He knows he is going to lose her. Like Mabel, he is just waiting for time to pass.

One day, Mabel is there before Norma Jean gets home from work, and Leroy finds himself confiding in her. Mabel, he realizes, must know Norma Jean better than he does.

"I don't know what's got into that girl," Mabel says. "She used to go to bed with the chickens. Now you say she's up all hours. Plus her a-smoking. I like to died."

"I want to make her this beautiful home," Leroy says, indicating the Lincoln Logs. "I don't think she even wants it. Maybe she was happier with me gone."

"She don't know what to make of you, coming home like this."

"Is that it?"

Mabel takes the roof off his Lincoln Log cabin. "You couldn't get *me* in a log cabin," she says. "I was raised in one. It's no picnic, let me tell you."

"They're different now," says Leroy.

"I tell you what," Mabel says, smiling oddly at Leroy.

"What?"

"Take her on down to Shiloh. Y'all need to get out together, stir a little. Her brain's all balled up over them books."

Leroy can see traces of Norma Jean's features in her mother's face. Mabel's worn face has the texture of crinkled cotton, but suddenly she looks pretty. It occurs to Leroy that Mabel has been hinting all along that she wants them to take her with them to Shiloh.

"Let's all go to Shiloh," he says. "You and me and her. Come Sunday."

Mabel throws up her hand in protest. "Oh, no, not me. Young folk want to be by theirselves."

When Norma Jean comes in with groceries, Leroy says excitedly, "Your mama here's been dying to go to Shiloh for thirty-five years. It's about time we went, don't you think?"

"I'm not going to butt in on anybody's second honeymoon," Mabel says.

"Who's going on a honeymoon, for Christ's sake?" Norma Jean says loudly.

"I never raised no daughter of mine to talk that-a-way," Mabel says.

"You ain't seen nothing yet," says Norma Jean. She starts putting away boxes and cans, slamming cabinet doors.

"There's a log cabin at Shiloh," Mabel says. "It was there during the battle. There's bullet holes in it."

"When are you going to *shut up* about Shiloh, Mama?" asks Norma Jean.

"I always thought Shiloh was the prettiest place, so full of history," Mabel goes on. "I just hoped y'all could see it once before I die, so you could tell me about it." Later, she whispers to Leroy, "You do what I said. A little change is what she needs."

"Your name means 'the king,' " Norma Jean says to Leroy that evening. He is trying to get her to go to Shiloh, and she is reading a book about another century.

"Well, I reckon I ought to be right proud."

"I guess so."

"Am I still king around here?"

Norma Jean flexes her biceps and feels them for hardness. "I'm not fooling around with anybody, if that's what you mean," she says.

"Would you tell me if you were?"

"I don't know."

"What does *your* name mean?"

"It was Marilyn Monroe's real name."

"No kidding!"

"Norma comes from the Normans. They were invaders," she says. She closes her book and looks hard at Leroy. "I'll go to Shiloh with you if you'll stop staring at me."

On Sunday, Norma Jean packs a picnic and they go to Shiloh. To Leroy's relief, Mabel says she does not want to come with them. Norma Jean drives, and Leroy, sitting beside her, feels like some boring hitchhiker she has picked up. He tries some conversation, but she answers in in monosyllables. At Shiloh, she drives aimlessly through the park, past bluffs and trails and steep ravines. Shiloh is an immense place, and Leroy cannot see it as a battleground. It is not what he expected. He thought it would look like a golf course. Monuments are everywhere, showing through the thick clusters of trees. Norma Jean passes the log cabin Mabel mentioned. It is surrounded by tourists looking for bullet holes.

"That's not the kind of log house I've got in mind," says Leroy apologetically.

"I know *that.*"

"This is a pretty place. Your mama was right."

"It's O.K.," says Norma Jean. "Well, we've seen it. I hoped she's satisfied."

They burst out laughing together.

At the park museum, a movie on Shiloh is shown every half hour, but they decide that they don't want to see it. They buy a souvenir Confederate flag for Mabel, and then they find a picnic spot near the cemetery. Norma Jean has brought a picnic cooler, with pimiento sandwiches, soft drinks, and Yodels. Leroy eats a sandwich and then smokes a joint, hiding it behind the picnic cooler. Norma Jean has quit smoking altogether. She is picking cake crumbs from the cellophane wrapper, like a fussy bird.

Leroy says, "So the boys in gray ended up in Corinth. The Union soldiers zapped 'em finally. April 7, 1862."

They both know that he doesn't know any history. He is just talking about some of the historical plaques they have read. He feels awkward, like a boy on a date with an older girl. They are still just making conversation.

"Corinth is where Mama eloped to," says Norma Jean.

They sit in silence and stare at the cemetery for the Union dead and, beyond, at a tall cluster of trees. Campers are parked nearby, bumper to bumper, and small children in bright clothing are cavorting and squealing. Norma Jean wads up the cake wrapper and squeezes it tightly in her hand. Without looking at Leroy, she says, "I want to leave you."

Leroy takes a bottle of Coke out of the cooler and flips off the cap. He holds the bottle poised near his mouth but cannot remember to take a drink. Finally he says, "No, you don't."

"Yes, I do."

"I won't let you."

"You can't stop me."

"Don't do me that way."

Leroy knows Norma Jean will have her own way. "Didn't I promise to be home from now on?" he says.

"In some ways, a woman prefers a man who wanders," says Norma Jean. "That sounds crazy, I know."

"You're not crazy."

Leroy remembers to drink from his Coke. Then he says, "Yes, you *are* crazy. You and me could start all over again. Right back at the beginning."

"We *have* started all over again," says Norma Jean. "And this is how it turned out."

"What did I do wrong?"

"Nothing."

"Is this one of those women's lib things?" Leroy asks.

"Don't be funny."

The cemetery, a green slope dotted with white markers, looks like a subdivision site. Leroy is trying to comprehend that his marriage is breaking up, but for some reason he is wondering about white slabs in a graveyard.

"Everything was fine till Mama caught me smoking," says Norma Jean, standing up. "That's set something off."

"What are you talking about?"

"She won't leave me alone—*you* won't leave me alone." Norma Jean seems to be crying, but she is looking away from him. "I feel eighteen again. I can't face that all over again." She starts walking away. "No, it *wasn't* fine. I don't know what I'm saying. Forget it."

Leroy takes a lungful of smoke and closes his eyes as Norma Jean's words sink in. He tries to focus on the fact that thirty-five hundred soldiers died on the grounds around him. He can only think of that war as a board game with plastic soldiers. Leroy almost smiles, as he compared the Confederates' daring attack on the Union camps and Virgil Mathis's raid on the bowling alley. General Grant, drunk and furious, shoved the Southerners back to Corinth, where Mabel and Jet Beasley were married years later, when Mabel was still thin and good-looking. The next day, Mabel and Jet visited the battleground, and then Norma Jean was born, and then she married Leroy and they had a baby, which they lost, and now Leroy and Norma Jean are here at the same battleground. Leroy knows he is leaving out a lot. He is leaving out the insides of history. History was always just names and dates to him. It occurs to him that building a house out of logs is similarly empty—too simple. And the real inner workings of a marriage, like most of history, have escaped him. Now he sees that building a log house is the dumbest idea he could have had. It was clumsy of him to think Norma Jean would want a log house. It was a crazy idea. He'll have to think of something else, quickly. He will wad the blueprints into tight balls and fling them into the lake. Then he'll get moving again. He opens his eyes. Norma Jean has moved away and is walking through the cemetery, following a serpentine brick path.

Leroy gets up to follow his wife, but his good leg is asleep and his bad leg still hurts him. Norma Jean is far away, walking rapidly toward the bluff by the river, and he tries to hobble toward her. Some children run past him, screaming noisily. Norma Jean has reached the bluff, and she is looking out over the Tennessee River. Now she turns toward Leroy and waves her arms. Is she beckoning to him? She seems to be doing an exercise for her chest muscles. The sky is unusually pale—the color of the dust ruffle Mabel made for their bed.

Reflections

Private Exploration

1. Copy a key passage from "Shiloh" and explore it in your notebook. How does the passage illuminate your understanding of the story as a whole?
2. Without telling us directly, Mason contrasts Norma Jean's values with Leroy's. Draw a line down the center of the page of your notebook. On one side jot down specific actions, words, or phrases that reveal Leroy's values. On the other, do the same for Norma Jean. After you've finished, scan the specifics you've listed and consider what they reveal about each character's values. What appears to be the source of conflict in their marriage?
3. What's really going on here as Leroy attempts to convince Norma Jean of his intention to build her a cabin?

   'You and me together could lift those logs. It's just like lifting weights.' Norma Jean doesn't answer. Under her breath, she is counting. Now she's marching through the kitchen. She is doing goose steps.

Public Exploration

Consider this excerpt:

> For those of us who write, it is necessary to scrutinize not only the truth of what we speak, but the truth of that language by which we speak it. For others, it is to share

and spread also those words that are meaningful to us. But primarily for all, it is necessary to teach by living and speaking those truths which we believe and know beyond understanding. Because in this way alone we can survive, by taking part in a process of life that is creative and continuing, that is growth.

—AUDRE LORDE

First, explore your reactions and feelings privately in your reading notebook. In what possible ways could Lorde's views speak to Bobby Ann Mason's story? In what ways might those truths be of value to us all? After you've had an opportunity to draft several ideas of your own, join your class or group and take turns sharing responses, discussing and questioning the ideas that surface.

Private Reflection

Consider the title, "Shiloh." Check an encyclopedia for more information. Review the story to find specific instances when Shiloh is mentioned. Consider whether the title gathers meaning as the story progresses. Reflect especially on the final scene at Shiloh when Norma Jean stands on the bluff waving her arms.

Piki

WILLIAM LEAST HEAT MOON

Dirty and hard, the morning light could have been old concrete. Twenty-nine degrees inside. I tried to figure a way to drive down the mountain without leaving the sleeping bag. I was stiff—not from the cold so much as from having slept coiled like a grub. Creaking open and pinching toes and fingers to check for frostbite, I counted to ten (twice) before shouting and leaping for my clothes. Shouting distracts the agony. Underwear, trousers, and shirt so cold they felt wet.

I went outside to relieve myself. In the snow, with the hot stream, I spelled out *alive.* Then to work chipping clear the windows. Somewhere off this mountain, people still lay warm in their blankets and not yet ready to get up to a hot breakfast. So what if they spent the day selling imprinted ballpoint pens? Weren't they down off mountains?

Down. I had to try it. And down it was, Utah 14 a complication of twists and drops descending the west side more precipitately than the east. A good thing I hadn't attempted it in the dark. After a mile, snow on the pavement became slush, then water, and finally at six thousand feet, dry and sunny blacktop.

Cedar City, a tidy Mormon town, lay at the base of the mountains on the edge of the Escalante Desert. Ah, desert! I pulled in for gas, snow still melting off my rig. "See you spent the night in the Breaks," the attendant said. "You people never believe the sign at the bottom."

"I believed, but it said something about winter months. May isn't winter."

"It is up there. You Easterners just don't know what a mountain is."

I didn't say anything, but I knew what a mountain was: a high pile of windy rocks with its own weather.

In the cafeteria of Southern Utah State College, I bought a breakfast of scrambled eggs, pancakes, bacon, oatmeal, grapefruit, orange juice, milk, and a cinnamon roll. A celebration of being alive. I was full of victory.

Across the table sat an Indian student named Kendrick Fritz, who was studying chemistry and wanted to become a physician. He had grown up in Moenkopi, Arizona, just across the highway from Tuba City. I said, "Are you Navajo or Hopi?"

"Hopi. You can tell by my size. Hopis are smaller than Navajos."

His voice was gentle, his words considered, and smile timid. He seemed open to questions. "Fritz doesn't sound like a Hopi name."

"My father took it when he was in the Army in the Second World War. Hopis usually have Anglo first names and long Hopi last names that are hard for other people to pronounce."

I told him of my difficulty in rousing a conversation in Tuba City. He said, "I can't speak for Navajos about prejudice, but I know Hopis who believe we survived Spaniards, missionaries, a thousand years of other Indians, even the BIA. But tourists?" He smiled. "Smallpox would be better."

"Do you—yourself—think most whites are prejudiced against Indians?"

"About fifty-fifty. Half show contempt because they saw a drunk squaw at the Circle K. Another half think we're noble savages—they may be worse because if an Indian makes a mistake they hate him for being human. Who wants to be somebody's ideal myth?"

"My grandfather used to say the Big Vision made the Indian, but the white man invented him."

"Relations are okay here, but I wouldn't call them good, and I'm not one to go around looking for prejudice. I try not to."

"Maybe you're more tolerant of anglo ways than some others."

"Could be. I mean, I *am* studying to be a doctor and not a medicine man. But I'm no apple Indian—red outside and white underneath. I lived up in Brigham City, Utah, when I went to the Intermountain School run by the BIA. It was too easy though. Too much time to goof around. So I switched to Box Elder—that's a public school. I learned there. And I lived in Dallas a few months. What I'm saying is that I've lived on Hopi land and I've lived away. I hear Indians talk about being red all the way through criticizing others for acting like Anglos, and all the time they're sitting in a pickup at a drive-in. But don't tell them to trade the truck for a horse."

"The Spanish brought the horse."

He nodded. "To me, being Indian means being responsible to my people. Helping with the best tools. Who invented penicillin doesn't matter."

"What happens after you finish school?"

"I used to want out of Tuba, but since I've been away, I've come to see how our land really is our Sacred Circle—it's our strength. Now, I want to go back and practice general medicine. At the Indian hospital in Tuba where my mother and sister are nurse's aides, there aren't any Indian M.D.'s, and that's no good. I don't respect people who don't help themselves. Hopi land is no place to make big money, but I'm not interested anyway."

"You don't use the word *reservation.*"

"We don't think of it as a reservation since we were never ordered there. We found it through Hopi prophecies. We're unusual because we've always held onto our original land—most of it anyway. One time my grandfather pointed out the old boundaries to me. We were way up on a mesa. I've forgotten what they are except for the San Francisco Peaks. But in the last eighty years, the government's given a lot of our land to Navajos, and now we're in a hard spot—eight thousand Hopis are surrounded and outnumbered twenty-five to one. I don't begrudge the Navajo anything, but I think Hopis should be in on making the decisions. Maybe you know that Congress didn't even admit Indians to citizenship until about nineteen twenty. Incredible—live someplace a thousand years and then find out you're a foreigner."

"I know an Osage who says, 'Don't Americanize me and I won't Americanize you.' He means everybody in the country came from someplace else."

"Hopi legends are full of migrations."

"Will other Hopis be suspicious of you when you go home as a doctor?"

"Some might be, but not my family. But for a lot of Hopis, the worst thing to call a man is *kahopi,* 'not Hopi.' Nowadays, though, we all have to choose either the new ways or the Hopi way, and it's split up whole villages. A lot of us try to find the best in both places. We've always learned from other people. If we hadn't, we'd be extinct like some other tribes."

"Medicine's a pretty good survival technique."

"Sure, but I also like Jethro Tull and the Moody Blues. That's not survival."

"Is the old religion a survival technique?"

"If you live it."

"Do you?"

"Most Hopis follow our religion, at least in some ways, because it reminds us who we are and it's part of the land. I'll tell you, in the rainy season when the desert turns green, it's beautiful there. The land is medicine too."

"If you don't mind telling me, what's the religion like?"

"Like any religion in one way—different clans believe different things."

"There must be something they all share, something common."

"That's hard to say."

"Could you try?"

He thought a moment. "Maybe the idea of harmony. And the way a Hopi prays. A good life, a harmonious life, is a prayer. We don't just pray for ourselves, we pray for all things. We're famous for the Snake Dances, but a lot of people don't realize those ceremonies are prayers for rain and crops, prayers for life. We also pray for rain by sitting and thinking about rain. We sit and picture wet things like streams and clouds. It's sitting in pictures."

He picked up his tray to go. "I could give you a taste of the old Hopi Way. But maybe you're too full after that breakfast. You always eat so much?"

"The mountain caused that." I got up. "What do you mean by 'taste'?"

"I'll show you."

We went to his dormitory room. Other than several Kachina dolls he had carved from cottonwood and a picture of a Sioux warrior, it was just another collegiate dorm room—maybe cleaner than most. He pulled a shoebox from under his bed and opened it carefully. I must have been watching a little wide-eyed because he said, "It isn't live rattlesnakes." From the box he took a long cylinder wrapped in waxed paper and held it as if trying not to touch it. "Will you eat this? It's very special." He was smiling. "If you won't, I can't share the old Hopi Way with you."

"Okay, but if it's dried scorpions, I'm going to speak with a forked tongue."

"Open your hands." He unwrapped the cylinder and ever so gently laid across my palms an airy tube the color of a thunderhead. It was about ten inches long and an inch in diameter. "There you go," he said.

"You first."

"I'm not having any right now."

So I bit the end off the blue-gray tube. It was many intricately rolled layers of something with less substance than butterfly wings. The bite crumbled to flakes that stuck to my lips. "Now tell me what I'm eating."

"Do you like it?"

"I think so. Except it disappears like cotton candy just as I get ready to chew. But I think I taste corn and maybe ashes."

"Hopis were eating that before horses came to America. It's piki. Hopi bread you might say. Made from blue-corn flour and ashes from greasewood or sagebrush. Baked on an oiled stone by my mother. She sends piki every so often. It takes time and great skill to make. We call it Hopi cornflakes."

"Unbelievably thin." I laid a piece on a page of his chemistry book. The words showed through.

"We consider corn our mother. The blue variety is what you might call our compass—wherever it grows, we can go. Blue corn directed our migrations. Navajos cultivate a yellow species that's soft and easy to grind, but ours is hard. You plant it much deeper than other corns, and it survives where they would die. It's a genetic variant the Hopi developed."

"Why is it blue? That must be symbolic."

"We like the color blue. Corn's our most important ritual ingredient."

"The piki's good, but it's making me thirsty. Where's a water fountain?"

When I came back from the fountain. Fritz said, "I'll tell you what I think the heart of our religion is—it's the Four Worlds."

Over the next hour, he talked about the Hopi Way, and showed pictures and passages from *Book of the Hopi*. The key seemed to be emergence. Carved in a rock near the village of Shipolovi is the ancient symbol for it:

With variations, the symbol appears among other Indians of the Americas. Its lines represent the course a person follows on his "road of life" as he passes through birth, death, rebirth. Human existence is essentially a series of journeys, and the emergence symbol is a kind of map of the wandering soul, an image of a process; but it is also, like most Hopi symbols and ceremonies, a reminder of cosmic patterns that all human beings move in.

The Hopi believes mankind has evolved through four worlds: the first a shadowy realm of contentment; the second a place so comfortable the people forgot where they had come from and began worshipping material goods. The third world was a pleasant land too, but the people, bewildered by their past and fearful for their future, thought only of their own earthly plans. At last, the Spider Grandmother, who oversees the emergences, told them: "You have forgotten what you should have remembered, and now you have to leave this place. Things will be harder." In the fourth and present world, life is difficult for mankind, and he struggles to remember his source because materialism and selfishness block a greater vision. The newly born infant comes into the fourth world with the door of his mind open (evident in the cranial soft spot), but as he ages, the door closes and he must work at remaining receptive to the great forces. A human being's grandest task is to keep from breaking with things outside himself.

"A Hopi learns that he belongs to two families," Fritz said, "his natural clan and that of all things. As he gets older, he's supposed to move closer to the greater family. In the Hopi Way, each person tries to recognize his part in the whole."

"At breakfast you said you hunted rabbits and pigeons and robins, but I don't see how you can shoot a bird if you believe in the union of life."

"A Hopi hunter asks the animal to forgive him for killing it. Only life can feed life. The robin knows that."

"How does robin taste, by the way?"

"Tastes good."

"The religion doesn't seem to have much of an ethical code."

"It's there. We watch what the Kachinas say and do. But the Spider Grand-

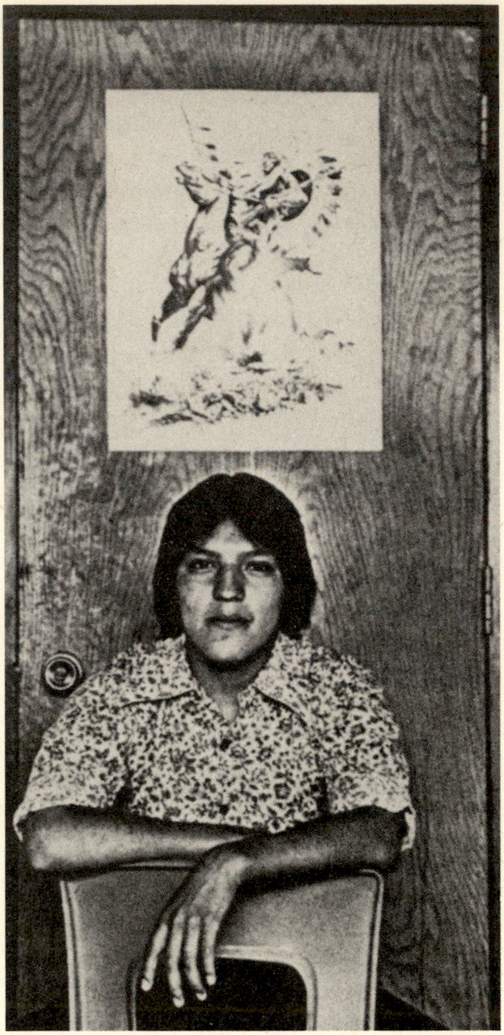

mother did give two rules. To all men, not just Hopis. If you look at them, they cover everything. She said, 'Don't go around hurting each other,' and she said, 'Try to understand things.' "

"I like them. I like them very much."

"Our religion keeps reminding us that we aren't just will and thoughts. We're also sand and wind and thunder. Rain. The seasons. All those things. You learn to respect everything because you *are* everything. If you respect yourself, you respect all things. That's why we have so many songs of creation to remind us where we came from. If the fourth world forgets that, we'll disappear in the wilderness like the third world, where people decided they had created themselves."

"Pride's the deadliest of the Seven Deadly Sins in old Christian theology."

"It's *kahopi* to set yourself above things. It causes divisions."

Fritz had to go to class. As we walked across campus, I said, "I guess it's hard to be a Hopi in Cedar City—especially if you're studying biochemistry."

"It's hard to be a Hopi anywhere."

"I mean, difficult to carry your Hopi heritage into a world as technological as medicine is."

"Heritage? My heritage is the Hopi Way, and that's a way of the spirit. Spirit can go anywhere. In fact, it has to go places so it can change and emerge like in the migrations. That's the whole idea."

Reflections

Personal Exploration

1. What do you make of this sentence:

   A good life, a harmonious life, is a prayer.

2. Ponder the Hopi's "old religion" and its values in terms of survival. In what ways does it reveal its harmonious nature? What do you find surprising or mysterious or fascinating about these beliefs? What truths does the Hopi religion reveal? How does it feel to think about a religion or belief different from your own? Why is it surprising?
3. Think about the significance of the Hopi's description of man's evolution. Consider what the various stages suggest about man, his values, and survival. Drawing from your own culture, can you point out other descriptions of man's evolution that resemble the Hopi's four stages of emergence? What is the value of realizing such similarities?

Public Exploration

The Spider Grandmother says "You have forgotten what you should have remembered, and now you have to leave this place. Things will be harder." Others have expressed similar viewpoints supporting this legendary grandmother. The philosopher Stern has written that "In a country without memory anything can happen." Author Patricia Hampl has commented, ". . . it is a grave error not to inhabit memory. There may be no more pressing intellectual need in our culture than for people to become sophisticated about the function of memory." Reflect on the value of memory in terms of human survival. For instance, why should we remember the Holocaust, the Soetu massacre in South Africa, the Viet Nam war, the 1989 Chinese Student revolution in Tienanmen Square, or the fall of the Berlin Wall? What is the danger of forgetting these events? If you are unfamiliar with them now, what is the danger of remaining in darkness?

Personal Reflection

1. Consider this statement:

   A human being's grandest task is to keep from breaking with things outside himself.

2. Fritz shares his "Hopi cornflakes" with Heat Moon, but the bread obviously represents more than a source of nourishment. Consider its larger significance: what it represents to the Hopis and what it represents to Fritz when he shares it. Think about your own family traditions. Perhaps you had a grandmother who made Moravian cookies or her own special Stollen from a recipe passed on from one generation to the other. Consider some part of your heritage which has become significant to you and your family over the years—or which has been lost—and explore its value.

Chike's School Days

CHINUA ACHEBE

Sarah's last child was a boy, and his birth brought great joy to the house of his father, Amos. The child received three names at his baptism—John, Chike, Obiajulu. The last name means "the mind at last is at rest." Anyone hearing this name knew at once that its owner was either an only child or an only son. Chike was an only son. His parents had had five daughters before him.

Like his sisters Chike was brought up "in the ways of the white man," which meant the opposite of traditional. Amos had many years before bought a tiny bell with which he summoned his family to prayers and hymn-singing first thing in the morning and last thing at night. This was one of the ways of the white man. Sarah taught her children not to eat in their neighbours' houses because "they offered their food to idols." And thus she set herself against the age-old custom which regarded children as the common responsibility of all so that, no matter what the relationship between parents, their children played together and shared their food.

One day a neighbour offered a piece of yam to Chike, who was only four years old. The boy shook his head haughtily and said, "We don't eat heathen food." The neighbour was full of rage, but she controlled herself and only muttered under her breath that even an *Osu* was full of pride nowadays, thanks to the white man.

And she was right. In the past an *Osu* could not raise his shaggy head in the presence of the free-born. He was a slave to one of the many gods of the clan. He was a thing set apart, not to be venerated but to be despised and almost spat on. He could not marry a free-born, and he could not take any of the titles of his clan. When he died, he was buried by his kind in the Bad Bush.

Now all that had changed, or had begun to change. So that an *Osu* child could even look down his nose at a free-born, and talk about heathen food! The white man had indeed accomplished many things.

Chike's father was not originally an *Osu*, but had gone and married an *Osu* woman in the name of Christianity. It was unheard of for a man to make himself *Osu* in that way, with his eyes wide open. But then Amos was nothing if not mad. The new religion had gone to his head. It was like palm-wine. Some people drank it and remained sensible. Others lost every sense in their stomach.

The only person who supported Amos in his mad marriage venture was Mr. Brown, the white missionary, who lived in a thatch-roofed, red-earth-walled parsonage and was highly respected by the people, not because of his sermons, but because of a dispensary he ran in one of his rooms. Amos had emerged from Mr. Brown's parsonage greatly fortified. A few days later he told his widowed mother, who had recently been converted to Christianity and had taken the name of Elizabeth. The shock nearly killed her. When she recovered, she went down on her knees and begged Amos not to do this thing. But he would not hear; his ears had been nailed up. At last, in desperation, Elizabeth went to consult the diviner.

This diviner was a man of great power and wisdom. As he sat on the floor of his hut beating a tortoise shell, a coating of white chalk round his eyes, he saw not only the present, but also what had been and what was to be. He was called "the man of the four eyes." As soon as old Elizabeth appeared, he cast his stringed cowries and told her what she had come to see him about. "Your son has joined the white man's religion. And you too in your old age when you should know better. And do you wonder that he is stricken with insanity? Those who gather ant-infested faggots must be prepared for the visit of lizards." He cast his cowries a number of times and wrote with a finger on a bowl of sand, and all the while his *nwifulu*, a talking calabash, chatted to itself. "Shut up!" he roared, and it immediately held its peace. The diviner then muttered a few incantations and rattled off a breathless reel of proverbs that followed one another like the cowries in his magic string.

At last he pronounced the cure. The ancestors were angry and must be appeased with a goat. Old Elizabeth performed the rites, but her son remained insane and married an *Osu* girl whose name was Sarah. Old Elizabeth renounced her new religion and returned to the faith of her people.

We have wandered from our main story. But it is important to know how Chike's father became an *Osu*, because even today when everything is upside down, such a story is very rare. But now to return to Chike who refused heathen food at the tender age of four years, or maybe five.

Two years later he went to the village school. His right hand could now reach across his head to his left ear, which proved that he was old enough to tackle the mysteries of the white man's learning. He was very happy about his new slate and pencil, and especially about his school uniform of white shirt and brown khaki shorts. But as the first day of the new term approached, his young mind dwelt on the many stories about teachers and their canes. And he remembered the song his elder sisters sang, a song that had a somewhat disquieting refrain:

Onye nkuzi ewelu itali piagbusie umuaka.

One of the ways an emphasis is laid in Ibo is by exaggeration, so that the teacher in the refrain might not actually have flogged the children to death. But there was no doubt he did flog them. And Chike thought very much about it.

Being so young, Chike was sent to what was called the "religious class" where they sang, and sometimes danced, the catechism. He loved the sound of words and he loved rhythm. During the catechism lesson the class formed a ring to dance the teacher's question. "Who was Caesar?" he might ask, and the song would burst forth with much stamping of feet.

Siza bu eze Rome
Onye nachi enu uwa dum.

It did not matter to their dancing that in the twentieth century Caesar was no longer ruler of the whole world.

And sometimes they even sang in English. Chike was very fond of "Ten Green Bottles." They had been taught the words but they only remembered the first and the last lines. The middle was hummed and hie-ed and mumbled:

Ten grin botr angin on dar war,
Ten grin botr angin on dar war,
Hm, hm hm hm hm
Hm, hm hm hm hm hm,
An ten grin botr angin on dar war.

In this way the first year passed. Chike was promoted to the "Infant School," where work of a more serious nature was undertaken.

We need not follow him through the Infant School. It would make a full story in itself. But it was no different from the story of other children. In the Primary School, however, his individual character began to show. He developed a strong hatred for arithmetic. But he loved stories and songs. And he liked particularly the sound of English words, even when they conveyed no meaning at all. Some of them simply filled him with elation. "Periwinkle" was such a word. He had now forgotten how he learned it or exactly what it was. He had a vague private meaning for it and it was something to do with fairyland. "Constellation" was another.

Chike's teacher was fond of long words. He was said to be a very learned man. His favourite pastime was copying out jaw-breaking words from his *Chambers' Etymological Dictionary*. Only the other day he had raised applause from his class by demolishing a boy's excuse for lateness with unanswerable erudition. He had said: "Procrastination is a lazy man's apology." The teacher's erudition showed itself in every subject he taught. His nature study lessons were memorable. Chike would always remember the lesson on the methods of seed dispersal. According to teacher, there were five methods: by man, by animals, by water, by wind, and by explosive mechanism. Even those pupils who forgot all the other methods remembered "explosive mechanism."

Chike was naturally impressed by teacher's explosive vocabulary. But the fairyland quality which words had for him was of a different kind. The first sentences in his *New Method Reader* were simple enough and yet they filled him with a vague exultation: "Once there was a wizard. He lived in Africa. He went to China to get a lamp." Chike read it over and over again at home and then made a song of it. It was a meaningless song. "Periwinkles" got into it, and also "Damascus." But it was like a window through which he saw in the distance a strange, magical new world. And he was happy.

Reflections

Private Exploration

1. Explore the changes Chike and his family have undergone in order to thrive under the ways of the white man. What evidence does Achebe provide to reveal the confusion and struggle the family experiences as it attempts to bridge old traditions and beliefs with new? How successful are they? Consider how their values are changed. Just what has the white man accomplished?
2. Achebe writes with the lightness of wind on water. We marvel at the rhythm of his sentences, the words and patterns he uses to pull us inside Chike's world. Explore Achebe's use of language and the feelings you experience reading this story. How does it feel to hear words like "Osu," and "niwifulu"? Just for the fun of it (and to remind yourself what it feels like to speak and learn a new language) read the following passage out loud: "Onye nkuzi ewelu itali piabusisumuaka." What new physical sensations do you experience as you read? Try to describe the sensations as well as your thoughts and feelings regarding them.
3. What do you make of this passage?

    > But it [Chike's song] was like a window through which he saw a strange, magical new world. And he was happy.

4. If English is meaningful only for its sound, and not its meaning, how is it valuable?

Public Exploration

1. Author Ursula Le Guin writes that "There have been many civilizations that did not use the wheel, but there has never been a civilization that did not tell stories." How might story telling and imagination be regarded as resources for survival? Discuss this in terms of the individual (private survival) and in terms of others (public survival or the survival of a culture).
2. What is the relationship between language and values?

Personal Reflection

We once lived in a small fishing village outside Lisbon, Portugal. We couldn't speak or read Portuguese. We tried to learn by listening to tapes and reading study manuals, but we were never successful. The Portuguese words continued to pass over our heads like the sound of the sea—ish-ish, ish-ish. Somehow we survived, but our lives and our values were never the same. Focus on any experience you've had in a different culture or with different languages. You don't need to travel as far as Europe to experience such a shift. If you've ever lived in the West and traveled East, or moved from the South to the North, you know what we mean. Write about your experience, focusing particularly on language or the culture conflicts you experienced. What is the value of such exposure? How did your experience affect your thinking, your perception of the world?

The Ignored Lesson of Anne Frank

BRUNO BETTELHEIM

When the world first learned about the Nazi concentration and death camps, most civilized people felt the horrors committed in them to be so uncanny as to be unbelievable. It came as a severe shock that supposedly civilized nations could stoop to such inhuman acts. The implication that modern man has such inadequate control over his cruel and destructive proclivities was felt as a threat to our views of ourselves and our humanity. Three different psychological mechanisms were most frequently used for dealing with the appalling revelation of what had gone on in the camps:

1. its applicability to man in general was denied by asserting—contrary to evidence—that the acts of torture and mass murder were committed by a small group of insane or perverted persons;

2. the truth of the reports was denied by declaring them vastly exaggerated and ascribing them to propaganda (this originated with the German government, which called all reports on terror in the camps "horror propaganda"—*Greuel-propaganda*);

3. the reports were believed, but the knowledge of the horror repressed as soon as possible.

All three mechanisms could be seen at work after liberation of those prisoners remaining. At first, after the discovery of the camps and their death-dealing, a wave of extreme outrage swept the Allied nations. It was soon followed by a general repression of the discovery in people's minds. Possibly this reaction was due to something more than the blow dealt to modern man's narcissism by the realization that cruelty is still rampant among men. Also present may have been the dim but extremely threatening realization that the modern state now has available the means for changing personality, and for destroying millions it deems undesirable. The ideas that in our day a people's personalities might be changed against their will by the state, and that other populations might be wholly or partially exterminated, are so fearful that one tries to free oneself of them and their impact by defensive denial, or by repression.

The extraordinary world-wide success of the book, play, and movie *The Diary of Anne Frank* suggests the power of the desire to counteract the realization of the personality-destroying and murderous nature of the camps by concentrating all attention on what is experienced as a demonstration that private and intimate life can continue to flourish even under the direct persecution by the most ruthless totalitarian system. And this although Anne Frank's fate demonstrates how efforts at disregarding in private life what goes on around one in society can hasten one's own destruction.

What concerns me here is not what actually happened to the Frank family, how they tried—and failed—to survive their terrible ordeal. It would be very wrong to take apart so humane and moving a story, which aroused so much well-merited compassion for gentle Anne Frank and her tragic fate. What is at issue is the universal and uncritical response to her diary and to the play and movie based on it, and what this reaction tells about our attempts to cope with the feelings her fate—used by us to serve as a symbol of a most human reaction to Nazi terror—arouses in us. I believe that the world-wide acclaim given her story cannot be explained unless we recognize in it our wish to forget the gas chambers, and our effort to do so by glorifying the ability to retreat into an extremely private, gentle, sensitive world, and there to cling as much as possible to what have been one's usual daily attitudes and activities, although surrounded by a maelstrom apt to engulf one at any moment.

The Frank family's attitude that life could be carried on as before may well have been what led to their destruction. By eulogizing how they lived in their hiding place while neglecting to examine first whether it was a reasonable or an effective choice, we are able to ignore the crucial lesson of their story—that such an attitude can be fatal in extreme circumstances.

While the Franks were making their preparations for going passively into hiding, thousands of other Jews in Holland (as elsewhere in Europe) were trying to escape to the free world, in order to survive and/or fight. Others who could not escape went underground—into hiding—each family member with, for example, a different gentile family. We gather from the diary, however, that the chief desire of the Frank family was to continue living as nearly as possible in the same fashion to which they had been accustomed in happier times.

Little Anne, too, wanted only to go on with life as usual, and what else could she have done but fall in with the pattern her parents created for her existence? But hers was not a necessary fate, much less a heroic one; it was a terrible but also a senseless fate. Anne had a good chance to survive, as did many Jewish children in Holland. But she would have had to leave her parents and go live with a gentile Dutch family, posing as their own child, something her parents would have had to arrange for her.

Everyone who recognized the obvious knew that the hardest way to go underground was to do it as a family; to hide out together made detection by the SS most likely; and when detected, everybody was doomed. By hiding singly, even when one got caught, the others had a chance to survive. The Franks, with their excellent connections among gentile Dutch families, might well have been able to hide out singly, each with a different family. But instead, the main principle of their planning was continuing their beloved family life—an understandable desire, but highly unrealistic in those times. Choosing any other course would have meant not merely giving up living together, but also realizing the full measure of the danger to their lives.

The Franks were unable to accept that going on living as a family as they had done before the Nazi invasion of Holland was no longer a desirable way of life, much as they loved each other; in fact, for them and others like them, it was most dangerous behavior. But even given their wish not to separate, they failed to make appropriate preparations for what was likely to happen.

There is little doubt that the Franks, who were able to provide themselves with so much while arranging for going into hiding, and even while hiding, could have provided themselves with some weapons had they wished. Had they had a gun, Mr. Frank could have shot down at least one or two of the "green police" who came for them. There was no surplus of such police, and the loss of an SS with every Jew arrested would have noticeably hindered the functioning of the police state. Even a butcher knife, which they certainly could have taken with them into hiding, could have been used by them in self-defense. The fate of the Franks wouldn't have been very different, because they all died anyway except for Anne's father. But they could have sold their lives for a high price, instead of walking to their death. Still, although one must assume that Mr. Frank would have fought courageously, as we know he did when a soldier in the first World War, it is not everybody who can plan to kill those who are bent on killing him, although many who would not be ready to contemplate doing so would be willing to kill those who are bent on murdering not only them but also their wives and little daughters.

An entirely different matter would have been planning for escape in case of discovery. The Franks' hiding place had only one entrance; it did not have any other exit. Despite the fact, during their many months of hiding, they did not try to devise one. Nor did they make other plans for escape, such as that one of the family members—as likely as not Mr. Frank—would try to detain the police in the narrow entrance way—maybe even fight them, as suggested above—thus giving other members of the family a chance to escape, either by reaching the roofs of adjacent houses, or down a ladder into the alley behind the house in which they were living.

Any of this would have required recognizing and accepting the desperate straits in which they found themselves, and concentrating on how best to cope with them. This was quite possible to do, even under the terrible conditions in which the Jews found themselves after the Nazi occupation of Holland. It can be seen from many other accounts, for example from the story of Marga Minco, a girl of about Anne Frank's age who lived to tell about it. Her parents had planned that when the police should come for them, the father would try to detain them by arguing and fighting with them, to give the wife and daughter a chance to escape through a rear door. Unfortunately it did not quite work out this way, and both parents got killed. But their short-lived resistance permitted their daughter to make her escape as planned and to reach a Dutch family who saved her.

This is not mentioned as a criticism that the Frank family did not plan or behave along similar lines. A family has every right to arrange their life as they wish or think best, and to take the risks they want to take. My point is not to criticize what the Franks did, but only the universal admiration of their way of coping, or rather of not coping. The story of little Marga who survived, every bit as touching, remains totally neglected by comparison.

Many Jews—unlike the Franks, who through listening to British radio news were better informed than most—had no detailed knowledge of the extermination camps. Thus it was easier for them to make themselves believe that complete compliance with even the most outrageously debilitating and degrading Nazi orders might offer a chance for survival. But neither tremendous anxiety that inhibits clear thinking and with it well-planned and determined action, nor ignorance about what happened to those who responded with passive waiting for being rounded up for their extermination, can explain the reaction of audiences to the play and movie retelling Anne's story, which are all about such waiting that results finally in destruction.

I think it is the fictitious ending that explains the enormous success of this play and movie. At the conclusion we hear Anne's voice from the beyond, saying, "In spite of everything, I still believe that people are really good at heart." This improbable sentiment is supposedly from a girl who had been starved to death, had watched her sister meet the same fate before she did, knew that her mother had been murdered, and had watched untold thousands of adults and children being killed. This statement is not justified by anything Anne actually told her diary.

Going on with intimate family living, no matter how dangerous it might be to survival, was fatal to all too many during the Nazi regime. And if all men are good, then indeed we can all go on with living our lives as we have been accustomed to in times of undisturbed safety and can afford to forget about Auschwitz. But Anne, her sister, her mother, may well have died because her parents could not get themselves to believe in Auschwitz.

While play and movie are ostensibly about Nazi persecution and destruction, in actuality what we watch is the way that, despite this terror, lovable people manage to continue living their satisfying intimate lives with each other. The heroine grows from a child into a young adult as normally as any other girl would, despite the most abnormal conditions of all other aspects of her existence, and that of her family. Thus the play reassures us that despite the destructiveness of Nazi racism and tyranny in general, it is possible to disregard it in one's private life much of the time, even if one is Jewish.

True, the ending happens just as the Franks and their friends had feared all along: their hiding place is discovered, and they are carried away to their doom. But the fictitious declaration of faith in the goodness of all men which concludes the play falsely reassures us since it impresses on us that in the combat between Nazi terror and continuance of intimate family living the latter wins out, since Anne has the last word. This is simply contrary to fact, because it was she who got killed. Her seeming survival through her moving statement about the goodness of men releases us effectively of the need to cope with the problems Auschwitz presents. That is why we are so relieved by her statement. It explains why millions loved play and movie, because while it confronts us with the fact that Auschwitz existed it encourages us at the same time to ignore any of its implications. If all men are good at heart, there never really was an Auschwitz; nor is there any possibility that it may recur.

The desire of Anne Frank's parents not to interrupt their intimate family living, and their inability to plan more effectively for their survival, reflect the failure of all too many others faced with the threat of Nazi terror. It is a failure that deserves close examination because of the inherent warnings it contains for us, the living.

Submission to the threatening power of the Nazi state often led both to the disintegration of what had once seemed well-integrated personalities and to a return to an immature disregard for the dangers of reality. Those Jews who submitted passively to Nazi persecution came to depend on primitive and infantile thought processes: wishful thinking and disregard for the possibility of death. Many persuaded themselves that they, out of all the others, would be spared. Many more simply disbelieved in the possibility of their own death. Not believing in it, they did not take what seemed to them desperate precautions, such as giving up everything to hide out singly; or trying to escape even if it meant risking their lives in doing so; or preparing to fight for their lives when no escape was possible and death had become an immediate possibility. It is true that defending their lives in active combat before they were rounded up to be transported into the camps might have hastened their deaths, and so, up to a point, they were protecting themselves by "rolling with the punches" of the enemy.

But the longer one rolls with the punches dealt not by the normal vagaries of life, but by one's eventual executioner, the more likely it becomes that one will no longer have the strength to resist when death becomes imminent. This is particularly true if yielding to the enemy is accompanied not by a commensurate strengthening of the personality, but by an inner disintegration. We can observe such a process among the Franks, who bickered with each other over trifles, instead of supporting each other's ability to resist the demoralizing impact of their living conditions.

Those who faced up to the announced intentions of the Nazis prepared for the worst as a real and imminent possibility. It meant risking one's life for a self-chosen purpose, but in doing so, creating at least a small chance for saving one's own life or those of others, or both. When Jews in Germany were restricted to their homes, those who did not succumb to inertia took the new restrictions as a warning that it was high time to go underground, join the resistance movement, provide themselves with forged papers, and so on, if they had not done so long ago. Many of them survived.

Some distant relatives of mine may furnish an example. Early in the war, a young man living in a small Hungarian town banded together with a number of other Jews to prepare against a German invasion. As soon as the Nazis imposed curfews on the Jews, his group left for Budapest—because the bigger capital city with its greater anonymity offered chances for escaping detection. Similar groups from other towns converged in Budapest and joined forces. From among themselves they selected typically "Aryan" looking men who equipped themselves with false papers and immediately joined the Hungarian SS. These spies were then able to warn of impending persecution and raids.

Many of these groups survived intact. Furthermore, they had also equipped themselves with small arms, so that if they were detected, they could put up enough of a fight for the majority to escape while a few would die fighting to make the escape possible. A few of the Jews who had joined the SS were discovered and immediately shot, probably a death preferable to one in the gas chambers. But most of even these Jews survived, hiding within the SS until liberation.

Compare these arrangements not just to the Franks' selection of a hiding place that was basically a trap without an outlet but with Mr. Frank's teaching typically academic high-school subjects to his children rather than how to make a getaway: a token of his inability to face the seriousness of the threat of death. Teaching high-school subjects had, of course, its constructive aspects. It relieved the ever-present anxiety about their fate to some degree by concentrating on different matters, and by implication it encouraged hope for a future in which such knowledge would be useful. In this sense such teaching was purposeful, but it was erroneous in that it took the place of much more pertinent teaching and planning: how best to try to escape when detected.

Unfortunately the Franks were by no means the only ones who, out of anxiety, became unable to contemplate their true situation and with it to plan accordingly. Anxiety, and the wish to counteract it by clinging to each other, and to reduce its sting by continuing as much as possible with their usual way of life incapacitated many, particularly when survival plans required changing radically old ways of living that they cherished, and which had become their only source of satisfaction.

My young relative, for example, was unable to persuade other members of his family to go with him when he left the small town where he had lived with them. Three times, at tremendous risk to himself, he returned to plead with his relatives, pointing out first the growing persecution of the Jews, and later the fact that transport to the gas chambers had already begun. He could not convince these Jews to leave their homes and break up their families to go singly into hiding.

As their desperation mounted, they clung more determinedly to their old living arrangements and to each other, became less able to consider giving up the possessions they had accumulated through hard work over a lifetime. The more severely their freedom to act was reduced, and what little they were still permitted to do restricted by insensible and degrading regulations imposed by the Nazis, the more did they become unable to contemplate independent action. Their life energies drained out of them, sapped by their ever-greater anxiety. The less they found strength in themselves, the more they held on the little that was left of what had given them security in the past—their old surroundings, their customary way of life, their possessions—all these seemed to give their lives some permanency, offer some symbols of security. Only what had once been symbols of security now endangered life, since they were excuses for avoiding change. On each successive visit the young man found his relatives more incapacitated, less willing or able to take his advice, more frozen into inactivity, and with it further along the way to the crematoria where, in fact, they all died.

Levin renders a detailed account of the desperate but fruitless efforts made by small Jewish groups determined to survive to try to save the rest. She tells how messengers were "sent into the provinces to warn Jews that deportation meant death, but their warnings were ignored because most Jews refused to contemplate their own annihilation." I believe the reason for such refusal has to be found in their inability to take action. If we are certain that we are helpless to protect ourselves against the danger of destruction, we cannot contemplate it. We can consider the danger only as long as we believe there are ways to protect ourselves, to fight back, to escape. If we are convinced none of this is possible for us, then there is no point in thinking about the danger; on the contrary, it is best to refuse to do so.

As a prisoner in Buchenwald, I talked to hundreds of German Jewish prisoners who were brought there as part of the huge pogrom in the wake of the murder of vom Rath in the fall of 1938. I asked them why they had not left Germany, given the utterly degrading conditions they had been subjected to. Their answer was: How could we leave? It would have meant giving up our homes, our work, our sources of income. Having been deprived by Nazi persecution and degradation of much of their self-respect, they had become unable to give up what still gave them a semblance of it: their earthly belongings. But instead of using possessions, they became captivated by them, and this possession by earthly goods became the fatal mask for their possession by anxiety, fear, and denial.

How the investment of personal property with one's life energy could make people die bit by bit was illustrated throughout the Nazi persecution of the Jews. At the time of the first boycott of Jewish stores, the chief external goal of the Nazis was to acquire the possessions of the Jews. They even let Jews take some things out of the country at that time if they would leave the bulk of their property behind. For a long time the intention of the Nazis, and the goal of their first discriminatory laws, was to force undesirable minorities, including Jews, into emigration.

Although the extermination policy was in line with the inner logic of Nazi racial ideology, one may wonder whether the idea that millions of Jews (and other foreign nationals) could be submitted to extermination did not partially result from seeing the degree of degradation Jews accepted without fighting back. When no violent resistance occurred, persecution of the Jews worsened, slow step by slow step.

Many Jews who on the invasion of Poland were able to survey their situation and draw the right conclusions survived the Second World War. As the Germans approached, they left everything behind and fled to Russia, much as they distrusted and disliked the Soviet system. But there, while badly treated, they could at least survive. Those who stayed on in Poland believing they could go on with life-as-before sealed their fate. Thus in the deepest sense the walk to the gas chamber was only the last consequence of these Jews' inability to comprehend what was in store; it was the final step of surrender to the death instinct, which might also be called the principle of inertia. The first step was taken long before arrival at the death camp.

We can find a dramatic demonstration of how far the surrender to inertia can be carried, and the wish not to know because knowing would create unbearable anxiety, in an experience of Olga Lengyel. She reports that although she and her fellow prisoners lived just a few hundred yards from the crematoria and the gas chambers and knew what they were for, most prisoners denied knowledge of them for months. If they had grasped their true situation, it might have helped them save either the lives they themselves were fated to lose, or the lives of others.

When Mrs. Lengyel's fellow prisoners were selected to be sent to the gas chambers, they did not try to break away from the group, as she successfully did. Worse, the first time she tried to escape the gas chambers, some of the other selected prisoners told the supervisors that she was trying to get away. Mrs. Lengyel desperately asks the question: How was it possible that people denied the existence of the gas chambers when all day long they saw the crematoria burning and smelled the odor of burning flesh? Why did they prefer ignoring the extermination to fighting for their very own lives? She can offer no explanation, only the observation that they resented anyone who tried to save himself from the common fate, because they lacked enough courage to risk action themselves. I believe they did it because they had given up their will to live and permitted their death tendencies to engulf them. As a result, such prisoners were in the thrall of the murdering SS not only physically but also psychologically, while this was not true for those prisoners who still had a grip on life.

Some prisoners even began to serve their executioners, to help speed the death of their own kind. Then things had progressed beyond simple inertia to the death instinct running rampant. Those who tried to serve their executioners in what were once their civilian capacities were merely continuing life as usual and thereby opening to door to their death.

For example, Mrs. Lengyel speaks of Dr. Mengele, SS physician at Auschwitz, as a typical example of the "business as usual" attitude that enabled some prisoners, and certainly the SS, to retain whatever balance they could despite what they were doing. She described how Dr. Mengele took all correct medical precautions during childbirth, rigorously observing all aseptic principles, cutting the umbilical cord with greatest care, etc. But only half an hour later he sent mother and infant to be burned in the crematorium.

Having made his choice, Dr. Mengele and others like him had to delude themselves to be able to live with themselves and their experience. Only one personal document on the subject has come to my attention, that of Dr. Nyiszli, a prisoner serving as "research physician" at Auschwitz. How Dr. Nyiszli deluded himself can be seen, for example, in the way he repeatedly refers to himself as working in Auschwitz as a physician, although he worked as the assistant of a criminal murderer. He speaks of the Institute for Race, Biological, and Anthropological Investigation as "one of the most qualified medical centers of the Third Reich," although it was devoted to proving falsehoods. That Nyiszli was a doctor didn't alter the fact that he—like any of the prisoner foremen who served the SS better than some SS were willing to serve it—was a participant in the crimes of the SS. How could he do it and live with himself?

The answer is: by taking pride in his professional skills, irrespective of the purpose they served. Dr. Nyiszli and Dr. Mengele were only two among hundreds of other—and far more prominent—physicians who participated in the Nazis' murderous pseudo-scientific human experiments. It was the peculiar pride of these men in their professional skill and knowledge, without regard for moral implications, that made them so dangerous. Although the concentration camps and crematoria are no longer here, this kind of pride still remains with us; it is characteristic of a modern society in which fascination with technical competence has dulled concern for human feelings. Auschwitz is gone, but so long as this attitude persists, we shall not be safe from cruel indifference to life at the core.

I have met many Jews as well as gentile anti-Nazis, similar to the activist group in Hungary described earlier, who survived in Nazi Germany and in the occupied countries. These people realized that when a world goes to pieces and inhumanity reigns supreme, man cannot go on living his private life as he was wont to do, and would like to do; he cannot, as the loving head of a family, keep the family living together peacefully, undisturbed by the surrounding world; nor can he continue to take pride in his profession or possessions, when either will deprive him of his humanity, if not also of his life. In such times, one must radically reevaluate all of what one has done, believed in, and stood for in order to know how to act. In short, one has to take a stand on the new reality—a firm stand, not one of retirement into an even more private world.

If today, Negroes in Africa march against the guns of a police that defends *apartheid*—even if hundreds of dissenters are shot down and tens of thousands rounded up in camps—their fight will sooner or later assure them of a chance for liberty and equality. Millions of the Jews of Europe who did not or could

not escape in time or go underground as many thousands did, could at least have died fighting as some did in the Warsaw ghetto at the end, instead of passively waiting to be rounded up for their own extermination.

Reflections

Private Exploration

1. Select a key passage from Bettleheim and use it to explore the essay's argument as you see it. Are you persuaded? Are you affected most by logic here or by emotion? Does Bettleheim require you to reevaluate your thinking? Do you find yourself agreeing or resisting?
2. Consider the following as a starting point for evaluating Bettleheim.

> A man must see, do and think things for himself, in the face of those who are sure that they have already been over all the ground.
>
> —JACOB BRONOWSKI

3. Bettelheim criticizes the Franks for choosing to live as a family rather than separating and resisting. Had they defended themselves, he believes "they could have sold their lives for a higher price, instead of walking to their death." Explore your own thoughts regarding this choice, the price one places on life of the individual vs. the life of the family. Would their deaths have been more dignified by their separate active resistance? If you found yourself in a similar situation can you speculate on the choice you would make? How might it feel to be confronted with such a decision?

Public Exploration

1. Share with your group or class your initial experiences with Bettleheim's essay, as you've written about them in your notebook. Consider other's initial responses. Use several of these to explore the different kinds of values that Bettleheim argues are necessary for survival in situations of great crises. If there is disagreement, take time for silent reflection and use part of that time to explore your own feelings further in your notebook.
2. Bruno Bettleheim criticizes the line, "In spite of everything, I still believe that people are really good at heart." Anne Frank did not actually make such a statement in her diary. Bettleheim claims that as a consequence of inserting such a fiction into the play and movie, we are presented with an unrealistic and dangerous sentiment. Bettelheim argues that such a belief ". . . releases us effectively of the need to cope with the problems Auschwitz presents . . . it encourages us to ignore any of its implications."

   But Anne Frank *did* write that ". . . we still love life, we haven't yet forgotten the voice of nature, we still hope, hope about everything."

   Another survivor, Vaclav Havel, a Czechoslovakian writer who endured years of persecution and imprisonment for his resistance to totalitarianism, has expressed his belief that hope is necessary to overcome the forces of oppression:

> The more unpropitious the situation in which we demonstrate hope, the deeper that hope is. Hope is definitely not the same thing as optimism. It is not the conviction that something will turn our well, but the certainty that something makes sense, regardless of how it turns out.

Compare Bettleheim's concerns with Havel's philosophy. At what point does hope become dangerous? At what point might it appear as a necessary resource for human survival?

Personal Reflection

1. If you've had the opportunity to write about and to discuss Bettelheim's essay with others, probe further into your own thoughts and feelings. Consider what Bettleheim might teach us about survival. Do you agree or disagree that fighting assures "a chance for liberty and equality"? What qualities of personal character are required? Would you have them if the situation called for it? If possible, draw from recent historical events or from other readings as you explore your response.
2. Think back on any time when you either acted or failed to act regarding the persecution of an individual or a group. Retell the story of the incident and the role you played. Reflect on your response. What motivated you to act as you did? Try to be as honest as possible here (i.e., consider how family, culture, or other factors might have influenced your response, as well as personal idealism or personal fear). Try to recall your feelings, the thoughts that ran through your mind. Did the consequences of that experience change your thinking or your feelings? Does anything in Bettleheim cast a new light on your actions?

It Is Raining on the House of Anne Frank

LINDA PASTAN

It is raining on the house
of Anne Frank
and on the tourists
herded together under the shadow
of their umbrellas,
on the perfectly silent
tourists who would rather be
somewhere else
but who wait here on stairs
so steep they must rise
to some occasion
high in the empty loft,
in the quaint toilet,

in the skeleton
of a kitchen
or on the map—
each of its arrows
a barb of wire—
with all the dates, the expulsions,
the forbidding shapes
of continents.
And across Amsterdam it is raining
on the Van Gogh Museum
where we will hurry next
to see how someone else
could find the pure
center of light
within the dark circle
of his demons.

Reflections

Private Exploration

1. Begin by jotting down your initial impression. What does the poem mean to you on a first reading? This deceptively simple poem demands careful attention. As you read it a second time, make marginal notations on verbs, adjectives, or images that seem to imply more than is stated. Consider what those words or phrases reveal about the tourists or what may be implied about the speaker.
2. If you're not familiar with Van Gogh (or with Anne Frank for that matter), you'll want to check a reference work in your library. Take notes in your notebook on the information you find there, and consider how it illuminates the poem as a whole.

Public Exploration

After someone in your class or group has read the poem aloud, take turns sharing your initial summary and response to the poem. If you looked up material in the library on Van Gogh or on Anne Frank, share that information and reflect on the connections between the two. Discuss the differences in perception that arise in your group, and how different backgrounds or different historical perspectives might affect your responses. Consider especially what you feel is implied by the final metaphor.

Private Reflection

If you've had an opportunity to hear others discuss Pastan's poem, return now to your original reactions and consider how they may have changed or modified. You might want to focus especially on references to "demons" and "the center of light in a dark circle." How might the metaphor be extended to the speaker and her own position in the "herd" of tourists?

Thriving as an Outsider, Even as an Outcast, in Smalltown America

LOUIE CREW

From 1973 to 1970, my spouse and I lived in Fort Valley, a town of 12,000 people, the seat of Peach County, sixty miles northeast of Plains, right in the geographic center of Georgia. I taught English at a local black college and my spouse was variously a nurse, hairdresser, choreographer for the college majorettes, caterer, and fashion designer.

The two of us have often been asked how we survived as a gay, racially integrated couple living openly in that small town. We are still perhaps too close to the Georgia experience and very much caught up in our similar struggles in central Wisconsin to offer a definite explanation, but our tentative conjectures should interest anyone who values the role of the dissident in our democracy.

Survive we did. We even throve before our departure. Professionally, my colleagues and the Regents of the University System of Georgia awarded me tenure, and the Chamber of Commerce awarded my spouse a career medal in cosmetology. Socially, we had friends from the full range of the economic classes in the community. We had attended six farewell parties in our honor before we called a halt to further fetes, especially several planned at too great a sacrifice by some of the poorest folks in the town. Furthermore, I had been away only four months when the college brought me back to address an assembly of Georgia judges, mayors, police chiefs, and wardens. We are still called two to three times a week by scores of people seeking my spouse's advice on fashion, cooking, or the like.

It was not always so. In 1974 my spouse and I were denied housing which we had "secured" earlier before the realtor saw my spouse's color. HUD documented that the realtor thought that "the black man looked like a criminal." Once the town was up in arms when a bishop accused the two of us of causing a tornado which had hit the town early in 1975, an accusation which appeared on the front page of the newspaper. "This is the voice of God. The town of Fort Valley is harboring Sodomists. Would one expect God to keep silent when homosexuals are tolerated? We remember what He did to Sodom and Gomorrah" (*The Macon Herald*, March 20, 1975: 1). A year later my Episcopal vestry asked me to leave the parish, and my own bishop summoned me for discipline for releasing to the national press correspondence related to the vestry's back-room maneuvers. Prompted in part by such officials, the local citizens for years routinely heckled us in public, sometimes threw rocks at our apartment, trained their children to spit on us from their bicycles if we dared to jog, and badgered us with hate calls on an average of six to eight times a week.

One such episode offers a partial clue to the cause of our survival. It was late summer, 1975 or 1976. I was on my motorcycle to post mail at the street-side box just before the one daily pickup at 6:00 P.M. About fifty yards away, fully audible to about seventy pedestrians milling about the court house and other public buildings, a group of police officers, all men, began shouting at me from the steps of their headquarters: "Louise! Faggot! Queer!"

Anyone who has ever tried to ease a motorcycle from a still position without revving the engine knows that the feat is impossible: try as I did to avoid the suggestion, I sounded as if I were riding off in a huff. About half-way up the street, I thought to myself, "I'd rather rot in jail than feel the way I do now." I turned around, drove back—the policemen still shouting and laughing—and parked in the lot of the station. When I walked to the steps, only the lone black policeman remained.

"Did you speak to me?" I asked him.

"No, sir," he replied emphatically.

Inside I badgered the desk sergeant to tell her chief to call me as soon as she could locate him, and I indicated that I would press charges if necessary to prevent a recurrence. I explained that the police misconduct was an open invitation to more violent hoodlums to act out the officers' fantasies with impunity in the dark. Later, I persuaded a black city commissioner and a white one, the latter our grocer and the former our mortician, to threaten the culprits with suspension if ever such misconduct occurred again.

Over a year later, late one Friday after his payday, a black friend of my spouse knocked at our door to offer a share of his Scotch to celebrate his raise—or so he said. Thus primed, he asked me, "You don't recognize me, do you?"

"No," I admitted.

"I'm the lone black policeman that day you were heckled. I came by really because I thought you two might want to know what happened inside when Louie stormed up to the sergeant."

"Yes," we said.

"Well, all the guys were crouching behind the partition to keep you from seeing that they were listening. Their eyes bulged when you threatened to bring in the F.B.I. and such. Then when you left, one spoke for all when he said, 'But sissies aren't supposed to do things like that!' "

Ironically, I believe that a major reason for our thriving on our own terms of candor about our relationship has been our commitment to resist the intimidation heaped upon us. For too long lesbians and gay males have unwillingly encouraged abuses against ourselves by serving advance notice to any bullies, be they the barnyard-playground variety, or the Bible-wielding pulpiteers, that we would whimper or run into hiding when confronted with even the threat of exposure. It is easy to confuse sensible nonviolence with cowardly nonresistance.

In my view, violent resistance would be counter-productive, especially for lesbians and gays who are outnumbered 10 to 1 by heterosexuals, according to Kinsey's statistics. Yet our personal experience suggests that special kinds of creative nonviolent resistance are a major source of hope if lesbians and gay males are going to reverse the physical and mental intimidation which is our daily portion in this culture.

Resistance to oppression can be random and spontaneous, as in part was my decision to return to confront the police hecklers, or organized and sustained, as more typically has been the resistance by which my spouse and I have survived. I believe that only organized and sustained resistance offers much hope for long-range change in any community. The random act is too soon forgotten or too easily romanticized.

Once we had committed ourselves to one another, my spouse and I never gave much thought for ourselves to the traditional device most gays have used for survival, the notorious "closet" in which one hides one's identity from all but a select group of friends. In the first place, a black man and a white man integrating a Georgia small town simply cannot be inconspicuous. More importantly, the joint checking account and other equitable economies fundamental to the quality of our marriage are public, not private acts. Our denial of the obvious would have secured closet space only for our suffocation; we would have lied, "We are ashamed and live in secret."

All of our resistance stems from our sense of our own worth, our conviction that we and our kind do not deserve the suffering which heterosexuals continue to encourage or condone for sexual outcasts. Dr. Martin Luther King used to say, "Those who go to the back of the bus, deserve the back of the bus."

Our survival on our own terms has depended very much on our knowing and respecting many of the rules of the system which we resist. We are not simply dissenters, but conscientious ones.

For example, we are both very hard workers. As a controversial person, I know that my professionalism comes under far more scrutiny than that of others. I learned early in my career that I could secure space for my differences by handling routine matters carefully. If one stays on good terms with secretaries, meets all deadlines, and willingly does one's fair share of the busy work of institutions, one is usually already well on the way towards earning collegial space, if not collegial support. In Georgia, I routinely volunteered to be secretary for most committees on which I served, thereby having enormous influence in the final form of the groups' deliberations without monopolizing the forum as most other molders of policy do. My spouse's many talents and sensibilities made him an invaluable advisor and confidante to scores of people in the community. Of course, living as we did in a hairdresser's salon, we knew a great deal more about the rest of the public than that public knew about us.

My spouse and I are fortunate in the fact that we like the enormous amount of work which we do. We are not mere opportunists working hard only as a gimmick to exploit the public for lesbian and gay issues. Both of us worked intensely at our professional assignments long before we were acknowledged dissidents with new excessive pressures to excel. We feel that now we must, however unfairly, be twice as effective as our competitors just to remain employed at all.

Our survival has also depended very much on our thorough knowledge of the system, often knowledge more thorough than that of those who would use the system against us. For example, when my bishop summoned me for discipline, I was able to show him that his own canons give him no authority to discipline a lay person except by excommunication. In fact, so hierarchical have the canons of his diocese become, that the only laity who exist worthy of their mention are the few lay persons on vestries.

Especially helpful has been our knowledge of communication procedures. For example, when an area minister attacked lesbians and gays on a TV talk show, I requested equal time; so well received was my response that for two more years I was a regular panelist on the talk show, thereby reaching most residents of the entire middle Georgia area as a known gay person, yet one speaking not just to sexual issues, but to a full range of religious and social topics.

When I was occasionally denied access to media, as in the parish or diocese or as on campus when gossip flared, I knew the value of candid explanations thoughtfully prepared, xeroxed, and circulated to enough folks to assure that the gossips would have access to the truthful version. For example, the vestry, which acted in secret, was caught by surprise when I sent copies of their hateful letter to most other parishioners, together with a copy of a psalm which I wrote protesting their turning the House of Prayer into a Court House. I also was able to explain that I continued to attend, not in defiance of their withdrawn invitation, but in obedience to the much higher invitation issued to us all by the real head of the Church. In January, 1979, in the first open meeting of the parish since the vestry's letter of unwelcome three years earlier, the entire parish voted to censure the vestry for that action and to extend to me the full welcome which the vestry had tried to deny. Only three voted against censure, all three of them a minority of the vestry being censured.

My spouse and I have been very conscious of the risks of our convictions. We have viewed our credentials—my doctorate and his professional licenses—not as badges of comfortable respectability, but as assets to be invested in social change. Dr. King did not sit crying in the Albany jail, "Why don't these folks respect me? How did this happen? What am I doing here?" When my spouse and I have been denied jobs for which we were the most qualified applicants, we have not naively asked how such things could be, nor have we dwelt overly long on self-pity, for we have known in advance the prices we might have to pay, even if to lose our lives. Our realism about danger and risk has helped us to preserve our sanity when everyone about us has seemed insane. I remember the joy which my spouse shared with me over the fact that he had just been fired for his efforts to organize other black nurses to protest their being treated as orderlies by the white managers of a local hospital.

Never, however, have we affirmed the injustices. Finally, we simply cannot be surprised by any evil and are thus less likely to be intimidated by it. Hence, we find ourselves heirs to a special hybrid of courage, a form of courage too often ignored by the heterosexual majority, but widely manifest among sexual outcasts, not the courage of bravado on battlegrounds or sportsfields, but the delicate courage of the lone person who patiently waits out the stupidity of the herd, the cagey courage that has operated many an underground railway station.

Our survival in smalltown America has been helped least, I suspect, by our annoying insistence that potential friends receive us not only in our own right, but also as members of the larger lesbian/gay and black communities of which we are a part. Too many whites and heterosexuals are prepared to single us out as "good queers" or "good niggers," offering us thereby the "rewards" of their friendship only at too great a cost to our integrity. My priest did not whip up the vestry against me the first year we lived openly together. He was perfectly happy to have one of his "clever queers" to dress his wife's hair and the other to help him write his annual report. We became scandalous only when the two of us began to organize the national group of lesbian and gay-male Episcopalians, known as INTEGRITY; then we were no longer just quaint. We threatened his image of himself as the arbiter of community morality, especially as he faced scores of queries from brother priests elsewhere.

Many lesbians and gay males are tamed by dependencies upon carefully selected heterosexual friends with whom they have shared their secret, often never realizing that in themselves alone, they could provide far more affirmation and discover far more strength than is being cultivated by the terms of these "friendships." Lesbians and gay males have always been taught to survive on the heterosexuals' terms, rarely on one's own terms, and almost never on the terms of a community shared with other lesbians and gay males.

Heterosexuals are often thus the losers. The heterosexual acquaintances close to us early on when we were less visible who dropped us later as our notoriety spread were in most cases folks of demonstrably much less character strength than those heterosexuals who remained our friends even as we asserted our difference with thoughtful independence.

My spouse and I have never been exclusive nor aspired to move to any ghetto. In December, 1978, on the night the Macon rabbi and I had successfully organized the area's Jews and gays to protest a concert by Anita Bryant, I returned home to watch the videotape of the march on the late news in the company of eight house guests invited by my spouse for a surprise party, not one of them gay (for some strange reason nine out of ten folks are not), not one of them obligated to be at the earlier march, and not one of them uneasy, as most of our acquaintances would have been a few years earlier before we had undertaken this reeducation together.

Folks who work for social change need to be very careful to allow room for it to happen, not to allow realistic appraisals of risks to prevent their cultivation of the very change which they germinate.

Our survival has been helped in no small way by our candor and clarity in response to rumor and gossip, which are among our biggest enemies. On my campus in Georgia, I voluntarily spoke about sexual issues to an average of

50 classes per year outside my discipline. Initially, those encounters sharpened my wits for tougher national forums, but long after I no longer needed these occasions personally for rehearsal, I continued to accept the invitations, thereby reaching a vast majority of the citizens of the small town where we continued to live. I used to enjoy the humor of sharing with such groups facts which would make my day-to-day life more pleasant. For example, I routinely noted that when a male student is shocked at my simple public, "Hello," he would look both ways to see who might have seen him being friendly with the gay professor. By doing this he is telling me and all other knowledgeable folks far more new information about his own body chemistry than he is finding out about mine. More informed male students would reply, "Hello" when greeted. With this method I disarmed the hatefulness of one of their more debilitating weapons of ostracism.

All personal references in public discussions inevitably invade one's privacy, but I have usually found the invasion a small price to pay for the opportunity to educate the public to the fact that the issues which most concern sexual outcasts are not genital, as the casters-out have so lewdly imagined, but issues of justice and simple fairness.

Resistance is ultimately an art which no one masters to perfection. Early in my struggles, I said to a gay colleague living openly in rural Nebraska, "We must stamp on every snake." Wisely he counseled, "Only if you want to get foot poisoning." I often wish I had more of the wisdom mentioned in *Ecclesiastes*, the ability to judge accurately, "The time to speak and the time to refrain from speaking." Much of the time I think it wise to pass public hecklers without acknowledging their taunts, especially when they are cowardly hiding in a crowd. When I have faced bullies head-on, I have tried to do so patiently, disarming them by my own control of the situation. Of course, I am not guaranteed that their violence can thus be aborted every time.

Two major sources of our survival are essentially very private—one, the intense care and love my spouse and I share, and the other, our strong faith in God as Unbounding Love. To these we prefer to make our secular witness, more by what we do than by what we say.

In conclusion, I am not masochist enough to choose the hard lot of sexual outcast in smalltown America. Had I the choice to change myself but not the world, I would choose the easiest roles and return as a white male heterosexual city-slicker millionaire, not because whites, males, heterosexuals, city-slickers, and millionaires are better, but because they have fewer difficulties. Yet, given only the choice of changing the world more easily than changing my color, my biological plumbing, my locale, or my inherited bank account, I am grateful for the opportunity to be a dissident in a country which preserves at least the ideal of freedom even if it denies freedom in scores of specific instances. I was not told in my eighth-grade civics class in Alabama what a high price one would have to pay for exercising freedom of speech, as when what one speaks is radically confronting the docile and ignorant majority, but I am grateful that I had a good eighth-grade civics class, learning thoroughly the mechanisms one must use to change this government.

Sometimes I think a society's critics must appreciate the society far more than others, for the critics typically take very seriously the society's idle promises and forgotten dreams. When I occasionally see them, I certainly don't find many of my heterosexual eighth-grade classmates probing much farther than the issues of our common Form 1040 headaches and the issues as delivered by the evening news. Their lives seem often far duller than ours and the main adventures in pioneering they experience come vicariously, through television, the movies, and for a few, through books. In defining me as a criminal, my society may well have hidden a major blessing in its curse by forcing me out of lethargy into an on-going, rigorous questioning of the entire process. Not only do I teach *The Adventures of Huckleberry Finn*, my spouse and I have in an important sense had the chance to be Huck and Jim fleeing a different form of slavery and injustice in a very real present.

Reflections

Personal Exploration

1. Consider this statement:

> Those who go to the back of the bus, deserve the back of the bus.
>
> —MARTIN LUTHER KING, JR.

2. Throughout his essay, Louie Crew analyzes his own resources for private and public survival. What is the value of distinguishing between private and public resources? Are any of them limited only to dissenters? Evaluate each of them, considering especially whether their usefulness might enhance the quality of your own life.

Public Exploration

Explore your attitudes toward each of the three following questions:

a. How do you view gays, lesbians, radical feminists, black Islamic militants, white neo-Nazis, those who burn American flags?

b. How do you view the following?

- an inventor who sets off to create what everyone says is impossible
- a student who challenges the administration on residence hall policies which almost everyone else seems to find acceptable
- a mother who has left her family behind to travel around the country protesting lax laws on drunk driving because her own son died after being killed by an intoxicated driver
- a teacher who refuses to use textbooks because they stifle his or her own approach to a subject

c. Having considered a and b above, what do you make of this passage?

> Independence, originality, and therefore dissent: these words show the progress, they stamp the character of our civilization as once they did that of

Athens in flower. From Luther in 1517 to Spinoza grinding lenses, from Huguenot weavers and Quaker ironmasters to the Puritans funding Harvard, and from Newton's heresies to the calculated universe of Eddington, the profound movements of history have been begun by unconforming men. . . . For dissent is also native in any society which is still growing. Has there ever been a society which has died of dissent? Several have died of conformity in our lifetime. . . . Dissent is not in itself an end; it is the surface mark of a deeper value. Dissent is the mark of freedom, as originality is the mark of independence of mind.

—JACOB BRONOWSKI

Private Reflection

1. If you've had a chance to discuss Crew's essay with others, and if different views emerged, reflect thoughtfully on those differences in attitudes and feelings. Consider the possible influences behind them such as language, culture, history, or differences in personal experience. Have you found out anything important about yourself or those around you in discovering these differences?
2. Have you ever considered yourself a dissident, outcast, or outsider? Explore your experience, focusing sharply on an incident or series of incidents, as Crew does in his essay. Reflect on your own resources for survival, both private and public. Having read Crew's essay, which of his resources might have helped you thrive? Which would have proved useless?

• Daystar •

RITA DOVE

She wanted a little room for thinking:
but she saw diapers steaming on the line,
a doll slumped behind the door.
So she lugged a chair behind the garage
to sit out the children's naps.

Sometimes there were things to watch—
the pinched armor of a varnished cricket,
a floating maple leaf. Other days
she stared until she was assured
when she closed her eyes
she'd see only her own vivid blood.

She had an hour, at best, before Liza appeared
pouting from the top of the stairs.
And just *what* was mother doing
out back with the field mice? Why,

building a palace. Later
that night when Thomas rolled over and
lurched into her, she would open her eyes
and think of the place that was hers
for an hour—where
she was nothing,
pure nothing, in the middle of the day.

Reflections

Private Exploration

1. After you've read "Daystar" several times, jot down your most immediate response to the speaker's thoughts and actions. Try to pinpoint specific words and lines that led to your reaction.
2. Explore the title. Does it offer any insight into the poem? You might want to check the *Oxford English Dictionary* to find additional meanings. Do additional meanings add dimension to the poem?

Public Exploration

After a member of your class or group has read the poem aloud, explore the speaker's concept of "pure nothing in the middle of the day." What is the speaker suggesting? Is there an implicit or explicit criticism of family and husband here? Or are there other possibilities? If someone in your group has privately explored the title, "Daystar," consider how it might relate to the poem as a whole. What kind of values are implied by the poem?

Private Reflection

What is your Daystar? And why? Or, if you don't have one, explore your own way of finding peace in yourself, escaping pressures, or dreaming of a different life. Consider whether by the nature of your choice, your own Daystar reflects a different set of values from that of Rita Dove in "Daystar."

The Palace of the Moorish Kings

EVAN S. CONNELL

Often we wondered why he chose to live as he did, floating here and there like a leaf on a pond. We had talked about this without ever deciding that we understood, although each of us had an opinion. All we could agree upon was that he never would marry. In some way he was cursed, we thought. One of those uncommon men who follow dim trails around the world hunting a fulfillment they couldn't find at home. Early in a man's life this may not be unnatural, but years go by and finally he ought to find a wife and raise children so that by the time his life ends he will have assured the continuation of life. To us that seemed the proper pattern because it was traditional, and we were holding to it as best we could. Only J.D. had not.

From the capitals and provinces of Europe he had wandered to places we had scarcely heard of—Ahmedabad, Penang, the Sulu archipelago. From the Timor coast he had watched the moon rise above the Arafura Sea. He had slept like a beggar beside the red fort in Old Delhi and had seen the Ajanta frescoes. Smoke from funeral pyres along the Ganges at Varanasi had drifted over him, and he'd been doused with brilliant powders during the festival of Bahag Bihn.

Three hundred miles south of Calcutta, he had told us, is a 13th century Hindu temple known as the Black Pagoda of Konorak which is decorated with thousands of sculptured sandstone figures—lions, bulls, elephants, deities, musicians, dancing girls and frankly explicit lovers. Its vegetable-shaped peak, the *sikhara,* collapsed a long time ago, but the *mandapa* is still there, rising in three stages. It represents the chariot of the sun. This fantastic vehicle is drawn by a team of elaborately carved horses and century after century it rolls toward the Bay of Bengal. Nothing equals it, he said. Nothing. The temple complex at Khajuraho is marvelous, but Konorak—and he gestured as he did whenever he could not articulate his feelings.

What he was after, none of us knew. Seasons turned like the pages of a familiar album while he traveled the byways of the world. He seemed to think his life was uncircumscribed, as though years were not passing, as though he might continue indefinitely doing whatever he pleased. Perhaps he thought he would outlive not only us but our children, and theirs beyond them.

We ourselves had no such illusions. We could see the clean sweep of youth sagging. Not that we had considered ourselves old, or even badly middle-aged, just that there was some evidence in the mirror. And there was other evidence. Zobrowski's son, for example, was in Asia fighting a war that had begun secretly, deceptively, like a disease, had gotten inside of us and was devouring us before we understood its course. We who had fought in the Second World War had gone along confidently supposing that if war broke out again we would be recalled for duty, but now the government ignored us. It was somewhat embarrassing, as if we were at fault. Young Dave Zobrowski did the fighting while all we did was drive to the office. A boy hardly old enough for long pants had been drafted.

The war offered a deep and bitter paradox. We had succeeded. Beyond all possible question we had succeeded: we had defeated the enemy, yet we had failed. Davy, too, attacked the riddle, unaware at his age that an insoluble problem existed, just as it had existed for us and as it existed for our fathers after the war they called The Great War. Maybe young Dave was more conscious of this than we had been, because we were more knowing than our fathers; still, not much had been changed by our evident sophistication. One conflict ended. Another began. Awareness was irrelevant.

So, against this, we were helpless. We could only hope that our bewilderment and dismay were misplaced. The acid we tasted while listening to newscasts and hearing the casualty figures—"body count" the Pentagon secretaries chose to call it—we could only hope that these falsified and shameful statistics would soon be forgotten. During the Second World War we would have thought it degenerate to gloat over corpses. Now this had become official practice. Apparently it was meant to reassure and persuade us that the government's cause was just.

The slow spectacle of ourselves aging, a dubious war, the decay of our presumably stable nation—these matters were much on our minds when J.D. wrote that he had decided to stop traveling. He was planning to come home. Furthermore, he intended to get married.

We were, of course, astonished. At an age when his friends might become grandfathers he had concluded that perhaps he should stop amusing himself like a college boy in the summertime.

Our wives were not surprised. They considered marriage inevitable and they were relieved that J.D. had at last come to his senses. They were merely irritated that he had waited so long. They regarded his solitary wandering as some kind of pretext for taking advantage of women all over the world. If we were in charge, they seemed to say, he'd have been suitably married years ago. The news affected them quite differently than it affected Zobrowski and Al Bunce and the others who used to play football and marbles with J.D. in those tranquil days when it was safe to walk the streets, and the air in the city was almost as sweet as it was on a farm.

Then we didn't think of our city the way we do now. Sometimes in winter or when the earth was soft after a rain we would find deer tracks across a vacant lot, and occasionally we caught a glimpse of what we thought must be a strange dog vanishing into the shrubbery—only to realize that it was a fox. Now we go about our business in a metropolis. The sizeable animals have disappeared, nobody knows quite where; but we don't see them, not even their prints. Gray squirrels once in a while, some years a good many, but little else. Robins, jays, bluebirds, cardinals, thrashers—we used to sprinkle breadcrumbs on the snowy back porch just to watch a parliament of birds arrive. Today our luncheon guests are the ubiquitous sparrows who can put up with anything.

Smoke fouls the sky and we find ourselves constantly interrupted by the telephone. Billboards, wires, garbage. We have difficulty accepting these everyday truths. How can we admit that the agreeable past, which we thought was permanent and inviolable, has slipped away like a Mississippi steamboat? We like to think that one morning we will see again those uncultivated fields thick with red clover, streams shaded by cottonwood and willow, and butterflies flickering through the sunlight as clearly as illustrations in the heroic books we read when we were eight.

We used to discuss what we would do when we grew up. We made splendid plans. First, of course, we would be rich. Next, we would marry beautiful exciting women with names like Rita, Hedy or Paulette. We would race speedboats and monoplanes, become as famous as Sir Malcolm Campbell and Colonel Roscoe Turner, or perhaps become wild animal trainers like Clyde Beatty, or hunters like Frank Buck, or great athletes like Glenn Cunningham and Don Budge. There were jungles to be explored, mountain peaks that had never been scaled, cities buried in the sand.

One after another these grandiose ideas acquired the patina of dreams. We could perceive as we grew older that we had not been realistic, so it was natural for Bunce to stop talking about an all-gold motorcycle. Art Stevenson would laugh when reminded of his vow to climb Mount Everest. But there were less ambitious adventures which still seemed reasonable. It's not so hard, for instance, to visit the ruins of Babylon; apparently you can go by jet to Baghdad to hire a taxi.

All of us intended to travel—we agreed on that—just as soon as matters could be arranged. As soon as we finished school. As soon as we could afford a long vacation. As soon as the payments were made on the house and the car. As soon as the children were old enough to be left alone. Next year, or the year after, everything would be in order.

Only J.D. had managed to leave. Surabaja. Brunei. Kuala Lumpur. The islands of Micronesia. He had sent us postcards and occasionally a letter describing where he had been or where he thought he might go next, so in a sense we knew what the world was like.

Once he had returned for a visit. Just once. He stayed not quite three days. We felt obscurely insulted, without being able to explain our resentment. He was not obligated to us. We had played together, gone through school together and exchanged the usual juvenile confidences, but no pacts were signed. We couldn't tell him to come home at Christmas, or insist that he stop fooling around and get a job. Nevertheless, we wished he would; bitterness crept into our talk because we knew he meant more to us than we meant to him. We suspected he seldom thought about us. He could guess where we would be at almost any hour; he could have drawn the outline of our lives day after day and year after year. Why should he think about us? Who thinks about a familiar pair of shoes?

Nor could we explain why we so often discussed him. Perhaps we were annoyed by his indifference toward our values. The work we did was as meaningless to him as the fact that our children were growing up. To us nothing was more significant than our jobs and our families, but to J.D. these vital proceedings had less substance than breadcrumbs in the snow. When he wrote, usually to Zobrowski, he never asked what we were doing. He considered us to have a past—a childhood involved with his own—but a transitory nebulous present and a predictable future.

During his visit we questioned him as if we might not ever talk to him again. We asked about Africa—if he had seen Mount Kilimanjaro. He said yes, he had been there, but you seldom see much of Kilimanjaro for the clouds.

Millicent asked if he had shot anything. He said no, he was not a hunter. But he had met an Englishman who did some sort of office work in Bristol and every year came down to hunt, and they had sat up all night drinking gin and talking while the clouds opened and closed and opened again to reveal different aspects of Kilimanjaro in the moonlight, and it sounded as though the lions were only a few yards away. This was as close as he had gotten to hunting the big game of Africa he told her with mock seriousness. Unless you counted the flies, which were savage brutes.

Nairobi, he said, was a delightful town, surprisingly clean, and the weather was decent. We had assumed that it was filthy and humid.

The Masai lives not far from Nairobi, he said, and you can visit their compounds if you care to. They eat cheese and drink the blood of cattle and have no use for 20th century marvels, except for ceramic beads with which they make rather attractive bracelets and necklaces. Their huts are plastered with animal dung, yet you can tell from watching a Masai warrior that once they were the lords of this territory just as you see in Spanish faces the memory of an age when Spaniards ruled Europe. But it's embarrassing to visit the Masai, he said, because they start to dance whenever a tourist shows up.

I should guess they look forward to the tips, Zobrowski remarked.

They get paid, J.D. said, but you don't tip a Masai. And nobody needs to tell you.

Barbara asked how he liked Ethiopia. He said he'd been there but hadn't stayed long because of the cholera and the mud. He mentioned this Ethiopian mud twice. We thought it strange that his principal memory of such an exotic country should be something as prosaic as mud.

Nor did we understand why he chose to cross and recross a world of dung-smeared huts, lepers, starvation and cholera. No doubt he had seen rare and wonderful sights, he must have met a good many unusual people, and he had tasted fruits we weren't apt to taste. Granted the entertainment value, what else is there? His pursuit of ephemeral moments through peeling back streets struck us as aimless. He is Don Quixote, Zobrowski observed later, without a lance, an opponent or an ideal.

Perhaps J.D. knew what he wanted, perhaps not. We wondered if the reason for his travels could be negative—ridiculing the purpose and substance of our lives. In any event, we had assumed that he would continue trudging from continent to continent as deluded as Quixote until death overtook him in a squalid cul de sac. We were wrong.

He was planning to settle down. Evidently he had decided to emulate us. When we recognized this we felt a bit more tolerant. After all, what sweeter compliment is there? Then, too, it should be interesting to learn what the Black Forest was like. Dubrovnik. Kabul. Goa. The South Seas. At our leisure we would be able to pick the richest pockets of his experience.

Leroy Hewitt was curious about Moslem Africa and meant to ask if there were minarets and cool gardens, and if it was indeed true that the great square at Marrakesh is filled with storytellers, dancers, acrobats and sorcerers just as it was hundreds of years ago. Once J.D. had traveled from Marrakesh to the walled city of Taroudent, rimmed by dark gold battlements, and he had gone over the Atlas mountains to Tiznit and to Goulimine to the lost Islamic world of women wearing long blue veils and of bearded warriors armed with jeweled daggers.

From there we had no idea where he went. Eventually, from Cairo, had come a torn postcard—a cheap colored photo of a Nile steamer. The penciled message told us that he had spent a week aboard this boat and the afternoon was hot and he was drinking lemonade. How far up the Nile he had traveled we didn't know, or whether he had come down from Uganda.

Next he went to some Greek island, from there to Crete, and later, as closely as we could reconstruct his path, to Cyprus. He wrote that the grapes on Cyprus were enormous and sweet and hard, like small apples, and he had bought an emerald which turned out to be fraudulent, and was recuperating from a blood infection which he'd picked up on the Turkish coast. Months passed before we heard any more. He wrote next from Damascus. The following summer he was in Iraq, thinking he might move along to Shiraz, wondering if he could join a camel train across the plateau. He wanted to visit Karachi. What little we knew of these places we had learned from melodramatic movies and the *National Geographic.*

But what brought J.D. unexpectedly into focus was the Indo-China war. We saw him the way you suddenly see crystals in a flask of treated water. Dave Zobrowski was killed.

When we heard that Davy was dead, that his life had been committed to the future of our nation, we perceived for the first time how J.D. had never quite met the obligations of citizenship. During the Second World War he had been deferred because his father was paralyzed by a stroke and his mother had always been in poor health, so he stayed home and worked in the basement of Wolferman's grocery. Nobody blamed him. Not one of us who went into the service blamed him, nor did any of us want to trade places with him. But that was a long time ago and one tends to forget reasons while remembering facts. The fact that now came to mind most readily concerning J.D. and the war was just that he had been deferred. We resented it. We resented it no more than mildly when we recalled the circumstances; nevertheless we had been drafted and he hadn't. We also knew that we had accomplished very little, if anything, while we were in uniform. We were bored and sometimes terrified, we shot at phantoms and made absurd promises to God. That was about the extent of our contribution toward a better world. It wasn't much, still there was the knowledge that we had walked across the sacrificial block.

After the war we began voting, obeying signs, watering the grass in summer, sowing ashes and rock salt in winter, listening to the six o'clock news and complaining about monthly bills. J.D. had not done this either. As soon as his sister graduated from secretarial school and got a job he packed two suitcases and left. He had a right to his own life; nobody denied that. Nobody expected him to give up everything for his parents' comfort. But he had left with such finality.

Problems sprang up around us like weeds, not just family difficulties but national and international dilemmas that seemed to need our attention, while J.D. loitered on one nutmeg-scented island after another. Did it matter to him, for instance, that America was changing with the malevolent speed of a slap in the face? Did it make any difference to him that American politicians now ride around smiling and waving from bullet-proof limousines? We wondered if he had an opinion about drugs, ghettos, riots, extremists and the rest of it. We suspected that these threatening things which were so immediate to us meant less to him than the flavor of a Toulouse strawberry. And now young Dave was among the thousands who had been killed in an effort to spread democracy—one more fact that meant nothing to J.D. He was out to lunch forever, as Bruce remarked.

While we waited for him to return we argued uncertainly over whether or not it was a man's privilege to live as he pleased. Wasn't J.D. obligated to share with us the responsibility of being human? We knew our responsibilities, which were clear and correct, and hadn't disclaimed them. Maybe our accomplishments were small, but we took pride in them. We might have no effect on these staggering days, no more than we had affected the course of the war, but at least we participated.

We waited through days charged with electric events which simultaneously shocked and inured us, shocking us until we could feel very few shocks, until even such prodigious achievements as flights to the moon appeared commonplace. At the same time our lives continued turning as slowly and methodically as a water wheel: taxes, business appointments, bills, promotions, now and then a domestic squabble. This was why we so often found ourselves talking about J.D.—the only one whose days dropped from a less tedious calendar. He had gone to sleep beside the Taj Mahal while we occupied ourselves with school bonds, mortgages, elections, auto repairs, stock dividends, cocktail parties, graduations and vacations and backyard barbecues.

Because we had recognized adolescent fantasies for what they are, and had put them away in the attic like childhood toys, we felt he should have done the same. What was he expecting? Did he hope somehow to seize the rim of life and force it to a stop? Implausibly, romantically, he had persisted—on his shoulders a rucksack stuffed with dreams.

He drifted along the Mediterranean littoral like a current, pausing a month or so in Yugoslavia or Greece, frequently spending Easter on the Costa del Sol; and it was after one of these sojourns in Spain that he came back to see us. His plans then concerned the Orient—abandoned temples in a Cambodian rain forest, Singapore, Macao, Burma, Sikkim, Bhutan. He talked enthusiastically, youthfully, as though you could wander about these palaces as easily as you locate them on a map.

He had met somebody just back from the foothills of the Himalayas who told him that at Gangtok you see colors more luminous than any you could imagine—more brilliant, more hallucinatory than the wings of tropical butterflies. The idea fascinated him. We asked what sense it made, quite apart from the danger and the trouble, to go such a long distance for a moment of surprise. He wasn't sure. He agreed that perhaps it didn't make sense.

He'd heard about prayer flags posted on bamboo sticks, the waterways of Kashmir, painted houseboats, mango trees on the road to Dharamasala. He thought he'd like to see these things. and there was a building carved from a cliff near Aurangabad. And there was a fortified city called Jaisalmer in the Rajasthan desert.

Then he was gone. Like a moth that flattens itself against a window and mysteriously vanishes, he was gone.

A friend of Art Stevenson's, a petroleum engineer who was sent to the Orient on business, told Art that he happened to see J.D. sitting under a tree on the outskirts of Djakarta. He did not appear to be doing anything, the engineer said; and as he, the engineer, was pressed for time he didn't stop to say hello. But there could be no doubt, he told Art, that it was indeed J.D. dressed in faded khaki and sandals, doing absolutely nothing there in the baking noonday heat of Indonesia. He is mad, Zobrowski commented when we heard the story.

This, of course, was an overstatement. Yet by the usual standards his itinerant and shapeless life was, at the very least, eccentric; and the word 'madness' does become appropriate if one sits long enough beneath a tree.

However, some lunacy afflicts our own temperate and conservative neighborhood. We meet it on the front page every morning—a catalogue of outrageous crimes and totally preposterous incidents as incomprehensible as they are unremitting. What can be done? We look at each other and shrug and wag our heads as though to say well, suppose we just wait and maybe things will get back to normal. At the same time we know this isn't likely. So it could be argued that Zobrowski's judgment was a trifle narrow.

Anyway, regardless of who was made, we waited impatiently for J.D. When he arrived we would do what we could to help him get settled, not without a trace of malicious satisfaction. But more important, we looked forward to examining him. We needed to know what uncommon kernel had made him different. This, ultimately, was why we had not been able to forget him.

Our wives looked forward to his return for another reason: if he was planning to get married they wanted to have a voice in the matter. They thought it would be foolish to leave the choice of a wife entirely up to him. They were quite in league about this. They had a few suitable divorcees picked out, and there were several younger women who might be acceptable.

We knew J.D. had spent one summer traveling around Ireland with a red-haired movie actress, and we had heard indirectly about an affair with a Greek girl who sang in nightclubs along the Riviera. How many others there had been was a subject for speculation. It seemed to us that he amused himself with women, as though the relationship between a man and a woman need be no more permanent than sea foam. Leroy Hewitt suggested, perhaps to irritate the ladies, that their intricate plans might be a waste of time because J.D. probably would show up with a Turkish belly dancer. But the ladies, like Queen Victoria, were not amused.

We tried to remember which girls interested him when we were in school. All of us agreed that he had been inconstant. It was one girl, then another. And as we thought back to those days it occurred to us that he had always been looking for somebody unusual—some girl with a reputation for brilliance, individuality or beauty. The most beautiful girl in school was Helen Louise Sawyer. J.D. would take her on long drives through the country or to see travel films, instead of to a dance where she herself could be seen. This may have been the reason they broke up. Or it might have been because she was conceited and therefore rather tiresome—a fact which took J.D. some time to admit.

For a while he dated the daughter of a Congregational minister who, according to the story, had been arrested for prostitution. Almost certainly there was no truth in it, but this rumor isolated her and made her a target. J.D. was the only one with enough nerve to date her publicly, and the only one who never boasted about what they had done.

His other girls, too, were somehow distinctive. Gwyneth, who got a dangerous reputation for burning her dates with a lighted cigarette at intimate moments. A cross-eyed girl named Grace who later became a successful fashion designer in New York. Mitzi McGill, whose father patented a vending machine that supposedly earned him a million dollars. The Lundquist twins, Norma and Laura. To nobody's surprise J.D. went out with both of them.

Rarities excited him. The enchanted glade. The sleeping princess. Avalon. We, too, had hoped for and in daydreams anticipated such things, but time taught us better. He was the only one who never gave up. As a result he was a middle-aged man without a trade, without money or security of any sort, learning in the August of life that he shouldn't have despised what might be called average happiness—3% down the years, so to speak. It wasn't exhilarating, not even adventurous, but it was sufficient.

Now, at last, J.D. was ready to compromise.

I've expected this, Zobrowski said. He's our age. He's beginning to get tired.

He's lonely, said Millicent. He wants a home.

Are we echoing each other? Zobrowski asked

On Thanksgiving Day he telephoned from Barcelona. He knew we would all be at Zobrowski's; we gathered there every Thanksgiving, just as it was customary to drop by the Hewitts' for eggnog on Christmas Eve, and to spend New Year's Day at the Stevensons'.

It was midnight in Barcelona when he called. Having gorged ourselves to the point of dyspepsia we were watching football on television, perfectly aware that we were defaulting on a classic autumn afternoon. Somebody in the next block was burning leaves, the air was crisp and through the picture window we could see a maple loaded like a treasure galleon with red gold. But we had prepared for the feast by drinking too much and by accompanying this with too many tidbits before sitting down to the principal business—split-pea soup, a green salad with plenty of Roquefort, dry heavy salty slices of sugar-cured Jackson County ham as well as turkey with sage and chestnut and onion dressing, mushroom and giblet gravy, wild rice, sweet potatoes, creamed asparagus, corn on the cob, hot biscuits with fresh country butter and honey that would hardly flow from the spoon. For dessert there were dense flat triangles of black mince pie topped with rum sauce. Nobody had strength enough to step outside.

As somnolent as glutted snakes we sprawled in Zobrowski's front room smoking cigars, sipping brandy and nibbling peppermints and mixed nuts while the women cleared the table. Embers snapped in the fireplace as group after group of helmeted young Trojans rushed across the miniature gridiron. It was toward such completed days that we had worked. For the moment we'd forgotten J.D.

His call startled us, though we were not surprised that he was in Spain again. He had gone back there repeatedly, as though what he was seeking he'd almost found in Spain. Possibly he knew the coast between Ayamonte and Port-Bou better than we knew the shore of Lake Lotawana. He had been to Gijón and Santander and famous cities like Seville. He'd followed baroque holy processions and wandered through orange groves in Murcia. During his visit he spoke fervently of this compelling, strict, anachronistic land—of the apple wine *manzanilla*, fringed silk shawls, bloody saints, serrated mountains, waterless valleys, burnt stony plateaus, thistles as tall as trees lining the road to Jaén.

We remembered his description of goat bells tinkling among rocky Andalusian hills and we could all but feel the sea breeze rise from Gibraltar. One afternoon he ate lunch in a secluded courtyard beside a fountain—bread, a ball of cheese and some sausage the color of an old boot. He insisted he'd never eaten better.

He imitated the hoarse voices of singing gypsies—a strident unforgotten East beneath their anguished music—and told us about a cataract of lavender blossoms pouring across the ruined palace of the Moorish kings at Málaga. As young as another Byron he had brought back these foreign things.

There's a town called Ronda which is built along a precipice, and he told us that when he looked over the edge he could feel his face growing damp. He was puzzled because the sky was blue. Then he realized that spray was blowing up the cliff from the river. It was so quiet, he said, that all he heard was wind through the barranca and he was gazing down at two soaring hawks.

He thought Granada might be Spain's most attractive city. He had told us it was the last Arab bastion on the peninsula and it fell because of rivalry between the Abencerrages and Zegris families—information anybody could pick up in a library. But for him this was more than a musty fact. He said that if you look through a certain grate beneath the floor of the cathedral you can actually see the crude iron coffins containing the bodies of Ferdinand and Isabella; or if you go up a certain street near the Alhambra you pass a shop where an old man with one eye sits at a bench day after day meticulously fitting together decorative little boxes of inlaid wood. And he liked to loiter in the Plaza España, particularly while the sun was going down, when swallows scour the twilight for insects.

He had ridden the night train to San Sebastián along with several members of the Guardia Civil in Napoleonic leather hats who put their machine guns on an empty seat and played cards, with the dignity and sobriety peculiar to Spaniards, beneath the faltering light of a single yellow bulb. Outside a station in the mountains where the train paused to build up compression there was a gas lamp burning with vertical assurance, as though a new age had not begun. Wine bottles rolled in unison across the warped floor of the frayed Edwardian couch when the train creaked around a curve late at night, and the soldiers ignored a young Spaniard who began to speak of liberty. Liberty would come to Spain the young man believed—even though Franco's secret police were as common as rats in a sewer.

From everything J.D. said about Spain we thought it must be like one of those small dark green olives, solid as leather, with a lasting taste.

He returned to Barcelona more than to any other city, although it was industrial and enormous. He liked the Gothic *barrio*, the old quarter. He enjoyed eating outside a restaurant called *La Magdalena* which was located in an alley just off the Ramblas. Whenever a taxi drove through the alley the diners had to stand up and push their chairs against the wall so it could squeeze past. Whores patrolled the *barrio*, two by two, carrying glossy handbags. Children who should have been at home asleep went from cafe to cafe peddling cigarettes. Lean old men wearing flat-brimmed black hats and women in polka dot dresses snapped their fingers and clapped and danced furiously with glittering eyes on cobblestones that were worn smooth when the Armada sailed toward England.

Flowers, apple wine, moonlight on distant plazas, supper in some ancient alley, Arabs, implications, relics—that was how he had lived while we went to work.

Now he was calling to us from a boarding house in the cheap section of Barcelona. He was alone, presumably, in the middle of the night while we were as surfeited, prosperous and unrepentant as could be. It was painful to compare his situation with ours.

So, Zobrowski said to him on the telephone, you're there again.

J.D. said yes, he was in the same boarding house—*pensión*, he called it—just off Via Layetana. He usually stayed at this place when he was in Barcelona because it had a wonderful view. You could understand Picasso's cubism, he said with a laugh, if you looked across these rooftops.

I'm afraid my schedule won't permit it, Zobrowski remarked. What a pity, said J.D.

Zobrowski took a fresh grip on the telephone. It would appear, he said, that Spain continues to stimulate your imagination.

Actually no, J.D. answered. That's why I'm coming back.

Then he explained. He wasn't altogether clear, but it had to do with progress. With jet planes and credit cards and the proliferation of luxury hotels and high rise apartments you could hardly tell whether you were in Barcelona or Chicago. Only the street signs were different. It wasn't just Barcelona, it was everyplace. Even the villages had begun to change. They were putting television sets in bars where you used to hear flamenco. You could buy *Newsweek* almost as soon as it was published. The girls had started wearing blue jeans. There was a Playboy club in Torremolinos.

Years ago he had mentioned a marble statue of a woman in one of the Barcelona plazas and he had said to us, with an excess of romantic enthusiasm, that she would always be there waiting for him.

Zobrowski asked about this statue. J.D. replied that she was growing a bit sooty because of the diesel trucks and cabs and motorbikes.

He said he had recently been up north. The mountain beyond Torrelavega was completely obscured by factory smoke and there was some sort of yellowish chemical or plastic scum emptying into the river with a few half-dead fish floating through it.

The first time he was in Spain he had walked from Santillana del Mar to Altamira to have a look at the prehistoric cave paintings. There wasn't a tourist in sight. He had passed farmers with long-handled scythes, larks were singing, the sky was like turquoise, and he waded through fields of flowers that reached to his knees. Now, he said, he was afraid to go back. He might get run over by a John Deere tractor, or find a motel across the road from the caves.

That bullfighting poster you had, Zobrowski said, the one with Manolete's name on it. Reproductions of that poster are for sale at a number of department stores.

You're flogging me, J.D. said after a pause.

I suppose I am, Zobrowski said.

However, I do get the point, J.D. said. Another decade and the world's going to be as homogenized as a bottle of milk.

Millicent is here, Zobrowski said. She would like a word with you.

J.D.! Millie exclaimed. How marvelous to hear you're coming home! You remember Kate Van Dusen, of course. Ray Van Dusen's sister?—tall and slim with absolutely gorgeous eyes.

J.D. admitted that he did.

She married Barnett Thomas of Thomas Bakery Products, but things just didn't work out and they've separated.

There was no response. Millie seemed about to offer a trans-Atlantic summary of the marriage. Separated was a euphemism, to say the least. Kate and Barnett were in the midst of a reckless fight over property and the custody of their children.

She's asked about you, Millie went on. She heard you might be coming back.

I'm engaged, J.D. said.

We didn't realize that, said Millie without revealing the horror that flooded the assembled women. We simply understood that you were considering marriage. Who is she?

Margaret Hobbs, he said.

Marbaret Hobbs? Millie sounded uncertain. Is she British?

You know her, J.D. answered. She's been teaching kindergarten in Philadelphia.

Oh! Oh, my God! Millie said.

We had gone to grammar school with Margaret Hobbs. She was a pale dumpy child with a screeching voice. Otherwise she was totally undistinguished. Her parents had moved to Philadelphia while we were in the sixth grade and none of us had heard of her since. Her name probably hadn't been mentioned for twenty-five years.

We met by accident last summer, J.D. said. Margaret and some other schoolteachers were on a tour and we've been corresponding since then. I guess I've always had a special feeling for her and it turns out she's always felt that way about me. She told me she used to wonder what I was doing and if we'd ever meet again. It's as though in a mysterious way we'd been communicating all these years.

How interesting, Millie said.

It really is, isn't it! J.D. said. Anyhow, I'm anxious for all of you to make her acquaintance again. She's amazingly well informed and she remembers everybody.

I think it's just wonderful, Millie said. We're so pleased. I've always wished I could have known Margaret better. Now here's Leroy.

Is that you, young fellow? Leroy asked.

Hello, said J.D. You don't sound much different.

Leroy chuckled and asked if he'd been keeping himself busy. J.D. said he supposed so.

Great talking to you, Leroy said. We'll have a million yarns to swap when you get home. Hang on, here's Aileen.

We look forward to hearing of your adventures, Aileen said. When do you arrive?

J.D. didn't know exactly. He was going to catch a freighter from Lisbon.

Aileen mentioned that last month's *Geographic* had an article on the white peacocks.

After a moment J.D. replied that the connection must be bad because it sounded as if she was talking about peacocks.

Have you been to Estoril? Aileen almost shouted.

Estoril? Yes, he'd been to Estoril. The casino was jammed with tourists. Germans and Americans, mostly. He liked southern Portugal better—the Algarve. Faro, down by the cape.

Faro, Aileen repeated, memorizing the name. Then she asked if he would stop in Philadelphia before coming home.

J.D. was vague. The freighter's first two ports of call were Venezuela and Curaçao. Next it went to Panama. He thought he might hop a bus from Panama, or maybe there would be a boat of some sort heading for British Honduras or Yucatán or maybe New Orleans.

Aileen began to look bewildered. She was sure that he and Margaret would be able to coordinate their plans and it had been a pleasure chatting. She gave the phone to Art Stevenson.

Art said a lot of water had flowed under the bridge and J.D. might not recognize him because he had put on a pound or two. J.D. answered that he himself had been losing some hair. Art proposed that they try to work out a deal.

Neither of them knew what to say next. Art gave the phone to Barbara.

Barbara asked if he and Margaret would be interested in joining the country club. If so, she and Al would be delighted to sponsor them.

Not at first, J.D. said. Maybe later. Let me talk to Dave again.

He was thinking of buying a car in Europe because he had heard he could save money that way, and he wanted Zobrowski's advice. He had never owned a car.

Zobrowski suggested that he wait until he got back. Bunce's brother-in-law was a Chevrolet dealer and should be able to arrange a price not far above wholesale. Zobrowski also pointed out that servicing foreign cars in the United States can be a problem. Then, too, you're better off buying from somebody you know.

J.D. inquired about jobs.

We had never learned how he supported himself abroad. As far as we could determine he lived from day to day. There have always been individuals who manage to do this, who discover how to operate the levers that enable them to survive while really doing nothing. It's a peculiar talent and it exasperates people who live conventionally.

A job could be found for him, that wasn't the issue. What disturbed us was that he had no bona fide skills. Zobrowski was a respected surgeon. Bunce was vice-president of the Community National Bank and a member of the Board of Education. Art Stevenson was director and part-owner of an advertising agency. Leroy Hewitt was a successful contractor, and so on. One or another of J.D.'s friends could find him a place, but there would be no way to place him on equal terms. He could speak French, Italian, Spanish, German and Portuguese well enough to make himself understood, besides a few necessary phrases of Arabic and Swedish and Hindi and several others, but language schools want instructors who are fluent. He knew about inexpensive restaurants and hotels throughout Europe, and the best way to get from Izmir to Aleppo. No doubt he knew about changing money in Port Said. Now he would be forced to work as a stock clerk or a Western Union messenger, or perhaps as some sort of trainee competing with another generation. The idea made us uncomfortable.

Margaret would soon find a job. Excluding the fact that Bunce was on the Board of Education, she was evidently an experienced teacher with the proper credentials. She could do private tutoring until there was a full-time position. But J.D. in his coat of many colors couldn't do anything professionally.

I have a suggestion, Zobrowski said to him on the telephone. This will sound insulting, but you've got to face facts. Your capacities, such as they are, don't happen to be widely appreciated.

I'm insulted, J.D. said.

Zobrowski cleared his throat before continuing: Fortunately, our postmaster is related by marriage to one of the cardiologists on the staff of Park Lane Hospital. I have never met this man—the postmaster, that is—but, if you like, I will speak to the cardiologist and explain your situation. I cannot, naturally, guarantee a thing. However, it's my feeling that this fellow might be able to take you on at the post office. It wouldn't be much, mind you.

Well, said J.D. from a great distance, please have a talk with that cardiologist. I'm just about broke.

I'm sorry, Zobrowski said, although not surprised. You enjoyed yourself for a long time while the rest of us went to an office day after day, whether we liked it or not. I won't belabor this point, but I'm sure you recall the fable of the grasshopper and the ant.

J.D. had never cared for lectures, and in the face of this we thought he might hang up. But we all heard him say yes, he remembered the fable.

If I sound harsh, forgive me, Zobrowski said. It's simply that you have lived as the rest of us dreamt of living, which is not easy for us to accept.

J.D. didn't answer.

Now, as we wait to greet him, we feel curiously disappointed. The end of his journey suggests that we were right, therefore he must have been wrong, and it follows that we should feel gratified. The responsibilities we assumed were valid, the problems with which we occupy ourselves are not insignificant and the values we nourish will flower one day—if not tomorrow. His return implies this judgment. So the regret we feel, but try to hide, seems doubly strange. Perhaps without realizing it we trusted him to keep our youth.

Reflections

Personal Exploration

1. Copy a key passage from Connell's story in your notebook and explore how you see it illuminating the work as a whole.
2. Consider how the parable of the grasshopper and the ant might relate to Connell's story. Does anything justify the grasshopper's behavior? Would his life be better if he had imitated the ant's way of living? And what about the ant? What does the parable suggest about choices we make for survival? Was Thoreau right when he wrote that most of us "live meanly as ants"?
3. Focus your attention on the Thanksgiving scene (p. 594). Why does Connell give such a precise description of the holiday? Consider what is revealed about the values and the choices these people have made that make all the difference between their lives and J.D.'s. Why should they feel resentment toward J.D.? Why, with so much fullness in their lives, do they find it hard to accept J.D.'s behavior?

Public Exploration

Is it our privilege to live as we please or is that privilege superseded by a responsibility to family, friends, and country? What would your mother or father say? What about your pastor or priest? What about your friends? Can you truthfully make a decision for yourself in this matter? Can you make a decision that might go against the grain?

Personal Reflection

1. What do you make of this statement: "We ourselves had no illusions."
2. J.D.'s friends made a choice about their own survival as J.D. did about his. Reflect on the differences between their choices and the consequence of those choices. How can a judgment be made as to their "rightness" or "wrongness"? How can any of us determine at the end of our lives whether our choice has been the right one?

3. Is scientist Lewis Thomas only being a Romantic when he writes the following:

> We are not like the social insects. They have only the one way of doing things, and they will do it forever, coded for that way. We are coded differently, not just for binary chores, *go* or *no-go*. We can go four ways at once, depending on how the air feels: *go, no go*, but also *maybe*, plus *what the hell let's give it a try*. We are in for one surprise after another if we keep at it and keep alive. We can build structures for human society never seen before, music never heard before.

The Transformation of Silence into Language and Action

AUDRE LORDE

I have come to believe over and over again that what is most important to me must be spoken, made verbal and shared, even at the risk of having it bruised or misunderstood. That the speaking profits me, beyond any other effect. I am standing here as a Black lesbian poet, and the meaning of all that waits upon the fact that I am still alive, and might not have been. Less than two months ago I was told by two doctors, one female and one male, that I would have to have breast surgery, and that there was a 60 to 80 percent chance that the tumor was malignant. Between that telling and the actual surgery, there was a three-week period of the agony of an involuntary reorganization of my entire life. The surgery was completed, and the growth was benign.

But within those three weeks, I was forced to look upon myself and my living with a harsh and urgent clarity that has left me still shaken but much stronger. This is a situation faced by many women, by some of you here today. Some of what I experienced during that time has helped elucidate for me much of what I feel concerning the transformation of silence into language and action.

In becoming forcibly and essentially aware of my mortality, and of what I wished and wanted for my life, however short it might be, priorities and omissions became strongly etched in a merciless light, and what I most regretted were my silences. Of what had I *ever* been afraid? To question or to speak as I believed could have meant pain, or death. But we all hurt in so many different ways, all the time, and pain will either change or end. Death, on the other hand, is the final silence. And that might be coming quickly, now, without regard for whether I had ever spoken what needed to be said, or had only betrayed myself into small silences, while I planned someday to speak, or waited for someone else's words. And I began to recognize a source of power within myself that comes from the knowledge that while it is most desirable not to be afraid, learning to put fear into a perspective gave me great strength.

I was going to die, if not sooner then later, whether or not I had ever spoken myself. My silences had not protected me. Your silence will not protect you. But for every real word spoken, for every attempt I had ever made to speak those truths for which I am still seeking, I had made contact with other women while we examined the words to fit a world in which we all believed, bridging our differences. And it was the concern and caring of all those women which gave me strength and enabled me to scrutinize the essentials of my living.

The women who sustained me through that period were Black and white, old and young, lesbian, bisexual, and heterosexual, and we all shared a war against the tyrannies of silence. They all gave me a strength and concern without which I could not have survived intact. Within those weeks of acute fear came the knowledge—within the war we are all waging with the forces of death, subtle and otherwise, conscious or not—I am not only a casualty, I am also a warrior.

What are the words you do not yet have? What do you need to say? What are the tyrannies you swallow day by day and attempt to make your own, until you will sicken and die of them, still in silence? Perhaps for some of you here today, I am the face of one of your fears. Because I am woman, because I am Black, because I am lesbian, because I am myself—a Black woman warrior poet doing my work—come to ask you, are you doing yours?

And of course I am afraid, because the transformation of silence into language and action is an act of self-revelation, and that always seems fraught with danger. But my daughter, when I told her of our topic and my difficulty with it, said, "Tell them about how you're never really a whole person if you remain silent, because there's always that one little piece inside you that wants to be spoken out, and if you keep ignoring it, it gets madder and madder and hotter and hotter, and if you don't speak it out one day it will just up and punch you in the mouth from the inside."

In the cause of silence, each of us draws the face of her own fear—fear of contempt, of censure, or some judgment, or recognition, of challenge, of annihilation. But most of all, I think, we fear the visibility without which we cannot truly live. Within this country where racial difference creates a constant, if unspoken, distortion of vision, Black women have on one hand always been highly visible, and so, on the other hand, have been rendered invisible through the depersonalization of racism. Even within the women's movement, we have had to fight, and still do, for that very visibility which also renders us most vulnerable, our Blackness. For to survive in the mouth of this dragon we call america, we have had to learn this first and most vital lesson—that we were never meant to survive. Not as human beings. And neither were most of you here today, Black or not. And that visibility which makes us most vulnerable is that which also is the source of our greatest strength. Because the machine will try to grind you into dust anyway, whether or not we speak. We can sit in our corners mute forever while our sisters and our selves are wasted, while our children are distorted and destroyed, while our earth is poisoned; we can sit in our safe corners mute as bottles, and we will still be no less afraid.

In my house this year we are celebrating the feast of Kwanza, the African-american festival of harvest which begins the day after Christmas and lasts for seven days. There are seven principles of Kwanza, one for each day. The first principle is Umoja, which means unity, the decision to strive for and maintain unity in self and community. The principle for yesterday, the second day, was Kujichagulia—self-determination—the decision to define ourselves, name ourselves, and speak for ourselves, instead of being defined and spoken for by others. Today is the third day of Kwanza, and the principle for today is Ujima—collective work and responsibility—the decision to build and maintain ourselves and our communities together and to recognize and solve our problems together.

Each of us is here now because in one way or another we share a commitment to language and to the power of language, and to the reclaiming of that language which has been made to work against us. In the transformation of silence into language and action, it is vitally necessary for each one of us to establish or examine her function in that transformation and to recognize her role as vital within that transformation.

For those of us who write, it is necessary to scrutinize not only the truth of what we speak, but the truth of that language by which we speak it. For others, it is to share and spread also those words that are meaningful to us. But primarily for us all, it is necessary to teach by living and speaking those truths which we believe and know beyond understanding. Because in this way alone we can survive, by taking part in a process of life that is creative and continuing, that is growth.

And it is never without fear—of visibility, of the harsh light of scrutiny and perhaps judgment, of pain, of death. But we have lived through all of those already, in silence, except death. And I remind myself all the time now that if I were to have been born mute, or had maintained an oath of silence my whole life long for safety, I would still have suffered, and I would still die. It is very good for establishing perspective.

And where the words of women are crying to be heard, we must each of us recognize our responsibility to seek those words out, to read them and share them and examine them in their pertinence to our lives. That we not hide behind the mockeries of separations that have been imposed upon us and which so often we accept as our own. For instance, "I can't possibly teach Black women's writing—their experience is so different from mine." Yet how many years have you spent teaching Plato and Shakespeare and Proust? Or another, "She's a white woman and what could she possibly have to say to me?" Or, "She's a lesbian, what would my husband say, or my chairman?" Or again, "This woman writes of her sons and I have no children." And all the other endless ways in which we rob ourselves of ourselves and each other.

We can learn to work and speak when we are afraid in the same way we have learned to work and speak when we are tired. For we have been socialized to respect fear more than our own needs for language and definition, and while we wait in silence for that final luxury of fearlessness, the weight of that silence will choke us.

The fact that we are here and that I speak these words is an attempt to break that silence and bridge some of those differences between us, for it is not difference which immobilizes us, but silence. And there are so many silences to be broken.

Reflections

Private Exploration

1. Select and copy out any passage from Lorde's essay you find particularly illuminating, infuriating, or confusing. Explore your reaction in your reading notebook. Confront your reaction. What do you think and feel? And why?
2. Write about a time in your life when an event or set of circumstances led you to look on yourself and your life with such clarity that it motivated you to act. Tell the story of what happened to you. Consider how you responded and the results of those actions. In what way, if any, did the choices and actions you undertook reflect some kind of value?
3. Has there ever been a time in your life when you were silent but wish you'd spoken out? What motivated you to keep silent? What truth were you repressing? Reflect on what happened or did not happen as a result. In looking back now, would you have made a different choice?

Public Exploration

As a group select the most controversial campus, local, or national issue of the moment. How many of you have spoken out? How many have remained silent? Consider any "truths" that are being repressed. Would speaking out contribute to a solution? Would it only inflame the issue? Would your own personal survival be enhanced or placed in jeopardy by choosing to speak? Should it matter? Do you have to wait for "certain death" before you have courage? Before you can choose to speak the truth as you really see it?

Private Reflection

We admire Audre Lorde's honesty, her willingness to admit she is afraid because "the transformation of silence is an act of self-revelation" that always seems "fraught with danger." If you had an opportunity to explore Lorde's essay with your class or group, reflect on the thoughts and feelings you experienced as you participated.

What did you reveal about yourself? What position did you take? What were your contributions? Were you honest? Did working in the group or with your class intimidate you from speaking out? Did you feel encouraged to speak because others were open and committed to some kind of action? Consider the experience in terms of what it revealed about yourself.

If you did not explore Lorde's essay with others, apply the same questions to any issue in your neighborhood or community which challenged you: an abortion protest, a racist incident, a public march through the streets by gays and lesbians, the destruction of a historic building, the raising of taxes, or whatever. Did you speak out? Did you ignore it? Consider your response to the experience in terms of what it revealed about yourself.

CONNECTIONS

Although your best writing will usually emerge from insights already under development in your reading notebook, here are some additional possibilities for exploring relationships between and among various works of literature.

1. In an essay, "On Self-Respect," Joan Didion makes the following claim:

   > . . . character—the willingness to accept responsibility for one's own life—is the source from which self-respect springs.

   With this in mind, reflect on several of the readings in this chapter, using details from them for an essay in which you explore the value of individual responsibility and its relationship to survival.
2. "Survival" is a key word that appears in several writings about native Americans throughout this text. Read, or reread, "Blue Winds Dancing" (p. 184), "Piki" (p. 555), and "Landscape, History and the Pueblo Imagination" (p. 276). Write an essay in which you compare and contrast the various perspectives of survival that surface in these readings. (Be sure to introduce and document your sources. See the Appendix if you need help.) As you conclude your paper, reflect on the value of these readings in terms of resources for your own survival.
3. Read *The Diary of Anne Frank* and evaluate Bruno Bettelheim's criticism of the decisions Anne's father took to preserve his family. Consider whether the alternatives Bettelheim proposes were in fact choices that might have bettered the family's chances for survival, and whether "survival" was the sole fact Anne's father had in mind.
4. A number of authors collected here have written about the value of speaking out and the dangers confronted. Write an essay focusing on the value of transforming silence into language and action. You might want to use ideas from any of the following: Crew's "Living as an Outsider, Even as an Outcast, in Small Town America" (p. 578), Kingston's "The Quiet Girl" (p. 470), Thoreau's "On the Duty of Civil Disobedience" (p. 496), Lorde's "The Transformation of Silence" (p. 601), and either or both Sophocles' and Jean Anouilh's version of *Antigone* (p. 688).
5. One of our objectives in writing this book has been to encourage you to become more aware of your values and the choices you make. We have touched on a few important ones: *imagination*, *love*, *perception*, and *work*. Yet each of the readings touches on still other values: *knowledge*, *creativity*, *self-respect*, *commitment*, *integrity*. Select several of the readings in this chapter which strike you as important and write an essay focusing on the link between a specific value and survival—a value that makes the difference between merely existing and living a meaningful life.
6. In "Thriving as an Outsider in Small Town America," (p. 578) Louie Crew writes, "Our survival on our own terms had depended very much on our knowing and respecting many of the rules of the system which we resist." Use Crew's statement as a starting point to explore the idea of conformity and nonconformity as it relates to individual survival. (You might also want to read Thoreau's "Civil Disobedience" (p. 496) for a contrasting position.)
7. Many of the writers included in this book, survivors in their own right, have over-

come obstacles and succeeded in spite of them: Martin Luther King, Bruno Bettelheim, Audre Lorde, William Least Heat Moon, Isak Dineson, Virginia Woolf, Flannery O'Connor, Alice Walker, Anne Morrow Lindbergh, Leslie Silko, Elie Wiesel, Tillie Olsen. Write an investigative research paper on any one of these individuals who interests you. Limit biographical information to a paragraph or so. Focus your primary attention on the obstacle the individual has struggled to overcome and how it was accomplished. Consider actions, values, attitudes, and cultural influences. (You might want to check the Appendix for suggestions about reference sources and guides to articles on each writer.)

Photograph by Andreas Feininger

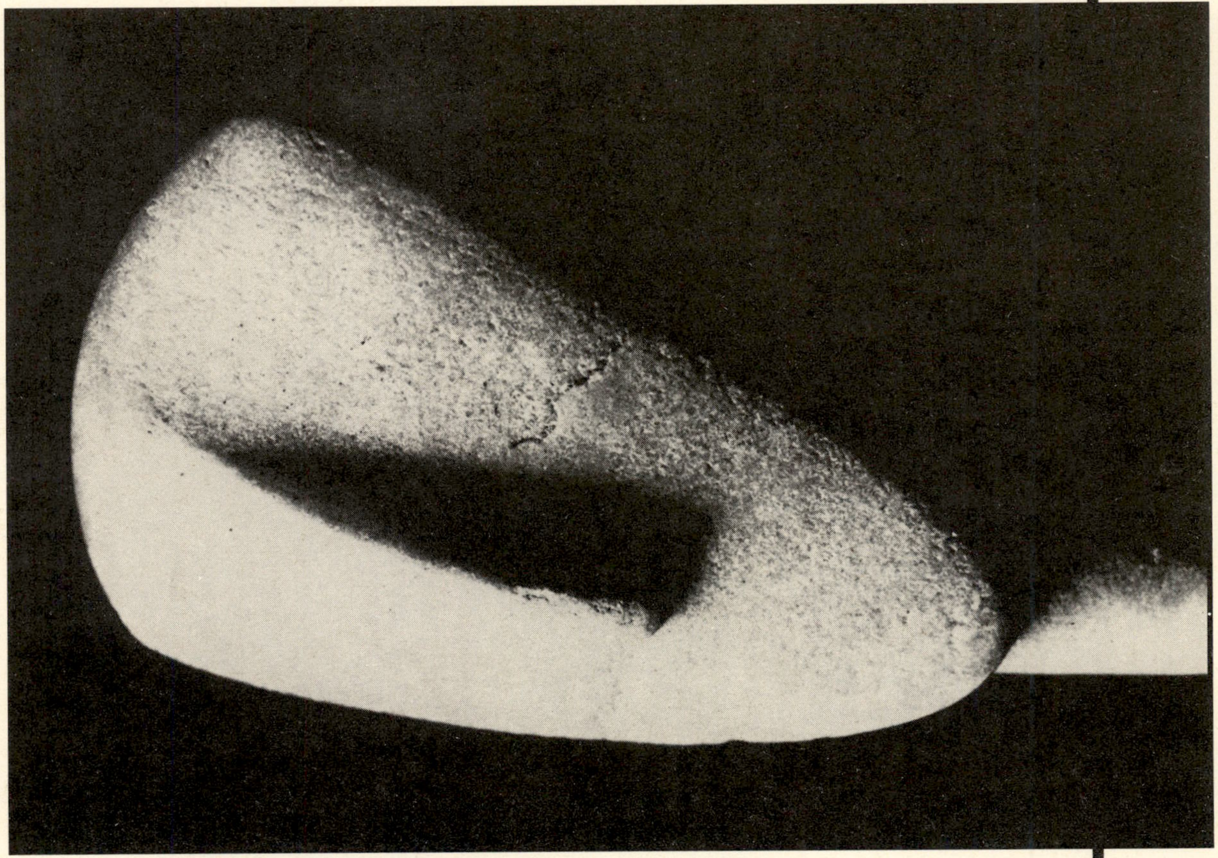

PART 3

Larger Perspectives

CHAPTER 12

ROWING TOWARD EDEN

As we decide and choose, so are our lives formed.

Uncle Russell might have devoted himself to any musical instrument—piano, cello, flute, even the harmonica—but for some reason he chose the fiddle. He's taken lessons for years. Each time we visit, he invites us into the living room for a performance. Uncle Russell sits upright in a straight back chair, Reeboks firmly planted on the carpet, the shiny fiddle tucked beneath his chin. Aunt Mildred positions herself at the old blonde spinet to accompany him. Her fingers sweep a trickle of furious chords that begin in a flourish at one end of the piano and end in a flood at the other. Then Uncle Russell closes his eyes. He lifts his bow in a high arc, gracefully lowers it to the strings, and begins his own studied rendition of "Go Tell Aunt Rhody." The notes stagger like a stiff-legged hen, each string aching to be forgotten by everyone except Uncle Russell. Contented as a kid goat ruminating in a field of clover, he is swept away in his own private reverie.

Watching him from across the room, we can hardly contain ourselves. Yet the profound pleasure Uncle Russell takes in his own playing demands reverence and respect. We watch and listen with the same attentiveness demanded by the Julliard String Quartet playing a Bach Fugue at Lincoln Center. Old Uncle Russell is transfigured by his music. It is for him, and for us, a hallowed moment.

Once again we realize how clearly our choices affect the meaning of our lives. We decide what work we will do, what work we refuse to do. We open ourselves to perceptions of the world that are different from our own, or we remain closed. We hold onto traditions and avoid change, or we question the relevance of traditions and try to adapt to new conditions. We ask questions: What do I want for myself? What do I want for the world I live in?

In this final chapter we've gathered several novellas and full-length plays. Each is concerned with complex and difficult choices that shape lives, destroy lives, delineate values. Whether reading Joyce Carol Oates' *Theft* or Jean Anouilh's contemporary version of Sophocles' *Antigone,* we encourage you to be sensitive to the problems individual characters confront, the decisions they make, and the results of those decisions. The choices are never simple or clear, yet the consequences are always profound.

Old Uncle Russell made a choice that seems, on the surface, almost trivial: he would play the fiddle instead of the harmonica. But we have a friend who has chosen to spend her life in Maine studying the reproductive cycle of sharks. To do so, she and her husband, whose work keeps him in Georgia, must live a thousand miles apart. A student we know has decided to postpone graduate school in order to teach English in Kenya. His parents fear he may lose the opportunity to enter the best schools that are open to him now. Each of these individuals has made a choice, each hoping it may prove to be the right one, each rowing toward what he or she hopes will be some distant Eden, some ideal that will give life meaning and value.

Theft

JOYCE CAROL OATES

The semester Marya became acquainted with Imogene Skillman, a thief suddenly appeared in Maynard House, where Marya was rooming in her sophomore year at Port Oriskany: striking at odd, inspired, daring hours, sometimes in the early morning when a girl was out of her room and showering in the bathroom just down the corridor, sometimes late at night when some of the girls sat in the kitchen, drinking coffee, their voices kept low so that the resident adviser would not hear. (The kitchen was supposed to close officially at midnight. Maynard House itself "closed" at midnight—there were curfews in those days, in the women's residences.) A wristwatch stolen from one room, seven dollars from another, a physics textbook from yet another . . . the thief was clearly one of the residents, one of the twenty-six girls who roomed in the house, but no one knew who it was; no one wanted to speculate too freely. Naturally there were wild rumors, cruel rumors. Marya once heard the tail end of a conversation in which her own name—"Knauer"—was mentioned. She had brushed by, her expression neutral, stony. She wanted the girls to know she had heard—she scorned even confronting them.

One Saturday morning in November Marya returned to her room after having been gone less than five minutes—she'd run downstairs to check the mail, though she rarely received letters—to see, with a sickening pang, that the door was ajar.

Her wallet had been taken from her leather bag, which she'd left carelessly in sight, tossed on top of her bed.

Her lips shaped empty, angry prayers—Oh God please *no*—but of course it was too late. She felt faint, sickened. She had just cashed a check for forty-five dollars—a week's part-time wages from the university library—and she'd had time to spend only a few dollars; she needed the money badly. "No," she said aloud, baffled, chagrined. "God damn it, *no*."

Someone stood in the opened doorway behind her saying Marya? Is something wrong? but Marya paid her no notice. She was opening the drawers of her bureau one by one; she saw, disgusted, frightened, that the thief had been there too—rooting around in Marya's woollen socks and sweaters and frayed underwear. And her fountain pen was gone. She kept it in the top drawer of the bureau, a prize of her own, a handsome black Parker pen with a thick nub . . . now it was gone.

She had to resist the impulse to yank the drawer out and throw it to the floor—to yank all the drawers out—to give herself up to rage. A flame seemed to pass through her, white-hot, scalding. It was so unfair: she needed that money, every penny of that money, she'd worked in the library in that flickering fluorescent light until she staggered with exhaustion, and even then she'd been forced to beg her supervisor to allow her a few more hours. Her scholarships were only for tuition; she needed that money. And the pen—she could never replace the pen.

It was too much: something in her chest gave way: she burst into tears like an overgrown child. She had never heard such great gulping ugly sobs. And the girl in the doorway—Phyllis, whose room was across the hall—shy, timid, sweet-faced Phyllis—actually tried to hold her in her arms and comfort her. It's so unfair, it's so unfair, Marya wept, what am I going to *do*. . . .

Eventually the wallet was returned to Marya, having been found in a trash can up the street. Nothing was missing but the money, as it turned out: nothing but the money! Marya thought savagely. The wallet itself—simulated crocodile, black, with a fancy brass snap—now looked despoiled, worn, contemptible. It had been a present from Emmett two years before and she supposed she'd had it long enough.

She examined it critically inside and out. She wondered what the thief had thought. Marya Knauer's things, Marya Knauer's "personal" possessions: were they worth stealing, really?

For weeks afterward Marya dreaded returning to her room. Though she was careful to lock the door all the time now it always seemed, when she stepped inside, that someone had been there . . . that something was out of place. Sometimes when she was halfway up the long steep hill to Stafford Hall she turned impulsively and ran back to her dormitory seven blocks away, to see if she'd remembered to lock the door. You're breaking down, aren't you, she mocked herself as she ran, her heart pumping, perspiration itching beneath her arms,—this is how it begins, isn't it: cracking up.

In the early years of the century Maynard House must have been impressive: a small Victorian mansion with high handsome windows, a wide veranda rimmed with elaborate fretwork, a cupola, a half-dozen fireplaces, walnut paneling in several of the downstairs rooms. But now it had become dim and shabby. The outside needed painting; the wallpaper in most of the rooms was discolored. Because it was so far from the main campus, and because its rooms were so cramped (Marya could stand at her full height on only one side of her room, the ceiling on the other slanted so steeply) it was one of the lowest priced residences for women. The girls who roomed there were all scholarship students like Marya, and, like Marya, uneasily preoccupied with studies, grades, part-time employment, finances of a minute and degrading nature. They were perhaps not so humorless and unattractive as Maynard House's reputation would have it, but they did share a superficial family resemblance—they might have been cousins, grimly energetic, easily distracted, a little vain (for they *were* scholarship winners after all, competition for these scholarships was intense throughout the state), badly frightened at the prospect of failure. They were susceptible to tears at odd unprovoked moments, to eating binges, to outbursts of temper; several, including Marya, were capable of keeping their doors closed for days on end and speaking to no one when they did appear.

Before the theft Marya had rather liked Maynard House; she prized her cubbyhole of a room because it was *hers*; because in fact she could lock the door for days on end. The standard university furniture didn't displease her—the same minimal bed, desk, chair, bureau, bedside table, lamp in each room—and the sloped ceiling gave the room a cavelike, warmly intimate air, especially at night when only her desk lamp was burning. Though she couldn't really afford it Marya had bought a woven rug for the floor—Aztec colors, even more fierce than those in hers and Alice's rug at home—and a new lampshade edged with a festive gold braid; she had bought a Chagall print for ninety-eight cents (marked down because it was slightly shopworn) at the University Store. The walls were decorated with unframed charcoal drawings she had done, sketches of imaginary people, a few glowering self-portraits: when she was too tense or excited to sleep after hours of studying, or after having taken an exam, she took up a stick of charcoal and did whatever it seemed to wish to do—her fingers empowered with a curious sort of energy, twitchy, sporadic, often quite surprising. From the room's walls smudged and shadowy variants of her own sober face contemplated her. Strong cheekbones, dark eyes, thick dark censorious brows. . . . She had made the portraits uglier than she supposed she really was; that provided some comfort, it might be said to have been a reverse vanity. Who is *that*? one of the girls on the floor once asked, staring at Marya's own image,—is it a man?—a woman?

Marya prized her aloneness, her monastic isolation at the top of the house, tucked away in a corner. She could stay up all night if she wished, she could skip breakfast if she wished, she could fall into bed after her morning classes and sleep a heavy drugged sleep for much of the afternoon; and no one knew or cared. It seemed extraordinary to her now that for so many years—for all of her lifetime, in fact—she had had to submit to the routine schedule of Wilma's household: going to bed when she wasn't sleepy, getting up when the others did, eating meals with them, living her life as if it were nothing more than an extension of theirs. She loved to read for pleasure once her own assignments were completed: the reading she did late at night acquired an aura, a value, a mysterious sort of enchantment, that did not usually belong to daylight. It was illicit, precious beyond estimation. It seemed to her at such times that she was capable of slipping out of her own consciousness and into that of the writer's . . . into the very rhythms of another's prose. Bodiless, weightless, utterly absorbed, she traversed the landscape of another's mind and found it like her own yet totally unlike—surprising and jarring her, enticing her, leading her on. It was a secret process yet it was not criminal or forbidden—she made her way with the stealth of the thief, elated, subdued, through another's imagination, risking no harm, no punishment. The later the hour and the more exhausted she was, the greater, oddly, her powers of concentration; nothing in her resisted, nothing stood aside to doubt or ridicule; the books she read greedily seemed to take life through her, by way of her, with virtually no exertion of her own. It scarcely seemed to matter what she read, or whom—Nietzsche, William James, the Brontës, Wallace Stevens, Virginia Woolf, Stendhal, the early Greek philosophers—the experience of reading was electrifying, utterly mesmerizing, beyond anything she could recall from the past. She'd been, she thought severely, a superficial person in the past—how could anything that belonged to Innisfail, to those years, matter?

A writer's authentic self, she thought, lay in his writing and not in his life; it was the landscape of the imagination that endured, that was really real. Mere life was the husk, the actor's performance, negligible in the long run. . . . How could it be anything more than the vehicle by which certain works of art were transcribed. . . ? The thought frightened her, exhilarated her. She climbed out of her bed and leaned out her window as far as she could, her hair whipping in the wind. For long vacant minutes she stared at the sky; her vision absorbed without recording the illuminated water tower two miles north of the campus, the flickering red lights of a radio station, the passage of clouds blown livid across the moon. Standing in her bare feet, shivering, her head fairly ringing with fatigue and her eyes filling with tears, she thought her happiness almost too exquisite to be borne.

The first time Imogene Skillman climbed, uninvited, to Marya's room at the top of the old mansion, she stood in the doorway and exclaimed in her low throaty amused voice, "So *this* is where you hide out! . . . this depressing little hole."

Imogene was standing with her hands on her hips, her cheeks flushed, her eyes moving restlessly about. Why, Marya's room was a former maid's room, wasn't it, partitioned off from the others on the floor; and it had only that one window—no wonder the air was stale and close; and that insufferable Chagall print!—wasn't Marya aware that everyone on campus had one? And it was a poor reproduction at that. Then Imogene noticed the charcoal sketches; she came closer to investigate; she said, after a long moment, "At least these are interesting, I wouldn't mind owning one or two of them myself."

Marya had been taken by surprise, sitting at her desk, a book opened before her; she hadn't the presence of mind to invite Imogene in, or to tell her to go away.

"So this is where Marya Knauer lives," Imogene said slowly. Her eyes were a pellucid blue, blank and innocent as china. "All alone, of course. Who would *you* have roomed with—?"

The loss of the money and the Parker fountain pen was so upsetting to Marya, and so bitterly ironic, partly because Marya herself had become a casual thief.

She thought, I deserve this.

She thought, I will never steal anything again.

Alice had led her on silly little shoplifting expeditions in Woolworth's: plastic combs, spools of thread, lipsticks, useless items (hairnets, thumbtacks) pilfered for the sheer fun of it. Once, years ago, when she was visiting Bonnie Michalak, she made her way stealthily into Mrs. Michalak's bedroom and took—what had it been?—a button, a thimble, two or three pennies?—from the top of her dresser. A tube of much-used scarlet lipstick from the locker of a high school friend; a card-sized plastic calendar (an advertisement from a stationer's in town) from Mr. Schwilk's desk; stray nickels and dimes, quarters, fifty-cent pieces. . . . One of her prizes, acquired with great daring and trepidation, was a (fake) ruby ring belonging to someone's older sister, which Marya had found beneath carelessly folded clothing in a stall in the women's bathroom at Wolf's Head Lake, but had never dared to wear. The thefts were always impulsive and rather pointless. Marya saw her trembling hand dart out, saw the fingers close . . . and in that instant, wasn't the object hers?

There was a moment when an item passed over from belonging to another person to belonging to Marya; that moment interested her greatly. She felt excitement, near-panic, elation. A sense of having triumphed, in however petty a fashion.

(It had come to seem to her in retrospect that she'd stolen Father Shearing's wristwatch. She seemed to recall . . . unless it was a particularly vivid dream . . . she seemed to recall slipping the watch from his table into her bookbag, that old worn soiled bookbag she'd had for years. Father Shearing was asleep in his cranked-up bed. Though perhaps not . . . perhaps he was watching her all along through his eyelashes. Marya? Dear Marya? A common thief?)

Since coming to Port Oriskany she felt the impulse more frequently but she knew enough to resist. It was a childish habit, she thought, disgusted,—it wasn't even genuine theft, intelligently committed. Presumably she wanted to transgress; even to be punished; she *wanted* to be sinful.

Odd, Marya thought uneasily, that no one has ever caught me. When I haven't seemed to care. When I haven't seemed to have *tried.*

It happened that, in her classes, she found herself gazing at certain individuals, and at their belongings, day after day, week after week. What began as simple curiosity gradually shaded into intense interest. She might find herself, for instance, staring at a boy's spiral notebook in a lecture class . . . plotting a way to getting it for herself, leafing through it, seeing what he'd written. (For this boy, like Marya, was a daydreamer; an elaborate and tireless doodler, not without talent.) There was an antique opal ring belonging to a girl in her English literature class: the girl herself had waist-long brown hair, straight and coarse, and Marya couldn't judge whether she was striking, and very good-looking, or really quite repulsive. (Marya's own hair was growing long again—long and wavy and unruly—but it would never be that length again; the ends simply broke off.) Many of the students at Port Oriskany were from well-to-do families, evidently, judging from their clothes and belongings: Marya's eye moved upon handtooled leather bags, and boots, and wristwatches, and earrings, and coats (suede, leather, fur-trimmed, camel's hair) half in scorn and half in envy. She did not want to steal these items, she did not *want* these items, yet, still, her gaze drifted onto them time and again, helplessly. . . .

She studied faces too, when she could. Profiles. That blonde girl in her political science class, for instance: smooth clear creamy skin, china-blue mocking eyes, a flawless nose, mouth: long hair falling over one shoulder. Knee-high leather boots, kid gloves, a handsome camel's hair coat, a blue cashmere muffler that hadn't been cleaned in some time. An engagement ring with a large square-cut diamond. . . . But it was the girl's other pieces of jewelry that drew Marya's interest. Sometimes she wore a big silver ring with a turquoise stone; and a long sporty necklace made of copper coins; and a succession of earrings in her pierced ears—gold loops that swung and caught the light, tiny iridescent-black stones, ceramic disks in which gold-burnished reds and blues flashed. Marya stared and stared, her heart quickening with—was it envy?—but envy of precisely what? It could not have been these expensive trinkets she coveted.

Imogene Skillman was a theatre arts major; she belonged to one of the sororities on Masefield Avenue; Marya had even been able to discover that she was from Laurel Park, Long Island, and that she was engaged to a law student who had graduated from Port Oriskany several years ago. After she became acquainted with Imogene she would have been deeply humiliated if Imogene had known how much Marya knew of her beforehand. Not only her background, and her interest in acting, but that big leather bag, those boots, the silver ring, the ceramic earrings. . . .

It might have been Imogene's presence in class that inspired Marya to speak as she frequently did; answering their professor's questions in such detail, in such self-consciously structured sentences. (Marya thought of herself as shy, but, as it turned out, she could often speak at length if required—she became, suddenly, articulate and emphatic—even somewhat combative. The tenor of her voice caused people to turn around in their seats and often surprised, when it did not disconcert, her professors.) It wasn't that she spoke her mind—she rarely offered opinions—it seemed to her necessary to consider as many sides of an issue as possible, as many relevant points, presenting her case slowly and clearly and forcefully, showing no sign of the nervousness she felt. It was not simply that most of her professors solicited serious discussion—gave evidence, in fact, of being greatly dependent upon it to fill up fifty minutes of class time—or even that (so Marya reasoned, calculated) her precious grade might depend upon such contributions; she really became caught up in the subjects themselves. Conflicting theories of representative democracy, property rights, civil disobedience . . . the ethics of propaganda . . . revolution and counterrevolution . . . whether in fact terrorism might ever be justified. . . . Even when it seemed, as it sometimes did, that Marya's concern for these issues went beyond that of the professor's, she made her point; she felt a grudging approval throughout the room; and Imogene Skillman turned languidly in her seat to stare at her.

One afternoon Imogene left behind a little handwoven purse that must have slipped out of her leather bag. Marya snatched it up as if it were a prize. She followed after Imogene—followed her out of the building—that tall blonde girl in the camel's hair coat—striding along, laughing, in a high-spirited conversation with her friends. Marya approached her and handed her the purse, saying only, "You dropped this," in a neutral voice; she turned away without waiting for Imogene's startled thanks.

Afterward she felt both elated and unaccountably fatigued. As if she had experienced some powerful drain on her energy. As if, having returned Imogene's little purse to her, she now regretted having done so; and wondered if she had been a fool.

Marya's friendship with Imogene Skillman began, as it was to end, with a puzzling abruptness.

One day Imogene simply appeared beside Marya on one of the campus paths, asking if she was walking this way?—and falling comfortably in step with her. It was done as easily and as effortlessly as if they were old friends; as if Imogene had been reading Marya's most secret thoughts.

She began by flattering her, telling her she said "interesting" things in class; that she seemed to be the only person their professor really listened to. Then, almost coyly: "I should confess that it's your voice that really intrigues me. What if—so I ask myself, I'm always trying things on other people!—what if *she* was playing Hedda—Hedda Gabler—with that remarkable voice—and not mine—*mine* is so reedy—I've heard myself on tape and can barely stop from gagging. And there's something about your manner too—also your chin—when you speak—it looks as if you're gritting your teeth but you *are* making yourself perfectly audible, don't be offended! The thing is, I'm doing Hedda myself, I can't help but be jealous of how you might do her in my place though it's all *my* imagination of course. Are you free for lunch? No? Yes? We could have it at my sorority—no, better out—it's not so claustrophobic, out. We'll have to hurry, though, Marya, is it?—I have a class at one I don't *dare* cut again."

It gave Marya a feeling of distinct uneasiness, afterward, to think that Imogene had pursued *her.* Or, rather, that Imogene must have imagined herself the pursuer; and kept up for weeks the more active, the more charitably outgoing and inquisitive, of their two roles. (During their first conversation, for instance, Marya found herself stammering and blushing as she tried to answer Imogene's questions—Where are you from, what are you studying, where do you live on campus, what do you *think* of this place, isn't it disappointing?—put in so candid and ingenuous a manner, with that wide blue-eyed stare, Marya felt compelled to reply. She also felt vaguely criminal, guilty—as if she'd somehow drawn Imogene to her by the very intensity of her own interest, without Imogene's conscious knowledge.)

If Imogene reached out in friendship, at the beginning, Marya naturally drew back. She shared the Knauers' peasant shrewdness, or was it meanspiritedness: what does this person want from *me,* why on earth would this person seek out *me*? It was mysterious, puzzling, disconcerting. Imogene was so pretty, so popular and self-assured, a dominant campus personality; Marya had only a scattering of friends—friendly acquaintances, really. She hadn't, as she rather coolly explained to Imogene, time for "wasting" on people.

She also disapproved of Imogene's public manner, her air of flippancy, carelessness. In fact Imogene was quite intelligent—her swiftness of thought, her skill at repartee, made that clear—but she played at seeming otherwise, to Marya's surprise and annoyance. Imogene was always *Imogene,* always *on.* She was a master of sudden dramatic reversals: sunny warmth that shaded into chilling mockery; low-voiced serious conversations, on religion, perhaps (Imogene was an agnostic who feared, she said, lapsing into Anglicanism—it ran in her family), that deteriorated into wisecracks and bawdy jokes simply because one of her theatre friends appeared. While Marya was too reserved to ask Imogene about herself, Imogene was pitiless in her interrogation of Marya, once the formality of their first meeting was out of the way. Has your family *always* lived in that part of the state, do you mean your father was really a *miner,* how old were you when he died, how old were you when your mother died, do you keep in touch with your high school friends, are you happy here, are you in love with anyone, have you ever been in love, are you a virgin, do you have any plans for this summer, what will you do after graduation?—what do you think your *life* will be? Marya was dazed, disoriented. She answered as succinctly and curtly as she dared, never really telling the truth, yet not precisely lying; she had the idea that Imogene could detect a lie; she'd heard her challenge others when she doubted the sincerity of what they said. Half-truths went down very well, however. Half-truths, Marya had begun to think, were so much more reasonable—so much more convincing—than whole truths.

For surely brazen golden-haired Imogene Skillman didn't really want to know the truth about Marya's family—her father's death (of a heart attack, aged thirty-nine, wasn't that a possibility?—having had rheumatic fever, let's say, as a boy); her mother's disappearance that was, at least poetically, a kind of death too (automobile accident, Marya ten at the time, no one to blame). Marya was flattered, as who would not be, by Imogene's intense *interest* and *sympathy* ("You seem to have had such a hard life. . . .") but she was shrewd enough to know she must not push her friend's generosity of spirit too far: it was one thing to be moved, another thing to be repulsed.

So she was sparing with the truth. A little truth goes a long way, she thought, not knowing if the remark was an old folk saying, or something she'd coined herself.

She told herself that she resented Imogene's manner, her assumption of an easygoing informality that was all one-sided, or nearly; at the same time it couldn't be denied that Marya Knauer visibly brightened in Imogene Skillman's presence. She saw with satisfaction how Imogene's friends—meeting them in the student union, in the pub, in the restaurants and coffee shops along Fairfield Street—watched them with curiosity, and must have wondered who Imogene's new friend was.

Marya Knauer: but who is *she*?—where did Imogene pick up *her*?

Marya smiled cynically to herself, thinking that she understood at last the gratification a man must feel, in public, in the company of a beautiful woman. Better, really, than being the beautiful woman yourself.

They would have quarrelled, everything would have gone abrasive and sour immediately, if Marya hadn't chosen (consciously, deliberately) to admire Imogene's boldness, rather than to be insulted by it. (*Are you happy, are you lonely, have you even been in love, are you a virgin?*—no one had ever dared ask Marya such questions. The Knauers were reticent, prudish, about such things as personal feelings: Wilma might haul off and slap her, and call her a little shit, but she'd have been convulsed with embarrassment to ask Marya if she was happy or unhappy, if she loved anyone, if, maybe, she knew how Wilma loved *her*. Just as Lee and Everard might quarrel, and Lee might dare to tell his brawny hot-tempered father to go to hell, but he'd never have asked him—he'd never have even imagined asking him—how much money he made in a year, how much he had in the bank, what the property was worth, did he have a will, did he guess that, well, Lee sort of looked up to *him*, loved *him*, despite all these fights?)

Marya speculated that she'd come a great distance from Innisfail and the Canal Road—light-years, really, not two hundred miles—and she had to be careful, cautious, about speaking in the local idiom.

Imogene was nearly as tall as Marya, and her gold-gleaming hair and ebullient manner made her seem taller. Beside her, Marya knew herself shabby, undramatic, unattractive; it was not *her* perogative to take offense, to recoil from her friend's extreme interest. After all—were so very many people interested in her, here in Port Oriskany? Did anyone really care if she lied, or told the truth, or invented ingenious half-truths . . . ? In any case, despite Imogene's high spirits, there was usually something harried about her. She hadn't studied enough for an exam, play rehearsals were going badly, she'd had an upsetting telephone call from home the night before, what in Christ's name was she to *do*? . . . Marya noted that beautiful white-toothed smile marred by tiny tics of vexation. Imogene was always turning the diamond ring round and round her finger, impatiently; she fussed with her earrings and hair; she was always late, always running—her coat unbuttoned and flapping about her, her tread heavy. Her eyes sometimes filled with tears that were, or were not, genuine.

Even her agitation, Marya saw, was enviable. There are certain modes of unhappiness with far more style than happiness.

Imogene insisted that Marya accompany her to a coffee shop on Fairfield—pretentiously called a coffee "house"—where all her friends gathered. These were her *real* friends, apart from her sorority sisters and her fraternity admirers. Marya steeled herself against their critical amused eyes; she didn't want to be one of their subjects for mimicry. (They did devastating imitations of their professors and even of one another—Marya had to admit, laughing, that they were really quite good. If only she'd known such people back in Innisfail!—in high school!—she might have been less singled out for disapproval; she might have been less lonely.)

Marya made certain that she gave her opinions in a quick flat unhesitating voice, since opinions tenuously offered were usually rejected. If she chose to talk with these people at all she made sure that she talked fast, so that she wouldn't be interrupted. (They were always interrupting one another, Imogene included.) With her excellent memory Marya could, if required, quote passages from the most difficult texts; her vocabulary blossomed wonderfully in the presence of a critical, slightly hostile audience she knew she *must* impress. (For Imogene prided herself on Marya Knauer's brilliance, Marya Knauer's knowledge and wit. Yes, that's right, she would murmur, laughing, nudging Marya in the ribs, go on, go *on,* you're absolutely right—you've got them now!) And Marya smoked cigarettes with the others, and drank endless cups of bitter black coffee, and flushed with pleasure when things went well . . . though she was wasting a great deal of time these days, wasn't she? . . . and wasn't time the precious element that would carry her along to her salvation?

The coffee shop was several blocks from the University's great stone archway, a tunnellike place devoid of obvious charm, where tables were crowded together and framed photographs of old, vanished athletes lined the walls. Everyone—Imogene's "everyone"—drifted there to escape from their living residences, and to sit for hours, talking loudly and importantly, about Strindberg, or Whitman, or Yeats, or the surrealists, or Prufrock, or Artaud, or *Ulysses,* or the Grand Inquisitor; or campus politics (who was in, who was out); or the theater department (comprised half of geniuses and saints, half of losers). Marya soon saw that several of the boys were in love with Imogene, however roughly they sometimes treated her. She didn't care to learn their names but of course she did anyway—Scott, and Andy, and Matthew (who took a nettlesome sort of dislike to Marya); there was a dark ferret-faced mathematics student named Brian whose manner was broadly theatrical and whose eyeglasses flashed with witty malice. The other girls in the group were attractive enough, in fact quite striking, but they were no match for Imogene when she was most herself.

Of course the love, even the puppyish affection, went unrequited. Imogene was engaged—the diamond ring was always in sight, glittering and winking; Imogene occasionally made reference to someone named Richard, whose opinion she seemed to value highly. (What is Imogene's fiancé like, Marya asked one of the girls, and was told he was "quiet"—"watchful"—that Imogene behaved a little differently around him; she was quieter herself.)

One wintry day when Marya should have been elsewhere she sat with Imogene's friends in a booth at the smoky rear of the coffee house, half-listening to their animated talk, wondering why Imogene cared so much for them. Her mind drifted loose; she found herself examining one of the photographs on the walls close by. It was sepia-tinted, and very old: the 1899 University rowing team. Beside it was a photograph of the 1902 football team. How young those smiling athletes must have felt, as the century turned, Marya thought. It must have seemed to them . . . *theirs.*

She was too lazy to excuse herself and leave. She was too jealous of Imogene. No, it was simply that her head ached; she hadn't slept well the night before and wouldn't sleep well tonight. . . . Another rowing team. Hopeful young men, standing so straight and tall; their costumes slightly comical; their haircuts bizarre. An air of team spirit, hearty optimism, doom. Marya swallowed hard, feeling suddenly strange. She really should leave . . . She really shouldn't be here. . . .

Time had been a nourishing stream, a veritable sea, for those young men. Like fish they'd swum in it without questioning it—without knowing it was the element that sustained them and gave them life. And then it had unaccountably withdrawn and left them exposed . . . Forever youthful in those old photographs, in their outdated costumes; long since aged, dead, disposed of.

Marya thought in a panic that she must leave; she must return to her room and lock the door.

But when she rose Imogene lay a hand on her arm and asked irritably what was wrong, why was she always jumping up and down: couldn't she for Christ's sake sit *still?*

The vehemence of Imogene's response struck them all, it was in such disproportion to Marya's behavior. Marya herself was too rushed, too frightened, to take offense. She murmured, "Good-bye, Imogene," without looking at her; and escaped.

It was that night, not long before curfew, that Imogene dropped by for the first time at Maynard House. She rapped on Marya's door, poked her head in, seemed to fill the doorway, chattering brightly as if nothing were wrong; as if they'd parted amiably. Of course she *was* rather rude about the room—Marya hadn't realized it must have been a maid's room, in the house's earliest incarnation—but her rudeness as always passed by rather casually, in a sort of golden blue. She looked so pretty, flushed with cold, her eyes inordinately damp. . . .

Tell me about these drawings, she said,—I didn't know you were an artist. These are *good.*

But Marya wasn't in a mood for idle conversation. She said indifferently that she *wasn't* an artist; she was a student.

But Imogene insisted she was an artist. Because the sketches were so rough, unfinished, yet they caught the eye, there was something unnerving about them. "Do you see yourself like this, though?—Marya?" Imogene asked almost wistfully. "So stern and ugly?—it *isn't* you, is it?"

"It isn't anyone," Marya said. "It's a few charcoal strokes on old paper."

She was highly excited that Imogene Skillman had come to her room: had anyone on the floor noticed?—had the girl downstairs at the desk, on telephone duty, noticed? At the same time she wished her gone, it was an intrusion into her privacy, insufferable. She had never invited Imogene to visit her—she never would.

"So this is where you live," Imogene said, drawing a deep breath. Her eyes darted mercilessly about; she would miss nothing, forget nothing. "You're alone and you don't mind, that's *just* like you. You have a whole other life, a sort of secret life, don't you," she said, with a queer pouting downward turn of her lips.

Friendship, Marya speculated in her journal,—the most enigmatic of all relationships.

In a sense it flourished unbidden; in another, it had to be cultivated, nurtured, sometimes even forced into existence. Though she was tirelessly active in most aspects of her life she'd always been quite passive when it came to friendship. She hadn't time, she told herself; she hadn't energy for something so . . . ephemeral.

Nothing was worthwhile, really worthwhile, except studying; getting high grades; and her own reading, her own work. Sometimes Marya found herself idly contemplating a young man—in one of her classes, in the library; sometimes, like most of her female classmates, she contemplated one or another of her male professors. But she didn't want a lover, not even a romance. To cultivate romance, Marya thought, you had to give over a great deal of time for daydreaming: she hadn't time to waste on *that.*

Since the first month of her freshman year Marya had acquired a reputation for being brilliant—the word wasn't hers but Imogene's: Do you know everyone thinks you're brilliant, everyone is afraid of you?—and it struck Marya as felicitous, a sort of glass barrier that would keep other people at a distance. . . . And then again she sometimes looked up from her reading, and noted that hours had passed; where was she and what was she doing to herself? (Had someone called her? Whispered her name? Marya, Marya. . . . You little savage, Marya. . . .) Suddenly she ached with the desire to see Wilma, and Everard; and her brothers; even Lee. She felt as if she must leave this airless little cubbyhole of a room—take a Greyhound bus to Innisfail—see that house on the Canal Road—sit at the kitchen table with the others—tell them she loved them, she loved them and couldn't help herself; what was happening?

Great handfuls of her life were being stolen from her and she would never be able to retrieve them.

To counteract Imogene Skillman's importance in her life, Marya made it a point to be friendly—if not, precisely, to *become friends*—with a number of Maynard House girls. She frequently ate meals with them in the dining hall a few blocks away, though she was inclined (yes, it was rude) to bring along a book or two just in case. And if the conversation went nowhere Marya would murmur, Do you mind?—I have so much reading to do.

Of course they didn't mind. Catherine or Phyllis or Sally or Diane. They too were scholarship students; they too were frightened, driven.

(Though Marya knew they discussed her behind her back. She was the only girl in the house with a straight-A average and they were waiting . . . were they perhaps hoping? . . . for her to slip down a notch or two. They were afraid of her sarcasm, her razorish wit. Then again, wasn't she sometimes very funny?—If you liked that sort of humor. As for the sorority girl Imogene Skillman: what did Marya see in *her*?—what did *she* see in Marya? It was also likely, wasn't it, that Marya was the house thief? For the thief still walked off with things sporadically. These were mean, pointless thefts—a letter from a mailbox, another textbook, a single angora glove, an inexpensive locket on a tarnished silver chain. Pack-rat sort of thievery, unworthy, in fact, of any girl who roomed in Maynard.)

When Marya told Imogene about the thief and the money she'd lost, Imogene said indifferently that there was a great deal of stealing on campus, and worse things too (this, with a sly twist of her lips), but no one wanted to talk about it; the student newspaper (the editors were all friends of hers, she knew such things) was forever being censored. For instance, last year a girl committed suicide by slashing her wrists in one of the off-campus senior houses and the paper wasn't allowed to publish the news, not even to *hint* at it, and the local newspaper didn't run anything either, it was all a sort of totalitarian kindergarten state, the university. As for theft: "*I've* never stolen anything in my life," Imogene said, smiling, brooding, "because why would I want anything that somebody else has already had?—something second-hand, used?"

Your friend Imogene, people began to say.

Your friend Imogene: she dropped by at noon, left this note for you.

Marya's pulses rang with pleasure, simple gratitude. She was flattered but—well, rather doubtful. Did she even *like* Imogene? Were they really friends? In a sense she liked one or two of the girls in Maynard better than she liked Imogene. Phyllis, for instance, a mathematics major, very sharp, very bright, though almost painfully shy; and a chunky farm girl named Diane from a tiny settlement north of Shaheen Falls, precociously matronly, with thick glasses and a heavy tread on the stairs and a perpetual odor of unwashed flesh, ill-laundered clothes. . . . But Diane was bright, very bright; Marya thought privately that here was her real competition at Port Oriskany, encased in baby fat, blinking through those thick lenses. (The residence buzzed with the rumor, however, that Diane was doing mysteriously poorly in her courses, had she a secret grief?—an unstated terror?) Marya certainly liked Phyllis and Diane, she recognized them as superior individuals, really much nicer, much kinder, than Imogene. Yet she had to admit it would not have deeply troubled her if she never saw them again. And the loss of Imogene would have been a powerful blow.

She went twice to see the production of *Hedda Gabler* in which Imogene starred. For she really did star, it was a one-woman show. That hard slightly drawling slightly nasal voice, that mercurial manner (cruel, seductive, mock-sweet, languid, genuinely anguished by turns), certain odd tricks and mannerisms (the way she held her jaw, for instance: had she pilfered that from Marya?)—Imogene was *really* quite good; really a success. And they'd made her up to look even more beautiful on stage than she looked in life: her golden hair in a heavy Victorian twist, her cheeks subtly rouged, her eyes enormous. Only in the tense sparring scene with Judge Brack, when Hedda was forced to confront a personality as strong as her own, did Imogene's acting falter: her voice went strident, her manner became too broadly erotic.

Marya thought, slightly dazed,—Is she really talented? Is there some basis for her reputation, after all?

Backstage, Marya didn't care to compete for Imogene's attention; let the others hug and kiss her and shriek congratulations if they wished. It was all exaggerated, florid, embarrassing . . . so much emotion, such a *display*. . . . And Imogene looked wild, frenzied, her elaborate makeup now rather clownish, seen at close quarters. "Here's Marya," she announced, "—Marya will tell the truth—here's Marya—shut up, you idiots!—she'll tell the truth—*was* I any good, Marya?—*was* I really Hedda?" She pushed past her friends and gripped Marya's hands, staring at her with great shining painted eyes. She smelled of greasepaint and powder and perspiration; it seemed to Marya that Imogene towered over her.

"Of course you were good," Marya said flatly. "You know you were good."

Imogene gripped her hands tighter, her manner was feverish, outsized. "What are you saying?—you didn't care for the performance? It wasn't right? I failed?"

"Don't be ridiculous," Marya said, embarrassed, trying to pull away. "You don't need me to assess you, in any case. You *know* you were—"

"You didn't like it! Did you!"

"—you were perfect."

"Perfect!" Imogene said in hoarse stage voice, "—but that doesn't sound like one of your words, Marya—you don't *mean* it."

It was some seconds before Marya, her face burning with embarrassment and resentment, could extricate her hands from Imogene's desperate grip. No, she couldn't come to the cast party; she had to get back to work. And yes, yes, for Christ's sake, *yes*—Imogene had been "perfect": or nearly.

Friendship, Marya wrote in her journal, her heart pounding with rage,—play-acting of an amateur type.

Friendship, she wrote,—a puzzle that demands too much of the imagination.

So she withdrew from Imogene, tried even to stop thinking about her, looking for her on campus. (That blue muffler, that camel's hair coat. And she had a new coat too: Icelandic shearling, with a black fur collar.) She threw herself into her work with more passion than before. Exams were upon her, papers were due, she felt the challenge with a sort of eager dread, an actual greed, knowing she could do well even if she didn't work hard; and she intended to work very, very hard. Even if she got sick, even if her eyes went bad.

Hour after hour of reading, taking notes, writing, rewriting. In her room, the lamp burning through the night; in one or another of her secret places in the library; in a corner of an old brick mansion a quarter-mile away that had been converted into the music school, where she might read and scribble notes and daydream, her heartbeat underscored by the muffled sounds of pianos, horns, violins, cellos, flutes, from the rows of practice rooms. The sounds—the various musics—were all rather harmonious, heard like this, in secret. Marya thought, closing her eyes: If you could only *be* music.

At the same time she had her job in the library, her ill-paid job, a drain on her time and spirit, a terrible necessity. She explained that she'd lost her entire paycheck—the money had been stolen out of her wallet—she *must* be allowed to work a little longer, to clock a few more hours each week. She intended (so she explained to her supervisor) to make up the loss she'd suffered by disciplining herself severely, spending no extra money if she could avoid it. She *must* be allowed a few hours extra work. . . . (The Parker pen could never be replaced, of course. As for the money: Marya washed her hair now once a week, and reasoned that she did not really need toothpaste, why did anyone *need* toothpaste?—she was sparing with her toiletries in general, and, if she could, used other girls', left in the third floor bathroom. She was always coming upon lost ballpoint pens, lost notebooks, even loose change; she could appropriate—lovely word, "appropriate"—cheap mimeograph paper from a supply room in the library; sometimes she even found half-empty packs of cigarettes—though her newest resolution was to stop smoking, since she resented every penny spent on so foolish a habit. Her puritan spirit blazed; she thought it an emblem of her purity, that the waistbands of her skirts were now too loose, her underwear was a size too large.)

After an evening of working in the library—her pay was approximately $1 an hour—she hurried home to Maynard, exhausted, yet exhilarated, eager to get to her schoolwork. Once she nearly fainted running up the stairs and Diane, who happened to be nearby, insisted that she come into her room for a few minutes. You look terrible, she said in awe—almost as bad as I do. But Marya brushed her aside, Marya hadn't time. She was light-headed from the stairs, that was all.

One night Imogene telephoned just before the switchboard was to close. What the hell was wrong, Imogene demanded, was Marya angry at her? She hurried out of class before Imogene could say two words to her—she never came down to Fairfield Street any longer—was she secretly in love?—was she working longer hours at the library?—would she like to come to dinner sometime this week, at the sorority?—or next week, before Christmas break?

Yes, thought Marya, bathed in gratitude, in golden splendor, "No," she said aloud, quietly, chastely, "—but thank you very much."

Schopenhauer, Dickens, Marx, Euripides. Oscar Wilde. Henry Adams. Sir Thomas More. Thomas Hobbes. And Shakespeare—of course. She read, she took notes, she daydreamed. It sometimes disturbed her that virtually nothing of what she read had been written by women (except Jane Austen, dear perennial Jane, *so* feminine!) but in her arrogance she told herself *she* would change all that.

Is this how it begins, she wondered, half-amused. Breaking down. Cracking up.

Why breaking *down* . . . but cracking *up* . . . ?

Her long periods of intense concentration began to be punctuated by bouts of directionless daydreaming, sudden explosions of *feeling*. At such times Shakespeare was too dangerous to be read closely—Hamlet whispered truths too cruel to be borne, every word in *Lear* hooked in flesh and could not be dislodged. As for Wilde, Hobbes, Schopenhauer . . . even cynicism, Marya saw, can't save you.

At such times she went for walks along Masefield Avenue, past the enormous sorority and fraternity houses. They too were converted mansions but had retained much of their original glamor and stateliness. Imogene's, for instance, boasted pretentious white columns, four of them, in mock-Southern Colonial style. The cryptic Greek letters on the portico struck an especially garish and irrelevant note. What did such symbols mean, what did it mean (so Marya wondered, not quite bitterly) to be *clubbable*—? In the winter twilight, in the cold, these outsized houses appeared especially warm and secretive; every window of their several storeys blazed. Marya thought, Why don't I feel anything, can't I even feel envy. . . ? But the sororities were crudely discriminatory (one was exclusively for Catholic girls, another exclusively for Jewish girls, the sixteen others had quotas for Catholics and blackballed all Jews who dared cross their threshold: the procedure was that blunt, that childish). Dues and fees were absurdly high, beyond the inflated price for room and board; the meetings involved pseudoreligious "Greek" rituals (handshakes, secret passwords, special prayers). Imogene complained constantly, was always cutting activities and being fined ($10 fine for missing a singing rehearsal!—the very thought made Marya shiver in disbelief), always mocking the alumns, those well-to-do matrons with too much time on their hands. Such assholes, all of them, Imogene said loftily, such *pretentious* assholes. It was part of Imogene's charm that she could be both contemptuous of pretension and marvelously—shamelessly—pretentious herself.

Time is the element in which we exist, Marya noted solemnly in her journal,—We are either borne along by it, or drowned in it.

It occurred to her with a chilling certitude that *every moment not consciously devoted to her work* was an error, a blunder. As if you can kill time, Thoreau said, without injuring Eternity.

Lying drowsily and luxuriously in bed after she'd wakened . . . conversations with most people, or, indeed *all* people . . . spending too long in the shower, or cleaning her room, or staring out the window, or eating three meals a day (unless of course she brought along a book to read) . . . daydreaming and brooding about Innisfail, or the Canal Road, or that wretched little tarpaper-roofed shanty near Shaheen Falls that had been her parents' house . . . crying over the past (though in fact she rarely cried these days) as if the past were somehow present. In high school she had been quite an athlete, especially at basketball and field hockey; in college she hadn't time, hadn't the slightest interest. It pleased her that she always received grades of A but at the same time she wondered,—Are these *really* significant grades, do I *really* know anything?—or is Port Oriskany one of the backwaters of the world, where nothing, even "excellence," greatly matters? She needed high grades in order to get into graduate school, however; beyond that she didn't allow herself to think. Though perhaps she wouldn't go to graduate school at all . . . perhaps she would try to write . . . her great problem being not that she hadn't anything to write about but that she had too much.

Unwisely, once, she confided in Imogene that she halfway feared to write anything that wasn't academic or scholarly or firmly rooted in the real world: once she began she wouldn't be able to stop: she was afraid of sinking too deep into her own head, cracking up, becoming lost.

Imogene said it once that Marya was just the type to be excessive, she needed reining in. "I know the symptoms," she said severely. Anyway, what good would academic success—or any kind of success—do her, if she destroyed her health?

"*You're* concerned about my health?" Marya asked increduously.

"Of course. Yes, I *am.* Why shouldn't I be," Imogene said, "—aren't I a friend of yours?"

Marya stared at her, unable to reply. It struck her as wildly incongruous that Imogene Skillman, with her own penchant for abusing her health (she drank too much at fraternity parties, she stayed up all night doing hectic last-minute work) should be worrying about Marya.

"Aren't I a friend of yours?" Imogene asked less certainly. "Don't I have the right . . . ?"

Marya turned away with an indifferent murmur, perhaps because she was so touched.

"My health isn't of any use to me," she said, "if I don't get anything accomplished. If I fail."

Of course it was possible, Marya saw, to ruin one's health and fail anyway.

Several of her fellow residents in Maynard House were doing poorly in their courses, despite their high intelligence and the goading terror that energized them. One of them was Phyllis, who was failing an advanced calculus class; another, a chronically withdrawn and depressed girl named Mary, a physics major, whose deeply shadowed eyes and pale grainy skin, as well as her very name, struck a superstitious chord of dread in Marya—she avoided her as much as possible, and had the idea that Mary avoided *her.*

The University piously preached an ethic of knowledge for its own sake—knowledge and beauty being identical—the "entire person" was to be educated, not simply the mind; but of course it acted swiftly and pragmatically upon another ethic entirely. Performance was all, the grade-point average *was* everything. Marya, no idealist, saw that this was sound and just; but she felt an impatient sort of pity for those who fell by the wayside, or who, like the scholarship girls, in not being *best,* were to be judged *worthless,* and sent back home. (Anything below a B was failing for them.) She wanted only to be best, to be outstanding, to be . . . defined to herself as extraordinary . . . for, apart from being extraordinary, had she any essence at all?

The second semester of her freshman year she had come close to losing her perfect grade-point average. Unwisely, she signed up for a course in religion, having been attracted to the books on the syllabus and the supplementary reading list (the *Upanishads*; the *Bhagavad-Gītā*; the *Bible*; the *Koran*; *Hymns of the Rigveda*; books on Gnosticism, and Taoism, and medieval Christianity, and the Christian heresies, and animism, magic, witchcraft, Renaissance ideas of Platonic love). It was all very promising, very heady stuff; quite the antidote to the catechismal Catholicism in which Marya no longer believed, and for which she had increasingly less tolerance. The professor, however turned out to be an ebullient balding popinjay who lectured from old notes in a florid and self-dramatizing style, presenting ideas in a melange clearly thrown together from others' books and articles. He wanted nothing more than these ideas (which were fairly simple, not at all metaphysical or troubling) given back to him on papers and examinations; and he did not encourage questions from the class. Marya would surely have done well—she transcribed notes faultlessly, even when contemptuous of their content—but she could not resist sitting in stony silence and refusing to laugh when the professor embarked upon one or another of his jocular anecdotes. It was a classroom mannerism of his, almost a sort of tic, that each time he alluded to something female he lowered his voice and added, as if off the cuff, a wry observation, meant not so much to be insulting as to be mildly teasing. He was a popular lecturer, well-liked by most, not taken seriously by the better students; even the girls laughed at his jokes, being grateful, as students are, for something—anything—to laugh at. Marya alone sat with her arms folded, her brow furrowed, staring. It was not until some years later that she realized, uncomfortably, how she must have appeared to that silly perspiring man—a sort of gorgon in the midst of his amiable little sea of admirers.

So it happened that, though Marya's grades for the course were all A's, the grade posted for her final examination was C; and the final grade for the course—a humiliating B+.

Marya was stunned, Marya was sickened—she would have had to reach back to her childhood—or to the night of that going-away party—for an episode of equal mortification. That it was petty made it all the more mortifying.

I can forget this insult and forget him, Marya instructed herself,—or I can go to him and protest. To forget it seemed in a way noble, even Christian; to go to the man's office and humble herself in trying to get the grade raised (for she knew very well she hadn't written a C exam) somehow childish, degrading.

Of course she ran up to his office, made an appointment to see him; and, after a few minutes' clucking and fretting (he pretended she had failed to answer the last question, she hadn't handed in both examination booklets, but there the second booklet was, at the bottom of a heap of papers—ah, what a surprise!), he consented to raise the grade to A. And smiled roguishly at her, as if she had been caught out in mischief, or some sort of deception; for which he was forgiving her. "You seem like a rather grim young woman," he said, "you never smile—you look so *preoccupied.*" Marya stared at his swinging foot. He was a satyrish middle-aged man, red-brown tufts of hair in his ears, a paunch straining against his shirt front, a strangely vulnerable smile; a totally mediocre personality in every way—vain, uncertain, vindictive—yet Marya could see why others liked him; he was predictable, safe, probably decent enough. But she hated him. She simply wished him dead.

He continued as if not wanting to release her, waiting for her smile of blushing gratitude and her meek *thank you*—which assuredly was not going to come; he said again, teasing, "Are you *always* such an ungiving young woman, Miss Knauer?"—and Marya swallowed hard, and fixed her dark loathing stare on him, and said: "My mother is sick. She's been sick all semester. I know I shouldn't think about it so much . . . I shouldn't depress other people . . . but sometimes I can't help it. She isn't expected to live much longer, the cancer has metastasized to the brain. . . . I'm sorry if I offended you."

He stared at her; then began to stammer his apologies, rising from his desk, flushing deeply—the very image of chagrin and repentance. In an instant the entire atmosphere between them changed. He was sorry, he murmured, so very sorry . . . of course he couldn't have known. . . .

A minute later Marya was striding down the corridor, her pulse beating hot, in triumph. In her coat pocket was the black fountain pen she had lifted from the man's cluttered desk.

An expensive pen, as it turned out. A Parker, with a squarish blunt nub, and the engraved initials E. W. S.

Marya used the pen to take notes in her journal, signing her name repeatedly, hypnotically: *Marya, Marya Knauer, Marya Marya Marya Marya Knauer,* a name that eventually seemed to have been signed by someone else, a stranger.

The shame of having humbled herself before the ignorant man had been erased by the shame—what should have been shame—of theft.

So Marya speculated, thinking of that curious episode in her life. Eventually the pen ran out of ink and she didn't indulge herself in buying more—it was so old-fashioned a practice, a luxury she couldn't afford.

Phyllis began staying out late, violating curfew, returning to the residence drunk, dishevelled, tearful, angry—she couldn't stand the four walls of her room any longer, she told Marya; she couldn't stand shutting the door upon herself.

One night she didn't return at all. It was said afterward that she had been picked up by Port Oriskany police, wandering downtown, miles away, dazed and only partly clothed in the bitter cold—the temperature had gone as low as −5°F. She was taken at once to the emergency room of the city hospital; her parents, who lived upstate, were called; they came immediately the next morning to take her back home. No one at Maynard House was ever to see her again.

All the girls in the residence talked of Phyllis, somewhat dazed themselves, frightened. How quickly it had happened—how quickly Phyllis had disappeared. Marya was plied with questions about Phyllis (how many subjects she was failing, who were the boys she'd gone out with) but Marya didn't know; Marya grew vague, sullen.

And then the waters close over your head.—This phrase ran through Marya's mind repeatedly.

They talked about Phyllis for two or three days, then forgot her.

The following Saturday, however, Phyllis's mother and older sister arrived to pack up her things, clean out her room, fill out a half-dozen university forms. The resident advisor accompanied them; they looked confused, nervous, rather lost. Both women had Phyllis's pale blond limp hair, her rather small, narrow face. How is Phyllis, some of the girls asked, smiling, cautious, and Mrs. Myer said without looking at anyone, Oh Phyllis is fine, resting and eating and sleeping right again, sleeping good hours, she said, half-reproachfully, as if sleeping right hadn't been possible in Maynard House; and they were all to blame. Marya asked whether she might be returning second semester. No, not that soon, Mrs. Myer said quickly. She and the silent older sister were emptying drawers, packing suitcases briskly. Marya helped with Phyllis's books and papers, which lay in an untidy heap on her desk and on the floor surrounding the desk. There were dust balls everywhere. A great cobweb in which the dessicated corpses of insects hung, including that of the spider itself. Stiffened crumpled Kleenex wadded into balls, everywhere underfoot. An odor of grime and despair. . . . Marya discovered a calculus bluebook slashed heavily in red with a grade of D.; a five-page paper on a subject that made no sense to her—Ring theory?—with a blunt red grade of F. It seemed to Marya that Phyllis was far more real now, more present, than she had been in the past . . . even when she'd tried to comfort Marya by taking her in her arms.

Marya supposed she had been Phyllis's closest friend at Port Oriskany. Yet Phyllis's mother and sister hadn't known her name, had no message for her . . . clearly Phyllis had never mentioned her to them at all. It was disappointing, sobering.

And the waters close over your head, Marya thought.

Then something remarkable happened: Marya rose from Phyllis's closet, a pile of books in her arms, her hair in her face, when she happened to see Mrs. Myer dumping loose items out of a drawer into a suitcase: a comb, ballpoint pens, coins, loose pieces of jewelry,—and her black fountain pen. *The* pen, unmistakable.

My God, Marya whispered.

No one heard. Marya stood rooted to the spot, staring, watching as her prize disappeared into Phyllis's suitcase, hidden now by a miscellany of socks and underwear. *The* pen—the emblem of her humiliation and triumph—disappearing forever.

It wasn't until months later that someone in Maynard made the observation that the thefts seemed to have stopped. . . . Since Phyllis moved out. . . . And the rest of the girls (they were at breakfast, eight or ten of them at a table) took it up, amazed, reluctant, wondering. Was it possible . . . *Phyllis* . . . ?

Marya said quietly that they shouldn't say such things since it couldn't be proved; that constituted slander.

Wednesday dinner, a "formal" dinner, in Imogene's sorority house, and Marya is seated beside Imogene, self-conscious, unnaturally shy, eating her food without tasting it. She *can* appreciate the thick slabs of roast beef, the small perfectly cooked parsley potatoes, the handsome gilt-edged china, the white linen tablecloth ("Oh it's Portuguese—from Portugal"), the crystal water goblets, the numerous tall candles, the silvery-green silk wallpaper, the house mother's poised social chatter at the head table . . . and the girls' stylized animation, their collective stylized beauty. For they *are* beautiful, without exception, as unlike the girls of Maynard House as one species is unlike another.

Imogene Skillman, in this dazzling context, isn't Marya's friend; she is clearly a sorority girl; even wearing her pin with its tiny diamonds and rubies just above her left breast. Her high delicate laughter echoes, that of the others', . . . she isn't going to laugh coarsely here, or say anything witty and obscene . . . she can be a little mischievous, just a little cutting, at best. Marya notes how refined her table manners have become for the occasion; how practiced she is at passing things about, summoning one of the houseboys for assistance without quite looking at him. (The houseboy in his white uniform!—one of a subdued and faintly embarrassed little squadron of four or five boys, he turns out to be an acquaintance of Marya's from her Shakespeare class, who resolutely avoids her eye throughout the prolonged meal.)

Marya makes little effort to take part in the table's conversation, which swings from campus topics to vacation plans—Miami Beach, Sarasota, Bermuda, the Barbados, Trinidad, Switzerland ("for skiing"). Where are you going, Imogene asks Marya brightly, and Marya, with a pinched little smile says she will spend a few days at home, then return to school; she has work to do that must be done here. And Imogene's friends gaze upon her with faint neutral smiles. Is this the one Imogene boasted of, who is so intelligent and so well-spoken . . . ? So *witty* . . . ?

For days Marya has been anticipating this dinner, half in dread and half in simple childish excitement. She feared being ravenous with hunger and eating too much out of anxiety; she feared having no appetite at all. But everything is remote, detached, impersonal. Everything is taking place at a little distance from her. A mistake, my coming here, she thinks, my being invited. But she doesn't feel any great nervousness or discomfort. Like the uniformed houseboys who stand with such unnatural stiffness near the doorway to the kitchen, Marya is simply waiting for the meal to end.

She finds herself thinking of friendship, in the past tense. Phyllis, and Diane, and one or two others at Maynard; and, back in Innisfail, Bonnie Michalak, Erma Dietz. She *might* have been a close friend to any of these girls but of course she wasn't, isn't. As for Imogene—she knows she is disappointing Imogene but she can't seem to force herself to care. She halfway resents Imogene for having invited her—for having made a fool out of *herself*, in bringing Marya Knauer to dinner.

How pretty you look, Imogene said, very nearly puzzled, when Marya arrived at six-thirty,—what have you *done* to yourself?

Marya flushed with annoyance; then laughed; with such exuberance that Imogene laughed with her. For it *was* amusing, wasn't it?—Marya Knauer with her hair attractively up in a sort of French twist; Marya Knauer with her lips reddened, and her eyebrows plucked ("pruned," she might have said), Marya Knauer in a green-striped jersey dress that fitted her almost perfectly. A formal dinner meant high heels and stockings, which Marya detested; but she was wearing them nonetheless. And all for Imogene.

Yet now, seated beside Imogene, she pays very little attention to her friend's chatter; she feels subdued, saddened; thinking instead of old friendships, old half-friendships, that year or so during which she'd imagined herself extraordinary, because it had seemed that Emmett Schroeder loved her. She had not loved him—she wasn't capable, she supposed, of loving anyone—but she had certainly basked in the sunny intensity of *his* love: she'd lapped it up eagerly, thirstily (so she very nearly saw herself, a dog lapping water) as if convinced that it had something to do with her. And now Imogene's friendship, which she knows she cannot keep for very long . . . Imogene who has a reputation for being as recklessly improvident with her female friends as with her male friends. . . . Why make the effort, Marya reasons, when all that matters in life is one's personal accomplishment? Work, success, that numbing grade-point average . . . that promise of a future, any future. . . .

While Imogene and several of the others are discussing (animatedly, severely) a sorority sister not present, Marya studies her face covertly; recalls an odd remark Imogene made some weeks ago. The measure of a person's love for you is the depth of his hurt at your betrayal; *that's* the only way you can know how much, or how little, you matter.

Imogene's face had fairly glowed in excited triumph, as she told Marya this bit of wisdom. Marya thought,—She knows from experience, the bitch. She knows her own value.

Imogene is telling a silly convoluted story about a dear friend of hers (it turns out to be Matthew, devoted Matthew) who "helped" her with her term paper on Chekhov: she'd given him a messy batch of notes, he was kind enough to "arrange" them and "expand upon them" and "shape them into an 'A' paper." He's a saint, Imogene says sighing, laughing,—so sweet and so patient; so pathetic, really. But now Imogene is worried ("terrified") that their professor will call her into his office and interrogate her on her own paper, which she hadn't the time to read in its entirety; it was thirty pages long and heavy with footnotes. The girls assure her that if he marked it "A" it *is* an "A"; he'd never ask to see it again. Yes, says Imogene, opening her eyes wide,—but wait until he reads my final exam, and I say these ridiculous things about Chekhov!

Part of this is play-acting, Marya knows, because Imogene is quite intelligent enough, on the subject of Chekhov or anything else connected with drama; so Marya says, though not loudly enough for the entire table to hear: "That wasn't a very kind thing for *you* to do, was it?—and not very honest either."

Imogene chooses not to hear the tone of Marya's remark; she says gaily: "Oh you mean leading poor Matt on? Making him think—? But otherwise he wouldn't have written so *well*, there wouldn't have been so many impressive *footnotes*."

Marya doesn't reply. Marya draws her thumbnail hard against the linen tablecloth, making a secret indentation.

Imogene says, making a joke of it: "Marya's such a puritan—I know better than to ask help of *her*."

Marya doesn't rise to the bait; the conversation shifts onto other topics; in another fifteen minutes the lengthy dinner is over.

"You aren't going home immediately, are you?" Imogene says, surprised. She is smiling but there are strain lines around her mouth. "Come upstairs to my room for a while. Come on, we haven't had a chance to talk."

"Thank you for everything," says Marya. "But I really have to leave. I'm pressed for time these days. . . ."

"You *are* angry?—about that silly Matthew?" Imogene says.

Marya shrugs her shoulders, turns indifferently away.

"Well—are *you* so honest?" Imogene cries.

Marya gets her coat from the closet, her face burning. (Are *you* so honest! *You!*) Imogene is apologizing, talking of other things, laughing, while Marya thinks calmly that she will never see Imogene Skillman again.

"There's no reason why you shouldn't take this coat, it's a perfectly good coat," Imogene said in her "serious" voice—frank, level, unemphatic. "I don't want it any longer because I have so many coats, I never get to wear it and it *is* perfectly lovely, it shouldn't just hang in the closet. . . . Anyway here it is; I think it would look wonderful on you."

Marya stared at the coat. it was the camel's hair she had long admired. Pleasantly scratchy beneath her fingers, belted in back, with a beautiful silky-beige lining: she estimated it would have cost $250 or more, new. And it was almost new.

(Marya's coat, bought two or three years before in Innisfail, had cost $45 on sale.)

Imogene insisted, and Marya tried on the coat, flicking her hair out from inside the collar, studying herself critically in Imogene's full-length mirror. Imogene was saying, "If you're worrying that people will know it's my coat—it *was* my coat—don't: camel's hair coats all look alike. Except they don't look like wool imitations."

Marya met Imogene's frank blue gaze in the mirror. "What about your parents, your mother?—won't someone wonder where the coat has gone?"

Imogene puckered her forehead quizzically. "What business is it of theirs?" she asked. "It's *my* coat. My things are mine, I do what I want with them."

Marya muttered that she just couldn't *take* the coat, and Imogene scolded her for talking with her jaw clenched, and Marya protested in a louder voice, yet still faintly, weakly. . . . "It's a beautiful coat," she said. She was thinking: It's too good for me, I can't accept and I can't refuse and I hate Imogene for this humiliation.

Imogene brought the episode to an end by saying rather coldly: "You'll hurt my feelings, Knauer, if you refuse it. If you're weighing your pride against mine, don't bother—mine is far, far more of a burden."

"So you are—Marya," Mrs. Skillman said in an ambiguous voice (warm? amused? doubtful?) in the drab front parlor of Maynard House, as Marya approached. She and Mr. Skillman and Imogene were taking Marya out to dinner, downtown at the Statler Chop House, one of the area's legendary good restaurants. "We've heard so much about you from Imogene," Mrs. Skillman said, "I think we were expecting someone more. . . ."

"Oh Mother, what on earth—!" Imogene laughed sharply.

". . . I was going to say *taller,* perhaps *older,*" Mrs. Skillman said, clearly annoyed by her daughter's interruption.

Marya shook hands with both the Skillmans and saw to her relief that they appeared to be friendly well-intentioned people, attractive enough, surely, and very well-dressed, but nothing like their striking daughter. *She* might have been their daughter, brunette and subdued. (Except she hadn't dared wear the camel's hair coat, as Imogene had wanted. She was wearing her old plaid wool and her serviceable rubberized boots.)

In their presence Imogene was a subtly different person. Rather more disingenuous, childlike, sweet. Now and then at dinner Marya heard a certain self-mocking tone in her friend's voice ("am I playing this scene correctly?—how is it going down?") but neither of the Skillmans took notice; and perhaps it was Marya's imagination anyway.

Then, near the end of the meal, Imogene got suddenly high on white wine and said of her father's business: "It's a sophisticated form of theft."

She giggled, no one else laughed; Marya kept her expression carefully blank.

". . . I mean it *is,* you know . . . it's indirect. . . . 'Savings and Loans' . . . and half the clients blacks who want their Dee-troit cars financed," Imogene said.

"Imogene, you aren't funny," Mrs. Skillman said.

"She's just teasing," Mr. Skillman said. "My little girl likes to tease."

"I do like to tease, don't I?—Marya knows." Imogene said, nudging her. Then, as if returning to her earlier sobriety, she said: "*I never mean a word of what I say and everybody knows it.*"

The subject leapt to Imogene's negligence about writing letters, or even telephoning home. "If we try to call," Mrs. Skillman said, "the line at the residence is busy for hours; and when we finally get through you aren't in; you're *never* in. And you never return our calls. . . ."

Imogene said carelessly that her sorority sisters were bad at taking down messages. Most of them were assholes, actually—

"Imogene!" Mrs. Skillman said.

"Oh Mother you know they *are,*" Imogene said in a childlike voice.

After an awkward pause Mr. Skillman asked about Richard: Richard had evidently telephoned *them,* asking if something was wrong with Imogene because he couldn't get through to her either. "Your mother and I were hoping there wasn't some sort of . . . misunderstanding between you."

Imogene murmured that there weren't any misunderstandings at all between them.

"He seemed to think . . . to wonder . . ." Mrs. Skillman said. "That is, as long as we were driving up to visit. . . ."

Imogene finished off her glass of white wine and closed her eyes ecstatically. She said: "I really don't care to discuss my private matters in a restaurant.—

Anyway Marya is here: why don't we talk about something lofty and intellectual? *She's* taking a philosophy course—if she can't tell us the meaning of life no one can."

"You and Richard haven't quarrelled, have you?" Mrs. Skillman said.

Imogene raised her left hand and showed the diamond ring to her mother, saying, "*Please* don't worry, I haven't given it back, it's safe." To Marya she said lightly: "Mother would be mortified if Dickie demanded it back. It's somebody's old dead socialite *grandmother's*."

"Imogene," Mr. Skillman said, his voice edged with impatience, "you really shouldn't tease so much. I've just read that teasing is a form of aggression . . . did you know that?"

"Not that I'd give it back if Dickie *did* demand it," Imogene laughed. "It's mine, I've earned it, let him *sue* to get it back—right, Marya?—he's going to be a hotshot lawyer after all. Let him *practice*."

Everyone, including Marya, laughed as if Imogene had said something unusually witty; and Imogene, in the cool voice she used to summon the houseboys at her sorority, asked a passing waiter for more wine.

Richard.

"Dickie."

Am I jealous of someone called "Dickie," Marya wondered, lying sprawled and slovenly across her bed. She was doing rough, impatient charcoal sketches of imaginary faces—beetle-browed, glowering, defiantly ugly—that inevitably turned out to be forms of her own.

In Imogene's cluttered room on the second floor of the baronial sorority house Marya had come upon, to her astonishment, copies of *Bride* magazine. She leafed through them, jeering, while Imogene hid her face in laughing protestation. Wedding gowns! Satin and pearls! Veils made of antique lace! Orange blossoms! Shoes covered in white silk! And what is this, Marya said, flapping the pages in Imogene's direction,—a wedding-cake bridegroom to go with it all?—standing a little out of the range of the camera's focus, amiable and blurred.

"Ah, but you'll have to be a bridesmaid," Imogene said dryly. "Or a maid of honor."

Imogene showed her snapshots of the legendary Richard, flicking them like playing cards. Marya saw that, yes, Richard was a handsome young man—dark strong features, a slightly heavy chin, intelligent eyes. He was demanding, perhaps; an excellent match for Imogene. But it was difficult, Marya thought, to believe that the person in the snapshots—*this* person, standing with his hands on his hips, his hair lifting in the wind—would be capable of loving Imogene as much as she required being loved.

Imogene threw herself across her bed, lay on her back, let her long hair dangle to the floor. Her belly was stretched flat; her pelvic bones protruded. She smoothed her shirt across her abdomen with long nervous fingers. ". . . The first time I came with him," she said hesitantly, but with a breathy laugh, "it wasn't . . . you know . . . it wasn't with him inside me, the way you're supposed to . . . I was afraid of that then, I thought I might get pregnant. And he was so big, I thought he'd hurt me, they're *very* big compared to . . . compared to us. The first time it worked for me he was, well, you know, kissing me there . . . he'd gotten all crazy and wild and I couldn't stop him, and I never thought I would let anyone do that . . . I'd *heard* about that . . . because . . . oh Marya, am I embarrassing you? . . . because afterward,'' she said, laughing shrilly, ''they only want to kiss you: and it's disgusting.''

She rolled over amidst the tumble of things strewn on her bed and hid her face from Marya.

After a long time she said, her breath labored, her face still turned away: ''Am I embarrassing you?''

Marya's throat and chest were so constricted, she couldn't reply.

A Marya Knauer anecdote, told by Imogene with peals of cruel ribald laughter. . . .

Imogene insisted that Marya accompany her on a date, yes a ''date,'' an actual ''date'' (though it was generally thought that Marya shunned men because she imagined they weren't *serious* enough). Her escort was Matthew Fein, of all people—Matthew who had seemed to dislike Marya but who in fact (so Imogene revealed) had simply been afraid of her.

''Afraid of me?—you're being ridiculous,'' Marya said. She hardly knew whether to be hurt or flattered.

''Of course he's afraid of you, or was,'' Imogene said. ''And my poor sorority sisters!—they told me afterward they'd never seen such eyes as yours—taking them all in and condemning them! *Those assholes!*''

It would be an ordinary evening, Imogene promised, no need to dress up, no *need* for the high-heels-stockings routine, though it was perfectly all right (so Imogene said innocently) if Marya wanted to comb her hair. Imogene's date for the evening was a senior in business administration and advertising whose name Marya never caught, or purposefully declined to hear. They drove out to a suburban mall to see a movie—in fact it was a pretentious French ''film''—and then they went to a local Italian restaurant where everyone, excepting of course Marya, drank too much; and then they drove to the water-tower hill where numerous other cars were parked, their headlights off. Marya stiffened. Matthew had not yet touched her but she knew that he would be kissing her in another minute; and she had no idea of how to escape gracefully.

''. . . Few minutes?'' Imogene murmured from the front seat.

She was sending them away!—Marya saw with disbelief that, by the time she and Matthew climbed out of the car, Imogene and her date were locked in a ravenous embrace. One would have thought the two of them lovers; one would have thought them at least fond of each other. Marya's heart was beating frantically. That bitch! That bitch! Marya worried that she might suffocate—she couldn't seem to catch her breath.

Matthew took her cold unresisting hand. He slipped his arm around her shoulders.

They were meant to stroll for a few minutes along the darkened path, to contemplate, perhaps, the view of Port Oriskany below, all sparkling winking lights. A romantic sight, no doubt. Beautiful in its way. Matthew was saying something rather forced—making a joke of some kind—about the French movie?—about Imogene's reckless behavior?—but Marya interrupted. "Isn't she supposed to be engaged?" she asked. "Yes, I suppose so," Matthew said in resignation, "but she does this all the time. It's just Imogene." "She does this all the *time*?" Marya said, "but why—?" Matthew laughed uncomfortably. He was not quite Marya's height and his dark eyes shied away from hers. "I don't know," he said defensively, "—as I said, it's just Imogene, it's her business. Why shouldn't she do what she wants to do? Don't be angry with *me*."

He was nervous yet keenly excited; Marya sensed his sexual agitation. Behind them, parked along the gravelled drive, were lovers' cars, one after another; from this distance, the car in which Imogene and her "date" were pawing at each other was undistinguishable from the others.

"You might not approve," Matthew said, his voice edged now with an air of authority, "—but Imogene is a free soul, she does what she wants, I don't suppose she actually *lies* to her fiancé. He'd have to allow her some freedom, you know, or she'd break off the engagement."

"You know a lot about her," Marya said.

"Imogene is a close friend of mine, we've worked together . . . I was stage manager for *Hedda Gabler*, don't you remember?"

"It's all so . . . trivial," Marya said slowly. "So degrading."

"What do you mean?"

"Oh—this."

"This—?"

Marya indicated the cars parked along the drive. Her expression was contemptuous.

"You take an awfully superior attitude, don't you," Matthew said, with an attempt at jocular irony. He tightened his arm around her shoulders; he drew nearer. Marya could hear his quickened breathing.

Is this idiot really going to kiss me, Marya wondered. Her heart was still beating heavily; she could see Imogene's profile, the cameo-clear outline of her face, illuminated for an instant as the headlights were extinguished. Then she moved into the young man's embrace, she kissed him, slid her arms around his neck. . . .

"Does she make love with them?" Marya asked.

"Them—?"

"Different boys. Men. One week after another."

"I don't know," Matthew said resentfully. "I suppose so—if she wants to."

"I thought *you* were in love with her," Marya said mockingly.

"We're just friends," Matthew said, offended.

"Oh no," said Marya, "—everyone knows you're in *love* with her."

Matthew drew away from Marya and walked beside her without speaking. There was nothing for them to do, suddenly; not a thing left to say. It was still March and quite cold. Their footsteps sounded dully on the crusted snow. Marya thought, The various ways we seek out our humiliations. . . .

After a few minutes Matthew said something conciliatory about the night, the stars, the city lights, "infinity," certain remarks of Pascal's; but Marya made no effort to listen. She kept seeing Imogene kissing that near-stranger, Imogene locking her arms about his neck *as if he mattered. As if they were lovers.*

She was going to observe aloud, cynically, that making love was as good a way as any of passing the time, if you hadn't anything better to do, when Matthew, brave Matthew, turned to her and took hold of her shoulders and tried to kiss her. It was a desperate gesture—his breath smelled of sweet red wine—but Marya would have none of it. She shoved him roughly in the chest.

"Marya, for Christ's sake grow up," Matthew said angrily. "You're a big girl now—"

"Why should you *kiss* me?" Marya said, equally angry, "—when you don't even *like* me? When you know I don't like you in the slightest, when we haven't anything to say to each other, when we're just waiting for the evening to get finished!—in fact we've been made fools of, both of us. And now you want to kiss me," she said, jeering, "—just for something to do."

He began to protest but Marya dismissed him with a derisory wave of her hand. She was going to walk back to the residence, she said; she was through with them all. Especially Imogene.

Matthew followed along behind her for a few minutes, trying to talk her into coming back to the car. It was almost midnight, he said; the campus was two miles away; what if something happened to her. . . . Marya ignored him and walked faster, descending the hill past a slow stream of cars that were ascending it, their headlights blinding her eyes. She lowered her head, tried to hide her face, her hands thrust deep in the pockets of her camel's hair coat. At first she was furious—almost sick with fury—her head rang with accusations against Imogene—but the cold still night air was so invigorating, so wonderfully cleansing, she felt quite good by the time she got to Maynard House, not very long after midnight. She felt *very* good.

Next day, Sunday, Imogene stood at the downstairs desk ringing Marya's buzzer repeatedly, one two three four, one two three four, and then one long rude ring, until Marya appeared at the top of the stairs, her hair in a towel. "Who the hell—?" she called down. She and Imogene stared at each other. Then Imogene said contemptuously, "Here's your purse, you left your purse in the car, Knauer. D'you know, Knauer, your behavior is getting eccentric; it isn't even amusing, just what if something had happened to you last night—walking back here all alone—a college girl, in some of those neighborhoods!—don't you think Lyle and Matt and I would feel responsible? But *you*," she said, her voice rising, "—*you* haven't the slightest sense of—of responsibility to other people—"

"Just leave the purse," Marya said, leaning over the bannister. "Leave it and go back to screwing what's-his-name—that's *your* responsibility—"

"Go screw yourself!" Imogene shouted. "Go fuck yourself!"

"Go fuck *yourself!*" Marya shouted.

As the stories sifted back to Marya, over a period of a week or ten days, they became increasingly disturbing, ugly.

In one version Marya Knauer had been almost attacked—that is, raped—in a black neighborhood near the foot of Tower Hill; and had run back to her residence hall, hysterical and sobbing. It was an even graver insult that her purse had been taken from her—her purse and all her money.

In another version, Marya was so panicked at being simply touched by her date (she was a virgin, she was frigid, she'd never been kissed before) that she ran from the car, hysterical and panting . . . ran all the way back to campus. The boy was a blind date, someone in drama, or maybe business administration, it was all a total surprise to him that Marya Knauer was so . . . crazy.

In a third improbable version it was Imogene Skillman's fiancé who offered to take Marya back to the residence, because she was so upset—having a breakdown of some kind—and when they were halfway there she threw herself on him in the car *while he was actually driving.* And then, ashamed, she opened the car door and jumped out *while the car was still in motion.*

"It's Imogene," Marya said, licking her numbed lips. "She's making these things up . . . Why is she *doing* this to me . . . !"

There were vague rumors too that Marya had borrowed small sums of money from Imogene. And items of clothing as well—the camel's hair coat, for instance. (Because she hadn't a coat of her own. Because her coat had literally gone to shreds. Because she was so *poor,* a scholarship student from the hills, practically a *hillbilly.* . . .) As far as she was concerned, Imogene was reported saying, Marya Knauer could keep the coat if she was that desperate. Imogene no longer wanted it back.

Marya telephoned Imogene and accused her of telling lies, of telling slanderous tales. "Do you think I don't know who's behind this?" Marya cried. But Imogene hung up at once: Imogene was too wise to reply.

Marya began to see how people watched her . . . smiling covertly as she passed. They were pitying her, yet merciless. They knew. Marya Knauer with all her pretensions, Marya Knauer who had made a fool of herself with another girl's fiancé, Marya Knauer who was cracking up. . . .

In the fluorescent-lit dining hall she sat alone in an alcove, eating quickly, her head-bowed; it was too much trouble to remove her plates and glass of water from the tray. Two boys passed near and she heard them laugh softly. . . . *That* the one? There? one of them whispered. She turned back to her book (. . . *the thought of suicide is a strong consolation, one can get through many a bad night with it*) but the print danced crazily in her eyes.

"Do you think I don't know who's behind this,—who's responsible?" Marya asked aloud, in anguish, in the privacy of her room. She tried to lock her door from the inside—as if there were any danger of being interrupted, invaded—but the doors in Maynard, as in university housing generally, did not lock in that direction.

At about this time Marya was notified that a short story she had submitted to a national competition had placed first; and, not long afterward—within a week or ten days, in fact—she learned that another story, sent out blindly and naively to a distinguished literary magazine, was accepted for publication.

She thought of telephoning Wilma and Everard . . . she thought of telephoning Imogene . . . running along the corridors of Maynard House, knocking on doors, sharing her good news. But her elation was tempered almost at once by a kind of sickened dread—she was going to be unequal to the task of whatever it was (so her panicked thoughts raced, veered) she might be expected to do.

Lately her "serious" writing frightened her. Not just the content itself—though the content was often wild, disturbing, unanticipated—but the emotional and psychological strain it involved. She could write all night long, sprawled across her bed, taking notes, drafting out sketches and scenes, narrating a story she seemed to be hearing in a kind of trance; she could write until her hand ached and her eyes filled with tears and she felt that another pulsebeat would push her over the brink—into despair, into madness, into sheer extinction. Nothing is worth this, she told herself very early one morning, nothing can be worth this, she thought, staring at herself in the mirror of the third floor bathroom,—a ghastly hollowed-eyed death's head of a face, hardly recognizable as Marya, as a girl of nineteen.

Give up. Don't risk it. *Don't* risk it.

So she cautioned herself, so she gave and took warning. There was another kind of writing—highly conscious, cerebral, critical, discursive—which she found far easier; far less dangerous. She was praised for it lavishly, given the highest grades, the most splendid sort of encouragement. She should plan, her professors said, to go on to graduate school . . . they would advise her, help her get placed, help her make her way. . . . Don't risk this, she told herself, the waters will suck you down and close over your head: I know the symptoms.

And she did, she did. As if she had lived a previous life and could recall vividly the anguish of . . . whatever it was that might happen.

One windy morning at the end of March she saw Imogene Skillman walking with several of her friends. Imogene in sunglasses, her hair blowing wild, her laughter shrill and childish, Imogene in tight-fitting jeans and a bulky white ski sweater, overlong in the sleeves. That slatternly waifish affect. . . . Marya stood watching. Staring. Poor Marya Knauer, staring. Why did you lie about me! she wanted to cry. Why did you betray me! But she stood silent, paralyzed, watching. No doubt a figure of pathos—or of comedy—her snarled black hair blowing wild as Imogene's, her skin grainy and sallow.

Of course Imogene saw her; but Imogene's eyes were discreetly hidden by the dark-tinted glasses. No need for her to give any sign of recognition. No need.

Marya wrote Imogene a muddled little note, the first week in April.

Things aren't going well for me, I missed a philosophy exam & have no excuse & can't make myself lie. I don't know . . . am I unhappy (is it that simple?) Why don't you drop by & see me sometime . . . or I could come over there & see you. . . .

Yet she felt a revulsion for Imogene; she *really* disliked her. That lazy drunken dip of her head, her lipstick smeared across her face, sliding her arms around the neck of . . . whoever it had been: kissing open-mouthed, simulating passion. Would you two let us alone for a few minutes, Imogene drawled,—Would you two like to go for a stroll, for a few minutes?

I'll come over there, Marya wrote, *and strangle you with that pretentious braid of yours.*

In all she wrote a dozen notes, some by hand and some on the typewriter. But she sent only the first ("why don't you drop by & see me sometime . . . or I could come over there & see you"), not expecting, and not receiving, an answer.

What is fictitious in a friendship, Marya pondered, and what is "real": the world outside the head, the world *inside*: but whose world?—from whose point of view?

If Imogene died. . . .

If Imogene were dying. . . .

She wouldn't lift a hand to prevent that death!—so she thought.

At the same time she quizzed herself about how to respond, should Imogene really ask her to be a bridesmaid. (She had declined being a bridesmaid at Alice's wedding; but then she had the excuse of schoolwork, distance.) Imogene's wedding was going to be a costly affair held in Long Beach, New York sometime the following year. The bridesmaid's dress, the shoes . . . the shoes alone . . . would be staggeringly expensive.

I can't afford it, Marya would say.

I can't afford *you.*

Though they hadn't any classes together this semester Marya learned that Imogene had been absent from one of her lectures for three days running. So she simply went, one rainy April afternoon, to Imogene's residence—to that absurd white-columned "house" on Masefield Avenue—and rapped hard on Imogene's door; and let herself in before Imogene could call out sleepily, who is it . . . ?

The shades were crookedly drawn. Clothes and towels and books were strewn about. Imogene lay half-undressed on the bed with the quilted spread pulled over her; the room smelled of something acrid and medicinal.

"Oh Marya," Imogene said guiltily.

"Are you sick?" Marya asked.

They had both spoken at the same time.

". . . a headache, cramps, nothing worth mentioning," Imogene said hoarsely. ". . . the tail-end of this shitty flu that's been going around."

Marya stood with her hands on her hips, regarding Imogene in bed. Imogene's skin looked oddly coarse, her hair lay in spent greasy tangles on the pillow, spilling off the edge of the bed; her body was flat, curiously immobile. Without makeup she looked both young and rather ravaged. "If you're really sick, if you need a doctor, your sorority sisters will see to it," Marya said half-mockingly.

"I'm not really sick," said Imogene at once. "I'm resting."

After a long pause Marya said, as if incidentally: ''You told so many lies about me.''

Imogene coughed feebly. ''They weren't exactly *lies*, there was an essence. . . .''

''They were lies,'' Marya said. ''I wanted to strangle you.''

Imogene lay without moving, her hands flat on her stomach. She said in a childish vague voice: ''Oh nobody believed anything, it was just . . . talk . . . spinning tales. . . . You know, thinking ''What if'' . . . that sort of thing. Anyway there was an *essence* that was true.''

Marya was pacing about the room, the balls of her feet springy, the tendons of her calves strained. ''I don't intend to let you destroy me,'' she said softly. ''I don't even intend to do poorly in my courses.'' She brushed her hair out of her face and half-smiled at Imogene—a flash of hatred. ''You won't make me lose my perfect record,'' she said.

''Won't I,'' said Imogene.

Marya laughed. She said: ''But why did you concoct a story about your fiancé and me?—you know I've never even met him; I don't have any interest in meeting him.''

''Yes you do,'' Imogene said, a little sharply. ''You're jealous of him—of him and me.''

''You're angry that I'm not jealous *enough*,'' Marya said. ''Do you think I'd want to sleep with your precious, 'Dickie'?''

''You think so goddam fucking highly of yourself, don't you,'' Imogene said, sitting up, adjusting a pillow impatiently behind her. ''*You* can't be cracked open, can you?—a nut that can't be cracked,'' she said, laughing, yawning. ''A tight little virgin, I suppose. And Catholic too!—what a joke! Very very proud of yourself.''

''Why didn't you talk to me on the phone, why didn't you answer my note?'' Marya asked quietly.

''Why did you avoid me on campus?''

''Avoid you when?''

''Why do you always look the other way?''

''Look the other way *when*—?''

''All the time.''

Marya was striking her hands, her fists, lightly together. She drew a deep shaky breath. ''As for the coat—you *gave* me the coat. Your precious Salvation Army gesture. You *gave* me the coat, you *forced* it on me.''

''Oh Knauer, nobody forces anything on *you*,'' Imogene said, sneering, ''What bullshit—!''

''I want to know why you've been spreading lies about me and ridiculing me behind my back,'' Marya said levelly.

Imogene pulled at her hair in a lazy, mawkishly theatrical gesture. ''Hey. Did I tell you. I'm transferring out of here next year,'' she said. ''I'm going to school somewhere in New York, N.Y.U. probably. The drama courses are too *restrained* here, there's too much crap about *tradition*. . . .''

''I said I want to know *why*.''

"Oh for Christ's sweet sake what are you talking about!" Imogene cried. "I'm sick, my head is spinning, if you don't leave me alone I'm going to puke all over everything. I haven't been to a class in two weeks and I don't give a damn but I refuse to give *you* the satisfaction. . . . Transfer to New York, Marya, why don't you: you know you think you're too good for us *here*."

Marya stared at her, trembling. She had a vision of running at her friend and pummelling her with her fists—the two of them fighting, clawing, grunting in silence.

"Your jealousy, your morbid possessiveness. . . ." Imogene was saying wildly, her eyes wide, ". . . the way you sat in judgment of my parents . . . my poor father trying so hard to be *nice* to you, to be *kind*, because he felt *sorry* for you . . . and my mother too. . . . 'Is she one of your strays and misfits?' Mother said, 'another one of that gang that will turn on you'. . . . As for my sorority sisters. . . ."

Marya said slowly, groping: "And what about you? You're spoiled, you're vicious. . . . And you don't even act that well: people here baby you, lie to you, tell you the kind of crap you want to hear."

At this Imogene threw herself back against the flattened pillows, laughing, half-sobbing. "Yes," she said. "Good. Now leave me alone."

"Do you think they tell you anything else?—anything else but crap?" Marya said carelessly, "—people who are in love with you? People who don't even know who you *are*?"

Imogene pawed at the bedspread and pulled it roughly over herself. She lay very still but Marya could hear her labored breath. ". . . I took some aspirin before you came in, I want to sleep, maybe you'd better let me alone. I think you'd better let me alone."

She closed her eyes, she waved Marya away with a languid gesture.

"Good-bye, Marya!" she whispered.

On the sidewalk outside the house Marya took out the earrings boldly to examine them.

The Aztec ones, the barbarian-princess ones, bronze and red and blue, burnishing, gleaming. . . . Marya had seen her hand reach out to take them but she did not remember *taking* them from the room.

She tossed them in the palm of her hand as she strode along Masefield Avenue, smiling, grinning. No one, she thought in triumph, can keep me from my perfect record.

She went that day to an earring shop down on Fairfield Street; asked to have her ears pierced and Imogene's splendid earrings inserted. But the proprietor told her that wasn't the procedure; first, gold studs are inserted . . . then, after a few weeks, when the wounds are healed. . . .

No, Marya insisted, put in *these*. I don't have time to waste.

But there was the danger of infection, she was told. Everything has to be germ-free, antiseptic. . . .

"I don't give a damn about that," Marya said fiercely. "These earrings *are* gold. Put antiseptic on *them.* . . . Just pierce my ears and put them in and I'll pay you and that's all.''

''Do you have five dollars?'' the young man said curtly.

Crossing the quadrangle between Stafford Hall and the chapel one cold May afternoon, Marya caught sight of Imogene approaching her. It had been approximately two weeks since the theft of the earrings—two weeks during which Marya had worn the earrings everywhere, for everyone to see, to comment upon, to admire. She and Imogene had frequently noticed each other, usually at a distance, though once in rather close quarters on a crowded stairway; and Marya had been amused at Imogene's shocked expression; and the clumsy way she'd turned aside, pretending she hadn't seen Marya and Marya's new earrings.

Not a very good actress after all, Marya thought.

Now, however, Imogene was approaching her head-on, though her movements were rather forced, wooden. Marya didn't slacken her pace; she was headed for the library. She wore her raincoat half-unbuttoned, her head was bare, her hair loose, the earrings swung heavily as she walked, tugged at her earlobes. (Yes, her earlobes *were* sore. Probably infected, Marya thought indifferently, waking in the night to small stabs of pain.)

Imogene's face was dead white, and not very attractive. Something horsy about that face, after all, Marya thought. Her mouth was strained, and the tendons in her neck were clearly visible as, suddenly, she ran at Marya. She was screaming something about ''hillbilly bitch''—''thief''—She grabbed at Marya's left ear, she would have ripped the earring out of Marya's flesh, but Marya was too quick for her: she knew instinctively what Imogene would try to do.

She struck Imogene's hand aside, and gave her a violent shove; Imogene slapped her hard across the face; Marya slapped *her.* ''You bitch!'' Imogene cried. ''You won't get away with this! *I know you!*''

All their books had fallen to the sidewalk, Imogene's leather bag was tripping her up, passers-by stopped to stare, incredulous. What a sight, Imogene Skillman and Marya Knauer fighting, in front of the chapel,—both in blue jeans, both livid with rage. Marya was shouting, ''Don't you touch me, you! What do you mean, touching *me*!'' She was the better fighter, crouching with her knees bent, like a man, swinging at Imogene, striking her on the jaw. Not a slap but an actual punch: Marya's fist was unerring.

The blow was a powerful one, for Marya struck from the shoulder. Imogene's head snapped back—blood appeared on her mouth—she staggered backward and swayed, almost lost her balance. ''Oh, Marya,'' she said.

Marya snatched up her things and turned away. Her long fast stride and the set of her shoulders, the set of her head, must have indicated confidence; angry assurance; but in fact she was badly shaken . . . it was some time before she could catch her breath. When she turned to look back Imogene was sitting on the ground and a small crowd had gathered around her. You'll be all right, Marya thought, someone will always take care of *you.*

After that, very little happened.

Marya kept the earrings, though her ears *were* infected and she had to give up wearing them; Imogene Skillman never approached her again, never pressed charges; nor did anyone dare bring the subject up to either of the girls.

Marya's record remained perfect but Imogene did poorly at the end of the semester, failing two subjects; and, in place of transferring to another university she quit college altogether.

That fall, Marya learned that Imogene was living in New York City. She had broken off her engagement over the summer; she had joined a troupe of semiprofessional actors, and lived in an apartment off St. Mark's Square. It was said that she had a small role in an off-Broadway play scheduled to open sometime that winter but Marya never learned the title of the play, or when, precisely, it opened; or how successful it was.

One of Us

DORIS LESSING

Christmas ended, and Ben was two and a few months old. Paul was sent to a little nursery school down the road, to get him away from Ben. The naturally high-spirited and friendly child was becoming nervous and irritable. He had fits of tears or of rage, throwing himself on the floor screaming, or battering at Harriet's knees, trying to get her attention, which never seemed to leave Ben.

Dorothy went off to visit Sarah and her family.

Harriet was alone with Ben during the day. She tried to be with him as she had with the others. She sat on the floor with building blocks and toys you could push about. She showed him colourful pictures. She sang him little rhymes. But Ben did not seem to connect with the toys, or the blocks. He sat among the litter of bright objects and might put one block on another, looking at Harriet to see if this was what he should do. He stared hard at pictures held out to him, trying to decipher their language. He would never sit on Harriet's knees, but squatted by her, and when she said, "That's a bird, Ben, look—just like that bird on that tree. And that's a flower," he stared, and then turned away. Apparently it was not that he could not understand how this block fitted into that or how to make a pile of them, rather that he could not grasp the point of it all, nor of the flower, nor the bird. Perhaps he was too advanced for this sort of game? Sometimes Harriet thought he was. His response to her nursery pictures was that he went out into the garden and stalked a thrush on the lawn, crouching down and moving in a low fast run—and he nearly did catch the thrush. He tore some primroses off their stems, and stood with them in his hands, intently staring at them. Then he crushed them in his strong little fists and let them drop. He turned his head and saw Harriet looking at him: he seemed to be thinking that she wanted him to do something, but what? He stared at the spring flowers, looked up at a blackbird on a branch, and came slowly indoors again.

One day, he talked. Suddenly. He did not say, "Mummy," or "Daddy," or his own name. He said, "I want cake." Harriet did not even notice, at first, that he was talking. Then she did, and told everyone, "Ben's talking. He's using sentences." As their way was, the other children encouraged him: "That's very good, Ben," "Clever Ben!" But he took no notice of them. From then on he announced his needs. "I want that." "Give me that." "Go for a walk now." His voice was heavy and uncertain, each word separate, as if his brain were a lumber-house of ideas and objects, and he had to identify each one.

The children were relieved he was talking normally. "Hello, Ben," one would say. "Hello," Ben replied, carefully handing back exactly what he had been given. "How are you, Ben?" Helen asked. "How are you?" he replied. "No" said Helen, "now you must say, 'I'm very well, thank you,' or, 'I'm fine.' "

Ben stared while he worked it out. Then he said clumsily, "I'm very well."

He watched the children, particularly Luke and Helen, all the time. He studied how they moved, sat down, stood up; copied how they ate. He had understood that these two, the older ones, were more socially accomplished than Jane; and he ignored Paul altogether. When the children watched television, he squatted near them and looked from the screen to their faces, for he needed to know what reactions were appropriate. If they laughed, then, a moment later, he contributed a loud, hard, unnatural-sounding laugh. What was natural to him, it seemed, in the way of amusement was his hostile-looking teeth-bared grin, that looked hostile. When they became silent and still with attention, because of some exciting moment, then he tensed his muscles, like them, and seemed absorbed in the screen—but really he kept his eyes on them.

Altogether, he was easier. Harriet thought: Well, any ordinary child is at its most difficult for about a year after it gets to its feet. No sense of self-preservation, no sense of danger: they hurl themselves off beds and chairs, launch themselves into space, run into roads, have to be watched every second. . . . And they are also, she added, at their most charming, delightful, heartbreakingly sweet and funny. And then they gradually become sensible and life is easier.

Life had become easier . . . but this was only as she saw it, as Dorothy brought home to her.

Dorothy came back to this household after what she called "a rest" of some weeks, and Harriet could see her mother was preparing for a "real talk" with her.

"Now, girl, would you say that I am interfering? That I give you a lot of unwanted advice?"

They were sitting at the big table, mid-morning, with cups of coffee. Ben was where they could watch him, as always. Dorothy was trying to make what she said humorous, but Harriet felt threatened. Her mother's honest pink cheeks were bright with embarrassment, her blue eyes anxious.

"No," said Harriet. "You aren't. You don't."

"Well, now I'm going to have my say."

But she had to stop: Ben began banging a stone against a metal tray. He did this with all his force. The noise was awful, but the women waited until Ben stopped: interrupted, he would have raged and hissed and spat.

"You have five children," Dorothy said. "Not one. Do you realise that I might just as well be the mother of the others when I'm here? No, I don't believe you do, you've got so taken over by . . ."

Ben again banged the tray with his stone, in a frenzy of exulting accomplishment. It looked as if he believed he was hammering metal, forging something: one could easily imagine him, in the mines deep under the earth, with his kind. . . . Again they waited until he stopped the noise.

"It's not right," said Dorothy. And Harriet remembered how her mother's "That's not right!" had regulated her childhood.

"I'm getting on, you know," said Dorothy. "I can't go on like this, or I'll get ill."

Yes, Dorothy was rather thin, even gaunt. Yes, Harriet thought, full of guilt as usual, she should have noticed.

"And you have a husband, too," said Dorothy, apparently not knowing how she was turning the knife in her daughter's heart. "He's very good, you know, Harriet. I don't know how he puts up with it."

The Christmas after Ben became three only partly filled the house. A cousin of David's had said, "I've been inspired by you, Harriet! After all, I've got a home, too. It's not as big as yours, but it's a nice little house." Several of the family went there. But others said they were coming: made a point of coming, Harriet realised. These were the near relations.

Again a pet was brought. This time it was a big dog, a cheerful boisterous mongrel, Sarah's children's friend, but most particularly Amy's. Of course all the children loved him, but Paul most of all, and this made Harriet's heart ache, for they could have no dog or cat in their home. She even thought: Well, now Ben is more sensible, perhaps . . . But she knew it was impossible. She watched how the big dog seemed to know that Amy, the loving little child in the big ugly body, needed gentleness: he moderated his exuberance for her. Amy would sit by the dog with her arm around his neck, and if she was clumsy with him, he lifted his muzzle and gently pushed her away a little, or gave a small warning sound that said, "Be careful." Sarah said this dog was like a nursemaid to Amy. "Just like Nana in *Peter Pan*," the children said. But if Ben was in the room, the dog watched him carefully and went to lie in a corner, his head on his paws, stiff with attention. One morning when people were sitting around having breakfast, Harriet for some reason turned her head and saw the dog, asleep, and Ben going silently up to him in a low crouch, hands held out in front of him. . . .

"Ben!" said Harriet sharply. She saw those cold eyes turn towards her, caught a gleam of pure malice.

The dog, alerted, scrambled up, and his hair stood on end. He whined anxiously, and came into the part of the room where they all were, and lay down under the table.

Everyone had seen this, and sat silent, while Ben came to Dorothy and said, "I want milk." She poured him some, and he drank it down. Then he looked at them all staring at him. Again he seemed to be trying to understand them. He went into the garden, where they could see him, a squat little gnome, poking with a stick at the earth. The other children were upstairs somewhere.

Around the table sat Dorothy, with Amy on her lap, Sarah, Molly, Frederick, James, and David. Also Angela, the successful sister, "the coper," whose children were all normal.

The atmosphere made Harriet say defiantly, "All right, then, let's have it."

She thought it not without significance, as they say, that it was Frederick who said, "Now look here, Harriet, you've got to face it, he's got to go into an institution."

"Then we have to find a doctor who says he's abnormal," said Harriet. "Dr. Brett certainly won't."

"Get another doctor," said Molly. "These things can be arranged." The two large haystacky people, with their red well-fed faces, were united in determination, nothing vague about them now they had decided there was a crisis, and one that—even indirectly—threatened them. They looked like a pair of judges after a good lunch, Harriet thought, and glanced at David to see if she could share this criticism with him; but he was staring down at the table, mouth tight. He agreed with them.

Angela said, laughing, "Typical upper-class ruthlessness."

No one could remember that note being struck, or at least not so sharply, at this table before. Silence, and then Angela softened it with "Not that I don't agree."

"Of course you agree," said Molly. "Anyone sensible would have to."

"It's the way you said it," said Angela.

"What does it matter how it is said?" enquired Frederick.

"And who is going to pay for it?" asked David. "I can't. All I can do is to keep the bills paid, and that is with James's help."

"Well, James is going to have to bear the brunt of this one," said Frederick, "but we'll chip in." It was the first time this couple had offered any financial help. "Mean, like all their sort," the rest of the family had agreed; and now this judgement was being remembered. They would come for a stay of ten days and contribute a pair of pheasants, a couple of bottles of very good wine. Their "chipping in," everyone knew, wouldn't amount to much.

Full of division, the family sat silent.

Then James said, "I'll do what I can. But things are not as good as they were. Yachts are not everyone's priority in hard times.

Silence again, and everyone was looking at Harriet.

"You are funny people," she said, setting herself apart from them. "You've been here so often and you *know*—I mean, *you* really know what the problem is. What are we going to say to the people who run this institution?"

"It depends on the institution," said Molly, and her large person seemed full of energy, conviction: as if she had swallowed Ben whole and was digesting him, thought Harriet. She said, mildly enough, though she trembled, "You mean, we have to find one of those places that exist in order to take on children families simply want to get rid of?"

"Rich families," said Angela, with a defiant little sniff.

Molly, confronting impertinence, said firmly, "Yes. If there is no other kind of place. But one thing is obvious: if something isn't done, then it's going to be catastrophic."

"It *is* catastrophic," said Dorothy, firmly taking her position. "The other children . . . they're suffering. You're so involved with it, girl, that you don't see it."

"Look," said David, impatient and angry because he could not stand this, fibres tangled with Harriet, with his parents, being tugged and torn. "Look, I agree. And some time Harriet is going to have to agree. And as far as I am concerned, that time is now. I don't think I can stick it any longer." And now he did look at his wife, and it was a pleading, suffering look. *Please,* he was saying to Harriet. *Please.*

"Very well," said Harriet. "If some place can be found that . . ." And she began to cry.

Ben came in from the garden and stood watching them, in his usual position, which was apart from everyone else. He wore brown dungarees and a brown shirt, both in strong material. Everything he wore had to be thick, because he tore his clothes, destroyed them. With his yellowish stubbly low-growing hair, his stony unblinking eyes, his stoop, his feet planted apart and his knees bent, his clenched held-forward fists, he seemed more than ever like a gnome.

"She is crying," he remarked, of his mother. He took a piece of bread off the table and went out.

"All right," said Harriet, "what *are* you going to tell them?"

"Leave it to us," said Frederick.

"Yes," said Molly.

"My God!" said Angela, with a kind of bitter appreciation of them. "Sometimes when I'm with you, I understand everything about this country."

"Thank you," said Molly.

"Thank you," said Frederick.

"You aren't being fair, girl," said Dorothy.

"*Fair,*" said Angela, and Harriet, and Sarah, her daughters, almost all at once.

And then everyone but Harriet laughed. In this way was Ben's fate decided.

A few days later, Frederick rang to say that a place had been found and a car was coming for Ben. At once. Tomorrow.

Harriet was frantic: the haste of it, the—yes, ruthlessness! And the doctor who had authorised this? Or would? A doctor who had not even seen Ben? She said all this to David, and knew from his manner that a good deal had gone on behind her back. His parents had talked to him at his office. David had said something like "Yes, I'll see to it" when Molly, whom suddenly Harriet hated, had said, "You'll have to be firm with Harriet."

"It's either him or us," said David to Harriet. He added, his voice full of cold dislike for Ben, "He's probably just dropped in from Mars. He's going back to report on what he's found down here." He laughed—cruelly, it seemed to Harriet, who was silently taking in the fact—which of course she had half known already—that Ben was not expected to live long in this institution, whatever it was.

"He's a little child," she said. *"He's our child."*

"No, he's not," said David, finally. "Well, he certainly isn't mine."

They were in the living-room. Children's voices rose sharp and distant from the dark winter garden. On the same impulse, David and Harriet went to the window and pulled back the heavy curtains. The garden held dim shapes of tree and shrub, but the light from this warm room reached across the lawn to a shrub that was starkly black with winter, lit twiggy growths that showed a glitter of water, and illuminated the white trunk of a birch. Two small figures, indistinguishably unisex in their many-coloured padded jackets, trousers, woollen caps, emerged from the black under a holly thicket, and came forward. They were Helen and Luke, on some adventure. Both held sticks and were prodding them here and there into last year's leaves.

"Here it is!" Helen's voice rose in triumph, and the parents saw, emerging into the light on the end of the stick, the summer's lost red-and-yellow plastic ball. It was dirtied and squashed, but whole. The two children began a fast stamping dance around and around, the rescued ball held aloft in triumph. Then, suddenly, for no obvious reason, they came racing up to the French doors. The parents sat down on a sofa, facing the doors, which burst inwards, and there they were, two slight, elegant little creatures, with flaring red, frost-burned cheeks and eyes full of the excitements of the dark wilderness they had been part of. They stood breathing heavily, their eyes slowly adjusting to reality, the warm, lit family room and their parents sitting there looking at them. For a moment it was the meeting of two alien forms of life: the children had been part of some old savagery, and their blood still pounded with it; but now they had to let their wild selves go away while they rejoined their family. Harriet and David shared this with them, were with them in imagination and in memory, from their own childhoods: they could see themselves clearly, two adults, sitting there, tame, domestic, even pitiable in their distance from wildness and freedom.

Seeing their parents there alone, no other children around, and above all, no Ben, Helen came to her father, Luke to his mother, and Harriet and David embraced their two adventurous little children, *their* children, holding them tight.

Next morning the car, which was a small black van, came for Ben. Harriet had known it was coming, because David had not gone to work. He had stayed so as to "handle" her! David went upstairs, and brought down suitcases and holdalls that he had packed quietly while she was giving the children breakfast.

He flung these into the van. Then, his face set hard, so that Harriet hardly knew him, he picked Ben up from where he sat on the floor in the living-room, carried him to the van, and put him in. Then he came fast to Harriet, with the same hard set face, and put his arm around her, turned her away from the sight of the van, which was already on its way (she could hear yells and shouts coming from inside it), and took her to the sofa, where—still holding her tight—he said, over and over again, "We have to do it, Harriet. We have to." She was weeping with the shock of it, and with relief, and with gratitude to him, who was taking all the responsibility.

When the children came home, they were told Ben had gone to stay with someone.

"With Granny?" asked Helen, anxious.

"No."

Four pairs of suspicious, apprehensive eyes became suddenly full of relief. Hysterical relief. The children danced about, unable to help themselves, and then pretended it was a game they had thought up then and there.

At supper they were overbright, giggling, hysterical. But in a quiet moment Jane asked shrilly. "Are you going to send us away, too?" She was a stolid, quiet little girl. Dorothy in miniature, never saying anything unnecessary. But now her large blue eyes were fixed in terror on her mother's face.

"No, of course we aren't," said David, sounding curt.

Luke explained, "They are sending Ben away because he isn't really one of us."

In the days that followed, the family expanded like paper flowers in water. Harriet understood what a burden Ben had been, how he had oppressed them all, how much the children had suffered; knew that they had talked about it much more than the parents had wanted to know, had tried to come to terms with Ben. But now Ben was gone their eyes shone, they were full of high spirits, and they kept coming to Harriet with little gifts of a sweet or a toy, "This is for you, Mummy." Or they rushed up to kiss her, or stroke her face, or nuzzle to her like happy calves or foals. And David took days off from work to be with them all—to be with her. He was careful with her, tender. As if I were ill, she decided rebelliously. Of course she thought all the time of Ben, who was a prisoner somewhere. What kind of a prisoner? She pictured the little black van, remembered his cries of rage as he was taken away.

The days went by, and normality filled the house. Harriet heard the children talking about the Easter holidays. "It will be all right now that Ben isn't here," said Helen.

They had always understood so much more than she had wanted to acknowledge.

While she was part of the general relief, and could hardly believe she had been able to stand such strain, and for so long, she could not banish Ben from her mind. It was not with love, or even affection, that she thought of him, and she disliked herself for not being able to find one little spark of normal feeling: it was guilt and horror that kept her awake through the nights. David knew she was awake, though she did try to hide it.

Then one morning she started up out of sleep, out of a bad dream, though she did not know what, and she said, "I'm going to see what they are doing to Ben."

David opened his eyes, and lay silent, staring over his arm at the window.

He had been dozing, not asleep. She knew he had feared this, and there was something about him then that said to her: Right, then that's it, it's enough.

"David, I've got to."

"Don't," he said.

"I simply have to."

Again she knew from the way he lay there, not looking at her, and did not say anything more than that one syllable, that it was bad for her, that he was making decisions as he lay there. He stayed where he was for a few minutes, and then got out of bed, and went out of the room and downstairs.

When she had got her clothes on, she rang Molly, who was at once coldly angry. "No, I'm not going to tell you where it is. Now you've done it, then leave it alone."

But at last she did give Harriet the address.

Again Harriet was wondering why she was always treated like a criminal. Ever since Ben was born it's been like this, she thought. Now it seemed to her the truth, that everyone had silently condemned her. I have suffered a misfortune, she told herself; I haven't committed a crime.

Ben had been taken to a place in the North of England; it would be four or five hours' drive—perhaps more, if she was unlucky with the traffic. There was bad traffic, and she drove through grey wintry rain. It was early afternoon when she approached a large solid building of dark stone, in a valley high among moors she could hardly see for grey drifting rain. The place stood square and upright among dismal dripping evergreens, and its regular windows, three rows of them, were barred.

She entered a small entrance lobby that had a handwritten card tacked on the inner door: "Ring for Attendance." She rang, and waited, and nothing happened. Her heart was beating. She still surged with the adrenaline that had given her the impetus to come, but the long drive had subdued her, and this oppressive building was telling her nerves, if not her intelligence—for, after all, she had no facts to go on—that what she had feared was true. Yet she did not know exactly what that was. She rang again. The building was silent: she could hear the shrill of a bell a long way off in its interior. Again, nothing, and she was about to go around to the back when the door abruptly opened to show a slatternly girl wearing jerseys, cardigans, and a thick scarf. She had a pale little face under a mass of curly yellow hair that had a blue ribbon holding a queue like a sheep's tail. She seemed tired.

"Yes?" she asked.

Harriet saw, understanding what this meant, that people simply did not come here.

She said, already stubborn, "I'm Mrs. Lovatt and I've come to see my son."

It was evident that these were words this institution, whatever it was, did not expect to meet.

The girl stared, gave an involuntary little shake of the head that expressed incapacity, and then said, "Dr. MacPherson isn't here this week." She was Scottish, too, and her accent was strong.

"Someone must be deputising for him," said Harriet decisively.

The girl fell back before Harriet's manner, smiling uncertainly, and very worried. She muttered, "Wait here, then," and went inside. Harriet followed her before the big door was shut to exclude her. The girl did glance around, as if she planned to say, You must wait outside, but instead she said, "I'll fetch someone," and went on into the dark caverns of a corridor that had small ceiling lights all along it, hardly disturbing the gloom. There was a smell of disinfectant. Absolute silence. No, after a time Harriet became aware of a high thin screaming that began, and stopped, and went on again, coming from the back of the building.

Nothing happened. Harriet went out into the vestibule, which was already darkening with the approaching night. The rain was now a cold deluge, silent and regular. The moors had disappeared.

She rang again, decisively, and returned to the corridor.

Two figures appeared, a long way off under the pinpoints of the ceiling lights, and came towards her. A young man, in a white coat that was not clean, was followed by the girl, who now had a cigarette in her mouth and was screwing up her eyes from the smoke. Both looked tired and uncertain.

He was an ordinary young man, though worn down in a general way; taken bit by bit, hands, face, eyes, he was unremarkable, but there was something desperate about him, as if he contained anger, or hopelessness.

"You can't be here," he said, in a flurried indecisive way. "We don't have visiting days here." His voice was South London, flat and nasal.

"But I am here," said Harriet. "I am here to see my son Ben Lovatt."

And suddenly he took in a breath, and looked at the girl, who pursed her lips together and raised her eyebrows.

"Listen," said Harriet. "I don't think you understand. I'm not just going away, you know. I've come to see my son, and that is what I am going to do."

He knew she meant it. He slowly nodded, as if saying, Yes, but that isn't the point. He was looking hard at her. She was being given a warning, and from someone who was taking the responsibility for it. He might be a rather pitiable young man, and certainly an overtired and inadequately fed one, doing this job because he could not get another, but the weight of his position—the unhappy weight of it—was speaking through him, and his expression and his reddened, smoke-tired eyes were severe, authoritative, to be taken seriously.

"When people dump their kids here, they don't come and see them after," he said.

"You see, you don't understand at all," said the girl.

Harriet heard herself explode with "I'm sick of being told I don't understand this and that. I'm the child's mother. I'm Ben Lovatt's mother. Do *you* understand that?"

Suddenly they were all three together in understanding, even in desperate acceptance of some kind of general fatality.

He nodded, and said, "Well, I'll go and see . . ."

"And I am coming, too," she said.

This really did alert him. "Oh no," he exclaimed, "you are *not*!" He said something to the girl, who began running surprisingly fast down the corridor. "You stay here," he said to Harriet, and strode after the girl.

Harriet saw the girl turn right and disappear, and without thinking she opened a door at her right hand. She saw the young man's arm raised in imprecation, or warning, while what was behind that door reached her.

She was at the end of a long ward, which had any number of cots and beds along the walls. In the cots were—monsters. While she strode rapidly through the ward to the door at the other end, she was able to see that every bed or cot held an infant or small child in whom the human template had been wrenched out of pattern, sometimes horribly, sometimes slightly. A baby like a comma, great lolling head on a stalk of a body . . . then something like a stick insect, enormous bulging eyes among stiff fragilities that were limbs . . . a small girl all blurred, her flesh guttering and melting . . . a doll with chalky swollen limbs, its eyes wide and blank, like blue ponds, and its mouth open, showing a swollen little tongue. A lanky boy was skewed, one half of his body sliding from the other. A child seemed at first glance normal, but then Harriet saw there was no back to its head; it was all face, which seemed to scream at her. Rows of freaks, nearly all asleep, and all silent. They were literally drugged out of their minds. Well, nearly silent: there was a dreary sobbing from a cot that had its sides shielded with blankets. The high intermittent screaming, nearer now, still assaulted her nerves. A smell of excrement, stronger than the disinfectant. Then she was out of the nightmare ward and in another corridor, parallel to the one she had first seen, and identical. At its end she saw the girl, followed by the young man, come a little way towards her and then again turn right. . . . Harriet ran fast, hearing her feet thud on the boards, and turned where they did, and was in a tiny room holding trolleys of medicines and drugs. She ran through this and was now in a long cement-floored passage that had doors with inspection grilles in them all along the wall facing her. The young man and the girl were opening one of these doors as she arrived beside them. All three were breathing heavily.

"Shit," said the young man, meaning her being there.

"Literally," said Harriet as the door opened on a square room whose walls were of white shiny plastic that was buttoned here and there and looked like fake expensive leather upholstery. On the floor, on a green foam-rubber mattress, lay Ben. He was unconscious. He was naked, inside a strait-jacket. His pale yellow tongue protruded from his mouth. His flesh was dead white, greenish. Everything—walls, the floor, and Ben—was smeared with excrement. A pool of dark yellow urine oozed from the pallet, which was soaked.

"I told you not to come!" shouted the young man. He took Ben's shoulders and the girl Ben's feet. From the way they touched the child, Harriet saw they were not brutal; that was not the point at all. They lifted Ben thus—for in this way they had to touch very little of him—out of this room, along the corridor a little way, and through another door. She followed, and stood watching. This was a room that had sinks all along one wall, an immense bath, and a sloping cement shelf with plugs all along it. They put Ben on this shelf, unwound the strait-jacket, and, having adjusted the temperature of the water, began washing him down with a hose that was attached to one of the taps. Harriet leaned against the wall, watching. She was shocked to the point where she felt nothing at all. Ben did not move. He lay like a drowned fish on the slab, was turned over several times by the girl, when the young man interrupted the hosing process for the purpose, and was finally carried by them both to another slab, where they dried him and then took a clean strait-jacket from a pile and put it on him.

"Why?" demanded Harriet, fierce. They did not answer.

They took the child, trussed, unconscious, his tongue lolling, out of the room, down the corridor, and into another room that had a cement shelf like a bed in it. They put Ben on it, and then both stood up and sighed: "Phew."

"Well, there he is," said the young man. He stood for a moment, eyes closed, recovering from the ordeal, and then lit a cigarette. The girl put out her hand for one; he gave it to her. They stood smoking, looking at Harriet in an exhausted, defeated way.

She did not know what to say. Her heart was hurting as it would for one of her own, real children, for Ben looked more ordinary than she had ever seen him, with those hard cold alien eyes of his closed. Pathetic: she had never seen him as pathetic before.

"I think I'll take him home," she said.

"It's up to you," said the young man shortly.

The girl was looking curiously at Harriet, as if she were part of the phenomenon that was Ben, of the same nature. She asked, "What are you going to do with him?" She added, and Harriet recognised fear in her voice, "He's so strong—I've never seen anything like it."

"None of us have seen anything like it," said the young man.

"Where are his clothes?"

Now he laughed, scornful, and said, "You're going to put his clothes on and take him home, just like that?"

"Why not? He was wearing clothes when he came."

The two attendants—nurses, orderlies, whatever they were—exchanged looks. Then both took a drag on their cigarettes.

He said, "I don't think you understand, Mrs. Lovatt. How far have you got to go, for a start?"

"Four or five hours' driving."

He laughed again, at the impossibility of it—of *her*, Harriet—and said, "He's going to come round on the journey, and then what?"

"Well, he'll see me," she said, and saw from their faces that she was being stupid. "All right, then, what do you advise?"

"Wrap him in a couple of blankets, over the strait-jacket," said the girl.

"And then drive like hell," he said.

The three now stood in silence, looking at each other, a long, sober look.

"You try doing this job," said the girl suddenly, full of rage against fate. "You just try it. Well, I'm leaving at the end of this month."

"And so am I, no one sticks it longer than a few weeks," said the man.

"All right," said Harriet. "I'm not going to complain, or anything."

"You'll have to sign a form. We have to be covered," he said.

But they could not easily find the form. At last, after a lot of rummaging about in a filing cabinet, they produced a slip of paper, mimeographed years ago, that said Harriet acquitted the institution of all responsibility.

Now she picked Ben up, touching him for the first time. He was deadly cold. He lay heavy in her arms, and she understood the words "a dead weight."

She went out into the corridor, saying, "I'm not going through that ward again."

"Who could blame you?" said the young man, wearily sarcastic. He had got hold of a load of blankets, and they wrapped Ben in two, carried him out to the car, laid him on the back seat, and piled more blankets over him. Only his face showed.

She stood with the two young people by the car. They could hardly see each other. Apart from the car lights, and the lights of the building, it was dark. Water squelched under foot. The young man took out of his overall pocket a plastic package containing a syringe, a couple of needles, and some ampules.

"You had better take these," he said.

Harriet hesitated, and the girl said, "Mrs. Lovatt, I don't think you realise—"

She nodded, took the package, got in.

"You can give him up to four shots a day, not more," said the young man.

As she was about to let the clutch pedal out, she asked, "Tell me, how long do you think he would have lasted?"

Their faces were white patches in the gloom, but she could see that he shook his head, turning away. The girl's voice came: "None of them last long. But this one . . . he's very strong. He's the strongest any of us have seen."

"Which means he would have lasted longer?"

"No," he said. "No, that's not it at all. Because he's so strong, he fights all the time, and so he has to have bigger shots. It kills them."

"All right," said Harriet. "Well, thank you both."

They stood watching as she drove off, but almost at once vanished into the wet dark. As she rounded the drive, she saw them standing in the dimly lit porch, close together, as if reluctant to go in.

She drove as fast as she could through the wintry rain, avoiding the main roads, keeping an eye on the heap of blankets behind her. About half-way home she saw the blankets heave and convulse, and Ben woke with a bellow of rage, and thrashed about, landing on the floor of the car, where he began to scream, not like the thin high automatic screaming she had heard at the institution but screams of fear that vibrated through her. She stuck it out for half an hour, feeling the thuds that Ben made vibrate through the car. She was looking for a lay-by that had no other car in it, and when she found one, she stopped, let the engine run, and took out the syringe. She knew how to use it, from some illness of the other children. She broke open the capsule, which had no brand name on it, and filled the syringe. Then she leaned over the back of the seat. Ben, naked except for the strait-jacket, and blue with cold, was heaving and struggling and bellowing. His eyes looked up at her in a glare of hate. He didn't recognise her, she thought. She did not dare unwind the jacket. She was afraid of injecting him anywhere near his neck. At last she managed to grab, and hold, an ankle, jabbed the needle into the lower part of his calf, and waited until he went limp: it took a few moments. What was this stuff?

Again she put him on the back seat under the blankets, and now she drove on the main roads home. She got there at about eight. The children would be sitting around the kitchen table. And David would be with them: he would not have gone to work.

With Ben a mound of blankets in her arms, his face covered, she went into the living-room, and looked over the low wall to where they all sat around the big table. Luke. Helen. Jane. Little Paul. And David, his face set and angry. And very tired.

She remarked, "They were killing him," and saw that David would not forgive her for saying this in front of the children. All showed fear.

She went straight up the stairs to the big bedroom, and through it to "the baby's room," and put Ben on the bed. He was waking up. And then it began, the fighting, the heaving, the screaming. Again he was on the floor, rolling around on it, and again he flexed and bent and thrashed, and his eyes were pure hate.

She could not take off the strait-jacket.

She went down into the kitchen, and got milk and biscuits while her family sat and watched her in total silence.

The Antigone of Sophocles

An English version by Dudley Fitts & Robert Fitzgerald

Characters

ANTIGONE
ISMENE
EURYDICE
CREON
HAIMON
TEIRESIAS
A SENTRY
A MESSENGER
CHORUS

SCENE. *Before the palace of Creon, King of Thebes. A central double door, and two lateral doors. A platform extends the length of the façade, and from this platform three steps lead down into the "orchestra," or chorus-ground.*

TIME. *Dawn of the day after the repulse of the Argive army from the assault on Thebes.*

PROLOGUE

[*Antigone and Ismene enter from the central door of the palace.*]

Antigone. Ismene, dear sister,
You would think that we had already suffered enough
For the curse on Oedipus.
I cannot imagine any grief
That you and I have not gone through. And now—
Have they told you of the new decree of our King Creon?

Ismene. I have heard nothing: I know
That two sisters lost two brothers, a double death
In a single hour; and I know that the Argive army
Fled in the night; but beyond this, nothing.

Antigone. I thought so. And that is why I wanted you
To come out here with me. There is something we must do.

Ismene. Why do you speak so strangely?

Antigone. Listen, Ismene:
Creon buried our brother Eteocles
With military honors, gave him a soldier's funeral,
And it was right that he should; but Polyneices,
Who fought as bravely and died as miserably,—
They say that Creon has sworn
No one shall bury him, no one mourn for him,
But his body must lie in the fields, a sweet treasure
For carrion birds to find as they search for food.
That is what they say, and our good Creon is coming here
To announce it publicly; and the penalty—
Stoning to death in the public square!
There it is,
And now you can prove what you are:
A true sister, or a traitor to your family.

Ismene. Antigone, you are mad! What could I possibly do?

Antigone. You must decide whether you will help me or not.

Ismene. I do not understand you. Help you in what?

Antigone. Ismene, I am going to bury him. Will you come?

Ismene. Bury him! You have just said the new law forbids it.

Antigone. He is my brother. And he is your brother, too.

Ismene. But think of the danger! Think what Creon will do!

Antigone. Creon is not strong enough to stand in my way.

Ismene. Ah sister!
Oedipus died, everyone hating him
For what his own search brought to light, his eyes
Ripped out by his own hand; and Iocaste died,
His mother and wife at once: she twisted the cords
That strangled her life; and our two brothers died,

Each killed by the other's sword. And we are left:
But oh, Antigone,
Think how much more terrible than these
Our own death would be if we should go against Creon
And do what he has forbidden! We are only women,
We cannot fight with men, Antigone!
The law is strong, we must give in to the law
In this thing, and in worse. I beg the Dead
To forgive me, but I am helpless: I must yield
To those in authority. And I think it is dangerous business
To be always meddling.

Antigone. If that is what you think,
I should not want you, even if you asked to come.
You have made your choice, you can be what you want to be.
But I will bury him; and if I must die,
I say that this crime is holy: I shall lie down
With him in death, and I shall be as dear
To him as he to me.
It is the dead,
Not the living, who make the longest demands:
We die for ever . . .
You may do as you like,
Since apparently the laws of the gods mean nothing to you.

Ismene. They mean a great deal to me; but I have no strength
To break laws that were made for the public good.

Antigone. That must be your excuse, I suppose. But as for me,
I will bury the brother I love.

Ismene. Antigone,
I am so afraid for you!

Antigone. You need not be:
You have yourself to consider, after all.

Ismene. But no one must hear of this, you must tell no one!
I will keep it a secret, I promise!

Antigone. O tell it! Tell everyone!
Think how they'll hate you when it all comes out
If they learn that you knew about it all the time!

Ismene. So fiery! You should be cold with fear.

Antigone. Perhaps, But I am doing only what I must.

Ismene. But can you do it? I say that you cannot.

Antigone. Very well: when my strength gives out,
I shall do no more.

Ismene. Impossible things should not be tried at all.

Antigone. Go away, Ismene:
I shall be hating you soon, and the dead will too,
For your words are hateful. Leave me my foolish plan.
I am not afraid of the danger; if it means death,
It will not be the worst of deaths—death without honor.

Ismene. Go then, if you feel that you must.
You are unwise,
But a loyal friend indeed to those who love you.

[*Exit into the palace.* Antigone *goes off, left. Enter the Chorus.*]

PARODOS

Strophe 1

Chorus. Now the long blade of the sun, lying
Level east to west, touches with glory
Thebes of the Seven Gates. Open, unlidded
Eye of golden day! O marching light
Across the eddy and rush of Dirce's stream,
Striking the white shields of the enemy
Thrown headlong backward from the blaze of morning!
Choragos. Polyneices their commander
Roused them with windy phrases,
He the wild eagle screaming
Insults above our land,
His wings their shields of snow,
His crest their marshalled helms.

Antistrophe 1

Chorus. Against our seven gates in a yawning ring
The famished spears came onward in the night;
But before his jaws were sated with our blood,
Or pinefire took the garland of our towers,
He was thrown back; and as he turned, great Thebes—
No tender victim for his noisy power—
Rose like a dragon behind him, shouting war.
Choragos. For God hates utterly
The bray of bragging tongues;
And when he beheld their smiling,
Their swagger of golden helms,
The frown of his thunder blasted
Their first man from our walls.

Strophe 2

Chorus. We heard his shout of triumph high in the air
Turn to a scream; far out in a flaming arc
He fell with his windy torch, and the earth struck him.
And others storming in fury no less than his
Found shock of death in the dusty joy of battle.
Choragos. Seven captains at seven gates
Yielded their clanging arms to the god

That bends the battle-line and breaks it.
These two only, brothers in blood,
Face to face in matchless rage,
Mirroring each the other's death,
Clashed in long combat.

Antistrophe 2

Chorus. But now in the beautiful morning of victory
Let Thebes of the many chariots sing for joy!
With hearts for dancing we'll take leave of war:
Our temples shall be sweet with hymns of praise,
And the long nights shall echo with our chorus.

SCENE I

Choragos. But now at last our new King is coming:
Creon of Thebes, Menoikeus' son.
In this auspicious dawn of his reign
What are the new complexities
That shifting Fate has woven for him?
What is his counsel? Why has he summoned
The old men to hear him?

[*Enter* Creon *from the palace, center. He addresses the* Chorus *from the top step.*]

Creon. Gentlemen: I have the honor to inform you that our Ship of State, which recent storms have threatened to destroy, has come safely to harbor at last, guided by the merciful wisdom of Heaven. I have summoned you here this morning because I know that I can depend upon you: your devotion to King Laïos was absolute; you never hesitated in your duty to our late ruler Oedipus; and when Oedipus died, your loyalty was transferred to his children. Unfortunately, as you know, his two sons, the princes Eteocles and Polyneices, have killed each other in battle; and I, as the next in blood, have succeeded to the full power of the throne.

I am aware, of course, that no Ruler can expect complete loyalty from his subjects until he has been tested in office. Nevertheless, I say to you at the very outset that I have nothing but contempt for the kind of Governor who is afraid, for whatever reason, to follow the course that he knows is best for the State; and as for the man who sets private friendship above the public welfare,—I have no use for him, either. I call God to witness that I saw my country headed for ruin, I should not be afraid to speak out plainly; and I need hardly remind you that I would never have any dealings with an enemy of the people. No one values friendship more highly than I; but we must remember that friends made at the risk of wrecking our Ship are not real friends at all.

These are my principles, at any rate, and that is why I have made the following decision concerning the sons of Oedipus: Eteocles, who died as a man should die, fighting for his country, is to be buried with full military honors, with all the ceremony that is usual when the greatest heroes die; but his brother Polyneices, who broke his exile to come back with fire and sword against his native city and the shrines of his fathers' gods, whose one idea was to spill the blood of his blood and sell his own people into slavery—Polyneices, I say, is to have no burial: no man is to touch him or say the least prayer for him; he shall lie on the plain, unburied; and the birds and the scavenging dogs can do with him whatever they like.

This is my command and you can see the wisdom behind it. As long as I am King, no traitor is going to be honored with the loyal man. But whoever shows by word and deed that he is on the side of the State,—he shall have my respect while he is living and my reverence when he is dead.

Choragos. If that is your will, Creon son of Menoikeus,
You have the right to enforce it: we are yours.

Creon. That is my will. Take care that you do your part.

Choragos. We are old men: let the younger ones carry it out.

Creon. I do not mean that: the sentries have been appointed.

Choragos. Then what is it that you would have us do?

Creon. You will give no support to whoever breaks this law.

Choragos. Only a crazy man is in love with death!

Creon. And death it is; yet money talks, and the wisest
Have sometimes been known to count a few coins too many.

[*Enter* Sentry *from left.*]

Sentry. I'll not say that I'm out of breath from running, King, because every time I stopped to think about what I have to tell you, I felt like going back. And all the time a voice kept saying, "You fool, don't you know you're walking straight into trouble?"; and then another voice: "Yes, but if you let somebody else get the news to Creon first, it will be even worse than that for you!" But good sense won out, at least I hope it was good sense, and here I am with a story that makes no sense at all; but I'll tell it anyhow, because, as they say, what's going to happen's going to happen and—

Creon. Come to the point. What have you to say?

Sentry. I did not do it. I did not see who did it. You must not punish me for what someone else has done.

Creon. A comprehensive defense! More effective, perhaps, If I knew its purpose. Come: what is it?

Sentry. A dreadful thing . . . I don't know how to put it—

Creon. Out with it!
Sentry. Well, then;
The dead man—
Polyneices—

[*Pause. The* Sentry *is overcome, fumbles for words. Creon waits impassively.*]

out there—
someone,—
New dust on the slimy flesh!

[*Pause. No sign from* Creon.]

Someone has given it burial that way, and
Gone . . .

[*Long pause.* Creon *finally speaks with deadly control.*]

Creon. And the man who dared do this?
Sentry. I swear I
Do not know! You must believe me!
Listen:
The ground was dry, not a sign of digging, no,
Not a wheeltrack in the dust, no trace of anyone.
It was when they relieved us this morning: and one of them,
The corporal, pointed to it.
There it was,
The strangest—
Look:
The body, just mounded over with light dust: you see?
Not buried really, but as if they'd covered it
Just enough for the ghost's peace. And no sign
Of dogs or any wild animal that had been there.

And then what a scene there was! Every man of us
Accusing the other: we all proved the other man did it,
We all had proof that we could not have done it.
We were ready to take hot iron in our hands,
Walk through fire, swear by all the gods,
It was not I!
I do not know who it was, but it was not I!

[Creon's *rage had been mounting steadily, but the* Sentry *is too intent upon his story to notice it.*]

And then, when this came to nothing, someone said
A thing that silenced us and made us stare
Down at the ground: you had to be told the news,
And one of us had to do it! We threw the dice,
And the bad luck fell to me. So here I am,
No happier to be here than you are to have me:
Nobody likes the man who brings bad news.

Choragos. I have been wondering, King: can it be that the gods have done this?

Creon. (*furiously*) Stop!
Must you doddering wrecks
Go out of your heads entirely? "The gods"!
Intolerable!
The gods favor this corpse? Why? How had he served them?
Tried to loot their temples, burn their images,
Yes, and the whole State, and its laws with it!
Is it your senile opinion that the gods love to honor bad men?
A pious thought!—
No, from the very beginning
There have been those who have whispered together,
Stiff-necked anarchists, putting their heads together,
Scheming against me in alleys. These are the men,
And they have bribed my own guard to do this thing.
(*Sententiously.*) Money!
There's nothing in the world so demoralizing as money.
Down go your cities,
Homes gone, men gone, honest hearts corrupted,
Crookedness of all kinds, and all for money!
(*To* Sentry.) But you—
I swear by God and by the throne of God,
The man who has done this thing shall pay for it!
Find that man, bring him here to me, or your death
Will be the least of your problems: I'll string you up
Alive, and there will be certain ways to make you
Discover your employer before you die;
And the process may teach you a lesson you seem to have missed:
The dearest profit is sometimes all too dear:
That depends on the source. Do you understand me?
A fortune won is often misfortune.

Sentry. King, may I speak?

Creon. Your very voice distresses me.

Sentry. Are you sure that it is my voice, and not your conscience?

Creon. By God, he wants to analyze me now!

Sentry. It is not what I say, but what has been done, that hurts you.

Creon. You talk too much.

Sentry. Maybe; but I've done nothing.

Creon. Sold your soul for some silver: that's all you've done.
Sentry. How dreadful it is when the right judge judges wrong!
Creon. Your figures of speech
May entertain you now; but unless you bring me the man,
You will get little profit from them in the end.

[*Exit* Creon *into the palace.*]

Sentry. "Bring me the man"—!
I'd like nothing better than bringing him the man!
But bring him or not, you have seen the last of me here.
At any rate, I am safe!

[*Exit* Sentry.]

ODE I

Strophe 1

Chorus. Numberless are the world's wonders, but none
More wonderful than man; the stormgray sea
Yields to his prows, the huge crests bear him high;
Earth, holy and inexhaustible, is graven
With shining furrows where his plows have gone
Year after year, the timeless labor of stallions.

Antistrophe 1

The lightboned birds and beasts that cling to cover,
The lithe fish lighting their reaches of dim water,
All are taken, tamed in the net of his mind;
The lion on the hill, the wild horse windy-maned,
Resign to him; and his blunt yoke has broken
The sultry shoulders of the mountain bull.

Strophe 2

Words also, and thought as rapid as air,
He fashions to his good use; statecraft is his,
And his the skill that deflects the arrows of snow,
The spears of winter rain: from every wind
He has made himself secure—from all but one:
In the late wind of death he cannot stand.

Antistrophe 2

O clear intelligence, force beyond all measure!
O fate of man, working both good and evil!
When the laws are kept, how proudly his city stands!

When the laws are broken, what of his city then?
Never may the anárchic man find rest at my hearth,
Never be it said that my thoughts are his thoughts.

SCENE II

[*Reenter* Sentry *leading* Antigone.]

Choragos. What does this mean? Surely this captive woman
Is the Princess, Antigone. Why should she be taken?
Sentry. Here is the one who did it! We caught her
In the very act of burying him.—Where is Creon?
Choragos. Just coming from the house

[*Enter* Creon, *center.*]

Creon. What has happened?
Why have you come back so soon?
Sentry. (*expansively*) O King,
A man should never be too sure of anything:
I would have sworn
That you'd not see me here again: your anger
Frightened me so, and the things you threatened me with;
But how could I tell then
That I'd be able to solve the case so soon?
No dice-throwing this time: I was only too glad to come!
Here is this woman. She is the guilty one:
We found her trying to bury him.
Take her, then; question her; judge her as you will.
I am through with the whole thing now, and glad of it.
Creon. But this is Antigone! Why have you brought her here?
Sentry. She was burying him, I tell you!
Creon. (*severely*) Is this the truth?
Sentry. I saw her with my own eyes. Can I say more?
Creon. The details: come, tell me quickly!
Sentry. It was like this:
After those terrible threats of yours, King,
We went back and brushed the dust away from the body.
The flesh was soft by now, and stinking,
So we sat on a hill to windward and kept guard.
No napping this time! We kept each other awake.
But nothing happened until the white round sun
Whirled in the center of the round sky over us:
Then, suddenly,
A storm of dust roared up from the earth, and the sky

Went out, the plain vanished with all its tress
In the stinging dark. We closed our eyes and endured it.
The whirlwind lasted a long time, but it passed;
And then we looked, and there was Antigone!
I have seen
A mother bird come back to a stripped nest, heard
Her crying bitterly a broken note or two
For the young ones stolen. Just so, when this girl
Found the bare corpse, and all her love's work wasted,
She wept, and cried on heaven to damn the hands
That had done this thing.
And then she brought more dust
And sprinkled wine three time for her brother's ghost.

We ran and took her at once. She was not afraid,
Not even when we charged her with what she had done.
She denied nothing.
And thus was a comfort to me,
And some uneasiness: for it is a good thing
To escape from death, but it is no great pleasure
To bring death to a friend.
Yet I always say
There is nothing so comfortable as your own safe skin!

Creon. (*slowly, dangerously*) And you, Antigone,
You with your head hanging,—do you confess this thing?

Antigone. I do. I deny nothing.

Creon. (*to* Sentry) You may go.

[*Exit* Sentry.]

(*To* Antigone.) Tell me, tell me briefly:
Had you heard my proclamation touching this matter?

Antigone. It was public. Could I help hearing it?

Creon. And yet you dared defy the law.

Antigone. I dared.
It was not God's proclamation. That final Justice
That rules the world below makes no such laws.

Your edict, King, was strong,
But all your strength is weakness itself against
The immortal unrecorded laws of God.
They are not merely now: they were, and shall be,
Operative for ever, beyond man utterly.

I knew I must die, even without your decree:
I am only mortal. And if I must die

Now, before it is my time to die,
Surely this is no hardship: can anyone
Living, as I live, with evil all about me,
Think Death less than a friend? This death of mine
Is of no importance; but if I had left my brother
Lying in death unburied, I should have suffered.
Now I do not.
You smile at me. Ah Creon,
Think me a fool, if you like; but it may well be
That a fool convicts me of folly.

Choragos. Like father, like daughter: both headstrong, deaf to reason!
She has never learned to yield:

Creon. She has much to learn.
The inflexible heart breaks first, the toughest iron
Cracks first, and the wildest horses bend their necks
At the pull of the smallest curb.
Pride? In a slave?
This girl is guilty of a double insolence,
Breaking the given laws and boasting of it.
Who is the man here,
She or I, if this crime goes unpunished?
Sister's child, or more than sister's child,
Or closer yet in blood—she and her sister
Win bitter death for this!
(*To* Servants.) Go, some of you,
Arrest Ismene. I accuse her equally.
Bring her: you will find her sniffing in the house there.

Her mind's a traitor: crimes kept in the dark
Cry for light, and the guardian brain shudders;
But how much worse than this
Is brazen boasting of barefaced anarchy!

Antigone. Creon, what more do you want than my death?

Creon. Nothing.
That gives me everything.

Antigone. Then I beg you: kill me.
This talking is a great weariness: your words
Are distasteful to me, and I am sure that mine
Seem so to you. And yet they should not seem so:
I should have praise and honor for what I have done.
All these men here would praise me
Were their lips not frozen shut with fear of you.
(*Bitterly.*) Ah the good fortune of kings,
Licensed to say and do whatever they please!

Creon. You are alone here in that opinion.

Antigone. No, they are with me. But they keep their tongues in leash.

Creon. Maybe. But you are guilty, and they are not.
Antigone. There is no guilt in reverence for the dead.
Creon. But Eteocles—was he not your brother too?
Antigone. My brother too.
Creon. And you insult his memory?
Antigone. (*softly*) The dead man would not say that I insult it.
Creon. He would: for your honor a traitor as much as him.
Antigone. His own brother, traitor or not, and equal in blood.
Creon. He made war on his country. Eteocles defended it.
Antigone. Nevertheless, there are honors due all the dead.
Creon. But not the same for the wicked as for the just.
Antigone. Ah Creon, Creon
Which of us can say what the gods hold wicked?
Creon. An enemy is an enemy, even dead.
Antigone. It is my nature to join in love, not hate.
Creon. (*finally losing patience*) Go join them then; if you must have your love,
Find it in hell!
Chorágos. But see, Ismene comes:

[*Enter* Ismene, *guarded.*]

Those tears are sisterly, the cloud
That shadows her eyes rains down gentle sorrow.
Creon. You too, Ismene,
Snake in my ordered house, sucking my blood
Stealthily—and all the time I never knew
That these two sisters were aiming at my throne!
Ismene,
Do you confess your share in this crime, or deny it?
Answer me.
Ismene. Yes, if she will let me say so. I am guilty.
Antigone. (*coldly*) No, Ismene. You have no right to say so.
You would not help me, and I will not have you help me.
Ismene. But now I know what you meant; and I am here
To join you, to take my share of punishment.
Antigone. The dead man and the gods who rule the dead
Know whose act this was. Words are not friends.
Ismene. Do you refuse me, Antigone? I want to die with you:
I too have a duty that I must discharge to the dead.
Antigone. You shall not lessen my death by sharing it.
Ismene. What do I care for life when you are dead?
Antigone. Ask Creon. You're always hanging on his opinions.
Ismene. You are laughing at me. Why, Antigone?
Antigone. It's a joyless, laughter, Ismene.
Ismene. But can I do nothing?
Antigone. Yes. Save yourself. I shall not envy you.
There are those who will praise you; I shall have honor, too.

Ismene. But we are equally guilty!
Antigone. No more, Ismene.
You are alive, but I belong to Death.
Creon. (*to the* Chorus) Gentlemen, I beg you to observe these girls:
One has just now lost her mind; the other
It seems, has never had a mind at all.
Ismene. Grief teaches the steadiest minds to waver, King.
Creon. Yours certainly did, when you assumed guilt with the guilty!
Ismene. But how could I go on living without her?
Creon. You are.
She is already dead.
Ismene. But your own son's bride!
Creon. There are places enough for him to push his plow.
I want no wicked women for my sons!
Ismene. O dearest Haimon, how your father wrongs you!
Creon. I've had enough of your childish talk of marriage!
Choragos. Do you really intend to steal this girl from your son?
Creon. No; Death will do that for me.
Choragos. Then she must die?
Creon. (*ironically*) You dazzle me.
—But enough of this talk!
(*To* Guards.) You, there, take them away and guard them well:
For they are but women, and even brave men run
When they see Death coming.

[*Exeunt* Ismene, Antigone, *and* Guards.]

ODE II

Strophe I

Chorus. Fortunate is the man who has never tasted God's vengeance!
Where once the anger of heaven has struck, that house is shaken
For ever: damnation rises behind each child
Like a wave cresting out of the black northeast,
When the long darkness under sea roars up
And bursts drumming death upon the windwhipped sand.

Antistrophe 1

I have seen this gathering sorrow from time long past
Loom upon Oedipus' children: generation from generation
Takes the compulsive rage of the enemy god.
So lately this last flower of Oedipus' line
Drank the sunlight! but now a passionate word
And a handful of dust have closed up all its beauty.

Strophe 2

What mortal arrogance
Transcends the wrath of Zeus?
Sleep cannot lull him nor the effortless long months
Of the timeless gods: but he is young for ever,
And his house is the shining day of high Olympos.
All that is and shall be,
And all the past, is his.
No pride on earth is free of the curse of heaven.

Antistrophe 2

The straying dreams of men
May bring them ghosts of joy:
But as the drowse, the waking embers burn them;
Or they walk with fixed eyes, as blind men walk.
But the ancient wisdom speaks for our own time:
Fate works most for woe
With Folly's fairest show.
Man's little pleasure is the spring of sorrow.

SCENE III

Choragos. But here is Haimon, King, the last of all your sons.
Is it grief for Antigone that brings him here,
And bitterness at being robbed of his bride?

[*Enter* Haimon.]

Creon. We shall soon see, and no need of diviners.
—Son,
You have heard my final judgment on that girl:
Have you come here hating me, or have you come
With deference and with love, whatever I do?

Haimon. I am your son, father. You are my guide.
You make things clear for me, and I obey you.
No marriage means more to me than your continuing wisdom.

Creon. Good. That is the way to behave: subordinate
Everything else, my son, to your father's will.
This is what a man prays for, that he may get
Sons attentive and dutiful in his house.
Each one hating his father's enemies,
Honoring his father's friends. But if his sons
Fail him, if they turn out unprofitably,
What has he fathered but trouble for himself
And amusement for the malicious?
So you are right

Not to lose your head over this woman.
Your pleasure with her would soon grow cold, Haimon,
And then you'd have a hellcat in bed and elsewhere.
Let her find her husband in Hell!
Of all the people in this city, only she
Has had contempt for my law and broken it.
Do you want me to show myself weak before the people?
Or to break my sworn word? No, and I will not.
The woman dies.
I suppose she'll plead "family ties." Well, let her.
If I permit my own family to rebel,
How shall I earn the world's obedience?
Show me the man who keeps his house in hand,
He's fit for public authority.
I'll have no dealings
With lawbreakers, critics of the government:
Whoever is chosen to govern should be obeyed—
Must be obeyed, in all things, great and small,
Just and unjust! O Haimon,
The man who knows how to obey, and that man only,
Knows how to give commands when the time comes.
You can depend on him, no matter how fast
The spears come: he's a good soldier, he'll stick it out.

Anarchy, anarchy! Show me a greater evil!
This is why cities tumble and the great houses rain down,
This is what scatters armies!
No, no: good lives are made so by discipline.
We keep the laws then, and the lawmakers,
And no woman shall seduce us. If we must lose,
Let's lose to a man, at least! Is a woman stronger than we?

Choragos. Unless time has rusted my wits,
What you say, King, is said with point and dignity.

Haimon. (*boyishly earnest*) Father:
Reason is God's crowning gift to man, and you are right
To warn me against losing mine. I cannot say—
I hope that I shall never want to say!—that you
Have reasoned badly. Yet there are other men
Who can reason, too; and their opinions might be helpful.
You are not in a position to know everything
That people say or do, or what they feel:
Your temper terrifies—everyone
Will tell you only what you like to hear.
But I, at any rate, can listen; and I have heard them
Muttering and whispering in the dark about this girl.
They say no woman has ever, so unreasonably,

Died so shameful a death for a generous act:
"She covered her brother's body. Is this indecent?
She kept him from dogs and vultures. Is this a crime?
Death?—She should have all the honor that we can give her!"

This is the way they talk out there in the city.

You must believe me:
Nothing is closer to me than your happiness.
What could be closer? Must not any son
Value his father's fortune as his father does his?
I beg you, do not be unchangeable:
Do not believe that you alone can be right.
The man who thinks that,
The man who maintains that only he has the power
To reason correctly, the gift to speak, the soul—
A man like that, when you know him, turns out empty.
It is not reason never to yield to reason!

In flood time you can see how some trees bend,
And because they bend, even their twigs are safe,
While stubborn trees are torn up, roots and all.
And the same thing happens in sailing:
Make your sheet fast, never slacken,—and over you go,
Head over heels and under: and there's your voyage.
Forget you are angry! Let yourself be moved!
I know I am young; but please let me say this:
The ideal condition
Would be, I admit, that men should be right by instinct;
But since we are all too likely to go astray,
The reasonable thing is to learn from those who can teach.

Choragos. You will do well to listen to him, King,
If what he says is sensible. And you, Haimon,
Must listen to your father.—Both speak well.

Creon. You consider it right for a man of my years and experience
To go to school to a boy?

Haimon. It is not right
If I am wrong. But if I am young, and right,
What does my age matter?

Creon. You think it right to stand up for an anarchist?

Haimon. Not at all. I pay no respect to criminals.

Creon. Then she is not a criminal?

Haimon. The City would deny it, to a man.

Creon. And the City proposes to teach me how to rule?

Haimon. Ah. Who is it that's talking like a boy now?

Creon. My voice is the one voice giving orders in this City!

Haimon. It is no City if it takes orders from one voice.
Creon. The State is the King!
Haimon. Yes, if the State is a desert.

[*Pause.*]

Creon. This boy, it seems, has sold out to a woman.
Haimon. If you are a woman: my concern is only for you.
Creon. So? Your "concern"! In a public brawl with your father!
Haimon. How about you, in a public brawl with justice?
Creon. With justice, when all that I do is within my rights?
Haimon. You have no right to trample on God's right.
Creon. (*completely out of control*) Fool, adolescent fool! Taken in by a woman!
Haimon. You'll never see me taken in by anything vile.
Creon. Every word you say is for her!
Haimon. (*quietly, darkly*) And for you.
And for me. And for the gods under the earth.
Creon. You'll never marry her while she lives.
Haimon. Then she must die.—But her death will cause another.
Creon. Another?
Have you lost your senses? Is this an open threat?
Haimon. There is no threat in speaking to emptiness.
Creon. I swear you'll regret this superior tone of yours!
You are the empty one!
Haimon. If you were not my father,
I'd say you were perverse.
Creon. You girl-struck fool, don't play at words with me!
Haimons. I am sorry. You prefer silence.
Creon. Now, by God—
I swear, by all the gods in heaven above us,
You'll watch it, I swear you shall!
(*To the Servants.*) Bring her out!
Bring the woman out! Let her die before his eyes!
Here, this instant, with her bridegroom beside her!
Haimon. Not here, no; she will not die here, King.
And you will never see my face again.
Go on raving as long as you've a friend to endure you.

[*Exit* Haimon.]

Choragos. Gone, gone.
Creon, a young man in a rage is dangerous!
Creon. Let him do, or dream to do, more than a man can.
He shall not save these girls from death.
Choragos. These girls?

You have sentenced them both?

Creon. No, you are right.
I will not kill the one whose hands are clean.

Choragos. But Antigone?

Creon. (*somberly*) I will carry her far away
Out there in the wilderness, and lock her
Living in a vault of stone. She shall have food,
As the custom is, to absolve the State of her death.
And there let her pray to the gods of hell:
They are her only gods:
Perhaps they will show her an escape from death,
Or she may learn,
though late,
That piety shown the dead is pity in vain.

[*Exit* Creon.]

ODE III

Strophe

Chorus. Love, unconquerable
Waster of rich men, keeper
Of warm lights and all-night vigil
In the soft face of a girl:
Sea-wanderer, forest-visitor!
Even the pure Immortals cannot escape you,
And mortal man, in his one day's dusk,
Trembles before your glory.

Antistrophe

Surely you swerve upon ruin
The just man's consenting heart,
As here you have made bright anger
Strike between father and son—
And none has conquered but Love!
A girl's glance working the will of heaven:
Pleasure to her alone who mocks us,
Merciless Aphrodite.

SCENE IV

Choragos. (*as* Antigone *enters guarded*) But I can no longer stand in awe of this,
Nor, seeing what I see, keep back my tears.
Here is Antigone, passing to the chamber
Where all find sleep at last.

Strophe 1

Antigone. Look upon me, friends, and pity me
Turning back at the night's edge to say
Good-by to the sun that shines for me no longer;
Now sleepy Death
Summons me down to Acheron, that cold shore:
There is no bridesong there, nor any music.

Chorus. Yet not unpraised, not without a kind of honor,
You walk at last into the underworld;
Untouched by sickness, broken by no sword.
What woman has ever found your way to death?

Antistrophe 1

Antigone. How often I have heard the story of Niobe,
Tantalos' wretched daughter, how the stone
Clung fast about her, ivy-close: and they say
The rain falls endlessly
And sifting soft snow; her tears are never done.
I feel the loneliness of her death in mine.

Chorus. But she was born of heaven, and you
Are woman, woman-born. If her death is yours,
A mortal woman's, is this not for you
Glory in our world and in the world beyond?

Strophe 2

Antigone. You laugh at me. Ah, friends, friends,
Can you not wait until I am dead? O Thebes,
O men many-charioted, in love with Fortune,
Dear springs of Dirce, sacred Theban grove,
Be witnesses for me, denied all pity,
Unjustly judged! and think a word of love
For her whose path turns
Under dark earth, where there are no more tears.

Chorus. You have passed beyond human daring and come at last
Into a place of stone where Justice sits.
I cannot tell
What shape of your father's guilt appears in this.

Antistrophe 2

Antigone. You have touched it at last: that bridal bed
Unspeakable, horror of son and mother mingling:
Their crime, infection of all our family!
O Oedipus, father and brother!

Your marriage strikes from the grave to murder mine.
I have been a stranger here in my own land:
All my life
The blasphemy of my birth has followed me.
Chorus. Reverence is a virtue, but strength
Lives in established law: that must prevail.
You have made your choice,
Your death is the doing of your conscious hand.

Epode

Antigone. Then let me go, since all your words are bitter,
And the very light of the sun is cold to me.
Lead me to my vigil, where I must have
Neither love nor lamentation; no song, but silence.

[Creon *interrupts impatiently.*]

Creon. If dirges and planned lamentations could put off death,
Men would be singing for ever.
(To the Servants.) Take her, go!
You know your orders: take her to the vault
And leave her alone there. And if she lives or dies,
That's her affair, not ours: our hands are clean.
Antigone. O tomb, vaulted bride-bed in eternal rock,
Soon I shall be with my own again
Where Persephone welcomes the thin ghosts underground:
And I shall see my father again, and you, mother,
And dearest Polyneices—
dearest indeed
To me, since it was my hand
That washed him clean and poured the ritual wine:
And my reward is death before my time!

And yet, as men's hearts know, I have done no wrong,
I have not sinned before God. Or if I have,
I shall know the truth in death. But if the guilt
Lies upon Creon who judged me, then, I pray,
May his punishment equal my own.
Choragos. O passionate heart,
Unyielding, tormented still by the same winds!
Creon. Her guards shall have good cause to regret their delaying.
Antigone. Ah! That voice is like the voice of death!
Creon. I can give you no reason to think you are mistaken.
Antigone. Thebes, and you my fathers' gods,
And rulers of Thebes, you see me now, the last
Unhappy daughter of a line of kings,

Your kings, led away to death. You will remember
What things I suffer, and at what men's hands,
Because I would not transgress the laws of heaven.
(To the Guards, simply.) Come: let us wait no longer.

[*Exit* Antigone, *left, guarded.*]

ODE IV

Strophe 1

Chorus. All Danae's beauty was locked away
In a brazen cell where the sunlight could not come:
A small room still as any grave, enclosed her.
Yet she was a princess too,
And Zeus in a rain of gold poured love upon her.
O child, child,
No power in wealth or war
Or tough sea-blackened ships
Can prevail against untiring Destiny!

Antistrophe 1

And Dryas' son also, that furious king,
Bore the god's prisoning anger for his pride:
Sealed up by Dionysos in deaf stone,
His madness died among echoes.
So at the last he learned what dreadful power
His tongue had mocked:
For he had profaned the revels,
And fired the wrath of the nine
Implacable Sisters that love the sound of the flute.

Strophe 2

And old men tell a half-remembered tale
Of horror where a dark ledge splits the sea
And a double surf beats on the gráy shóres:
How a king's new woman, sick
With hatred for the queen he had imprisoned,
Ripped out his two sons' eyes with her bloody hands
While grinning Ares watched the shuttle plunge
Four times: four blind wounds crying for revenge,

Antistrophe 2

Crying, tears and blood mingled.—Piteously born,
Those sons whose mother was of heavenly birth!
Her father was the god of the North Wind

And she was cradled by gales,
She raced with young colts on the glittering hills
And walked untrammeled in the open light:
But in her marriage deathless Fate found means
To build a tomb like yours for all her joy.

SCENE V

[*Enter blind* Teiresias, *led by a boy. The opening speeches of* Teiresias *should be in singsong contrast to the realistic lines of* Creon.]

Teiresias. This is the way the blind man comes, Princes, Princes,
Lockstep, two heads lit by the eyes of one.
Creon. What new thing have you to tell us, old Teiresias?
Teiresias. I have much to tell you: listen to the prophet, Creon.
Creon. I am not aware that I have ever failed to listen.
Teiresias. Then you have done wisely, King, and ruled well.
Creon. I admit my debt to you. But what have you to say?
Teiresias. This, Creon: you stand once more on the edge of fate.
Creon. What do you mean? Your words are a kind of dread.
Teiresias. Listen, Creon:
I was sitting in my chair of augury, at the place
Where the birds gather about me. They were all a-chatter,
As is their habit, when suddenly I heard
A strange note in their jangling, a scream, a
Whirring fury; I knew that they were fighting,
Tearing each other, dying
In a whirlwind of wings clashing. And I was afraid.
I began the rites of burnt-offering at the altar,
But Hephaistos failed me: instead of bright flame,
There was only the sputtering slime of the fat thigh-flesh
Melting: the entrails dissolved in gray smoke,
The bare bone burst from the welter. And no blaze!

This was a sign from heaven. My boy described it,
Seeing for me as I see for others.

I tell you, Creon, you yourself have brought
This new calamity upon us. Our hearths and altars
Are stained with the corruption of dogs and carrion birds
That glut themselves on the corpse of Oedipus' son.
The gods are deaf when we pray to them, their fire
Recoils from our offering, their birds of omen
Have no cry of comfort, for they are gorged
With the thick blood of the dead.

O my son,
These are no trifles! Think: all men make mistakes,
But a good man yields when he knows his course is wrong,
And repairs the evil. The only crime is pride.

Give in to the dead man, then: do not fight with a corpse—
What glory is it to kill a man who is dead?
Think, I beg you:
It is for your own good that I speak as I do.
You should be able to yield for your own good.

Creon. It seems that prophets have made me their especial province.
All my life long
I have been a kind of butt for the dull arrows
Of doddering fortune-tellers!
No, Teiresias:
If your birds—if the great eagles of God himself
Should carry him stinking bit by bit to heaven,
I would not yield. I am not afraid of pollution:
No man can defile the gods.
Do what you will,
Go into business, make money, speculate
An India gold or that synthetic gold from Sardis,
Get rich otherwise than by my consent to bury him.
Teiresias, it is a sorry thing when a wise man
Sells his wisdom, lets out his words for hire!

Teiresias. Ah Creon! Is there no man left in the world—

Creon. To do what?—Come, let's have the aphorism!

Teiresias. No man who knows that wisdom outweighs any wealth?

Creon. As surely as bribes are baser than any baseness.

Teiresias. You are sick, Creon! You are deathly sick!

Creon. As you say: it is not my place to challenge a prophet.

Teiresias. Yet you have said my prophecy is for sale.

Creon. The generation of prophets has always loved gold.

Teiresias. The generation of kings has always loved brass.

Creon. You forget yourself! You are speaking to your King.

Teiresias. I know it. You are a king because of me.

Creon. You have a certain skill; but you have sold out.

Teiresias. King, you will drive me to words that—

Creon. Say them, say them!
Only remember: I will not pay you for them.

Teiresias. No, you will find them too costly.

Creon. No doubt. Speak:
Whatever you say, you will not change my will.

Teiresias. Then take this, and take it to heart!
The time is not far off when you shall pay back
Corpse for corpse, flesh of your own flesh.

You have thrust the child of this world into living night,
You have kept from the gods below the child that is theirs:
The one in a grave before her death, the other,
Dead, denied the grave. This is your crime:
And the Furies and the dark gods of Hell
Are swift with terrible punishment for you.

Do you want to buy me now, Creon?

Not many days,
And your house will be full of men and women weeping,
And curses will be hurled at you from far
Cities grieving for sons unburied, left to rot
Before the walls of Thebes.

There are my arrows, Creon: they are all for you.

(*To Boy.*) But come, child: lead me home.
Let him waste his fine anger upon younger men.
Maybe he will learn at last
To control a wiser tongue in a better head.

[*Exit* Teiresias.]

Choragos. The old man has gone, King, but his words
Remain to plague us. I am old, too,
But I cannot remember that he was ever false.
Creon. That is true. . . . It troubles me.
Oh it is hard to give in! but it is worse
To risk everything for stubborn pride.
Choragos. Creon: take my advice.
Creon. What shall I do?
Choragos. Go quickly: free Antigone from her vault
And build a tomb for the body of Polyneices.
Creon. You would have me do this!
Choragos. Creon, yes!
And it must be done at once: God moves
Swiftly to cancel the folly of stubborn men.
Creon. It is hard to deny that heart! But I
Will do it: I will not fight with destiny,
Choragos. You must go yourself, you cannot leave it to others.
Creon. I will go.
—Bring axes, servants:
Come with me to the tomb. I buried her, I
Will set her free.
Oh quickly!

My mind misgives—
The laws of the gods are mighty, and a man must serve them
To the last day of his life!

[*Exit* Creon.]

PAEAN

Strophe 1

Choragos. God of many names.
Chorus. O Iacchos
son
of Kadmeian Sémele
O born of the Thunder!
Guardian of the West
Regent
Of Eleusis' plain
O Prince of maenad Thebes
and the Dragon Field by rippling Ismenós:

Antistrophe 1

Choragos. God of many names
Chorus. the flame of torches
flares on our hills
the nymphs of Iacchos
dance at the spring of Castalia:
from the vine-close mountain
come ah come in ivy:
Evohé evohé! sings through the streets of Thebes

Strophe 2

Choragos. God of many names
Chorus. Iacchos of Thebes
heavenly Child
of Sémele bride of the Thunderer!
The shadow of plague is upon us:
come
with clement feet
oh come from Parnasos
down the long slopes
across the lamenting water

Antistrophe 2

Choragos. Io Fire! Chorister of the throbbing stars!
O purest among the voices of the night!
Thou son of God, blaze for us!

Chorus. Come with choric rapture of circling Maenads
Who cry *Io Iacche*!
God of many names!

EXODUS

[*Enter* Messenger *from left.*]

Messenger. Men of the line of Kadmos, you who live
Near Amphion's citadel,
I cannot say
Of any condition of human life "This is fixed,
This is clearly good, or bad." Fate raises up,
And Fate casts down the happy and unhappy alike:
No man can foretell his Fate.
Take the case of Creon:
Creon was happy once, as I count happiness:
Victorious in battle, sole governor of the land,
Fortunate father of children nobly born.
And now it has all gone from him! Who can say
That a man is still alive when his life's joy fails?
He is a walking dead man. Grant him rich,
Let him live like a king in his great house:
If his pleasure is gone, I would not give
So much as the shadow of smoke for all he owns.
Choragos. Your words hint at sorrow: what is your news for us?
Messenger. They are dead. The living are guilty of their death.
Choragos. Who is guilty? Who is dead? Speak!
Messenger. Haimon.
Haimon is dead; and the hand that killed him
Is his own hand.
Choragos. His fathers'? or his own?
Messenger. His own, driven mad by the murder his father had done.
Choragos. Teiresias, Teiresias, how clearly you saw it all!
Messenger. This is my news: you must draw what conclusions you can from it.
Choragos. But look: Eurydice, our Queen:
Has she overheard us?

[*Enter* Eurydice *from the palace, center.*]

Eurydice. I have heard something, friends:
As I was unlocking the gate of Pallas' shrine,
For I needed her help today, I heard a voice
Telling of some new sorrow. And I fainted

There at the temple with all my maidens about me.
But speak again: whatever it is, I can bear it:
Grief and I are no strangers.
Messenger. Dearest Lady,
I will tell you plainly all that I have seen.
I shall not try to comfort you: what is the use,
Since comfort could lie only in what is not true?
The truth is always best.
I went with Creon
To the outer plain where Polyneices was lying,
No friend to pity him, his body shredded by dogs.
We made our prayers in that place to Hecate
And Pluto, that they would be merciful. And we bathed
The corpse with holy water, and we brought
Fresh-broken branches to burn what was left of it,
And upon the urn we heaped up a towering barrow
Of the earth of his own land.
When we were done, we ran
To the vault where Antigone lay on her couch of stone.
One of the servants had gone ahead,
And while he was yet far off he heard a voice
Grieving within the chamber, and he came back
And told Creon. And as the King went closer,
The air was full of wailing, the words lost,
And he begged us to make all haste. "Am I a prophet?"
He said, weeping, "And must I walk this road,
The saddest of all that I have gone before?
My son's voice calls me on. Oh quickly, quickly!
Look through the crevice there, and tell me
If it is Haimon, or some deception of the gods!"

We obeyed; and in the cavern's farthest corner
We saw her lying:
She had made a noose of her fine linen veil
And hanged herself. Haimon lay beside her,
His arms about her waist, lamenting her,
His love lost under ground, crying out
That is father had stolen her away from him.

When Creon saw him the tears rushed to his eyes
And he called to him: "What have you done, child? Speak to me.
What are you thinking that makes your eyes so strange?
O my son, my son, I come to you on my knees!"
But Haimon spat in his face. He said not a word,
Staring—
And suddenly drew his sword

And lunged. Creon shrank back, the blade missed; and the boy,
Desperate against himself, drove it half its length
Into his own side, and fell. And as he died
He gathered Antigone close in his arms again,
Choking, his blood bright red on her white cheek.
And now he lies dead with the dead, and she is his
At last, his bride in the house of the dead.

[*Exit* Eurydice *into the palace.*]

Choragos. She has left us without a word. What can this mean?
Messenger. It troubles me, too; yet she knows what is best,
Her grief is too great for public lamentation,
And doubtless she has gone to her chamber to weep
For her dead son, leading her maidens in his dirge.

[*Pause.*]

Choragos. It may be so: but I fear this deep silence.
Messenger. I will see what she is doing. I will go in.

[*Exit* Messenger *into the palace.*]

[*Enter* Creon *with attendants, bearing* Haimon's *body.*]

Choragos. But here is the king himself: oh look at him,
Bearing his own damnation in his arms.
Creon. Nothing you say can touch me any more.
My own blind heart has brought me
From darkness to final darkness. Here you see
The father murdering, the murdered son—
And all my civic wisdom!

Haimon my son, so young, so young to die,
I was the fool, not you; and you died for me.
Choragos. That is the truth; but you were late in learning it.
Creon. This truth is hard to bear. Surely a god
Has crushed me beneath the hugest weight of heaven,
And driven me headlong a barbaric way
To trample out the thing I held most dear.

The pains that men will take to come to pain!

[*Enter* Messenger *from the palace.*]

Messenger. The burden you carry in your hands is heavy,
But it is not all: you will find more in your house.

Creon. What burden worse than this shall I find there?
Messenger. The Queen is dead.
Creon. O port of death, deaf world,
Is there no pity for me? And you, Angel of evil,
I was dead, and your words are death again.
Is it true, boy? Can it be true?
Is my wife dead? Has death bred death?
Messenger. You can see for yourself.

[*The doors are opened and the body of* Eurydice *is disclosed within.*]

Creon. Oh pity!
All true, all true, and more than I can bear!
O my wife, my son!
Messenger. She stood before the altar, and her heart
Welcomed the knife her own hand guided,
And a great cry burst from her lips for Megareus[25] dead,
And for Haimon dead, her sons; and her last breath
Was a curse for their father, the murderer of her sons.
And she fell, and the dark flowed in through her closing eyes.
Creon. O God, I am sick with fear.
Are there no swords here? Has no one a blow for me?
Messenger. Her curse is upon you for the deaths of both.
Creon. It is right that it should be. I alone am guilty.
I know it, and I say it. Lead me in,
Quickly, friends.
I have neither life nor substance. Lead me in.
Choragos. You are right, if there can be right in so much wrong.
The briefest way is best in a world of sorrow.
Creon. Let it come,
Let death come quickly, and be kind to me.
I would not ever see the sun again.
Choragos. All that will come when it will; but we, meanwhile,
Have much to do. Leave the future to itself.
Creon. All my heart was in that prayer!
Choragos. Then do not pray any more: the sky is deaf.
Creon. Lead me away. I have been rash and foolish.
I have killed my son and my wife.
I look for comfort; my comfort lies here dead.
Whatever my hands have touched has come to nothing.
Fate has brought all my pride to a thought of dust.

[*As* Creon *is being led into the house, the* Choragos *advances and speaks directly to the audience.*]

Choragos. There is no happiness where there is no wisdom;
No wisdom but in submission to the gods.
Big words are always punished,
And proud men in old age learn to be wise.

Antigone

JEAN ANOUILH

CHORUS
ANTIGONE
NURSE
ISMENE
HAEMON
CREON
FIRST GUARD (*JONAS*)
SECOND GUARD (*A CORPORAL*)
THIRD GUARD
MESSENGER
PAGE
EURYDICE

[Antigone, *her hands clasped round her knees, sits on the top step. The* Three Guards *sit on the steps, in a small group, playing cards. The* Chorus *stands on the top step.* Eurydice *sits on the top step, just left of center, knitting. The* Nurse *sits on the second step, left of* Eurydice. Ismene *stands in front of arch, left, facing* Haemon, *who stands left of her.* Creon *sits in the chair at right end of the table, his arms over the shoulder of his* Page, *who sits on the stool beside his chair. The* Messenger *is leaning against the downstage portal of the right arch.*]

[*The curtain rises slowly; then the* Chorus *turns and moves downstage.*]

Chorus. Well, here we are.

These people are about to act our for you the story of Antigone.

That thin little creature sitting by herself, staring straight ahead, seeing nothing, is Antigone. She is thinking. She is thinking that the instant I finish telling you who's who and what's what in this play, she will burst forth as the tense, sallow, willful girl whose family would never take her seriously and who is about to rise up alone against Creon, her uncle, the King.

Another thing that she is thinking is this: she is going to die. Antigone is young. She would much rather live than die. But there is no help for it. When your name is Antigone, there is only one part you can play; and she will have to play hers through to the end.

From the moment the curtain went up, she began to feel that inhuman forces were whirling her out of this world, snatching her away from her sister Ismene, whom you see smiling and chatting with that young man; from all of us who sit or stand here, looking at her, not in the least upset ourselves—for we are not doomed to die tonight.

[Chorus *turns and indicates* Haemon.]

The young man talking to Ismene—to the gay and beautiful Ismene—is Haemon. He is the King's son, Creon's son. Antigone and he are engaged to be married. You wouldn't have thought she was his type. He likes dancing, sports, competition; he likes women, too. Now look at Ismene again. She is certainly more beautiful than Antigone. She is the girl you'd think he'd go for. Well . . . There was a ball one night. Ismene wore a new evening frock. She was radiant. Haemon danced every dance with her. And yet, that same night, before the dance was over, suddenly he went in search of Antigone, found her sitting alone—like that, with her arms clasped round her knees—and asked her to marry him. We still don't know how it happened. It didn't seem to surprise Antigone in the least. She looked up at him out of those solemn eyes of hers, smiled sort of sadly and said "yes." That was all. The band struck up another dance. Ismene, surrounded by a group of young men, laughed out loud. And . . . well, here is Haemon expecting to marry Antigone. He won't, of course. He didn't know, when he asked her, that the earth wasn't meant to hold a husband of Antigone, and that this princely distinction was to earn him no more than the right to die sooner than he might otherwise have done.

[Chorus *turns toward* Creon.]

That gray-haired, powerfully built man sitting lost in thought, with his little page at his side, is Creon, the King. His face is lined. He is tired. He practices the difficult art of a leader of men. When he was younger, when Oedipus was King and Creon was no more than the King's brother-in-law, he was different. He loved music, bought rare manuscripts, was a kind of art patron. He would while away whole afternoons in the antique shops of this city of Thebes. But Oedipus died. Oedipus' sons died. Creon had to roll up his sleeves and take over the kingdom. Now and then, when he goes to bed weary with the day's work, he wonders whether this business of being a leader of men is worth the trouble. But when he wakes up, the problems are there to be solved; and like a conscientious workman, he does his job.

Creon has a wife, a Queen. Her name is Eurydice. There she sits, the old lady with the knitting, next to the Nurse who brought up the two girls. She will go on knitting all through the play, till the time comes for her to go to her room and die. She is a good woman, a worthy, loving soul. But she is no help to her husband. Creon has to face the music alone. Alone with his Page, who is too young to be of any help.

The others? Well, let's see.

[*He points toward the* Messenger.]

That pale young man leaning against the wall is the Messenger. Later on he will come running in to announce that Haemon is dead. He has a premonition of catastrophe. That's what he is brooding over. That's why he won't mingle with the others.

As for those three red-faced card players—they are the guards. One smells of garlic, another of beer; but they're not a bad lot. They have wives they are afraid of, kids who are afraid of them; they're bothered by the little day-to-day worries that beset us all. At the same time—they are policemen: eternally innocent, no matter what crimes are committed; eternally indifferent, for nothing that happens can matter to them. They are quite prepared to arrest anybody at all, including Creon himself, should the order be given by a new leader.

That's the lot. Now for the play.

Oedipus, who was the father of the two girls, Antigone and Ismene, had also two sons, Eteocles and Polynices. After Oedipus died, it was agreed that the two sons should share his throne, each to reign over Thebes in alternate years.

[*Gradually, the lights on the stage have been dimmed.*]

But when Eteocles, the elder son, had reigned a full year, and time had come for him to step down, he refused to yield up the throne to his younger brother. There was civil war. Polynices brought up allies—six foreign princes; and in the course of the war he and his foreigners were defeated, each in front of one of the seven gates of the city. The two brothers fought, and they killed one another in single combat just outside the city walls. Now Creon is King.

[Chorus *is leaning, at this point, against the left proscenium arch. By now the stage is dark, with only the cyclorama bathed in dark blue. A single spot lights up the face of* Chorus.]

Creon has issued a solemn edict that Eteocles, with whom he had sided, is to be buried with pomp and honours, and that Polynices is to be left to rot. The vultures and the dogs are to bloat themselves on his carcass. Nobody is to go into mourning for him. No gravestone is to be set up in his memory. And above all, any person who attempts to give him religious burial will himself be put to death.

[*While* Chorus *has been speaking the characters have gone out one by one.* Chorus *disappears through the left arch.*]

[*It is dawn, gray and ashen, in a house asleep.* Antigone *steals in from out-of-doors, through the arch, right. She is carrying her sandals in her hand. She pauses, looking off through the arch, taut, listening, then turns and moves across downstage. As she reaches the table, she sees the* Nurse *approaching through the arch, left. She runs quickly toward the exit. As she reaches the steps, the* Nurse *enters through arch and stands still when she sees* Antigone.]

Nurse. Where have you been?

Antigone. Nowhere. It was beautiful. The whole world was gray when I went out. And now—you wouldn't recognize it. It's like a post card: all pink, and green, and yellow. You'll have to get up earlier, Nurse, if you want to see a world without color.

Nurse. It was still pitch black when I got up. I went to your room, for I thought you might have flung off your blanket in the night. You weren't there.

Antigone [*comes down the steps*]. The garden was lovely. It was still asleep. Have you ever thought how lovely a garden is when it is not yet thinking of men?

Nurse. You hadn't slept in your bed. I couldn't find you, I went to the back door. You'd left it open.

Antigone. The fields were wet. They were waiting for something to happen. The whole world was breathless, waiting. I can't tell you what a roaring noise I seemed to make alone on the road. It bothered me that whatever was waiting wasn't waiting for me. I took off my sandals and slipped into a field. [*She moves down to the stool and sits.*]

Nurse [*kneels at* Antigone's *feet to chafe them and put on the sandals*]. You'll do well to wash your feet before you go back to bed, Miss.

Antigone. I'm not going back to bed.

Nurse. Don't be a fool! You get some sleep! And me, getting up to see if she hasn't flung off her blanket; and I find her bed cold and nobody in it!

Antigone. Do you think that if a person got up every morning like this, it would be just as thrilling every morning to be the first girl out-of-doors?

[Nurse *puts* Antigone's *left foot down, lifts her other foot and chafes it.*]

Nurse. Morning my grandmother! It was night. It still is. And now, my girl, you'll stop trying to squirm out of this and tell me what you were up to. Where've you been?

Antigone. That's true. It was still night. There wasn't a soul out of doors but me, who thought that it was morning. Don't you think it's marvelous—to be the first person who is aware that it is morning?

Nurse. Oh, my little flibbertigibbet! Just can't imagine what I'm talking about, can she? Go on with you! I know that game. Where have you been, wicked girl?

Antigone [*soberly*]. No. Not wicked.

Nurse. You went out to meet someone, didn't you? Deny it if you can.

Antigone. Yes. I went out to meet someone.

Nurse. A lover?

Antigone. Yes, Nurse. Yes, the poor dear. I have a lover.

Nurse [*stands up; bursting out*]. Ah, that's very nice now, isn't it? Such goings-on! You, the daughter of a king, running out to meet lovers. And we work our fingers to the bone for you, we slave to bring you up like young ladies! [*She sits on chair, right of table.*] You're all alike, all of you. Even you—who never used to stop to primp in front of a looking glass, or smear your mouth with rouge, or dindle and dandle to make the boys ogle you, and you ogle back. How many times I'd say to myself, "Now that one, now: I wish she was a little more of a coquette—always wearing the same dress, her hair tumbling round her face. One thing's sure," I'd say to myself, "none of the boys will look at her while Ismene's about, all curled and cute and tidy and trim. I'll have this one on my hands for the rest of my life." And now, you see? Just like your sister, after all. Only worse: a hypocrite. Who is the lad? Some little scamp, eh? Somebody you can't bring home and show to your family, and say, "Well, this is him, and I mean to marry him and no other." That's how it is, is it? Answer me!

Antigone [*smiling faintly*]. That's how it is. Yes, Nurse.

Nurse. Yes, says she! God save us! I took her when she wasn't that high. I promised her poor mother I'd make a lady of her. And look at her! But don't you go thinking this is the end of this, my young 'un. I'm only your nurse and you can play deaf and dumb with me; I don't count. But your Uncle Creon will hear of this! That, I promise you.

Antigone [*a little weary*]. Yes. Creon will hear of this.

Nurse. And we'll hear what he has to say when he finds out that you go wandering alone o' nights. Not to mention Haemon. For the girl's engaged! Going to be married! Going to be married, and she hops out of bed at four in the morning to meet somebody else in a field. Do you know what I ought to do to you? Take you over my knee the way I used to do when you were little.

Antigone. Please, Nurse, I want to be alone.

Nurse. And if you so much as speak of it, she says she wants to be alone!

Antigone. Nanny, you shouldn't scold, dear. This isn't a day when you should be losing your temper.

Nurse. Not scold, indeed! Along with the rest of it, I'm to like it. Didn't I promise your mother? What would she say if she was here? "Old Stupid!" That's what she'd call me. "Old Stupid. Not to know how to keep my little girl pure! Spend your life making them behave, watching over them like a mother hen, running after them with mufflers and sweaters to keep them warm, and eggnogs to make them strong; and then at four o'clock in the morning, you who always complained you never could sleep a wink, snoring in your bed and letting them slip out into the bushes." That's what she'd say, your mother. And I'd stand there, dying of shame if I wasn't dead already. And all I could do would be not to dare look her in the face; and "That's true," I'd say. "That's all true what you say, Your Majesty."

Antigone. Nanny, dear. Dear Nanny. Don't cry. You'll be able to look Mamma in the face when it's your time to see her. And she'll say, "Good morning, Nanny. Thank you for my little Antigone. You did look after her so well." She knows why I went out this morning.

Nurse. Not to meet a lover?

Antigone. No. Not to meet a lover.

Nurse. Well, you've a queer way of teasing me, I must say! Not to know when she's teasing me! [*Rises to stand behind* Antigone.] I must be getting awfully old, that's what it is. But if you loved me, you'd tell me the truth. You'd tell me why your bed was empty when I went along to tuck you in. Wouldn't you?

Antigone. Please, Nanny, don't cry any more. [Antigone *turns partly toward* Nurse, *puts an arm up to* Nurse's *shoulder. With her other hand,* Antigone *caresses* Nurse's *face.*] There now, my sweet red apple. Do you remember how I used to rub your cheeks to make them shine? My dear, wrinkled red apple! I didn't do anything tonight that was worth sending tears down the little gullies of your dear face. I am pure, and I swear that I have no other lover than Haemon. If you like, I'll swear that I shall never have any other lover than Haemon. Save your tears, Nanny, save them, Nanny dear; you may still need them. When you cry like that, I become a little girl again; and I mustn't be a little girl today. [Antigone *rises and moves upstage.*]

[Ismene *enters through arch, left. She pauses in front of arch.*]

Ismene. Antigone! What are you doing up at this hour? I've just been to your room.

Nurse. The two of you, now! You're both going mad, to be up before the kitchen fire has been started. Do you like running about without a mouthful of breakfast? Do you think it's decent for the daughters of a king? [*She turns to* Ismene.] And look at you, with nothing on, and the sun not up! I'll have you both on my hands with colds before I know it.

Antigone. Nanny dear, go away now. It's not chilly, really. Summer's here. Go and make us some coffee. Please, Nanny, I'd love some coffee. It would do me so much good.

Nurse. My poor baby! Her head's swimming, what with nothing on her stomach, and me standing here like an idiot when I could be getting her something hot to drink. [*Exit* Nurse.]

[*A pause.*]

Ismene. Aren't you well?

Antigone. Of course I am. Just a little tired. I got up too early. [Antigone *sits on a chair, suddenly tired.*]

Ismene. I couldn't sleep, either.

Antigone. Ismene, you ought not to go without your beauty sleep.

Ismene. Don't make fun of me.

Antigone. I'm not, Ismene, truly. This particular morning, seeing how beautiful you are makes everything easier for me. Wasn't I a miserable little beast when we were small? I used to fling mud at you, and put worms down your neck. I remember tying you to a tree and cutting off your hair. Your beautiful hair! How easy it must be never to be unreasonable with all that smooth silken hair so beautifully set round your head.

Ismene [*abruptly*]. Why do you insist upon talking about other things?

Antigone [*gently*]. I am not talking about other things.

Ismene. Antigone, I've thought about it a lot.

Antigone. Have you?

Ismene. I thought about it all night long. Antigone, you're mad.

Antigone. Am I?

Ismene. We cannot do it.

Antigone. Why not?

Ismene. Creon will have us put to death.

Antigone. Of course he will. That's what he's here for. He will do what he has to do, and we will do what we have to do. (He is bound to put us to death. We are bound to go out and bury our brother.) That's the way it is. What do you think we can do to change it?

Ismene [*releases* Antigone's *hand; draws back a step*]. I don't want to die.

Antigone. I'd prefer not to die, myself.

Ismene. Listen to me, Antigone. I thought about it all night. I'm older than you are. I always think things over, and you don't. You are impulsive. You get a notion in your head and you jump up and do the thing straight off. And if it's silly, well, so much the worse for you. Whereas, *I* think things out.

Antigone. Sometimes it is better not to think too much.

Ismene. I don't agree with you! [Antigone *looks at* Ismene, *then turns and moves to chair behind table.* Ismene *leans on end of table top, toward* Antigone.] Oh, I know it's horrible. And I pity Polynices just as much as you do. But all the same, I sort of see what Uncle Creon means.

Antigone. I don't want to "sort of see" anything.

Ismene. Uncle Creon is the king. He has to set an example!

Antigone. But I am not the king; and I don't have to set people examples. Little Antigone gets a notion in her head—the nasty brat, the willful, wicked girl; and they put her in a corner all day, or they lock her up in the cellar. And she deserves it. She shouldn't have disobeyed!

Ismene. There you go, frowning, glowering, wanting your own stubborn way in everything. Listen to me. I'm right oftener than you are.

Antigone. I don't want to be right!

Ismene. At least you can try to understand.

Antigone. Understand! The first word I ever heard out of any of you was that word "understand." Why didn't I "understand" that I must not play with water—cold, black, beautiful flowing water—because I'd spill it on the palace tiles. Or with earth, because earth dirties a little girl's frock. Why didn't I "understand" that nice children don't eat out of every dish at once; or give everything in their pockets to beggars; or run in the wind so fast that they fall down; or ask for a drink when they're perspiring; or want to go swimming when it's either too early or too late, merely because they happen to feel like swimming. Understand! I don't want to understand. There'll be time enough to understand when I'm old. . . . If I ever *am* old. But not now.

Ismene. He is stronger than we are, Antigone. He is the king. And the whole city is with him. Thousands and thousands of them, swarming through all the streets of Thebes.

Antigone. I am not listening to you.

Ismene. His mob will come running, howling as it runs. A thousand arms will seize our arms. A thousand breaths will breathe into our faces. Like one single pair of eyes, a thousand eyes will stare at us. We'll be driven in a tumbrel through their hatred, through the smell of them and their cruel, roaring laughter. We'll be dragged to the scaffold for torture, surrounded by guards with their idiot faces all bloated, their animal hands clean-washed for the sacrifice, their beefy eyes squinting as they stare at us. And we'll know that no shrieking and no begging will make them understand that we want to live, for they are like slaves who do exactly as they've been told, without caring about right or wrong. And we shall suffer, we shall feel pain rising in us until it becomes so unbearable that we *know* it must stop. But it won't stop; it will go on rising and rising, like a screaming voice. Oh, I can't, I can't, Antigone!

[*A pause.*]

Antigone. How well have you thought it all out.

Ismene. I thought of it all night long. Didn't you?

Antigone. Oh, yes.

Ismene. I'm an awful coward, Antigone.

Antigone. So am I. But what has that to do with it?

Ismene. But, Antigone! Don't you want to go on living?

Antigone. Go on living! Who was it that was always the first out of bed because she loved the touch of the cold morning air on her bare skin? Who was always the last to bed because nothing less than infinite weariness could wean her from the lingering night? Who wept when she was little because there were too many grasses in the meadow, too many creatures in the field, for her to know and touch them all?

Ismene [*clasps* Antigone's *hands, in a sudden rush of tenderness*]. Darling little sister!

Antigone [*repulsing her*]. No! For heaven's sake! Don't paw me! And don't let us start sniveling! You say you've thought it all out. The howling mob—the torture—the fear of death. . . . They've made up your mind for you. Is that it?

Ismene. Yes.

Antigone. All right. They're as good excuses as any.

Ismene. Antigone, be sensible. It's all very well for men to believe in ideas and die for them. But you are a girl!

Antigone. Don't I know I'm a girl? Haven't I spent my life cursing the fact that I was a girl?

Ismene [*with spirit*]. Antigone! You have everything in the world to make you happy. All you have to do is reach out for it. You are going to be married; you are young; you are beautiful——

Antigone. I am not beautiful.

Ismene. Yes, you are! Not the way other girls are. But it's always you that the little boys turn to look back at when they pass us in the street. And when you go by, the little girls stop talking. They stare and stare at you, until we've turned a corner.

Antigone [*a faint smile*]. "Little boys—little girls."

Ismene [*challengingly*]. And what about Haemon?

[*A pause.*]

Antigone. I shall see Haemon this morning. I'll take care of Haemon. You always said I was mad; and it didn't matter how little I was or what I wanted to do. Go back to bed now, Ismene. The sun is coming up, and, as you see, there is nothing I can do today. Our brother Polynices is as well guarded as if he had won the war and were sitting on his throne. Go along. You are pale with weariness.

Ismene. What are you going to do?

Nurse [*calls from off-stage*]. Come along, my dove. Come to breakfast.

Antigone. I don't feel like going to bed. However, if you like, I'll promise not to leave the house till you wake up. Nurse is getting me breakfast. Go and get some sleep. The sun is just up. Look at you: you can't keep your eyes open. Go.

Ismene. And you will listen to reason, won't you? You'll let me talk to you about this again? Promise?

Antigone. I promise. I'll let you talk. I'll let all of you talk. Go to bed, now. [Ismene *goes to arch; exit.*] Poor Ismene!

Nurse [*enters through arch, speaking as she enters*]. Come along, my dove. I've made you some coffee and toast and jam. [*She turns toward arch as if to go out.*]

Antigone. I'm not really hungry, Nurse.

[Nurse *stops, looks at* Antigone, *then moves behind her.*]

Nurse [*very tenderly*]. Where is your pain?

Antigone. Nowhere, Nanny dear. But you must keep me warm and safe, the way you used to do when I was little. Nanny! Stronger than all fever, stronger than any nightmare, stronger than the shadow of the cupboard that used to snarl at me and turns into a dragon on the bedroom wall. Stronger than the thousand insects gnawing and nibbling in the silence of the night. Stronger than the night itself, with the weird hooting of the night birds that frightened me even when I couldn't hear them. Nanny, stronger than death. Give me your hand, Nanny, as if I were ill in bed, and you sitting beside me.

Nurse. My sparrow, my lamb! What is it that's eating your heart out?

Antigone. Oh, it's just that I'm a little young still for what I have to go through. But nobody but you must know that.

Nurse [*places her other arm around* Antigone's *shoulder*]. A little young for what, my kitten?

Antigone. Nothing in particular, Nanny. Just—all this. Oh, it's so good that you are here. I can hold your callused hand, your hand that is so prompt to ward off evil. You are very powerful, Nanny.

Nurse. What is it you want me to do for you, my baby?

Antigone. There isn't anything to do, except put your hand like this against my cheek [*She places the* Nurse's *hand against her cheek. A pause, then, as* Antigone *leans back, her eyes shut.*] There! I'm not afraid any more. Not afraid of the wicked ogre, nor of the sandman, nor of the dwarf who steals little children. [*A pause.* Antigone *resumes on another note.*] Nanny . . .

Nurse. Yes?

Antigone. My dog, Puff . . .

Nurse [*straightens up, draws her hand away*]. Well?

Antigone. Promise me that you will never scold her again.

Nurse. Dogs that dirty up a house with their filthy paws deserve to be scolded.

Antigone. I know. Just the same, promise me.

Nurse. You mean you want me to let her make a mess all over the place and not say a thing?

Antigone. Yes, Nanny.

Nurse. You're asking a lot. The next time she wets my living-room carpet, I'll——

Antigone. Please, Nanny, I beg of you!

Nurse. It isn't fair to take me on my weak side, just because you look a little peaked today. . . . Well, have it your own way. We'll mop up and keep our mouth shut. You're making a fool of me, though.

Antigone. And promise me that you will talk to her. That you will talk to her often.

Nurse [*turns and looks at* Antigone]. Me, talk to a dog!

Antigone. Yes. But mind you: you are not to talk to her the way people usually talk to dogs. You're to talk to her the way I talk to her.

Nurse. I don't see why both of us have to make fools of ourselves. So long as you're here, one ought to be enough.

Antigone. But if there was a reason why I couldn't go on talking to her——

Nurse [*interrupting*]. Couldn't go on talking to her! And why couldn't you go on talking to her? What kind of poppycock——?

Antigone. And if she got too unhappy, if she moaned and moaned, waiting for me with her nose under the door as she does when I'm out all day, then the best thing, Nanny, might be to have her mercifully put to sleep.

Nurse. Now what *has* got into you this morning? [Haemon *enters through arch*]. Running around in the darkness, won't sleep, won't eat—[Antigone *sees* Haemon.]—and now it's her dog she wants killed. I never.

Antigone [*interrupting*]. Nanny! Haemon is here. Go inside, please. And don't forget that you've promised me. [Nurse *goes to arch; exit.* Antigone *rises.*] Haemon, Haemon! Forgive me for quarreling with you last night.

[*She crosses quickly to* Haemon *and they embrace.*] Forgive me for everything. It was all my fault. I beg you to forgive me.

Haemon. You know that I've forgiven you. You had hardly slammed the door, your perfume still hung in the room, when I had already forgiven you. [*He holds her in his arms and smiles at her. Then draws slightly back.*] You stole that perfume. From whom?

Antigone. Ismene.

Haemon. And the rouge? and the face powder? and the frock? Whom did you steal them from?

Antigone. Ismene.

Haemon. And in whose honor did you get yourself up so elegantly?

Antigone. I'll tell you everything. [*She draws him closer.*] Oh, darling, what a fool I was! To waste a whole evening! A whole, beautiful evening!

Haemon. We'll have other evenings, my sweet.

Antigone. Perhaps we won't.

Haemon. And other quarrels, too. A happy love is full of quarrels, you know.

Antigone. A happy love, yes. Haemon, listen to me.

Haemon. Yes?

Antigone. Don't laugh at me this morning. Be serious.

Haemon. I am serious.

Antigone. And hold me tight. Tighter than you have ever held me. I want all your strength to flow into me.

Haemon. There! With all my strength.

[*A pause.*]

Antigone [*breathless*]. That's good. [*They stand for a moment, silent and motionless.*] Haemon! I wanted to tell you. You know—the little boy we were going to have when we were married?

Haemon. Yes?

Antigone. I'd have protected him against everything in the world.

Haemon. Yes, dearest.

Antigone. Oh, you don't know how I should have held him in my arms and given him my strength. He wouldn't have been afraid of anything, I swear he wouldn't. Not of the falling night, nor of the terrible noonday sun, nor of all the shadows, or all the walls in the world. Our little boy, Haemon! His mother wouldn't have been very imposing: her hair wouldn't always have been brushed; but she would have been strong where he was concerned, so much stronger than all those real mothers with their real bosoms and their aprons around their middle. You believe that, don't you, Haemon?

Haemon [*soothingly*]. Yes, yes, my darling.

Antigone. And you believe me when I say that you would have had a real wife?

Haemon. Darling, you are my real wife.

Antigone [*pressing against him and crying out*]. Haemon, you loved me! You did love me that night, didn't you? You're sure of it!

Haemon [*rocking her gently*]. What night, my sweet?

Antigone. And you are very sure, aren't you, that that night, at the dance, when you came to the corner where I was sitting, there was no mistake? It was me you were looking for? It wasn't another girl? And you're sure that never, not in your most secret heart of hearts, have you said to yourself that it was Ismene you ought to have asked to marry you?

Haemon [*reproachfully*]. Antigone, you are idiotic. You might give me credit for knowing my own mind. It's you I love, and no one else.

Antigone. But you love me as a woman—as a woman wants to be loved, don't you? Your arms around me aren't lying, are they? Your hands, so warm against my back—they're not lying? This warmth that's in me; this confidence, this sense that I am safe, secure, that flows through me as I stand here with my cheek in the hollow of your shoulder: they are not lies, are they?

Haemon. Antigone, darling, I love you exactly as you love me. With all of myself.

[*They kiss.*]

Antigone. I'm sallow, and I'm scrawny. Ismene is pink and golden. She's like a fruit.

Haemon. Look here, Antigone——

Antigone. Ah, dearest, I am ashamed of myself. But this morning, this special morning, I must know. Tell me the truth! I beg you to tell me the truth! When you think about me, when it strikes you suddenly that I am going to belong to you—do you have the feeling that—that a great empty space is being hollowed out inside you, that there is something inside you that is just—dying?

Haemon. Yes, I do, I do.

[*A pause.*]

Antigone. That's the way I feel. And another thing. I wanted you to know that I should have been very proud to be your wife—the woman whose shoulder you would put your hand on as you sat down to table, absent-mindedly, as upon a thing that belonged to you. [*After a moment, draws away from him. Her tone changes.*] There! Now I have two things more to tell you. And when I have told them to you, you must go away instantly, without asking any questions. However strange they may seem to you. However much they may hurt you. Swear that you will!

Haemon [*beginning to be troubled*]. What are these things that you are going to tell me?

Antigone. Swear, first, that you will go away without one word. Without so much as looking at me. [*She looks at him, wretchedness in her face.*] You hear me, Haemon. Swear it, please. This is the last mad wish that you will ever have to grant me.

[*A pause.*]

Haemon. I swear it, since you insist. But I must tell you that I don't like this at all.

Antigone. Please, Haemon. It's very serious. You must listen to me and do as I ask. First, about last night, when I came to your house. You asked me a moment ago why I wore Ismene's dress and rouge. It was because I was stupid. I wasn't very sure that you loved me as a woman; and I did it—because I wanted you to want me. I was trying to be more like other girls.

Haemon. Was *that* the reason? My poor——

Antigone. Yes. And you laughed at me. And we quarreled; and my awful temper got the better of me and I flung out of the house. . . . The real reason was that I wanted you to take me; I wanted to be your wife before——

Haemon. Oh, my darling——

Antigone [*shuts him off*]. You swore you wouldn't ask any questions. You swore, Haemon. [*Turns her face away and goes on in a hard voice.*] As a matter of fact, I'll tell you why. I wanted to be your wife last night because I love you that way very—very strongly. And also because—— Oh, my darling, my darling, forgive me; I'm going to cause you quite a lot of pain. [*She draws away from him.*] I wanted it also because I shall never, never be able to marry you, never! [Haemon *is stupefied and mute; then he moves a step towards her.*] Haemon! You took a solemn oath! You swore! Leave me quickly! Tomorrow the whole thing will be clear to you. Even before tomorrow: this afternoon. If you please, Haemon, go now. It is the only thing left that you can do for me if you still love me. [*A pause as* Haemon *stares at her. Then he turns and goes out through the arch.* Antigone *stands motionless, then moves to a chair at end of table and lets herself gently down on it. In a mild voice, as of calm after storm.*] Well, it's over for Haemon, Antigone.

[Ismene *enters through arch, pauses for a moment in front of it when she sees* Antigone, *then crosses behind table.*]

Ismene. I can't sleep. I'm terrified. I'm so afraid that, even though it is daylight, you'll still try to bury Polynices. Antigone, little sister, we all want to make you happy—Haemon, and Nurse, and I, and Puff whom you love. We love you, we are alive, we need you. And you remember what Polynices was like. He was our brother, of course. But he's dead; and he never loved you. He was a bad brother. He was like an enemy in the house. He never thought of you. Why should you think of him? What if his soul does have to wander through endless time without rest or peace? Don't try something that is beyond your strength. You are always defying the world, but you're only a girl, after all. Stay at home tonight. Don't try to do it, I beg you. It's Creon's doing, not ours.

Antigone. You are too late, Ismene. When you first saw me this morning, I had just come in from burying him. [*Exit* Antigone *through arch.*]

[*The lighting, which by this time has reached a point of early morning sun, is quickly dimmed out, leaving the stage bathed in a light blue color.* Ismene *runs out after* Antigone. *On* Ismere's *exit the lights are brought up suddenly to suggest a later period of the day.* Creon *and* Page *enter through curtain upstage.* Creon *stands on the top step; his* Page *stands at his right side.*]

Creon. A private of the guards, you say? One of those standing watch over the body? Show him in.

[*The* Page *crosses to arch; exit.* Creon *moves down to end of table.* Page *re-enters, preceded by the* First Guard, *livid with fear.* Page *remains on upstage side of arch.* Guard *salutes.*]

Guard. Private Jonas, Second Battalion.

Creon. What are you doing here?

Guard. It's like this, sir. Soon as it happened, we said: "Got to tell the chief about this before anybody else spills it. He'll want to know right away." So we tossed a coin to see which one would come up and tell you about it. You see, sir, we thought only one man had better come, because, after all, you don't want to leave the body without a guard. Right? I mean, there's three of us on duty, guarding the body.

Creon. What's wrong about the body?

Guard. Sir, I've been seventeen years in the service. Volunteer. Wounded three times. Two mentions. My record's clean. I know my business and I know my place. I carry out orders. Sir, ask any officer in the battalion; they'll tell you. "Leave it to Jonas. Give him an order: he'll carry it out." That's what they'll tell you, sir. Jonas, that's me—that's my name.

Creon. What's the matter with you, man? What are you shaking for?

Guard. By rights it's the corporal's job, sir. I've been recommended for a corporal, but they haven't put it through yet. June, it was supposed to go through.

Creon [*interrupts*]. Stop chattering and tell me why you are here. If anything has gone wrong, I'll break all three of you.

Guard. Nobody can say we didn't keep our eye on that body. We had the two-o'clock watch—the tough one. You know how it is, sir. It's nearly the end of the night. Your eyes are like lead. You've got a crick in the back of your neck. There's shadows, and the fog is beginning to roll in. A fine watch they give us! And me, seventeen years in the service. But we was doing our duty all right. On our feet, all of us. Anybody says we were sleeping is a liar. First place, it was too cold. Second place—— [Creon *makes a gesture of impatience.*] Yes, sir. Well, I turned around and looked at the body. We wasn't only ten feet away from it, but that's how I am. I was keeping my eye on it. [*Shouts.*] Listen, sir, I was the first man to see it! Me! They'll tell you. I was the one let out that yell!

Creon. What for? What was the matter?

Guard. Sir, the body! Somebody had been there and buried it. [Creon *comes* *down a step on the stair. The* Guard *becomes more frightened.*] It wasn't much, you understand. With us three there, it couldn't have been. Just covered over with a little dirt, that's all. But enough to hide it from the buzzards.

Creon. By God, I'll——! [*He looks intently at the* Guard.] You are sure that it couldn't have been a dog, scratching up the earth?

Guard. Not a chance, sir. That's kind of what we hoped it was. But the earth was scattered over the body just like the priests tell you you should do it. Whoever did that job knew what he was doing, all right.

Creon. Who could have dared? [*He turns and looks at the* Guard.] Was there anything to indicate who might have done it?

Guard. Not a thing, sir. Maybe we heard a footstep—I can't swear to it. Of course we started right in to search, and the corporal found a shovel, a kid's shovel no bigger than that, all rusty and everything. Corporal's got the shovel for you. We thought maybe a kid did it.

Creon [*to himself*]. A kid! [*He looks away from the* Guard.] I broke the back of the rebellion; but like a snake, it is coming together again. Polynices' friends, with their gold, blocked by my orders in the banks of Thebes. The leaders of the mob, stinking of garlic and allied to envious princes. And the temple priests, always ready for a bit of fishing in troubled waters. A kid! I can imagine what he is like, their kid: a baby-faced killer, creeping in the night with a toy shovel under his jacket. [*He looks at his* Page.] Though why shouldn't they have corrupted a real child? Very touching! Very useful to the party, an innocent child. A martyr. A real white-faced baby of fourteen who will spit with contempt at the guards who kill him. A free gift to their cause: the precious, innocent blood of a child on my hands. [*He turns to the* Guard.] They must have accomplices in the Guard itself. Look here, you. Who knows about this?

Guard. Only us three, sir. We flipped a coin, and I came right over.

Creon. Right. Listen, now. You will continue on duty. When the relief squad comes up, you will tell them to return to barracks. You will uncover the body. If another attempt is made to bury it, I shall expect you to make an arrest and bring the person straight to me. And you will keep your mouths shut. Not one word of this to a human soul. You are all guilty of neglect of duty, and you will be punished; but if the rumor spreads through Thebes that the body received burial, you will be shot—all three of you.

Guard [*excitedly*]. Sir, we never told nobody, I swear we didn't! Anyhow, I've been up here. Suppose my pals spilled it to the relief; I couldn't have been with them and here too. That wouldn't be my fault if they talked. Sir, I've got two kids. You're my witness, sir, it couldn't have been me. I was here with you. I've got a witness! If anybody talked, it couldn't have been me! I was——

Creon [*interrupting*]. Clear out! If the story doesn't get around, you won't be shot. [*The* Guard *salutes, turns, and exits at the double.* Creon *turns and paces upstage, then comes down to end of the table.*] A child! [*He looks at* Page.] Come along, my lad. Since we can't hope to keep this to ourselves, we shall have to be the first to give out the news. And after that, we shall have to clean up the mess. [Page *crosses to side of* Creon. Creon *puts his hand on* Page's *shoulder.*] Would you be willing to die for me? Would you defy the Guard with your little shovel? [Page *looks up at* Creon.] Of course you would. You would do it, too. [*A pause.* Creon *looks away from* Page *and murmurs*] A child!

[Creon *and* Page *go slowly upstage center to top step.* Page *draws aside the curtain, through which exit* Creon *with* Page *behind him.*]

[*As soon as* Creon *and* Page *have disappeared,* Chorus *enters and leans against the upstage portal or arch, left. The lighting is brought up to its brightest point to suggest mid-afternoon.* Chorus *allows a a pause to indicate that a crucial moment has been reached in the play, then moves slowly downstage, center. He stands for a moment silent, reflecting, and then smiles faintly.*]

Chorus. The spring is wound up tight. It will uncoil of itself. That is what is so convenient in tragedy. The least little turn of the wrist will do the job. Anything will set it going: a glance at a girl who happens to be lifting her arms to her hair as you go by; a feeling when you wake up on a fine morning that you'd like a little respect paid to you today, as if it were as easy to order as a second cup of coffee; one question too many, idly thrown out over a friendly drink—and the tragedy is on.

The rest is automatic. You don't need to lift a finger. The machine is in perfect order; it has been oiled ever since time began, and it runs without friction. Death, treason, and sorrow are on the march; and they move in the wake of storm, of tears, of stillness. Every kind of stillness. The hush when the executioner's ax goes up at the end of the last act. The unbreathable silence when, at the beginning of the play, the two lovers, their hearts bared, their bodies naked, stand for the first time face to face in the darkened room, afraid to stir. The silence inside you when the roaring crowd acclaims the winner—so that you think of a film without a sound track, mouths agape and no sound coming out of them, a clamor that is no more than a picture; and you, the victor, already vanquished, alone in the desert of your silence. That is tragedy.

Tragedy is clean, it is restful, it is flawless. It has nothing to do with melodrama—with wicked villains, persecuted maidens, avengers, sudden revelations, and eleventh-hour repentances. Death, in a melodrama, is really horrible because it is never inevitable. The dear old father might so easily have been saved; the honest young man might so easily have brought in the police five minutes earlier.

In a tragedy, nothing is in doubt and everyone's destiny is known. That makes for tranquility. There is a sort of fellow-feeling among characters in a tragedy: he who kills is as innocent as he who gets killed: it's all a matter of what part you are playing. Tragedy is restful; and the reason is that hope, that foul, deceitful thing, has no part in it. There isn't any hope. You're trapped. The whole sky has fallen on you, and all you can do about it is to shout.

Don't mistake me: I said "shout": I did not say groan, whimper, complain. That, you cannot do. But you can shout aloud; you can get all those things said that you never thought you'd be able to say—or never even knew you had it in you to say. And you don't say these things because it will do any good to say them: you know better than that. You say them for their own sake; you say them because you learn a lot from them.

In melodrama you argue and struggle in the hope of escape. That is vulgar; it's practical. But in tragedy, where there is no temptation to try to escape, argument is gratuitous: it's kingly.

[*Voices of the* Guards *and scuffling sound heard through the archway.* Chorus *looks in that direction; then, in a changed tone:*]

The play is on. Antigone has been caught. For the first time in her life, little Antigone is going to be able to be herself.

[*Exit* Chorus *through arch. A pause, while the offstage voices rise in volume, then the* First Guard *enters, followed by* Second *and* Third Guards, *holding the arms of* Antigone *and dragging her along. The* First Guard, *speaking as he enters, crosses swiftly to end of the table. The* Two Guards *and* Antigone *stop downstage.*]

First Guard [*recovered from his fright*]. Come on, now, Miss, give it a rest. The chief will be here in a minute and you can tell him about it. All I know is my orders. I don't want to know what you were doing there. People always have excuses; but I can't afford to listen to them, see. Why, if we had to listen to all the people who want to tell us what's the matter with this country, we'd never get our work done. [*To the* Guards.] You keep hold of her and I'll see that she keeps her face shut.

Antigone. They are hurting me. Tell them to take their dirty hands off me.

First Guard. Dirty hands, eh? The least you can do is try to be polite, Miss. Look at me: I'm polite.

Antigone. Tell them to let me go. I shan't run away. My father was King Oedipus. I am Antigone.

First Guard. King Oedipus' little girl! Well, well, well! Listen, Miss, the night watch never picks up a lady but they say, you better be careful: I'm sleeping with the police commissioner.

[*The* Guards *laugh.*]

Antigone. I don't mind being killed, but I don't want them to touch me.

First Guard. And what about stiffs, and dirt, and such like? You wasn't afraid to touch them, was you? "Their dirty hands!" Take a look at your own hands. [Antigone, *handcuffed, smiles despite herself as she looks down at her hands. They are grubby.*] You must have lost your shovel, didn't you? Had to go at it with your fingernails the second time, I'll bet. By God, I never saw such nerve! I turn my back for about five seconds; I ask a pal for a chew; I say "thanks"; I get the tobacco stowed away in my cheek—the whole thing don't take ten seconds; and there she is, clawing away like a hyena. Right out in broad daylight! And did she scratch and kick when I grabbed her! Straight for my eyes with them nails she went. And yelling something fierce about, "I haven't finished yet; let me finish!" She ain't got all her marbles!

Second Guard. I pinched a nut like that the other day. Right on the main square she was, hoisting up her skirts and showing her behind to anybody that wanted to take a look.

First Guard. Listen, we're going to get a bonus out of this. What do you say we throw a party, the three of us?

Second Guard. At the old woman's? Behind Market Street?

Third Guard. Suits me. Sunday would be a good day. We're off duty Sunday. What do you say we bring our wives?

First Guard. No. Let's have some fun this time. Bring your wife, there's always something goes wrong. First place, what do you do with the kids? Bring them, they always want to go to the can just when you're right in the middle of a game of cards or something. Listen, who would have thought an hour ago that us three would be talking about throwing a party now? The way I felt when the old man was interrogating me, we'd be lucky if we got off with being docked a month's pay. I want to tell you, I was scared.

Second Guard. You sure we're going to get a bonus?

First Guard. Yes. Something tells me this is big stuff.

Third Guard [*to* Second Guard]. What's-his-name, you know—in the Third Battalion? He got an extra month's pay for catching a firebug.

Second Guard. If we get an extra month's pay, I vote we throw the party at the Arabian's.

First Guard. You're crazy! He charges twice as much for liquor as anybody else in town. Unless you want to go upstairs, of course. Can't do that at the old woman's.

Third Guard. Well, we can't keep this from our wives, no matter how you work it out. You get an extra month's pay, and what happens? Everybody in the battalion knows it, and your wife knows it too. They might even line up the battalion and give it to you in front of everybody, so how could you keep your wife from finding out?

First Guard. Well, we'll see about that. If they do the job out in the barrack yard—of course that means women, kids, everything.

Antigone. I should like to sit down, if you please.

[*A pause, as the* First Guard *thinks it over.*]

First Guard. Let her sit down. But keep hold of her. [*The two* Guards *start to lead her toward the chair at end of table. The curtain upstage opens, and* Creon *enters, followed by his* Page. First Guard *turns and moves upstage a few steps, sees* Creon.] 'Tenshun! [*The three* Guards *salute.* Creon, *seeing* Antigone *handcuffed to* Third Guard, *stops on the top step, astonished.*]

Creon. Antigone! [*To the* First Guard.] Take off those handcuffs! [First

Guard *crosses above table to left of* Antigone.] What is this? [Creon *and his* Page *come down off the steps.*]

[First Guard *takes key from his pocket and unlocks the cuff on* Antigone's *hand.* Antigone *rubs her wrist as she crosses below table toward chair at end of table.* Second *and* Third Guards *step back to front of arch.* First Guard *turns upstage toward* Creon.]

First Guard. The watch, sir. We all came this time.
Creon. Who is guarding the body?
First Guard. We sent for the relief.

[Creon *comes down.*]

Creon. But I gave orders that the relief was to go back to barracks and stay there! [Antigone *sits on chair at left of table.*] I told you not to open your mouth about this!
First Guard. Nobody's said anything, sir. We made this arrest, and brought the party in, the way you said we should.
Creon [*to* Antigone]. Where did these men find you?
First Guard. Right by the body.
Creon. What were you doing near your brother's body? You knew what my orders were.
First Guard. What was she doing? Sir, that's why we brought her in. She was digging up the dirt with her nails. She was trying to cover up the body all over again.
Creon. Do you realize what you are saying?
First Guard. Sir, ask these men here. After I reported to you, I went back, and first thing we did, we uncovered the body. The sun was coming up and it was beginning to smell, so we moved it up on a little rise to get him in the wind. Of course, you wouldn't expect any trouble in broad daylight. But just the same, we decided one of us had better keep his eye peeled all the time. About noon, what with the sun and the smell, and as the wind dropped and I wasn't feeling none too good, I went over to my pal to get a chew. I just had time to say "thanks" and stick it in my mouth, when I turned round and there she was, clawing away at the dirt with both hands. Right out in broad daylight! Wouldn't you think when she saw me come running she'd stop and leg it out of there? Not her! She went right on digging as fast as she could, as if I wasn't there at all. And when I grabbed her, she scratched and bit and yelled to leave her alone, she hadn't finished yet, the body wasn't all covered yet, and the like of that.
Creon [*to* Antigone]. Is this true?
Antigone. Yes, it is true.
First Guard. We scraped the dirt off as fast as we could, then we sent for the relief and we posted them. But we didn't tell them a thing, sir. And we

brought in the party so's you could see her. And that's the truth, so help me God.

Creon [*to* Antigone.] And was it you who covered the body the first time? In the night?

Antigone. Yes, it was. With a toy shovel we used to take to the seashore when we were children. It was Polynices' own shovel; he had cut his name in the handle. That was why I left it with him. But these men took it away; so the next time, I had to do it with my hands.

First Guard. Sir, she was clawing away like a wild animal. Matter of fact, first minute we saw her, what with the heat haze and everything, my pal says, "That must be a dog," he says. "Dog!" I says, "that's a girl, that is!" And it was.

Creon. Very well. [*Turns to the* Page.] Show these men to the anteroom. [*The* Page *crosses to the arch, stands there, waiting.* Creon *moves behind the table. To the* First Guard.] You three men will wait outside. I may want a report from you later.

First Guard. Do I put the cuffs back on her, sir?

Creon. No. [*The* Three Guards *salute, do an about-turn, and exeunt through arch, right.* Page *follows them out. A pause.*] Had you told anybody what you meant to do?

Antigone. No.

Creon. Did you meet anyone on your way—coming or going?

Antigone. No, nobody.

Creon. Sure of that, are you?

Antigone. Perfectly sure.

Creon. Very well. Now listen to me. You will go straight to your room. When you get there, you will go to bed. You will say that you are not well and that you have not been out since yesterday. Your nurse will tell the same story. [*He looks toward arch, through which the* Guards *have gone out.*] And I'll get rid of those three men.

Antigone. Uncle Creon, you are going to a lot of trouble for no good reason. You must know that I'll do it all over again tonight.

[*A pause. They look one another in the eye.*]

Creon. Why did you try to bury your brother?

Antigone. I owed it to him.

Creon. I had forbidden it.

Antigone. I owed it to him. Those who are not buried wander eternally and find no rest. If my brother were alive, and he came home weary after a long day's hunting, I should kneel down and unlace his boots, I should fetch him food and drink, I should see that his bed was ready for him. Polynices is home from the hunt. I owe it to him to unlock the house of the dead in which my father and my mother are waiting to welcome him. Polynices has earned his rest.

Creon. Polynices was a rebel and a traitor, and you know it.

Antigone. He was my brother.

Creon. You heard my edict. It was proclaimed throughout Thebes. You read my edict. It was posted up on the city walls.

Antigone. Of course I did.

Creon. You knew the punishment I decreed for any person who attempted to give him burial.

Antigone. Yes, I knew the punishment.

Creon. Did you by any chance act on the assumption that a daughter of Oedipus, a daughter of Oedipus' stubborn pride, was above the law?

Antigone. No, I did not act on that assumption.

Creon. Because if you had acted on that assumption, Antigone, you would have been deeply wrong. Nobody has a more sacred obligation to obey the law than those who make the law. You are a daughter of lawmakers, a daughter of kings, Antigone. You must observe the law.

Antigone. Had I been a scullery maid washing my dishes when the law was read aloud to me, I should have scrubbed the greasy water from my arms and gone out in my apron to bury my brother.

Creon. What nonsense! If you had been a scullery maid, there would have been no doubt in your mind about the seriousness of that edict. You would have known that it meant death; and you would have been satisfied to weep for your brother in your kitchen. But you! You thought that because you come of the royal line, because you were my niece and were going to marry my son, I shouldn't dare have you killed.

Antigone. You are mistaken. Quite the contrary. I never doubted for an instant that you would have me put to death.

[*A pause, as* Creon *stares fixedly at her.*]

Creon. The pride of Oedipus! Oedipus and his headstrong pride all over again. I can see your father in you—and I believe you. Of course you thought that I should have you killed! Proud as you are, it seemed to you a natural climax in your existence. Your father was like that. For him as for you human happiness was meaningless; and mere human misery was not enough to satisfy his passion for torment. [*He sits on stool behind the table.*] You come of people for whom the human vestment is a kind of straitjacket: it cracks at the seams. You spend your lives wriggling to get out of it. Nothing less than a cosy tea party with death and destiny will quench your thirst. The happiest hour of your father's life came when he listened greedily to the story of how, unknown to himself, he had killed his own father and dishonored the bed of his own mother. Drop by drop, word by word, he drank in the dark story that the gods had destined him first to live and then to hear. How avidly men and women drink the brew of such a tale when their names are Oedipus—and Antigone! And it is so simple, afterwards, to do what your father did, to put out one's eyes and take one's daughter begging on the highways.

Let me tell you, Antigone: those days are over for Thebes. Thebes has a right to a king without a past. My name, thank God, is only Creon. I stand here with both feet firm on the ground; with both hands in my pockets; and I have decided that so long as I am king—being less ambitious than your father was—I shall merely devote myself to introducing a little order into this absurd kingdom; if that is possible.

Don't think that being a king seems to me romantic. It is my trade; a trade a man has to work at every day; and like every other trade, it isn't all beer and skittles. But since it is my trade, I take it seriously. And if, tomorrow, some wild and bearded messenger walks in from some wild and distant valley—which is what happened to your dad—and tells me that he's not quite sure who my parents were, but thinks that my wife Eurydice is actually my mother, I shall ask him to do me the kindness to go back where he came from; and I shan't let a little matter like that persuade me to order my wife to take a blood test and the police to let me know whether or not my birth certificate was forged. Kings, my girl, have other things to do than to surrender themselves to their private feelings. [*He looks at her and, smiles.*] Hand *you* over to be killed! [*He rises, moves to end of table and sits on the top of table.*] I have other plans for you. You're going to marry Haemon; and I want you to fatten up a bit so that you can give him a sturdy boy. Let me assure you that Thebes needs that boy a good deal more than it needs your death. You will go to your room, now, and do as you have been told; and you won't say a word about this to anybody. Don't fret about the guards: I'll see that their mouths are shut. And don't annihilate me with those eyes. I know that you think I am a brute, and I'm sure you must consider me very prosaic. But the fact is, I have always been fond of you, stubborn though you always were. Don't forget that the first doll you ever had came from me. [*A pause.* Antigone *says nothing, rises, and crosses slowly below the table toward the arch.* Creon *turns and watches her; then*] Where are you going?

Antigone [*stops downstage. Without any show of rebellion*]. You know very well where I am going.

Creon [*after a pause*]. What sort of game are you playing?

Antigone. I am not playing games.

Creon. Antigone, do you realize that if, apart from those three guards, a single soul finds out what you have tried to do, it will be impossible for me to avoid putting you to death? There is still a chance that I can save you; but only if you keep this to yourself and give up your crazy purpose. Five minutes more, and it will be too late. You understand that?

Antigone. I must go and bury my brother. Those men uncovered him.

Creon. What good will it do? You know that there are other men standing guard over Polynices. And even if you did cover him over with earth again, the earth would again be removed.

Antigone. I know all that. I know it. But that much, at least, I can do. And what a person can do, a person ought to do.

[*Pause.*]

Creon. Tell me, Antigone, do you believe all that flummery about religious burial? Do you really believe that a so-called shade of your brother is condemned to wander for ever homeless if a little earth is not flung on his corpse to the accompaniment of some priestly abracadabra? Have you ever listened to the priests of Thebes when they were mumbling their formula? Have you ever watched those dreary bureaucrats while they were preparing the dead for burial—skipping half the gestures required by the ritual, swallowing half their words, hustling the dead into their graves out of fear that they might be late for lunch?

Antigone. Yes, I have seen all that.

Creon. And did you never say to yourself as you watched them, that if someone you really loved lay dead under the shuffling, mumbling ministrations of the priests, you would scream aloud and beg the priests to leave the dead in peace?

Antigone. Yes, I've thought all that.

Creon. And you still insist upon being put to death—merely because I refuse to let your brother go out with that grotesque passport; because I refuse his body the wretched consolation of that mass-production jibber-jabber, which you would have been the first to be embarrassed by if I had allowed it. The whole thing is absurd!

Antigone. Yes, it's absurd.

Creon. Then why, Antigone, why? For whose sake? For the sake of them that believe in it? To raise them against me?

Antigone. No.

Creon. For whom then if not for them and not for Polynices either?

Antigone. For nobody. For myself.

[*A pause as they stand looking at one another.*]

Creon. You must want very much to die. You look like a trapped animal.

Antigone. Stop feeling sorry for me. Do as I do. Do your job. But if you are a human being, do it quickly. That is all I ask of you. I'm not going to be able to hold out for ever.

Creon [*takes a step toward her*]. I want to save you, Antigone.

Antigone. You are the king, and you are all-powerful. But that you cannot do.

Creon. You think not?

Antigone. Neither save me nor stop me.

Creon. Prideful Antigone! Little Oedipus!

Antigone. Only this can you do: have me put to death.

Creon. Have you tortured, perhaps?

Antigone. Why would you do that? To see me cry? to hear me beg for mercy? Or swear whatever you wish, and then begin over again?

[*A pause.*]

Creon. You listen to me. You have cast me for the villain in this little play of yours, and yourself for the heroine. And you know it, you damned little mischiefmaker! But don't you drive me too far! If I were one of your preposterous little tyrants that Greece is full of, you would be lying in a ditch this minute with your tongue pulled out and your body drawn and quartered. But you can see something in my face that makes me hesitate to send for the guards and turn you over to them. Instead, I let you go on arguing; and you taunt me, you take the offensive. [*He grasps her left wrist.*] What are you driving at, you she devil?

Antigone. Let me go. You are hurting my arm.

Creon [*gripping her tighter*]. I will not let you go.

Antigone [*moans*]. Oh!

Creon. I was a fool to waste words. I should have done this from the beginning. [*He looks at her.*] I may be your uncle—but we are not a particularly affectionate family. Are we, eh? [*Through his teeth, as he twists.*] Are we? [Creon *propels* Antigone *round below him to his side.*] What fun for you, eh? To be able to spit in the face of a king who has all the power in the world; a man who has done his own killing in his day; who has killed people just as pitiable as you are—and who is still soft enough to go to all this trouble in order to keep you from being killed.

[*A pause.*]

Antigone. Now you are squeezing my arm too tightly. It doesn't hurt any more.

[Creon *stares at her, then drops her arm.*]

Creon. I shall save you yet. [*He goes below the table to the chair at end of table, takes off his coat, and places it on the chair.*] God knows, I have things enough to do today without wasting my time on an insect like you. There's plenty to do, I assure you, when you've just put down a revolution. But urgent things can wait. I am not going to let politics be the cause of your death. For it is a fact that this whole business is nothing but politics: the mournful shade of Polynices, the decomposing corpse, the sentimental weeping, and the hysteria that you mistake for heroism—nothing but politics.

Look here. I may not be soft, but I'm fastidious. I like things clean, shipshape, well scrubbed. Don't think that I am not just as offended as you are by the thought of that meat rotting in the sun. In the evening, when the breeze comes in off the sea, you can smell it in the palace, and it nauseates me. But I refuse even to shut my window. It's vile; and I can tell you what I wouldn't tell anybody else: it's stupid, monstrously stupid. But the people of Thebes have got to have their noses rubbed into it a little longer. My God! If it was up to me, I should have had them bury your brother long ago as a mere matter of public hygiene. I admit that what I am doing is childish. But if the featherheaded rabble I govern are to understand what's what, that stench has got to fill the town for a month!

Antigone [*turns to him*]. You are a loathsome man!

Creon. I agree. My trade forces me to be. We could argue whether I ought or ought not to follow my trade; but once I take on the job, I must do it properly.

Antigone. Why do you do it at all?

Creon. My dear, I woke up one morning and found myself King of Thebes. God knows, there were other things I loved in life more than power.

Antigone. Then you should have said no.

Creon. Yes. I could have done that. Only, I felt that it would have been cowardly. I should have been like a workman who turns down a job that has to be done. So I said yes.

Antigone. So much the worse for you, then. I didn't say yes. I can say no to anything I think vile, and I don't have to count the cost. But because you said yes, all that you can do, for all your crown and your trappings, and your guards—all that you can do is to have me killed.

Creon. Listen to me.

Antigone. If I want to. I don't have to listen to you if I don't want to. You've said your *yes.* There is nothing more you can tell me that I don't know. You stand there, drinking in my words. [*She moves behind chair.*] Why is it that you don't call your guards? I'll tell you why? You want to hear me out to the end; that's why.

Creon. You amuse me.

Antigone. Oh, no, I don't. I frighten you. That is why you talk about saving me. Everything would be so much easier if you had a docile, tongue-tied little Antigone living in the palace. I'll tell you something, Uncle Creon: I'll give you back one of your own words. You are too fastidious to make a good tyrant. But you are going to have to put me to death today, and you know it. And that's what frightens you. God! Is there anything uglier than a frightened man!

Creon. Very well. I am afraid, then. Does that satisfy you? I am afraid that if you insist upon it, I shall have to have you killed. And I don't want to.

Antigone. I don't have to do things that I think are wrong. If it comes to that, you didn't really want to leave my brother's body unburied, did you? Say it! Admit that you didn't.

Creon. I have said it already.

Antigone. But you did it just the same. And now, though you don't want to do it, you are going to have me killed. And you call that being a king!

Creon. Yes, I call that being a king.

Antigone. Poor Creon! My nails are broken, my fingers are bleeding, my arms are covered with the welts left by the paws of your guards—but I am a queen!

Creon. Then why not have pity on me, and live? Isn't your brother's corpse, rotting there under my windows, payment enough for peace and order in Thebes? My son loves you. Don't make me add your life to the payment. I've paid enough.

Antigone. No, Creon! You said yes, and made yourself king. Now you will never stop paying.

Creon. But God in heaven! Won't you try to understand me! I'm trying hard enough to understand you! There had to be one man who said yes. Somebody had to agree to captain the ship. She had sprung a hundred leaks; she was loaded to the water line with crime, ignorance, poverty. The wheel was swinging with the wind. The crew refused to work and were looting the cargo. The officers were building a raft, ready to slip overboard and desert the ship. The mast was splitting, the wind was howling, the sails were beginning to rip. Every man jack on board was about to drown—and only because the only thing they thought of was their own skins and their cheap little day-to-day traffic. Was that a time, do you think, for playing with words like yes and no? Was that a time for a man to be weighing the pros and cons, wondering if he wasn't going to pay too dearly later on; if he wasn't going to lose his life, or his family, or his touch with other men? You grab the wheel, you right the ship in the face of a mountain of water. You shout an order, and if one man refuses to obey, you shoot straight into the mob. Into the mob, I say! The beast as nameless as the wave that crashes down upon your deck; as nameless as the whipping wind. The thing that drops when you shoot may be someone who poured you a drink the night before; but it has no name. And you, braced at the wheel, you have no name, either. Nothing has a name—except the ship, and the storm. [*A pause as he looks at her.*] Now do you understand?

Antigone. I am not here to understand. That's all very well for you. I am here to say no to you, and die.

Creon. It is easy to say no.

Antigone. Not always.

Creon. It is easy to say no. To say yes, you have to sweat and roll up your sleeves and plunge both hands into life up to the elbows. It is easy to say no, even if saying no means death. All you have to do is to sit still and wait. Wait to go on living; wait to be killed. That is the coward's part. *No* is one of your man-made words. Can you imagine a world in which trees say *no* to the sap? In which beasts say *no* to hunger or to propagation? Animals are good, simple, tough. They move in droves, nudging one another onwards, all traveling the same road. Some of them keel over, but the rest go on; and no matter how many may fall by the wayside, there are always those few left that go on bringing their young into the world, traveling the same road with the same obstinate will, unchanged from those who went before.

Antigone. Animals, eh, Creon! What a king you could be if only men were animals!

[*A pause.* Creon *turns and looks at her.*]

Creon. You despise me, don't you? [Antigone *is silent.* Creon *goes on, as if to himself.*] Strange. Again and again, I have imagined myself holding this conversation with a pale young man I have never seen in the flesh. He would have come to assassinate me, and would have failed. I would be trying to find out from him why he wanted to kill me. But with all my logic and all my powers of debate, the only thing I could get out of him would be that he despised me. Who would have thought that the white-faced boy would turn out to be you? And that the debate would arise out of something so meaningless as the burial of your brother?

Antigone [*repeats contemptuously.*] Meaningless!

Creon [*earnestly, almost desperately*]. And yet, you must hear me out. My part is not an heroic one, but I shall play my part. I shall have you put to death. Only, before I do, I want to make one last appeal. I want to be sure that you know what you are doing as well as I know what I am doing. Antigone, do you know what you are dying for? Do you know the sordid story to which you are going to sign your name in blood, for all time to come?

Antigone. What story?

Creon. The story of Eteocles and Polynices, the story of your brothers. You think you know it, but you don't. Nobody in Thebes knows that story but me. And it seems to me, this afternoon, that you have a right to know it too. [*A pause as* Antigone *moves to chair and sits.*] It's not a pretty story. [*He turns, gets stool from behind the table and places it between the table and the chair.*] You'll see. [*He looks at her for a moment.*] Tell me, first. What do you remember about your brothers? They were older than you, so they must have looked down on you. And I imagine that they tormented you—pulled your pigtails, broke your dolls, whispered secrets to each other to put you in a rage.

Antigone. They were big and I was little.

Creon. And later on, when they came home wearing evening clothes, smoking cigarettes, they would have nothing to do with you; and you thought they were wonderful.

Antigone. They were boys and I was a girl.

Creon. You didn't know why, exactly, but you knew that they were making your mother unhappy. You saw her in tears over them; and your father would fly into a rage because of them. You heard them come in, slamming doors, laughing noisily in the corridors—insolent, spineless, unruly, smelling of drink.

Antigone [*staring outward*]. Once, it was very early and we had just got up. I saw them coming home, and hid behind a door. Polynices was very pale and his eyes were shining. He was so handsome in his evening clothes. He saw me, and said: "Here, this is for you"; and he gave me a big paper flower that he had brought home from his night out.

Creon. And of course you still have that flower. Last night, before you crept out, you opened a drawer and looked at it for a time, to give yourself courage.

Antigone. Who told you so?

Creon. Poor Antigone! With her night club flower. Do you know what your brother was?

Antigone. Whatever he was, I know that you will say vile things about him.

Creon. A cheap, idiotic bounder, that is what he was. A cruel, vicious little voluptuary. A little beast with just wit enough to drive a car faster and throw more money away than any of his pals. I was with your father one day when Polynices, having lost a lot of money gambling, asked him to settle the debt; and when your father refused, the boy raised his hand against him and called him a vile name.

Antigone. That's a lie!

Creon. He struck your father in the face with his fist. It was pitiful. Your father sat at his desk with his head in his hands. His nose was bleeding. He was weeping with anguish. And in a corner of your father's study, Polynices stood sneering and lighting a cigarette.

Antigone. Thats a lie.

[*A pause.*]

Creon. When did you last see Polynices alive? When you were twelve years old. *That's* true, isn't it?

Antigone. Yes, that's true.

Creon. Now you know why. Oedipus was too chicken-hearted to have the boy locked up. Polynices was allowed to go off and join the Argive army. And as soon as he reached Argos, the attempts upon your father's life began—upon the life of an old man who couldn't make up his mind to die, couldn't bear to be parted from his kingship. One after another, men slipped into Thebes from Argos for the purpose of assassinating him, and every killer we caught always ended by confessing who had put him up to it, who had paid him to try it. And it wasn't only Polynices. That is really what I am trying to tell you. I want you to know what went on in the back room, in the kitchen of politics; I want you to know what took place in the wings of this drama in which you are burning to play a part.

Yesterday, I gave Eteocles a State funeral, with pomp and honors. Today, Eteocles is a saint and a hero in the eyes of all Thebes. The whole city turned out to bury him. The schoolchildren emptied their saving boxes to buy wreaths for him. Old men, orating in quavering, hypocritical voices, glorified the virtues of the great-hearted brother, the devoted son, the loyal prince. I made a speech myself; and every temple priest was present with an appropriate show of sorrow and solemnity in his stupid face. And military honors were accorded the dead hero.

Well, what else could I have done? People had taken sides in the civil war. Both sides couldn't be wrong; that would be too much. I couldn't have made them swallow the truth. Two gangsters was more of a luxury than I could afford. [*He pauses for a moment.*] And this is the whole point of my story. Eteocles, that virtuous brother, was just as rotten as Polynices. That great-hearted son had done his best, too, to procure the assassination of his father. That loyal prince had also offered to sell out Thebes to the highest bidder.

Funny, isn't it? Polynices lies rotting in the sun while Eteocles is given a hero's funeral and will be housed in a marble vault. Yet I have absolute proof that everything that Polynices did, Eteocles had plotted to do. They were a pair of blackguards—both engaged in selling out Thebes, and both engaged in selling out each other; and they died like the cheap gangsters they were, over a division of the spoils.

But, as I told you a moment ago, I had to make a martyr of one of them. I sent out to the holocaust for their bodies; they were found clasped in one another's arms—for the first time in their lives, I imagine. Each had been spitted on the other's sword, and the Argive cavalry had trampled them down. They were mashed to a pulp, Antigone. I had the prettier of the two carcasses brought in and gave it a State funeral; and I left the other to rot. I don't know which was which. And I assure you, I don't care.

[*Long silence, neither looking at the other.*]

Antigone [*in a mild voice*]. Why do you tell me all this?

Creon. Would it have been better to let you die a victim to that obscene story?

Antigone. It might have been. I had my faith.

Creon. What are you going to do now?

Antigone [*rises to her feet in a daze*]. I shall go up to my room.

Creon. Don't stay alone. Go and find Haemon. And get married quickly.

Antigone [*in a whisper*]. Yes.

Creon. All this is really beside the point. You have your whole life ahead of you—and life is a treasure.

Antigone. Yes.

Creon. And you were about to throw it away. Don't think me fatuous if I say that I understand you; and that at your age I should have done the same thing. A moment ago, when we were quarreling, you said I was drinking in your words. I was. But it wasn't you I was listening to; it was a lad named Creon who lived here in Thebes many years ago. He was thin and pale, as you are. His mind, too, was filled with thoughts of self-sacrifice. Go and find Haemon. And get married quickly, Antigone. Be happy. Life flows like water, and you young people let it run away through your fingers. Shut your hands; hold on to it, Antigone. Life is not what you think it is. Life is a child playing around your feet, a tool you hold firmly in your grip, a bench you sit down upon in the evening, in your garden. People will tell you that that's not life, that life is something else. They will tell you that because they need your strength and your fire, and they will want to make use of you. Don't listen to them. Believe me, the only poor consolation that we have in our old age is to discover that what I have just said to you is true. Life is nothing more than the happiness that you get out of it.

Antigone [*murmurs, lost in thought*]. Happiness . . .

Creon [*suddenly a little self-conscious*]. Not much of a word, is it?

Antigone [*quietly*]. What kind of happiness do you foresee for me? Paint me the picture of your happy Antigone. What are the unimportant little sins that I shall have to commit before I am allowed to sink my teeth into life and tear happiness from it? Tell me: to whom shall I have to lie? Upon whom shall I have to fawn? To whom must I sell myself? Whom do you want me to leave dying, while I turn away my eyes?

Creon. Antigone, be quiet.

Antigone. Why do you tell me to be quiet when all I want to know is what I have to do to be happy? This minute; since it is this very minute that I must make my choice. You tell me that life is so wonderful. I want to know what I have to do in order to be able to say that myself.

Creon. Do you love Haemon?

Antigone. Yes, I love Haemon. The Haemon I love is hard and young, faithful and difficult to satisfy, just as I am. But if what I love in Haemon is to be worn away like a stone step by the tread of the thing you call life, the thing you call happiness, if Haemon reaches the point where he stops growing pale with fear when I grow pale, stops thinking that I must have been killed in an accident when I am five minutes late, stops feeling that he is alone on earth when I laugh and he doesn't know why—if he too has to learn to say yes to everything—why, no, then, no! I do not love Haemon!

Creon. You don't know what you are talking about!

Antigone. I do know what I am talking about! Now it is you who have stopped understanding. I am too far away from you now, talking to you from a kingdom you can't get into, with your quick tongue and your hollow heart. [*Laughs.*] I laugh, Creon, because I see you suddenly as you must have been at fifteen: the same look of impotence in your face and the same inner conviction that there was nothing you couldn't do. What has life added to you, except those lines in your face, and that fat on your stomach?

Creon. Be quiet, I tell you!

Antigone. Why do you want me to be quiet? Because you know that I am right? Do you think I can't see in your face that what I am saying is true? You can't admit it, of course; you have to go on growling and defending the bone you call happiness.

Creon. It is your happiness, too, you little fool!

Antigone. I spit on your happiness! I spit on your idea of life—that life that must go on, come what may. You are all like dogs that lick everything they smell. You with your promise of a humdrum happiness—provided a person doesn't ask too much of life. I want everything of life, I do; and I want it now! I want it total, complete: otherwise I reject it! I will *not* be moderate. I will *not* be satisfied with the bit of cake you offer me if I promise to be a good little girl. I want to be sure of everything this very day; sure that everything will be as beautiful as when I was a little girl. If not, I want to die!

Creon. Scream on, daughter of Oedipus! Scream on, in your father's own voice!

Antigone. In my father's own voice, yes! We are of the tribe that asks questions, and we ask them to the bitter end. Until no tiniest chance of hope remains to be strangled by our hands. We are of the tribe that hates your filthy hope, your docile, female hope; hope, your whore——

Creon [*grasps her by her arms*]. Shut up! If you could see how ugly you are, shrieking those words!

Antigone. Yes, I am ugly! Father was ugly, too. [Creon *releases her arms, turns and moves away. Stands with his back to* Antigone.] But Father became beautiful. And do you know when? [*She follows him to behind the table.*] At the very end. When all his questions had been answered. When he could no longer doubt that he *had* killed his own father; that he *had* gone to bed with his own mother. When all hope was gone, stamped out like a beetle. When it was absolutely certain that nothing, nothing could save him. Then he was at peace; then he could smile, almost; then he became beautiful. . . . Whereas you! Ah, those faces of yours, you candidates for election to happiness! It's you who are the ugly ones, even the handsomest of you—with that ugly glint in the corner of your eyes, that ugly crease at the corner of your mouths. Creon, you spoke the word a moment ago: the kitchen of politics. You look it and you smell of it.

Creon [*struggles to put his hand over her mouth*]. I order you to shut up! Do you hear me?

Antigone. *You* order me? Cook! Do you really believe that you can give me orders?

Creon. Antigone! The anteroom is full of people! Do you want them to hear you?

Antigone. Open the doors! Let us make sure that they can hear me!

Creon. By God! You shut up, I tell you!

[Ismene *enters through arch.*]

Ismene [*distraught*]. Antigone!

Antigone [*turns to* Ismene]. You, too? What do you want?

Ismene. Oh, forgive me, Antigone. I've come back. I'll be brave. I'll go with you now.

Antigone. Where will you go with me?

Ismene [*to* Creon]. Creon! If you kill her, you'll have to kill me too.

Antigone. Oh, no, Ismene. Not a bit of it. I die alone. You don't think I'm going to let you die with me after what I've been through? You don't deserve it.

Ismene. If you die, I don't want to live. I don't want to be left behind, alone.

Antigone. You chose life and I chose death. Now stop blubbering. You had your chance to come with me in the black night, creeping on your hands and knees. You had your chance to claw up the earth with your nails, as I did; to get yourself caught like a thief, as I did. And you refused it.

Ismene. Not any more. I'll do it alone tonight.

Antigone [*turns round toward* Creon]. You hear that, Creon? The thing is catching! Who knows but that lots of people will catch the disease from me! What are you waiting for? Call in your guards! Come on, Creon! Show a little courage! It only hurts for a minute! Come on, cook!

Creon [*turns toward arch and calls*]. Guard!

[Guard *enter through arch.*]

Antigone [*in a great cry of relief*]. At last, Creon!

[Chorus *enters through left arch.*]

Creon [*to the* Guards]. Take her away! [Creon *goes up on top step.*]

[Guards *grasp* Antigone *by her arms, turn and hustle her toward the arch, right, and exeunt.* Ismene *mimes horror, backs away toward the arch, left, then turns and runs out through the arch. A long pause, as* Creon *moves slowly downstage.*]

Chorus [*behind* Creon. *Speaks in a deliberate voice*]. You are out of your mind, Creon. What have you done?

Creon [*his back to* Chorus]. She had to die.

Chorus: You must not let Antigone die. We shall carry the scar of her death for centuries.

Creon. She insisted. No man on earth was strong enough to dissuade her. Death was her purpose, whether she knew it or not. Polynices was a mere pretext. When she had to give up that pretext, she found another one—that life and happiness were tawdry things and not worth possessing. She was bent upon only one thing: to reject life and to die.

Chorus. She is a mere child, Creon.

Creon. What do you want me to do for her? Condemn her to live?

Haemon [*calls from offstage*]. Father! [Haemon *enters through arch, right.* Creon *turns toward him.*]

Creon. Haemon, forget Antigone. Forget her, my dearest boy.

Haemon. How can you talk like that?

Creon [*grasps* Haemon *by the hands*]. I did everything I could to save her, Haemon. I used every argument. I swear I did. The girl doesn't love you. She could have gone on living for you; but she refused. She wanted it this way; she wanted to die.

Haemon. Father! The guards are dragging Antigone away! You've got to stop them! [*He breaks away from* Creon.]

Creon [*looks away from* Haemon]. I can't stop them. It's too late. Antigone has spoken. The story is all over Thebes. I cannot save her now.

Chorus. Creon, you must find a way. Lock her up. Say that she has gone out of her mind.

Creon. Everybody will know it isn't so. The nation will say that I am making an exception of her because my son loves her. I cannot.

Chorus. You can still gain time, and get her out of Thebes.

Creon. The mob already knows the truth. It is howling for her blood. I can do nothing.

Haemon. But, Father, you are master in Thebes!

Creon. I am master under the law. Not above the law.

Haemon. You cannot let Antigone be taken from me. I am your son!

Creon. I cannot do anything else, my poor boy. She must die and you must live.

Haemon. Live, you say! Live a life without Antigone? A life in which I am to go on admiring you as you busy yourself about your kingdom, make your persuasive speeches, strike your attitudes? Not without Antigone. I love Antigone. I will not live without Antigone!

Creon. Haemon—you will have to resign yourself to life without Antigone. [*He moves to left of* Haemon.] Sooner or later there comes a day of sorrow in each man's life when he must cease to be a child and take up the burden of manhood. That day has come for you.

Haemon [*backs away a step*]. That giant strength, that courage. That massive god who used to pick me up in his arms and shelter me from shadows and monsters—was that you, Father? Was it of you I stood in awe? Was that man you?

Creon. For God's sake, Haemon, do not judge me! Not you, too!

Haemon [*pleading now*]. This is all a bad dream, Father. You are not yourself. It isn't true that we have been backed up against a wall, forced to surrender. We don't have to say *yes* to this terrible thing. You are still king. You are still the father I revered. You have no right to desert me, to shrink into nothingness. The world will be too bare, I shall be too alone in the world, if you force me to disown you.

Creon. The world *is* bare, Haemon, and you *are* alone. You must cease to think your father all-powerful. Look straight at me. See your father as he is. That is what it means to grow up and be a man.

Haemon [*stares at* Creon *for a moment*]. I tell you that I will not live without Antigone. [*Turns and goes quickly out through arch.*]

Chorus. Creon, the boy will go mad.

Creon. Poor boy! He loves her.

Chorus. Creon, the boy is wounded to death.

Creon. We are all wounded to death.

[First Guard *enters through arch, right, followed by* Second *and* Third Guards *pulling* Antigone *along with them.*]

First Guard. Sir, the people are crowding into the palace!

Antigone. Creon, I don't want to see their faces. I don't want to hear them howl. You are going to kill me; let that be enough. I want to be alone until it is over.

Creon. Empty the palace! Guards at the gates!

[Creon *quickly crosses toward the arch; exit. Two* Guards *release* Antigone; *exeunt behind* Creon. Chorus *goes out through arch, left. The lighting dims so that only the area about the table is lighted. The cyclorama is covered with a dark blue color. The scene is intended to suggest a prison cell, filled with shadows and dimly lit.* Antigone *moves to stool and sits. The* First Guard *stands upstage. He watches* Antigone, *and as she sits, he begins pacing slowly downstage, then upstage. A pause.*]

Antigone [*turns and looks at the* Guard]. It's you, is it?

Guard. What do you mean, me?

Antigone. The last human face that I shall see. [*A pause as they look at each other, then* Guard *paces upstage, turns, and crosses behind table.*] Was it you that arrested me this morning?

Guard. Yes, that was me.

Antigone. You hurt me. There was no need for you to hurt me. Did I act as if I was trying to escape?

Guard. Come on now, Miss. It was my business to bring you in. I did it. [*A pause. He paces to and fro upstage. Only the sound of his boots is heard.*]

Antigone. How old are you?

Guard. Thirty-nine.

Antigone. Have you any children?

Guard. Yes. Two.

Antigone. Do you love your children?

Guard. What's that got to with you? [*A pause. He paces upstage and downstage.*]

Antigone. How long have you been in the Guard?

Guard. Since the war. I was in the army. Sergeant. Then I joined the Guard.

Antigone. Does one have to have been an army sergeant to get into the Guard?

Guard. Supposed to be. Either that or on special detail. But when they make you a guard, you lose your stripes.

Antigone [*murmurs*]. I see.

Guard. Yes. Of course, if you're a guard, everybody knows you're something special; they know you're an old N.C.O. Take pay, for instance. When you're a guard you get your pay, and on top of that you get six months' extra pay, to make sure you don't lose anything by not being a sergeant any more. And of course you do better than that. You get a house, coal, rations, extras for the wife and kids. If you've got two kids, like me, you draw better than a sergeant.

Antigone [*barely audible*]. I see.

Guard. That's why sergeants, now, they don't like guards. Maybe you noticed they try to make out they're better than us? Promotion, that's what it is. In the army, anybody can get promoted. All you need is good conduct. Now in the Guard, it's slow, and you have to know your business—like how to make out a report and the like of that. But when you're an N.C.O. in the Guard, you've got something that even a sergeant-major ain't got. For instance——

Antigone [*breaking him off*]. Listen.

Guard. Yes, Miss.

Antigone. I'm going to die soon.

[*The* Guard *looks at her for a moment, then turns and moves away.*]

Guard. For instance, people have a lot of respect for guards, they have. A guard may be a soldier, but he's kind of in the civil service, too.

Antigone. Do you think it hurts to die?

Guard. How would I know? Of course, if somebody sticks a saber in your guts and turns it round, it hurts.

Antigone. How are they going to put me to death?

Guard. Well, I'll tell you. I heard the proclamation all right. Wait a minute. How did it go now? [*He stares into space and recites from memory.*] "In order that our fair city shall not be pol-luted with her sinful blood, she shall be im-mured—immured." That means, they shove you in a cave and wall up the cave.

Antigone. Alive?

Guard. Yes. . . . [*He moves away a few steps.*]

Antigone [*murmurs*]. O tomb! O bridal bed! Alone! [Antigone *sits there, a tiny figure in the middle of the stage. You would say she felt a little chilly. She wraps her arms round herself.*]

Guard. Yes! Outside the southeast gate of the town. In the Cave of Hades. In broad daylight. Some detail, eh, for them that's on the job! First they thought maybe it was a job for the army. Now it looks like it's going to be the Guard. There's an outfit for you! Nothing the Guard can't do. No wonder the army's jealous.

Antigone. A pair of animals.

Guard. What do you mean, a pair of animals?

Antigone. When the winds blow cold, all they need do is to press close against one another. I am all alone.

Guard. Is there anything you want? I can send out for it, you know.

Antigone. You are very kind. [*A pause.* Antigone *looks up at the* Guard.] Yes, there is something I want. I want you to give someone a letter from me, when I am dead.

Guard. How's that again? A letter?

Antigone. Yes, I want to write a letter; and I want you to give it to someone for me.

Guard [*straightens up*]. Now, wait a minute. Take it easy. It's as much as my job is worth to go handing out letters from prisoners.

Antigone [*removes a ring from her finger and holds it out toward him*]. I'll give you this ring if you will do it.

Guard. Is it gold? [*He takes the ring from her.*]

Antigone. Yes, it is gold.

Guard [*shakes his head*]. Uh-uh. No can do. Suppose they go through my pockets. I might get six months for a thing like that. [*He stares at the ring, then glances off right to make sure that he is not being watched.*] Listen, tell you what I'll do. You tell me what you want to say, and I'll write it down in my book. Then, afterwards, I'll tear out the pages and give them to the party, see? If it's in my handwriting, it's all right.

Antigone [*winces.*]. In your handwriting? [*She shudders slightly.*] No. that would be awful. The poor darling! In your handwriting.

Guard [*offers back the ring*]. O.K. It's no skin off my nose.

Antigone [*quickly*]. Of course, of course. No, keep the ring. But hurry. Time is getting short. Where is your notebook? [*The* Guard *pockets the ring, takes* *his notebook and pencil from his pocket, puts his foot up on chair, and rests the notebook on his knee, licks his pencil.*] Ready? [*He nods.*] Write, now. "My darling . . ."

Guard [*writes as he mutters*]. The boy friend, eh?

Antigone. "My darling. I wanted to die, and perhaps you will not love me any more . . ."

Guard [*mutters as he writes*] ". . . will not love me any more."

Antigone. "Creon was right. It is terrible to die."

Guard [*repeats as he writes*] ". . . terrible to die."

Antigone. "And I don't even know what I am dying for. I am afraid . . ."

Guard [*looks at her*]. Wait a minute! How fast do you think I can write?

Antigone [*takes hold of herself*]. Where are you?

Guard [*reads from his notebook*]. "And I don't even know what I am dying for."

Antigone. No. Scratch that out. Nobody must know that. They have no right to know. It's as if they saw me naked and touched me, after I was dead. Scratch it all out. Just write: "Forgive me."

Guard [*looks at* Antigone]. I cut out everything you said there at the end, and I put down, "Forgive me"?

Antigone. Yes. "Forgive me, my darling. You would all have been so happy except for Antigone. I love you."

Guard [*finishes the letter*] ". . . I love you." [*He looks at her.*] Is that all?

Antigone. That's all.

Guard [*straightens up, looks at notebook*]. Damn funny letter.

Antigone. I know.

Guard [*looks at her*]. Who is it to? [*A sudden roll of drums begins and continues until after* Antigone's *exit. The* First Guard *pockets the notebook and shouts at* Antigone.] O.K. That's enough out of you! Come on!

[*At the sound of the drum roll,* Second *and* Third Guards *enter through the arch.* Antigone *rises.* Guards *seize her and exeunt with her. The lighting moves up to suggest late afternoon.* Chorus *enters.*]

Chorus. And now it is Creon's turn.

[Messenger *runs through the arch, right.*]

Messenger. The Queen . . . the Queen! Where is the Queen?

Chorus. What do you want with the Queen? What have you to tell the Queen?

Messenger. News to break her heart. Antigone had just been thrust into the cave. They hadn't finished heaving the last block of stone into place when Creon and the rest heard a sudden moaning from the tomb. A hush fell over us all, for it was not the voice of Antigone. It was Haemon's voice that came forth from the tomb. Everybody looked at Creon; and he howled like a man demented: "Take away the stones! Take away the stones!" The slaves leaped at the wall of stones, and Creon worked with them, sweating and tearing at the blocks with his bleeding hands. Finally a narrow opening was forced, and into it slipped the smallest guard.

Antigone had hanged herself by the cord of her robe, by the red and golden twisted cord of her robe. The cord was round her neck like a child's collar. Haemon was on his knees, holding her in his arms and moaning, his face buried in her robe. More stones were removed, and Creon went into the tomb. He tried to raise Haemon to his feet. I could hear him begging Haemon to rise to his feet. Haemon was deaf to his father's voice, till suddenly he stood up of his own accord, his eyes dark and burning. Anguish was in his face, but it was the face of a little boy. He stared at his father. Then suddenly he struck him—hard; and he drew his sword. Creon leaped out of range. Haemon went on staring at him, his eyes full of contempt—a glance that was like a knife, and that Creon couldn't escape. The King stood trembling in the far corner of the tomb, and Haemon went on staring. Then, without a word, he stabbed himself and lay down beside Antigone, embracing her in a great pool of blood.

[*A pause as* Creon *and* Page *enter through arch on the* Messenger's *last words.* Chorus *and the* Messenger *both turn to look at* Creon; *then exit the* Messenger *through curtain.*]

Creon. I have had them laid out side by side. They are together at last, and at peace. Two lovers on the morrow of their bridal. Their work is done.

Chorus. But not yours, Creon. You have still one thing to learn. Eurydice, the Queen, your wife——

Creon. A good woman. Always busy with her garden, her preserves, her sweaters—those sweaters she never stopped knitting for the poor. Strange, how the poor never stop needing sweaters. One would almost think that was all they needed.

Chorus. The poor in Thebes are going to be cold this winter, Creon. When the Queen was told of her son's death, she waited carefully until she had finished her row, then put down her knitting calmly—as she did everything. She went up to her room, her lavender-scented room, with its embroidered doilies and its pictures framed in plush; and there, Creon, she cut her throat. She is laid out now in one of those two old-fashioned twin beds, exactly where you went to her one night when she was still a maiden. Her smile is still the same, scarcely a shade more melancholy. And if it were not for that great red blot on the bed linen by her neck, one might think she was asleep.

Creon [*in a dull voice*]. She, too. They are all asleep. [*Pause.*] It must be good to sleep.

Chorus. And now you are alone, Creon.

Creon. Yes, all alone. [*To* Page.] My lad.

Page. Sir?

Creon. Listen to me. They don't know it, but the truth is the work is there to be done, and a man can't fold his arms and refuse to do it. They say it's dirty work. But if we didn't do it, who would?

Page. I don't know, sir.

Creon. Of course you don't. You'll be lucky if you never find out. In a hurry to grow up, aren't you?

Page. Oh, yes, sir.

Creon. I shouldn't be if I were you. Never grow up if you can help it. [*He is lost in thought as the hour chimes.*] What time is it?

Page. Five o'clock, sir.

Creon. What have we on at five o'clock?

Page. Cabinet meeting, sir.

Creon. Cabinet meeting. Then we had better go along to it.

[*Exeunt* Creon *and* Page *slowly through arch, left, and* Chorus *moves downstage.*]

Chorus. And there we are. It is quite true that if it had not been for Antigone they would all have been at peace. But that is over now. And they are at peace. All those who were meant to die have died: those who believed one thing, those who believed the contrary thing, and even those who believed nothing at all, yet were caught up in the web without knowing why. All dead: stiff, useless, rotting. And those who have survived will now begin quietly to forget the dead: they won't remember who was who or which was which. It is all over. Antigone is calm tonight, and we shall never know the name of the fever that consumed her. She has played her part.

[*Three* Guards *enter, resume their places on steps as at the rise of the curtain, and begin to play cards.*]

A great melancholy wave of peace now settles down upon Thebes, upon the empty palace, upon Creon, who can now begin to wait for his own death.

Only the guards are left, and none of this matters to them. It's no skin off their noses. They go on playing cards.

[Chorus *walks toward the arch, left, as the curtain falls.*]

APPENDIX

PREPARING A MANUSCRIPT

QUESTIONS AND ANSWERS

Here are answers to questions students often ask when writing essays. For more detailed information, see the *MLA Handbook for Writers* available in most college bookstores and libraries.

1. QUESTIONS ABOUT FINDING ADDITIONAL INFORMATION

**** Where can I find information about someone's life and work?***
Check the Reference Department of your library. Here are selected examples of what might be available.

- For information about notable people no longer living:

  Dictionary of American Biography
  Dictionary of National Biography (British)
  Notable American Women (1607–1950)

- For information about distinguished people still living:

  Contemporary Author's Autobiographical Series
  Current Biography
  Dictionary of Literary Biography
  International Who's Who
  Who's Who in America

- For information focusing on the lives of writers:

  American Authors 1600–1900
  British Authors before 1800
  British Authors 1900
  Contemporary Authors
  Contemporary Novelists
  Contemporary Poets
  Contemporary Dramatists
  Twentieth Century Authors
  World Authors 1950–1970

- For specific biographies and works of criticism, the card catalog or computer terminal in the library will help you locate books and special reference works. You may check for information by author, title, or subject.

If you're fortunate enough to have a library that allows you to enter the stacks, old-fashioned browsing sometimes pays off. Let's say you've read something by Anton Chekhov and are interested in learning more about his work as a physician. You might check under his name in the computer catalog or under a more general subject like Russian Literature. Once you have call numbers, you can go to the shelves and glance through the tables-of-contents and indexes of various biographies or works of criticism for information on Chekhov's work as a physician. Browsing can also trigger new interests and topics you might not have considered.

**** Where can I find information not available in books?***
Check the Periodicals Department of your library for the *Reader's Guide to Periodicals Index.* This index includes articles from popular magazines such as *Newsweek, Time, Harpers,* and *The New Yorker.*

Begin by looking up the subject you're interested in and copy all the information provided to help you locate articles on the subject. Check inside the front cover of the index for an explanation of all abbreviations. Once you have the information on the source, check the "Library Holdings List" to determine whether your library subscribes to that particular source. If it does, the listing will provide you with a call number or direct you to the microfilm section.

**** What if I need more specialized information?***
The reference department contains numerous specialized indexes on art, religion, history, and music. Most of these index scholarly and professional journals. Look especially for the following:

- *The Humanities Index* (1974–present) covers archeology, history, classics, literature, performing arts, philosophy, and religion.
- *The Essay and General Literature Index* covers essays written about authors and their work.
- *Book Review Digest* indexes articles, reviews and critiques.

**** Where can I find information on the history of a word?***

- *The Oxford English Dictionary* (*OED*) describes the history of words. If you look up "bank," for example, you'll find that it originated from the word "shelf" or "bench;" in other words, the term refers to the table or counter over which a money changer conducted his business.
- For words used today, check the *Webster's Third International Dictionary of English,* usually considered the authoritative work, although *The American Heritage Dictionary* is also good.

2. QUESTIONS ABOUT EVALUATING SOURCES

**** How can I know whether articles and books I find are the best ones for my research?***
With the article or book in hand, ask yourself the following before taking notes:

a) *Is the work relevant to my focus?*
Titles can be misleading. The actual work may not provide the information hoped for, and sometimes, as you gather information, your intended approach changes. For books, make a quick survey of the table of contents and the index, looking for key words that point to your focus. For journal

or magazine articles, skim subtitles throughout the essay (if any), or quickly skim the first and last sentences of each paragraph.

b) *Is the source itself comprehensive or narrowly focused?*
Scanning the contents, indexes, and subheadings helps you determine how broad or narrow the source is. Until you're sure of your focus, begin with works that give an overview of the subject. This is where books may serve you best. Once you've narrowed your topic, you'll probably find that journal articles may be more useful.

c) *When was the article or book written?*
Most of the time you'll want to use the most current information. Scholarly research and attitudes change over the decades. An essay on marriage published in the 1990s will often take a dramatically different approach from one published in the 1950s or 1850s. Scientific data and theories change almost yearly, as does research in psychology and sociology. However, using appropriate historical sources would be expected if you're tracing a subject over a period of time. Certainly, any "classic" source (especially those other authors refer to frequently) should prove useful.

d) *Does the source contain a bibliography?*
A bibliography, especially if it contains a brief description of the works the author has consulted, can assure you that the information within the book is current and has been well-documented. It may also lead to additional useful sources.

e) *What can I do If I can't find what I need?*
When all else fails, consult any reference librarian for guidance, or ask your instructor for advice. They may direct you to standard works or specialized indexes—or to an expert on the subject.

3. QUESTIONS ABOUT TAKING NOTES

* *What is plagiarism?*

Anytime you use other people's words, data, ideas, or even patterns of organization as your own, without quoting the material and giving credit to the author or source, you are plagiarizing. Most colleges and universities consider plagiarism the equivalent of cheating, punishable with failure for the paper or even the course.

* *How can I avoid plagiarism?*

Two techniques will help.

a) Both paraphrased and quoted information taken from any source must be documented. Before taking notes, jot down all the information you'll need later for the Works Cited page (author, title, place of publication, publisher, date, and page numbers).

b) Once you begin taking notes, avoid the lazy technique of copying out information word for word from the source. In order to paraphrase (and summarize) you must translate or restate relevant information *in your own words.* The best way to do that is to first scan the source, reread sections you want to paraphrase, then turn away from the original. You may want to cover the original with a sheet of paper or push it out of sight if necessary. Write down from memory the information you want to retain, without looking back at the original. Then feel free to reread the source to make sure your paraphrase is complete and accurate. Make sure you've noted the exact pages.

And remember, even a paraphrase must be credited either in the text itself or in a parenthetical in-text documentation. (See *Questions about Quotations or Paraphrases below.*)

4. QUESTIONS ABOUT QUOTATIONS OR PARAPHRASES

**** How do I introduce a quotation?***

Although you'll want to paraphrase more than you quote, the use of quotations can give vibrancy to your writing and heighten interest in your discussion. Keep in mind, however, that both quotations and paraphrases without introductions may seem meaningless to readers. In general, the first time you use a source, provide the full name of the author and text:

- In her essay "The Angel in the House" Virginia Woolf. . . .
- According to Virginia Woolf, writing in "The Angel in the House," . . . .
- "The Angel in the House," an essay by Virginia Woolf, explores the condition of. . . .
- The obstacles women must confront are made clear in Virginia Woolf's "The Angel in the House."

In later references, use of the last name only is sufficient; however, you'll still need to clarify the general context from which a quotation or paraphrase is taken.

- Even after becoming a successful writer, Woolf continued to find that she was "haunted by the phantom" (412).

**** How do I incorporate quotations from other sources?***

At some point during your writing, you may want to incorporate material from other texts. Contemporary documentation methods (see pp. 732–733) require you to provide only a parenthetical citation that includes the last name of the author and a page number (this in turn would refer the reader to the complete citation on the Works Cited page). This method, however, creates weak and sometimes confusing prose. A stronger method is to signal the reader that material from another source is being used by incorporating the author's full name (and sometimes brief information about the author along with at least an abbreviated title).

- *weak:* Although Parris argues that minorities should be willing to be absorbed by the majority culture, there are dissenting views. "When an individual gives up his native language, he loses his childhood, his parents, his roots that may go back thousands of years" (Garcia-Sancho 513).

- *stronger:* Although Parris argues that minorities should be willing to be absorbed by the majority culture, there are dissenting views. Rafela Garcia-Sancho, professor of anthropology at Stanford, writing in the journal *Human Reflections,* encourages minorities to create their own subcultures within the larger whole: "When an individual gives up his native language, he loses his childhood, his parents, his roots that may go back thousands of years" (513).

**** What punctuation should I use to introduce a quotation?***

Usually a comma follows a brief introduction.

- According to Stein, "Women may unknowingly give up their own values in order to be accepted by men" (268).

A colon may be used when your introduction to the quotation is a complete thought.

- Sloan believes women writers will continue to struggle: "They are impeded by the extreme conventionality of the other sex" (267).

Sometimes no punctuation is needed if your introduction blends into the syntax and flow of the quotation:

- When Langer argues against marriage, she assumes that "there are needs more important than sex and less significant than friendship for celibacy" (12).

**** Do periods and commas go inside or outside the quotation mark?***

Commas and periods are placed inside the quotation mark.

- "I've seen all this before," he argued.
- He argued: "I've seen all this before."

Exception:

If a parenthetical citation is used, the period goes outside the final parenthetical mark.

- According to Hampl, "We only store in memory images we value" (99).

**** How do I use only part of a quotation?***

Use an ellipsis, three spaced periods (. . .) to show that words or phrases within a sentence have been omitted.

- Jess follows their vision and for a brief moment sees something: "Framed by glossy black hair, a face appeared, the features blurred by a veil yet familiar to me . . . then there was no face" (182).

To omit words from the end of a quotation, or to leave out a complete sentence from the interior of a quotation, use four spaced periods (. . . .).

- Rodriguez reveals a disintegrating relationship with his father when he writes, "The very first chance that I got, I evaded his grasp . . . . "
- Journalist Ellen Goodman has commented that "What makes me happy is rewriting . . . . It's like cleaning house, getting rid of all your junk, getting things in the right order, tightening things up."

**** How do I insert a word or phrase to clarify the quotation?***
Square brackets may be used to indicate changes, to clarify, or to correct an error in the original. You may need to clarify a vague pronoun reference, or change the tense of the quotation to keep it consistent with your own.

- According to Alvarez, "He [Mark Twain] greatly exaggerated the flaws in Cooper's prose style" (155).
- While the four men wait for Jake's response, "all eyes [turn] to Muriel" (19).

**** How do I handle a long quotation?***
Quotations of more than four or five typed lines should be used judicially. Too many long quotations can overpower your own writing or create the impression that you're trying to pad your paper. If using a long quotation is unavoidable, begin a new line, approximately ten spaces in from the left margin, omit the quotation marks and type the quotation double spaced. This is called blocking.

- William Manchester describes a battlefield on Okinawa:

  > All greenery had vanished; as far as one could see, heavy shellfire had denuded the scene of shrubbery. What was left resembled a crater moonscape. But the craters were vanishing, too thin even to dig foxholes. (467)

  Years later, the landscape had changed dramatically. Nature had replenished the scene with a growth of heavy jungle.

NOTE:
When a block quotation includes a parenthetical page citation at the end, the period appears before the parenthesis—the only exception to the rule.

5. QUESTIONS ABOUT DOCUMENTING SOURCES

**** Why should I give credit for a source?***
Giving credit to an author for words and ideas is a fair and courteous act. To claim someone else's ideas as your own is intellectual thievery.

**** What do I need to document?***
All information, ideas, concepts, phrases, and even organizational patterns taken from primary and secondary sources, whether quoted, paraphrased, or

summarized, must be credited. However, common or "general knowledge," information the average reader should know or which can be found in numerous sources (such as the date Columbus landed in the Americas), is not documented. If you're unsure about what to document, remember its always safer to document than to risk plagiarism.

*** How do I provide credit for a source?***

For papers written in the humanities, follow a three-step process derived from the Modern Language Association guidelines.

- First, interweave the author and title of the source into your text as you write.
- Second, add a parenthetical page citation for the source when you've completed the paraphrase or quotation.
- Third, provide complete bibliographic information for each source you've used on a Works Cited list (a sample Works Cited is shown on pp. 735–737).

Here are examples of different ways to interweave author and title of a source with a following parenthetical page citation (steps one and two).

- Marie Winn, author of "The Plug-In Drug," probes the effects of television on American families (122).
- In her essay, "The Plug-In Drug," Marie Winn probes the effects of television on American families (122).
- Marie Winn probes the effects of television on American families in her essay "The Plug-In Drug" (122).
- "The Plug-In Drug," an essay by Marie Winn, probes the effects of television on American families (122).

*** Do I always need to integrate the author and title of a source into the text?***

No. The MLA style sheet does not require it. You have the option of citing the author's last name and the page number in the parenthetical citation.

- The effect of television on American families can create an unconscious shift in family values (Winn 122).

However, we recommend integrating as much documentary information as possible or necessary into your text the *first* time you introduce a source. It will add strength and clarity for your reader.

*** How do I credit a work without an author?***

Use a shortened version of the title.

title cited in text	In *Women in Literature* Kate Millett states that *Villette* reads like a long meditation (74).
short version of title used in citation	Kate Millett states that *Villette* reads like a meditation from a prisoner (*Women* 74).

**** How do I credit a play?***
If the play is in verse, MLA recommends that you include the act, scene, and line numbers.

- Hamlet's soliloquy, "To be, or not to be . . . ," provides our first interior view of his dilemma (3.1.56–89).

6. QUESTIONS ABOUT STYLE

**** Do I underline or quote my own title?***
Neither. Your title is your own. Do not underline or use quotation marks unless you include in it the title of the work you're writing about. For example:

- Common Threads in Chappell's *I Am One of You Forever* [an original title including the novel being discussed]
- A Native Experience: "Blue Winds Dancing" [an original title combined with story or essay title being discussed]

**** When should an author's title be underlined?***
Generally, the title of a whole work, or larger work, is indicated by italics or by underlining.

novels	*The Scarlet Letter*
plays	*Hamlet*
collected works	*Classics of Modern Poetry*
magazines	*Newsweek*
newspapers	*Los Angeles Times*
journals	*Journal of American Medicine*
television programs	*Saturday Night Live*
films	*Gone With the Wind*

**** When should an author's title be placed in quotation marks?***
Use quotation marks for titles of works which appear within larger works.

essays	"Corporate Man"
short stories	"Inheritance"
poems	"Ox Cart Man"
an article	"A Visit with Eudora"

Exceptions: Titles of sacred writings are never underlined or placed in quotations.

Koran
Genesis
Talmud
Bible

**** Do I use the author's first or last name as I'm writing?***
For the sake of clarity and out of respect, use the author's full name the first

time you mention it. Afterwards, use the last name only (omit Mr., Mrs., or Ms.).

- *first occurrence:* Sally Youngblood's novel focuses on the life of a young girl growing up in New Mexico.
- *thereafter:* Youngblood shows her character in a variety of poignant situations.
- *inappropriate:* Sally shows her character in a variety of poignant situations.

**** What tense should I use?***
Use simple present tense when discussing the content of any printed text still in existence. Although Plato wrote several thousand years ago, his words continue to exist in front of us as we read them. Shakespeare may be dead, but Hamlet continues to walk up and down the stage today.

- Plato argues that we prefer blindness to the harsh light of truth.
- Hamlet watches his uncle closely looking for signs of guilt.

**** What's the difference between a dash and a hyphen?***
A dash is indicated by two marks (- -); a hyphen by one (-).

Use a dash (- -) to indicate a sudden break in thought or to insert additional information.

- Louise Rosenblatt believes that reading for a vicarious experience is acceptable: "This is a perfectly valid way of responding to literature—in some ways the most valid, since it means that the work has profound importance to the reader" (206).

Use a hyphen (-) to divide words at the end of a line:

- Samuel Johnson believed "great works are performed, not by strength but by perseverance."

Or use a hyphen to join compound words:

- He has announced that he's a pro-choice candidate.

7. QUESTIONS ABOUT THE WORKS CITED LISTING

**** Is a Works Cited list the same as the old Bibliography page?***
Not exactly. Only sources cited in your paper can appear, not works merely consulted. Every entry in the works cited list must refer back to at least one parenthetical citation. The MLA style also prefers "Works Cited" to the more limited title "Bibliography" (literally "description of books") because it accommodates a variety of sources—films, articles, computer software—that may be cited.

**** What form do I use for my Works Cited list?***
List sources alphabetically according to the author's last name, or by title, if no author is given. The MLA organizes information for each source in this order:

- author's name
- title
- place of publication
- name of publisher
- year published
- and for works in anthologies, introductions, articles, and news stories, the inclusive page numbers.

Sample Entries for Books

*** A book by one author:**
Robinson, Marilynne. *Housekeeping.* New York: Bantam, 1981.

*** A book by two authors:**
Strunk, W., Jr., and E. B. White. *The Elements of Style.* 4th ed. New York: Macmillan, 1983.

*** A book by three or more authors:**
Helsinger, Elizabeth K. *et al. The Woman Question: Society and Literature in Britain and America 1837–1883.* Chicago: U of Chicago P, 1989.

*** A book with an anonymous author:**
Literary Marketplace: The Directory of American Book Publishing. 1985 ed. New York: Bowker, 1984.

*** A book with an editor:**
Vicinus, Martha, ed. *A Widening Sphere.* Bloomington: Indiana UP, 1977.

*** A translation:**
Tolstoy, Leo. *War and Peace.* Trans. Constance-Garnett. London: Pan, 1972.

*** An essay or story in an anthology:**
Faulkner, William. "Dry September." *Literature: The Human Experience.* Ed. Richard Abcarian and Marvin Klotz. New York: St. Martin's, 1983. 549–557.

*** An introduction, preface, foreword, or afterword.**
Brown, Robert McAfee. Preface. *Night.* By Elie Wiesel. New York: Bantam, 1986.

Sample Entries for Articles

* **An entry in a reference book** (no author given):
"Brown, John." *The Concise Columbia Encyclopedia.* 1983.
"Paranoia." *American Heritage Dictionary.* 1984 ed.

* **An entry in a reference book** (with an author):
Kearns, Catherine. "Lee Smith." *Dictionary of Literary Biography Yearbook:* 1983. Ed. Mary Bruccoli and Jean W. Ross. Detroit: Gale, 1984. 314–324.

Harrison, Robert. "Poetic Form, Part 1." *The Bookman* 60.4. (1920): 2 65-278. In "English Poets," *Nineteenth-Century Literature Criticism.* Vol. 12. Ed. Martin B. Hicks. Detroit: Gale, 1985. 77.

* **An article in a popular magazine:**
MacLeish, William H. "Where do we go from here?" *Smithsonian* April 1990: 59–68.

* **An article in a journal:**
Fulwiler, Toby. "How Well Does Writing Across the Curriculum Work?" *College English* 46 (1984): 113–25.

* **An article in a newspaper:**
"Revisiting Yellowstone." *New York Times* 20 April 1989: 46.

* **A book review:**
Updike, John. "Cohn's Doom." Rev. of *God's Grace,* by Bernard Malamud. *New Yorker* 8 Nov. 1982: 167–70.

8. HOW DO I PREPARE MY FINAL MANUSCRIPT?

We recommend the form described by the Modern Language Association (MLA). The following pages show three excerpts from Tracy Gilbert's paper (provided in full on p. 117) which illustrate Manuscript Form, In-text Documentation, and the Works Cited list.

Sample First Page

Tracy Gilbert

Prof. Bertagnolli

Freshman Writing 101

28 Mar 1991

KILLING THE PHANTOMS

My Victorian grandmother believed that a woman's place is in the home, a myth she passed on to my mother, and one my mother would have liked to pass on to my sisters and me. But by the time we reached adulthood, things had changed. More and more women, married or not, were working outside the home, doing pretty much as they pleased. My sisters and I would never have accepted the restricted life my mother and my grandmother conformed to. We had minds of our own—something my mother continues to blame on my Italian father and incompatible blood lines.

Reading Virginia Woolf's speech, "Angel in the House," reminded me of the roles my grandmother and mother had accepted without question. Even after the second reading, I didn't find anything especially insightful or startlingly new about women and work. I'd heard most of it before. Woolf's speech seems to speak to a different generation of women. Surely today most women think for themselves, and surely

Sample Page Illustrating In-Text Documentation

Gilbert 3

Carol Christ's essay, "Victorian Masculinity and the Angel in the House," from A Widening Sphere, gave me some helpful background information. The phrase "angel in the house" was first used as the title of a domestic epic poem by Conventry Patmore, a prominent Victorian poet. It describes the courtship and marriage of Honoria, the perfect lady—the angel—who is unselfish, gentle, simple noble. During the Victorian period, she came to represent the ideal woman (146). The angel in the house existed to protect men from evil, and in order to accomplish that a woman needed to be pure and lovely and unselfish (149). According to Sandra Gilbert and Susan Garbar in The Madwoman in the Attic, numerous books printed during the Victorian period describe the proper conduct for ladies reminding them to be submissive, modest, and self-less (23). Women were meant to please men and knowing how made them angelic (24).

According to Bonnie Anderson and Judith Zinsser in A History of Their Own, it was generally agreed that Victorian women would have a more positive impact if they stayed at home and were good wives and mothers. "If a woman remained traditionally subservient and deferential to men and did not challenge

Sample Works Cited Page

Gilbert 6

WORKS CITED

Anderson, Bonnie S. and Judith P. Zinsser. A History of Their Own. 2 Vols. New York: Harper, 1988. Vol. 2.

Christ, Carol. "Victorian Masculinity and the Angel in the House." A Widening Sphere. Ed. by Martha Vicinus. Bloomington: Indiana UP, 1977. 146-162.

Gilbert, Sandra M. and Susan Gubar. The Madwoman in the Attic. New Haven: Yale UP, 1979.

Helsinger, Elizabeth K., et al., eds. The Woman Question: Society and Literature in Britain and America, 1837-1883. 3 vols. Chicago: U of Chicago Press, 1989. Vol. 2.

"Traditional." The American Heritage Dictionary Second College Edition. 1982.

Woolf, Virginia. "The Angel in the House." The Conscious Reader. Ed. by Caroline Shrodes, Harry Finestone, and Michael Shugrue. 4th ed. New York: Macmillan, 1988. 264-268.

Acknowledgments

Chapter 2

"Marrakech." Excerpt from "Marrakech" in *Such, Such Were the Joys* by George Orwell, copyright © 1953 by Sonia Brownell Orwell and renewed 1981 by Mrs. George K. Perutz, Mrs. Miriam Gross, Dr. Michael Dickson, Executors of the Estate of Sonia Brownell Orwell. Reprinted by permission of Harcourt Brace Jovanovich, Inc.

Chapter 3

"The Iguana." From *Out of Africa*, by Isak Dinesen. Copyright © 1937 by Random House, Inc., and renewed by Rungstedlundfonden. Reprinted by permission of Random House.

"Paper Pills." From *Winesburg, Ohio* by Sherwood Anderson. Copyright © 1919 by B. W. Huebsch. Copyright renewed 1947 by Eleanor Copenhaver Anderson. Reprinted by permission of the publisher, Viking Penguin, a division of Penguin Books, a division of Penguin Books USA, Inc.

Chapter 4

"Angel in the House." "Professions for Women." From *The Death of the Moth and Other Essays* by Virginia Woolf, copyright © 1942 by Harcourt Brace Jovanovich, Inc., and renewed 1970 by Marjorie T. Parsons. Reprinted by permission of the publisher.

Chapter 5

"Metaphors." Reprinted by permission of Faber and Faber, Ltd., and HarperCollins Publishers, Inc., from *The Collected Poems of Sylvia Plath.*

"Ars Poetica." Reprinted by permission of Curtis Brown, Ltd. Copyright © 1961 by X. J. Kennedy.

"The Picnic." Copyright © 1989 by John Logan and reprinted from *John Logan: The Collected Poems* with the permission of BOA Editions, Ltd., 92 Park Ave., Brockport, NY 14420.

"The House Was Quiet and the World Was Calm." Copyright © 1947 by Wallace Stevens. Reprinted from *The Collected Poems of Wallace Stevens*, by permission of Alfred A. Knopf, Inc.

Chapter 6

"Sight into Insight." Excerpt from *Pilgrim at Tinker Creek* by Annie Dillard. Copyright © 1974 by Annie Dillard. Reprinted by permission of HarperCollins Publishers, Inc.

"Seeing and Knowing." From *The Unknown Craftsman*, published by Kodansha International Ltd. Copyright © 1972. Reprinted by permission. All rights reserved.

"Good Contry People." From *A Good Man Is Hard to Find and Other Stories*, copyright © 1955 by Flannery O'Connor and renewed 1983 by Regina O'Connor. Reprinted by permission of Harcourt Brace Jovanovich, Inc.

"Memory's Glass." By permission. Originally appeared in *The Christian Science Monitor.* Copyright © 1984.

"Beauty: When the Other Dancer Is the Self." From *In Search of Our Mothers' Gardens*, copyright © 1983 by Alice Walker. Reprinted by permission of Harcourt Brace Jovanovich, Inc.

"Channeled Whelk." From *Gift of the Sea* by Anne Morrow Lindbergh. Copyright © 1955 by Anne Morrow Lindbergh. Reprinted by permission of Pantheon Books, a division of Random House, Inc.

"Rattler, Alert." Copyright © by Brewster Ghiselin, 1946, 1969, 1980. By permission of Brewster Ghiselin.

"Snake." From *The Complete Poems of D. H. Lawrence*, edited by Vivian De Sola Pinto and F. Warren Roberts. Copyright © 1964, 1971 by Angelo Ravagli and C. M. Weekley, executors of the Estate of Frieda Lawrence Ravagli. Reprinted by permission of the publisher, Viking Penguin, a division of Penguin Books USA, Inc.

"The Barn and the Bees." From *Having Everything Right* by Kim Stafford. Copyright © 1986 by Kim Stafford. Reprinted by permission of Confluence Press.

Chapter 7

"Memory and Imagination." Copyright © 1985 by Patricia Hampl. Appeared in *The Dolphin Reader* (Houghton Mifflin Co.) Reprinted by permission of Rhoda Weyr Agency, New York.

"Why Are Americans Afraid of Dragons." Copyright © 1974 by Ursula K. Le Guin. Reprinted by permission of the author and the author's agent, Virginia Kidd.

"How Wang-Fo Was Saved." From *Oriental Tales* by Marguerite Yourcenar. Translation copyright © 1983, 1985 by Alberto Manguel. Originally published in French under the title *Nouvelles Orientales*, copyright © 1938 by Librairie Gallimard. Reprinted by permission of Farrar, Straus and Giroux, Inc.

"The Imaginative Mind in Art." From *The Visionary Eye* by Jacob Bronowski, published by the MIT Press.

"The Force That Through the Green Fuse . . ." From *Poems of Dylan Thomas.* Copyright © 1939 by New Directions Publishing Corporation. From *The Poems* by Dylan Thomas, published by Dent. Reprinted by permission of David Higham Associates.

"Provide, Provide." From *The Poetry of Robert Frost* edited by Edward Connery Lathem. Copyright © 1930, 1939, 1969 by Holt, Rinehart and Winston. Copyright © 1936, 1958 by Robert Frost; copyright © 1964, 1967 by Lesley Frost Ballantine. Reprinted by permission of Henry Holt and Company, Inc.

"Landscape, History, and the Pueblo Imagination." Copyright © 1986 by Leslie Marmon Silko. Reprinted by permission of the author.

"Psalm Concerning the Castle." From *Poems: 1960–1967* by Denise Levertov. Copyright © 1966 by Denise Levertov Goodman. Reprinted by permission of New Directions Publishing Corporation.

"The Creation of the Inaudible." Copyright © 1986 by Pattiann Rogers. Reprinted from *The Tattooed Lady in the Garden* by permission of Wesleyan University Press.

"Johnson Gibbs." "The Telegram" and "The Good Times" reprinted by permission of Louisiana State University Press from *I Am One of You Forever* by Fred Chappell. Copyright © 1985 by Fred Chappell.

"Portrait of a Drummer at the Edge of Magic." Excerpts from *Drumming at the Edge of Magic* by Mickey Hart with Jay Stevens. Copyright © 1990 by Mickey Hart and Jay Stevens. Reprinted by permission of HarperCollins Publishers, Inc.

"The Beginning." From *Nine Women* by Shirley Ann Grau. Copyright © 1985 by Shirley Ann Grau. Reprinted by permission of Alfred A. Knopf, Inc.

Chapter 8

"The Unromantic Generation." Copyright © 1987 by The New York Times Company. Reprinted by permission.

"Sex Without Love." From *The Dead and the Living* by Sharon Olds. Copyright © 1983 by Sharon Olds. Reprinted by permission of Alfred A. Knopf, Inc.

"Love or Marriage." Copyright © 1962 by *Harper's Magazine.* All rights reserved. Reprinted from the May issue by special permission.

"How I Met My Husband." From *Something I've Been Meaning to Tell You* by Alice Munro. Copyright © 1974 by Alice Munro. Originally published by McGraw-Hill Ryerson Limited. Reprinted by arrangement with Virginia Barber Literary Agency. All rights reserved.

"Where Is the Love?" Copyright © 1990 by June Jordan.

"Marriage Amulet." Reprinted from *Carpenter of the Sun* by Nancy Willard, by permission of Liveright Publishing Corporation. Copyright © 1974 by Nancy Willard.

"Hemispheres." Grace Shulmans' books of poems include *Hemispheres* and *Burn Down the Icons.* She is author of *Marianne Moore: The Poetry of Engagement.*

"What We Talk About When We Talk About Love." Copyright © 1981 by Raymond Carver. Reprinted from *What We Talk About When We Talk About Love* by Raymond Carver, by permission of Alfred A. Knopf, Inc.

"The Likeness of Atonement (At-one-ment)." From "Discipline and Hope" in *A Continuous Harmony,* copyright © 1972, 1970 by Wendell Berry. Reprinted by permission of Harcourt Brace Jovanovich, Inc.

"Bridging." From *Free Agents* by Max Apple. Copyright © 1984 by Max Apple. Reprinted by permission of HarperCollins Publishers, Inc.

"This Is a Poem to My Son Peter." Reprinted from *The Night Train and the Golden Bird* by Peter Meinke, by permission of the University of Pittsburgh Press. Copyright © 1977 by Peter Meinke.

"A Prologue to Parallel Lives." From *Parallel Lives: Five Victorian Marriages* by Phyllis Rose. Copyright © 1983 by Phyllis Rose. Reprinted by permission of Alfred A. Knopf, Inc.

"The Necessary Enemy." From *The Collected Essays and Occasional Writings of Katherine Anne Porter.* Copyright © 1970 by Katherine Anne Porter. Reprinted by permission of Houghton

Mifflin Company/Seymour Lawrence. All rights reserved.

"On Love." Reprinted from *Rilke on Love and Other Difficulties: Translations and Considerations of Rainer Maria Rilke* by John J. L. Mood, by permission of W. W. Norton & Company, Inc. Copyright © 1975 by W. W. Norton & Company, Inc.

Chapter 9

"I Stand Here Ironing." From *Tell Me a Riddle* by Tillie Olsen, copyright © 1956, 1957, 1960, 1961 by Tillie Olsen. Used by permission of Delacorte Press/Seymour Lawrence, a division of Bantam, Doubleday, Dell Publishing.

"The Value of Working." Copyright 1981 Time, Inc. Reprinted by permission.

"The Importance of Work." From *Outrageous Acts and Everyday Rebellions* by Gloria Steinem. Copyright © 1983 by Gloria Steinem. Reprinted by arrangement of Henry Holt and Company, Inc.

"Work in an Alienated Society." From *The Sane Society* by Eric Fromm. Copyright © 1955, 1983 by Erich Fromm. Reprinted by permission of Henry Holt and Company, Inc.

"The Inheritance of Tools." Copyright © 1986 by Scott Russell Sanders; first appeared in *The North American Review*, reprinted by permisison of the author and the author's agent, Virginia Kidd.

"Digging." From *Poems: 1965–1975* by Seamus Heaney. Copyright © 1966, 1969, 1972, 1975, 1980 by Seamus Heaney. Reprinted by permission of Farrar, Straus and Giroux, Inc.

"Maintenance." Originally appeared in *The Georgia Review*, Volume XLIV, Nos. 1 and 2 (Spring/Summer 1990), copyright © 1990 by The University of Georgia, © 1990 by Naomi Shihab Nye. Reprinted by permission of Naomi Shihab Nye and *The Georgia Review*.

"Exploring the Managed Heart." Arlie Hochschild. *Managed Heart: Commercialization of Human Feeling*, pp. 3–9 and 17–23. Copyright © 1983 The Regents of the University of California.

"The Myth of Sisyphus." From *The Myth of Sisyphus and Other Essays* by Albert Camus, translated by Justin O'Brien. Copyright © 1955 by Alfred A. Knopf, Inc. Reprinted by permission of the publisher.

"Ox Cart Man." Reprinted by permission. Copyright © 1977 The New Yorker Magazine, Inc.

Chapter 10

"A Summons at Buchenwald." Excerpt from *Night* by Elie Wiesel. Translation copyright © 1960 by MacGibbon & Kee. Reprinted by permission of Hill and Wang, a division of Farrar, Straus and Giroux, Inc.

"Leningrad Cemetery." Reprinted by permission. Copyright © 1981 Sharon Olds. Originally appeared in *The New Yorker* magazine.

"Shame." From *Nigger: An Autobiography* by Dick Gregory, with Robert Lipsyte. Copyright © 1964 by Dick Gregory Enterprises, Inc. Reprinted by permission of the publisher, E. P. Dutton, an imprint of Penguin Books USA, Inc.

"Three Thousand Dollar Death Song." Copyright © 1980 Malki Museum Press.

"Six Feet of the Country." From *Six Feet of the Country* by Nadine Gordimer. Copyright © 1956, 1961, 1964, 1965, 1975, 1977, 1983 by Nadine Gordimer. Reprinted by permission of the publisher, Viking Penguin, a division of Penguin Books USA, Inc.

"The Quiet Girl. From *The Woman Warrior: Memoirs of a Girlhood Among Ghosts* by Maxine Hong Kingston. Copyright © 1975, 1976 by Maxine Hong Kingston. Reprinted by permission of Alfred A. Knopf, Inc.

"The Greatest Man in the World." Copyright © 1935 James Thurber. Copyright © 1963 Helen Thurber and Rosemary A. Thurber. From *The Middle-Aged Man and the Flying Trapeze*, published by HarperCollins Publishers, Inc.

"Letter from Birmingham Jail." From *Why We Can't Wait* by Martin Luther King, Jr. Copyright © 1963, 1964 by Martin Luther King, Jr.

New Year's Day Address. Copyright © 1990 by The New York Times Company. Reprinted by permission.

"Gooseberries." Reprinted by permission of T. Litvinov.

"Those Winter Sundays." Reprinted from *Angle of Ascent: New and Selected Poems* by Robert Hayden, by permission of Liveright Publishing Corporation. Copyright © 1975, 1972, 1970, 1966 by Robert Hayden.

Chapter 11

"The Library Card." From *Black Boy* by Richard Wright. Copyright © 1937, 1942, 1944, 1945 by Richard Wright. Reprinted by permission of HarperCollins Publishers, Inc.

"Shiloh." From *Shiloh and Other Stories* by Bobbie Ann Mason. Copyright © 1982 by Bobbie Ann Mason. Reprinted by permission of HarperCollins Publishers, Inc.

"Piki." From *Blue Highways: A Journey Into America* by William Least Heat Moon. Copyright © 1982 by William Least Heat Moon. By permission of Little, Brown and Company.

"Chike's School Days." Excerpts from *Girls at War and Other Stories* by Chinua Achebe, copyright © 1972, 1973 by Chinua Achebe. Used by permission of Doubleday, a division of Bantam Doubleday Dell Publishing Group, Inc., and Harold Ober Associates Incorporated.

"The Ignored Lesson of Anne Frank." From *Surviving and Other Essays* by Bruno Bettleheim. Copyright 1952, © 1960, 1962, 1976, 1979 by Bruno Bettleheim and Trude Bettleheim as trustees. Reprinted by permission of Alfred A. Knopf, Inc.

"It Is Raining on the House of Anne Frank." Reprinted from *The Five Stages of Grief* by Linda Pastan, by permission of W. W. Norton & Company, Inc. Copyright © 1978 by Linda Pastan.

"The Achievement of Desire." From *Hunger of Memory* by Richard Rodriguez. Reprinted by permission of David R. Godine, Publisher.

"Thriving As an Outsider." Robert P. Wolensky and Edward S. Miller (eds.), *The Small City and Regional Community*, Proceedings of the 1980 Conference, University of Wisconsin–Steven's Point: Foundation Press, Inc.

"Daystar." Reprinted from *Thomas and Beulah* by Rita Dove. By permission of Carnegie Mellon University Press, copyright © 1986.

"The Palace of the Moorish Kings." Excerpted from *St. Augustine's Pigeon*, copyright © 1980 by Evan S. Connell. Published by North Point Press and reprinted by permission.

"The Transformation of Silence into Language and Action." From *The Cancer Journals*, copyright © 1980 by Audre Lorde. Reprinted by permission of Aunt Lute Books (415) 558-8116.

Chapter 12

"Theft." Copyright 1986 by The Ontario Review, Inc. Originally appeared as Chapter 6 of *Marya: A Life* by Joyce Carol Oates.

"I Sing the Body Electric." Reprinted by permisison of Don Congdon Associates, Inc. Copyright © 1969 by Ray Bradbury.

"Swimmer in the Secret Sea." Reprinted by permission of William Kotzwinkle. Copyright 1975 by William Kotzwinkle.

"One of Us." From *The Fifth Child* by Doris Lessing. Copyright © 1988 by Doris Lessing. Reprinted by permission of Alfred A. Knopf, Inc.

"Antigone." From *The Antigone of Sophocles: An English Version* by Dudley Fitts and Robert Fitzgerald, copyright © 1939 by Harcourt Brace Jovanovich, Inc., and renewed 1967 by Dudley Fitts and Robert Fitzgerald, reprinted by permission of the publisher.

"Antigone." From *Antigone*, by Jean Anouilh, adapted and translated by Lewis Galantiere. Copyright © 1946 by Random House, Inc., renewed 1974 by Lewis Galantiere. Reprinted by permission of Random House, Inc.

ILLUSTRATION CREDITS

p. xx, The Griot by Willie Nash. Courtesy of the artist; p. 168, Courtesy of Robert Sawers/Pacific Asia Museum, Pasadena; p. 183 (left, top) Frank Scherschel/*Life* Magazine)/© Time Warner, Inc.; (left, bottom) Lisa Larsen/*Life* Magazine/© Time Warner, Inc.; (right) AP/ Wide World Photos; p. 239, *Green Violinist* by Marc Chagall. Solomon R. Guggenheim Museum, New York. Gift, Solomon R. Guggenheim, 1937. Photograph by Robert E. Mates; p. 302, *The Kiss* by Constantin Brancusi. Copyright 1912. Philadelphia Museum of Art, the Louise and Walter Arensberg Collection; p. 381, *The Sower* by Jean-Francois Millet. Museum of Fine Arts, Boston. Gift of Quincy Adams Shaw through Quincy A. Shaw, Jr., and Mrs. Marian Shaw Haughton; p. 447, Plate from 13 *Grabados* bv David Alfaro Siqueiros, 1931. Woodcut, printed in black, block: 5 1/8 x 3 7/16 in. Collection, The Museum of Modern Art, New York, Inter-American Fund; p. 534, *The Sun and Moon* from "Genesis" by Paul Nash, London, Nonesuch Press, 1924. Woodcut, printed in black, page size: 10 1/2 x 7 9/16 in. Collection, The Museum of Modern Art, New York. A Conger Goodyear Fund; p. 610, *Father Mueller* by Ernst Ludwig Kirchner, 1917. Woodcut, printed in color, block: 2 15/16 X 13 3/8 in. Collection, The Museum of Modern Art, New York. Gift of Victor S. Riesenfeld.

INDEX